MONTGOMERY WARD
Fashions of the Twenties

EDITED AND WITH AN INTRODUCTION BY
JOANNE OLIAN

14 G 116
All Silk
De Luxe
Flat Crepe
$13⁷⁵

DOVER PUBLICATIONS, INC.
MINEOLA, NEW YORK

Planet Friendly Publishing
✓ Made in the United States
✓ Printed on Recycled Paper
Text: 10%   Cover: 10%
Learn more: www.greenedition.org

GREEN
EDITION

At Dover Publications we're committed to producing books in an earth-friendly manner and to helping our customers make greener choices.

Manufacturing books in the United States ensures compliance with strict environmental laws and eliminates the need for international freight shipping, a major contributor to global air pollution.

And printing on recycled paper helps minimize our consumption of trees, water and fossil fuels. The text of *Montgomery Ward Fashions of the Twenties* was printed on paper made with 10% post-consumer waste (text), 10% post-consumer waste (insert) and the cover was printed on paper made with 10% post-consumer waste. According to Environmental Defense's Paper Calculator, by using this innovative paper instead of conventional papers, we achieved the following environmental benefits:

Trees Saved: 7 • Air Emissions Eliminated: 598 pounds
Water Saved: 2,878 gallons • Solid Waste Eliminated: 175 pounds

For more information on our environmental practices, please visit us online at www.doverpublications.com/green

Bibliographical Note

This Dover edition, first published in 2010, contains a new selection of pages from *Montgomery Ward & Co., Catalogue Number 107, Fall and Winter 1927–28,* Baltimore. Some pages refer to catalog pages that are not included in this edition.

Library of Congress Cataloging-in-Publication Data

Montgomery Ward fashions of the twenties / edited and with an introduction by JoAnne Olian.
      p. cm.
   ISBN-13: 978-0-486-47281-2 (pbk.)
   ISBN-10: 0-486-47281-7 (pbk.)
      1. Clothing and dress—United States—History—20th century—Catalogs.
2. Montgomery Ward—Catalogs. 3. Nineteen twenties. I. Olian, JoAnne.
GT615.M65 2009
391.00973'09042—dc22

2009052284

Manufactured in the United States by Courier Corporation
47281701
www.doverpublications.com

INTRODUCTION

Show me the clothes of a country and I can write history.

—Anatole France

A beloved chronicle of Americana, the mail-order catalog is a quintessential element of our country's history. As early as 1744 Benjamin Franklin, the first mail-order merchant, issued a list of 600 books to be sold by mail. As both mirror and record of the people, no other book has served to the same degree. The catalog kept pace with improvements in technology and changes in fashion, fanning the flame of consumer demand and enabling it to offer standardized, reliable items for the comfort of even the most isolated farmers in the land. The democratization of clothing in America owes a great deal to the mail-order industry, which made reasonably priced, good quality garments available to a broad spectrum of consumers. Economically, socially, and geographically catalogs allowed everybody to participate as a culture of consumption.

Sometimes called the "Farmer's Bible," the catalog occupied a place of honor in the farm kitchen, while the actual Bible was relegated to the seldom-used parlor. The first of these publications was the Montgomery Ward catalog, which predated Sears by fourteen years. Affectionately dubbed the "Wish Book," the Grolier Club, a distinguished society of bibliophiles, named it in 1946 "one of the hundred most influential books on American life." They claimed that "No idea ever mushroomed so far from so small a beginning, or had so profound an influence on the economics of a continent, as the concept, original to America, of direct selling by mail, for cash...the mail-order catalog has been perhaps the greatest single influence in increasing the standard of American middle-class living. It brought the benefit of wholesale prices to city and hamlet, to the crossroads and the prairies; it indicated cash payment as against crippling credit; it urged millions of housewives to bring into their homes and place upon their backs and on their shelves and on their floors creature comforts which otherwise they could never have hoped for and above all, it substituted sound quality for shoddy."

Aaron Montgomery Ward had worked in a barrel factory for 25 cents a day, stacked bricks for 30 cents, been a country storekeeper and a traveling salesman for Chicago department stores in several rural areas, acquainting him with farmers' needs and giving him the idea to sell to members of Grange societies by mail. Robert Hendrickson, author of *The Grand Emporiums* says, "Ward found that farmers were objecting bitterly to the prices they paid for goods at the traditional but obsolescent country stores.... Not only were prices high and storekeepers often dishonest, but the choice of goods was frequently limited at the inefficient general store, and if the farmer complained, the storekeeper—honestly or not—advised that he had to buy what his wholesaler offered at his wholesaler's prices." In 1872, with $1,600 in savings, Ward founded his mail-order business. His first mailing was a one-page price list of 163 items mostly priced at a dollar, sent primarily to members of the Grange—a political organization founded by farmers to combat discriminatory laws and practices by big business against small individual farmers.

The first bound catalog, issued in 1875, was 3 x 5 inches and consisted of 32 pages with illustrations. Ward boasted, "Give me your age and describe your general build, and we will in nine cases out of ten, give you a fit." On the inside cover he explained how he was able to sell for such low prices by buying directly from manufacturers, eliminating the middleman, and keeping his overhead low, claiming to save customers "40 to 100 percent which are the profits of the middlemen." Just five years later sales exceeded $10 million. Much of his success was due to being appointed official supply house for the Illinois Grange, which he used in his advertising, as "The Original Grange Supply House selling to Grangers, other farmers and mechanics at the lowest wholesale prices," and for his policy of "Satisfaction Guaranteed or Your Money Back." Ward's was dedicated to providing creature comforts for life on the prairies. In its early days the company was held in such high esteem that it was thought to be able to supply the gamut of merchandise from "love powders" to embalming fluid. Everything necessary to farmers' existence was available, from groceries to liniment, while most of the non-essentials were for their wives. Every item was clearly illustrated and the first mail-order picture of a woman's dress was published in the Montgomery Ward catalog for 1878.

By the 1893 Columbian exposition in Chicago the catalog had mushroomed into a two pound, 544-page volume. It was already widely used in rural schools as a textbook to teach everything from arithmetic to drawing. It was employed to drill children in reading and spelling; they practiced arithmetic by filling out orders and totaling them. They copied the illustrations in the catalog and they used postal zone maps as an aid in learning geography. Girls cut out the pictures in old catalogs for paper dolls.

Most importantly, farm families learned what was happening in the wider world. In spite of the fact that they were widely separated geographically and often ethnically, emigrating from many different countries, the catalog helped create a land of homogenous people who all desired the same material things pictured in the mail-order catalogs. Customers were invited to write to Ward's in twelve different foreign languages, including Czech and Russian. With the increase in railroad routes and the introduction of Rural Free Delivery in 1896 and parcel post in 1913, no home was beyond the reach of the mail-order merchant.

Dwight Hoover's memoir, *A Good Day's Work,* recalls his boyhood on an Iowa farm in the early 1930s, providing invaluable insight into farm life and the way in which clothing was worn:

"The daily routine was almost always the same. My father would awaken me at five or five-thirty to do the morning chores. I would descend the stairs in my flannel pajamas to dress behind the dining room stove, shivering until I put on my long winter underwear and my first layer of clothes (a long-sleeve cotton or wool flannel shirt and denim overalls, not jeans). The myth that farm children were sewed into their underwear at the beginning of winter and cut out in the spring was just that, a myth. No one I knew had that done, but they, like me, changed their underwear infrequently. I put on a clean pair at least every week. For special occasions I would change more often.

"Having fully dressed with my sheepskin coat and galoshes, I would go to the barn with my father by the light of a kerosene lantern—until 1937 when the farm was electrified.

"I had gotten my school clothes in September; among these were usually a new pair of overalls and a new pair of galoshes, the four-buckle kind. (Somehow the buckles rarely lasted for more than a season.) If I had outgrown my shoes, I received a new pair of high-top work shoes. In the later thirties I would have gotten a pair of felt inserts for galoshes that would cover several pairs of woolen socks. The inserts proved effective for keeping my feet warm during days of walking on frozen ground. Not every season but irregularly I would get either a sheepskin coat or a mackinaw. The sheepskin had a fleece lining and collar, with a canvas outer shell. It was utilitarian and could take hard use; it was not a fancy dress coat as today's can be. The canvas might be ripped and torn by protruding nails or pieces of wood jutting out from unexpected places. The mackinaw was usually wool and more likely to be worn on dressy occasions."

In 1920 the farm population was about 32 million, 30 percent of the U.S. total. When evangelist Aimee Semple McPherson walked out on the stage of her Foursquare Gospel Church in Los Angeles with a full milk pail and asked how many had ever lived on a farm, the entire audience rose. As late as 1935 only one farm home in ten was wired for electricity and most had no running water. Household appliances such as washers and vacuum cleaners were available for use with electricity, steam, or hand operation. The automobile was gaining in popularity, still farm families continued to rely heavily on the catalog. Unpaved roads were often impassable due to snowdrifts during the winter and mud in the spring. However, a segment of the population who formerly shopped by mail could now drive into town and visit a retail establishment where garments could be seen, tried on, paid for, and carried out without waiting for parcel post to deliver them. Thus, the customer base for catalog fashion was dwindling, limited increasingly to the most isolated. Nevertheless, the president of the company, in his introduction to the 1927–28 catalog, stated that eight million people were customers in the preceding year, representing an increase of three million over the preceding three years. While practical clothing and farm equipment accounted for much of the volume, Ward's also attempted to woo the fashion conscious customer with "New Idea" shops, which sold "only designs from Paris or New York—the twin style centers of the world," claiming that "the business of our New Fashion shops is probably the fastest growing in the United States."

Ward provided fashionable attire for the women whose sole arbiter was the catalog. Glamour was lent to apparel by ascribing it to Paris or New York. Typically, "Everything about this frock suggests its Fifth Avenue origin," or "This frock follows a Paquin creation." The names of prominent French designers were habitually invoked. Hollywood had also begun to exert its influence. Ziegfeld Follies star Billie Burke is mentioned in connection with both a pair of women's pajamas (page 31) and one for girls (page 42).

Allusions to the twenties inevitably evoked a string of clichés—flapper, Jazz Age, Roaring Twenties, etc. Judging by the contents of the catalog, its customers' leisure hours were spent largely at home entertaining themselves by playing the banjo, mouth organ, ukulele, and accordion or listening to such favorites as "Ain't She Sweet" and "Lil' Liza Jane" on a Melophonic console phonograph. *A Girl of the Limberlost** by Gene Stratton-Porter, the Tarzan series,*** and *Arrowsmith* by Sinclair Lewis were bestsellers. The number of Masonic and Eastern Star rings shown in the catalog attests to the popularity of fraternal organizations. The state fair was an annual event of importance to farmers and their children who displayed their Future Farmers of America or 4-H Club projects. The catalog offered much in the way of childhood pastimes. Children amused themselves with many of the same toys still beloved today such as model trains, Tinkertoys, bicycles, sports equipment for boys, and baby dolls and doll carriages for their sisters.

The decade was marked by larger than life sports personalities. With the exception of Charlie Chaplin, Tom Mix, and Charles Lindbergh, the most popular names of the decade were sports figures such as Babe Ruth who had just hit his sixtieth home run for the New York Yankees, "Red" Grange, Bobby Jones, Jack Dempsey, and "Big Bill" Tilden. Sportswomen were so celebrated that when Gertrude Ederle successfully swam the English channel in 1928, she was

*Available as a Dover reprint.
**Tarzan of the Apes* is available as a Dover reprint.

honored with a ticker-tape parade down Broadway. That same year Amelia Earhart flew solo across the Atlantic. Helen Wills, "Queen Helen," the several time U.S. Lawn Tennis Association women's singles champion, known equally for her style and prowess on the courts, was a vocal proponent of short skirts, sleeveless blouses, and bare legs as essential to an effective tennis game. In order to promote their towns during the Florida land boom of the 1920s, chambers of commerce even sponsored women's basketball and swimming teams. As the first modern sports celebrities, these women exerted a profound influence on the modern ideal of physical beauty.

College added an aura of glamour and a sporty look. A "jaunty tomboy coat" for women (page 6) of fur whose "shaggy appearance is characteristic of expensive raccoon," sold for the sizable sum of $125. References such as "Hollywood model" and "Collegiate Overcoat in Popular Yale Blue" appeared in copy for young men's clothing. Even high school girls, no longer content with gingham frocks and cotton stockings, demanded silk dresses and silk stockings.

World War I had a profound influence on fashion as women replaced men in factories, drove buses and even ambulances overseas, creating the need for less constricting garments. More importantly, greater freedom for women helped lead to the passage of the woman suffrage amendment in 1920. As straight lines replaced curves in fashion as well as in architecture, the ideal body type became androgynous. Rounded hips, small waists, ample busts, and long hair, all traditional feminine attributes, were superseded by their antithesis—a boyish flatness and a short, almost mannish hairstyle.

Long tresses, considered a woman's crowning glory, were shorn and bobbed hair became the norm. In 1927 the electric waving machine, invented several decades earlier by Charles Nessler, became a sensation. Makeup was no longer considered a sign of loose morals and respectable women were applying cosmetics to enhance their appearance. Montgomery Ward sold rouge, face powder, lipstick, mascara, and eyelash curlers from companies such as Max Factor and Maybelline, may of whom are still in business. A compact to powder one's nose was an essential purse accessory and appeared as a gift suggestion on the same page as silver thimbles.

The twenties was a decade of minimal clothing for women, as the boyish figure replaced the full-blown matron of previous decades. Ward's proved equal to the challenge, offering a large number of pure silk dresses at the price of $13.75, especially remarkable considering their plethora of details—tucks, pleats, and draping. Dressy fashions, however, unlike those of the French couture, were almost never sleeveless. The waist, at its natural place at the start of the decade, fell until it settled on the hips in 1927. Conversely, from hems at mid-calf in 1920, skirts climbed gradually to their zenith in 1927, when they barely covered the knee, displaying a flash of shiny flesh-color stocking. Ward's offered fashionable stockings in light of the pared-down clothing in fashion, there are several pages of heavy-duty corsets in the 1927–28 catalog. All wool wrap coats with fur shawl collars ranged in price from $8.98 to $49.95, to a fox-collared muskrat fur at $198.75. Fur trims ranged from Manchurian wolf dog and moufflon (a small wild sheep from Asia Minor) to coney (rabbit) dyed to resemble numerous other animals including beaver. Since Ward advertised its willingness to buy raw furs from trappers, these collars may have been made from furs purchased directly by the company. Coats were available in sizes and styles to fit bust sizes from 34 to 53 inches, the "fuller figure" starting at 39 inches; proportioned sizes for 5'3" and under; and "misses" 14 through 20 years of age, bust sizes 32 to 38 inches. Girls from 7 to 14 could be kept warm for as little as $3.98 in a basic untrimmed coat or in a coat "Fit for a Princess" of all wool velour with fur collar and cuffs for $13.98. Millinery for women and girls occupied several pages. Most of the styles were based on a deep crowned cloche, which complemented the streamlined silhouette and necessitated short hair.

In spite of the pages of girls' coats and hats, there are relatively few dresses for girls below high school age. According to *Middletown*, the seminal study of a middle-America town in the 1920s by Robert and Helen Lynd, older girls competed for popularity through dress, hence a homemade garment was unthinkable and a disproportionate amount of the family budget went toward that end. However, little girls habitually wore homemade dresses, as well as hand-me-downs from their more fashionable sisters. The comparative ease and low cost of sewing a cotton dress by machine accounts for the number of pages devoted to brightly colored, inexpensive printed cotton piece goods suitable for the home sewer.

Boys' suits were sold with a choice of knickers or "longies," the former in sizes up to 12 years and the long pants version up to 16 years. Boys from 3 to 8 years of age could choose suits consisting of waist and shorts in a variety of styles including sailor, Eton, and lumberjack. Hats for men and boys, both functional and dressy, occupy several pages. Nobody went bareheaded. Hats, scarves, mittens, and gloves were often birthday or Christmas gifts. Men's coats were equal to harsh winters and their dress shirts were sold by neck size only. Sleeves came in one length, adjustable with sleeve garters.

The mail order industry catered to the needs of the entire family. The catalog was an illustrated encyclopedia of American life. It was a force for assimilation of immigrants of diverse nationalities into Americans. If indeed clothes make the man, Americans were both identifiable and united by their purchases. William C. Browning, an early twentieth century clothing manufacturer, while not limiting his remarks to the mail-order industry, summed up its effect on American society: "And if it be true…that the condition of a people is indicated by its clothing, America's place in the scale of civilized lands is a high one. We have provided not alone abundant clothing at a moderate cost for all classes of citizens, but we have given them at the same time that style and character in dress that is essential to the self-respect of a free, democratic people."

JoAnne Olian
Sands Point, New York

Here Again Are Fashion's Newest

TYPICAL OF THE HIGH STANDARDS
OF THIS GREATER STYLE SERVICE

Our Finest Sports Coat

*Sumptuously Furred
All Wool Plaid*

In tribute to our Newer Coat Shop—the smart Sports Mode sends this distinctly swagger style! Modeled to the moment, for the better informed tailored woman.

A very distinctive model—beautifully tailored from a sportive new All Wool Plaid Coating—of warm, drifting pattern, pleasingly soft to the eye. A very superior coating woven from Pure Virgin Wool, with soft nap closely resembling the expensive Camel's Hair.

Topped like the best of sports styles—with big mushroom collar of finest selected Manchurian Wolf Dog Skins, long haired and glistening.

Swagger ease in every line—from the smooth saddle shoulders to the hip-tab panels, set on at a new slant above the insert pockets. Rich velvet pipings strengthen the warm color tones.

The coat is carefully finished with a beautiful lining of rich All Silk Crepe—above a warm interlining. Length, about 44 inches.

WOMEN'S SIZES: 34, 36, 38, 40, 42, 44-inch bust. State bust measure. Read "How to Order" on Page 51. Ship. wt., 5 lbs. 8 oz.

10 G 20—Black and gray plaid with black fur
10 G 22—Brown and tan plaid with red fox color fur $22⁹⁸

Our Handsomest Coat

Exact Reproduction of a Costly Import

Luxuriously rich—magnificently styled—the original of this model was the supreme choice of our Fashion Experts—from among the many beautiful imports from Paris. The exact reproduction—a wealth of coat beauty—is yours from the New Coat Shop for less than half the price of its costly original.

Tailored with infinite care from beautiful All Wool Duv-Bloom; a fabric of velvet softness, which tailors with rare charm. Luxuriously furred with long haired, gleaming Manchurian Wolf Dog—the finest selected pelts—closely resembling the costly fox. The same fur makes sumptuous mushroom collar and deep, set up cuffs, and borders the swinging over-flounces, softly shirred on below rows of rich floss stitching—which adorn the fronts.

Youthfully straight untrimmed back. Under a rich lining of beautiful All Silk Crepe, the coat is warmly interlined. Length, about 44 inches.

WOMEN'S SIZES: 34, 36, 38, 40, 42-inch bust. State bust measure. Read "How to Order" on Page 51. Shipping weight, 4 lbs. 13 oz.

10 G 26—Beaver brown
10 G 28—Grackle blue $49⁵⁰

The Two-Piece Frock—As Paris Glorifies It

All Silk De Luxe Crepe Satin With Filmy Georgette and Embroidery

Reproduced from the costly Paris original for the best judge of style in the world—the Typical American Woman!

The lovely overblouse is draped, front and back, to modishly swathe the hips by means of soft shirrings. Radiant sleeve puffs of contrasting All Silk Georgette Crepe are set on under an exquisite bead-like "flower-and-pearl" embroidery. The georgette daintily tips the rippling plaited skirt tiers, while a piquant flower carries the contrasting theme to the shoulder. Lithe and straight at back, the skirt is attached to a rich bodice of All Silk Crepe.

A beautiful exponent of our NEW IDEA in Fashions—richly developed in gleaming All Silk "De Luxe" Crepe Satin—and reasonably priced for all!

WOMEN'S SIZES: 34, 36, 38, 40, 42, 44-inch bust. Lengths from back of neck to bottom of hem, 43 and 45 inches only. State bust measure and length. Read "How to Order" on Page 51. Shipping weight, 1 lb. 12 oz.

14 G 90—Black with rose pink
14 G 92—Balsam (dark) green with bisque
14 G 94—Marron glace (cocoa brown) with French beige $17⁹⁸

Only designs from Paris or New York

1

New Idea Coats
A Never-Ending Marvel and Delight to Particular Women

Very Rich Coat
Buxkin Suede
All Wool
Lavishly Furred With
Smartly Dyed Mandel
New Side Panels

10 G 250 New bolster shawl collar, deep gauntlet shaped cuffs, unusual grouping of plaits below the hipline. These are features which make this coat one of the outstanding fashions of the year. Such original styling would not be developed in anything but the finest fabric.

This All Wool Buxkin Suede deserves both the fashion features which have been incorporated in it and the skillful tailoring required to bring out each smart detail. Women will be especially pleased with the clever way in which the side panel effects, with their cordings and silk stitchery, ease the line, without in any way disturbing the slender silhouette. Richly lined, over a warm interlining, with fine All Silk Crepe. Inside pocket finished with plaiting. Length, about 45 inches.

WOMEN'S SIZES: 34, 36, 38, 40, 42, 44, 46-inch bust. State bust measure. Read "How to Order" on Page 51. Shipping weight, 6 pounds 2 ozs.
10 G 250—Reindeer tan. Mink dyed Mandel fur.
10 G 252—Gracklehead (medium) blue. Raccoon dyed Mandel fur.
10 G 254—Brickdust. Mink dyed Mandel fur. **$29.95**

Mandel Fur

French Coney Fur

Mandel Fur

10 G 262
All Wool
Vel-Suede
$19.98

10 G 250
All Wool
Buxkin
Suede
$29.95

10 G 256
All Wool
Velour
$12.98

Mandel Fur

Manchurian Wolf Dog Fur

Heavy All Wool Velour
With French Coney Fur
Conservatively Styled

10 G 256 A triumph in coat values! At a minimum cost, less than you would expect to pay for such a dressy, fur-trimmed style, you can have this warm, serviceable coat. Of a pleasing quality, winter weight, All Wool Velour, it is lined throughout with strong, high grade mercerized fabric that will give very satisfactory wear; warmly interlined, too. Points of the arrow shaped insets under the arms, leading down to the inverted plait, are smartly stitched with silk floss. The inverted plait is outlined by a slenderizing corded tuck which extends to the hem of coat.

In all our New Idea coats you will note these little details of improved tailoring.

The large and attractive mushroom collar of silky French Coney fur to match the cuffs, may be buttoned up high around the neck for added protection against cold winter weather. Convenient inside pocket is pleasing addition. A dignified looking coat, cut on smartly conservative lines that will please both in style and lasting comfort. It would undoubtedly retail for more. Length, about 45 inches.

WOMEN'S SIZES: 34, 36, 38, 40, 42, 44, 46-inch bust. State bust measure. Read "How to Order" on Page 51. Shipping weight, 4 pounds 15 ounces.
10 G 256—Reindeer (dark) tan.
10 G 258—Gracklehead (medium) blue.
10 G 260—Brickdust. **$12.98**

10 G 274
Seal
Bloom
Bolivia
$21.98

All Wool Vel-Suede
Fluffy Mandel Fur
Diagonal Tucking

10 G 262 The style and quality of this coat are above reproach! The chic, diagonal lines of the tucked and button trimmed side panel insets are heightened by a silk stitched diamond on each point. Fluffy Mandel fur makes a flattering frame for the face in the large mushroom collar, and is used for the wide cuffs.

The high grade, smooth finish, winterweight All Wool Vel-Suede is unique for its beauty and excellent wearing qualities. Rayon Faced Jacquard lining, with inside pocket. Warmly interlined. Made with no-seam facing and saddle shoulders. Length, about 45 inches.

WOMEN'S SIZES: 34, 36, 38, 40, 42, 44, 46-inch bust. State bust measure. Read "How to Order" on Page 51. Shipping weight, 5 pounds 10 ounces.
10 G 262—Dark brown. Mink dyed Mandel fur.
10 G 264—Gracklehead (medium) blue. Raccoon dyed Mandel fur.
10 G 266—Cranberry red. Mink dyed Mandel fur. **$19.98**

10 G 268
All Wool
Buxkin Suede
$32.50

New York Elegance—Regal Quality
Characteristic of the New Fashion Idea
All Wool Buxkin Suede—Manchurian Wolf Dog

10 G 268 One glance at this coat and you will appreciate the extent to which a carefully styled—carefully selected coat serves to bring out the natural figure grace. A distinguished model; its fabric and fur rich, its workmanship expert.

The fine, long-haired black Manchurian Wolf-dog used for the handsome collar and cuffs, is a suitable accompaniment for the lovely material of which the coat is made—All Wool Buxkin Suede, delightfully smooth in texture and velvety in appearance with a glove-like finish. An unusually stunning effect is formed by the insets and folds at the sides, with points of silk floss stitching to further emphasize its smartness. Smooth fitting saddle shoulders. Lined with a fine quality of All Silk Crepe over a warm interlining. Convenient inner pockets. Length, about 45 inches.

WOMEN'S SIZES: 34, 36, 38, 40, 42, 44, 46-inch bust. State size. Read "How to Order" on Page 51. Shipping weight, 6 pounds.
10 G 268—Reindeer (dark) tan.
10 G 270—Taupe gray.
10 G 272—Gracklehead (medium) blue. **$32.50**

The "New Idea"—Popular in New York
This Handsome Example of Seal Bloom Bolivia
Has Mushroom Collar of Fluffy Mandel Fur

10 G 274 Hundreds of women who live in large cities, now buy here because they have proved to themselves that for much smaller expenditure, the "New Idea" in Fashions gives them the same style and quality exhibited in the expensive smart shops of the larger cities.

Here is a typical example. A smart New York coat, its straight, slenderizing lines accentuated by cordings and folds at each side. A mushroom collar of soft, fluffy Mandel fur enhances the richness of the velvety Seal Bloom Bolivia, appropriately used for this dressy model. It has just enough cotton to make it durable. A no-seam facing and trim-fitting saddle shoulders are proof of the expert workmanship employed in every detail. A convenient pocket has been placed on the Rayon faced Jacquard lining. Warmly interlined. Length, about 45 inches.

WOMEN'S SIZES: 34, 36, 38, 40, 42, 44, 46-inch bust. State size. Read "How to Order" on Page 51. Shipping weight, 5 pounds 8 ounces.
10 G 274—Beaver brown. Mink dyed Mandel fur.
10 G 276—Black. Raccoon dyed Mandel fur.
10 G 278—Gracklehead (medium) blue. Raccoon dyed Mandel fur. **$21.98**

Smartest of Fashion Notes
~Careful Quality Making

Genuine Vicuna

Mandel Fur

French Coney Fur

10 G 104
All Wool Chamo Suede
$34.95

10 G 110
All Wool Vel-Suede
$19.98

10 G 116
All Wool Velour
$11.50

Mandel Fur

10 G 122
All Wool Vel-Suede
$18.98

Genuine Vicuna

10 G 128
All Wool Chamo Suede
$39.95

Fashion Applied To Strict Economy
All Wool Velour With Silky French Coney Fur An Unusual Value

10 G 116 "I never imagined it possible that $11.50 could go so far!" you'll say. And it's certain—the more you wear this Coat of All Wool Velour, the more you'll marvel at its splendid value. You'd search a long, long time before you could find a coat of better material—more carefully styled and finished—for the same low price!

A clever, conservative style which you will find equal to the smartest occasion —as well as practical for everyday wear. Generously furred with soft French Coney. The snug mushroom collar may be buttoned close or worn graciously open; deep cuffs set on with the same expert care. Very neat trim underarm panels suggest fashionable height, in their arrangement of diagonal cord tucking aslant the dressy panel of vertical cord tucking. In addition to its warm winter weight, the coat is interlined beneath its durable mercerized twill lining, finished with convenient inside pocket. Length, about 45 inches.

Our New Hat Shop offers many New Idea models—in a surpassingly smart collection, from which you may order just the ideal hat to complete your costume.

WOMEN'S SIZES: 34, 36, 38, 40, 42, 44, 46-inch bust. State bust measure. Read "How to Order" on Page 51. Shipping weight, 4 pounds 15 ounces.

10 G 116—Reindeer brown.
10 G 118—Gracklehead (medium) blue.
10 G 120—Brickdust.   **$11.50**

Novelty New Fabric Exclusively Tailored
All Wool Chamo Suede Richly Trimmed With Genuine Vicuna Fox Fur

10 G 104 Beautiful exponent of our New Idea in Fashions! A Coat that will fulfill your highest expectations and give you more than one season of beautiful service.

Exclusive Fifth Avenue shows decided favor for this remarkably lovely winter-weight coating—All Wool Chamo Suede. With such velvety warmth and softness— no wonder it takes its place among the best! Warmly interlined, and has a rich lining of heavy All Silk Crepe, finished with a convenient inside pocket.

Lovely mushroom collar and cuffs of genuine brown Vicuna Fox—very rich and attractive; resembling the costly fox. Stunning side panels and fan-flare cord tucking were copied from a beautiful import. A similar touch distinguishes the dressy sleeves. Length, about 45 inches.

WOMEN'S SIZES: 34, 36, 38, 40, 42, 44, 46-inch bust. State bust measure. Be sure to read "How to Order" Instructions on Page 51.

10 G 104—Medium brown.
10 G 106—Gracklehead (medium) blue.
10 G 108—Cranberry red.   **$34.95**

A "New Idea" Beauty And Very Fine Value
New All Wool Vel-Suede With Mandel Fur Many Dressy Features

10 G 110 An excellent example of what a small sum will do when wisely spent on a "New Idea" Coat. This model is worth much more. Its splendid weight and glove-smooth weave merit highest approval for this All Wool Vel-Suede—one of the most popular new coatings. The coat also carries a warm interlining, and is attractively lined with a Rayon Faced Jacquard, which will give two seasons of satisfactory service.

Slenderizing plaited panels are set up on the sides between dressy half-moon stitching and self covered buttons. Newest double band cuffs match the large mushroom collar of thick, fluffy Mandel Fur. Tailored according to our exacting "New Idea" standards; a supreme value for small expenditure. Convenient inner pocket. Length, about 45 inches.

WOMEN'S SIZES: 34, 36, 38, 40, 42, 44, 46-inch bust. State bust measure. Read "How to Order" on Page 51. Ship.wt., 5 lbs. 2 oz.

10 G 110—Reindeer (dark) tan. Mink dyed Mandel fur.
10 G 112—Gracklehead (medium) blue. Raccoon dyed Mandel fur.
10 G 114—Cranberry red, Mink dyed Mandel fur.   **$19.98**

Smart All Wool Vel-Suede
"New Idea" Quality—Modest Price Warmly Trimmed with Mandel Fur

10 G 122 Newest features distinguish this inexpensive Coat of All Wool Vel Suede, the fabric which goes into many higher-priced coats! Firmly woven and of velvet-smooth texture; warm and responsive to expert tailoring. Interlined for added warmth; practically lined with lustrous Satin de Chine.

Splendidly collared and cuffed with thick, soft Mandel Fur. Smartly swung from easy saddle shoulders. Very new cord tucks start with tailor arrow heads at yoke depth in back, and swing in semi-cape outline to the trim panel fronts. Inside pocket. Length, about 45 inches.

WOMEN'S SIZES: 34, 36, 38, 40, 42, 44, 46-inch bust. State bust measure. Read "How to Order" on Page 51. Shipping weight, 5 pounds 10 ounces.

10 G 122—Dark brown. Mink dyed Mandel fur.
10 G 124—Gracklehead (medium) blue; Raccoon dyed Mandel fur.
10 G 126—Cranberry red, Mink dyed Mandel fur.   **$18.98**

A Superb New Wrap Around
Glove-Smooth All Wool Chamo Suede Richly Furred With Brown Vicuna

10 G 128 A gem among many, typical of our supreme New Idea in Coat Fashions! All Wool Chamo Suede incomparably smooth and firm—which tailors with unusual distinction. Its beautiful fur alone would ordinarily bring a high price, for it is the genuine Brown Vicuna, long haired, brilliant; resembling fox. A lavish collar of dressy shawl depth, with deep cuffs to match.

Within these wrap-around lines the figure is sure to appear more youthful. Self material bands admirably sweep the overlapping front, and strap the sleeves. Warm interlining; dressy silk mixed Brocaded Faille lining, good for two seasons of beautiful service. Inside pockets. A wrap to satisfy you in every detail. Length, about 45 inches.

WOMEN'S SIZES: 34, 36, 38, 40, 42, 44, 46-inch bust. State bust measure. Read "How to Order" on Page 51. Shipping weight, 5 pounds 8 ounces.

10 G 128—Copper brown.
10 G 130—Medium tan.
10 G 132—Lipstick red.   **$39.95**

3

If You Are 5 Feet 3 Inches or Less~These Coats Will Fit You
Specially Proportioned Lines~Sleeves~Body~Length

Coats for Little Women

You will be delighted, as have been the Fashion experts, over this newer phase of the New Idea. Now, The New Coat Shop brings special sizes, a perfect fit, for the short woman about 5 feet 3 inches—or less—in height. Original designs, special lines, truly proportioned to her figure. No need for alterations—for the sleeves are shorter than average and the length in exact accord. The short woman will glory in this new service, to her exact requirements. Take your measurements from information on Page 51.

Special Sizes	33½	35½	37½	39½	41½	43½	45½
Bust, Inches	34	36	38	40	42	44	46
Length, Inches	40	41	42	43	43	44	45

Mendoza Beaver Fur

Mandel Fur

Mandel Fur

10 G 416
All Wool Buxkin Suede
$19.98

10 G 422
All Wool Chamo Suede
$22.98

10 G 428
All Wool Suede Velour
$15.98

Mandel Fur

10 G 434
All Wool Buxkin Suede
$24.95

Genuine Vicuna

10 G 440
Seal Bloom Bolivia
$29.98

Straight Line Coat
Warmly, Modishly Furred With Mendoza Beaver

10 G 416 A smart and tailored model with lines well suited to the short woman. It is a dress coat that will give excellent wearing service for it is made of All Wool Buxkin Suede of a high grade winter weight with a soft glovelike finish. The deep shawl collar with its becoming neck line, and the full deep cuffs are of Mendoza Beaver Fur made of selected coney skins, sheared and dyed to resemble genuine Beaver. Attractive panels are formed at the side by cord tucking and ornaments of heavy silk floss twist. The coat is carefully tailored and well interlined for added warmth and comfort. Rayon faced Jacquard makes a pretty, serviceable lining for two seasons of faithful service. Convenient inner pocket. SPECIAL SIZES FOR LITTLE WOMEN: 33½ to 45½. Lengths, 40 to 45 inches. See size scale above. State size wanted. Ship. wt., 5 lbs. 6 oz.
10 G 416—Reindeer (dark) tan.
10 G 418—Gracklehead (medium) blue.
10 G 420—Cranberry red. **$19.98**

Beautifully Styled
Incomparably Tailored and Generously Furred

10 G 434 Designed particularly for women who cannot reasonably wear the models made for their taller sisters. Length of body, sleeves and general lines are for her especially. All Wool Buxkin Suede with a glove-smooth finish.
Pretty mushroom collar and cuffs of popular Mandel Fur, thick and soft. Underarm panels and single fold plait with buttons add smartness. Cord tucks and stitching to match side panels trim the sleeves, cut with saddle shoulders. A distinctly novel finish, much admired in New York. Silk faced Rayon Jacquard that will wear two seasons. Extra warmth interlining. An excellent value. Inside pocket.
SPECIAL SIZES FOR LITTLE WOMEN: 33½ to 45½. Lengths, 40 to 45 inches. See size scale above. State size wanted. Ship. wt., 5 lbs. 8 oz.
10 G 434—Reindeer (dark) tan. Mink dyed Mandel fur.
10 G 436—Gracklehead (medium) blue. Raccoon dyed Mandel fur.
10 G 438—Brickdust. Mink dyed Mandel fur. **$24.95**

Chamo Suede
New Panel Lined Popular Mandel Fur

10 G 422 A youthful style for little women. This smart coat is made of the lovely soft and pliable Chamo Suede an All Wool fabric of good winter weight. The mushroom collar and cuffs, set up from the edge of the sleeves, are of Mandel fur. Heavy cord tucks in an attractive arrangement decorate the fronts and each side of the back. Each tuck finished with silk floss stitched arrowheads. Saddle shoulders give a comfortable fit. Rayon faced Jacquard that will give two seasons' wear lines the coat and added warmth is given by interlining. Button and loop front closing and inside pocket.
SPECIAL SIZES FOR LITTLE WOMEN: 33½ to 45½. Lengths, 40 to 45 inches. See special size scale above. State size wanted. Shipping weight, 5 pounds 2 ounces.
10 G 422—Copper brown. Mink dyed Mandel fur.
10 G 424—Gracklehead (medium) blue. Raccoon dyed Mandel fur.
10 G 426—Medium tan. Mink dyed Mandel fur. **$22.98**

Luxurious Model
Gracious New Lines Genuine Vicuna Fur

10 G 440 Deep-piled Seal Bloom Bolivia fabric, with just enough cotton in its weave to give it durable wearing qualities. The large luxurious shawl collar and deep cuffs are of genuine brown Vicuna Fur. It is longhaired, very full and closely resembles the expensive fox.
A smart and fashionable feature is the insertion of self material that runs around the entire body of the coat and fastens in front with a large button and loop. The sleeves also have insertions of reversed material to harmonize. Saddle shoulders give an easy fit. Extra warmth is given by an interlining; convenient inner pocket. All Silk Satin lining will wear two years. This model is carefully tailored and possesses both style and quality.
SPECIAL SIZES FOR LITTLE WOMEN: 33½ to 45½. Lengths, 40 to 45 inches. See size scale above. State size wanted. Ship. wt., 5 lbs. 6 oz.
10 G 440—Beaver brown.
10 G 442—Gracklehead (medium) blue.
10 G 444—Black. **$29.98**

Attractive Dress Coat
Firm Smooth Fabric—Fur Collar—Attractive Panels

10 G 428 Attractive coat of All Wool Suede Velour. Its glove-like finish and pliant texture makes it especially adaptable to fine tailoring. The full mushroom collar, becomingly shaped, is of fluffy Mandel Fur and can be worn open or fastened close about the neck. Insertions of self material smartly trim the sides of the coat and are finished with diamond shaped clusters of Silk Floss stitching. Corresponding inserts are on the sleeves. Saddle shoulders and tailored turnback cuffs. Lining of high grade mercerized fabric that will give two seasons' wear. Inside pocket. An interlining for extra warmth.
SPECIAL SIZES FOR LITTLE WOMEN: 33½ to 45½. Lengths, 40 to 45 in. Size scale above. State size. Ship. wt., 5 lbs. 8 oz.
10 G 428—Reindeer (dark) tan. Mink dyed Mandel fur.
10 G 430—Gracklehead (medium) blue. Raccoon dyed Mandel fur.
10 G 432—Cranberry red. Mink dyed Mandel fur. **$15.98**

The Fuller Figure Finds Slender Lines
In This Proper New Designing

French Coney Fur

Manchurian Wolf Dog

Mandel Fur

Mandel Fur

10 G 394
Silk Seal Plush
$23.98

10 G 382
All Wool Polaire
$9.98

10 G 386
Silk Seal Plush
$32.98

10 G 388
All Wool Suede Velour
$16.98

Manchurian Wolf Dog Fur

10 G 0396
Seal Bloom Bolivia
$29.98

A Value Masterpiece
Extra Warm—Serviceable Tailored Wool Polaire

10 G 382 It's hard to realize, isn't it, that such Coat value is actually to be had at only $9.98! At Ward's only—and nowhere else, we believe—can you find such style value!

Everyone knows the sturdy qualities of a good All Wool Polaire, and this is an extra heavy winter weight, lined with a durable mercerized twill. Notice its smart conservative lines—especially slenderizing. The underarm panels follow a very trim hip line, marked with dressy buttons. Plaits, cord tucks and stitchery panel are evidence of good tailoring. Two button closing, and warm slot pockets.

The full convertible collar and deep cuffs of lustrous French Coney—which you could not ordinarily get in a coat of this price. Length, about 47 inches.
EXTRA SIZES: 39, 41, 43, 45, 47, 49, 51, 53-inch bust. State bust measure. Read "How to Order" on Page 51. Ship. wt., 6 lbs. 12 oz.
10 G 382—Dark brown.
10 G 384—Reindeer (dark) Tan $9.98

Queenly Winter Model
With a Luxury of Warmth in the Silk Seal Plush

10 G 386 Manchurian Wolf Dog—the fur of long haired brilliant beauty—against the soft pile of gleaming Silk Seal Plush, makes this a quality coat; as warm and serviceable as it is luxuriously rich and beautiful!

The best of everything that enters into its making—that's the secret of this coat's outstanding value! Its styling—superbly simple; its finish—a tribute to our newer standard of perfect tailoring. Warm, as you know, yet for double protection, a cozy interlining. Charmingly lined with a Silk Mixed Jacquard of dressy pattern, carefully protected with a kicker lining of black Sateen.

Full roomy lines, youthfully straight; with soft sweep of shawl collar to the dressy button and loop closing. Two slot pockets; deep turned back cuffs with button trimmed points. Length, about 47 inches.
EXTRA SIZES: 39, 41, 43, 45, 47, 49, 51, 53-inch bust. State bust. Read "How to Order" on Page 51. Ship. wt., 6 oz.
10 G 386—Black only. $32.98

A Worthwhile Bargain
Service Counts With Style in This Wool Suede Velour

10 G 388 "Remarkable," you'll say, "in style and finish for a Coat priced so moderately!" Particularly youthful, because of its stunning convertible "Johnny" collar of fluffy Mandel fur.

All Wool Suede Velour—the fabric with a fine finish and firm weave, indicative of long, and satisfactory service. Interlined for extra warmth and practically lined with a lustrous high grade mercerized fabric, good for two seasons. Convenient inside pocket. Carefully tailored, with graceful saddle shoulders, ample sleeve room, and neat turn back cuffs. Very dressy slender side panels, outlined in dome shape by tailor cord tucks and worked in a rich panel motif of silk floss. Length, about 47 inches.
EXTRA SIZES: 39, 41, 43, 45, 47, 49, 51, 53-inch bust. State bust measure. Read "How to Order" on Page 51. Ship. weight, 6 pounds.
10 G 388—Dark brown. Mink dyed Mandel fur.
10 G 390—Gracklehead (medium) blue. Raccoon dyed Mandel fur.
10 G 392—Rust. Mink dyed Mandel fur. $16.98

Unusually Low Priced
For a Silk Seal Plush Coat With Mandel Fur Trimming

10 G 394 Indeed lovely! It comes in All Black Silk Seal Plush of smooth glossy pile, heightened by a most attractive large convertible collar with fashionable cuffs to match of fluffy Mandel fur, dyed to smartly resemble the more expensive raccoon.

A coat to serve you well and long, adding a distinct note of conservative richness to your every costume. Carefully made; with sleeves well set in and roomy, for fuller figure ease. The lines are youthfully straight—though ample everywhere, and the single button closing is graciously soft. Warmly interlined.

Attractively lined with a durable Silk Mixed Jacquard, with deep kicker lining of Sateen for added protection. Inside pocket. Length, about 47 inches.
EXTRA SIZES: 39, 41, 43, 45, 47, 49, 51, 53-inch bust. State bust measure. Read "How to Order" on Page 51. Ship. wt., 5 lbs. 12 oz.
10 G 394—Black only. $23.98

Rich—Conservative—Dressy
Carefully Priced New Idea Model Typical of our Superior Values

10 G 0396 Those who know this smooth lovely Seal Bloom Bolivia are enthusiastic about its deep pile and velvety warm texture. Has just enough cotton for long wear. Those who know the cost of a good, dependable fur will be delighted with the full mushroom collar of long, brilliant-haired Manchurian Wolf Dog; carefully selected pelts, set on with expert care.

Carefully tailored on slenderizing, conservative lines, with distinctive side panels of the reverse material, inset with deep single side plaits, and enriched with stitching and fine cord tucks. Smooth-fitting saddle shoulders. Warm interlining, beneath the attractive Silk Mixed Brocade lining, which will give two seasons of service. Convenient inner pocket. Length, about 47 inches.
EXTRA SIZES: 39, 41, 43, 45, 47, 49, 51, 53-inch bust. State bust. Read "How to Order" on Page 51. Shipping weight, 6 lbs. 2 oz.
10 G 0396—Black.
10 G 0398—Dark brown.
10 G 0400—Gracklehead (medium) blue $29.98

5

Fur Brings Style
Warmth and Luxury at Modest Prices

Brown Fox Collar

810 G 346 Same Model Self Collar $184.50

Brown Fox Collar

810 G 350 Same Model Self Collar $89.50

Mendoza Beaver
Mushroom Collar of Fox or Self Pelts

810 G 348 Now, at our low price, every woman can gratify her longing to be wrapped in luxurious fur. A fine Fur Coat is really economical, for, besides its additional warmth and beauty, it wears many seasons longer than the average cloth. The Mendoza Beaver, a rich, full furred Coney, sheared and dyed to resemble beaver, is stayed (specially reinforced) which prevents ripping and greatly increases its strength.

Here are the fashionable wrap-around lines preferred by well-dressed New York women. Mushroom collar of self fur, or for just a few dollars more of handsome, long haired Genuine Brown Fox! Lined with a heavy quality, silk mixed Poplin, and warmly interlined. An attractive little pocket is placed in the lining for your convenience. Finished with wide, turnback cuffs of Mendoza Beaver, and fastened with two attractive buttons and loops. Length, about 45 inches.

WOMEN'S SIZES: 34, 36, 38, 40, 42, 44-inch bust. State bust measure. Read "How to Order" on Page 51. Shipping weight, 5 pounds.

810 G 348—Brown Mendoza beaver with brown fox collar. $99.75
810 G 350—Brown Mendoza beaver with self collar. $89.50

810 G 348 Mendoza Beaver Fox Collar $99.75

810 G 342 American Opossum $125.00

810 G 344 Genuine Muskrat Fox Collar $198.75

10 G 31 Raccooney $49.95

10 G 352 Silverette Coney
10 G 354 Mink Dyed Coney $49.95

Jaunty Tomboy Coat
In Natural Opossum Popular Everywhere

810 G 342 The swagger style so much in evidence on college campuses—the Tomboy Coat with the jaunty, youthful air admired by every woman and miss! Full-furred, selected American Opossum skins, with the heavy, shaggy appearance characteristic of expensive raccoon which can stand much rough usage without showing signs of wear.

An important feature of this coat—and additional proof of its superior quality—is the long roll shawl collar, furred on both sides so it can be turned up high around the head when wintry winds demand additional protection. Sporty, double-breasted style, with deep slot pockets and smart leather buttons. Lined below waist with All Wool Plaid in an attractive pattern; bottom and yoke lined with Skinner's satin. Interlined.

This handsome coat will amply repay you, in pleasure and comfort, for the money invested. It will wear beautifully for years, and considering its fine quality and workmanship, is a real bargain. Length, about 45 inches.

WOMEN'S SIZES: 34, 36, 38, 40, 42, 44-inch bust. State bust measure. Read "How to Order" on Page 51. Shipping weight, 5 pounds.

810 G 342—American Opossum (raccoon shade). $125.00

Genuine Muskrat
Our Finest Fur Coat Style and Quality at a Saving

810 G 344 Sumptuously warm and lovely—this beautiful Fur Coat is the pride of our infinitely Finer Coat Shop. It brings you our new message of Quality and Finer Workmanship which assures lasting, beautiful style.

Genuine Muskrat in all its natural ombre shading. Only perfectly matched, selected skins are used in herring bone effect. Every skin reinforced with exacting care to prevent pulling apart.

Buying from our New Coat Shop, you receive superior quality—even though you pay much less here than you would elsewhere. You may select the large mushroom collar, in Natural Muskrat to match the coat or, for a few dollars more, in long-haired Genuine Fox, dyed a rich brown shade. Full cut on straight, slender lines and closes with two buttons. Well interlined, under its rich lining of long-wearing, All Silk Flat Crepe. Useful pocket in lining, strengthened at bottom with Chenille. Length, about 45 inches.

WOMEN'S SIZES: 34, 36, 38, 40, 42, 44-inch bust. State bust measure wanted. Read "How to Order" on Page 51. Shipping weight, 6 pounds.

810 G 344—Muskrat with brown fox collar. $198.75
810 G 346—Muskrat with self collar. $184.50

All the Appearance of an Expensive Coat
Everybody Thinks It's Natural Raccoon

10 G 31 Enjoy the pleasure and extra warmth of a beautiful, real Fur Coat, for hardly more than the price of a presentable cloth, if you choose this fashionable Genuine Raccooney. The large dark thick-furred coney skins, skillfully dyed to represent the expensive raccoon—are jointed with the utmost care to bring out their full beauty, and are firmly stayed (specially reinforced) to prevent separating. Large mushroom collar of Genuine Raccooney. The coat is finished expertly in every detail and lined, over a good warm interlining, with an attractive, serviceable, silk-mixed brocade. Protective wind shields are provided at the wrists. Two smart buttons and loops. Length, about 45 inches.

WOMEN'S SIZES: 34, 36, 38, 40, 42, 44, 46-inch bust. State bust measure. Read "How to Order" on Page 51. Shipping weight, 5 pounds.

10 G 31—Raccooney (resembling raccoon). $49.95

Extraordinary Value for Dressy Wear
Truly a Marvel at the Price

10 G 352 The exceedingly pretty stripings of Silverette Coney and Mink Dyed Coney rival the beauty of natural muskrat, in this coat. Roomy, wrap-around style is smart, and twice as warm in front. You'll be proud to throw the coat back to show the handsome two-color, silk-mixed Jacquard lining with its plaited inside pocket and bright silk braid. Large mushroom collar of self fur protects you from cold. Interlined, of course, for extra warmth. Two buttons, front closing. All skins firmly stayed, a special reinforcement to prevent separating. Length, about 45 inches.

WOMEN'S SIZES: 34, 36, 38, 40, 42, 44, 46-inch bust. State bust measure. Read "How to Order" on Page 51. Shipping weight, 5 lbs.

10 G 352—Silverette coney.
10 G 354—Mink dyed coney. $49.95

Luxurious Furs Sheer Beauty
All The Dependable Qualities

Marmot Fur and Silk Seal Plush

Charmingly Dignified Rich Brocade Lining

10 G 332 Sure to please—because it combines attractive appearance—sturdy wearing qualities—and comfort giving warmth—the "one, two, three" of what the thoughtful woman desires in her coat!

An excellent example of our New Idea Coats, which have gained thousands of friends and permanent patrons within the short space of a year.

Rich deep pile Silk Seal Plush, carefully tailored throughout. The charming mushroom collar and cuffs are of selected Marmot Fur, beautiful in quality and pleasing in combination with the gleaming Plush. Set-in sleeves are cut to give perfect fit and comfort and the sweeping revers end in a dressy button-and-loop closing. Well interlined, which gives it abundant warmth, sure protection against cold weather. The lining of Silk Mixed Brocade in an attractive pattern, will wear at least two seasons. There is a convenient little inner pocket. Length, about 46 inches. **WOMEN'S SIZES:** 34, 36, 38, 40, 42, 44, 46-inch bust. State bust measure. Read "How to Order" on Page 51. Ship. wt., 6 pounds 8 ounces. **10 G 332**—Black only. **$29.95**

Marmot Fur

Moufflon Fur

Mandel Fur

10 G 332 Silk Seal Plush $29.95

Moufflon Fur

Manchurian Wolf Dog

10 G 334 Caracul Fur Fabric $14.50

10 G 336 Silk Seal Plush $24.98

Caracul Fur Fabric
Practical—Inexpensive

Warm and Comfortable Splendidly Tailored

10 G 334 The thrifty woman who takes into consideration style, material and wearing qualities as well as price will be quick to appreciate this particularly fine value! What wonderful style and comfort she'll receive for her small investment.

Caracul Fur Fabric that strongly resembles the expensive Caracul Fur, of sturdy texture—warmth giving and enduring. An interlining gives greater protection against the cold. Convertible collar of soft Raccoon dyed Moufflon Fur can be worn open or closed about the neck. Simulated cuffs; button and loop front closing. Coat is cut on straight youthfully slenderizing lines. Fancy Sateen makes an attractive and durable lining, with inner pocket for convenience. Length, about 46 inches. **WOMEN'S SIZES:** 34, 36, 38, 40, 42, 44, 46-inch bust. State bust measure. Read "How to Order" on Page 51. Ship. wt., 5 lbs. 12 oz. **10 G 334**—Black only. **$14.50**

Silk Seal Plush
With Shawl Collar

Collar and Cuffs of Mandel Fur

10 G 336 For Milady who knows quality—this model of high grade deep pile fabric Silk Seal Plush, so warm, comfortable and rich in appearance! The long shawl collar and cuffs are of soft Mandel Fur dyed a Raccoon shade in smart contrast to the body of the coat.

Exceptionally well cut and beautifully tailored—as you see. Fastened with dressy button and loop. An attractive lining of Silk Mixed Jacquard with a kicker of Sateen will give two seasons' attractive wear. An interlining gives additional warmth, making the coat doubly protective against cold weather. Inner pocket for convenience. Has much of the warmth and appearance of a real fur coat. Length, about 46 inches. **WOMEN'S SIZES:** 34, 36, 38, 40, 42, 44, 46-inch bust. State bust measure. Read "How to Order Information" on Page 51. Shipping weight, 5 pounds 14 ounces. **10 G 336**—Black only. **$24.98**

10 G 338 Silk Seal Plush $18.98

10 G 340 Hudson Seal Plush $49.95

Silk Seal Plush—Fashionable Moufflon Fur
A Beautiful and Enduring Economy

10 G 338 Handsome—very inexpensive—and its service record will make it an unusually practical buy. A high grade deep-pile fabric Silk Seal Plush. The warm interlining will prove its comfort when the mercury drops. Large mushroom collar and cuffs of fluffy gray Moufflon Fur are sure to be becoming to the wearer.

Coat closes with a button and loop fastening. Exceedingly pretty lining of Silk Mixed Jacquard will give two seasons' wear. Inside pocket—a convenience to hold small articles. Exceptionally big value for the money—a coat you will wear and wear with the utmost satisfaction. Length, about 46 inches. **WOMEN'S SIZES:** 34, 36, 38, 40, 42, 44, 46-inch bust. State bust measure. Read "How to Order" on Page 51. Shipping weight, 5 pounds 10 ounces. **10 G 338**—Black only. **$18.98**

Hudson Seal Plush—Incomparable Fur Substitute
Sumptuously Dressed with Manchurian Wolf Dog

10 G 340 Quality in style, fine fabric and workmanship that will delight the woman who is looking for value! This high grade model is of Hudson Seal Plush—an unusually deep-pile fabric closely resembling the expensive genuine seal fur. This smart and attractive garment with its high luster appearance and assured wearing qualities will be a constant joy to the wearer. The deep shawl collar and cuffs are of Black Manchurian Wolf Dog—a rich long haired fur. Excellent cut and set in sleeves assure an easy fit. A fine interlining gives added warmth. A lining of Brocaded Silk Mixed Faille will give two seasons' wear. Inner pocket. About everything you'll find in a fur coat—appearance, warmth, comfort. Length, about 46 inches. **WOMEN'S SIZES:** 34, 36, 38, 40, 42, 44, 46-inch bust. State bust measure. Read "How to Order" on Page 51. Shipping weight, 7 pounds 6 ounces. **10 G 340**—Black only. **$49.95**

For Misses ~ Great Style Authorities Contribute to the New Idea ~

SPONSORED by Miss New York who sees the world and sets the youthful fashion pace! Our "New Idea" Coats for Misses are an education—a revelation!

They train her swiftly developing eye for truer style and finish, her touch for finer fabric quality, and turn her mind toward the wisdom of economy through value received.

In all our Newer Coats she will find the buoyant lines of Youth, wrought with the ineffable charm of simplicity, which should characterize every youthful style.

Mandel Fur

10 G 446
All Wool Suede Velour
$19.98

Beaverette Fur

10 G 452
All Wool Sports Tweed
$14.95

Mandel Fur

Mandel Fur

10 G 456
Wool Velour
$9.98

10 G 462
All Wool Buxkin Suede
$19.75

Beaverette Fur

Of Simple Beauty
All Wool Suede Velour Mandel Fur Trimmed

10 G 446 The miss who selects this beautiful Coat will feel the luxury of its warmth equally with the pride of its moderate cost. All Wool Suede Velour, smooth and soft, yet firmly woven. It tailors to perfection and is remarkably warm. Beneath its dressy lining of Rayon Faced Jacquard, strong enough for two seasons, is a warm interlining.

A superior quality Mandel Fur—soft and very fluffy—makes the beautiful deep shawl collar and dressy cuffs. Very smart side panel lines with attractive over-strape of self material, button trimmed. Lining pocket. Length, about 43 inches.
MISSES' SIZES: 14, 16, 18, 20 years: 32, 34, 36, 38-inch bust. State size wanted. Read "How to Order" on Page 51. Ship. wt., 3 lbs. 10 oz.
10 G 446—Reindeer brown. Mink dyed Mandel fur.
10 G 448—Gracklehead (medium) blue. Raccoon dyed Mandel fur.
10 G 450—Cranberry red. Mink dyed Mandel fur.
$19.98

↑A Knockabout Coat
All Wool Sports Tweed With Big Johnny Collar

10 G 452 For all her knockabout wear, here is the swagger choice of the campus girls and New York business girls who brave all weathers.

Big Woolly warm model in an All Wool Sports Tweed Coating of heavy winter weight, savoring of the jaunty English sports weaves. Typical belted sports style, with big Johnny collar, easy raglan shoulders, turnback tab cuffs and big patch pockets. Snappy buttons, detachable self belt with novelty buckle. Warmly interlined, under its lustrous durable Satin de Chine lining. Length, about 43 inches.
MISSES' SIZES: 14, 16, 18, 20 years: 32, 34, 36, 38-inch bust. State size wanted. Read "How to Order" on Page 51. Shipping weight, 3 pounds 12 ounces.
10 G 452—Tan mixture.
10 G 454—Gray mixture. **$14.95**

Dressy—Priced Low
Wool Velour with Smart Contrasting Trim

10 G 456 A beautiful economy Coat. Warm smooth faced Wool Velour with a small amount of sturdy cotton in its weave to make it wear longer. Remarkably dressy big cuffs, pocket inserts and deep simulated button-holes of contrasting Velour. Topped with a billowy mushroom collar of soft silky Mandel Fur. Practical mercerized twill lining; warmly interlined. Length, about 43 inches.
MISSES' SIZES: 14, 16, 18, 20 years; 32, 34, 36, 38-inch bust. State size wanted. Read "How to Order" on Page 51. Shipping weight, 3 pounds 6 ounces.
10 G 456—Reindeer (dark) tan. Mink dyed Mandel fur, dark brown trimmed.
10 G 458—Gracklehead (medium) blue. Raccoon dyed Mandel fur, navy blue trimming.
10 G 460—Cranberry red. Mink dyed Mandel fur, brickdust trimming. **$9.98**

All Wool Velour
Value for Your Money In Style—Fabric—Finish ←

10 G 468 Maintaining the best possible quality for the price, this Coat will entirely satisfy you for a surprisingly small sum! Well tailored from a smooth face All Wool Velour, with a warm interlining and a lustrous durable mercerized lining, which will serve you well for two seasons. Convenient inner pocket. Dressy mushroom collar and cuffs are of silky Beaverette Fur (sheared coney). Trim smart inverted plait side panels, with stitching and cloth covered buttons. Length, about 43 inches.
MISSES' SIZES: 14, 16, 18, 20 years; 32, 34, 36, 38-inch bust. State size wanted. Read "How to Order" instructions on top of Page 51. Shipping weight, 3 pounds 6 ounces.
10 G 468—Reindeer (dark) tan.
10 G 470—Brickdust.
10 G 472—Gracklehead (medium) blue. **$12.75**

A Distinctive Style
Novel Stitching All Wool Buxkin Suede ↑

10 G 462 Beautiful Dress Coat of fine All Wool Buxkin Suede. Warm winter weight; superior glove-smooth weave. Lovely new side panel treatments. Rich fat flares of floss stitching spreading to arrowheads above slender inverted plaits. A single row for the dressy wide revers below the billowy collar of Mandel Fur. Stunning big turnback cuffs. Warm interlining. Dressy lining of Rayon faced Jacquard will wear two seasons. Length, about 43 inches. Inner pocket.
MISSES' SIZES: 14, 16, 18, 20 years; 32, 34, 36, 38-inch bust. State size wanted. Read "How to Order" on Page 51. Shipping weight, 3 pounds 2 ounces.
10 G 462—Reindeer (dark) tan. Mink dyed Mandel fur.
10 G 464—Rose. Mink dyed Mandel fur.
10 G 466—Canton (dark Copenhagen) blue. Raccoon dyed Mandel fur. **$19.75**

10 G 468
All Wool Velour
$12.75

Economy and Value Are in This Coat
All Wool Velour With Dressy Beaverette Fur →

10 G 474 Not a soul will guess that the Miss who wears this Coat is practicing strict economy—for it really looks dollars more than its moderate cost. Carefully tailored from smooth All Wool Velour, and dressed up with a soft warm half shawl collar and deep cuffs of silky Beaverette fur (sheared coney). Warmly interlined; well lined with lustrous mercerized fabric, good for two seasons. Inside lining pocket. Trim neat side panels—with side plaits finished with silky floss arrowheads. Length, about 43 inches.
MISSES' SIZES: 14, 16, 18, 20 years; 32, 34, 36, 38-inch bust. State size wanted. Read "How to Order" on Page 51. Shipping weight, 3 pounds 6 ounces.
10 G 474—Reindeer (dark) tan.
10 G 476—Gracklehead blue.
10 G 478—Brickdust. **$11.98**

10 G 474
All Wool Velour
$11.98

Style Satisfaction~
This New High Standard
of Excellence
Makes It Sure~

Lyons Velvet—Rayon Facing

$2.98 **512G106**—Will fit heads 21¼ to 22 inches. Ship. wt., 1 lb. 14 oz.
COLORS: Black; monkey skin (rose tan); golden brown; Copenhagen blue; meadow pink; almond green. State color wanted.

What a perfect combination of dignity and charming femininity in this handsome Hat! The season's vogue for tall, distinguished lines is cleverly achieved by a cuff of Lyons Velvet, tipped with a bright Rayon facing, extending above the sectional crown. A wide band of harmonizing, lustrous Rayon satin ribbon softly drapes the hat and ties in a gracious bow. Rayon lining.

Smartly Blocked Wool Felt

$1.69 **512G108**—Will fit heads about 20¾ to 21½ inches. Shipping weight, 1 pound 14 ounces.
COLORS: Black; monkey skin (rose tan); Copenhagen blue; gooseberry (light) green; Castilian red; sand; gull gray (pearl). State color wanted.

Fifth Avenue shops display Hats of this type at prices which emphasize this value at our price! This All Wool Felt has the same custom-tailored front brim and hand-draped crown as an expensive hat; the two-tone Rayon grosgrain band and cocarde are just as carefully matched, in spite of the modest price. Finished with sweatband.

The New Felt "Cavalier"

$1.79 **512G110**—Will fit heads 21½ to 22¼ inches. Ship. wt., 2 lbs. 5 oz.
COLORS: Black; sand; wild honey (light wood brown); Copenhagen blue; navy blue. State color wanted.

Always in good taste for tailored wear, sports or travel; and, most important of all, becoming to all types. Of All Wool felt, the new creased crown banded with a clever, metal-buckled belt.

Same Model—Fur Velour

$3.29 **512G112**—Colors and sizes same as above. State color.

For better wear, silky velour with grosgrain band and bow, and colorful vagabond feather.

Modish Close-Fitting Cloche

$2.48 **152G114**—Will fit heads 21¼ to 22 inches. Ship. wt., 2 lbs. 4 oz.
COLORS: Sand with wild honey (light wood brown); Castilian red with black; gull gray (pearl) with navy blue; Copenhagen blue with dark Copenhagen blue; also all black. State color.

Snappy lines, jaunty trimming, fashionable colors! This is just the Hat for the particular miss and young woman who keep abreast of the times. Of double-faced All Wool felt, with a dashing quill the color of the upper brim. Bands of Rayon grosgrain ribbon circle the elaborately tucked close-fitting crown, and form the circlet through which the jainty quill is thrust.

Modified Ripple Brim

$2.29 **512G128**—Will fit heads 20¾ to 21½ inches. Ship. wt., 2 lbs. 4 oz.
COLORS: Sand and wood brown; black; gull gray (pearl); golden brown; al o Copenhagen blue with navy blue or almond green with balsam (dark) green. State color wanted.

For the woman or miss whose features require softer curves than are afforded by severe tailored Hats—a ripple brim model blocked of All Wool Handkerchief Felt that is much in vogue! The creased crown with its tam-effect fold at the back also favors softer contours. The Rayon belting band is embellished with flat, corner tacked bow. An exceptional value, as this fine new Felt is soft and non-crushable. Sweatband. A New Idea Hat in quality and finish.

Two Head Sizes

Lyons Velvet and Satin Tam

$2.98 **512G116**—Will fit heads 21¾ to 22½ inches.
512G118—Will fit heads 22¼ to 23½ inches.
Ship. wt., 2 pounds 5 ounces.
COLORS: Black with crabapple; black with Copenhagen blue; golden brown with sand; Canton (bright) blue with gray; or balsam (dark) green with gooseberry green. State color wanted.

The popularity of this medium-sized mushroom Hat is accounted for in the flattering sweep of its curves. Contrasting color of Rayon taffeta facing sheds a bright glow over the face. Lyons velvet, alternately placed around brim and crown, with tam effect of corded satin is drawn down by a jeweled pin over fluted, fan shaped moire ribbon trimming at the right. Rayon lining.

New Mode in Lyons Velvet

$2.98 **512G120**—Will fit heads 21¼ to 22 inches.
512G122—Will fit heads 22¼ to 23 inches.
Ship. wt., 1 pound 14 ounces.
COLORS: Black; golden brown; sand; Castilian red; navy blue; Copenhagen blue. All with assorted color ribbons to harmonize. State color wanted.

A pleasing product of our newer, better millinery—the New Idea! Lustrous Lyons velvet, without the usual stiffening to pucker and break; it may be depended upon to hold its becoming lines. New plaited-side brim rolls smartly off the face. Tri-color crescent insets in crown, caught with double-headed, jeweled pin, match Rayon grosgrain cocarde and band.

Two Head Sizes

Rich Lyons Velvet Model

$2.48 **512G124**—Will fit heads 21¼ to 22 inches.
512G126—Will fit heads 22¼ to 23 inches. Ship. wt., each, 1 lb. 14 oz.
COLORS: Black; balsam (dark) green; monkey skin (rose tan); golden brown; Copenhagen blue. State color wanted.

A band of harmonizing Rayon grosgrain ribbon, bordered with a metallic brocade, joins the narrow satin brim—shading the eyes in front, and rolling gracefully up at back—to the semi-tam crown of rich Lyons velvet. A fancy metal pin completes the trimming. This attractive French model is reproduced at a fraction of its import cost.

Be Sure to Send Exact Head Size *See Page 33*

Mirrored Velvet and Rayon

$1.89 **512G130**—Will fit heads 22¼ to 23 inches. Shipping weight, 2 pounds 13 ounces.
COLORS: Black with Copenhagen blue; black with Crabapple; meadow pink (rose); Copenhagen blue; Castilian red; wild honey (light wood brown) with sand. State color.

Amazing value for dress wear—such a handsome picture Hat for the small sum of $1.89! Enjoy the luxury of hats to match your frocks when you can complete a perfect costume at small expense. Mirrored Velvet and Rayon with draped crown. A festoon of Rayon ribbon and applique flowers across front. Mercerized facing in matching or contrasting colors. Full lined.

Lyons Velvet—Rayon Taffeta

$3.48 **512G132**—Will fit heads 21¾ to 22½ inches. Shipping weight, 1 pound 14 ounces.
COLORS: Black with Copenhagen blue; wild honey (light wood brown) with coral; navy blue with Castilian red; monkey skin (rose tan) with wood brown; also all black with contrasting flower. State color wanted.

Artistically blended colors in the unusual velvet flower appliques—in the silk hand stitchery against a background of velvet and Rayon taffeta—in the alternating shades of rich Lyons velvet of the draped crown—give this flattering turban an air of subtle charm. Equally appropriate with dressy frock or tailored costume! Rayon lined.

Lyons Velvet and Satin

$2.98 **512G134**—Will fit heads 21¼ to 22 inches.
COLORS: Black; golden brown; balsam (dark) green; monkey skin (rose tan). State color wanted. Ship. wt., 1 lb. 14 oz.

True Parisian chic characterizes this little Hat with its snug fitting, new panelled crown in which the dull surface of deep pile Lyons velvet is a soft contrast for the gleaming satin.

Its coquettish lines will appeal irresistibly to the woman who appreciates individuality. From the satin faced brim of velvet, a soft feather tassel droops caressingly against the cheek. The Rayon satin ribbon which encircles the crown is plaited into a smart cocarde above the feather. Rayon lined.

Every Hat We Show Is Designed
Either in Paris or New York

Gleaming Satin with Wool Felt

$1.98 **512 G 52**—Will fit heads 21 to 21¼ inches. Ship. wt., 1 lb. 14 oz.
COLORS: Black; red banana (light claret); balsam (dark) green; royal blue (Canton); monkey skin (rose tan).
State color wanted.

A close fitting model in the stunning new combination of gleaming Satin and soft smooth Felt Cloth. Satin for the "Melon" sectional tip crown, with deep helmet cuff of satin-piped felt cloth. Narrow little droop brim, disappearing at right under the chic contrasting flower, is caught up at left side back, giving a cut-away effect. Rayon lined. Everyone will think you paid much more for a Hat so remarkably stylish.

Wool Felt of Unusual Design

$2.39 **512 G 54**—Will fit heads 20¾ to 21½ inches. Shipping weight, 1 lb. 14 oz.
COLORS: Sand with wood brown; black with Copenhagen blue; Copenhagen blue with navy blue; almond green with balsam (dark) green.
State color wanted.

"It's different"—she knows in her heart—this fine soft Wool Felt Hat, with entirely new inverted tuck creases in crown. Slide crown slashed and laced with grosgrain ribbons in two-tone effect, to match both hat and contrasting band. Sweatband.

A Swagger Knockabout Felt

$2.98 **512 G 58**—Will fit heads 21¼ to 22 inches. Shipping weight 2 lbs. 4 oz.
COLORS: Sand with black; Copenhagen blue with navy blue; all black; monkey skin (rose tan) with dark brown; gooseberry (light) green with balsam (dark) green. State color wanted.

Glorifying the hatband, Paris raises it to its new height, almost atop the crown. So stunning and youthful, everyone wants to wear it. Will not crush but banishes its creases as only a very fine Felt can do. Wide contrasting belting ribbon band with fashionable dangle pendant, is interlaced through high crown slashes, above rows of matching stitching in the band tone. The soft brim is set on underneath for smart new ripple. Rayon lined.

Felt Cloth—A Smart New Model

$1.95 **512 G 56**—Will fit heads 21¼ to 22 inches. Ship. wt., 1 lb. 14 oz.
COLORS: Black with crabapple; monkey skin (rose tan) with wood brown; navy blue with Copenhagen blue; gooseberry (light) green with sand; Castilian red with sand. State color wanted.

Expensive Fifth Avenue Hats feature this new model, with the piquant slashed brim. Fashioned of Felt Cloth with crown richly embroidered in a harmonizing shade of Ribbonzene Braid, softly gathered at the top and creased across the back to fit the head snugly. The brim, which has many rows of self color machine stitching, tapers off the back, and is finished with six metallic ball buttons at right. Rayon lined.

Two Head Sizes

Send Us Exact Head Size
See Page 33

Rich Lyons Velvet and Satin

$3.29 **512 G 64**—Will fit heads 21¾ to 22½ inches.
512 G 464—Will fit heads 22¾ to 23½ inches.
COLORS: Black with crabapple or Copenhagen blue; marron glace (cocoa brown) with monkey skin (rose tan) facing. State color wanted. Shipping weight, 2 pounds 5 ounces.

Beautifully made! The materials alternate in the smooth barrel crown; upper brim of satin flanged with velvet. A contrasting Rayon underbrim facing repeats the hue of the flower finishing the band and bow of double faced ribbon. Rayon lined.

Lyons Velvet—Diagonally Tucked

$2.98 **512 G 66**—Will fit heads 21 to 21¾ in. Ship. wt., 1 lb. 14 oz.
COLORS: All Black. Also monkey skin (rose tan) with coral; gooseberry green; Castilian red; golden brown; Canton (medium) blue with sand. State color wanted.

Interesting Hat of fine soft Lyons Velvet tucked in diagonal effect. The dressy crown has a fan flare of velvet, piped in the contrasting tone of the brim insertion, and edged with a fluting of grosgrain Rayon Ribbon to match the band. Off-the-face brim of Rayon faced with velvet, cutaway at back. Rayon lined.

Two Head Sizes

Popular Semi-Poke Velvet

$2.39 **512 G 70**—Will fit heads 21¼ to 22½ inches.
512 G 470—Will fit heads 23¼ to 24 inches.
Ship. wt., 2 lbs. 5 oz.
COLORS: Black with crabapple; golden brown with sand; Copenhagen blue; Castilian red; or monkey skin (rose tan). State color wanted.

Another very fine value! For those who can best wear the flattering cup brim and semi-soft drape crown. Well made from a good quality soft, dressy velvet, with a self tone or contrasting Rayon underfacing for the poke brim, cutaway at back.

The front crown is enriched with a radiant fruit and flower applique, starred with points of ribbonzene. Narrow grosgrain Rayon ribbon makes the dressy little band with slant loop bow. We doubt if you could duplicate this value. Rayon lined.

New York Pays Twice the Price for This Swagger Sports Hat

$1.59 **512 G 68**—Will fit heads 21 to 21¼ inches. Ship. wt., 2 lbs. 4 oz.
COLORS: Black; sand; wild honey (light wood brown); gull gray (pearl); red banana (light claret); Canton (bright) blue. State color wanted.

To verify the unquestioned quality in which we are offering our new and finer Hats, we are making an example of this stunning model for only $1.59.

Smooth, soft Wool Felt—non-crushable—may be rolled and carried any way you like. Just the style New York is showing in its exclusive shops. Roomy, comfortable, light; delightful for sports or any informal wear. Its swagger droop brim ripples faintly toward its shorter back. Stunning adjustable self "buckle belt." Sweatband.

Two Head Sizes

Swagger Sports Comfort

$1.98 **512 G 72**—Will fit heads 21¼ to 22½ inches.
512 G 74—Will fit heads 22¾ to 23½ inches.
COLORS: Monkey skin (rose tan) with dark brown; black; red banana (light claret); sand with dark brown; Copenhagen blue. State color wanted. Shipping weight, 2 pounds 4 ounces.

Notice the size range in this good looking model of smooth wool felt. Large roomy lines; wider rolling brim, turned up at back. Center crown ridge with entirely new horseshoe crease, leaving the front plain and smooth. A very unusual cigarette-and-tuck fancy finishes the wide grosgrain band. Sweatband.

Close-Fitting—Very Chic

$1.99 **512 G 76**—Fits heads 21¼ to 22½ inches.
512 G 476—Fits heads 22¾ to 23½ inches.
COLORS: Black; monkey skin (rose tan); red banana (light claret); balsam (dark) green; rose. State color wanted. Ship. wt., 1 lb. 14 oz.

Carefully made of lustrous Satin. Unadorned save for the gleaming buckle-effect ornament which clasps the little self-tone grosgrain ribbon band. Groups of fine cord tucks dress the sloping side crown. The same finish for the chic narrow droop brim, rolled up at back and caught under a clever loop fancy of ribbon. Rayon lined.

Velvet and Rayon—With Gay Gypsy Air

$2.98 **512 G 78**—Will fit heads 21¼ to 22 inches. Ship. wt., 1 pound 4 ounces.
COLORS: Black; monkey skin (rose tan); golden brown; Copenhagen blue; red banana (light claret).
State color wanted.

A Hat of such evident quality that you'll consider it one of the very finest selections you've made at anything like the price.

Radiant Gypsy stripes in bright Rayon alternate with the rich Lyons Velvet used throughout this splendid model. Velvet tip crown, cuff, and narrow droop brim rolling softly up at back to meet the crown drape. Stunning high-color ornament at front. Grosgrain Rayon band. Rayon lined. Tremendously smart in New York!

Paris and NewYork Contribute Their Ideas Here

Again the New Hat Shop Leads
Women Everywhere Voice Their Approval
of This Finer Quality

"Hats They Are Wearing on Fifth Avenue and The Bois"
—Oh, Magic Words of Fashion!

DIRECT from Paris or New York comes every charming design in the New Hat Shop. Here women may choose with the same joyous knowledge of what is smart on Fifth Avenue as though they actually journeyed to New York. For every hat was inspired by the very artists who originate the lovelier, smarter things—the styles that make the mode! Each conforms to this superb New Idea—of quality—of finer materials—of nicer workmanship—of all details—even to soft silky linings.

It is the Triumph of the New Idea! You women from coast to coast who have received the New Hat Shop with such acclaim—who have recommended it to your friends—who have written us joyously of your amazement at our "wonderful hats"—it is your triumph as well as ours! We are doubly proud to offer you again this season—the newer, finer Millinery Fashions.

**Be Sure to Give
Your Correct Head Size
Read below at right**

Fine Imported Handkerchief Felt

$3 48 **512 G 44**—Will fit heads 21¼ to 22 inches. Ship. weight, 1 lb. 14 oz.
COLORS: Black; Liberty (royal) blue; balsam (dark) green; red banana (light claret); monkey skin (rose tan). State color wanted.

Among the hundreds of new Hats sent us from Paris, it would be hard to find a lovelier one than this, with such charming, simple, molded-to-the-head lines. The hand-tucked crown could have no more flattering complement than the fine coque feather, dropping from its close-fitting, up-turned brim to caress the neck. So great is the popularity of this new feather trimming, that only by reserving great numbers of them could we be sure of enough to fill the orders of our many customers.

Fine Kerchief Felt—New Ripple Brim

$3 98 **512 G 46**—Will fit heads 21¼ to 22½ inches. Shipping weight, 2 pounds 4 ounces.
COLORS: Black; monkey skin (rose tan); balsam (dark) green; Royal blue; red banana (light claret). State color.

If you were to step into one of New York's most "English" shops which supplies noted club and sports women with their tailored hats—you would find this Hat, but at several times our price. Blocked of an Imported Handkerchief Felt in the wide, slightly rippled brim sanctioned for this type of hat, with an entirely new and decidedly different crown—fashionably creased and entirely covered with tiny French knots of yarn. A tailored model of unusual smartness from the New Quality Hat Shop, for our friends and customers who are pleased with nothing less than the best.

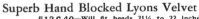

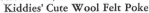

Superb Hand Blocked Lyons Velvet

$5 50 **512 G 40**—Will fit heads 21¼ to 22 inches. Shipping weight, 1 pound 14 ounces.
COLORS: Dark brown with monkey skin (rose tan); black; navy blue with gray; balsam (dark) green with almond green; Canton (medium) blue with Copenhagen blue. State color wanted.

A Hat in which every minute detail enhances the classic perfection of its skillfully molded lines! A distinguished style, identical with hats that sell for several times this price in the exclusive shops of Fifth Avenue. Its crown is of a superior quality Lyon's Velvet, hand-blocked and sure to retain its smooth lines. The brim, a triumph of the milliner's art, is of stiff belting ribbon, folding sharply off the face, tapering to a narrow turned-up back, and dipping gracefully down at the right. Three grosgrain ribbon stripes to match the brim continue its clever upward line, and finish base of crown. Rayon lined.

Kiddies' Cute Wool Felt Poke

$1 49 **512 G 42**—Will fit heads 19½ to 20¼ inches. Shipping weight, 2 pounds 3 ounces.
COLORS: Navy blue; Copenhagen blue; Castilian red; sand; black with Copenhagen blue. State color wanted.

How proud she is of her new poke Hat—just as smart as mother's. All Wool Felt with a new creased crown like a grown-up's, with a wide band of Rayon Grosgrain in checkerboard plaiting at front and a tailored finish of ends stitched up on the crown, and long flowing streamers in back. Sweatband.

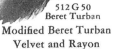

↑
512 G 48
Chatter Box
Felt

512 G 50
Beret Turban

Tailored Wool Felt
The New "Chatter Box"

$2 29 **512 G 48**—Will fit heads 21¼ to 22 inches. Ship. weight, 1 pound 14 ounces.
COLORS: All black; sand with wood brown; Copenhagen blue with dark Copenhagen blue; Castilian red with claret red; gooseberry (light) green with almond green. State color wanted.

Two of the season's most popular millinery modes combine to give this Hat added chic. First, the two helmet tucks that cross the crown from ear to ear; then the new "chatter box" brim, with the contrasting shade (except the all black) of the double-faced All Wool Felt uppermost, slashed and turned up to give the flat, brimless effect in front—folded down at the left and back. A smartly attractive pearl pin fastens the upper brim to the crown, which is banded with Rayon ribbon ending in a cocarde at right. Rayon lined.

Modified Beret Turban
Velvet and Rayon

$1 95 **512 G 50**—Will fit heads 21¼ to 22½ inches. Ship. weight, 1 pound 14 ounces.
COLORS: Wood brown with sand; almond green with gooseberry (light) green; monkey skin (rose tan); Copenhagen blue with gull gray (pearl); navy blue with sand; Castilian red with sand; all black. State color wanted.

Designed originally for the smart Parisian who understands how to make the most of her appearance, the Beret Turban is enthusiastically accepted by New York because it is so universally becoming. The pretty Velvet and Rayon Taffeta in blending or contrasting shades, or all black, are used to wonderful advantage in alternating bands, with the new corded tam effect draped over the cuddly feather pad. Rayon lined. At this remarkably low price you cannot afford to miss this value.

State Exact Head Size
Read How to Measur Below

Your Hat will be more becoming if it fits your head correctly. It is important that you give us your exact measurement. It is a simple matter to measure yourself by placing a tape line around the fullest part of your head, as shown. If you wear your hair coiled low at the neck, place the tape a trifle lower than would otherwise be necessary. Be sure the hat you order is listed in your headsize.

The New Idea Brings Misses' Hats For Every Hour of the Day~

Stunning Wool Felt

$1.59 512 G 192—Will fit heads 20¼ to 21½ inches. Shipping weight, 2 pounds 12 ounces.
COLORS: Sand with dark brown; balsam (dark) green; Castilian red; Copenhagen blue; black. State color.

Ready for smart wear with frock, suit or coat, this good looking Wool Felt Hat is appropriate for any informal wear. Has a swagger high crown, narrow turned up front brim, cutaway at back; and is strikingly finished with Rayon grosgrain band with stunning cocarde at right side. Sweatband.

Striking Two-Tone Felt

$2.49 512 G 194—Will fit heads 21¼ to 22 In. Shipping weight, 2 lbs. 4 oz.
COLORS: Sand with wild honey (wood brown); Copenhagen blue with dark Copenhagen blue; gull gray with navy blue; gooseberry green with balsam (dark) green; meadow pink with old rose. State color.

A Hat of dash and character. Two tone felt—the upper side of the droop brim carrying the second shade mentioned in colors above. New arched crown ridges caught with contrasting floss stitching. Brim turns up at back over a band of metallic stripe ribbon. Rayon lined.

Fine Soft Kerchief Felt

$2.69 512 G 196—Will fit heads 21¼ to 22 In. Ship. weight, 1 lb. 15 oz.
COLORS: Gooseberry (light) green with navy blue; Castilian red with navy blue; sand with wild honey; gull gray (pearl) with gobelin blue; or black. State color wanted.

Adopted by the smart New York Miss, it may well grace the smartest occasion. The fine soft "Kerchief" felt is impervious to crushing. Dressy little plaited brim frill of self color or contrasting belting ribbon, set on under a similar ribbon band with butterfly ends, at side. Colorful buttons. New drape-to-side crown. Rayon lined.

New Laced Brim

$1.98 512 G 198—Will fit heads 20¼ to 21½ inches. Shipping weight, 1 lb. 14 oz.
COLORS: Sand with wood brown ribbon; Castilian red with navy blue; Copenhagen blue with sand; almond green with gooseberry (light) green. Also solid black. State color.

Youthful little hood effect Hat of soft, pliable wool felt. Has its crown pinched in swirl effect; turns its cuff brim up very close, laces it with Rayon ribbon, and seals its chic with a clever lover's knot of self felt. Non-crushable. Lined with Rayon.

Lyons Velvet Poke

$2.98 512 G 200—Will fit heads 20½ to 21¼ in. 512 G 202—Will fit heads 21½ to 22¼ in. Ship. weight, 2 lbs. 5 oz.
COLORS: Black with Copenhagen blue or rose; wild honey (wood brown) with sand underbrim. Also rose; Copenhagen. State color.

Beautiful Lyons velvet; its draped crown gleaming with metallic braid and applique flowers. Contrasting streamer cocarde of Rayon ribbon. Cutaway poke brim, shirred above the Rayon facing. Rayon lined.

Velvet With Rayon Faille

$1.98 512 G 204—Will fit heads 21¼ to 22 In. Ship. weight, 2 lbs. 5 oz.
COLORS: Black with Copenhagen blue or rose; wood brown with sand; Castilian red; gooseberry green; meadow pink; gobelin blue; gull gray. State color.

Beautiful big Poke. Alternating of rich velvet and Rayon Faille—enriched with a radiant contrasting rose. Streamer band of grosgrain ribbon. Faille cutaway poke brim, with semiflange of velvet. Lined with Rayon.

Non-Crushable Wool Felt

$1.79 512 G 206—Will fit heads 20¼ to 21½ In. Shipping weight, 1 pound 14 ounces.
COLORS: Black; sand; rose; gobelin blue; golden brown. State color wanted.

So chic, soft and non-crushable, it may be tucked into your pocket or bag without a worry. Fine Wool Felt, charmingly molded to the head by means of a clever drape, held in place with a lovely gardenia. Just a touch of brim, alluringly rolled off the face. Rayon lined.

Wool Felt—Cuff Back

$1.98 512 G 208—Will fit heads 21 to 21¼ In. Ship. weight, 2 lbs. 5 oz.
COLORS: Black with Copenhagen; monkey skin (rose tan) with dark brown; gooseberry (light) green with balsam (dark) green; meadow pink with Burgundy red; Copenhagen with navy blue. State color.

Something different and very smart in a soft wool felt. Its slightly drooping narrow front brim turns up in a wider cuff effect at back. Bound with the same contrasting grosgrain Rayon ribbon which bands and laces the creased crown—up its sloping side—ends in a dashing little bow. Another two-tone effect. Sweatband.

Felt Comrade Hat

← **$1.98** 512 G 210—Will fit heads 20¾ to 21½ In. Shipping weight, 2 lbs. 5 ounces.
COLORS: Sand with dark brown; Copenhagen blue with navy blue; gooseberry (light) green with almond green; Castilian red with black. Also all black. State color wanted.

Little Comrade Hat—in delightful color combinations. Wonderfully soft smooth felt, with contrasting underbrim (second color in combinations above). Roll the soft brim as you like; it is comfortably short at back. Gypsy sash of two-tone softness.

Chic New York Felt

$2.39 512 G 214—Will fit heads 21 to 21¼ In. Shipping weight, 1 lb. 4 ounces. →
COLORS: Black; golden brown; sand; Castilian red; gobelin blue; meadow pink. State color wanted.

Another of those dashing soft wool felts which our style experts consider very unusual at the price. Molded to the head with sunburst of fine tailor tucks to mark its slight side drape. Very chic close rolled front brim, cut-in effect at back, and caught under the colorful spear pin. Lined with Rayon.

Felt Cloth Helmet Style

$1.00 512 G 216—Will fit heads 20¼ to 21½ In. Shipping weight, 1 pound 4 ounces.
COLORS: Castilian red with navy blue; sand with wild honey; Copenhagen blue with black; navy with sand; black with Castilian red. State color.

Fashion salutes the stunning Helmet Hat of feminine softness. For this is an unusually soft, non-crushable felt cloth, worth more than the $1.00 we are asking. Just as the New York Miss wears it, close fitting helmet fashion. Spear tucks to top its front crown; two-tone tab over the right ear. The same contrasting note is traced in the trio of self button appliques up the front.

This hat will serve you long after its low price has been forgotten.

Two Tones in Fine Felt ↑

$2.39 512 G 212—Will fit heads 21¼ to 22 In. Ship. wt., 2 lbs. 4 oz.
COLORS: Sand with wild honey (wood brown); Copenhagen blue with dark Copenhagen; gull gray (pearl) with Copenhagen; meadow pink with old rose; gooseberry (light) green with balsam (dark) green; black. State color.

Copied from a stunning import. Another revelation in two-tone wool felt—could anything be smarter? Entirely new chestnut-bur crease for the crown, underlined with two rows of the same bright silk floss button-hole stitching. A roguish little two-tone grosgrain ribbon cocarde finishes the double ribbon band which furthers the two-tone idea. Two-tone felt brim. Adjustable elastic back. Rayon lined.

Velvet and Rayon Tam

$1.95 512 G 218—Will fit heads 20¾ to 21½ In. Shipping weight, 1 lb. 14 oz.
COLORS: Golden brown with monkey skin (rose tan); navy blue with Castilian red; Copenhagen blue with gull gray; Castilian red with sand; black with Copenhagen blue. State color.

A quiet lovely style, to go with everything. The youthful semi-tam crown with its top of velvet, crisscrossed with gleaming soutache braid and side crown built up of alternating Rayon and velvet, sewed row on row. Modest little cuff brim of velvet, over which the crown drape is caught with a trig little Rayon ribbon—and buckle fancy. Rayon lined.

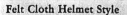

Little Daughter Also Finds Here
The Same High Standards

$1 39 512G246—Will fit heads 19¼ to 20½ in. Shipping weight, 2 lbs. 4 oz.
COLORS: Sand with Copenhagen or rose; Castilian red with navy; navy with sand; almond with sand. State color.
Dear little Poke with a ripple brim like Mother's. Of fine smooth felt cloth, with high sectional crown slashed over front—like the openwork picot-edge brim—to show the bright contrasting Rayon inserts. Same color band and full loop bow.

Imported Wool Felt
$1 45 512G248—Will fit heads 20 to 20¾ in. Shipping wt., 1 lb. 14 oz.
COLORS: Copenhagen blue; rose; Castilian red; sand; wild honey with sand; navy blue with Castilian red. State color.
Like Big Sister's and becoming, too. Dashing little model, with irregular brim turned up over left eye, slashed and turned down again, disappearing at back. Pliable imported wool felt with matching or contrasting band of Rayon grosgrain ribbon. Finished with sweatband. Equally appropriate for school or dress.

$1 19 512G250—Will fit heads 20¼ to 21 inches. Ship. wt., 1 lb. 13 oz.
COLORS: Sand; Copenhagen blue; meadow pink; Castilian red; navy blue; wild honey (light wood brown). State color.
Dressy little Hat of good quality velveteen, combined prettily with self tone Rayon, which makes the upturned brim; cutaway at back. Soft ruching of self color shirred Rayon ribbon, with band and fluttering streamer bow. Softly gathered medallion crown with colorful posy. Full lined.

Soft Felt Cloth
$1 19 512G252—Will fit heads 20½ to 21¼ in. Ship. wt., 1 lb. 14 oz.
COLORS: Sand with Copenhagen; Castilian red with navy; wild honey with sand; black with Castilian red; gooseberry (light) green with sand; navy blue with red. State color.
Soft pliable felt cloth. High sectional crown piped with the same contrasting felt which makes the upper picot edging for upturned brim. Novel coin circles, held with bright metal ornaments, alternate the combination colors. Full lined.

$1 39 512G254—Will fit heads 19¼ to 20½ in. Ship. wt., 1 lb. 14 oz.
COLORS: Sand with Copenhagen blue; Castilian red or Copenhagen blue with sand; wild honey with wood brown. State color.
Stunning little Hat with adjustable elastic back. Smooth felt cloth, with its crown fascinatingly criss-crossed with contrasting Rayon ribbon to match the graceful streamers. Velvet for the brim, with self picot edging. Full lined.

$1 59 512G256—Will fit heads 20½ to 21½ inches. Ship. wt., 1 lb. 14 oz.
COLORS: Sand; Copenhagen blue; meadow pink; Castilian red; or wild honey (wood brown). State color.
One of the smartest off-the-face Felts for the little Miss. Elastic insert at cutaway back makes it practical for the growing girl. Creased crown, with self-tone band and dressy loop under tiny felt flowers. **Ideal for school wear.**

$2 19 512G262—Will fit heads 20½ to 21¼ inches. Ship. wt., 2 lbs. 4 oz.
COLORS: Wild honey; Copenhagen; Castilian red; meadow pink; navy blue with red; black with Copenhagen or coral facing. State color.
Handsomest Dress Hat. Beautifully made from rich Lyons velvet, its shirred crown drawn into a charming wheel effect at side. Dainty poke brim (cutaway at back) faced with Rayon. Lovely streamer fancy; dainty floss stitched band.

Felt Cloth Hat
89¢ 512G258—Will fit heads 20½ to 21¼ in. Ship. wt., 1 lb. 13 oz.
COLORS: Sand; wild honey; Copenhagen blue; almond (green); Castilian red; navy blue. State color wanted.
For older sister, too—this wonder Hat of felt cloth, soft enough to tuck into her pocket. Popular skull cap style, gathered into a self covered crown button. A really "magic" picot edge brim, attached at back, adjustable over the front by means of a snappy buckle. Full lined.

Be Sure to Give Us Correct Head Size See Page 33

Soft Rich Velvet
$1 65 512G260—Will fit heads 20½ to 21¼ in. Ship. wt., 1 lb. 14 oz.
COLORS: Sand with rose; Castilian red or wood brown with sand; navy blue with Castilian red; Copenhagen blue with sand. State color wanted.
Lovely dress Hat of soft rich velvet, to flatter any little Miss. A chic streamer bow of Rayon ribbon catches the draped sectional tam crown at side. Dainty shirring of contrasting Rayon and colorful floss stitching finishes the pertly upturned brim. Full lined.

$1 98 512G264—Will fit heads 20½ to 21¼ inches. Ship. wt., 1 lb. 13 oz.
COLORS: Copenhagen blue; meadow pink; Castilian red; navy blue; sand; golden brown; all with trimming to harmonize. State color wanted.
Little Dress Hat she will love. Sectional crown and upper brim of rich mirrored velvet. Brim softly faced with shirred georgette crepe. Felt flower applique and chic rosette streamer. Elastic back.

$1 79 512G266—Will fit heads 20½ to 21¼ inches. Ship. wt., 2 lbs. 4 oz.
COLORS: Navy blue with red; wood brown with sand; sand with Copenhagen blue; balsam (dark) green with almond green; Copenhagen blue with sand; Castilian red. State color.
Soft lovely velvet with crown shirred to either side and caught under a cluster of posies. Coquettish brim, with upper facing of contrasting Rayon. Double ribbon band; two-tone effect.

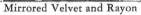

Bright Rayon at Its Loveliest
$1 69 512G268—Will fit heads 20¼ to 21½ inches. Ship. wt., 2 lbs. 4 oz.
COLORS: Copenhagen blue; meadow pink; sand; wild honey; Castilian red; navy blue. State color wanted.
Soft pretty velvet, and bright Rayon alternate in the draped tam-effect crown, to make this delightful hat, caught at side with circlet and streamer fancy of self tone Rayon ribbon. Piquant droop brim of Rayon edged with shirred Rayon ribbon.

Imported Wool Felt
$1 49 512G270—Will fit heads 20½ to 21¼ inches. Ship. wt., 2 lbs. 3 oz.
COLORS: Sand; Copenhagen blue; meadow pink; Castilian red; almond green; navy blue. State color.
A jaunty little Hat of fine soft imported wool felt, practical for school, but nice enough for dress. Carefully blocked into mushroom shape, with very smart crease from center front to back. A bright floss stitched spider spans its front and gay streamer fancy finishes its Rayon band. Drooped brim.

Mirrored Velvet and Rayon
$1 89 512G272—Will fit heads 20½ to 21¼ inches. Shipping weight, 1 lb. 13 oz.
COLORS: Sand with Copenhagen blue; meadow pink with sand; Castilian red with navy; black with pink; Copenhagen with sand. State color.
Distinctive style for her young Ladyship. Two tones double its smartness in bright mirrored velvet and lustrous Rayon. Velvet for the sectional crown. Rayon-shirred and corded for the little droop brim, its tone repeated in the front crown section latticed with narrow ribbon braid; also the band with full loop bow. Rayon lined.

Miss New York Wears Velvet
$1 95 512G274—Will fit heads 20¼ to 21 inches. Shipping weight, 2 pounds 4 ounces.
COLORS: Sand; Copenhagen blue; rose; Castilian red, also black with rose or Copenhagen underbrim and ribbon trimming. State color.
One of our loveliest Hats for her nicest occasions. This beautiful velvet takes its shirred crown with soft grace and it adds a delicate underbrim facing of shirred Rayon. The band with gay streamer bow adds a softening, youthful touch. Dainty forget-me-nots trace the outer brim. Full lined

13

Tucks—A New Fashion Feature

V Neck—Front Plaits—Geometric Tuckings

14 G 134 New York takes tucks in Fashion to produce this smartest Fifth avenue type of dress! Fine pin tuckings, used in innumerable ways to create modern geometric designs, make deep V-shaped yoke, front and back, in this Frock of All Silk "De Luxe" Flat Crepe. The collarless neckline, self piped, tapers toward the gay, bow knot flowing tie. An attractive grouping of knife and box plaits—a definitely smart feature—lends youthful grace and comfortable freedom to the skirt front. Wide tailored cuff holds the gathered sleeve. All around belt ornamented by trim pearl buckle. Sleeve openings are bound with self material and finished with utmost care, every detail giving further evidence of the superiority of the New Fashion Idea.

WOMEN'S SIZES: 34, 36, 38, 40, 42, 44-inch bust; lengths from back of neck to bottom of hem, 43 and 45 inches. State bust measure and length wanted. Read "How to Order Instructions" on top of Page 51. Shipping weight, 1 pound 12 ounces.
14 G 134—Canton (bright) blue.
14 G 136—English oak (rich brown). **$11.98**

14 G 128
All Silk
De Luxe
Crepe
Satin.
$15.00

14 G 134
All Silk
De Luxe
Flat Crepe
$11.98

See Size Scale on Page 48

14 G 156
All Silk
De Luxe
Crepe Satin
$14.98

Paquin Inspired

Uses Both Sides of the Material

14 G 128 Bright face, dull face, bright face, dull face—a dual role played by All Silk "De Luxe" Crepe Satin in this beautiful frock, following the dictates of famous French designers. The dull face, in the center panel of back, in the bands of sleeves, in the simulated front revers and the edge of the upper skirt tier, throws the bright face of the satin into glowing relief.

This frock follows a Paquin creation in its use of both sides of the fabric, and in the graceful flowing jabot of the skirt. Soft fichu effect collar of a contrasting All Silk Georgette is draped in center and finished with a long silk tassel to match. A handsome buckle gives a typical French touch between jabot and self material vestee.

WOMEN'S SIZES: 34, 36, 38, 40, 42, 44-inch bust; lengths from back of neck to bottom of wide basted hem, 43 inches. State bust measure. Read "How to Order" on Page 51. Ship. wt., 1 lb. 12 oz.
14 G 128—Black with flesh.
14 G 130—Claret red with beige. **$15.00**

Gracefully Feminine

Charmingly Trimmed With Reverse Side

14 G 140 Everything about this Frock suggests its Fifth avenue origin. Ever appealing to the American Woman who wisely chooses lines to enhance her feminine charm. All Silk "De Luxe" Crepe Satin is a glowing setting for the dull, reverse side of the fabric used in the V-shaped, waist length yokes of front and back. The tapering front is slashed for a triple V treatment of neckline, silk tasselled tie and open yoke. The dainty vestee and collar are of contrasting Silk Georgette piped with bright hued satin. A beautiful buckle, matching the tassel head in color and design, clasps an all around belt over the soft shirring of front peplum.

WOMEN'S SIZES: 34, 36, 38, 40, 42, 44-inch bust; lengths from back of neck to bottom of hem, 43 and 45 inches. State bust measure and length. Read "How to Order Instructions" on top of Page 51. Shipping weight, 1 pound 12 ounces.
14 G 140—Black with tan.
14 G 142—Mirador (dark brown) with tan. **$14.98**

14 G 140
All Silk
De Luxe
Crepe Satin
$14.98

14 G 146
All Wool
Poiret
Sheen
$11.50

Chic Suit Effect

Neatly Tailored Richly Embroidered

14 G 146 A skillful adaptation of the tailor-made suit for the more practical uses of a smart cloth frock. All Wool Poiret Sheen with vestee, collar and cuffs in a harmonizing shade of All Wool Rep. Vestee and collar are chain-stitch embroidered with Chinese medallions. Silky braid binds all edges and is set in a triple row across the front of contee effect. All around belt. Fancy buttons simulate front closing. Inverted tuckings at shoulders. The skirt has deep knife plaits at either side of front panel. Trim and practical—for business, and all smart daytime occasions.

WOMEN'S SIZES: 34, 36, 38, 40, 42, 44-inch bust; lengths from back of neck to bottom of hem, 43 and 45 inches. State bust measure and length. Read "How to Order" on Page 51. Ship. wt., 2 lbs. 1 oz.
14 G 146—Navy blue with tan.
14 G 148—Dark brown with tan. **$11.50**

14 G 150
All Silk
De Luxe
Flat Crepe
$12.98

Parisian Fashion

A French Idea—This New Two-Piece Frock

14 G 150 A double-faced beauty. Coming or going, this square-neck frock of All Silk "De Luxe" Flat Crepe is equally handsome, for the front and back are almost exactly alike, differing only with the streamer bows—Fashion's style note this season—at the front shoulder and hip, and the placing of the three inbot panels at the side front of skirt. Panels are attached to the blouse and sleeves by groups of self covered ball buttons. Skirt is attached to tub silk bodice top—Proud example of the New Idea!

WOMEN'S SIZES: 34, 36, 38, 40, 42, 44-inch bust; lengths from back of neck to bottom of hem, 43 and 45 inches. State bust measure and length. Read "How to Order Instructions" on top of Page 51. Shipping weight, 1 pound 12 ounces.
14 G 150—Marron glace (cocoa brown).
14 G 152—Black. **$12.98**

Stylish Side Drape

A Gown Chosen by New York's Smart Set

14 G 156 Typically New York—with an air of "savoir faire" that commands admiration everywhere. At formal receptions and important afternoon functions, women of the select inner circle are seen wearing gowns like this. With what dignity and grace the upper tier has been draped by three inverted tucks into a handkerchief cascade at the hip. How charmingly the band of the reversed Satin follows the line of the finely tucked contrasting georgette collared vestee, then ties smartly above the skirt.

A handsome buckle gives a brilliant finish to side drape. The dull surface of the All Silk "De Luxe" Crepe Satin is used in the deep V yoke of the back. Sleeves and tier of skirt bound with self material. Fancy buttons trim vest. Your pleasure in wearing this gown can not excel our pride in presenting a fashion so splendid!

WOMEN'S SIZES: 34, 36, 38, 40, 42, 44-inch bust; lengths from back of neck to bottom of basted hem, 43 and 45 inches. State bust measure and length. Read "How to Order" on Page 51. Ship. wt., 1 lb. 12 oz.
14 G 156—Black with flesh.
14 G 158—Marron glace (cocoa brown) with tawny birch (sand). **$14.98**

In One Year A New Standard Is Set
the Greatest Style Service Ever Inaugurated

Smartly Interpreting the New Fashion Idea
A Charming Combination of Satin and Crepe

14 G 180 Delightful—this Frock of All Silk "De Luxe" Crepe Satin that employs both sides of that lustrous material. The blouse is of the dull side of the material and the graceful jabot shows the gleaming surface of the Satin. The skirt, made of the Satin side, is cut out in an unique pointed effect above the soft folds of a side drape. A double collar adds distinction to the neck line. The detachable inner collar of Georgette can be worn open or fastened snugly about the throat. The cuffs are trimmed with Georgette. A fancy rhinestone buckle closes the pointed neck, and a row of cunning little buttons distinguish the side of this attractive dress. Inverted tucks at shoulders.
WOMEN'S SIZES: 34, 36, 38, 40, 42, 44-inch bust; lengths from back of neck to bottom of hem, 43 or 45 inches only. State bust measure and length. Read "How to Order" on Page 51. Shipping weight, 1 lb. 12 oz.
14 G 180—Black with tan.
14 G 182—Balsam (dark) green with tawny birch (sand). **$13.95**

14 G 180
All Silk
De Luxe
Crepe Satin
$13.95

14 G 186
All Silk
De Luxe
Crepe Satin
$12.98

14 G 162
All Silk
De Luxe
Crepe Satin
$14.95

14 G 168
All Silk
De Luxe
Flat Crepe
$13.98

14 G 174
All Silk
De Luxe
Flat Crepe
$14.50

14 G 192
All Silk
De Luxe
Flat Crepe
$12.95

Richly Embroidered
Uses Both Sides of the Lustrous Material

14 G 162 Dear to the heart of every woman is the Dress that can be charming and practical at the same time. Such a combination is found in this smart, tailored model of All Silk "De Luxe" Crepe Satin. Fashion never tires of a style so smartly simple—so adaptable. A dress you'll enjoy almost endlessly—because it's always smart—always suitable—for practically any occasion. The tie and pointed pockets are of All Silk Flat Crepe in a contrasting color; handsome embroidery in soft rich tones creates a note of distinction. A pleasing and striking effect is made by employing the reverse side of the material for the long revers, cuffs and box plaited panel on the skirt. Rows of fine tucks at the shoulder cause soft fullness across the front of the blouse, and the straight youthful back is crossed by a belt of Satin. In this dress you will find value—and style—demanded by discriminating women.
WOMEN'S SIZES: 34, 36, 38, 40, 42, 44-inch bust; lengths from neck to bottom of hem, 43 or 45 inches only. Read "How to Order" on Page 51. Ship. wt., 1 lb. 12 oz.
14 G 162—Black with tan.
14 G 164—English oak (rich brown) with tan. **$14.95**

New Square Cut Neck
Novel Applique Trimming Dashing Shoulder

14 G 168 A favorite of fashion this season—a graceful two-piece frock, cut on the latest lines that Paris and New York have sanctioned! All Silk "De Luxe" Flat Crepe, becoming and sufficiently dressy for semi-formal occasions. How Fashion smiles upon the new square neck! And how many times, too, she converts the dress material into soft bow ties for her smartest frocks.
A charming touch—the tie ends and cuffs of Flat Crepe in contrasting color. Little squares cut from the Crepe and applied to the blouse and sleeves are novel trimming, and a fancy ornament sparkles smartly at the waist. The skirt, attached to a Seco bodice, has a plaited front, each plait stitched part way down. A dress stunning in every detail—and ever so practical, too.
WOMEN'S SIZES: 34, 36, 38, 40, 42, 44-inch bust; lengths from back of neck to bottom of hem, 43 or 45 inches only. State bust measure and length. Read "How to Order" on Page 51. Shipping wt., 1 lb. 12 oz.
14 G 168—Black with white.
14 G 170—Claret red with beige. **$13.98**

Chic Tiers of Tucks
Rippling Rever in Newest French Fashion

14 G 174 A coat effect Dress of All Silk "De Luxe" Flat Crepe, delightful in style, fine fabric and workmanship. The skirt, with its front made of tiers of tucks, is fastened with a cameo pin above an inverted plait.
The blouse, opening over a tucked vestee of Georgette in contrasting color, is unusual and attractive with the right side forming rippling rever, and the opposite side straight. The pretty little snap cuffs match the vestee in color and material and add a pleasing note to the harmonious whole. A belt of the material starting from the sides, crosses the back and holds the slight fullness in place.
WOMEN'S SIZES: 34, 36, 38, 40, 42, 44-inch bust; lengths from back of neck to bottom of hem, 43 or 45 inches only. State bust measure and length. Read "How to Order" on Page 51. Shipping wt., 1 lb. 12 oz.
14 G 174—Navy blue with tan.
14 G 176—Black with gray. **$14.50**

A Prize Creation
Fringe—Embroidery Charmingly Combined

14 G 186 Alluring in every line is this beautiful All Silk "De Luxe" Crepe Satin Gown. The cord embroidery in a harmonizing tone following the graceful neck line is especially pretty, and the long silky fringe that edges the rounded cape in the back and the drapery in front helps to make this frock one of the loveliest creations of the season.
It appeals at once to those women who love beautiful things. There's charm in the way the pretty rhinestone buckle catches the soft shirring at the waistline. A flower of the material displays its dainty petals on the left shoulder. Another attractive feature is the sash that starts from the side and is tied at the back in a soft bow.
WOMEN'S SIZES: 34, 36, 38, 40, 42, 44-inch bust; lengths from back of neck to bottom of hem, 43 or 45 inches only. State bust measure and length. Read "How to Order" on Page 51. Ship. wt., 1 lb. 12 oz.
14 G 186—Black.
14 G 188—Balsam (dark) green.
14 G 190—Canton (medium) blue. **$12.98**

Surplice Style Dress
Two-Piece Effect Plaits and Sash Tie

14 G 192 New York fashion experts were delighted with the simple beauty in this new frock of All Silk "De Luxe" Flat Crepe. One of this season's most becoming models. Chic—and infinite charm—are expressed in the lines of the softly draped surplice. A two-piece effect—though in reality it is made all in one, for the skirt is attached to a bodice front over which the adjustable surplice blouse crosses and ties at the back in a lovely soft sash. Self material in contrasting color is used for the round-neck bodice, turned back cuffs and piping on the surplice.
A pretty flower at the shoulder adds a charming note of distinction to this stunning costume. Rows of silk covered buttons in a contrasting shade trim the loose panels of the front plaited skirt—a pleasing and unusual effect. A dress sure to delight the woman who loves fine things.
WOMEN'S SIZES: 34, 36, 38, 40, 42, 44-inch bust; lengths from back of neck to bottom of hem, 43 or 45 inches only. State bust measure and length. Read "How to Order" on Page 51. Shipping wt., 1 lb. 12 oz.
14 G 192—Black with white.
14 G 194—Navy blue with tan. **$12.95**

15

SELECTED AS THE BEST Both Paris and New York Contribute Their Finest to the New Idea

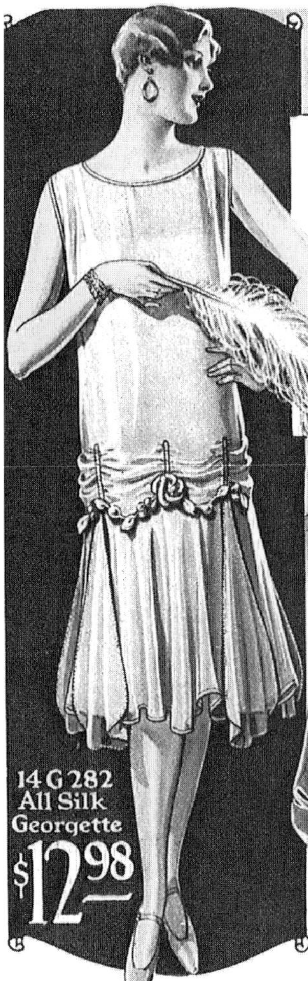

14 G 282
All Silk
Georgette
$12.98

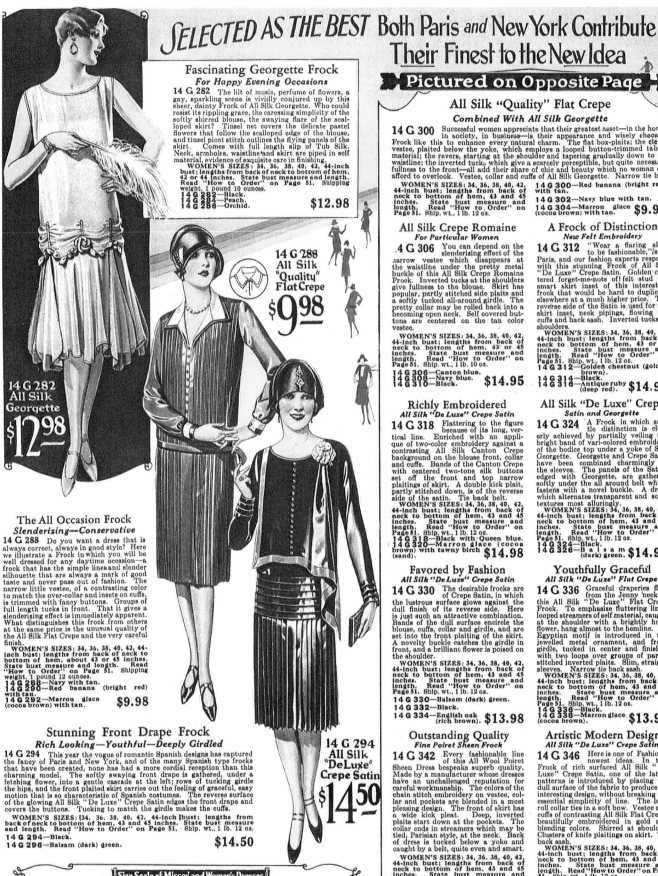

Fascinating Georgette Frock

For Happy Evening Occasions

14 G 282 The lilt of music, perfume of flowers, a gay, sparkling scene is vividly conjured up by this sheer, dainty Frock of All Silk Georgette. Who could resist its rippling grace, the caressing simplicity of the softly shirred blouse, the swaying flare of the scalloped skirt? Tinsel net covers the delicate pastel flowers that follow the scalloped edge of the blouse, and tinsel picot stitch outlines the flying panels of the skirt. Comes with full length slip of Tub Silk. Neck, armholes, waistline and skirt are piped in self material, evidence of exquisite care in finishing.
WOMEN'S SIZES: 34, 36, 38, 40, 42, 44-inch bust; lengths from back of neck to bottom of hem, 42 or 44 inches. State bust measure and length. Read "How to Order" on Page 51. Shipping weight, 1 pound 10 ounces.
14 G 282—Black.
14 G 284—Peach.
14 G 286—Orchid. **$12.98**

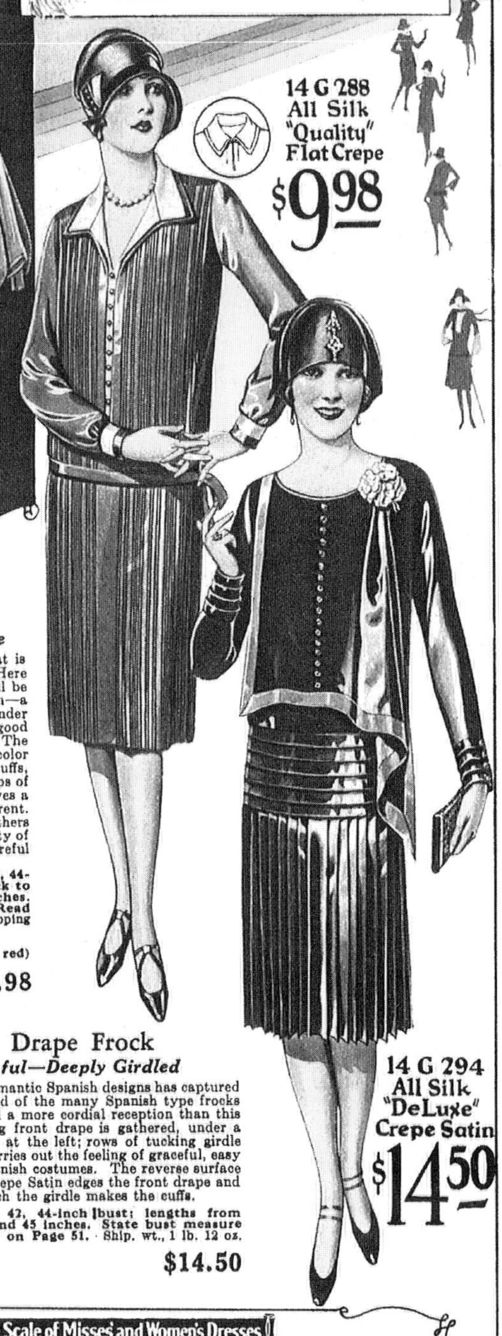

14 G 288
All Silk
"Quality"
Flat Crepe
$9.98

14 G 294
All Silk
"DeLuxe"
Crepe Satin
$14.50

The All Occasion Frock

Slenderizing—Conservative

14 G 288 Do you want a dress that is always correct, always in good style? Here we illustrate a Frock in which you will be well dressed for any daytime occasion—a frock that has the simple lines and slender silhouette that are always a mark of good taste and never pass out of fashion. The narrow little vestee, of a contrasting color to match the over-collar and insets on cuffs, is trimmed with fancy buttons. Groups of full length tucks in front. That it gives a slenderizing effect is immediately apparent. What distinguishes this frock from others at the same price is the unusual quality of the All Silk Flat Crepe and the very careful finish.
WOMEN'S SIZES: 34, 36, 38, 40, 42, 44-inch bust; lengths from back of neck to bottom of hem, about 43 or 45 inches. State bust measure and length. Read "How to Order" on Page 51. Shipping weight, 1 pound 12 ounces.
14 G 288—Navy with tan.
14 G 290—Red banana (bright red) with tan.
14 G 292—Marron glace (cocoa brown) with tan. **$9.98**

Stunning Front Drape Frock

Rich Looking—Youthful—Deeply Girdled

14 G 294 This year the vogue of romantic Spanish designs has captured the fancy of Paris and New York, and of the many Spanish type frocks that have been created, none has had a more cordial reception than this charming model. The softly swaying front drape is gathered, under a fetching flower, into a gentle cascade at the left; rows of tucking girdle the hips, and the front plaited skirt carries out the feeling of graceful, easy motion that is so characteristic of Spanish costumes. The reverse surface of the glowing All Silk "De Luxe" Crepe Satin edges the front drape and covers the buttons. Tucking to match the girdle makes the cuffs.
WOMEN'S SIZES: 34, 36, 38, 40, 42, 44-inch bust; lengths from back of neck to bottom of hem, 43 and 45 inches. State bust measure and length. Read "How to Order" on Page 51. Ship. wt., 1 lb. 12 oz.
14 G 294—Black.
14 G 296—Balsam (dark) green. **$14.50**

Size Scale of Misses' and Women's Dresses

Follow our instructions on Page 51. Allow nothing extra for fullness. Our Women's dresses are cut 4 inches larger in the hips than in the bust. Our Misses' dresses are cut 3 inches larger in the hips than in the bust. Our sizes are standard. They have been scaled by experts, who have worked out the exact relative figure proportions. Our dresses are designed to fit following measurements.

WOMEN'S DRESSES—PAGES 4 AND 43 TO 49, INCLUSIVE						
Bust measurement, inches	34	36	38	40	42	44
Proportionate hip measurement, inches	38	40	42	44	46	48
MISSES' DRESSES—PAGES 50 TO 52, INCLUSIVE						
Years	14	16	18	20	22	
Bust measurement, inches	32	34	36	38	40	
Proportionate hip measurement, inches	35	37	39	41	43	

If you measure 36 inches across the fullest part of the bust, and 40 inches hip, order a size 36. We have designed our dresses to fit—make no allowance.

Pictured on Opposite Page

All Silk "Quality" Flat Crepe

Combined With All Silk Georgette

14 G 300 Successful women appreciate that their greatest asset—in the home, in society, in business—is their appearance and wisely choose a Frock like this to enhance every natural charm. The flat box-plaits; the clever vestee, plaited below the yoke, which employs a looped button-trimmed tab of material; the revers, starting at the shoulder and tapering gradually down to the waistline; the inverted tucks which give a scarcely perceptible, but quite necessary fullness to the front—all add their share of chic and beauty which no woman can afford to overlook. Vestee, collar and cuffs of All Silk Georgette. Narrow tie belt.
WOMEN'S SIZES: 34, 36, 38, 40, 42, 44-inch bust; lengths from back of neck to bottom of hem, 43 and 45 inches. State bust measure and length. Read "How to Order" on Page 51. Ship. wt., 1 lb. 12 oz.
14 G 300—Red banana (bright red) with tan.
14 G 302—Navy blue with tan.
14 G 304—Marron glace (cocoa brown) with tan. **$9.98**

All Silk Crepe Romaine

For Particular Women

14 G 306 You can depend on the slenderizing effect of the narrow vestee which disappears at the waistline under the pretty metal buckle of this All Silk Crepe Romaine Frock. Inverted tucks at the shoulders give fullness to the blouse. Skirt has popular, partly stitched side plaits and a softly tucked all-around girdle. The pretty collar may be rolled back into a becoming open neck. Self covered buttons are centered on the tan color vestee.
WOMEN'S SIZES: 34, 36, 38, 40, 42, 44-inch bust; lengths from back of neck to bottom of hem, 43 or 45 inches. State bust measure and length. Read "How to Order" on Page 51. Ship. wt., 1 lb. 10 oz.
14 G 306—Canton blue.
14 G 308—Navy blue.
14 G 310—Black. **$14.95**

A Frock of Distinction

New Felt Embroidery

14 G 312 "Wear a flaring skirt to be fashionable," says Paris, and our fashion experts respond with this stunning Frock of All Silk "De Luxe" Crepe Satin. Golden centered forget-me-nots of felt stud the smart skirt inset of this interesting frock that would be hard to duplicate elsewhere at a much higher price. The reverse side of the Satin is used for the skirt inset, neck pipings, flowing tie, cuffs and back sash. Inverted tucks at shoulders.
WOMEN'S SIZES: 34, 36, 38, 40, 42, 44-inch bust; lengths from back of neck to bottom of hem, 43 or 45 inches. State bust measure and length. Read "How to Order" on Page 51. Ship. wt., 1 lb. 12 oz.
14 G 312—Golden chestnut (golden brown).
14 G 314—Black.
14 G 316—Antique ruby (deep red). **$14.98**

Richly Embroidered

All Silk "De Luxe" Crepe Satin

14 G 318 Flattering to the figure because of its long, vertical line. Enriched with an applique of two-color embroidery against a contrasting All Silk Canton Crepe background on the blouse front, collar and cuffs. Bands of the Canton Crepe with centered two-tone silk buttons set off the front and top narrow plaitings of skirt. A double kick plait, partly stitched down, is of the reverse side of the satin. Tie back belt.
WOMEN'S SIZES: 34, 36, 38, 40, 42, 44-inch bust; lengths from back of neck to bottom of hem, 43 and 45 inches. State bust measure and length. Read "How to Order" on Page 51. Ship. wt., 1 lb. 12 oz.
14 G 318—Black with Queen blue.
14 G 320—Marron glace (cocoa brown) with tawny birch (sand). **$14.98**

All Silk "De Luxe" Crepe

Satin and Georgette

14 G 324 A Frock in which subtle distinction is cleverly achieved by partially veiling the bright band of vari-colored embroidery of the bodice top under a yoke of Silk Georgette. Georgette and Crepe Satin have been combined charmingly in the sleeves. The panels of the Satin, edged with Georgette, are gathered softly under the all around belt which fastens with a novel buckle. A dress which alternates transparent and solid textures most alluringly.
WOMEN'S SIZES: 34, 36, 38, 40, 42, 44-inch bust; lengths from back of neck to bottom of hem, 43 and 45 inches. State bust measure and length. Read "How to Order" on Page 51. Ship. wt., 1 lb. 12 oz.
14 G 324—Black.
14 G 326—Balsam (dark) green. **$14.98**

Favored by Fashion

All Silk "De Luxe" Crepe Satin

14 G 330 The desirable frocks are of Crepe Satin, in which the lustrous surface glows against the dull finish of its reverse side. Here is just such an attractive combination. Bands of the dull surface encircle the blouse, cuffs, collar and girdle, and are set into the front plaiting of the skirt. A novelty buckle catches the girdle in front, and a brilliant flower is poised on the shoulder.
WOMEN'S SIZES: 34, 36, 38, 40, 42, 44-inch bust; lengths from back of neck to bottom of hem, 43 and 45 inches. State bust measure and length. Read "How to Order" on Page 51. Ship. wt., 1 lb. 12 oz.
14 G 330—Balsam (dark) green.
14 G 332—Black.
14 G 334—English oak (rich brown). **$13.98**

Youthfully Graceful

All Silk "De Luxe" Flat Crepe

14 G 336 Graceful draperies flow from the Jenny neck of this All Silk "De Luxe" Flat Crepe Frock. To emphasize fluttering lines, looped streamers of self material, caught at the shoulder with a brightly hued flower, hang almost to the hemline. An Egyptian motif is introduced in the jewelled metal ornament, and front girdle, tucked in center and finished with two loops over groups of partly stitched inverted plaits. Slim, straight sleeves. Narrow tie back sash.
WOMEN'S SIZES: 34, 36, 38, 40, 42, 44-inch bust; lengths from back of neck to bottom of hem, 43 and 45 inches. State bust measure and length. Read "How to Order" on Page 51. Ship. wt., 1 lb. 12 oz.
14 G 336—Black.
14 G 338—Marron glace (cocoa brown). **$13.98**

Outstanding Quality

Fine Poiret Sheen Frock

14 G 342 Every fashionable line of this All Wool Poiret Sheen Dress bespeaks superb quality. Made by a manufacturer whose dresses have an unchallenged reputation for careful workmanship. The colors of the chain stitch embroidery on vestee, collar and pockets are blended in a most pleasing design. The front of skirt has a wide kick pleat. Deep, inverted plaits start down at the pockets. The collar ends in streamers which may be tied, Parisian style, at the neck. Back of dress is tucked below a yoke and caught by a belt, quite even and smart.
WOMEN'S SIZES: 34, 36, 38, 40, 42, 44-inch bust; lengths from back of neck to bottom of hem, 43 and 45 inches. State bust measure and length. Read "How to Order" on Page 51. Ship. wt., 1 lb. 17 oz.
14 G 342—Navy blue only. **$12.98**

Artistic Modern Design

All Silk "De Luxe" Crepe Satin

14 G 346 Here is one of Fashion's newest ideas. In this Frock of rich surfaced All Silk "De Luxe" Crepe Satin, one of the latest patterns is introduced by placing the dull surface of the fabric to produce an interesting design, without breaking the essential simplicity of line. The long roll collar ties in a soft bow. Vestee and cuffs of contrasting All Silk Flat Crepe, beautifully embroidered in gold and blending colors. Shirred at shoulder. Clusters of knife plaitings on skirt. Tie back sash.
WOMEN'S SIZES: 34, 36, 38, 40, 42, 44-inch bust; lengths from back of neck to bottom of hem, 43 and 45 inches. State bust measure and length. Read "How to Order" on Page 51. Ship. wt., 1 lb. 12 oz.
14 G 346—Marron glace (cocoa brown) with tawny birch (sand).
14 G 348—Black with tan. **$14.95**

Fur Pieces Shown on Opposite Page

Handsome Thibetine Scarf

10 G 326 An unusually attractive Fur Piece. This large Thibetine Scarf is much sought by the well dressed woman because of its long silky hair. Scarf is about 32 inches in length, not including tail. Ship. wt., 1 lb. 4 oz.
10 G 326—Blue fox shade.
10 G 328—Beige tan. **$7.98**

Natural Red Fox Scarf

10 G 330 This genuine Red Fox Scarf with fur on both sides is made of full fur pelt famous for its wearing qualities and beauty. About 34 inches in length, not including the fine bushy tail, an added attraction. Ship. wt., 1 lb. 4 oz.
10 G 330—Natural red fox. **$12.98**

The Thrill and Joy of New York Style
With Every Assurance of Quality

14 G 312
All Silk
De Luxe
Crepe Satin
$14.98

14 G 300
Quality
All Silk
Flat Crepe
$9.98

14 G 306
All Silk
Crepe
Romaine
$14.95

10 G 326
Thibetine
Scarf
$7.98

14 G 318
All Silk
De Luxe
Crepe Satin
$14.98

14 G 324
All Silk
De Luxe
Crepe Satin
$14.98

14 G 330
All Silk
De Luxe
Crepe Satin
$13.98

10 G 330
Genuine
Red Fox
$12.98

14 G 336
All Silk
De Luxe
Flat Crepe
$13.98

14 G 342
All Wool
Poiret
Sheen
$12.98

14 G 346
All Silk
De Luxe
Crepe Satin
$14.95

*These Dresses are
also Furnished in
Each of the Colors
Described on
Opposite Page*

17

Again We Offer You This Greater Quality ~
Styled to the Minute

14 G 198
All Silk
Charmeuse
$9.98

Charming New York Style
Gleaming All Silk Charmeuse

14 G 198 A noteworthy feature of this Frock is the perfection of workmanship which brings out the marked distinction of its tailor-made lines. A fraction less attention to the cut and finish, less care in the tailoring would have fallen short of our New Idea "Quality" Standards. Here we have one of those handsome, dignified frocks, in a pleasing quality of lustrous All Silk Charmeuse, at a decidedly low price. Five rows of chain stitching follow the line and color of the band of contrasting All Silk Flat Crepe which faces the surplice of the slightly bloused front. The vestee is of the same contrasting shade of silk, and the cuffs are chain stitched like the waist. Skirt has deep knife plaits on either side of the panel front. Pearl buttons on belt.
WOMEN'S SIZES: 34, 36, 38, 40, 42, 44-inch bust; lengths from back of neck to bottom of hem, 43 and 45 inches only. State bust and length wanted. Read "How to Order" on Page 51. Shipping weight, 1 pound 12 ounces.
14 G 198—Black with tan.
14 G 200—Navy blue with beige.
$9.98

Coat Effect Frock
To Suit Your Thrift Budget
Two Tones in All Wool Crepe

14 G 204 Another evidence of the interesting values to be found in our newer Fashion Shop. One that makes Ward's new values the talk of the country, for nowhere else is such excellent quality obtainable at relatively low cost. This Dress of All Wool Crepe has its deep V-shaped pockets handsomely embroidered in harmonizing colors. The full length revers are piped in self material. A long panel of a contrasting shade of All Wool Crepe has the fashionable kick plait. Turn-back tailored cuffs, piped with self material, finish the close-fitting sleeves. All around belt, with metal buckle snapped in front. Flower ornament. New York wears this striking coat-effect style with a modish fur scarf, such as you will find shown on Page 49.
WOMENS' SIZES: 34, 36, 38, 40, 42, 44-inch bust; lengths from back of neck to bottom of hem, 43 and 45 inches only. State bust and length wanted. Read "How to Order" on Page 51. Ship. wt., 2 lbs. 1 oz.
14 G 204—Navy blue with tan.
14 G 206—Brown with tan. **$7.75**

14 G 204
All Wool
Crepe
$7.75

Neatly Tailored
Strikingly New

14 G 216 Tailor-made clothes have a decided appeal to the woman with an instinctive appreciation of style and quality. This smart cloth Frock will as surely win the instant approval of such discriminating women as its very moderate price will please their sense of thrift. The All Wool Poiret Sheen, soft to the touch, lends itself to the trim tailored lines of the coat dress which is here developed in a wrap-around effect. The notch collar and slashed cuffs have that tailored look which distinguishes made-to-order clothes. The double belts clasp with bright metal buckles. Vertical, inverted tucks give a pinched-in-waistline at back, slight fullness at the shoulders in front, and a soft graceful yokeline in back. Bright flower on the left lapel. A New Idea frock; quite superior to its modest price.
WOMEN'S SIZES: 34, 36, 38, 40, 42, 44-inch bust; length from back of neck to bottom of wide basted hem, about 43 inches. State bust measurement wanted. Read "How to Order" on Page 51. Shipping weight, 2 pounds 1 ounce.
14 G 216—Navy blue only. **$9.95**

14 G 216
All Wool
Poiret
Sheen
$9.95

Styled in Paris
Remarkably Rich

14 G 220 The yoke theme breaks the line, front and back, in this interesting Frock, without destroying the slender silhouette! Horizontal lines are used with telling effect against the long flowing lines of the graceful jabot drapes that hang from the left shoulder and hip. Three generous tucks give a two-piece effect to the front. A shaggy chrysanthemum of self material nods from the shoulder. Jabots and streamer cuffs are faced with a harmonizing shade of All Silk Flat Crepe. Trimmed with fancy buttons. Narrow belt ties in back.
WOMEN'S SIZES: 34, 36, 38, 40, 42, 44-inch bust; lengths from back of neck to bottom of hem, 43 and 45 in. State bust and length wanted. Read "How to Order" on Page 51. Ship. wt., 1 lb. 12 oz.
14 G 220—Marron glace (cocoa brown) with tan.
14 G 222—Navy with gray. **$12.98**

14 G 220
All Silk
De Luxe
Flat Crepe
$12.98

A New Paris Coat Frock
Tribute to Our New Idea

14 G 210 The coat dress is such a flattering mode that Paris and New York vie with each other in creating new variations of it. Here is a design in All Silk "De Luxe" Crepe Satin, worthy of a prize—an ensemble effect, as the kick plaits open and show the contrasting color All Silk Flat Crepe of the full length vestee. The fashionable long roll revers finish at the waist with a handsome pearl buckle. A narrow self belt is followed by tiers of tucks on the skirt front. Tasselled cord, to match the vestee.
WOMEN'S SIZES: 34, 36, 38, 40, 42, 44-inch bust; lengths from back of neck to bottom of hem, 43 and 45 inches only. State bust and length wanted. Read "How to Order" on Page 51. Shipping weight, 1 pound 2 ounces.
14 G 210—Black with tan.
14 G 212—Golden chestnut (golden brown) with tawny birch (sand). **$13.98**

14 G 210
All Silk
De Luxe
Crepe Satin
$13.98

Smartly Tailored Two-Piece Suit
For the Carefully Groomed Woman

14 G 226 This tailored suit of All Wool Poiret Sheen has a definite place in every wardrobe—one that nothing else can quite fill. Neat and most distinguished of all street costumes, it is also much in vogue as an indoor costume among business and professional women. The sleeveless waist, with the square Vionnet neckline, is of All Silk Crepe to match the lining of the jacket. Silk braid binds the pockets, cuffs, collar and lapels. Bright lapel boutonniere. Supremely tailored to meet the exactions of our higher New Idea Standard. In every way measuring up to the requirements of the woman accustomed to the very best.
WOMEN'S SIZES: 34, 36, 38, 40, 42, 44-inch bust; length from back of neck to bottom of wide basted hem, about 43 inches. State bust and length wanted. Read "How to Order" on Page 51. Shipping weight, 2 pounds 1 ounce.
14 G 226—Navy blue with silver gray only. **$15.00**

14 G 226
All Wool
Poiret
Sheen
$15.00

There Is No Question About It ~ The New Idea Assures You of Greater Quality

Slenderizing and Smart

Lovely All Silk De Luxe Flat Crepe
Pin Tucks, Box Plaits — Give Long Lines

14 G 580 Our fashion experts have been most discriminating in their choice of apparel for Madame who wears an extra size frock—most careful to choose up-to-the-minute designs that are correctly cut and proportioned to eliminate the curves which autocratic Dame Fashion has out-moded.

Here is a typical "larger" frock in All Silk "De Luxe" Flat Crepe. The two-piece overskirt, box plaited in alternating widths, would be quite as smart on a size 16, yet here, combined with the elongating pin tucks and rows of buttons on the blouse, it plainly says "long lines." A pin tucked band makes a smart division in front between waist and skirt and trims the sleeves. Long, self-material streamers are attached to the pin-tucked collar, and can be worn as a tie or crossed and thrown over the shoulders, scarf fashion.

EXTRA SIZES: 39, 41, 43, 45, 47, 49, 51, 53 inches bust; lengths from back of neck to bottom of basted hem, about 44 or 46 inches. State bust and length wanted. Read "How to Order" on Page 51. Ship. wt., 1 lb. 12 oz.
14 G 580—Navy blue.
14 G 582—Black.
14 G 584—Marron glace (cocoa brown). **$14.75**

14 G 580
All Silk
De Luxe
Flat Crepe
$14.75

Unusual Lines
An Economy Silk for Fuller Figures

14 G 586 An engaging Frock or All Silk Charmeuse with scalloped shawl revers outlining the dainty tucked vestee of All Silk Georgette in contrasting color. Groups of fancy buttons lead the eyes down, past an attractive metal buckle, to the wide, flat box plaits of the skirt. A narrow, self-material belt slips through loops at the sides and ties in back. The sleeve has a suggestion of a lantern puff, and is finished with a narrow cuff of the georgette over self material. A generous value at $9.98 you'll agree, when you see the frock!

EXTRA SIZES: 39, 41, 43, 45, 47, 49, 51, 53 inch bust; lengths from back of neck to bottom of hem, about 44 or 46 inches. State bust and length. Read "How to Order" on Page 51. Ship. wt., 1 pound 12 ounces.
14 G 586—Black with tan.
14 G 588—Navy blue with tan.
14 G 590—English oak (rich brown) with tan. **$9.98**

14 G 586
All Silk
Charmeuse
$9.98

Typically New York
Chic Button Trimmed Revers
Richly Embroidered Vestee

14 G 592 "Is that all you paid?" will be frequently heard when the proud owner of this beautiful Frock boasts of its low price. And she might well be proud of her choice, for this frock typifies the designing genius of America's style metropolis. Could anything be more charming than the long soft drape of the button-trimmed surplice revers? Or could dignity prove more luxurious than in the tan colored vestee embroidered in harmonizing shades! The wide knife plaits follow the youthful vogue of plaited skirts—and allow a comfortable freedom of movement. A beautiful buckle is centered on the self belt which ties softly in back. Nor has quality been neglected. The fabric—fashionable Silk "De Luxe" Flat Crepe, and the workmanship, are all that could be desired—more than should be expected—at the price!

EXTRA SIZES: 39, 41, 43, 45, 47, 49, 51, 53 inches bust; lengths from back of neck to bottom of hem, about 44 or 46 inches. State bust and length wanted. Read "How to Order" on Page 51. Ship. wt., 1 lb. 12 oz.
14 G 592—Black.
14 G 594—Marron glace (cocoa brown).
14 G 596—Navy blue. **$15.00**

14 G 592
All Silk
De Luxe
Flat Crepe
$15.00

Fashionable Economy
Warm All Wool Crepe Combines
Slim Appearance With Comfort

14 G 598 Very good looking, you can see at a glance! Wonderfully warm, too—and practical. Designed on the long slim lines, slenderizing for larger women. Of All Wool Crepe—a miracle of economy and service—sure to give many months of satisfactory wear. Bands of chain stitch embroidery, starting at the shoulder, lead down to the waist where the slenderizing line is continued by double, inverted plaits that are not only fashionable, but give plenty of walking freedom. The long revers that roll back from the self-material vestee are neatly bound with silk braid. Sleeves are gathered into the cuffs, which, like the long collar, are bordered with the embroidery. Belt ties in back. A better dress would be practically impossible to find at the price—for Ward's experts have sought and secured the best!

EXTRA SIZES: 39, 41, 43, 45, 47, 49, 51, 53 inches bust; lengths from back of neck to bottom of hem, about 44 or 46 inches. State bust and length. Read "How to Order" on Page 51. Ship. wt., 2 lbs. 2 oz.
14 G 598—Navy blue.
14 G 600—Brown. **$6.98**

14 G 598
All Wool
Crepe
$6.98

Slim Straight Lines
Stylish Pleated Flounce
Smart Tucks—Buttons

14 G 604 Fashion is ever on the lookout for new ways to convert simplicity into chic—and here she has attained her ideal, to perfection! An exceptionally good style for the stout figure, for its straight lines give a slenderizing effect. The material is All Silk "De Luxe" Flat Crepe—an unusual value for the price. A row of self-covered buttons and cord loops trim the side of the deep panel yoke on the blouse, and self-covered buttons finish the sleeves. There are rows of fine tucks on the long sleeves and on the wide band that forms the top of the front skirt flounce, the bottom of which is plaited. A fancy buckle on the belt of self-material gives a pretty finish to the dress. A model for the woman who is proud to find fashion—at a saving!

EXTRA SIZES: 39, 41, 43, 45, 47, 49, 51, 53 inches bust; lengths from back of neck to bottom of basted hem, about 44 or 46 inches. State bust and length wanted. Be sure to read the "How to Order Instructions" on top of Page 51. Shipping weight, 1 pound 12 ounces.
14 G 604—Marron glace (cocoa brown).
14 G 606—Black. **$12.98**

14 G 604
All Silk
De Luxe
Flat Crepe
$12.98

Exquisitely Simple
A Fashionable Union of
Crepe Satin and Georgette

14 G 610 The many women who have written congratulating us on the superiority of style and fabric which distinguish our newer fashions, will be delighted with this new Dress. The excellent quality of the shimmering "De Luxe" Crepe Satin can be relied upon to retain the slenderizing lines which skillful designing and expert tailoring have imparted, and the style is certain to be most suitable for the figure of larger proportions. Long, straight lines are accentuated by the finely plaited front panels of All Silk Georgette which sway open to reveal a band of richly embroidered metal braid. The metal braid also trims wide cuffs and collar, and adds its brightness to the V-opening of the neck, finished with diminutive satin tie. Self belt ties center back.

EXTRA SIZES: 39, 41, 43, 45, 47, 49, 51, 53 inches bust; lengths from back of neck to bottom of hem, about 44 or 46 inches. State bust and length. Read "How to Order" on Page 51. Ship. wt., 1 lb. 12 oz.
14 G 610—Black.
14 G 612—Marron glace (cocoa brown). **$14.75**

14 G 610
All Silk
De Luxe
Crepe Satin
and
Georgette
$14.75

FOR MISSES ~
Only the Newer ~More Exquisitely Graceful!

Only the Finest Can Meet the Demands of the "New Idea"

All Silk De Luxe Flat Crepe
Newer Style—Finer Quality

14 G 442 Fluted frills and partly stitched plaits make a charming Dress of All Silk "De Luxe" Flat Crepe, worthy of inclusion among the better fashions of our Newer, Finer Dress Shop. Fancy buttons are centered down the front panel. Perfectly tailored turn back cuffs and Eton Collar edged with contrasting Silk Crepe. Silk ribbon tie. Self belt with pearl buckle.
MISSES' SIZES: 14, 16, 18, 20, 22 years; 32, 34, 36, 38, 40-inch bust; length from back to bottom of hem, about 42 inches. State size wanted. Read "How to Order" on Page 51. Ship. wt., 1 lb. 12 oz.
14 G 442—Navy blue.
14 G 444—Claret red.
14 G 446—Marron glace (cocoa brown).
$12.95

Smart Velveteen Frock
Paisley Patterned Sleeves

14 G 448 A graceful model of Velveteen, with shirred raglan sleeves of All Silk Paisley patterned Crepe. The novel shoulder yoke is trimmed with two toned silk covered buttons. A corded girdle with silk tassel ties around the waist. Deep pointed cuffs of the velveteen finish the long graceful sleeves.
MISSES' SIZES: 14, 16, 18, 20, 22 years; 32, 34, 36, 38, 40-inch bust; length from back of neck to bottom of wide basted hem, about 42 inches. State size wanted. Read "How to Order" on Page 51. Ship. wt., 1 lb. 15 oz.
14 G 448—Dark brown.
14 G 450—Wine.
$7.95

14 G 442
All Silk De Luxe Flat Crepe
$12.95

14 G 448
Velveteen
$7.95

14 G 436
All Wool Crepe
$6.98

To Be Properly Fitted See Size Scale on Page 48

14 G 460
All Silk De Luxe Crepe Satin
$14.98

14 G 454
All Wool Flannel
$7.98

A College Favorite
Girlish Two-Piece Effect

14 G 436 Ideal for the school room or office is this All Wool Crepe Dress with the waistline prettily scalloped in front. The tie, collar facing, and insert on the sleeves are of All Wool Challis. The belt boasts a pretty buckle and the tie a fancy ornament. A practical, serviceable dress to stand hard wear. Regardless of this unusually low price, it is a New Idea Frock—the very best for your money.
MISSES' SIZES: 14, 16, 18, 20, 22 years; 32, 34, 36, 38, 40-inch bust; length from back of neck to bottom of hem, about 42 inches. State size wanted. Also be sure to read the "How to Order" instructions shown at the top of Page 51. Shipping weight, 1 pound 15 ounces.
14 G 436—Dark green.
14 G 438—Navy blue.
14 G 440—Brown.
$6.98

Stunning New Model
Square Bow Neck, Streamer Ties

14 G 466 A most youthful and flattering model is this Frock of All Silk Flat Crepe built on lines that fashion has decreed will be worn this season. The square cut neck is decidedly new and is given an unusual treatment in this dress. Another new touch seen is in the bow ties of the material falling softly across the front of the blouse at neck and waistline—a trimming that will be liked by those who desire girlish and graceful lines.
Pretty box plaits form the front of the skirt which is attached to a seco bodice. The slight fullness of the straight back is confined by a sash of the material. The long set-in sleeves are finished with a band of self material and have snap fasteners. Pretty silk-covered buttons of the same shade trim the cuffs. An ideal costume for afternoon wear or informal occasions, and the price is very remarkable.
MISSES' SIZES: 14, 16, 18, 20, 22 years; 32, 34, 36, 38, 40-inch bust; length from back of neck to bottom of hem, about 42 inches. State size wanted. Read "How to Order" on Page 51. Ship. wt., 1 lb. 12 oz.
14 G 466—Navy blue.
14 G 468—Golden chestnut (golden brown).
14 G 470—Red banana (bright red).
$7.98

14 G 466
All Silk Flat Crepe
$7.98

Two-Piece Frock
Richly Embroidered

14 G 460 You will be delighted with this lovely two-piece Frock of All Silk "De Luxe" Crepe Satin, with yoke and cuffs of contrasting color All Silk Flat Crepe and embroidery to match in tone. The blouse, hanging free in front, ties with a Satin sash at the back. There is a pretty shoulder flower harmonizing in color with the embroidery.
The skirt, box plaited in front, is attached to a bodice of tub silk. This is a dress that is pleasing to the eye and one that cannot fail to appeal to the most fastidious woman. She will recognize it as an exceptionally fine value, not only for its rich simplicity, but the beautiful care with which it is finished.
MISSES' SIZES: 14, 16, 18, 20, 22 years; 32, 34, 36, 38, 40-inch bust; length from back of neck to bottom of hem, about 42 inches. State size wanted. Read "How to Order" on Page 51. Ship. wt., 1 lb. 12 oz.
14 G 460—Black with peach.
14 G 462—Balsam (dark green) with tan. **$14.98**

14 G 472
All Silk Charmeuse
$8.98

Modish Two-Piece Effect
Contrasting Color and Braid

14 G 454 A softly tailored one-piece dress of All Wool Flannel trimmed with bands of self material in contrasting color, braid and buttons which serve to emphasize its smartness. Well arranged tucks on the shoulders give fullness across the front of blouse, while box and knife plaiting forming a front panel in the skirt allow ample freedom. Self material vestee.
MISSES' SIZES: 14, 16, 18, 20, 22 years; 32, 34, 36, 38, 40-inch bust; length from back of neck to bottom of hem, about 42 inches. State size wanted. Read "How to Order" on Page 51. Ship. wt., 1 lb. 15 oz.
14 G 454—Pine needle (light green) with carrara (dark green).
14 G 456—Light rosewood with dark rosewood. **$7.98**

Dressy Silk Frock
Daintily Lace Trimmed

14 G 472 A girlish Frock of All Silk Charmeuse, generously trimmed with a pretty patterned lace. The style of this model is most alluring and the wearer can always feel well dressed in it. The skirt flounce attached to the waist by deep shirring falls in soft, graceful lines. A self belt in front, with a fancy rhinestone ornament, ties at the back. The neck is cut in a point and trimmed with a wide band of the material in yoke effect.
A self bow tie makes a charming and becoming finish. There is ample fullness from the shoulder shirring. The long gathered-in sleeves are held by a band cuff and trimmed with an insert of lace that matches the lace on the flounce. A frock you will love to step into for any smart occasion. It will give good service. Another example of the satisfaction that our moderately priced frocks can give.
MISSES' SIZES: 14, 16, 18, 20, 22 years; 32, 34, 36, 38, 40-inch bust; length from back of neck to bottom of wide basted hem, about 42 inches. State size wanted. Be sure to read the "How to Order" instructions at the top of Page 51. Shipping weight, 1 pound 12 ounces.
14 G 472—Black.
14 G 474—Claret red. **$8.98**

20

Nation-Wide Fame Has Come To Our New Dress Shop In Less Than One Short Year
— Quality Did It!

STYLE, of course, played its part. Again this season, all designs are of Paris or New York; for no other cities, regardless of size, can give such authentic style guidance.

Wherever women gather—when talk turns to fashion, they praise this wonderful new style service. And they also say, that whatever you buy here, it is sure to be of that more dependable quality.

So we believe we can say to you fairly: These "New Idea" Dresses will give you more style and quality per dollar, than any dresses you can buy—ANYWHERE.

Latest Three-Piece Sports Frock

14 G 98 All Silk De Luxe Crepe Satin $17.50

14 G 104 All Wool Jersey and All Silk Crepe $15.00

14 G 116 All Silk De Luxe Flat Crepe $13.75

14 G 110 All Silk De Luxe Crepe Satin $14.98

14 G 122 All Silk De Luxe Flat Crepe $15.98

Exceptional Value
Latest Features in Every Line

14 G 98 An exceptionally charming Frock. A combination of fine material —All Silk "De Luxe" Crepe Satin—good workmanship, and style to please the most critical woman. Use of the reverse side of the material for trimming creates a delightful contrast. This scheme is carried out in the new pointed-neck yoke, soft bow tie, pointed cuffs, belt center and scalloped hem of the skirt.

A very rich splash of color to the blouse —the flower effect of velvet applique and hand embroidery above and below the inverted pocket. Smart little self covered buttons trim the cuffs of the sleeves. The blouse is gathered softly to the yoke in front and fulled slightly into the wide band that gives the dress a two-piece effect. The front of the skirt is finely plaited. The value of this dress will be recognized by the woman who knows and demands the best at a "true" price. We invite your critical comparison to similar models of its quality.
WOMEN'S SIZES: 34, 36, 38, 40, 42, 44-inch bust measure; lengths from back of neck to bottom of hem 43 and 45 inches only. State bust measure and length wanted. Read "How to Order" on Page 51. Ship. weight, 1 lb. 12 oz.
14 G 98—Marron glace (cocoa brown).
14 G 100—Black. $17.50

Three-Piece Frock
Delightfully Serviceable

14 G 104 This charming Frock can be worn with or without the jacket. It permits you to use the coat with other frocks or sport skirts. The plaited skirt and jacket are of fine quality All Wool Worsted jersey woven with the new process which prevents sagging—and the sleeveless blouse is of All Silk Crepe. The neck is cut square with a wide band of the same material in yoke effect that forms a soft bow tie at the center.

Slight gathers at the shoulders beneath the yoke supply a becoming fullness across the front. The belt of jersey is finished with loop buckles and rows of fancy stitching across the front plaited skirt hold the fullness in straight line effect. The jacket has two patch pockets and rows of stitching in band effect at the bottom. Buttons and button holes close the front.

A suit and frock combined. The rage with sports lovers on account of the convenience it gives them; always ready for sudden flurries of the thermometer.
WOMEN'S SIZES: 34, 36, 38, 40, 42, 44-inch bust; lengths from back of neck to bottom of hem, 43 and 45 inches only. State bust measure and length. Read "How to Order" on Page 51. Shipping weight, 1 pound 18 ounces.
14 G 104—Deauville sand
14 G 106—Rose luster (rust). $15.00

The New Flare-Skirt Frock
Rich All Silk "DeLuxe" Crepe Satin Crepe Face Trimming—Chic Buttons

14 G 110 A one-piece Dress of All Silk "DeLuxe" Crepe Satin, effectively trimmed with the reverse side of the material in the round yoke and sleeves and the plaited inserts on the skirt. Rows of self-covered buttons attached to inch lengths of silky cord decorate the sleeves and front panel effect on the blouse.

The skirt front is prettily developed in both sides of the material with a flare achieved by the circular cut and plaits. A satin sash ties at the back of the frock. A youthful and charming design.—a dress of exceptionally fine value that will be appreciated by the woman who knows.
WOMEN'S SIZES: 34, 36, 38, 40, 42, 44-inch bust; lengths from back of neck to bottom of hem 43 and 45 inches only. State bust measure and length. Read "How to Order" on Page 51. Shipping weight, 1 pound 12 ounces.
14 G 110—Black.
14 G 112—Golden chestnut (golden brown). $14.98

As Paris Wears Her Two-Piece Frock
Beautiful All Silk "DeLuxe" Flat Crepe Piquant Self Bows Over Sunburst Tucks

14 G 116 A two-piece dress in All Silk "De Luxe" flat crepe with a novel design of tucking on the blouse front—and soft bow ties of self material that fasten the neck opening and finish the slashed front at the waistline. The back of the blouse and sleeves are trimmed with rows of tucks—and the charming little narrow cuffs with loose ends are closed with buttons and button holes. Pipings of the same material edge the neck and partial front opening of the blouse. The vestee, and skirt which has a plaited front and sides in panel effect, are attached to a Seco Bodice. The plaits are stitched part way down from the waistline.
WOMEN'S SIZES: 34, 36, 38, 40, 42, 44-inch bust; lengths from back of neck to bottom of hem, 43 and 45 inches only. State bust measure and length. Read "How to Order" on Page 51. Shipping weight, 1 pound 12 ounces.
14 G 116—Navy blue.
14 G 118—Balsam (dark) green.
14 G 120—Marron glace (cocoa brown). $13.75

New York Welcomes This Two-Piece Effect
New Vionnet Neck — Modish Side Drape Fascinating Frills of Plaited Georgette

14 G 122 A distinctive frock in two-piece effect, of All Silk "De Luxe" Flat Crepe. Georgette in a contrasting color is used for the unusual collar and the pretty plaited cuffs, and ties with bands of the crepe and fancy stitching in the dress shade. Inverted tucks at the shoulder give fullness to the front. An all around band formed by wide tucks of the material gives the dress its two-piece effect. Fancy buckles at the belt and cuffs are attractive trimming. The plaits on the skirt front are stitched part way down—and a pointed drape attached with rows of shirring falls gracefully at the side.
WOMEN'S SIZES: 34, 36, 38, 40, 42, 44-inch bust; lengths from back of neck to bottom of hem, 43 and 45 inches only. State bust measure and length. Read "How to Order" on Page 51. Shipping weight, 1 pound 12 ounces.
14 G 122—Navy blue with white.
14 G 124—Black with tan. $15.98

Lovely New York Fashion
Smart and Becoming

14 G 244 A great favorite with our college girls. Appropriately simple and dressy for all their youthful occasions—this All Silk Flat Crepe Frock. The dainty over-collar, revers and turn-back cuffs of contrasting Georgette, the yoke front, the partly stitched plaits, all suggest an expensive frock. Self belt and vestee. Pearl buttons. MISSES' SIZES: 14, 16, 18, 20, 22 years; 32, 34, 36, 38, 40-inch bust; length from back of neck to bottom of hem, about 42 inches. State size wanted. Read "How to Order" on Page 51. Shipping weight, 1 pound 2 ounces.
14 G 244—Navy blue with tan.
14 G 246—Balsam (dark) green with beige.
14 G 248—Black with beige. **$7.98**

14 G 250
All Silk
Flat
Crepe

Two-Piece Scalloped Frock
Popular College Favorite

14 G 250 A most popular fashion with a particularly youthful scalloped blouse, gathered at sides under a pearl button trimmed band which is continued into a back-tied belt. The Peter Pan Collar and turn-back cuffs are of contrasting All Silk Flat Crepe. Skirt, with partly stitched plaits, attached to white seco silk bodice top. MISSES' SIZES: 14, 16, 18, 20, 22 years; 32, 34, 36, 38, 40-inch bust; length from back of neck to bottom of hem, about 42 inches. State size wanted. Read "How to Order" on Page 51. Shipping weight, 1 lb. 12 oz.
14 G 250—Navy blue with tan.
14 G 252—Claret red with beige.
14 G 254—Balsam (dark) green with beige. **$7.98**

14 G 244
All Silk
Flat
Crepe

14 G 238
All Silk
Flat
Crepe

To Be Properly Fitted
See Size Scale
on Page 48

14 G 262
All Silk
Flat
Crepe

New Yoke Frock
Collarless—Lovely

14 G 238 A charming model! Its Fifth Avenue origin is evident in the new, collarless yoke neckline, with its fine inverted tucks in back and dainty self tie. Just a suggestion of gathers below the yoke give a slight fullness that is charmingly gathered above the pockets into a soft blouse. The pocket flaps are accented with dainty pearl buttons. Deep side plaits below pockets. Tie back sash. The sleeves have chic dressy cuffs. MISSES' SIZES: 14, 16, 18, 20, 22 years; 32, 34, 36, 38, 40-in. bust; length from back of neck to bottom of hem, about 42 in. State size wanted. Read "How to Order" on Page 51. Ship. wt., 1 lb. 12 oz.
14 G 238—Claret red.
14 G 240—Canton (bright) blue.
14 G 242—Golden chestnut (golden brown). **$7.98**

A Stunning Model
All Silk Charmeuse

14 G 232 The self-confidence and poise that come from feeling well dressed will be enjoyed by wearers of this Frock. And they will have the added satisfaction of knowing that it cost so little. Made of lustrous, All Silk Charmeuse in a strictly tailored coat dress, with V-neck vestee and turn back cuffs of beige color All Silk Flat Crepe. Buttonholes and buttons on both vestee and dress front. Self belt, closed in front with fancy buckle. WOMEN'S SIZES: 34, 36, 38, 40, 42, 44-inch bust; length from back of neck to bottom of wide basted hem, about 43 inches. State bust measure. Read "How to Order" on Page 51. Shipping weight, 1 pound 12 ounces.
14 G 232—Black.
14 G 234—Canton blue. **$7.98**

14 G 232
All Silk
Charmeuse

14 G 274
All Silk
Flat
Crepe

Ideal Tailored Frock
Of Rich Simplicity

14 G 274 The coat effect Frock is chosen by many astute women for its flattering silhouette. This model has an extremely "fine" appearance, due to the narrow cord piping of contrasting All Silk Flat Crepe which outlines cuffs, collar and fronts and forms vestee. Ball buttons. Self reversible belt. Inverted tucks at shoulders. WOMEN'S SIZES: 34, 36, 38, 40, 42, 44-inch bust; lengths from back of neck to bottom of hem, about 43 and 45 in. State bust and length. Read "How to Order" on Page 51. Ship. weight, 1 lb. 12 oz.
14 G 274—Navy blue with tan.
14 G 276—Marron glace (cocoa brown) with beige.
14 G 278—Black with beige. **$7.98**

14 G 268
All Silk
Charmeuse

Two-Piece Effect
Youth in Every Line

14 G 268 This All Silk Charmeuse Dress would cost you several dollars more elsewhere. Our New Fashion Shop maintains both style and quality at $7.98. Two-piece effect is cleverly attained by a wide hip band of the Charmeuse. Contrasting Silk Crepe turnback cuffs and front panel. Self covered buttons. Skirt plaits partly stitched. WOMEN'S SIZES: 34, 36, 38, 40, 42, 44-inch bust; lengths from back of neck to bottom of hem, about 43 and 45 inches. State bust and length. Read "How to Order" on Page 51. Shipping weight, 1 pound 12 ounces.
14 G 268—Black with tan.
14 G 270—Navy blue with beige.
14 G 272—Brown with tan. **$7.98**

Smart Frock
All Silk Flat Crepe

14 G 262 Well made of firm textured, All Silk Flat Crepe with a tailored, self material tie slipping through the slot loop to finish the neckline. Fancy pearl buttons edge flaps of the pockets that are set above the knife plaitings on front of skirt. Tailored sleeves with narrow self cuffs. Narrow belt ties in back. WOMEN'S SIZES: 34, 36, 38, 40, 42, 44-inch bust; lengths from back of neck to bottom of hem, about 43 and 45 inches. State bust and length. Read "How to Order" on Page 51. Shipping weight, 1 lb. 12 oz.
14 G 262—Navy blue.
14 G 264—Marron glace (cocoa brown).
14 G 266—Black. **$7.98**

14 G 256
All Silk
Flat
Crepe

Typical French Frock
For Home—Club—Office

14 G 256 Have you longed for a French hand-made Frock? Here is an exact replica, with the same delicate tuckings and silk stitching (not hand-made, of course, but every bit as dainty) at a price which would hardly cover the cost of the material in a French frock. Two groups of pin tucks, placed between three wider tucks—double silk stitched—give a long front panel effect. Wide snap cuffs. Smart, four-in-hand tie of contrasting material. It would cost considerably more in a New York shop. WOMEN'S SIZES: 34, 36, 38, 40, 42, 44-inch bust; length from back of neck to bottom of wide basted hem, about 43 in. State bust and length. Read "How to Order" on Page 51. Shipping weight, 1 pound 12 ounces.
14 G 256—Navy blue.
14 G 258—Marron glace (cocoa brown).
14 G 260—Balsam (dark) green. **$7.98**

Useful Garments and Negligees for Leisure Hours
Priced for Savings

36 G 172 Broadcloth $1.84

36 G 47 Sateen Regular Sizes $1.00

Extra Sizes $1.19

Hand Embroidered

Brightly Trimmed Sateen Apron Dress
Practical for Housework Very Carefully Tailored

36 G 47—Standard Sateen for this practical Apron Dress of black with orange colored pipings; gayly stitched.
REGULAR SIZES: Small (34 to 36 bust); Medium (38 to 40 bust); Large (42 to 44 bust). State size.
Ship. wt., 1 pound.
36 G 47—Black only. $1.00
EXTRA SIZES: (46 to 48 bust) or (50 to 52 bust) State size. Ship. wt., 1 lb. 2 oz.
36 G 49—Black only. $1.19

Apron Dress
Attractive Style Embroidered Trimming

36 G 172—Hand embroidered! An Apron Dress comfortably designed for the home worker—and so pretty and appropriate that it will make home much more pleasant for the woman who wears it. Of good quality Mercerized Broadcloth that looks very dressy, and will give excellent service.

The collar forms a tie and the turned back cuffs have fancy stitching. There is a distinctive embroidered design on the front of dress that is most pleasing.

You'll be proud to wear a style so smart on the porch and street as well as in your home.
SIZES: Small (34 to 36 bust); medium (38 to 40 bust); or large (42 to 44 bust). State size wanted. Ship. wt., 1 lb.
36 G 172—Rose.
36 G 174—Copenhagen blue.
36 G 176—Lavender. $1.84

36 G 400 Chambray or Linene $1.69

INDIAN HEAD or Sateen $1.98

Japanese Kimono
Serpentine Crepe Colorful Figured Design

36 G 219—A colorful Serpentine Crepe Kimono in figured design, with Japanese sleeves. The collar is long and made of a contrasting color of the Crepe material. The pocket is topped with a plain band and the tie sash at the side is of the figured Crepe. A most charming kimono and one that will be pleasingly becoming.
SIZES: Small (34 to 36 bust); medium (38 to 40 bust); or large (42 to 44 bust). State size wanted. Shipping weight, 1 pound.
36 G 219—Rose.
36 G 221—Copen. blue. $1.98

36 G 219 Serpentine Cotton Crepe $1.98

36 G 178 Silk Crepe de Chine $6.95

36 G 190 Flannelette $1.69

Daintiest Negligee!
Our Finest Quality Lace Ruffle Trimmed

36 G 178—Beautifully chic and dainty—this Negligee will appeal to the eternal feminine love for soft frills. Of good quality All Silk Crepe de Chine, prettily frilled with rows of dainty lace. Has deep, flattering shawl collar and graceful sleeves in butterfly style. The sides are beautified with medallion ruffles of lace.
SIZES: Small (34 to 36 bust); medium (38 to 40 bust), or large (42 to 44 bust). State size wanted. Shipping weight, 1 pound.
36 G 178—Copenhagen blue.
36 G 180—Orchid pink.
36 G 182—Nile green. $6.95

Flannelette Kimono
Warmth and Comfort on Chilly Mornings

36 G 190—On cold mornings, this pretty Figured Flannelette Kimono will be appreciated by the woman who wants comfort! Of excellent material, in assorted patterns, and cut on attractive lines. Shirred bands of the cloth form the trimmings on collar and pocket. The elbow sleeves are finished with gathered ruffle of the same material. Adjustable side ties.
SIZES: Small (34 to 36 bust); medium (38 to 40 bust), or large (42 to 44 bust). State size wanted. Shipping weight, 1 pound 3 ounces.
36 G 190—Copen. blue.
36 G 192—Rose. $1.69

Tailored Uniform Dress
Choice of 4 Durable Materials Best for Lasting Service

36 G 400—For professional women and home workers. This trim Uniform Dress comes in Chambray, Linene, Indian Head or Sateen, trimly tailored. Deep yoke, front and back, with wide tucks for fullness. The collar can be worn open or closed. Set-in sleeves, finished with pointed cuffs. Pockets with tab trimmings.
WOMEN'S AND MISSES' SIZES: 34, 36, 38, 40, 42, 44, 46-inch bust; 16, 18, 20, 22 years. State size. Ship. wt., 1 lb.
36 G 400—Blue chambray.
36 G 402—White linene. $1.69
36 G 186—White Indian Head.
36 G 188—Black sateen. $1.98

Reversible Front Apron Dress
Unusual Quality for This Low Price Made of Lustrous Broadcloth

36 G 22—A triumph in quality and price. Our large purchases enable us to sell it for $1.19 when it ordinarily retails for much more. Of soft lustrous Broadcloth in many lovely shades, each trimmed with white, or you may buy it in all White. Wear it twice as long without laundering; for the reversible front closing gives double service and halves the laundry problem. Every home keeper or professional woman needs this practical garment—for those unavoidable surprise—emergency—occasions.
SIZES: Small (34 to 36 bust); medium (38 to 40 bust), or large (42 to 44 bust). State size wanted. Shipping weight, 14 ounces.
36 G 22—Copenhagen blue.
36 G 24—Rose.
36 G 26—Lavender.
36 G 28—Green.
36 G 30—White. $1.19

36 G 22 Broadcloth $1.19

FIFTH AVENUE Is Wearing Them

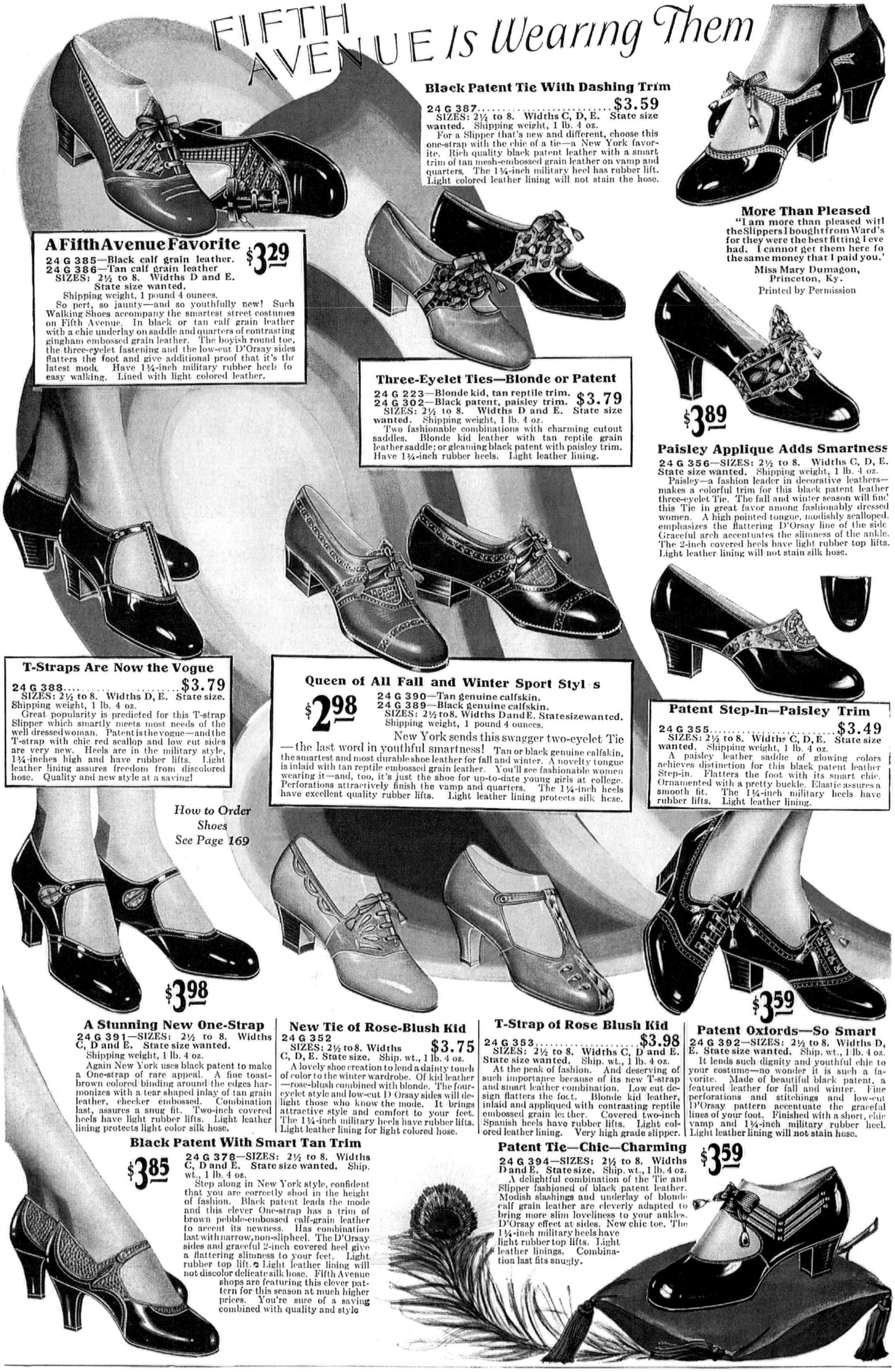

A Fifth Avenue Favorite

$3.29

24 G 385—Black calf grain leather.
24 G 386—Tan calf grain leather
SIZES: 2½ to 8. Widths D and E. State size wanted.
Shipping weight, 1 pound 4 ounces.

So pert, so jaunty—and so youthfully new! Such Walking Shoes accompany the smartest street costumes on Fifth Avenue. In black or tan calf grain leather with a chic underlay on saddle and quarters of contrasting gingham embossed grain leather. The boyish round toe, the three-eyelet fastening and the low-cut D'Orsay sides flatters the foot and give additional proof that it's the latest mode Have 1¾-inch military rubber heels fo easy walking. Lined with light colored leather.

Black Patent Tie With Dashing Trim

24 G 387.............................**$3.59**
SIZES: 2½ to 8. Widths C, D, E. State size wanted. Shipping weight, 1 lb. 4 oz.

For a Slipper that's new and different, choose this one-strap with the chic of a tie—a New York favorite. Rich quality black patent leather with a smart trim of tan mesh-embossed grain leather on vamp and quarters. The 1¾-inch military heel has rubber lift. Light colored leather lining will not stain the hose.

More Than Pleased

"I am more than pleased witl the Slippers I bought from Ward's for they were the best fitting I eve had. I cannot get them here fo the same money that I paid you.'

Miss Mary Dumagon,
Princeton, Ky.

Printed by Permission

Three-Eyelet Ties—Blonde or Patent

24 G 223—Blonde kid, tan reptile trim.
24 G 302—Black patent, paisley trim. **$3.79**
SIZES: 2½ to 8. Widths D and E. State size wanted. Shipping weight, 1 lb. 4 oz.

Two fashionable combinations with charming cutout saddles. Blonde kid leather with tan reptile grain leather saddle; or gleaming black patent with paisley trim. Have 1¾-inch rubber heels. Light leather lining.

$3.89

Paisley Applique Adds Smartness

24 G 356—SIZES: 2½ to 8. Widths C, D, E. State size wanted. Shipping weight, 1 lb. 4 oz.

Paisley—a fashion leader in decorative leathers—makes a colorful trim for this black patent leather three-eyelet Tie. The fall and winter season will find this Tie in great favor among fashionably dressed women. A high pointed tongue, modishly scalloped, emphasizes the flattering D'Orsay line of the side Graceful arch accentuates the slimness of the ankle. The 2-inch covered heels have light rubber top lifts. Light leather lining will not stain silk hose.

T-Straps Are Now the Vogue

24 G 388.............................**$3.79**
SIZES: 2½ to 8. Widths D, E. State size. Shipping weight, 1 lb. 4 oz.

Great popularity is predicted for this T-strap Slipper which smartly meets most needs of the well dressed woman. Patent is the vogue—and the T-strap with chic red scallop and low cut sides are very new. Heels are in the military style, 1¾-inches high and have rubber lifts. Light leather lining assures freedom from discolored hose. Quality and new style at a saving!

Queen of All Fall and Winter Sport Styl s

$2.98

24 G 390—Tan genuine calfskin.
24 G 389—Black genuine calfskin.
SIZES: 2½ to 8. Widths D and E. State size wanted.
Shipping weight, 1 pound 4 ounces.

New York sends this swagger two-eyelet Tie—the last word in youthful smartness! Tan or black genuine calfskin, the smartest and most durable shoe leather for fall and winter. A novelty tongue is inlaid with tan reptile embossed grain leather. You'll see fashionable women wearing it—and, too, it's just the shoe for up-to-date young girls at college. Perforations attractively finish the vamp and quarters. The 1¼-inch heels have excellent quality rubber lifts. Light leather lining protects silk hose.

Patent Step-In—Paisley Trim

24 G 355.............................**$3.49**
SIZES: 2½ to 8. Widths C, D, E. State size wanted. Shipping weight, 1 lb. 4 oz.

A paisley leather saddle of glowing colors achieves distinction for this black patent leather Step-in. Flatters the foot with its smart chic. Ornamented with a pretty buckle. Elastic assures a smooth fit. The 1¼-inch military heels have rubber lifts. Light leather lining.

How to Order Shoes See Page 169

$3.98

A Stunning New One-Strap

24 G 391—SIZES: 2½ to 8. Widths C, D and E. State size wanted.
Shipping weight, 1 lb. 4 oz.

Again New York uses black patent to make a One-strap of rare appeal. A fine toast-brown colored binding around the edges harmonizes with a tear shaped inlay of tan grain leather, checker embossed. Combination last, assures a snug fit. Two-inch covered heels have light rubber lifts. Light leather lining protects light color silk hose.

New Tie of Rose-Blush Kid

24 G 352 **$3.75**
SIZES: 2½ to 8. Widths C, D, E. State size. Ship. wt., 1 lb. 4 oz.

A lovely shoe creation to lend a dainty touch of color to the winter wardrobe. Of kid leather—rose-blush combined with blonde. The four-eyelet style and low-cut D Orsay sides will delight those who know the mode. It brings attractive style and comfort to your feet. The 1¾-inch military heels have rubber lifts. Light leather lining for light colored hose.

T-Strap of Rose Blush Kid

24 G 353.............................**$3.98**
SIZES: 2½ to 8. Widths C, D and E. State size wanted. Ship. wt., 1 lb. 4 oz.

At the peak of fashion. And deserving of such importance because of its new T-strap and smart leather combination. Low cut design flatters the foot. Blonde kid leather, inlaid and appliqued with contrasting reptile embossed grain le ther. Covered two-inch Spanish heels have rubber lifts. Light colored leather lining. Very high grade slipper.

$3.59

Patent Oxfords—So Smart

24 G 392—SIZES: 2½ to 8. Widths D, E. State size wanted. Ship. wt., 1 lb. 4 oz.

It lends such dignity and youthful chic to your costume—no wonder it is such a favorite. Made of beautiful black patent, a featured leather for fall and winter. Fine perforations and stitchings and low-cut D'Orsay pattern accentuate the graceful lines of your foot. Finished with a short, chic vamp and 1¾-inch military rubber heel. Light leather lining will not stain hose.

Black Patent With Smart Tan Trim

$3.85

24 G 378—SIZES: 2½ to 8. Widths C, D and E. State size wanted. Ship. wt., 1 lb. 4 oz.

Step along in New York style, confident that you are correctly shod in the height of fashion. Black patent leads the mode and this clever One-strap has a trim of brown pebble-embossed calf-grain leather to accent its newness. Has combination last with narrow, non-slipheel. The D'Orsay sides and graceful 2-inch covered heel give a flattering slimness to your feet. Light rubber top lift. Light leather lining will not discolor delicate silk hose. Fifth Avenue shops are featuring this clever pattern for this season at much higher prices. You're sure of a saving combined with quality and style

Patent Tie—Chic—Charming

$3.59

24 G 394—SIZES: 2½ to 8. Widths D and E. State size. Ship. wt., 1 lb. 4 oz.

A delightful combination of the Tie and Slipper fashioned of black patent leather. Modish slashings and underlay of blonde calf grain leather are cleverly adapted to bring more slim loveliness to your ankles. D'Orsay effect at sides. New chic toe. The 1¾-inch military heels have light rubber top lifts. Light leather linings. Combination last fits snugly.

Stylish Footwear at Economical Prices
The Cushion Insole Guarantees Their Comfort

NOW! Style is added to economical foot comfort. Approved by thousands—now thousands more are ordering them. A variety of pleasing styles—all with cushion insoles. Extremely low prices.

See Size Chart on Page 169

$2.79
Three-Button Strap—Soft Kid

24 G 312—SIZES: 2½ to 8. Widths D, E. State size wanted. Ship. wt., 1 lb. 6 oz. Neat style combined with real economy. Your feet will know the true meaning of comfort when you wear this neat Slipper. The cutout strap with three buttons fastens over the instep and hugs the shoe gently to your foot. Black genuine kid leather with full cushion insole, rubber heels and drill cloth lining.

$2.59
Side-Gore Pump—Black Kid

24 G 311—SIZES: 2½ to 8. Widths D, E. State size wanted. Ship. wt., 1 lb. 6 oz. Ward's low price brings you more good quality and fine appearance than you would ever expect. Select this Pump for its trim neatness and cushion insole foot comfort. Of soft black genuine kid leather with snug-fit elastic side gores. The vamp is smartly designed with cutouts. Full length cushion insole and 1¾-inch rubber heel. Drill lining—may be worn with light hose.

$2.79
Black Patent—Neat Strap

24 G 320—SIZES: 2½ to 8. Width E only. State size wanted. Ship. wt., 1 lb. 6 oz. Smart style—perfect comfort—fine fit—such as you'd expect only in more expensive shoes—yet this strap Slipper gives it to you for only $2.79. Of black patent leather overlaid with a neat cutout design on the sides and a wide gunmetal two-button twin strap. Full length cushion insole is a guarantee of comfort. Has 1¼-inch rubber heel. Light color cloth lining.

$2.69
Black Kid—Three-Eyelet Tie

24 G 310—SIZES: 2½ to 8. Widths D, E. State size wanted. Ship. wt., 1 lb. 6 oz. We're proud to offer this special value. It will delight the careful shopper who knows real value, because here style is combined with dependable quality, cushion insole comfort and low price. This three-eyelet openwork Tie is of soft black kid leather. Military heels have rubber top lifts. Full cushion insoles. Drill lining —can be worn with light hose.

Style–Cushion Sole Comfort

$2.69
Big Value—Of Soft Kid

24 G 317—SIZES: 2½ to 8. Widths D, E. State size wanted. Ship. wt., 1 lb. 6 oz. This Slipper is as outstanding an example of economy as you'll find anywhere. It combines the trim smartness necessary for the street with the comfort of a house slipper plus reliable materials and workmanship—at only $2.69. One-strap model of soft black kid leather with neatly designed vamp. Has a cushion insole and 1¾-inch rubber heel. Sturdy drill lining is fine for light hose.

$2.49
Two-Strap of Black Patent

24 G 313. SIZES: 2½ to 8. Widths D and E. State size wanted. Ship. wt., 1 lb. 6 oz. Neat, well fitting Slippers. You'll be exceedingly pleased with this big value. The chic, graceful style every woman wants, and the easeful shoe comfort your feet require. Black patent leather with neat cutouts. Cushion insole guarantees their comfort. Have 1¾-inch military rubber heels. Light color drill lining.

$2.59
Three-Eyelet Tie of Black Kid

24 G 319. SIZES: 2½ to 8. Width E only. State size wanted. Ship. wt., 1 lb. 6 oz. Now—style is added to economical foot comfort. You'll be happy with the smart appearance, genuine comfort and excellent saving which are yours when you purchase a pair of these Slippers. Of black kid leather with a snug-fitting three-eyelet cutout strap. Cushion insole from toe to heel and 1¼-inch rubber heel. Drill lining.

$2.49
Reptile Inlay—Black Patent

24 G 316—SIZES: 2½ to 8. Widths D, E. State size wanted. Ship. wt., 1 lb. 6 oz. Quality first! A youthful one-eyelet Tie that gives the foot a well groomed appearance and is perfectly comfortable because of the full length cushion insole. Fashionably made of black patent leather with gray lizard grain leather inlay at sides. The 1¼-inch heels have rubber top lift. Durable drill lining—can be worn with light colored hose.

Women's Service Shoes
Durable–Comfortable

$2.29
"Wonder-Wear" FiberSoles

24 G 902—SIZES: 2½ to 8. Width E only. State size wanted. Shipping weight, 1 lb. 12 oz. Every season more and more women are buying them. You'll understand the reason for their popularity the moment you put them on your feet. They're sturdy yet comfortable —ideal for house or street wear. The uppers are of fine brown grain leather, unlined. Flexible fiber soles, stitchdown sewed, are famous for their long wear. Low rubber heels.

House Slippers of Soft Kid

24 G 342—With strap............$1.29
24 G 341—Without strap........ 1.29
SIZES: 3 to 8. Width E. No half sizes. State size wanted. Shipping weight, 14 ounces. Two of our most popular House Slippers. Neat, very comfortable and splendid values at our price. Soft black genuine kid leather. Flexible oak leather soles and rubber heels give real foot comfort. Fluffy silk pompon.

For Service and Sports

24 G 195................$1.98
SIZES: 2½ to 8. Width E only. State size. Ship. wt., 1 lb. 12 oz. Service—neatness—soothing foot comfort—Big Saving—all yours in this Sports or everyday Oxford. Of soft, brown chrome leather (known as elkskin). Non-slip Wonder-Wear composition fiber soles—stitchdown sewed—are flexible and very tough—hard to wear out. Low rubber heels.

Service and Comfort
$2.98

24 G 1109—Widths: D, 2½ to 8; E, 2½ to 9. State size wanted. Shipping weight, 2 pounds. For many years this shoe has been giving thousands of our customers splendid service and real comfort for house and street wear. The uppers are soft, dull black gunmetal leather, full drill cloth lined. Has comfortable medium round toe and 1¾-inch military heel with rubber top lift.

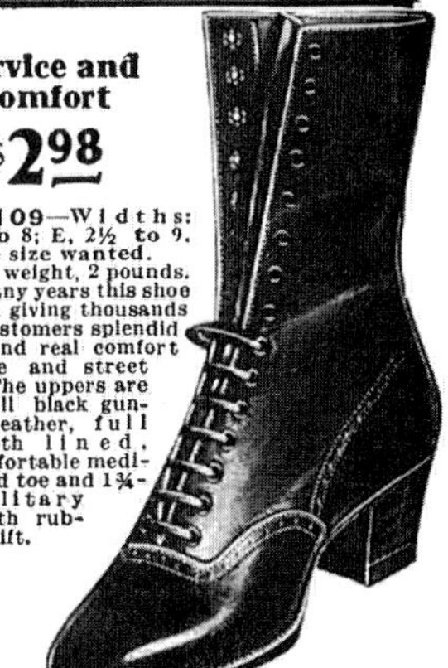

$2.98
And a Big Value at This Price

Soft, Heavy Black Kid

24 G 940...$2.98 SIZES: 2½ to 9. Width E only. State size wanted. Ship. wt., 1 lb. 10 oz. Assure yourself of an easy durable Shoe for work by ordering this one. Of heavy, soft, black, genuine kid leather with strong leather soles and rubber heels. Full cloth lined. Roomy shape is very comfortable.

Sturdy Gunmetal Work Shoe

24 G 1048. $2.98 SIZES: 2½ to 10 (except 9½). Width E. State size. Ship. weight, 2 lbs. Just the Work Shoe to stand the hard wear. Of black gunmetal grain leather—light weight but sturdy. Full drill lined, with leather insole and long wearing leather outsole. Rubber heels.

All Black Kid Leather

24 G 960................$2.98 SIZES: 2½ to 8. Widths D and E. Shipping weight, 1 pound 12 ounces. For fall and winter wear you'll need just such a Shoe as this. Comfortable for easy walking—gracefully proportioned to give to your feet the neatness you demand. Of black genuine kid, dressy and smooth fitting. The 1¾-inch military heel has a rubber lift. At $2.98 it saves you a goodly sum of money because of its reliable, serviceable quality and careful workmanship.

Fine 14-Inch Hiking Shoe

24 G 904.......$4.89 SIZES: 2½ to 8. Width E only. State size wanted. Shipping weight, 3 pounds. On crisp fall and winter days there's a world of healthful fun in long hikes. Here's a fine 14-inch moccasin vamp Hiking Boot of a design similar to those adopted by nationally known girls' clubs. Handy pocket fastens with buckle. Soft, golden tan leather (known as elkskin)—tough, durable, pliable. Goodyear welt soles, of strong viscolized (oiled) leather. Rubber heels.

25

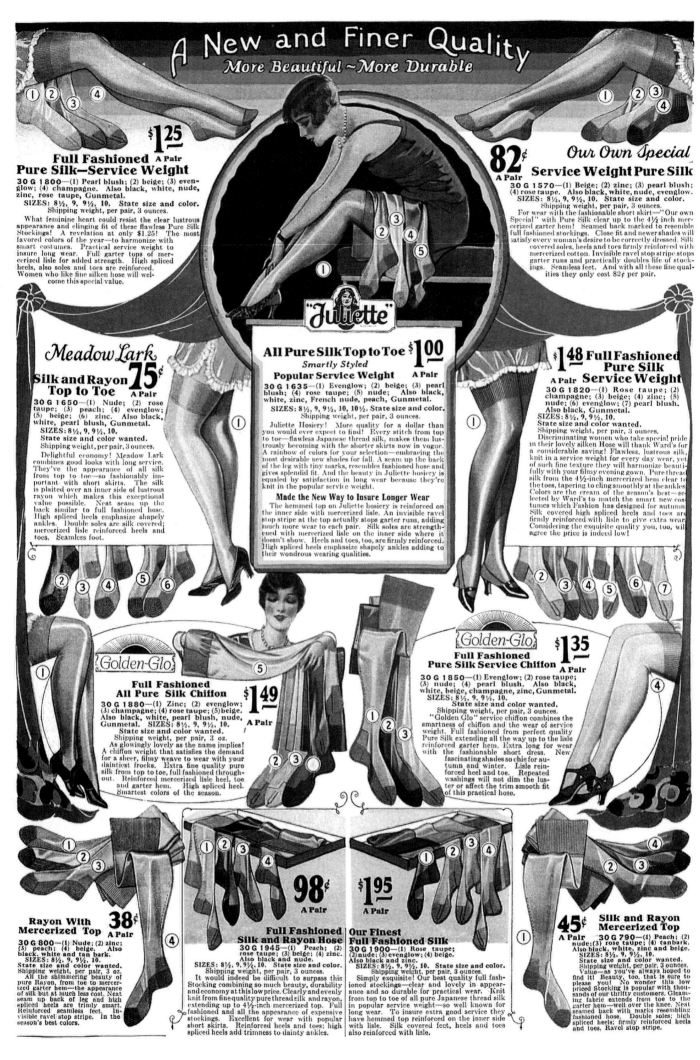

A New and Finer Quality
More Beautiful ~ More Durable

Full Fashioned $1.25 A Pair
Pure Silk—Service Weight

30 G 1800—(1) Pearl blush; (2) beige; (3) evenglow; (4) champagne. Also black, white, nude, zinc, rose taupe, Gunmetal.
SIZES: 8½, 9, 9½, 10. State size and color.
Shipping weight, per pair, 3 ounces.

What feminine heart could resist the clear lustrous appearance and clinging fit of these flawless Pure Silk Stockings! A revelation at only $1.25! The most favored colors of the year—to harmonize with smart costumes. Practical service weight to insure long wear. Full garter tops of mercerized lisle for added strength. High spliced heels, also sales and toes are reinforced. Women who like fine silken hose will welcome this special value.

82¢ A Pair — Our Own Special
Service Weight Pure Silk

30 G 1570—(1) Beige; (2) zinc; (3) pearl blush; (4) rose taupe. Also black, white, nude, evenglow.
SIZES: 8½, 9, 9½, 10. State size and color.
Shipping weight, per pair, 3 ounces.

For wear with the fashionable short skirt—"Our own Special" with Pure Silk clear up to the 4½-inch mercerized garter hem! Seamed back marked to resemble full fashioned stockings. Close fit and newer shades will satisfy every woman's desire to be correctly dressed. Silk covered soles, heels and toes firmly reinforced with mercerized cotton. Invisible ravel stop stripe stops garter runs and practically doubles life of stockings. Seamless feet. And with all these fine qualities they only cost 82¢ per pair.

Meadow Lark — Silk and Rayon Top to Toe 75¢ A Pair

30 G 1650—(1) Nude; (2) rose taupe; (3) peach; (4) evenglow; (5) beige; (6) zinc. Also black, white, pearl blush, Gunmetal.
SIZES: 8½, 9, 9½, 10.
State size and color wanted.
Shipping weight, per pair, 3 ounces.

Delightful economy! Meadow Lark combines good looks with long service. They've the appearance of all silk from top to toe—so fashionably important with short skirts. The silk is plaited over an inner side of lustrous rayon which makes this exceptional value possible. Neat seam up the back similar to full fashioned hose. High spliced heels emphasize shapely ankles. Double soles are silk covered; mercerized lisle reinforced heels and toes. Seamless foot.

"Juliette" — All Pure Silk Top to Toe $1.00 A Pair
Smartly Styled — Popular Service Weight

30 G 1635—(1) Evenglow; (2) beige; (3) pearl blush; (4) rose taupe; (5) nude. Also black, white, zinc, French nude, peach, Gunmetal.
SIZES: 8½, 9, 9½, 10, 10½. State size and color.
Shipping weight, per pair, 3 ounces.

Juliette Hosiery! More quality for a dollar than you would ever expect to find! Every stitch from top to toe—flawless Japanese thread silk, makes them lustrously becoming with the shorter skirts now in vogue. A rainbow of colors for your selection—embracing the most desirable new shades for fall. A seam up the back of the leg with tiny marks, resembles fashioned hose and gives splendid fit. And the beauty in Juliette hosiery is equaled by satisfaction in long wear because they're knit in the popular service weight.

Made the New Way to Insure Longer Wear

The hemmed top on Juliette hosiery is reinforced on the inner side with mercerized lisle. An invisible ravel stop stripe at the top actually stops garter runs, adding much more wear to each pair. Silk soles are strengthened with mercerized lisle on the inner side where it doesn't show. Heels and toes, too, are firmly reinforced. High spliced heels emphasize shapely ankles adding to their wondrous wearing qualities.

$1.48 A Pair — Full Fashioned Pure Silk Service Weight

30 G 1820—(1) Rose taupe; (2) champagne; (3) beige; (4) zinc; (5) nude; (6) evenglow; (7) pearl blush. Also black, Gunmetal.
SIZES: 8½, 9, 9½, 10.
State size and color wanted.
Shipping weight, per pair, 3 ounces.

Discriminating women who take special pride in their lovely silken Hose will thank Ward's for a considerable saving! Flawless, lustrous silk, knit in a service weight for every day wear, yet of such fine texture they will harmonize beautifully with your filmy evening gown. Pure thread silk from the 4½-inch mercerized hem clear to the toes, tapering to cling smoothly at the ankles. Colors are the cream of the season's best—selected by Ward's to match the smart new costumes which Fashion has designed for autumn. Silk covered high spliced heels and toes are firmly reinforced with lisle to give extra wear. Considering the exquisite quality you, too, will agree the price is indeed low!

Golden-Glo — Full Fashioned All Pure Silk Chiffon $1.49 A Pair

30 G 1880—(1) Zinc; (2) evenglow; (3) champagne; (4) rose taupe; (5) beige. Also black, white, nude, pearl blush, nude, Gunmetal. SIZES: 8½, 9, 9½, 10.
State size and color wanted.
Shipping weight, per pair, 3 oz.

As glowingly lovely as the name implies! A chiffon weight that satisfies the demand for a sheer, filmy weave to wear with your daintiest frocks. Extra fine quality pure silk from top to toe, full fashioned throughout. Reinforced mercerized lisle heel, toe and garter hem. High spliced heel. Smartest colors of the season.

Golden-Glo — Full Fashioned Pure Silk Service Chiffon $1.35 A Pair

30 G 1850—(1) Evenglow; (2) rose taupe; (3) nude; (4) pearl blush. Also black, white, beige, champagne, zinc, Gunmetal. SIZES: 8½, 9, 9½, 10.
State size and color wanted.
Shipping weight, per pair, 3 ounces.

"Golden Glo" service chiffon combines the smartness of chiffon and the wear of service weight. Full fashioned from perfect quality Pure Silk extending all the way up to the lisle reinforced garter top. Extra long for wear with the fashionable short dress. New fascinating shades so chic for autumn and winter. Lisle reinforced heel and toe. Repeated washings will not dim the luster or affect the trim smooth fit of this practical hose.

Rayon With Mercerized Top 38¢ A Pair

30 G 800—(1) Nude; (2) zinc; (3) peach; (4) beige. Also black, white and tan bark.
SIZES: 8½, 9, 9½, 10.
State size and color wanted.
Shipping weight, per pair, 3 oz.

All the shimmering beauty of pure Rayon, from top to mercerized garter hem—the appearance of silk but at much less cost. Neat seam up back of leg and high spliced heels are trimly smart. Reinforced seamless feet. Invisible ravel stop stripe. In the season's best colors.

Full Fashioned Silk and Rayon Hose 98¢ A Pair

30 G 1945—(1) Peach; (2) rose taupe; (3) beige; (4) zinc. Also black and nude.
SIZES: 8½, 9, 9½, 10. State size and color.
Shipping weight, per pair, 3 ounces.

It would indeed be difficult to surpass this Stocking combining so much beauty, durability and economy at this low price. Clearly and evenly knit from fine quality pure thread silk and rayon, extending up to 4½-inch mercerized top. Full fashioned and all the appearance of expensive stockings. Excellent for wear with popular short skirts. Reinforced heels and toes; high spliced heels add trimness to dainty ankles.

Our Finest Full Fashioned Silk $1.95 A Pair

30 G 1900—(1) Rose taupe; (2) rose taupe; (3) beige; (4) beige. Also black and zinc.
SIZES: 8½, 9, 9½, 10. State size and color.
Shipping weight, per pair, 3 ounces.

Simply exquisite! Our best quality full fashioned stockings—clear and lovely in appearance and so durable for practical wear. Knit from top to toe of all pure Japanese thread silk in popular service weight—so well known for long wear. To insure extra good service they have hemmed top reinforced on the inner side with lisle. Silk covered feet, heels and toes also reinforced with lisle.

Silk and Rayon Mercerized Top 45¢ A Pair

30 G 790—(1) Peach; (2) nude; (3) rose taupe; (4) tanbark. Also black, white, zinc and beige.
SIZES: 8½, 9, 9½, 10.
State size and color wanted.
Shipping weight, per pair, 3 ounces.

Value—as you've always hoped to find it! Beauty, too, that is sure to please you! No wonder this low priced Stocking is popular with thousands of our thrifty customers. Gleaming fabric extends from toe to the garter hem—well over the knee. Neat seamed back with marks resembling fashioned hose. Double soles; high spliced heels; firmly reinforced heels and toes. Ravel stop stripe.

26

Costume Slips and Bloomers
Economically Priced!

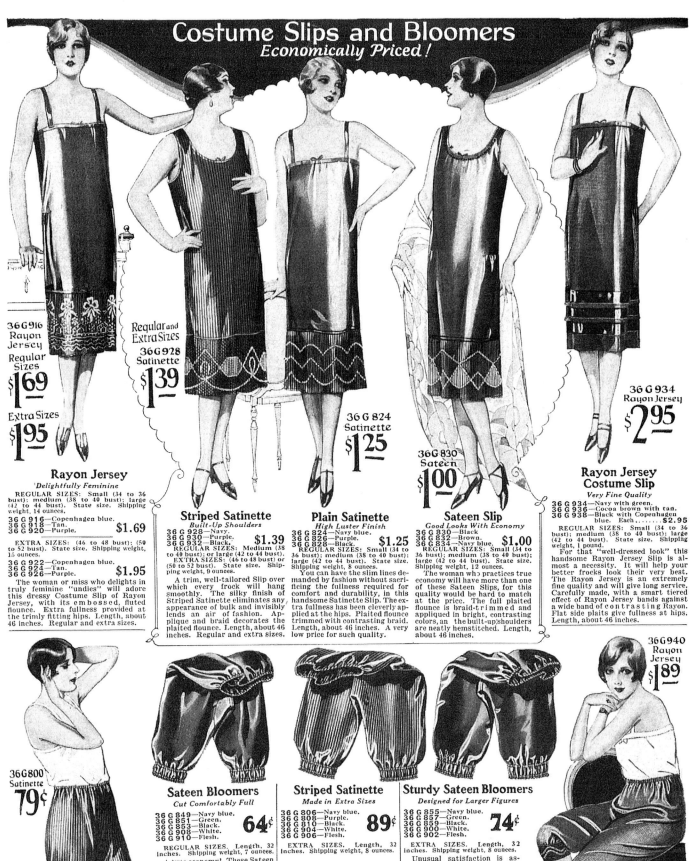

36 G 916
Rayon
Jersey
Regular
Sizes
$**1**69

Extra Sizes
$**1**95

Regular and
Extra Sizes
36 G 928
Satinette
$**1**39

36 G 824
Satinette
$**1**25

36 G 830
Sateen
$**1**00

36 G 934
Rayon Jersey
$**2**95

Rayon Jersey
Delightfully Feminine

REGULAR SIZES: Small (34 to 36 bust); medium (38 to 40 bust); large (42 to 44 bust). State size. Shipping weight, 14 ounces.

36 G 916—Copenhagen blue.
36 G 918—Tan.
36 G 920—Purple.   **$1.69**

EXTRA SIZES: (46 to 48 bust): (50 to 52 bust). State size. Shipping weight, 15 ounces.

36 G 922—Copenhagen blue.
36 G 924—Tan.
36 G 926—Purple.   **$1.95**

The woman or miss who delights in truly feminine "undies" will adore this dressy Costume Slip of Rayon Jersey, with its embossed, fluted flounce. Extra fullness provided at the trimly fitting hips. Length, about 46 inches. Regular and extra sizes.

Striped Satinette
Built-Up Shoulders

36 G 928—Navy.
36 G 930—Purple.
36 G 932—Black.   **$1.39**
REGULAR SIZES: Medium (38 to 40 bust); or large (42 to 44 bust).
EXTRA SIZES: (46 to 48 bust) or (50 to 52 bust). State size. Shipping weight, 9 ounces.

A trim, well-tailored Slip over which every frock will hang smoothly. The silky finish of Striped Satinette eliminates any appearance of bulk and invisibly lends an air of fashion. Applique and braid decorates the plaited flounce. Length, about 46 inches. Regular and extra sizes.

Plain Satinette
High Luster Finish

36 G 824—Navy blue.
36 G 826—Purple.
36 G 828—Black.   **$1.25**
REGULAR SIZES: Small (34 to 36 bust); medium (38 to 40 bust); large (42 to 44 bust). Shipping weight, 8 ounces.

You can have the slim lines demanded by fashion without sacrificing the fullness required for comfort and durability, in this handsome Satinette Slip. The extra fullness has been cleverly applied at the hips. Plaited flounce trimmed with contrasting braid. Length, about 46 inches. A very low price for such quality.

Sateen Slip
Good Looks With Economy

36 G 830—Black
36 G 832—Brown.
36 G 834—Navy blue.   **$1.00**
REGULAR SIZES: Small (34 to 36 bust); medium (38 to 40 bust); large (42 to 44 bust). State size. Shipping weight, 12 ounces.

The woman who practices true economy will have more than one of these Sateen Slips, for this quality would be hard to match at the price. The full plaited flounce is braid-trimmed and appliqued in bright, contrasting colors, an the built-up shoulders are neatly hemstitched. Length, about 46 inches.

Rayon Jersey Costume Slip
Very Fine Quality

36 G 934—Navy with green.
36 G 936—Cocoa brown with tan.
36 G 938—Black with Copenhagen blue. Each.......**$2.95**
REGULAR SIZES: Small (34 to 36 bust); medium (38 to 40 bust); large (42 to 44 bust). State size. Shipping weight, 1 pound.

For that "well-dressed look" this handsome Rayon Jersey Slip is almost a necessity. It will help your better frocks look their very best. The Rayon Jersey is an extremely fine quality and will give long service. Carefully made, with a smart tiered effect of Rayon Jersey bands against a wide band of contrasting Rayon. Flat side plaits give fullness at hips. Length, about 46 inches.

36 G 800
Satinette
79¢

32-Inch
Length

Sateen Bloomers
Cut Comfortably Full

36 G 849—Navy blue.
36 G 851—Green.
36 G 853—Black.
36 G 908—White.
36 G 910—Flesh.   **64¢**
REGULAR SIZES. Length, 32 inches. Shipping weight, 7 ounces.

A true economy! These Sateen Bloomers will give the utmost service. Generously cut, well made, reinforced where strength is most needed and finished with double elastic at knee and an elastic waistband.

Striped Satinette
Made in Extra Sizes

36 G 806—Navy blue.
36 G 808—Purple.
36 G 810—Black.
36 G 904—White.
36 G 906—Flesh.   **89¢**
EXTRA SIZES. Length, 32 inches. Shipping weight, 8 ounces.

For the fuller figure, a very smart, very practical, quite inexpensive Bloomer. The Striped Satinette is smooth fitting, a welcome feature for the larger woman. Reinforced at crotch.

Sturdy Sateen Bloomers
Designed for Larger Figures

36 G 855—Navy blue.
36 G 857—Green.
36 G 859—Black.
36 G 900—White.
36 G 902—Flesh.   **74¢**
EXTRA SIZES. Length, 32 inches. Shipping weight, 8 ounces.

Unusual satisfaction is assured the larger woman, in the long wearing quality and excellent make of these Sateen Bloomers. Made with reinforced seat, double elastic knee bands and elastic waistband.

36 G 940
Rayon
Jersey
$**1**89

Striped Satinette Bloomers
Looks and Feels Like Silk

36 G 800—Navy blue.
36 G 802—Purple.
36 G 804—Black.
36 G 912—White.
36 G 914—Flesh.   **79¢**
REGULAR SIZES. Length, 32 inches. Shipping weight; 7 ounces.

Because it looks and feels like silk, Striped Satinette is a favorite fabric for feminine undergarments. These Satinette Bloomers are of excellent make and fit, with double elastic at knee bands and elastic waistband.

Rayon Jersey

REGULAR SIZES. Length, 32 inches. Shipping weight, 12 ounces.
36 G 322—Navy blue.
36 G 324—Purple.
36 G 326—Black. $**1**39

EXTRA SIZES. Length, 32 inches. Shipping weight, 14 ounces.
36 G 328—Navy blue.
36 G 330—Purple.
36 G 332—Black. $**1**69

Every woman and miss will be delighted with the soft, clinging texture of these Rayon Jersey Bloomers for "best" wear. They are roomy, with double reinforced crotch. Double elastic knee bands. Elastic waistband.

Lustrous Rayon Jersey
As Beautiful as Pure Silk

36 G 940—Navy blue.
36 G 942—Purple.
36 G 944—Green.
36 G 946—Flesh. $**1**89
REGULAR SIZES. Length, 32 inches. Shipping weight, 14 ounces.

These Bloomers are just the thing to wear with tailored frocks or suits, to preserve smooth, slender lines. The plaited cuff, of an attractive, contrasting color trimmed with braid in color to harmonize, clasps snugly below the knee with a double row of elastic. Elastic also holds bloomers firmly at the waist. Strong, well-made, reinforced crotch. A garment that will give you that feeling of expensive luxury at small cost.

32-Inch
Length

for An Easy Smooth Figure

Supple Girdle

Smooth Back

MEASURE HERE

Popular Model $1.19
Light, Comfortable

32 G 1458—Flesh pink only.
SIZES: 24, 25, 26, 27, 28, 29, 30, 31, 32, 33, 34, 35, 36-inch waist only. Order actual waist measure over corset; also give hip measure.
Shipping weight, 1 pound.

Beauty experts are urging women to preserve their graceful figures with light girdles such as this. Made of good quality Rayon striped poplin with wide panels of supple elastic over hips. Wide band of elastic around top at sides and back. Light "Wont Rust" steels throughout. The front clasp is 7½ inches long with two retaining hooks below. Has four strong, adjustable hose supporters with rubber covered buttons.

MEASURE HERE

Keeps Diaphragm Flat

Holds Diaphragm $1.69
to Trim Lines

32 G 1486—Flesh pink only.
SIZES: 24, 25, 26, 27, 28, 29, 30, 31, 32, 33, 34, 35, 36-inch waist only. Order actual waist measure over corset; also give hip measure.
Shipping weight, 1 pound 2 ounces.

That slight extra support, that so many need across the diaphragm is cleverly provided by this very popular Corset. Designed a little higher in front to give a smooth flat line. Fine Rayon striped poplin with "Wont Rust" steels and with wide elastic panels over hips and an elastic strip at lower edge in back. Front clasp is 7½ inches long with three retaining hooks below; height above waist, 2 inches. Four adjustable hose supporters with rubber covered buttons.

$1.98

MEASURE HERE

Clasp-Around $1.98
for Supple Support

32 G 1599—Flesh pink only.
SIZES: 24, 25, 26, 27, 28, 29, 30, 31, 32, 33, 34, 35, 36-inch waist only. Order actual waist measure over corset; also give hip measure.
Shipping weight, 1 pound 2 ounces.

If you like your underthings to be dainty, you'll enjoy wearing this lustrous Rayon brocade Girdle trimmed with silky, colored braid. Looks as if it cost far more and will last surprisingly long. Pliable elastic panels over hips and at lower edge in back hold it close to the figure in smooth straight lines. Firmly boned with "Wont Rust" steels. Front clasp, 6¾ inches long with three retaining hooks below. Has four adjustable hose supporters with rubber covered buttons.

$2.98

Rayon Brocade

MEASURE HERE

Especially Rich $2.98
and Serviceable

32 G 1495—Flesh pink only.
SIZES: 24, 25, 26, 27, 28, 29, 30, 31, 32, 33, 34, 35, 36-inch waist only. Order actual waist measure over corset; also give hip measure.
Shipping weight, 1 pound 2 ounces.

Shows its rich quality in the fineness of its materials and in its careful finishing. Similar to girdles sold in exclusive city shops at prices almost double ours. Fancy shirred Rayon elastic all around top and extra wide elastic webbing panels over hips. Lustrous Rayon brocade back and front, lightly boned with "Wont Rust" steels and well reinforced with coutil. Four Rayon silk stripe adjustable hose supporters with rubber covered buttons.

16 INCHES

MEASURE HERE

Durolastic Girdle $1.9
"Style with Comfort"

SIZES: 24, 25, 26, 27, 28, 29, 30, 31, 32, 33, 34, 35 and 36-inch waist only.
32 G 1524—Pink only.
Length, 12 inches............$1.49
Sizes as above; also 38 and 40.
32 G 1526—Pink.
Length, 14 inches............$1.79
32 G 1529—Pink.
Length, 16 inches............1.89
Order actual waist measure over corset; also give hip measure.
Shipping weight, 1 pound 8 ounces.

Comfortable, pliable duro-elastic (heavy elastic) Girdle. Coutil front has 7½-inch clasp with two hooks below. "Wont Rust" steels covered with coutil. Dainty Rayon braid at top. Four Rayon striped hose supporters with rubber covered buttons.

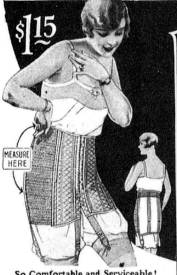

$1.15

MEASURE HERE

Smooth Back | Supple Restraint

So Comfortable and Serviceable!

32 G 1449—Flesh pink only........$1.15
SIZES: 24, 25, 26, 27, 28, 29, 30, 31, 32, 33, 34, 35, 36-inch waist only. Order actual waist measure over corset; also give hip measure.
Shipping weight, 1 pound 2 ounces.

Smartly designed Clasp-Around of sturdy figured coutil boned with "Wont Rust" steels. Elastic band at top and wide panels over hips. Front clasp, 7½ inches long has two hooks below. Back length, 14 inches. Four adjustable hose supporters.

$1.25

MEASURE HERE

Clasp-Around
32 G 1471—Flesh pink only.
SIZES: 24, 25, 26, 27, 28, 29, 30, 31, 32-inch waist only. Order actual waist measure over corset; also give hip measure.
Shipping weight, 1 pound.

Comfortably light, yet it will give firm support to the slender to average figure. The coutil and wide elastic webbing panels are of good wearing quality. Light "Wont Rust" steels. Front clasp, 6 inches long, has two retaining hooks below. Back length, 10½ inches. Four adjustable hose supporters.

Both Lined For Added Strength

BOTH OF SKINNER'S SATIN

Bandeau 98¢
Girdle $1.89

THIS GARMENT IS MADE OF WASHABLE
Skinner's Satin

College girls, their younger sisters and women who are still slender, all love to wear this Bandeau and Girdle. Daintily fashioned of lustrous Skinner's satin, these garments look so lovely and feel very soft and rich. Marvelous wearing and laundering quality. They are lined with firm, flesh colored batiste for extra strength. Cleverly designed to give the figure straight, flattering lines, yet retain all the naturally beautiful curves.

The Bandeau
32 G 1625—Flesh pink only........98¢
SIZES: 28, 30, 32, 34, 36, 38-inch bust only. State bust measure. Ship. wt., 4 ounces. Elastic inserts in back for easy adjustment. Rayon braid trimming. Fastens in back.

The Girdle........$1.89
32 G 1525—Flesh pink only.
SIZES: 24, 25, 26, 27, 28, 29, 30, 32, 34-inch waist only. Order actual waist measure over corset.
Shipping weight, 10 ounces.

Lightly boned 8-inch front section. Back is 10 inches long. Wide elastic side panels over hips. Four adjustable hose supporters.

$1.00

MEASURE HERE

Extraordinary
Clasp-Around Value $1.00

32 G 1523—Flesh pink only.
SIZES: 22, 23, 24, 25, 26, 27, 28, 29, 30, 31, 32, 33, 34, 35, 36-inch waist only. Order two inches smaller than waist measure over corset.
Shipping weight, 1 pound 4 ounces.

Serviceable coutil, well designed—a real bargain! Laced full length in back. Boned with "Wont Rust" steels. Front clasp, 7½ inches long, two retaining hooks. Four hose supporters.

"The Trig"
98¢

32 G 1741—Flesh pink only.
SIZES: 24, 25, 26, 27, 28, 29, 30, 31, 32-inch waist only. Order actual waist measure over corset.
Shipping weight, 7 ounces.

Smarter lines for your figure even though it needs scarcely any support. Good quality Rayon striped poplin with elastic panels; side opening. "Wont Rust" steels front and back. Four adjustable hose supporters.

Our "Supple Form"

$4.98

32 G 1537—SIZES: 26, 27, 28, 29, 30, 31, 32, 33, 34, 35, 36-inch waist only....$4.98
32 G 1538—EXTRA SIZES: 38 and 40-inch waist only....$5.25
Flesh pink only. Order actual waist measure over corset; also give hip measure. Ship. weight, each, 2 lbs.

You'll actually reduce your abdomen and diaphragm by wearing this specially designed Girdle. Marvelously durable coutil back and Rayon knitted elastic front panels. Two abdominal tabs of elastic and coutil with double loop supporters. Insert of shirred, silk striped elastic at lower edge of back. Heavy duplex "Wont Rust" steels. Front clasp, 7½ inches long with three hooks below. Back length, 14 inches. Four extra adjustable hose supporters.

MEASURE HERE

Prevents Corset Lines

Only 49¢

Smooth Back

"Golfette" for Sports and Everyday Wear
49¢

32 G 1736—Flesh pink only.
SIZES: 24, 25, 26, 27, 28, 29, 30, 32-inch waist only. Order actual waist measure over corset.
Shipping weight, 6 ounces.

Gives just enough restraint to the abdomen and makes garments hang smoothly over the hips. Sturdy figured coutil lightly boned in front; sides are of firm surgical elastic. Hooks at side front. Four adjustable hose supporters with rubber covered buttons.

A Big Purchase Cuts the Price!
Vests—Drawers—Bloomers
for Winter Wear

29 G 778 — **29 G 774**

29 G 813

29 G 809

Medium Heavy Fine Ribbed Cotton
White Only

Regular Sizes **49¢** A Garment

29 G 776

SIZES: 34, 36, 38-in. bust. State measure.
Shipping weight, each, 10 ounces.
29G774—High neck, long sleeve Vest ... 49¢
29G778—Dutch neck, elbow sleeve Vest 49¢
29G776—Ankle length Drawers .... 49¢

Extra Sizes **59¢** A Garment

SIZES: 40, 42, 44-inch bust. State bust measure.
Shipping weight, each, 12 ounces.
29 G 775—High neck, long sleeve Vest .... 59¢
29 G 779—Dutch neck, elbow sleeve Vest .... 59¢
29 G 777—Ankle length Drawers .... 59¢

Vests and Drawers that are deservedly popular because they offer dependable quality within the means of everyone. Fine ribbed knit in a medium heavy weight from good grade, durable cotton yarn. Lightly fleeced for warmth and real comfort. Choice of two vest styles—both have mercerized stitched down trim and mercerized drawtapes. Crocheted edge down front. All seams flatlocked. Shaped sides. Ankle length drawers have muslin waistband and convenient open seat. You can thoroughly depend upon their good qualities for excellent service after continuous wearing.

Raycrest

Fine Quality Rayon Striped Cotton
Cream Color Only

Regular Sizes **56¢** A Garment

SIZES: 34, 36, 38-inch bust.
State bust measure.
29 G 809—Low neck, sleeveless Vest ....56¢
29 G 810—Knee length Bloomers ....56¢
29 G 813—Dutch neck, elbow sleeve Vest ....56¢

Extra Sizes **65¢** A Garment

SIZES: 40, 42, 44-inch bust.
State bust measure.
29 G 811—Low neck, sleeveless Vest ....65¢
29 G 812—Knee length Bloomers ....65¢
29 G 814—Dutch neck, elbow sleeve Vest ....65¢

Shipping weight, each garment, 8 ounces.

When you see these Vests and Bloomers, you will marvel that we sell such attractive looking garments at so low a price. Splendid quality cotton, fine ribbed knit in a medium weight. Lustrous cross stripes of Rayon add elegance. Choice of sleeveless vest with tubular band neck and armholes, or Dutch neck style with short sleeves. Knee length bloomers have fresh elastic at waist and knee and large reinforced gusset in seat.

29 G 810

29 G 806

29 G 805

29 G 807

Lightly Fleeced Ribbed Knit Cotton
White Only
Double Extra Sizes 46, 48, 50 **85¢** A Garment

State bust measure. Shipping weight, each garment, 11 ounces.
29 G 805—Dutch neck, elbow sleeve Vest ....85¢
29 G 806—High neck, long sleeve Vest ....85¢
29 G 807—Ankle length Drawers ....85¢

Stout women all over the country have discovered that they can get perfect fitting underwear from Ward's. These Vests and Drawers are generously sized to insure satisfaction. Fine ribbed knit in a medium heavy weight from good quality cotton—slightly fleeced on the inside for warmth and softness. Choice of Dutch neck, elbow sleeve style or high neck, long sleeve style. Each finished with mercerized edging at neck and mercerized drawtape. Drawers are open seat style with wide flap to insure perfect closing. Strong muslin waistband. Button at sides with extra buttonholes for adjustment. All seams flatlocked.

Order All Drawers Same as Bust Measure

29 G 788

29 G 784

29 G 785

Extra Heavy Weight Thickly Fleeced Good Quality Cotton

29 G 836

29 G 802

Fine Quality Ribbed Knit Cotton
Heavy Weight—Lightly Fleeced

Regular Sizes **79¢** A Garment
White Only

SIZES: 34, 36, 38-inch bust. State bust measure. Shipping weight; each garment, 10 ounces.
29 G 784—High neck, long sleeve Vest ....79¢
29 G 785—Open seat style Drawers ....79¢
29 G 788—Dutch neck, elbow sleeve Vest ....79¢
29 G 808—Closed seat style Drawers ....79¢

Extra Sizes **88¢** A Garment
White Only

SIZES: 40, 42, 44-inch bust. State bust measure. Shipping weight; each garment, 12 ounces.
29 G 786—High neck, long sleeve Vest ....88¢
29 G 787—Open seat style Drawers ....88¢
29 G 790—Dutch neck, elbow sleeve Vest ....88¢
29 G 804—Closed seat style Drawers ....88¢

Excellent undergarments for cold weather wear—warm Vests and Drawers of heavy weight, fine ribbed knit of good quality cotton. Lightly fleeced for additional warmth and comfort. Vests have mercerized stitched down trim, mercerized tape, crocheted edge on front and reinforced shoulders. Ankle length drawers are in choice of open or closed seat with neat muslin waistband fastening at sides. All seams flatlocked for smooth comfort.

Closed Seat

29 G 808

White Only
Regular Sizes **77¢** A Garment

SIZES: 34, 36, 38-inch bust. State bust measure.
Shipping weight, each garment, 12 ounces.
29 G 800— High neck, long sleeve Vest ....77¢
29 G 836— Dutch neck, elbow sleeve Vest ....77¢
29 G 801—Open seat, Drawers ....77¢

Extra Sizes **89¢** A Garment

SIZES: 40, 42, 44-inch bust. State bust measure.
Shipping weight, each garment, 14 ounces.
29 G 802—High neck, long sleeve Vest ... 89¢
29 G 837—Dutch neck, elbow sleeve Vest .89¢
29 G 803—Open seat Drawers ....89¢

The woman who wants warm underwear for winter but does not care for wool, will find real protection in our heaviest weight cotton Vest and Drawers. They are fine elastic ribbed and have an extra thread knit in the back and brushed into a thick, warm fleecing. Vests have neat crocheted trimming around neck and down front opening. Drawers are ankle length and have strong muslin waistband with special tape adjustment in back.

Amazingly Serviceable!

Warmth and Service at Very Low Cost 49¢
32 G 114—Assorted stripes only.
SIZES: 34-36, 38-40, 42-44-inch bust only. State bust measure. Ship. wt., 10 oz.
Very careful buying makes possible the lowest price we have offered for years on a well made, good quality flannelette Gown. Round neck; short kimono sleeves hemstitched. Length, about 52 inches.

Dainty Floral Design Printed Flannelette 98¢
32 G 171—White with pink floral design.
32 G 182—Flesh pink; blue floral design.
SIZES: 34-36, 38-40, 42-44-inch bust only. State bust measure. Shipping weight, 12 ounces.
Dainty, attractive designs. Round neck; short kimono sleeves. Length, about 52 inches.

Dainty Plain Colors 89¢
32 G 145—White.
32 G 146—Flesh pink.
32 G 147—Peach.
SIZES: 34-36, 38-40, 42-44-inch bust only. State bust measure. Shipping weight, 14 ounces.
Marvelous value for women who prefer dainty solid color flannelette Gowns. Warm, durable quality with long sleeves and double yoke front and back. High round neck. Rayon embroidery and hemstitch trim. Length, about 52 inches.

Beautifully Embroidered 89¢
32 G 144—Assorted stripes only.
SIZES: 34-36, 38-40, 42-44-inch bust only. State bust measure. Shipping weight, 14 ounces.
You'll agree that we're offering you a remarkable bargain in this warm, carefully made flannelette Gown. Double yoke front and back is trimmed with embroidery and hemstitching in front. Long sleeves; felled seams throughout. Two-button closing. Length, 52 inches.

Embroidery Trim Our Best Seller $1.00
32 G 129—White.
32 G 130—Flesh pink.
32 G 131—Peach.
SIZES: 34-36, 38-40, 42-44-inch bust only. State bust measure. Ship. wt., 14 oz.
Flannelette Night Dress in solid colors. Double yoke front and back. Rayon embroidery and hemstitching trim. Felled seams throughout. Length, about 52 inches.

Extra Size Gowns

Unusual Value for Larger Women 89¢
32 G 161—Assorted stripes only.
EXTRA SIZES: 46, 48, 50, 52-inch bust only. State bust measure. Shipping weight, 14 ounces.
Seldom can you find stout size Nightgowns for such a low price! Good quality, too, with double yoke front and back for extra wear and warmth. Front trimmed with Rayon hemstitching. High round neck; long sleeves. Felled seams throughout. Length, about 52 inches.

Popular Plain Shades in Stout Sizes $1.00
32 G 135—White.
32 G 136—Flesh pink.
32 G 137—Peach.
EXTRA SIZES: 46, 48, 50, 52 bust only. State bust meas. Ship. wt., 15 oz.
Fine quality Gown that will be snug and warm for cold nights. Dainty plain colors in durable flannelette with double yoke front and back. Hemstitched in front. High V-neck. Felled seams throughout. Two buttons. Length, about 52 inches.

Trimmed With Embroidery and Hemstitching $1.49
32 G 138—Assorted stripes only.
EXTRA SIZES: 46, 48, 50 and 52-inch bust only. State bust measure. Ship. wt., 16 ounces.
Popular style in full, roomy sizes for the larger woman. Our best quality nationally known Amoskeag flannelette with high V-neck and double yoke front and back. Front has Rayon embroidery and hemstitching. Felled seams. Length, about 54 in.

Genuine Blendown Flannelette $1.45
32 G 155—Assorted stripes only.
SIZES: 34-36, 38-40, 42-44-inch bust only. State bust measures. Shipping weight, 16 ounces.
Famous quality—preferred by scores of women! Its unusual popularity is due to the warm woolen threads that are woven into its firm, soft texture, assuring extra comfort and coziness. Well made throughout with felled seams and carefully finished.
Yoke is made double front and back for extra warmth and service. Front finished in Rayon hemstitching. Three-button closing. Length, about 54 in.

BLENDOWN TRADE MARK APPLETON WOOL and COTTON

MADE OF AMOSKEAG FLANNELETTE

Misses Gown

Amoskeag Flannelette 89¢
32 G 186—Flesh pink.
32 G 187—Peach.
AGES: 14, 16 and 18 years. State age wanted. Ship. wt., each, 10 oz.
Warm, serviceable Gown for girls and misses. Good quality, Amoskeag flannelette. Has high round neck; long sleeves; double yoke front and back. Two rows of hemstitching trim the front.

Women's Flannelette Bloomers 39¢
REGULAR SIZES
LENGTHS: 25, 27 and 29 inches. State length.
32 G 176—Asst. gray stripes. Each .... 39¢
32 G 173—Peach.
32 G 174—Flesh. 49¢
EXTRA SIZES
LENGTHS: 25, 27, 29 in. State length wanted.
32 G 180—Assorted gray stripes. Each.... 49¢
Ship. wt., each, 8 ounces.
Elastic at waist and knee. Finished with ruffle. Full, roomy sizes.

Women's Warm Flannelette Nightwear

Regulation Style Striped $1.49
32 G 152—Assorted stripes only.
SIZES: 34-36, 38-40, 42-44-inch bust only. State bust measure. Shipping weight, 18 ounces.
Sleeping garments neatly made to give comfortable warmth without being bulky. You'll like this flannelette two-piece style with its smart coat, and pretty colored Rayon frogs. Has round neck, long sleeves and one pocket. Double yoke in back.

One-Piece "Billie Burke" $1.39
32 G 143 — Assorted stripes only.
SIZES: 34-36, 38-40, 42-44-inch bust only. State bust meas. Ship. wt., 14 oz.
Decidedly popular, particularly with younger women. Neatly trimmed and so comfortable. Soft, cozy flannelette with round neck and double yoke front and back. Front outlined with pretty colored hemstitching. Has one pocket and groups of shirring below yoke. Ankles finished with elastic and ruffle. Buttons down front and has button flap crotch. Well made with strong seams throughout.

Charming Style $1.89
32 G 141—Peach.
32 G 142—Flesh pink.
SIZES: 34-36, 38-40, 42-44-inch bust only. State bust measure. Shipping weight, each, 18 ounces.
Smart style as well as comfortable warmth and durability in this dainty Pajama Suit of Amoskeag flannelette. Jacket is cut on straight lines and finished with delicately colored Rayon braid around neck and pocket. Long sleeves, double yoke in back. Straight leg trousers fitted at waist with drawtape. Ankles hemmed.

79¢ Women's and Misses' Flannelette Slips
WOMEN'S SIZES: 34, 36, 38, 40, 42, 44-inch bust measure. State bust measure.
32 G 190—Assorted light stripes.
32 G 191—Assorted gray stripes. Each...... 79¢
MISSES' SIZES: AGES: 14, 16, 18 years. State age wanted.
32 G 194—Assorted light stripes. Each..... 69¢
Shipping weight, each, 10 oz.
Neck and built-up shoulders edged with shell crochet stitch. Two buttons in front. Flounce.

Misses' Sizes

Warmth and Service in This Attractive "Billie Burke" Style $1.49
32 G 172—Peach with blue designs only.
AGES: 14, 16, 18 years. State age. Shipping weight, 8 ounces.
Each $1.49
Girls like them because of their colorful floral designs. Double yoke front and back, with hemstitching design in front. High, comfortable round neck. Shirring below yoke. One pocket. Buttons down front and has drop seat. Legs finished with elastic and ruffle.

Cozy Eiderdown Bed Slippers 49¢
32 G 198—Gray.
32 G 199—Red.
WOMEN'S SIZES: 3, 5 and 7. State size. Shipping weight, each, 5 ounces.
Comfort and warmth in these soft, double eiderdown Slumber Slippers! Cuffs edged with fancy stitching, and finished with ribbon bows. Inexpensive for a gift, and sure to be appreciated.

39¢ Warm Petticoat Regular and Extra Sizes
REGULAR SIZES:
32 G 184—Dark gray stripes only. Each........ 39¢
EXTRA FULL SIZES:
32 G 185—Dark gray stripes only. Each........ 49¢
LENGTHS: 28, 30, 32, 34, 36 inches. State length. Shipping weight, each, 10 ounces.
Cozy warm, Petticoat made in full, roomy sizes. Good quality flannelette with tape draw at waist and flounce at bottom. Splendid durability even though it is priced so remarkably low.

MADE OF AMOSKEAG FLANNELETTE

31

Line O' Youth Corset Brassieres
Style With New Comfort

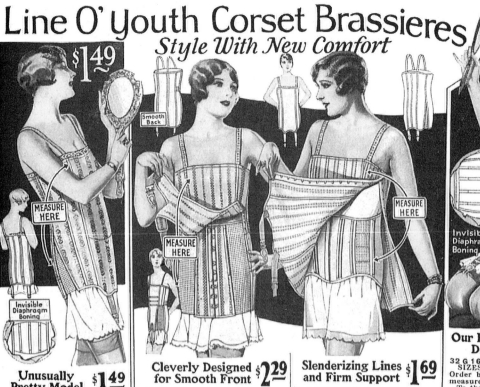

Trimline Self Adjusting Bust and Hip Sections

Laced Garments Come Fully Laced

MEASURE HERE

Smooth Back

Invisible Diaphragm Boning

Unusually Pretty Model $1.49

32 G 1734—Flesh pink only. SIZES: 32, 34, 36, 38, 40, 42, 44, 46-inch bust only. Order bust measure over fullest part; also give hip measure.

Shipping weight, 14 ounces.

You'll enjoy wearing this Corset Brassiere as its Rayon striped poplin is rich and silky and the white Val lace edging ever so pretty. You'll be amazed at the beauty it will bring to your figure—straight tailored lines, just gently curving.

There are firm "Wont Rust" steels full length in back, and elastic inserts over each hip. Concealed reinforced section, lightly boned, smoothly molds the diaphragm and abdomen. Fastens at side front. Four adjustable hose supporters with rubber covered buttons; fancy Rayon figured straps.

Cleverly Designed for Smooth Front $2.29

32 G 1688—Flesh pink only. SIZES: 32, 34, 36, 38, 40, 42, 44, 46, 48-inch bust only. Order actual bust measure over fullest part; also give hip measure.

Shipping weight, 1 pound 10 ounces.

New York fashion experts say this is one of the most successful Corset Brassieres ever designed for the average figure, just beginning to grow stout. Imagine the smooth unbroken line the lightly boned brassiere section will give as it extends over the abdomen with two hose supporters that hold it in place!

Firm "Wont Rust" steels extend full length in back. Made of rayon striped poplin with front elastic panels and "fit-well" elastic inserts at waistline of the brassiere section which fastens at side. Has 6½-inch girdle front clasp and three hooks. Two extra adjustable hose supporters; rubber covered buttons. Rayon figured shoulder straps.

Slenderizing Lines and Firm Support $1.69

32 G 1708—Flesh pink only. SIZES: 32, 34, 36, 38, 40, 42, 44, 46-inch bust only. Order actual bust measure over fullest part; also give hip measure.

Shipping weight, 14 ounces.

Gracious dignity and charming lines for the average to stout figure! With this 9½-inch inner belt of firmly boned jean cloth and elastic panels, the abdomen will be held in place smoothly, and actually reduced.

Fashioned of serviceable Rayon striped poplin with elastic inserts over the hips. You'll find the back restful as it is lightly boned with "Wont Rust" steels. Outer garment fastens at side front and belt in center front with concealed hooks and eyes. Four adjustable hose supporters with rubber covered buttons; Rayon figured shoulder straps.

Our Famous "Trimline" Model Designed for Perfect Fit $1.98

32 G 1694—Flesh pink only. SIZES: 32, 34, 36, 38, 40, 42, 44, 46-inch bust only. Order bust measure over fullest part; also give hip measure. Shipping weight, 16 ounces.

To the woman who thinks she is rather hard to fit, we highly recommend our popular "Trimline" model as a splendid foundation garment. Specially designed with supple panels of fine elastic above the waist in the back and over each hip, it will comfortably shape an average to stout figure into fashionable lines. Lacings in the back below waist make adjustment so very easy. The marvelous service it will give you is out of all proportion to its low price.

An invisible diaphragm section of firmly boned jean cloth fastened into the seams at the front insures youthful lines to the diaphragm and abdomen. Made of dependable Rayon striped poplin, boned full length in back with "Wont Rust" steels. Fastens at side with non-gapping hooks and eyes. Four adjustable hose supporters with rubber covered buttons. Rayon figured straps with elastic inserts.

Invisible Diaphragm Boning

Dainty Sylphline

MEASURE HERE

DIAPHRAGM CONTROL

32 G 1728

32 G 1649

Ideal for Figures Large Below the Waist $2.39

32 G 1665—Flesh pink only. SIZES: 32, 34, 36, 38, 40, 42, 44, 46-inch bust only. Order bust measure over fullest part; also give hip measure.

Shipping weight, 1 pound 6 ounces.

Flattering lines for the average to stout figure—especially for those who are large below the waist. Lacings below the waist in the back allow you to shape your figure into the fashionable lines that the new frocks require. Tailored of sturdy mercerized jacquard, with elastic webbing panels below the waist in front. Boned full length in back and lightly in front with "Wont Rust" steels.

Brassiere section fastens conveniently in center front with concealed hooks and eyes; girdle section has 6-inch front clasp and one retaining hook below. Four strong, adjustable hose supporters with rubber covered buttons. Fancy tape shoulder straps.

$1.59

32 G 1727—Elastic insert full length in back; no lacing. Flesh pink only.................

32 G 1728—Lacing below three-inch elastic insert in back. Flesh pink only..........$1.59

SIZES: 32, 34, 36, 38, 40, 42, 44, 46-inch bust. Order bust measure over fullest part; also give hip measure.

Shipping weight, 1 pound 6 ounces.

All the advantages of a well shaped Brassiere and a trimly fitting Girdle with the added convenience of a one-piece garment! And "Dainty Sylphline" gives such lovely lines to the average sized figure. Sturdy, figured coutil lightly boned full length in back and at sides with "Wont Rust" steels. Has below in front clasp. Brassiere section is stitched down on right side but free on the left and fastens with concealed hooks under the arm. Four adjustable hose supporters with rubber covered buttons. Tape straps.

Our Charming "Patricia" Model $3.98

32 G 1662—Flesh pink only. SIZES: 32, 34, 36, 38, 40, 42, 44, 46, 48-inch bust only. Order bust measure over fullest part; also give hip measure.

Shipping weight, 1 pound 6 ounces.

Fashionable city shops would ask about twice our price for such an up-to-date, lovely model! Its rich, costly materials look beautiful, last especially long and will feel so soft and fine. Silky Rayon jersey bust section gives the figure the natural beauty which is healthful and so stylish today.

Made of heavy Rayon brocade, with flexible "Wont Rust" steel boning in back and light boning across the abdomen. Strong, supple elastic silk striped webbing in front and over the hips assures a trim, perfect fit. Opens at side with concealed, non-gapping hooks and eyes. Rayon figured tape shoulder straps have elastic inserts. Four strong Rayon striped adjustable hose supporters with rubber covered buttons.

Light—Comfortable and Such a Bargain 98¢

32 G 1648—Smooth back, no lacing.............$ .98

32 G 1649—Laced full length in back............ 1.09

Flesh pink only. SIZES: 32, 34, 36, 38, 40, 42, 44, 46-inch bust only. Order bust measure over fullest part; also give hip measure.

Shipping weight, each, 12 ounces.

Perfectly amazing bargain—for it's serviceable and carefully designed even though it costs so little. Wearing a light support like this Corset Brassiere will preserve your slim girlish lines in a remarkable way. Very well made of finely woven poplin with dainty Rayon stripes. Supple elastic inserts over each hip allow perfect freedom and ease in any posture.

Three light "Wont Rust" steels effectively control diaphragm. Fastens at side front with concealed, non-gapping hooks and eyes that cannot touch the flesh. Four strong, adjustable hose supporters with protected rubber covered buttons. Tape shoulder straps.

Slim Lines Can Be Achieved So Comfortably $1.98

32 G 1705—Flesh pink only. SIZES: 32, 34, 36, 38, 40, 42, 44, 46-inch bust only. Order actual bust measure over fullest part; also give hip measure.

Shipping weight, 1 pound 2 ounces.

Perhaps you aren't used to wearing a Corset, yet realize that you need a little special restraint across the abdomen and a smooth fit over the hips! This carefully tailored garment will give you a slim, fashionable silhouette and it is so delightfully light and comfortable to wear.

Made of serviceable mercerized brocade with panels of elastic webbing at sides and back. The only boning is across the diaphragm and abdomen section—six flexible "Wont Rust" steels. You can see what a perfect choice it is for the active woman, it will allow her easy freedom in any position. Fastens at left side front with concealed, non-gapping hooks and eyes. Fancy Rayon tape shoulder straps. Four strong adjustable hose supporters with protected rubber covered buttons.

Summer Weight Garments *for Year Round Wear!*

29 G 402 **29 G 408** **29 G 410** **29 G 404** **29 G 584** **29 G 582**

WARDELLA UNION SUITS

Fine Ribbed Light Weight Cotton
White Only

Regular Sizes **45¢**	Extra Sizes **49¢**
Sizes: 34, 36, 38-inch bust. State bust measure.	Sizes: 40, 42, 44-inch bust. State bust measure.
29 G 400—Closed seat; wide knee; built-up shoulder.	29 G 401—Closed seat; wide knee; built-up shoulder.
29 G 402—Closed seat; wide knee; bodice top.	29 G 403—Closed seat; wide knee; bodice top.
29 G 404—Open seat; wide knee; built-up shoulder.	29 G 405—Open seat; wide knee; built-up shoulder.
29 G 408—Open seat; tight knee; built-up shoulder.	29 G 409—Open seat; tight knee; built-up shoulder.
29 G 410—Open seat; tight knee; bodice top.	29 G 411—Open seat; tight knee; bodice top.
Shipping weight, each, 6 oz.	Shipping weight, each, 6 oz.

Closed styles are made over the famous Triad pattern—full and roomy in the legs, yet smooth, close fitting over the hips. Women who do not require heavy weight underwear find these light ribbed cotton Union Suits excellent for year round wear. Knit of extra fine carded cotton, and finished throughout with painstaking care. Six styles for you to choose from—all have neat-tubular band finish at top and special reinforcement shields under arms. Hand finished buttonhole. Mercerized draw tape. Wide knee styles finished with mercerized shell edging. Bodice top styles have [mercerized lingerie tape straps. Reinforced gusset in crotch of tight knee styles.

Quality Combed Cotton
White Only

Regular Sizes **59¢**
Sizes: 34, 36, 38-inch bust. State bust measure. Ship. wt., ea., 6 oz.
29 G 580—Closed seat; wide knee.
29 G 582—Open seat; wide knee.
29 G 584—Open seat; tight knee.

Extra Sizes **65¢**
Sizes: 40, 42, 44-inch bust. State bust measure. Ship. wt., ea., 6 oz.
29 G 581—Closed style; wide knee.
29 G 583—Open seat; wide knee.
29 G 585—Open seat; tight knee.

Perfect fit and the utmost comfort—the two essentials of better quality garments are found in Wardella Union Suits. Closed seat style is cut over the famous Triad pattern, with an abundance of space in legs and close fitting hips. Knit of best grade combed cotton. All styles made with dainty picot edge, full tubular band tops. Mercerized draw tape; hand finished buttonhole in front. Reinforcing shields under arms; all seams flatlocked. Tight knee style has reinforced gusset in crotch. Open seat, wide knee style has mercerized shell edge bottom and shaped sides.

"Triad" **29 G 40 0** **Closed Seat** **29 G 580**

Rayon Striped Combed Cotton
White Only

Regular Sizes **69¢**
Sizes: 34, 36, 38-inch bust. State bust measure.Ship. wt., 6 oz.
29 G 708—Open seat; shaped sides; tight knee.
29 G 706—Closed seat; shell edged, wide knee.

Extra Sizes **79¢**
Sizes: 40, 42, 44-inch bust. State bust measure Ship. wt., 6 oz.
29 G 709—Open seat; shaped sides; tight knee.
29 G 707—Closed seat; shell edged; wide knee.

Fine ribbed cotton Union Suits with Rayon cross stripes for added attractiveness. Closed style cut over Triad pattern, famous for its comfort. Tight knee style shaped at sides and has double gusset in crotch. Flatlocked seams. Shields under arms.

29 G 706 **29 G 708**

29 G 711

Double Extra Sizes

29 G 710

62¢
Sizes: 46, 48, 50-inch Bust State bust measure. *White Only.*
29 G 710—Tight knee style.
29 G 711—Wide knee style.
Shipping weight, each, 8 ounces.

Carefully tailored over extra generous proportions, insuring perfect fit for women who need larger than average sizes. Fine ribbed knit from excellent quality cotton yarns in choice of two styles—tight knee, open seat with large double gusset in crotch, or wide knee, open seat, knees trimmed with mercerized shell edging. Both are finely finished in all details —built-up shoulders and armholes are edged with tubular band. Draw tape is lustrous mercerized. All seams flatlocked for comfort and longer wear.

Glove Silk **Cotton** **29 G 610**

Extra Quality Glove Silk Top
Pink Only

$1⁵⁹

29 G 610—Tight knee style; built-up shoulders.
29 G 611—Tight knee; bodice top.

EVEN SIZES: 34 to 44-inch bust. State size. Ship. wt., each, 6 ounces. A lovely Union Suit of fine appearance and comfort combined with the practical wearing qualities of cotton and at an economical price. The dainty glove silk top is very soft and comfortable; the fine ribbed combed cotton lower part is very serviceable. Two styles, both made with tight knee and reinforced in crotch. The built-up shoulder style has neat tubular band finish. Bodice top style has satin ribbon shoulder straps. Both have silk mixed ribbon draw tapes, and reinforced shields of silk under the arms. Wide lapped open seats. With this garment you can enjoy the pleasure of silk at a worthwhile saving.

29 G 611

Six Styles of Quality Cotton Vests—Every Price Saves You Money!

Mercerized Cotton

Lowest Priced Vests

SIZES: 34, 36, 38-inch bust. State bust measure. 29 G 628—White. **25¢**	SIZES: 34, 36, 38-inch bust. State bust measure. 29 G 614—White. **25¢**
SIZES: 40, 42, 44-inch bust. State bust measure. 29 G 629—White. **29¢**	SIZES: 40, 42, 44-inch bust. State bust measure. 29 G 615—White. **29¢**
Ship. weight, each, 4 oz. Built-up shoulder with tubular band finish around neck and armholes. Mercerized draw tape. Finished buttonhole.	Fine ribbed cotton, bodice style. Tubular band finish around top. Mercerized draw tape. Fancy lingerie tape straps

Fine Quality Vests

SIZES: 34, 36, 38-inch bust. State bust measure. 29 G 644—White only. **39¢**	SIZES: 34, 36, 38-inch bust. State bust measure. 29 G 622—White only. **39¢**
SIZES: 40, 42, 44-inch bust. State bust measure. 29 G 645—White only. **45¢**	SIZES: 40, 42, 44-inch bust. State bust measure. 29 G 623—White only. **45¢**
Ship. weight, each, 4 ounces. Fine ribbed bodice style. Tubular band finish at top. Mercerized draw tape. A very attractive Vest that will give good service.	Built-up shoulder style with tubular band finish around neck and armholes. Made of fine ribbed cotton. Mercerized draw tape. Very serviceable.

SIZES: 34, 36, 38-inch bust. State bust measure. 29 G 630—White. **42¢**	SIZES: 34, 36, 38-inch bust. State bust measure. 29 G 632—White. **42¢**
SIZES: 40, 42, 44-inch bust. State bust measure. 29 G 631—White. **47¢**	SIZES: 40, 42, 44-inch bust. State bust measure. 29 G 633—White. **47¢**
Ship. weight, each, 6 ounces. Dutch neck; short sleeves, shaped sides; draw tape at neck. Flatlocked seams. Pearl buttons.	Ship. weight, each, 6 ounces. Long sleeves; high neck; shaped sides. Draw tape at neck. Crochet edged front. Flatlocked seams. Pearl buttons.

Good Taste~Wonderful Style   Better Quality~The New Idea

All Wool Polaire
Contrasting Insertions

10 G 706 Polaire—for popularity—especially this excellent winter-weight All Wool weave! Your choice of three Fall shades, each with a stunningly blended convertible collar of fluffy Mandel Fur. Well tailored, with insertions of contrasting Velour to accent the slender side panel lines and smartly finish the cuffs. Warm interlining. Durable twill lining. GIRLS' SIZES: 8, 10, 12, 14 years. State size. Read "How to Order" Instructions on Page 27. Ship. wt., 4 lbs. 14 oz.
10 G 706—Reindeer (dark) tan; dark brown trim. Mink dyed Mandel fur.
10 G 708—Rust; cranberry red trim. Mink dyed Mandel fur.
10 G 710—Gracklehead (medium) blue; navy blue trim. Raccoon dyed Mandel fur. **$8.50**

Very Smart Model
Practical Velour Coating

10 G 718 We feel sure you could not duplicate this value elsewhere! Just enough sturdy cotton in its weave makes this smooth-faced Velour Coating even more durable. The coat is soft and warm — cozily interlined beneath its very durable mercerized twill lining. Dressy mushroom collar of soft, glossy Beaverette Fur (sheared coney). Insert pockets introduce the new side panels, alternating harmonizing buttons with groups of twin cord tucks. GIRLS' SIZES: 8, 10, 12, 14 years. State size wanted. Read "How to Order" on Page 27. Shipping weight, 4 lbs. 12 oz.
10 G 718—Reindeer (dark) tan.
10 G 720—Cranberry red.
10 G 722—Gracklehead (medium) blue. **$6.49**

10 G 712
All Wool Buxkin Suede
$11.98

10 G 712 All Wool Buxkin Suede of incomparably fine fabric of glove-like finish. Distinctive side panels, with bright floss stitching and self covered buttons. Smooth saddle shoulders sloping to the big collar of fluffy Mandel Fur. Warm interlining; high-lustre lining, good for two seasons.
GIRLS' SIZES: 8, 10, 12, 14 years. State size wanted. Read "How to Order" on Page 27. Ship. wt., 5 pounds.
10 G 712—Reindeer (dark tan). Mink dyed Mandel fur.
10 G 714—Canton (dark Copenhagen) blue. Raccoon dyed Mandel fur.
10 G 716—Rose. Mink dyed Mandel fur. **$11.98**

10 G 706
All Wool Polaire
$8.50

10 G 736
Wool Mixed Chinchilla
$8.98

10 G 718
Velour Coating
$6.49

10 G 700
Velour Coating
$7.98

10 G 724
All Wool Vel-Suede
$11.98

For Dressy Economy
An Excellent Choice

10 G 700 Primarily a service Coat, but smart enough for any purpose! Warm Velour Coating with a small amount of cotton in its sturdy weave. Wonderfully dressy collar and cuffs of glossy French Coney, for a coat of its price! New panel effect front, outlined with floss stitching, with "scallop" flaps above real insert pockets. Warm interlining; mercerized twill lining for long practical service. GIRLS' SIZES: 8, 10, 12, 14 years. State size. Read "How to Order" on Page 27. Shipping weight, 4 pounds 9 ounces.
10 G 700—Reindeer (dark) tan.
10 G 702—Rust.
10 G 704—Gracklehead (medium) blue. **$7.98**

All Wool Velour
for All Smart Wear

10 G 730 A smart, practical model for her All Purpose Coat. Warm soft-finish All Wool Velour, which carries its tailoring beautifully. An easy swinging style, with smooth saddle shoulder; finely tailored panels at side, which conceal deep insert pockets under button trimmed tab points. Big convertible collar and dressy cuffs of billowy Mandel Fur. Warmly interlined; lined with durable mercerized twill. GIRLS' SIZES: 8, 10, 12, 14 years. State size. Read "How to Order" on Page 27. Ship. wt., 4 lbs. 10 oz.
10 G 730—Medium brown. Mandel collar and cuffs, Mink dyed.
10 G 732—Brickdust. Mandel collar and cuffs, Mink dyed.
10 G 734—Gracklehead (medium) blue. Mandel collar and cuffs, Raccoon dyed. **$10.98**

10 G 730
All Wool Velour
$10.98

10 G 742
All Wool Velour
$8.49

10 G 736 Adopted by young New Yorkers! Wooly-warm Chinchilla with just enough cotton in its durable weave to make it even more practical. Swagger, mannish, double breasted; with notched lapels, flap pockets and turnback cuffs. Attractive lining of heavy Cotton Suede to double its warmth.
GIRLS' SIZES: 8, 10, 12, 14 years. State size. Read "How to Order" on Page 27. Shipping weight, 6 pounds 2 ounces.
10 G 736—Medium tan—tan Cotton Suede Lining.
10 G 738—Navy blue—red Cotton Suede Lining.
10 G 740—Copper brown—rust Cotton Suede Lining. **$8.98**

Stunning Model
All Wool Vel Suede

10 G 724 A New York beauty with lovely deep shawl collar of fluffy Mandel Fur—to grace this smooth fine All Wool Suede Velour. Beautifully tailored model, with easy saddle shoulders and pointed underarm panels, button trimmed above the tailor slot pockets. Smart cuffs. Warm interlining; highly mercerized lining—good for two seasons. GIRLS' SIZES: 8, 10, 12, 14 years. State size. Read "How to Order" on Page 27. Shipping weight, 5 pounds 14 ounces.
10 G 724—Medium Brown. Mink dyed Mandel fur.
10 G 726—Cranberry red. Mink dyed Mandel fur.
10 G 728—Gracklehead (medium) blue. Raccoon dyed Mandel fur. **$11.98**

Excellent Value
Lustrous Beaverette Fur

10 G 742 A surprisingly low price for such an attractive Coat! Well tailored along soft, youthful lines, from a very pleasing quality winter weight All Wool Velour. For added warmth there is a cozy interlining beneath the practical mercerized twill lining. She will like the dressy convertible collar and snug cuffs of soft lustrous Beaverette Fur (sheared coney). Smart new side pocket panels, with contrasting inserts stitched in harmonizing tones, and button trimmed. GIRLS' SIZES: 8, 10, 12, 14 years. State size. Read "How to Order" on Page 27. Ship. wt., 4 lbs. 5 oz.
10 G 742—Reindeer (dark) tan with dark brown trimming.
10 G 744—Brickdust with cranberry red trimming.
10 G 746—Gracklehead (medium) blue—navy blue trimming. **$8.49**

A Quality Never Before Known — At Such Money Saving Prices

Practical School Coat
of All Wool Polaire
10 G 774 All Wool Polaire—a soft, pliable material of good heavy weight and fine wearing qualities. The convertible collar of soft, warm Beaverette Fur (sheared Coney) buttons closely about the neck.
Patch pockets and turned back cuffs are trimmed with inserts of contrasting color Velour and buttons. The shoulders are cut in swinging Raglan style. Mercerized Twill lining for hard wear, and an interlining for warmth.
GIRLS' SIZES: 7, 8, 9 years. State size. See Girls' Size Scale on Page 27. Ship. wt., 4 lbs.
10 G 774—Reindeer (dark) tan, trimmed dark brown.
10 G 558—Cranberry red, trimmed brickdust.
10 G 560—Gracklehead (medium) blue, trimmed navy blue. **$5.48**

10 G 774
All Wool
Polaire
$5.48

10 G 782
All Wool
Velour
$5.98

Style and Charm
For the Little Miss
10 G 782 A well tailored Coat of charm and simplicity, modishly made of serviceable All Wool Velour. The convertible collar is of Beaverette Fur (sheared Coney). The simulated cuffs have pointed button trimmed tabs. Two welt pockets. Smart panels at the side are stitched with fancy floss and decorated with a row of buttons. If you wish to economize and still receive value in style, material and workmanship you will find this model the perfect answer to your needs! Mercerized twill lining; warm interlining.
GIRLS' SIZES: 7, 8, 9 yrs. State size. Size Scale on Page 27. Ship. wt., 4 lbs. 2 oz.
10 G 782—Reindeer (dark) tan.
10 G 784—Brickdust.
10 G 786—Gracklehead (medium) blue. **$5.98**

10 G 776
Velour
Coating
$3.98

Neat Tailored Model
10 G 776 A Coat well worth the money. Nice and warm, made of durable Velour Coating that has just enough cotton in its weave to give hard wear! The convertible collar and cuffs are trimmed with buttons and stitching. Twill lining. Warm interlining.
GIRLS' SIZES: 7, 8, 9 years. State size. See Girls' Size Scale on Page 27. Shipping weight, 4 pounds 2 ounces.
10 G 776—Dark brown.
10 G 778—Navy blue.
10 G 780—Cranberry red. **$3.98**

10 G 768
All Wool
Velour
$6.75

Very Smart
Priced Low
10 G 768 A charming Coat of durable All Wool Velour with collar of Mandel fur. The sleeves have saddle shoulders, and overstraps of self material faced with contrasting color to harmonize with the novel inserted pockets which have pretty buckles. The coat is lined with serviceable Mercerized Twill and interlined for additional warmth.
GIRLS' SIZES: 7, 8, 9 years. State size. See Girls' Size Scale on Page 27. Ship. wt., 4 lbs. 2 oz.
10 G 768—Reindeer (dark) tan. Mink dyed Mandel fur.
10 G 770—Brickdust. Mink dyed Mandel fur.
10 G 772—Gracklehead (medium) blue. Raccoon dyed Mandel fur. **$6.75**

10 G 794
All Wool
Buxkin Suede
$10.50

Smooth Buxkin Suede and Fur
10 G 794 A heavy weight All Wool Buxkin Suede of soft glove-like finish. Mandel fur makes the convertible collar; and self covered buttons with rat tail braid decorate the sleeves. High grade mercerized lining. Interlining.
GIRLS' SIZES: 7, 8, 9 years. State size. See Girls' Size Scale on Page 27. Shipping weight, 4 lbs. 8 oz.
10 G 794—Reindeer tan (dark tan). Mink dyed Mandel fur.
10 G 796—Canton (dark Copenhagen) blue. Raccoon dyed Mandel fur.
10 G 798—Rose. Mink dyed Mandel fur. **$10.50**

10 G 800
Velour
Coating
$4.98

Velour Coating
10 G 800 A pretty model of excellent material Velour Coating, cotton mixed to give hard wear! Convertible collar of Beaverette Fur. Inserted pockets in side panels, trimmed with buttons and self material inserts in contrasting shade. Stitching on panels and cuffs. Mercerized twill lining. Warm interlining.
GIRLS' SIZES: 7, 8, 9 years. State size. See Size Scale on Page 27. Shipping weight, 4 lbs. 2 oz.
10 G 800—Reindeer (dark) tan, trimmed dark brown.
10 G 802—Gracklehead (medium) blue, trimmed navy blue.
10 G 804—Cranberry red, trimmed rust. **$4.98**

10 G 806
All Wool
Velour
$5.98

Unusual Value and Style
10 G 806 A Coat of excellent value, you'll agree. Of fine All Wool Velour with mushroom collar of Beaverette fur (sheared Coney), and handsome embroidery on side panels and sleeves. The inserted pockets are quaint in design. Sturdy Mercerized Twill lining. Warm interlining.
GIRLS' SIZES: 7, 8, 9 years. State size. See Girls' Size Scale on Page 27. Shipping weight, 4 pounds 1 ounce.
10 G 806—Reindeer (dark) tan.
10 G 808—Brickdust.
10 G 810—Gracklehead (med.) blue. **$5.98**

10 G 812
All Wool
Vel Suede
$9.98

All Wool Vel Suede
10 G 812 Beautifully tailored from a glove-smooth fabric. Mushroom collar and cuffs of Mandel Fur. Attractive stitching and small metal ornaments. Saddle shoulders and inserted pockets. High grade mercerized lining; warm interlining.
GIRLS' SIZES: 7, 8, 9 years. State size. See Girls' Size Scale on Page 27. Shipping weight, 4 pounds.
10 G 812—Medium brown. Mink dyed Mandel fur.
10 G 814—Cranberry red. Mink dyed Mandel fur.
10 G 816—Gracklehead (medium) blue. Raccoon dyed Mandel fur. **$9.98**

10 G 788
Seal Bloom
Bolivia
$11.98

Seal Bloom Bolivia
Extra Style, Quality
10 G 788 She will love this Coat of smooth velvety Bolivia, with just enough cotton to make it durable, and whose handsome appearance speaks eloquently of its excellent quality and style. A convertible collar and cuffs of Mandel Fur, heavy cord tucks on front coat and sleeves and self covered buttons lend an air of smartness. Well interlined for warmth and has a high grade mercerized fabric for lining. Typical New Idea value!
GIRLS' SIZES: 7, 8, 9 years. State size. See Size Scale on Page 27. Ship. wt., 4 pounds 2 oz.
10 G 788—Golden brown. Mink dyed Mandel fur.
10 G 790—Cranberry red. Mink dyed Mandel fur.
10 G 792—Gracklehead (medium) blue. Raccoon dyed Mandel fur. **$11.98**

35

Your Child's Growing Feet
Need These Correctly Shaped Shoes

Sturdy Hi-cut for Sturdy Youngster

Children's Foot Health Goodyear Welt Shoes Flexible KORRY KROME Leather Soles

Six Hand Turned Sole Shoes for Children

These Three Styles Sizes 8½ to 11

Light Steel Arch

Tan Grain Leather

Healthy young children need such sturdy Hi-cuts as these for outdoor winter fun. Strong tan grain leather uppers with strap and buckle. Oak leather soles give good wear. Rubber heels. Made over the footform shape to keep young feet healthy. Shipping weight, 1 pound.
SIZES: 6 to 9. State size wanted.
24 G 2730 ....$1.59

Child's Warm Lined Shoe

$1.00 **Mothers— You Save Here**

Red Fleece Lined

Cozy in the Coldest Weather

Warm lined Hi-cuts, to keep your child's feet warm. Black kid leather vamp and felt top are red felt lined from top to toe. Sturdy leather soles. The higher tops give extra protection. Footform shape for growing feet. Shipping weight, 1 pound.
SIZES: 4 to 8. State size wanted.
24 G 2731 ....$1.00

Black Patent Leather

One of our finest and prettiest hand-turned Shoes for children. Vamps and quarters are of black patent; rose-blush leather top. Flexible hand-turned sole. Shipping weight, 1 pound.
SIZES: 8½ to 11.
State size wanted.
24 G 2751 ....$1.98

Very neat for little feet. Hand-turned soles are soft and flexible for your child's growing feet. Require no "breaking in." Of soft black patent leather. Shipping weight, 12 ounces.
SIZES: 8½ to 11.
State size wanted.
24 G 2601 ....$1.69

Colorful Paisley Trim

Child's dressy patent leather shoe with kid leather top. Has a pretty paisley applique on the vamp. The leather sole is hand-turned, flexible and easy underfoot. Spring heel. Shipping weight, 1 pound.
SIZES: 8½ to 11.
24 G 2750 ....$1.98

Rose Blush Top

Very new—and so dainty! Light flexible hand-turned sole is smooth inside and needs no "breaking in." Button style of black patent leather with a rose-blush leather top. FOOTFORM shape. Shipping weight, 1 pound.
SIZES: 4 to 8.
State size wanted.
24 G 2749 ....$1.59

Turn Sole

Very rich looking Button Shoes with black patent leather vamp and dull leather top. Flexible hand-turned leather soles are durable and easy on tender, growing feet. FOOTFORM shape. Leather heels. Ship. wt., 1 lb.
SIZES: 4 to 8.
State size wanted.
24 G 2748 ....$1.59

Two of the newest leathers make this child's pretty shoe. Brown patent leather with rose beige uppers. Soles are light, very flexible and smooth inside, because they are hand-turned. Foot-Shape. SIZES: 4 to 8. Ship. wt., 1 lb.
24 G 2747 ....$1.59

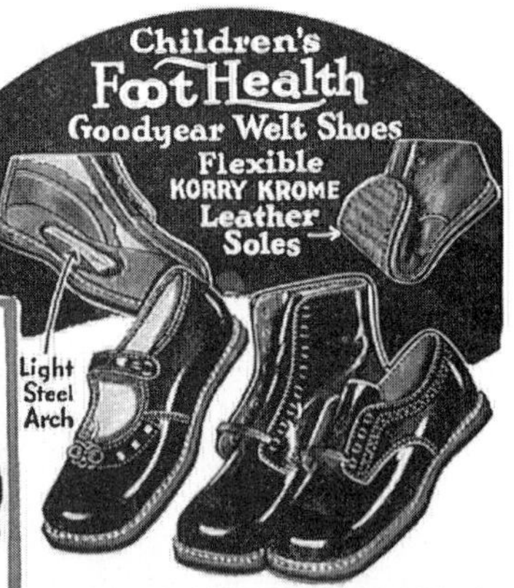

FOOT-HEALTH Shoes keep healthy feet strong, and help to strengthen weak feet. Every child can wear them with benefit. Rich black patent leather. Flexible KORRY-KROME leather soles. Goodyear welt. Notice construction features pictured above. They're $2.50 and $3 values. Best for growing feet. Shipping weight, 1 pound.
SIZES: 4 to 8. State size wanted.
24 G 2473—One-strap $1.69
24 G 2471—Blucher oxford.......1.98
24 G 2505—Blucher shoe........1.98

Copper Tips

Husky little fellows give the toe of their shoes extra wear. So we've capped this black gunmetal leather lace Shoe with a copper tip. Strong oak leather soles. Has rubber heel. Footform shape. Ship. wt., 1 lb.
SIZES: 6 to 9. State size wanted.
24 G 2746 ....$1.59

Children's Soft Kid Shoes

Here's Economy

$1.00 Only $1.00 a pair for these soft black, genuine kid leather Shoes! Footform shape is just right for little feet. Sturdy leather soles. Shipping weight, 1 pound.
SIZES: 4 to 8.
State size wanted.
24 G 2716—Button.
24 G 2717—Lace.
Per Pair ..$1.00

Soft Brown Kid

A fine opportunity to save! Choice of children's button or lace shoe at a special price. Soft, brown genuine kid leather uppers. Sturdy leather soles. Footform shape. Ship. wt., 1 pound.
SIZES: 4 to 8. State size.
24 G 2705—Button..........$1.19
24 G 2715—Lace............1.19

Hippity-Hop Shoes—Flexible Stitchdown Soles

Black patent leather and soft black leather tops. Footform shape, flexible stitchdown leather sole, cloth lining. Shipping weight, 1 pound.
SIZES: 4 to 8.
State size.
24G2507
$1.59

Hippity - Hop Shoes keep children's feet healthy. One-strap of black patent with blonde trimming. Flexible stitchdown soles. Ship. weight, 1 lb.
SIZES: 4 to 8.
State size.
24G2481
$1.98

IMPORTANT!
When you select the style Shoes for your child, be sure the size wanted is listed. Always measure the child's foot before ordering. See Chart on Page 169.

$1.59

Brown or Black Kid

Our Hippity-Hop Shoes are famous for their softness and flexibility. Of genuine kid leather, these have flexible, durable stitchdown leather soles—best for growing feet. Remarkably low priced. Shipping weight, 1 pound.
SIZES: 3 to 8. State size wanted.
24 G 2530—Brown kid.........$1.59
24 G 2531—Black kid..........1.59

Neat and Practical

Hippity-Hop Shoes are easy and flexible—the best for growing feet. Brown or black kid leather uppers. Stitchdown sewed soles are very flexible. Footform shape toe for growing feet. A bargain at our low price. Shipping weight, 1 pound.
SIZES: 3 to 8. State size.
24 G 2523—Brown.........$1.59
24 G 2522—Black 1.59

Neat Styles for Little Feet

For Dress-Up Time

$1.09 A very good quality Button Shoe for children. So practical, because it's very dressy, yet will wear a long time. Patent vamp and quarters. Blonde stitching trims the black leather uppers. Sturdy leather soles. Shipping weight, 1 pound.
SIZES: 4 to 8. State size.
24 G 2734
....$1.09

When They're Dressed In Their Best

$1.19 A pretty One-strap for children. Black patent, with vamp decoration of bright paisley leather. Ship. weight, 12 ounces.
SIZES: 4 to 8. State size.
24 G 2625 $1.19

$1.00 Mothers will save money on this neat patent leather Slipper. Colorful ornament. Good leather soles. Ship. wt., 12 oz.
SIZES: 4 to 8.
24 G 2614 $1.00

Flexible Stitchdown Soles

Dressy Styles

Excellent Values

Neat—of Brown Leather 95¢
FOOT-SHAPE Shoes form pliable young feet correctly because they're the shape of your child's feet. This sturdy brown leather Oxford has sturdy, flexible stitchdown leather soles. Shipping weight, 12 ounces.
24 G 2408—For children.
SIZES: 8½ to 13½....$1.15
24 G 2409—6 to 8..... .95

Has Pretty Reptile Trim

A pleasing Sandal of stylish new leathers. Black patent is trimmed with tan reptile. The FOOT-SHAPE toe correctly forms growing feet. Flexible leather soles are stitchdown sewed assuring a smooth inner surface. Our low price assures double satisfaction. Shipping weight, 12 ounces. State size wanted.
24 G 2459.....$1.49
SIZES: 8½ to 13½ $1.49
24 G 2460—SIZES: 6 to 8......1.39

Strong Fiber Soles

Soft, tan chrome leather (known as elk) Sandals. Children's feet will greatly benefit by their footform comfort. WONDER-WEAR composition soles wear long. Shipping weight, 12 ounces.
24 G 2475—SIZES: 11½ to 2......98¢
24 G 2476—8½ to 11....89¢
24 G 2477—6 to 8.....79¢

Dressy—Practical

This pretty dress-up Sandal is very popular with mothers because it will wear long. Black patent leather with flexible, stitchdown leather soles. Excellent values. Shipping weight, 14 oz. State size wanted.
24 G 2414—8½ to 13½.....$1.45
24 G 2415—6 to 8.....1.35

Brown Patent

A new and pretty T-strap Sandal, just like mother's. Beautiful brown patent leather with reptile trimming. Excellent leather soles. FOOT-SHAPE toe. Ship. wt., 12 oz. State size wanted.
24 G 2461—SIZES: 8½ to 13½....$1.59
24 G 2462—6 to 8....1.49

Gray Reptile Trim

A dressy, novel style for up-to-date youngsters. Black patent is trimmed with gray reptile embossed grain leather. Fine flexible leather soles are stitchdown sewed. FOOT-SHAPE too. Shipping weight, 12 ounces.
24 G 2463—SIZES: 8½ to 13½....$1.59
24 G 2464—6 to 8....1.49

New Tan Reptile Trim

Children will love the smart new style of this Sandal. One-eyelet Tie design with fancy, colorful silk laces. Rich, black patent leather is trimmed with tan reptile embossed grain leather. Stitchdown leather soles are flexible and smooth inside. Footform shape is healthiest for growing feet. Ship. wt., 12 oz. State size wanted.
24 G 2467—SIZES: 8½ to 13½....$1.49
24 G 2468—SIZES: 6 to 8......1.39

Tots' Very Warm Interlined Coats
3 to 6 Years
Unusually Low Prices for Such Quality

10 G 832 All Wool Velour $4.98

10 G 850 Velour Coating $3.98

10 G 826 All Wool Velour $4.98

10 G 838 All Wool Buckin Suede $8.75

10 G 844 All Wool Polaire $4.98

10 G 856 Velour Coating $3.98

10 G 862 Velour Coating $3.25

10 G 868 All Wool Vel-Suede $6.98

10 G 874 All Wool Velour $5.95

10 G 880 Velvety Plush $5.98

10 G 884 Seal Bloom Bolivia $8.98

10 G 890 All Wool Fancy Tweed $5.98

All Wool Velour

10 G 826 See my nice new Coat, she seems to say. And it is nice and warm and very sturdy. Good quality All Wool Velour, warmly interlined and lined with strong mercerized twill. Warm convertible collar of soft silky French Coney Fur. Scallop stitching and buttons on sleeves and front. Insert pockets.
GIRLS' SIZES : 3, 4, 5, 6 years. State size. See Size Scale on Page 27. Ship. wt., 3 pounds 8 ounces.
10 G 826—Reindeer (dark) tan.
10 G 828—Brickdust.
10 G 830—Gracklehead (medium) blue. **$4.98**

Another Big Value

10 G 832 Nice Little Coat of warm All Wool Velour, with soft dressy convertible collar of Beaverette fur (sheared coney). Has warm interlining and practical mercerized twill lining. Little puff sleeves and dressy front with bright stitching and buttons.
GIRLS' SIZES: 3, 4, 5, 6 yrs. State size. See on Page 27. Ship. wt., 3 lbs. 12 oz.
10 G 832—Med. brown.
10 G 834—Cranberry red.
10 G 836—Gracklehead (medium) blue. **$4.98**

For Best Dress

10 G 874 Dear little Dress Coat for such a modest sum! What mother wouldn't love to have her little girl dressed so sweetly? Soft, smooth All Wool Velour, of just right winter weight; but interlined for that extra warmth she needs, and nicely lined with high-luster mercerized twill for real service. Fluffy collar of warm Mandel fur, to close snugly about her throat. Smooth saddle shoulders. Dressy cord-tuck motif on sleeves and insert pockets.
GIRLS' SIZES: 3, 4, 5, 6 years. State size wanted. See Size Scale on Page 27. Ship. wt., 3 lbs. 8 oz.
10 G 874—Medium brown. Mink dyed Mandel fur.
10 G 876—Cranberry red. Mink dyed Mandel fur.
10 G 878—Gracklehead (medium) blue. Raccoon dyed Mandel fur. **$5.95**

Velvety Plush

10 G 880 Any little girl will adore this rich little Coat; and every Mother who has learned values, will know the sterling qualities of this soft velvety Plush. Made in fine French fashion; with quite dressy little collar, full length tuxedo front and turn back cuffs of the favored Gray Astrakhan Fur Fabric. Easy saddle shoulders and smart little slot pockets. Beautifully made; warmly interlined and carefully lined with a high luster serviceable fabric—good for two seasons' wear!
GIRLS' SIZES: 3, 4, 5, 6 years. State size wanted. See Size Scale on Page 27. Ship. wt., 3 lbs. 12 oz.
10 G 880 —Gracklehead (medium) blue.
10 G 882—Wine red. **$5.98**

A Dressy Coat for Miss Three to Six

10 G 838 Lucky the little Girl who gets this pretty Coat; firmly woven All Wool Buckin Suede of glovelike smoothness. Finished to delight mothers; from its fluffy Mandel fur collar, saddle shoulders, neatly stitched, and button trimmed pocket panel, to its warm interlining and sturdy lustrous lining, good for two season's wear.
GIRLS'-SIZES: 3, 4, 5, 6 years. State size wanted. See Girls' Size Scale on Page 27. Shipping weight, 4 pounds.
10 G 838—Reindeer tan. Mink dyed Mandel fur.
10 G 840—Canton blue (dark Copen). Raccoon dyed Mandel fur.
10 G 842—Cranberry red. Mink dyed Mandel fur. **$8.75**

Another Excellent Little Play Coat

10 G 844 A double service Coat—for play and better wear. A good warm winter weight All Wool Polaire, interlined for extra comfort and durably lined with highly mercerized twill. Has neat turn back cuffs and novel patch pockets welted with contrasting material. Bright metal buttons. Rich looking collar of soft Beaverette fur (sheared coney). Buttons close to neck.
GIRLS' SIZES: 3, 4, 5, 6 years. State size wanted. See Size Scale on Page 27. Shipping weight, 4 pounds.
10 G 844—Reindeer (dark) tan.
10 G 846—Cranberry red.
10 G 848—Gracklehead (medium) blue. **$4.98**

Warm Velour Coating for Strict Economy

10 G 862 Tailored like a high priced coat, from a winter weight Velour Coating with just enough cotton to make it durable. Warmly interlined and practically lined with strong mercerized twill. Nice little convertible collar buttons close to neck, and is stitched to match the button-trimmed insert side panels. Welt pockets.
GIRLS' SIZES: 3, 4, 5, 6 years. State size wanted. See Size Scale on Page 27. Shipping weight, 3 pounds 10 ounces.
10 G 862—Reindeer (dark) tan.
10 G 864—Gracklehead (medium) blue.
10 G 866—Cranberry red. **$3.25**

Fine Enough for Best Wear

10 G 868 All Wool Suede Velour—to keep her dressy and warm. Fine and suede-smooth, this fabric wonderfully exploits the little Coat's easy saddle shoulders, careful cord tucking, very smart sleeves and welt pocket motifs. Soft lustrous Beaverette fur (sheared coney) for convertible collar and cuffs. Warmly interlined; nicely lined with sturdy mercerized fabric. Good for two season's wear!
GIRLS' SIZES: 3, 4, 5, 6 years. State size wanted. See Girls' Size Scale on Page 27. Shipping weight, 3 pounds 10 ounces.
10 G 868—Reindeer (dark) tan.
10 G 870—Brickdust.
10 G 872—Gracklehead (medium) blue. **$6.98**

Warm Velour Coating

10 G 850 Much less than the shops are asking for this little Coat of warm Velour Coating, with a small amount of cotton in its sturdy weave. Snug convertible collar of silky French Coney. Fine cord tucking above the turnback cuffs. Patch pockets with cord tucking and buttons. Warm interlining; practical lining of high luster twill.
GIRLS' SIZES: 3, 4, 5, 6 years. State size. See Size Scale on Page 27. Ship. weight, 3 pounds 10 ounces.
10 G 850—Reindeer (dark) tan.
10 G 852—Cranberry red.
10 G 854—Gracklehead (medium) blue. **$3.98**

Dressy and Cozy

10 G 856 Big value in a dressy little all-service Coat of warm practical Velour Coating, with a small amount of cotton to strengthen its weave. Soft Beaverette fur (sheared coney) convertible collar buttons snugly about her neck. Puff sleeves with tab cuffs; useful insert pockets; neat stitching. Has interlining and strong high-luster twill lining. Worth more!
GIRLS' SIZES: 3, 4, 5, 6 years. State size. See Size Scale on Page 27. Ship. wt., 3 pounds 10 ounces.
10 G 856—Medium brown.
10 G 858—Gracklehead (medium) blue.
10 G 860—Cranberry red. **$3.98**

Seal Bloom Bolivia

10 G 884 Just like little Miss "New York" wears! One of our handsomest Coats for wee Fashionables. Beautifully made from soft velvety Seal Bloom Bolivia, lovely as her tiny self. Fluffy Mandel fur collar will button tight when she likes. Becoming, comfortable, saddle shoulders; slender underarm panels dotted with smart bright buttons. Warm, comfy slot pockets. Snugly interlined; carefully lined with high-luster fabric; good for two seasons' wear.
GIRLS' SIZES: 3, 4, 5, 6 years. See Girls' Size Scale on Page 27. State size wanted. Shipping weight, 3 pounds 14 ounces.
10 G 884—Golden brown. Mink dyed Mandel fur.
10 G 886—Gracklehead (medium) blue. Raccoon dyed Mandel fur.
10 G 888—Brickdust. Mink dyed Mandel fur. **$8.98**

All Wool Tweed

10 G 890 How sweet she will look in this Coat—cunning Miss Little-Tot! And how pleased Mother will be over the saving she'll make here! An adorable little girlish Check Tweed, every thread Wool, for just the right warmth during the cold winter of active outdoor play. And for added safety, there is a snug interlining beneath durable mercerized Sateen lining.
Stunning little Beaverette fur (sheared coney) collar that will button up tight over her throat. Three-button front, snappy patch pockets and Cranberry red Velour trimmings for contrast. A real bargain.
GIRLS' SIZES: 3, 4, 5, 6 years. See Girls' Size Scale on Page 27. State size wanted. Shipping weight, 3 pounds 14 ounces.
10 G 890—Medium tan. Only **$5.98**

37

A Greater Quality *With* Greater Style
Girls' Sizes 7 to 14 Years

15 G 802
Cotton
Flannel
$1.95

15 G 808
Rayon
$2.88

15 G 812
All Wool
"Ottorep"
$4.98

15 G 816
Velveteen
$4.95

15 G 822
All Wool
Crepe
$4.98

15 G 828
Chambray
and
Gingham
$1.98

15 G 832
All Silk
Taffeta
$4.98

15 G 834
All Silk
Crepe
de Chine

15 G 838
Mercerized
Broadcloth
$1.95

15 G 842
Velveteen
Corduroy
$3.69

15 G 782
All Wool
Serge
$2.98

Cotton Serge
$1.79

15 G 846
Wool Mixed
Plaid
$2.98

15 G 850
Wool
and Silk
Tweed
$3.95

15 G 854
All Wool
Serge
$2.89

*These Dresses are also
Furnished in Each of
the Colors Described
on Opposite Page*

15 G 856
All Wool
Jersey
$3.98

Balbriggan
For Smart Economy

15 G 762 In her choice of Copenhagen blue or deep rose! Comfortably warm Balbriggan, the popular, practical cotton jersey for mother's economy.

And here is the two-piece effect all the girls are wearing. Two snappy pockets set up over the blouse, where the sash belt starts from the sides. Gay little tie, held under an embroidered medallion slot. Two kick plaits suggest panel trimness and provide sufficient fullness for the skirt. Straight back. Snappy buttons.

GIRLS' SIZES: 7, 8, 10, 12, 14 years. State size. See size scale on Page 63. Ship. weight, 1 pound 5 ounces.

15 G 762—Copenhagen blue.
15 G 764—Deep rose.....$1.98

A Complete Line *for* School or Dress
Unusually Well Made
for Girls 7 to 14 Years

15 G 762 Cotton Balbriggan $1.98

15 G 770 All Silk Crepe de Chine $4.98

Fast Color Gingham
15 G 766 Mothers!—A very special purchase enables us to offer you this excellent Fast Color Plaid Gingham Dress for 98c—much less than you would be asked elsewhere. Gay assorted plaid in colors she likes, accented with plain gingham trimmings. Has a roomy neck vent; bright buttons; tie, and a self sash belt. Panel box plaits for the front skirt; straight youthful back.

GIRLS' SIZES: 7, 8, 10, 12, 14 years. State size. See size scale on Page 63. Ship. weight, 12 ounces.

15 G 766—Blue plaid.
15 G 768—Brown plaid.........98c

15 G 766 Plaid Gingham 98c

15 G 778 All Wool Serge $3.88

15 G 788 All Wool Blouse Wool Mixed Skirt $3.95

15 G 794 Mercerized Broadcloth $1.98

15 G 800 Worsted and Cotton $3.89

Party Frock
All Silk Crepe de Chine

15 G 770 Her fondest hopes will be realized in this lovely all Silk Crepe de Chine frock, in her choice of rose or Copenhagen blue or pure white. Daintily appropriate for dances and parties.

Girlish round neck with dainty streamer rosette; set in sleeves with frilly ruffles to match the fluffy skirt frills. And the skirt is very soft and lovely; shirred all around under a dainty heading. The ruffles are all picot-edged with a dainty contrasting color thread.

GIRLS' SIZES: 7, 8, 10, 12, 14 years. State size. See size scale on Page 63. Shipping weight, 1 pound 2 ounces.

15 G 770—Rose.
15 G 772—Copenhagen blue.
15 G 774—All white.......$4.98

Plain and Plaid Flannel
Appropriate for School Wear

15 G 788 Warm little Dress for general wear. Fine soft All Wool Flannel for the plain blouse. Sturdy Wool and Cotton Flannel for the box plaited skirt and trimmings. Black ribbon tie. Leatherette belt.

GIRLS' SIZES: 7, 8, 10, 12, 14 years. State size. See size scale on Page 63. Shipping weight, 1 pound 6 ounces.

15 G 788—Henna.
15 G 790—Copenhagen blue.
15 G 792—Green................$3.95

High Luster Broadcloth
Daintily Trimmed With Hand Stitching

15 G 794 One of our prettiest. Soft Mercerized Broadcloth with contrasting broadcloth collar and cuffs. Dainty two-tone hand stitching and pearl buttons. Clever two-color effect; sash back.

GIRLS' SIZES: 7, 8, 10, 12, 14 years. State size. See size scale on Page 63. Shipping weight, 1 pound 2 ounces.

15 G 794—Copenhagen blue.
15 G 796—Tan.
15 G 798—Rose.............$1.98

Wool or Cotton Serge
15 G 778 Typical Sailor Dress of inexpensive Cotton Serge or All Wool Serge. Popular co-ed Middy; cuff, emblem and tie. Plaited skirt attached to muslin lining.

GIRLS' SIZES: 7, 8, 10, 12, 14 years. State size. Size scale, Page 63. Ship. wt., 1 lb. 2 oz.

15 G 778—Navy blue All Wool serge..$3.88
15 G 780—Navy blue cotton serge.. 1.95

Worsted and Cotton Check
Bright Red Flannel Trimmed

15 G 800 Such a cheery little Frock of Worsted and Cotton Check, trimmed with bright red flannel for Hand Embroidered vestee effect and collar; with pocket tabs to match. Trim yoke-to-hem plaits and long set-in sleeves. Sash belt.

GIRLS' SIZES: 7, 8, 10, 12, 14 years. State size. See size scale on Page 63. Shipping weight, 1 pound 3 ounces.

15 G 800—Black and white check..$3.89

▶ Dresses Described Below Pictured on Opposite Page ◀

Wool or Cotton Serge
Slip-On Sailor Frock

15 G 782 We do not believe you can duplicate this value elsewhere. Good quality All Wool Serge, or inexpensive Cotton Serge. Popular slip-on Sailor Frock. The blouse buttons down front under plaits. Embroidered emblem on sleeve. Detachable belt and tie.

GIRLS' SIZES: 7, 8, 10, 12, 14 years. State size. See size scale on Page 63. Ship. wt., 1 pound 12 ounces.

15 G 782—Navy blue All Wool serge; gold braid...$2.98
15 G 784—Navy blue cotton serge; white braid.....1.79

Practical Cotton Flannel
In a Warm Colorful Plaid

15 G 802 Warm, colorful Cotton Flannel Frock. One-piece style, laid-in front box plaits which fall free below the pockets. Buckle belt ends in sash ties over the slender back. Fancy stitching is a bright finish for the plain-tone harmonizing collar and cuffs. Novelty embroidered motif.

GIRLS' SIZES: 7, 8, 10, 12, 14 years. State size. See size scale on Page 63. Ship. weight, 14 ounces.

15 G 802—Brown and red.
15 G 804—Blue and tan....$1.95

Gleaming Rayon
In Dainty Thread Check

15 G 806 This Frock of lustrous Rayon may be one of her best. A simple slip-on, with all the air of a bolero frock, with its piped slashes for the soft crush sash belt. Dressy fichu collar piped in the bright contrasting tone. Shirred skirt front; straight back.

GIRLS' SIZES: 7, 8, 10, 12, 14 years. State size. See size scale on Page 63. Shipping weight, 1 pound 2 ounces.

15 G 806—Peach.
15 G 808—Copen. blue.
15 G 810—Rose.........$2.88

All Wool Ottorep
Nicely Hand Embroidered

15 G 812 One of the loveliest Frocks for Girls we've ever offered at this price. All Wool Ottorep is noted for its fine smooth weave and beautiful sheen, and takes its tailoring perfectly. Every feature beautiful; trim panel waist plaits, finely plaited skirt panel, contrasting pipings, and hand embroidery. Sash belt.

GIRLS' SIZES: 7, 8, 10, 12, 14 years. State size. See size scale on Page 63. Ship. wt., 1 lb. 4 oz.

15 G 812—Henna.
15 G 814—Copen. blue..$4.98

Rich Velveteen
A Glimpse of Parisian Youth

15 G 816 Beautifully dressed she will be in this rich looking Frock of good quality Velveteen. Paris sponsors the two-tone shoulder bow, bright pipings, and streamer rosette over the right hip. Soft shirring at yoke, cuffs and girdle depth. Straight back. Shoulder closing. A very attractive model.

GIRLS' SIZES: 7, 8, 10, 12, 14 years. State size. See size scale on Page 63. Ship. wt., 1 lb. 10 oz.

15 G 816—Navy blue.
15 G 818—Brown.
15 G 820—Wine.........$4.95

All Wool Crepe
The Latest English Blouse

15 G 822 Fine little Frock for school or for best wear. A beautiful all Wool Crepe, fine and soft. One of Fifth Avenue's favorites, with deep shirred yoke effect, and waist softly bloused over a lining. The front skirt falls in immaculate box plaits. Straight sash back.

GIRLS' SIZES: 7, 8, 10, 12, 14 years. State size. See size scale on Page 63. Ship. weight, 1 pound 6 ounces.

15 G 822—Tan.
15 G 824—Copenhagen blue.
15 G 826—Wild rose.........$4.98

Chambray and Gingham
In New Two-Piece Effect

15 G 828 We do not believe you can find a prettier Frock anywhere for the price. Such a practical combination of Plain Chambray Blouse and Fancy Checked Gingham for the trim plaited skirt, with tie and cuffs to match. Fresh white pique collar; and two-tone hand stitching in front tab outline, accenting the two-piece effect. Straight sash back.

GIRLS' SIZES: 7, 8, 10, 12, 14 years. State size. See size scale on Page 63. Ship. wt., 1 lb. 2 oz.

15 G 828—Oxblood red.
15 G 830—Copenhagen blue.....$1.98

Choice of Two Materials
Or All Silk Crepe de Chine or Taffeta

15 G 832 Either choice will be lovely—the bouffant All Silk Taffeta, or rich soft All Silk Crepe de Chine. Bright contrasting pipings dress it up and suggest a smart bolero outline, and a similar thread picot the quaint rosettes and skirt ruches most effectively.

GIRLS' SIZES: 7, 8, 10, 12, 14 years. State size. See size scale on Page 63. Shipping weight, 1 pound 8 ounces.

15 G 832—Navy blue TAFFETA.....$4.98
SILK CREPE DE CHINE
15 G 834—Navy blue.
15 G 836—Palmetto green.........4.98

Lustrous Broadcloth
Dotted Sateen Trimming

15 G 838 All the girls will flock to this youthful Frock. Splendidly made from lustrous Broadcloth in plain soft tones, gayly finished with self tone Dotted Sateen. Girlish collar with artist's tie. Very trim inverted plaits mark a panel front, topped with catchy pockets. Youthful sash back. A bargain!

GIRLS' SIZES: 7, 8, 10, 12, 14 years. State size. See size scale on Page 63. Shipping weight, 1 pound 2 ounces.

15 G 838—Green.
15 G 840—Copenhagen blue......$1.95

Velveteen Corduroy
Bright Check Rayon Trim

15 G 842 This Velveteen Corduroy makes a modest, lovable Frock at remarkably low cost. A girlish slip-on with straight back and shirring below the belt. Bright check Rayon makes the collar, and the pipings—even the slot pocket 'kerchief. Smart alligator-grain belt. Bright metal buttons.

GIRLS' SIZES: 7, 8, 10, 12, 14 years. State size. See size scale on Page 63. Ship. weight, 1 pound 10 ounces.

15 G 842—Wine red.
15 G 844—Copen. blue.......$3.69

Cheery Tweed
Wool and Cotton Weave

15 G 846 For the School Girl's wardrobe. Neatly made from a serviceable Wool Mixed Tweed. Woven to resemble a two-tone plaid of more pretentious price. Assorted figured four-in-hand tie for the girlish slot. Buttons underline the slot pocket. Roomy box plaits for front skirt, below the snappy buckle belt.

GIRLS' SIZES: 7, 8, 10, 12, 14 years. State size. See size scale on Page 63. Ship. wt., 1 lb. 8 oz.

15 G 846—Brown.
15 G 848—Copen. blue.......$2.98

Wool and Silk Tweed
One of Our Smartest

15 G 850 A striking Dress of lovely Two-Toned All Wool and Silk Tweed. See how cleverly the embroidery stitching and pipings dress it up and accent its bright tones. Deep neck vent under the big Windsor tie. Chic little buckle belt sections above the panel skirt plaits. Sash back.

GIRLS' SIZES: 7, 8, 10, 12, 14 years. State size. See size scale on Page 63. Shipping weight, 1 pound.

15 G 850—Tan and tangerine.
15 G 852—Tan and green, henna trimmed.
green trimmed.........$3.95

All Wool Serge
Crisp, Snappy Style

15 G 854 Very smart economy Frock of good quality, double warp All Wool Serge. A very wide awake little style. Her favorite collar, with bright red buttons and dashing rayon tie. Military panel line and snappy pocket gayly marked off with fancy red braid. Flashing leatherette belt.

GIRLS' SIZES: 7, 8, 10, 12, 14 years. State size. See size scale on Page 63. Shipping weight, 1 pound 5 ounces.

15 G 854—Navy blue only...$2.89

All Wool Jersey
New York Favorite

15 G 856 Soft All Wool Jersey. Trim straight back, but the front takes on over-blouse lines above the shirred and plaited skirt. Contrasting All Wool Flannel makes the striking collar and cuffs, pipes the neck vent and blouse lines. Chic little self buckle belt; gay buttons and blouse ornament.

GIRLS' SIZES: 7, 8, 10, 12, 14 years. State size. See size scale on Page 63. Ship. wt., 1 pound 6 ounces.

15 G 856—Rust tan.
15 G 858—Cardinal red.
15 G 860—Copen. blue...$3.98

39

Value and Style for Girls
Ages 7 to 14 Years

15 G 746
Sateen
88¢

15 G 730
Wool Mixed Crepe
$2.98

15 G 734
Woven Cotton Check
$1.39

15 G 736
Linene
98¢

15 G 748
Linene
89¢
Broadcloth
$1.00

Neat Apron Frock
Good Quality Sateen
With Orange Piping

15 G 746 Of lustrous Sateen with pockets and cuffs of novelty assorted print. Orange piping down the front panel and a back sash complete it.

This will make a durable and serviceable Dress not only for the small girl but for big sister as well, as it comes in sizes from seven to fourteen years.

GIRLS' SIZES: 7, 8, 10, 12, 14 years. State size. See size scale at right. Shipping weight, 10 ounces.
15 G 746—Black only............88¢

Practical Crepe
Turned Back Cuffs
Hand Embroidered Collar

15 G 730 A Dress with tailored lines like mother's things. Neat, inexpensive wool mixed crepe model, with long sleeves and turned back cuffs. Side plaits in skirt give necessary fullness and freedom.

The hand embroidered collar, pointed pockets and silk ribbon tie add a note of charm. Sash back for nice finish.

GIRLS' SIZES: 7, 8, 10, 12, 14 years. State size. See size scale at right. Shipping weight, 1 pound 4 ounces.
15 G 730—Henna.
15 G 732—Navy......**$2.98**

Woven Cotton Check
Red Braid Trimming
Long Wear at Low Cost

15 G 734 Serviceable school Dress of Woven Cotton check in black and white with fancy red braid trimming collar, cuffs and pocket tabs. The sleeves are long and well tailored. Desirable fullness is given by inverted kick plaits. A red belt buckle and silk tie add a note of color. Neat, tailored looking and practical.

GIRLS' SIZES: 7, 8, 10, 12, 14 years. State size. See size scale at right. Shipping weight, 14 ounces.
15 G 734—Black and white check only......**$1.39**

Stylish Slip-On Frock
Good Quality Linene
Contrasting Collar

15 G 736 A smart slip-on Frock of crisp Linene at a low price. The material is durable, the workmanship fine. Novelty buttons blend with colorful embroidery and ribbon tie. Long sleeves with turned back cuffs, a collar of a contrasting color, and a kick plait give charm and style to this dress.

GIRLS' SIZES: 7, 8, 10, 12, 14 years. State size. See size scale at right. Shipping weight, 1 pound.
15 G 736—Copenhagen blue.
15 G 738—Rose.
......**98¢**

Little Sister's Smock
Linene or Broadcloth

15 G 748 Charming, practical little Smock to protect a nice school frock. Bright shades she will like. Roomy pockets. Cuffs may be rolled up.

GIRLS' SIZES: 7, 8, 10, 12, 14 years. State size. See size scale below. Shipping wt., 12 oz.
Crisp Linene
15 G 748—Copenhagen blue.
15 G 750—Rose.
15 G 752—Lavender. ....**89¢**
Lustrous Broadcloth
15 G 721—Copenhagen blue.
15 G 723—Rose.
15 G 725—Lavender..........**$1.00**

Size Scale
Girls' Dresses

Order size in chart below corresponding nearest to girl's chest measure. Be careful not to draw tape too tightly or let it slip. If she measures in between the sizes given order the next size larger.

Chest measure, in..	26	27	29	31	33
Size, years..........	7	8	10	12	14
Average dress length.	27	28	32	36	40

36 G 700
Blanket Cloth
$2.59

15 G 758
Chambray and Gingham
2 for 98¢

15 G 754
Cotton Gabardine
$1.69

15 G 717
Tupelo Home-Tex Cloth
88¢

Blanket Cloth Robe
In Gay Colors
Warm and Comfortable

36 G 700 Like a bright blanket for a little Indian Princess is this colorful Bathrobe with its two big pockets. Long sleeves and gay tasselled cord about the waist. Soft, cozy and warm.

SIZES: 7, 8, 10, 12, 14 years. LENGTHS: 34, 36, 40, 42, 46 inches. State size wanted. Shipping weight, 2 lbs. 10 oz.
36 G 700—Copenhagen blue.
36 G 702—Brown. Each............**$2.59**

Two Dresses for the Price of One
Plain Tone Chambray and Check Gingham
Attractive! Two Garments for Double Service

15 G 758 A real bargain! These two Dresses to be had for the price of one. Sold only in sets and offered at an exceptionally low price to wise mothers. Each dress is made with kimono sleeves and each has a back sash of self-material. The frock of plain Chambray is piped in a bright, check material. Ample fullness is achieved by use of a side plait. The checked dress is piped in plain self-toned chambray. Pointed pockets at belt and side plaits give added style and service.

GIRLS' SIZES: 7, 8, 10, 12, 14 years. State size. See size scale above at right. Shipping weight, 1 pound 12 ounces.
15 G 758—Blue chambray dress and blue checked gingham dress.
15 G 760—Pink chambray dress and pink check gingham dress.
Sold only in sets of one each......................**2 Dresses 98¢**

Cotton Gabardine
Scotch Plaid Trimming
Serviceable for School

15 G 754 Serviceable and colorful for school wear on cool days is this Cotton Gabardine Dress, with its rich Scotch plaid collar, sash and slot breast pocket. Long set in sleeves and panel side plaits make it practical and attractive. Roomy neck vent under tie.

GIRLS' SIZES: 7, 8, 10, 12, 14 years. State size. See size scale above. Shipping weight, 1 lb. 4 oz.
15 G 754—Navy blue.
15 G 756—Wine..........**$1.69**

Made for Hard Wear
Famous Dixie-Milled
Tupelo Home-Tex Cloth

15 G 717 Dresses of Tupelo Home-Tex Cloth are in constant demand by mothers who know. This sturdy material is firmly woven from selected cotton yarns, grown in Dixie and woven at a nearby Cotton Mill (which accounts for its low price).

It has a heavy thread stripe that contrasts well with the material of collar and inserts on the cuffs and front panels of blouse. Fancy buttons, pockets and kick plait finish this neat serviceable frock.

GIRLS' SIZES: 7, 8, 10, 12, 14 years. State size. See size scale above. Shipping weight, 14 ounces.
15 G 717—Tan with green.
15 G 719—Green with tan.........**88¢**

40

Girls' and Children's GOOD Shoes
for School, Dress or Play~ECONOMICAL

Handsome and Serviceable Brown or Black Grain Leather

Welcome news for mothers! Sturdy, good looking School or Dress Shoes for fall and winter that will give girls more than the ordinary service. Durable, brown or black calf grain leather uppers finished with neat perforations. Sturdy good weight soles of oak grain. Rubber heels. Their fine appearance will please girls who like to look tidy and well dressed. You can expect them to give months of wear. Ship.wt., 2 lbs.

SIZES: 2½ to 7. Width E. State size.

24 G 2889— $2.79
Brown calf grain leather
24 G 2890—Black calf grain leather .. 2.79

$2.49
Smart, New Black Oxford for Girls—Real Value

They're in style! Handsome D'Orsay Oxford Ties of black gunmetal leather with a boyish square toe and a low rubber heel. Just the sort of shoe that's so remarkably popular with young ladies everywhere. Your little girl will surely enjoy wearing them too. Soles of durable oak leather. Mothers who know real values will see at once that here is a very special offer that will save them money. Low rubber heels. Shipping weight, 1 pound 12 ounces.

SIZES: 2½ to 7. Width E. State size.
24 G 2986 ....$2.49

Sturdy Foot Form Shoes of Brown or Black Grain Leather

Your child will need fewer pairs if she wears these Shoes of sturdy brown grain leather or black gunmetal leather. Especially tanned for long service. Oak leather soles. FOOT-FORM shape permits youthful feet to grow naturally. Rubber heels. Ship. weight, 1 lb. 12 oz. State size wanted.

Brown Grain Leather
24 G 2868—For girls. 11½ to 2..... $2.39
24 G 2869—Children. 8½ to 11.... 1.98
Black Gunmetal Leather
24 G 2866—For girls. 11½ to 2..... $2.39
24 G 2867—Children. 8½ to 11.... 1.93

$2.39
Child's Pretty Two-Eyelet Tie

A smart two-eyelet Tie that's very durable. Tan or black grain leather; wears long. Oak leather soles. Rubber Heels. A splendid value. Ship. wt., 1 lb. 8 oz. State size wanted.

SIZES: 11½ to 2.
24 G 2908—Tan.
24 G 2909—Black.
Per pair. $2.39

Wonder School Shoes
$1.89

A great favorite with daughters and mothers for many years. They offer more real wearing quality at this low price than you would ever expect. Black box calf leather uppers are soft and durable. A wonder for comfort, service and value! Ship. wt., 2 pounds. State size.

24 G 2829—SIZES: 2½ to 8 ....$2.79
24 G 2830—SIZES: 11½ to 2 ...$1.98
24 G 2831—SIZES: 8½ to 11.... 1.89

Child's Black Patent D'Orsay Tie
$2.49

Quite the latest pattern for grownups, so the youngsters will like it too. A D'Orsay Tie of black patent leather with plenty of toe room for your child's growing feet. Durable leather soles. Rubber heels. A real bargain, you'll agree. Shipping weight, 1 lb. 8 oz. State size wanted.

SIZES: 11½ to 2.
24 G 2961 $2.49

See Shoe Size Chart Page 169

Goodyear Sewed BUCKROME Leather Soles

Special Value $2.69
Girls' Smart Oxford

Every mother will welcome the very low price of this good looking Oxford. Of brown side leather, in the popular D'Orsay style. Any girl will be delighted with its stylish appearance. Oak leather soles, specially tanned to give extra service, are hard to wear out. Rubber heels. Made over healthful last for growing feet. Ship. wt., 1 lb. 12 oz.

SIZES: 2½ to 7. State size.
24 G 3031 ....$2.69

Smart Tan Leather

Our finest for children. Handsome high quality Oxfords of tan calf grain leather. Soled with tough, flexible, Buckrome leather—It wears and wears—Goodyear sewed. Contrasting tan grain leather trim. Rubber heels. Shipping weight, 1 lb. 4 oz. State size wanted.

24 G 3026—11½ to 2 ....$2.79
24 G 3027—8½ to 11.... 2.49

Stylish Paisley Trim

Finer Shoes like these always prove their worth. Better materials—better construction. The tough, flexible Buckrome leather soles are Goodyear sewed. Black patent leather, with a colorful paisley leather trim. Rubber heels. Leather lining. Shipping weight, 1 lb. 4 oz. State size.

24 G 3024—11½ to 2....$2.79
24 G 3025—8½ to 11.... 2.49

New Paisley Inlay

Fine soft black patent with paisley inlay. Soled with Buckrome, the new, tough, flexible sole leather, Goodyear sewed. FOOT-FORM shape. White leather lining. Low rubber heels. Made in a factory that specializes in children's higher quality footwear. Ship. wt., 1 lb. 4 oz. State size.

24 G 3022—11½ to 2 ....$2.79
24 G 3023—8½ to 11.... 2.49

Clever Three-Eyelet Tie
$2.98

The young woman who takes note of the newest styles will want a pair of these three-eyelet Ties. they're of handsome, durable, black gunmetal leather, with a modishly contrasting trim of black patent leather. A shoe that promises to be one of the most popular of the new fall and winter styles, designed for wear with the smartest dresses. Oak leather soles are very long wearing. Rubber heels for comfortable walking. Shipping weight, 1 pound 12 ounces.

SIZES: 2½ to 7. Wide width. State size wanted.
24 G 3019 ....$2.98

Girls' Shoes With WonderWear Soles

They Reduce the Family Shoe Bill Because They Wear Longer

Girls' Sturdy Winter Hi-cut

Strong Brown Uppers
Popular Moccasin Toe

Sturdy for outdoor winter play. Brown retan (double tanned) leather uppers give extra long service. Uppers are of fine leather, with extra weight. Rubber heels. Moccasin toe. Shipping weight, 2 pounds. State size wanted.

24 G 2806—Height, 10 in. $3.69
SIZES: 2½ to 8
24 G 2807—Height, 9 in. 3.25
SIZES: 12½ to 2.
24 G 2808—Height, 8 in. 2.79
SIZES: 8½ to 12.

D'Orsay Oxford Tie

Young girls favor the Tie because It looks attractive. Uppers are of fine quality black gunmetal calf grain leather. Has the durable Wonder-Wear composition soles, famous for long service. Notice the non-slip ridges for sports wear. Rubber heels. Shipping weight, 1 pound 12 ounces.

SIZES: 2½ to 7. State size.
24 G 3028 ...... $2.98

Child's One Strap

A pretty dress Slipper that will wear unusually long because it has Wonder-Wear Inlay. Soled with Buckrome. Black patent composition soles. Black patent leather with fashionable trim of tan reptile embossed grain leather. Wide toe. Ship. wt., 1 lb. 4 oz.

SIZES: 11½ to 2. State size wanted. $2.49
24 G 3003

Longer Wear for Active Feet
Just the sort of School Shoes for running, hard playing children. The uppers are of durable and handsome black grain leather. Wonder-Wear composition soles give an unusual amount of service. A shoe that will materially reduce your shoe bill. Rubber heels. Leather insole. Healthy, broad toe last. Shipping weight, 2 pounds.
SIZES: 11½ to 2. State size wanted.
24 G 2812.. $2.69

Wear-Style-Value
$2.98

For school, sports, or everyday wear young girls prefer the Oxford style. It's practical, comfortable and always so good looking. Sturdy brown grain leather adorned with very pretty perforations. Stylish, square toe for growing feet. "Wonder-Wear" non-slip composition soles are extremely durable. Rubber heels. Ship. wt., 1 lb. 12 oz. State size.

SIZES: 2½ to 7. State size.
24 G 2970 ....$2.98

41

Roomier, Warmer~Lower Priced

Ages 2 to 14 Years

Princess Slip 31¢

AGES: 2, 4, 6 years. State age wanted. Ship. wt. each, 6 oz.
32 G 2344—Light ground assorted light stripes.
32 G 2345—Dark ground, assorted gray stripes.
Each................ **31¢**
AGES: 8, 10, 12, 14 years. State age. Ship. wt., each, 9 oz.
32 G 2346—Light ground, assorted light stripes.
32 G 2347—Dark ground, assorted gray stripes.
Each................ **55¢**
Well made of good quality flannelette. Armholes and round neck have neat shell crochet edging. Ruffle at bottom. Buttons in back.

Durable Pajamas 79¢

AGES: 2, 4, 6 years. State age. Shipping weight, each, 11 ounces.
32 G 2310—Assorted light stripes.
32 G 2311—White. Each..... **79¢**
AGES: 8, 10, 12, 14 years. State age. Shipping weight, each, 14 ounces.
32 G 2353—Assorted light stripes.
32 G 2354—White. Each..... **93¢**
Good looking Sleeping Suit of heavy quality flannelette. Smart Rayon frogs trim front opening. One pocket; drop seat. Reinforced seams.

Lowest Price in Years! 48¢

32 G 2302—Assorted light stripes only.
AGES: 2, 4 and 6 years. State age. Shipping weight, each, 8 ounces.
Our prices are amazingly low for these children's full cut Sleepers. Now you can have a good supply for the children without spending much money. Good quality flannelette in popular military style with high neck, long sleeves, and roomy warm feet. Buttons down back and has drop seat. Carefully made with all seams reinforced to give long service.

Novelty Print "Billie Burke" $1.29

32 G 2398—Flesh pink with figures.
AGES: 6, 8, 10, 12 years. State age. Shipping weight, 14 ounces.
Children always love wearing cute Billie Burkes like these with novelty print patterns. Trimly tailored of high-grade flannelette, they fit well, wear splendidly and are priced at a big saving. Double yoke front and back with two rows of hemstitching trimming in the front. Neat shirring finishes front at waistline on each side. One pocket; elastic at ankles.

Very Specially Priced 98¢ ← "Billie Burke"

32 G 2396—Assorted light stripes.
32 G 2397—White.
AGES: 6, 8, 10, 12 years. State age. Shipping weight, each, 13 ounces.
Decidedly popular with girls—they like the tailored smartness of these one-piece Billie Burkes. Reliable wearing quality, well made of warm, serviceable, heavy flannelette. Three dainty Rayon frogs trim the front. One pocket; neat shirring trims sleeves. Drop seat; reinforced seams. Elastic at ankles.

2 to 14 Years

AGES: 2, 4, 6 years. State age. Shipping weight, each, 7 ounces.
32 G 2340—Asst. light stripes.
32 G 2341—Asst. dark gray stripes. **53¢**
AGES: 8, 10, 12, 14 years. Ship. weight, each, 10 ounces.
32 G 2342—Asst. light stripes.
32 G 2343—Asst. dark gray stripes. **63¢**
Flannelette B'oomer Combination with shell crochet stitch trim. Buttoned front and drop seat. Elastic at knees. Well made; low priced.

For Ages 2 to 14

Special Value 58¢

AGES: 2, 4, 6 years. State age. Ship. wt., 10 oz.
32 G 2307—Assorted light stripes.. **58¢**
AGES: 8, 10, 12, 14 years. Ship. wt., 12 oz.
32 G 2350—Assorted light stripes.. **69¢**
Dependable quality, full cut Sleeping Suit priced at a genuine saving. Ever so carefully made of warm flannelette with high neck. Buttons down front and has drop seat. All seams reinforced for added strength.

Sturdy Quality 65¢

AGES: 2, 4, 6 years. State age. Ship. wt., 11 oz.
32 G 2308—Assorted light stripes.
32 G 2309—White. Each..... **65¢**
AGES: 8, 10, 12, 14 years. State age. Ship. wt., 14 oz.
32 G 2351—Assorted light stripes.
32 G 2352—White. Each..... **79¢**
Delightfully warm Pajamas of good quality flannelette—priced far below their real value! High neck; long sleeves and pocket. The feet insure perfect sleeping comfort for your children. Buttons down the front and has drop seat. Well made with reinforced seams.

Ages 2 to 12 Yrs. 79¢

AGES: 2, 4, 6 years. State age. Ship. weight, 12 ounces.
32 G 2381—White, with figures. Each..... **79¢**
AGES: 8, 10, 12, 14 years. Ship. weight, 14 ounces.
32 G 2382—White with figures. Each..... **97¢**
Sturdy flannelette Gown. Double yoke front and back; hemstitched front.

Plain Colors or Striped 53¢

AGES: 2, 4, 6 years. State age. Ship. wt., 11 oz.
32 G 2375—Assorted light stripes. Each.......... **53¢**
32 G 2376—Flesh pink.......65¢
32 G 2377—White...65¢
AGES: 8, 10, 12 years. State age. Ship. wt., 13 oz.
32 G 2378—Assorted light stripes. **63¢**
32 G 2379—Flesh pink.........79¢
32 G 2380—White...79¢
Amazing values—in children's good quality flannelette Gowns. Hemstitched trim. Double yoke front and back.

AMOSKEAG Flannelette

Trimmed With Rayon Frogs 83¢

32 G 2303—Assorted light stripes.
32 G 2304—White.
AGES: 2, 4, 6 years. State age wanted. Shipping weight, each, 10 ounces.
Extremely popular one-piece Sleeping Suits made of famous Amoskeag flannelette. Pretty Rayon frogs trim the front closing; one pocket; drop seat and warm feet. Full cut; reinforced seams.

Tots' Warm Sleepers 58¢

32 G 2300—Assorted light stripes.
32 G 2301—Plain white.
AGES: 1, 2, 3 years. State age wanted.
Shipping weight, each, 7 oz.
Amoskeag flannelette, famous for its warmth and resistance to hard wear, is used in this low priced one-piece Sleeper. Has cozy feet; high neck; long sleeves and pocket. Buttons down back and has drop seat. Reinforced seams. Roomy sizes.

Juvenile Design "Resta" Cloth 79¢

32 G 2305—Blue ground; novelty figures.
32 G 2306—Pink ground; novelty figures.
AGES: 2, 4 and 6 yrs. State age. Ship. wt., each, 10 ounces.
Cunning novelty one-piece Sleeping Suit of durable quality "Resta" cloth flannelette. Amusing juvenile designs that will delight the youngsters. Buttons in back. Has drop seat, pocket, and warm feet. Full cut; all seams are strongly reinforced.

Warm Knit Princess Slip $1.29

31 G 915—Cream white.
31 G 916—Gray with stripes.
AGES: 8 to 16 years. State age wanted.
Shipping weight, each, 10 ounces.
Every young miss should have at least one of these cozy garments for winter wear. They will keep her thoroughly warm when walking or riding, and will not look bulky under her nicest frocks. They are made attractively, too, from closely knit part wool yarns. Neck, armholes and bottom are finished with neat shell crochet edging, and the skirt is trimmed with pretty striping in contrasting color. Specially made so they won't rumple up at the knees. You'll find that they wash very easily, and give wonderful service. As usual, Ward's price is far below what you would expect to pay for such splendid quality!

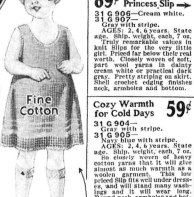

For Ages 8 to 16 Years

Fine Cotton **Part Wool**

Light Weight Princess Slip 79¢

31 G 917—Gray with stripe.
31 G 918—Cream white.
AGES: 8 to 16 years. State age wanted.
Ship. weight, each, 10 oz.
Although made of cotton yarns, it's so finely and closely woven that it will give ample warmth. A trimly fitting Slip, serviceable and surprisingly low priced. It will wash well and give long, satisfactory service. Neck, armholes and bottom are finished with neat shell crochet edging; neat striping on skirt.

Medium Weight Cozy Slip $1.09

31 G 994—Gray with stripe.
31 G 995—Camel tan with stripe.
AGES: 8 to 16 years. State age wanted.
Ship weight, each, 10 oz.
Growing girls need extra warmth and protection in cold weather and this closely knit, well fitting Princess Slip can be worn under their smartest dresses without spoiling their neat appearance. Made of soft part wool yarns; neck, armholes and bottom finished with neat shell crochet stitching.

Part Wool

Fine Cotton

Warm Slips for Ages 2 to 6

89¢ Little Girls' Princess Slip →

31 G 906—Cream white.
31 G 907—Gray with stripe.
AGES: 2, 4, 6 years. State age. Ship. weight, each, 7 oz.
Truly remarkable values in knit Slips for the very little girl. Priced far below their real worth. Closely woven of soft, part wool yarns in dainty cream white or practical dark gray. Pretty striping on skirt. Shell crochet edging finishes neck, armholes and bottom.

Cozy Warmth for Cold Days 59¢

31 G 904—Gray with stripe.
31 G 905—Navy blue with stripe.
AGES: 2, 4, 6 years. State age. Ship. weight, each, 7 oz.
So closely woven of heavy cotton yarns that it will give almost as much warmth as a woolen garment. This low priced Slip fits well under dresses, and will stand many washings and it will wear long. Round neck, armholes and bottom are edged with shell crochet stitching. Neat striping on skirt. A wonderful Ward value!

Worsted and Cotton

Carefully Made, Serviceable Garments *for* Children

Ages 2 to 14

FAMOUS *Kickaway* BLOOMERS

Ages 2 to 14

Kick-Proof—Comfortable
Ages 2 to 12
Famous because of their extra wear-resisting quality, their specially designed, reinforced concave saddle crotch, the comfortable, roomy seat and double stitched, bar-tacked seams.

Durable Sateen 45¢
AGES: 2, 4 and 6 years. Stage age. Ship. weight, 4 ounces.
32 G 2054—Black.
32 G 2055—White.....45¢
Each..........45¢
AGES: 8, 10 and 12 years. State age. Ship. weight, 6 ounces.
32 G 2056—Black.
32 G 2057—White.
Each..........49¢
Good quality durable sateen with all the famous Kickaway features described above.

Shadow Stripe Satinette 49¢
AGES: 2, 4 and 6 yrs. Ship. weight, 4 ounces.
32 G 2062—White.
32 G 2063—Black.
32 G 2064—Pink.
32 G 2065—Peach.
Each..........49¢
AGES: 8, 10 and 12 years. Ship. wt., 6 oz.
32 G 2066—White.
32 G 2067—Black.
32 G 2068—Pink.
32 G 2069—Peach.
Each..........59¢
State age wanted.
Soft satinette with all Kickaway features.

Lace Trim Princess Slip 59¢
32 G 2147—AGES: 2, 4 and 6 years. Ship. weight, 5 oz. 59¢
32 G 2148—AGES: 8, 10, 12 and 14 yrs. Ship. weight, 6 oz. 75¢
White only. State age.
Serviceable nainsook with pretty medallion and insertion in front. Neck, armholes and gathered ruffle edged with dainty Val lace.

Bloomer Combination 49¢
32 G 2168—AGES: 2, 4 and 6 years. Ship. weight, 5 oz. 49¢
32 G 2169—AGES: 8, 10 and 12 years. Ship. weight, 6 oz. 59¢
White only. State age.
Full sizes in good quality nainsook. Buttons in back; drop seat. Elastic and lace edging at knees.

Special Value Princess Slip 49¢
32 G 2175—AGES: 2, 4 and 6 years. Ship. weight, 5 oz. 49¢
32 G 2176—AGES: 8, 10, 12 and 14 years. Shipping weight, 6 oz. 59¢
White only. State age.
Firm nainsook with dainty Val lace at neck, armholes and on ruffle. Pin tucks trim ruffle.

How to Order Girls' Slips
Measure from shoulder to length desired; and order age corresponding nearest to length.

Age	Length
2 years	20 inches
4 years	23 inches
6 years	26 inches
8 years	28 inches
10 years	31 inches
12 years	35 inches
14 years	38 inches

Crepe Gown 79¢
AGES: 2, 4 and 6 yrs. Ship. wt., 6 oz.
32 G 2400—White.
32 G 2401—Pink.
32 G 2402—Peach.
Each..........79¢
AGES: 8, 10 and 12 years. Ship. wt., 7 oz.
32 G 2403—White.
32 G 2404—Pink.
32 G 2405—Peach.
Each..........89¢
State age wanted.
Children's Gown of crepe—easily washed; requires no ironing. Colored piping; shirred in front. Full sizes. Splendid value!

Cambric Pajamas 55¢
AGES: 2, 4 and 6 years. Shipping weight, 7 ounces.
32 G 2408—White only...55¢
AGES: 8, 10, 12 and 14 years. Shipping weight, 9 ounces.
32 G 2409—White only...68¢
State age wanted.
Neatly tailored of heavy cambric. Opens down front and closes in back with drop seat. Has one pocket, long sleeves and is ankle length. Wonderful value!

Specially Priced 42¢
AGES: 2, 4 and 6 years. Shipping weight, 6 ounces.
32 G 2406—White only...42¢
AGES: 8, 10 and 12 years. Shipping weight, 8 ounces.
32 G 2407—White only...49¢
State age wanted.
Pretty and long wearing Gown of good quality nainsook. Colored piping at neck and armholes and dainty shirring in front. Full sizes; well made.

Bodice Top Slip 65¢
Of Sateen
32 G 2158—Black.
32 G 2159—White.
32 G 2160—Flesh pink. 65¢
Shadow Stripe Satinette
32 G 2161—Black.
32 G 2162—White.
32 G 2163—Flesh pink. 89¢
AGES: 8, 10, 12 and 14 years. State age wanted. Shipping weight, each, 7 ounces.
Most exceptional values! Well made in full, roomy sizes in bodice top style; self material shoulder straps; ribbon draw.

SADDLE CROTCH

27¢ Sturdy Bloomers 29¢
for Ages 2 to 12 Years
Strongly made of dependable quality materials. Hand turned elastic at waist and knees; reinforced saddle crotch. All seams double stitched.

Firm Quality Plain Sateen
AGES: 2, 4 and 6 years. State age. Shipping weight, 4 ounces.
32 G 2072—Black.
32 G 2073—White. Each 27¢
AGES: 8, 10 and 12 years. State age. Shipping weight, 5 oz.
32 G 2051—Black.
32 G 2052—White. Each 35¢

Long-Wearing Striped Sateen
AGES: 2, 4 and 6 years. State age. Shipping weight, 4 ounces.
32 G 2082—Black.
32 G 2083—White. Each 29¢
AGES: 8, 10 and 12 years. State age. Shipping weight, 5 oz.
32 G 2084—Black.
32 G 2085—White. Each 37¢

Warm Flannelette 25¢
FLANNELETTE
32 G 2004—AGES: 2, 4 and 6 years. Shipping weight, 6 ounces....25¢
32 G 2005—AGES: 8, 10 and 12 years. Shipping weight, 8 ounces....35¢
Assorted light stripes. State age wanted.
The durability and warmth that children need are in these flannelette Bloomers. Double needle seams. Elastic at waistline and knee openings.

Built-Up Shoulder Style Princess Slip
Made in full sizes from good quality materials. Ruffle at bottom.

SATEEN OR SATINETTE

Good Quality Sateen
AGES: 2, 4 and 6 years. State age. Shipping weight, 6 ounces.
32 G 2150—Navy blue.
32 G 2151—White. Each 49¢
AGES: 8, 10, 12 and 14 years. State age.
32 G 2152—Navy blue.
32 G 2153—White. Each 59¢

Shadow Stripe Satinette
AGES: 2, 4 and 6 years. State age. Shipping weight, 6 ounces.
32 G 2154—Navy blue.
32 G 2155—White. Each 69¢
AGES: 8, 10, 12 and 14 years. Ship. wt., 8 ounces.
32 G 2156—Navy blue.
32 G 2157—White. Each 79¢

SATEEN OR SATINETTE

Sateen 49¢ / Satinette 69¢

Baby's Robe 98¢
Beacon Cloth
32 G 2702—Pink.
32 G 2703—Blue. Each..98¢
Blanket Cloth
32 G 2700—Pink.
32 G 2701—Blue. Each..79¢
Infants' size only. Shipping weight, 8 oz.
Good quality—soft, warm, genuine Beacon cloth or cotton blanket cloth with animal designs in white. Cords at neck and waist.

Beacon BLANKET / BLANKET CLOTH

For Boy or Girl $1.98
32 G 2706—Tan ground.
32 G 2707—Medium blue ground.
AGES: 2, 4 and 6 yrs. Ship. wt., 15 oz.
Carefully made, extra full cut Bathrobe of genuine Beacon Cloth—warm and durable. All-over floral design; satin ribbon trim on collar, cuffs and pocket. Rayon cords.

Warmth at Low Cost $1.49
32 G 2704—Tan ground.
32 G 2705—Blue ground.
AGES: 2, 4 and 6 yrs. Ship. wt., 13 oz.
Boys or girls will love this durable blanket cloth Bathrobe in interesting Navajo pattern. All edges finished with machine stitching. Tasseled cord in contrasting colors.

PURE GUM RUBBER

Sturdy Knit Waist 18¢
32 G 2001—White only.
AGES: 2, 4, 6, 8, 10, 12 years. State age. Shipping weight, 4 oz.
Closely knit combed cotton, strongly reinforced with tape. Plenty of bone buttons. Metal pin tubes at sides for supporters. Priced at a real saving.

35¢ Reinforced Knit Waist
32 G 2002—White only. AGES: 2, 4, 6, 8, 10, 12 years. State age wanted. Shipping weight, 5 ounces.
Especially well made of good quality combed cotton and strongly reinforced with banding of self materials. Bone buttons with tape loops around waistline for attaching other garments. Metal pin tubes for supporters.

Gingham Coverall 45¢
Checked Gingham
32 G 3450—Blue.
32 G 3451—Pink.
Novelty Prints
32 G 3452—Light ground, assorted prints. Each......45¢
AGES: 2, 4 and 6 years. Shipping weight, each, 6 oz.
Cute and very practical! Well-made Coverall Apron of sturdy materials. Circular collar, sleeves and pocket. Two-tone ruffles with white binding.

Slipover Style Apron 49¢
One Size for Ages 4, 6 and 8 Years
32 G 3250—Medium blue.
32 G 3251—Coral.
One Size for Ages 10 and 12 Years
32 G 3252—Medium blue.
32 G 3253—Coral.
Each......49¢
Shipping weight, each, 8 oz.
Heavy gum rubber in dainty shades. Contrasting two-tone ruffles. Wide shoulder back prevents slipping.

Reinforced Cambric Waist 25¢
32 G 2042—AGES: 2, 4 and 6 years......25¢
32 G 2043—AGES: 8, 10 and 12 years....29¢
State age wanted.
Shipping weight, each, 4 oz.
Child's Waist with double thickness under arms; all seams double stitched. Back closing. Taped bone buttons. Pin tubes for garters.

Baby's Waist 23¢
32 G 2012—White only.
AGES: 1, 2 and 3 years. State age. Shipping weight, 3 ounces.
Strong cambric, reinforced in front and back. Has stitched eyelets for pinning diapers and taped bone buttons. Back closing.

Skeleton Waist 35¢
32 G 2006—AGES: 2, 4 and 6 years. Ship. weight, 3 oz. Each..35¢
32 G 2007—AGES: 8, 10 and 12 years. Ship. wt., 5 oz. Each..39¢
State age wanted.
Boys' or girls' Skeleton Waist of heavy quality muslin. Wide tape front and back to hold waist in place. Taped bone buttons. Metal pin tubes for garters.

Little Wonder REG. U.S. PAT. OFF.

Heavy Muslin 35¢
32 G 2008—AGES: 2, 4 and 6 years. Ship. weight, 4 ounces. Each......35¢
32 G 2009—AGES: 8, 10 and 12 years. Ship. weight, 6 ounces. Each......39¢
State age wanted.
Reinforced Waist for girl or boy. Adjustable shoulder straps. Bone buttons on tape loops at waistline. Metal pin tubes for garters.

Nainsook Bloomers 25¢
32 G 2040—AGES: 2, 4 and 6 years. Ship. wt. 25¢
32 G 2041—AGES: 8, 10 and 12 years. Ship. wt., 4 oz. 35¢
White only. State age wanted.
An unchallenged bargain in good quality nainsook Bloomers carefully made to stand hard wear. Cut in full sizes with strong, double stitched seams. Hand turned durable elastic at waistline and elastic at knee.

Knickerbocker Drawers 35¢
32 G 2038—AGES: 2, 4 and 6 years. Each......35¢
32 G 2039—AGES: 8, 10 and 12 yrs. Each......39¢
White only. State age wanted. Shipping weight, 4 ounces.
Girls' sturdy cambric full cut Drawers. Reinforced placket. All seams double stitched. Embroidery at knees.

For Other Children's Lingerie See Pages 117 and 633

Better Fabrics~Sturdier Tailoring
Mean "LONGTIME" Service

$18⁹⁵

Always a Great Favorite
All Wool—Big Value

A favorite style for men who like a dignified, dressy Overcoat. This Chesterfield model is always in vogue—year after year men show their preference for it. Tailored of heavy All Wool overcoating—the long wearing LONGTIME quality that gives our customers a confidence which comes only from actual experience through months of wear. Fully lined with high-grade Venetian for extra warmth and service. In dark gray or black. Solid comfort goes way down into the warm flannel pockets, too. Neatly tailored velvet collar adds a desirable finish not usually found in coats priced so low.

This coat is a good example of the greater values Ward's is able to supply in a medium priced coat. Not only style, but sturdier fabric and more thorough workmanship, combine to produce a garment superior to overcoats usually sold for much higher prices. Average length, about 48 inches.

SIZES: Chest, 35, 36, 37, 38, 39, 40, 42, 44 inches. State chest measure. Read "How to Measure" on Page 238. Shipping weight, 8 pounds 4 ounces.

39 G 2607—Oxford gray.
39 G 2611—Black..... **$18.95**

Fine Quality All Wool
Navy Blue Chesterfield

Here's class, men—and value! This Fifth Avenue Coat is the Chesterfield model the best dressed men are wearing. Equally suitable for business or for dress wear. It is not a bulky, heavy coat, yet it will keep you warm on the coldest days as the cloth is an exceptionally closely woven All Wool Melton made of finely woven yarns. Ward's tremendous buying power and all year production enable us to offer you this exceptional value.

You will like the rich, dark, navy blue color. It's especially pleasing when combined with this smooth finished, sturdy overcoating usually found only in much higher priced garments. Venetian lining, too, is the good-looking, long wearing kind—in entire yoke and sleeves. All seams are taped for neatness and extra strength. Vent in back gives walking comfort and easy fit when you sit down.

Look at the picture and see how the square shoulders and broad lapels give the wearer an athletic appearance. The velvet collar adds a dressy finish specified by men of stylish inclinations. Measure about 46 inches from your collar down and you'll get an idea of the length of this coat.

SIZES: Chest, 34, 35, 36, 37, 38, 39, 40, 42 inches. State chest measure. Read "How to Measure" on Page 238. Shipping weight, 8 pounds.

39 G 2830—
Dark blue only......... **$22.50**

$22⁵⁰

Special

Cheviot
$18⁹⁵

Melton
$15⁰⁰

$23⁵⁰

$14⁹⁵

$13⁵⁰

Big Burly Ulster

Every year our sales of this big, burly Ulster gain by leaps and bounds. This means larger purchases year after year of this fine quality, soft All Wool cheviot overcoating, and as a result our prices are always lower. Now we are offering this overcoat, which many consider the equal of ones selling elsewhere for $25 and more, for only $18.95. You can't fully realize their roominess, their beautiful tailoring, their wonderful fit until you see one and wear it. Large convertible collar. Double breasted front; full belted back. Yoke and sleeves lined with satiny finished twilled Venetian. Full 48 inches long.

SIZES: Chest, 34 to 44 inches. Read "How to Measure" on Page 238. Shipping weight, 10 pounds.

39 G 2701—Dark brown mixture.
39 G 2705—Dark Warwick blue.
Each............. **$18.95**

Same Model in All Wool Melton

To those who want the same style, same length coat in the same sizes but at a lower price we recommend No. 39 G 2709—an All Wool Melton. Full lined. A substantial quality of tailoring and material and a surprising value at our low price. Shipping weight, 10 pounds.

39 G 2709—Dark brown only..... **$15.00**

Wind-Proof and Rain-Proof

This Fine Quality, good-looking Longtime Storm Coat comes down well over the legs (it's 48 inches long) protecting the entire body from cold, wind and rain. Combines three layers of warmth giving materials.

The outside is smooth finish, strength-tested 30 ounce All Wool Overcoating that will stand seasons of hard all-weather service. Lined with fancy worsted, an exceptionally durable fabric of much higher quality than linings generally used. Between the Overcoating and the Worsted lining is a layer of rain-proofed interlining that keeps out dampness and rain and won't let the wind blow through.

It's health protection at small cost, to wear this sturdily built, finely finished coat. Seams are strongly sewed and reinforced at all strain points. Convertible collar buttons closely around your neck for comfort and warmth. Flannel lined muff pockets. A rich, soft looking dark gray is the color. The style tailored into every line will last as long as the coat. You'll say you never saw such big all protecting roominess in an all weather garment.

SIZES: Chest, 35 to 48 inches. State chest measure. Read "How to Measure" on Page 238. Shipping weight, 11 lbs.

39 G 2739—Dark gray only.....**$23.50**

Heavy All Wool Melton

To the best of our knowledge this is the greatest $14.95 All Wool Overcoat value you could obtain anywhere. It is a garment that will give service and satisfaction out of all proportion to its small cost. A bargain made possible because we bought this heavy 32-ounce all wool overcoating when the market was low, at a price that was lower than the market value.

We made these coats in our own immense shops. Carefully and strongly tailored for appearance, comfort and long wear. Length about 44 inches, popular with men who walk a great deal or who wear an overcoat at work. All-around belt holds it close to body and keeps the wind out. Large sized collar that fits snugly around neck to shield you from the bitter cold.

The garment is fully and substantially lined for added warmth and wear. Seams are strongly sewed. Slip into one and you'll appreciate its all round comfort, especially at the low price we ask.

SIZES: Chest, 34 to 46 inches. State chest measurement wanted. Read "How to Measure" on Page 238. Shipping weight, 8 pounds 8 ounces.

39 G 2839—
Dark brown only..................**$14.95**

Gray or Black Melton

Do not judge the quality of this Coat by its price—unless you are an old customer of ours and know Ward's Values. For we know that wherever you may look, you couldn't find, at anywhere near this price, a Chesterfield coat as well tailored of such fine, smooth finished 85 per cent wool overcoating. You act wisely in selecting this model for the style has been a continuous favorite ever since it was first introduced many years ago. When you wear it note how many unusual features and points of dressiness we've put into it. Then you will get some idea of the everlasting effort we always make to give our customers more quality per dollar than they can find anywhere else.

The coat is fully lined with good quality twill and has a three button fly front. Large and warm side pockets and an inside breast pocket. Average length, about 46 inches.

SIZES: Chest, 35 to 44 inches. State chest measurement wanted. Read "How to Measure" on Page 238. Ship. weight, each, 7 pounds 4 ounces.

39 G 2601—Dark gray.
39 G 2603—Black. Each........ **$13.50**

All the New Ones Are Here

Stylish Wool Felt

539 G 315—Pearl gray. Blue band.
539 G 317—Tan. Brown band.
SIZES: 6¾, 6⅞, 7, 7⅛, 7¼, 7⅜, 7½.
State size. Read "How to Measure"
at bottom of page. Shipping weight, 2 pounds 4
ounces.
Here's a Hat bargain that deserves your most
careful consideration. The wool felt is of good
quality. Has a genuine leather sweatband and is
trimmed with an attractive band. The crown is
5⅝ inches, the brim 2⅝ inches—that's the right
style dimensions.

$1.98

Excellent Quality Styled Right

539 G 364—Pearl gray.
539 G 367—Tan.
539 G 368—Brown.
539 G 372—Black.
SIZES: 6¾, 6⅞, 7, 7⅛, 7¼, 7⅜, 7½, 7⅝, 7¾.
State size. Read "How to Measure" at bottom of page. Shipping weight, 2 lbs. 4 oz.
Nothing but the finer quality of genuine smooth finished fur felt would go for this Hat. This model has so much good sound style and is such an outstanding bargain that it would be considered a great value at $5 in the smartest shops. We took particular pains to find a manufacturer with a hand finishing process that would insure the style, smartness and snap so faithfully pictured here. Full satin lined and has a genuine leather sweatband. It's the new 2¾-inch curled brim and 5⅝-inch crown.

$3.95

Our Very Best Dress Hat

539 G 384—Pearl gray.
539 G 385—Steel gray.
539 G 388—Tan.
SIZES: 6¾, 6⅞, 7, 7⅛, 7¼, 7⅜,
7½, 7⅝, 7¾. State size wanted. Read "How to Measure" at bottom of page. Shipping weight, 2 pounds 4 ounces.
They typify the ideal for smartness and finish often sought but seldom found for less than $6. To make this exceptional Hat we picked a manufacturer with a long established reputation for producing only first quality headwear. He used extra fine quality, smooth finished fur felt. He styled it to satisfy the demands of the better dressed men of today. Full satin lined and the genuine leather sweatband is of A No. 1 quality. Neatly bound at the edge, which gives it that finished appearance so suitable for young or old. Crown is 5⅝ inches, brim 2⅝ inches.

$4.95

Exclusive Young Men's Style

539 G 375—Light gray.
539 G 376—Dark tan.
539 G 377—Black.
SIZES: 6¾, 6⅞, 7, 7⅛, 7¼, 7⅜,
7½. State size. Read "How to Measure" at bottom of page. Ship. wt., 2 lbs. 3 oz.
There is an air of distinction in these Hats. Both the welt edge brim and the attractive band are stylishly narrow. The smooth finished fine quality fur felt will retain its shape through months of service. The crown is 5⅝ inches, brim 2½ inches. Genuine leather sweatband.

$3.65

A Derby for Smart Wear

539 G 360—Black only.
SIZES: 6¾, 6⅞, 7, 7⅛,
7¼, 7⅜, 7½, 7⅝. State size.
Read "How to Measure"
at bottom of page. Ship. wt., 2 lbs. 2 oz.
Derbys are slated for another year of popularity. Men with good judgment about their clothes inevitably recognize the importance of the derby for dress and business wear. Then, too, they comfortably conform to most any type of head making the wearer appear at his best. Made of fine quality fur felt in the seasons latest style proportions—5-inch crown and 2¼-inch brim. The sweatband is of genuine leather.

$3.75

Style-Individuality

539 G 350—Pearl gray.
539 G 352—Tan.
539 G 354—Bluish gray.
SIZES: 6¾, 6⅞, 7, 7⅛, 7¼,
7⅜, 7½. State size. Read "How to Measure" at bottom of page. Shipping weight, 2 pounds 3 ounces.
The latest style trends have shown decided favoring of the lighter weight Hats—here's one made by one of the best manufacturers in America. The smooth finish fur felt comes in a shape particularly suited to both young and old. Sweatband is of genuine leather. The crown is 5⅝ inches, brim 2½ inches.

$3.69

Popular Trooper Style

539 G 328—Black.
539 G 332—Steel gray.
539 G 336—Dark brown.
SIZES: 6¾, 6⅞, 7, 7⅛, 7¼, 7⅜,
7½, 7⅝, 7¾. State size. Read "How to Measure" below. Shipping weight, 2 pounds 2 ounces.
Men who know and appreciate lasting style, good quality and outstanding value buy them season after season. Made entirely of genuine smooth finished fur felt, a surprising feature in a hat selling so low. The neatly bound brim is 2⅝ inches wide, the crown 5⅝ inches deep.

$2.98

Extra Fine-Light Weight

539 G 389—Pearl gray.
539 G 391—Light tan.
539 G 393—Copper brown.
SIZES: 6¾, 6⅞, 7, 7⅛,
7¼, 7⅜, 7½. State size. Read "How to Measure" below. Shipping weight, 2 pounds 2 ounces.
The most exclusive shops will sell these best quality Hats as feature values at from $6 to $7. Rakish—light—"easy looking"—that's the way the young fellows like them. Here's one you can dent on the side—put a crease in the middle—flip the brim down. No matter what you do to our soft light weight "Genuine Hares Fur Special" they will always be good looking. Crown is 5½ inches, brim 2⅝ inches.

$4.85

Conservative Style

539 G 338—Dark brown.
539 G 342—Black.
SIZES: 6¾, 6⅞, 7, 7⅛,
7¼, 7⅜, 7½. State size. Read "How to Measure" below. Shipping weight, 2 pounds 2 ounces.
Although this is our lowest price, good quality, smooth finished fur felt Hat, it represents a value you couldn't match elsewhere. Made in conservative trooper style—popular year in and year out. Full leather sweatband. Crown 5⅝ inches, brim 2⅝ inches.

$2.45

Popular Priced Snap Brim

539 G 339—Pearl gray.
539 G 340—Light brown.
539 G 341—Bluish gray.
SIZES: 6¾, 6⅞, 7, 7⅛, 7¼,
7⅜, 7½. State size. Read "How to Measure" below. Shipping weight, 2 pounds 3 ounces.
More good style, finish and quality couldn't be put into a Hat at this price. The quality of the smooth finished, fine fur felt makes this one of the best hat bargains ever offered anywhere. Genuine leather sweatband. The crown is 5⅝ inches, the brim 2½ inches.

$2.95

Wool Felt Roll Crusher

39 G 310—Pearl gray.
39 G 320—Black.
SIZES: 6¾, 6⅞, 7, 7⅛, 7¼, 7⅜, 7½, 7⅝, 7¾. State size. Read "How to Measure" below. Shipping weight, 10 ounces.
Intensely popular for all round wear. Made of good quality wool felt. The crown is 5 inches, the brim 2½ inches.

95¢

Lowest Priced Wool Felt

539 G 301—Pearl gray.
539 G 302—Light tan.
SIZES: 6¾, 6⅞, 7, 7⅛, 7¼, 7⅜, 7½. State size.
Read "How to Measure" below. Shipping weight, 2 pounds.
Made of good quality wool felt. Crown 5⅝ inches; brim 2⅝ inches. Has genuine leather sweatband.

$1.59

New Fall Shape

539 G 344—Pearl gray.
539 G 346—Tan.
539 G 348—Bluish gray.
SIZES: 6¾, 6⅞, 7, 7⅛, 7¼,
7⅜, 7½, 7⅝, 7¾. State size. Read "How to Measure" below. Shipping weight, 2 pounds 4 ounces.
Popular style in exceptional quality felt—this smart Snap Brim Hat is a value if there ever was one. The medium weight, smooth finished fur felt will give good service. Has genuine leather sweatband. Crown is 5½ inches, brim 2⅝ inches.

$3.45

The Very Newest Doeskin Felt

539 G 379—Pearl gray.
539 G 381—Brown.
539 G 383—Dark cadet blue.
SIZES: 6¾, 6⅞, 7, 7⅛, 7¼, 7⅜, 7½,
7⅝, 7¾. State size. Read "How to Measure" below. Shipping weight, 2 pounds 3 ounces.
Supreme in style, faultless in finish, unquestioned in quality is our new "Doeskin Special." The fine quality, genuine fur felt is so softly finished it feels like velvet. Full satin lined. Genuine leather sweatband. Crown 5½ inches, brim 2⅝ inches.

$3.85

Genuine Beaver Finish Fur Felt

539 G 395—Pearl gray.
539 G 397—Tan.
539 G 399—Medium brown.
SIZES: 6¾, 6⅞, 7, 7⅛, 7¼, 7⅜, 7½,
7⅝, 7¾. State size. Read "How to Measure" below. Shipping weight, 2 pounds 4 ounces.
The new fur napped beaver finish which is becoming so popular with better dressed men. Exclusively created for us by a manufacturer with thirty years experience in making the finest hats. Hand-made—hand-blocked and full satin lined. Genuine leather sweatband. The crown is 5½ in., the brim 2⅝ in.

$4.98

How to Measure for Hats and Caps

Measure around the head as shown in picture at the right, using an accurate tape measure or a strip of paper which can afterwards be measured. Then consult size chart at the right.

Head Measure Inches	Order Hat Size	Head Measure Inches	Order Hat Size
18⅝	6	21⅝	7
19	6⅛	22	7⅛
19⅜	6¼	22⅜	7¼
19¾	6⅜	22¾	7⅜
20⅛	6½	23⅛	7½
20½	6⅝	23½	7⅝
20⅞	6¾	23⅞	7¾
21¼	6⅞		

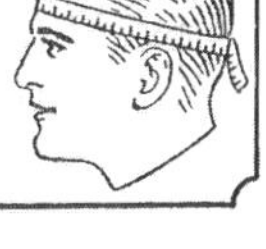

45

A Good Raincoat Saves Clothes

Men's Rubberized Topcoat for All-Purpose Wear

$8.95

You have raincoat protection plus topcoat style in this rain-proof All-Weather Coat. Will keep you warm on chilly days and dry in wet weather. A dressy combination garment that's always practical and at our moderate price it's indeed a big value. Made for you by the country's best manufacturer of rain clothing. Light in weight and absolutely wind-proof. Every detail of its construction lives up to a high standard of expert workmanship and fine quality materials. Sturdily made of fancy woven nearly half wool cassimere in a choice of two attractive overplaids—a medium tan and a medium blue-gray. Has rubber lining that will always remain soft and pliable as only the best rubber will. A good looking plaid is vulcanized right into the rubber lining—it can't wear off. All seams are sewed, cemented and finally strapped with silk to match lining, making the garment

Absolutely Rain-Proof

Buttons are reinforced with small stay buttons. Bottom of garment and collar edges are double stitched. Three ventilation eyelets under each arm. The vent in back closes with button. Turn up the collar in windy weather—it's convertible. Single breasted style. When you see it you'll be enormously pleased. The more wear you give it the more you will appreciate its sturdiness and all around practicability. Average length, 48 inches.

SIZES: Chest 34, 36, 38, 40, 42, 44, 46, 48 inches. State chest measure wanted. Read "How to Measure" on Page 238. Shipping weight, 3 pounds 12 ounces.

42 G 5343—Medium tan striped.
42 G 5345—Medium bluish-gray striped.

Each $8.95

Men's Size $6.75

Our Famous Leathertex

For Men—Youths—Boys

Looks like leather, feels like leather, but is lighter and more comfortable in weight—and costs only one-fourth as much. That's Leathertex, the popular, special processed rubber coated material used in these shower-proof Coats. The embossed surface has the effect of genuine leather. It is guaranteed not to harden in any temperature. Nor will it crack, scuff or peel. Gives more wear than ordinary raincoat materials. To clean spots on it, just wash with a wet cloth. The inside of Leathertex cloth is a napped cotton fabric with a suede cloth appearance.

Also Worn as Topcoat

It's dressy and also protects you from sudden showers. Double breasted with a half belt in back. Convertible collar. Two large outside patch pockets with flaps; vent in back. Buttons are reinforced with small stay buttons. Facings and all seams piped. Average length, men's sizes, 45 inches.

MEN'S SIZES: Chest 34, 36, 38, 40, 42, 44, 46, 48 inches. State chest measure wanted. Read "How to Measure" on Page 238. Shipping weight, 4 pounds 8 ounces.

42 G 5703—Black.
42 G 5707—Tan.
42 G 5709—Cordovan brown. Each $6.75

BOYS' AND YOUTHS' SIZES: 10, 12, 14, 16, 18 years. Ship. wt., 3 lbs. 6 oz.
42 G 5637—Maroon only $5.95

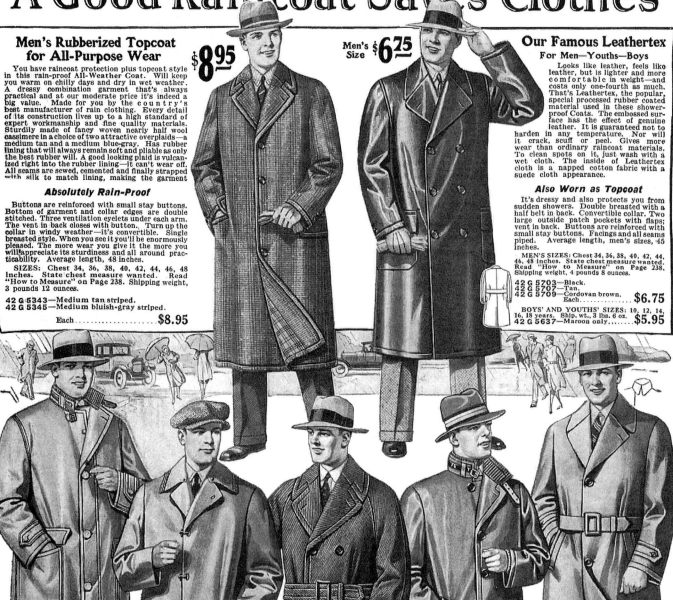

Popular College Slicker

$4.75

Thousands of men wear them! The popular College style Slicker Raincoat that originated on the college campus. Now worn everywhere by men who like this common sense garment. Light in weight and absolutely water-proof. Made by a company renowned for its manufacture of slicker clothing. Garment treated by process that makes it water-proof and wind-proof. Has a fly front that fastens with snap fasteners and buttons—a feature that gives double rain protection. Double thickness of slicker cloth in the sleeves and throughout body, extending 4 inches from the bottom of the coat. Storm tab on sleeves. Collar is corduroy faced and has four loops and leather strap to give close fit around neck. Two large outside patch pockets with flaps—roomy enough to carry several school books. Average length, 52 inches.

SIZES: Chest 34, 36, 38, 40, 42, 44, 46, 48 inches. State chest measure. Read "How to Measure" on Page 238. Shipping weight, 4 pounds 4 ounces.

42 G 5545—Yellow.
42 G 5547—Olive.
42 G 5549—Black. Each $4.75

Jean Cloth Rubber Lined

$7.85

You men who are outdoors in all sorts of weather require better protection than just an ordinary raincoat can give you. This excellent rain-proof garment is made from durable Jean cloth lined with the best black rubber that can be produced. The workmanship is in keeping with the material—the very best. It's sturdy enough for work! Neat enough for ordinary dress purposes. It's a top-notch value that defies duplication.

All seams are cemented and vulcanized. Collar is corduroy tipped with reinforced band collar riveted at each end. The corners of the pockets and top of vent are also reinforced with rivets. Double outside back with ventilation eyelets underneath. Inside yoke front and back of domet flannel. Neat single-breasted style with five buckles and slot fasteners. Average length, about 50 inches.

SIZES: Chest 36, 38, 40, 42, 44, 46, 48 inches. State chest measure. Read "How to Measure" on Page 238. Shipping weight, 4 lbs. 12 oz.

42 G 5479—Drab only $7.85

Dressy Style Plaid Back

$5.95

"I was surprised at the excellent quality and workmanship at the low price I paid," says Wm. H. McKean of Mansfield, Ohio.

This Raincoat is very popular as men appreciate the splendid protection it gives—for the small investment. Made from a diagonal print Asia cloth and lined with an attractive printed plaid material. Between these two cloths is an interlining of rubber which makes it absolutely rain-proof and wind-proof. In addition all seams are sewed, cemented and strapped; all facings piped. The accepted double breasted style with convertible collar. The all-around belt fastens with a metal buckle. Ventilation eyelets under each arm. Men, a coat of this undeniable good quality—selling at this low price is a value you will surely appreciate. Average length, 46 inches.

SIZES: Chest 34, 36, 38, 40, 42, 44, 46 inches. State chest measure. Read "How to Measure" on Page 238. Shipping weight, 3 pounds 6 ounces.

42 G 5309—Tan.
42 G 5311—Oxford gray. Each $5.95

Our Very Best Collegiate Model

$6.75

In style this Raincoat is like the popular college model Slicker. But instead of a slicker cloth, the outside is a specially patented rubber rain-proof coating, smooth finished and with a permanent luster. Guaranteed not to crack or lose its pliability. Made by the sole owner of the patent rights, the only company in the world that has this wonderful process.

Lining is sheeting, dyed to match the surface. Corduroy faced collar with loops and genuine patent leather strap; you'll appreciate its comfort and protection in rainy, windy weather. Set-in sleeves with storm wristlets inside of cuffs. Ventilation eyelets under each arm. Two inside patch pockets with flaps. Vent in back. All seams stitched, cemented and strapped. Average length, 50 inches.

SIZES: Chest 34, 36, 38, 40, 42, 44, 46, 48 inches. State chest measure. Read "How to Measure" on Page 238. Shipping weight, 3 pounds 9 ounces.

42 G 5491—Yellow.
42 G 5493—Olive.
42 G 5495—Black. Each. $6.75

Excellent Value Rubber Interlined

$3.98

Here's the Raincoat for men and young men who limit their expenditures and still demand good quality. This coat is one of our biggest sellers and while you can't expect the same fine points of style, thorough workmanship and longer wearing qualities of our very best coats—it will give a surprising amount of wear and service considering the low price.

Of good wearing Asia cloth, with a rubber interlining. The lining is a durable cotton cloth in an attractive plaid pattern. You are assured complete rain and wind protection. All seams are strapped and cemented for extra protection. Set-in sleeves; attractive all-around belt. It's just the right length, too, about 48 inches long. It carries our complete guarantee. You'll be mighty well pleased with all its fine features.

SIZES: Chest 34, 36, 38, 40, 42, 44, 46 inches. State chest measure. Read "How to Measure" on Page 238. Shipping weight, 3 pounds.

42 G 5317—Tan.
42 G 5319—Oxford gray. Each $3.98

46

Fur Brings Comfort and Adds Style
to These "**LONGTIME**" Quality Coats

$39.50
Horsehide
Fur

$29.75
Raccoon
Lined

Genuine Horsehide or Genuine Galloway

All the wealth of style, warmth and comfort that a coat could possibly give are here combined to make one of the leading Fur Coat values of all America. When it's blizzard time and icy cold, just wrap yourself inside this snug fur coat and you'll laugh at the worst kind of below-zero weather. Whether you're twenty or sixty years of age you'll appreciate this protection from wind and snow and cold. Thanks to fur clad college men from coast to coast everybody knows how to "bundle up" and at the same time to be correctly and stylishly dressed.

Whether driving in winter's ice and cold or walking along the snow banked highways, here's comfort that you'll always be thankful for and an investment you'll never regret. We've priced these attractively low at a saving of at least $15 less than you'd pay anywhere else. Not alone in price and value do these garments stand out of and above the crowd, but in quality as well. Only superior furs are used. We've chosen two of the country's foremost service-giving furs—brushed, dyed black HORSEHIDE and the ever-popular natural black GALLOWAY. Either will outwear any other fur that could be used in coats priced so low.

Constructed as only the best fur coat manufacturers know how to build them. Body and sleeves lined with black quilted satin—that adds another layer of warmth to these beautiful garments. Large shawl collar may be worn close around neck. Double knit wristlets. Arm shields to resist wear. Leather kicker straps. Inside breast pocket. Average length, about 50 in. SIZES: Chest 38, 40, 42, 44, 46, 48 inches. State chest measure. Read "How to Measure" on Page 238. Shipping weight, 13 pounds 2 ounces.
842 G 7157—
Black galloway............**$45.00**
842 G 7145........**$39.50**
Black horsehide.

All Wool—Fur Lined Raccoon or Marmot

Style and comfort demand fur lining in these "Longtime" quality Coats. They're our two most popular models and as dressy as those fine coats you see in the windows of the best fur shops. Judge their quality, by the excellent materials and workmanship in them—not by their moderate price. Both are of fine finished All Wool Melton cloth, for its resistance to wear.

The $42.50 garment is our very best fur lined coat and one you'll prize highly. It has a body lining of brown marmot fur. The large marmot collar is so deeply brown that it's almost black.

The $29.75 coat is lined throughout body with black pieced raccoon fur. Large collar is black coney fur. Every season adds to the popularity of this wonderful coat.

Both garments have an interlining that adds permanent shapeliness to style and service. Sleeves are lined with quilted sateen. Double arm shields of glove tanned leather. 18-inch back vent closes with button. The extra service, the comfortable warmth, the thorough workmanship, the correct modeling and the moderate prices of these coats will yield you a satisfaction you have never experienced before. Average length, 48 in. SIZES: Chest 36, 38, 40, 42, 44, 46, 48 inches. State chest measure. Read "How to Measure" on Page 238. Shipping weight, 10 pounds 12 ounces.

842 G 7017—Black with brown pieced marmot lining and dark **$42.50** brown marmot collar.......
842 G 7001—Black with black pieced Raccoon lining and black **$29.75** coney fur collar.............

Coney or Sealine Fur Collar. Warm Linings **$19.45**

Think of the comfort of the thick fur collar next to your face and neck when the winds blow cold. And consider the moderate price, the wonderful quality, the pleasing style, the long service you get for such a low price. They're the most remarkable values you could find anywhere.

These heavy black Ulsters are made of All Wool Frieze fabric, a quality usually found only in much higher priced garments. The $19.45 coat has an attractive Coney fur collar and is entirely lined with warm quilted sateen. The other garment is lined with plush and has a collar of sealine fur. Average length, about 50 inches. SIZES: Chest 35, 36, 37, 38, 39, 40, 42, 44, 46, 48 in. State chest measure. Read "How to Measure" on Page 238. Ship. wt., 9 lbs. 8 oz.
39 G 2967—Black with Coney fur collar, quilted sateen lining........**$19.45**
39 G 2971—Black with sealine fur collar, plush lining................**24.50**

Sheepskin Lined Brown Lambskin Collar **$19.95**

Winter comfort for the man who needs a warm Overcoat and still doesn't want to purchase an expensive garment. Warmed by its genuine sheepskin lining, cold winds will never bother you. Very popular because of its low price and high value. Of a good quality Melton overcoating, about 80 per cent wool. Has a large collar of electrified lambskin, not only warm and comfortable but extremely dressy. Body of garment lined with genuine sheepskin extending from base of the collar 30 inches down the inside of coat. Sheepskin lining gives wonderful warmth and service. Sleeve lining is chocolate brown tanned leather. Has single arm-shields, also of leather. Knit wristlets. Back of coat has stylish inverted pleat. Average length, about 46 inches.
SIZES: Chest 34, 36, 38, 40, 42, 44, 46 inches. State chest measure. Read "How to Measure" on Page 238. Ship. wt., 11 lbs. 8 oz.
42 G 6981—Brown only......**$19.95**

All Wool Melton Leather Lined **$18.95**

It's simply impossible for anybody to give you greater value in a leather lined Coat. Due to the nation-wide popularity of this coat, we're able to make quantity purchases which bring down the price to bedrock bottom. But don't judge the quality by the price—for it's far better than you'd reasonably expect in such a garment.

Made of ALL WOOL dark brown 30-ounce overcoating. Body and sleeves lined with chocolate color glove LEATHER. This lining starts at base of collar and extends 26 inches down inside of coat. The great Big Warm Collar is made of electrified lambskin. Knit wristlets keep out cold at sleeves. Has detachable three-piece belt. Inverted pleat in back. Average length, about 46 inches.
SIZES: Chest 34, 36, 38, 40, 42, 44, 46 inches. State chest measure. Read "How to Measure" on Page 238. Ship. wt., 11 lbs. 2 oz.
42 G 6992—Dark brown only......**$18.95**

Persian Lamb Collar Marmot Lined **$39.75**

It's tailored of heavy All Wool Melton, in the very popular shade of Oxford Gray and lined throughout the body with pieced marmot fur, in a rich shade of brown. The big collar is of Genuine Persian Lamb—a fur you'll see on many of the higher priced coats. The Melton fabric is famous for long wear —you won't need another overcoat for several seasons —when you do buy a new coat, you'll want another one just like this.

When you try to find this quality of fabric and fur in other garments, you'll see them only in coats that cost much more. Sleeves have quilted Satin lining for extra warmth and wear. For permanence of stylish shape, we have added a warm interlining.
SIZES: Chest 36, 38, 40, 42, 44, 46, 48 inches. State chest measure. Read "How to Measure" on Page 238. Ship. wt., 10 lbs. 12 oz.
842 G 7019—Oxford gray with brown pieced Marmot fur lining and black Persian lamb fur collar **$39.75**

47

We Talked With the Finer Tailors Everywhere ⇔ ⇔
We Consulted With America's Famous Woolen Mills—
Now STYLISH Suits Can Be GUARANTEED
One Full Year for Dress Wear

"Follow the words of this great offer—you are reading THE FIRST GUARANTEE OF ITS KIND EVER WRITTEN— a guarantee that gives to "Service" a new and greater meaning. We secured the ideas of expert tailors—we reached an agreement with one of the most famous woolen mills in the United States. We found that through special handling in our own Great Longtime Tailor Shops we could produce high character stylish suits of finest Virgin Wool Worsteds and offer them with a complete guarantee of one full year. And I say to you men who pride yourselves on quiet, successful dress and who have been paying $40 or more for custom made suits—before you buy another $40 suit for yourself—see these, for which you pay less than $25."

Manager Ward's Clothing Department

Dress Suit Guarantee

We guarantee that this Supreme Quality Longtime Suit will give you **ONE YEAR'S SERVICE** *when used for dress wear. Should it fail to wear you one year from date of purchase, for dress purposes, we will replace it with a new suit of the same kind, charging you for the number of days you have had the first suit, and crediting you for the number of days it failed to wear, in fulfillment of our One Year's Guarantee.*

Finest Worsted Fabrics
All Pure Virgin Wool

Matching the splendid tailoring are fabrics distinguished for their fine texture and durability—a texture that unmistakably says "FIRST QUALITY" and a durability that's GUARANTEED. The colors are rich looking, quiet and conservative, just such selections as men accustomed to the finest would choose. Fabrics like these—closely woven, heavy weight all Pure Virgin Wool worsteds—represent an entirely new standard of quality, never before associated with the price you pay here. But we bought more bolts of these remarkable fabrics than the combined requirements of hundreds of ordinary establishments so we can give you this superior quality, including the best of Longtime tailoring at a price you've been long awaiting.

The Tailoring Is Superb!

Both *The* **BROADWAY** and *The* **WALL STREET** are specially handled—hand finished and hand shaped to make them the finest and best suits that ever came out of our Great Longtime Tailor Shops!

Tailoring experts closely superintend every step to be sure that each suit has the cut—the style—the finish and all the quality marks that better dressed men and young men demand today. Construction—outside and inside—is superior. Haircloth and canvas shape the coat fronts to insure permanence. Durable Alpaca lining is tailored into the coats. All seams are sewed with silk thread and tape bound, as are the finest custom finishes. Every finished garment is rigidly inspected and released only when marked "Perfect."

EITHER SUIT WITH ONE OR TWO PANTS

The Broadway *for Young Men*
COAT HALF LINED WITH ALPACA

SIZES: Chest 34 to 42 inches. Waist 28 to 38 inches, Trousers inseam 28 to 33 inches. State chest, waist and trousers inseam measure. See size scale for young men on opposite page. Read "How to Measure" on Page 238.

ONE PANTS SUIT

Shipping weight, 6 pounds 4 ounces. — EACH $24.50
39 G 1663—Striped medium gray.
39 G 1667—Striped navy blue.
39 G 1671—Striped medium brown.
39 G 1673—Navy blue serge.

TWO PANTS SUIT

Shipping weight, 7 pounds 14 ounces. — EACH $32.00
39 G 1763—Striped medium gray.
39 G 1767—Striped navy blue.
39 G 1771—Striped medium brown.
39 G 1773—Navy blue serge.

The Wall Street *for Men*
COAT FULL ALPACA LINED

SIZES: Chest 35 to 44 inches. Waist 30 to 42 inches. Trousers inseam 28 to 33 inches. State chest, waist and trousers inseam measure. See size scale for men on opposite page. Read "How to Measure" on Page 238.

ONE PANTS SUIT

Shipping weight, 6 pounds 8 ounces. — EACH $24.50
39 G 1075—Navy blue serge.
39 G 1079—Banker's gray.
39 G 1183—Striped medium brown.

TWO PANTS SUIT

Shipping weight, 8 pounds. — EACH $32.00
39 G 1775—Navy blue serge.
39 G 1779—Banker's gray.
39 G 1783—Striped medium brown.

The Best Dressed Fellows

Just the Style You Want
Two Attractive Prices

$12.50 Part Wool $19.50 All Virgin Wool

Whether on the campus or in the business world, a fellow's friends measure him, to a great extent, by the judgment he displays in the choice of his Suits. The majority of well dressed young men do not wear expensive suits. The moderate priced model that combines good taste in style with a sturdy attractive pattern that will stand the gaff, is invariably the popular choice. That's just the reason why our LONGTIME models enjoy a decided preference today.

Our $19.50 suit is a big favorite. The popular trend of smartness and neatness is aptly tailored under rigid supervision, into the clean cut lines. The All Virgin Wool worsted, navy blue fabric of diagonal weave offers the very best obtainable in suits within the price range—in fact it is far superior to many in the more expensive models. You can be sure that it will stand up throughout the life of the suit and keep you neatly dressed at all times. It is half lined with alpaca. The double breasted style is distinctively broad shouldered and tapers slightly at the hips. The lapels are correctly shaped. The 5-button vest and the 19-inch cuff bottom trousers fittingly become the general style.

Our $12.50 suit is exactly the same in style as the one above with the same high grade tailoring and substantial construction. The sturdy diagonal weave navy blue material is one-third wool and full lined with strong twill.

State chest, waist and trouser inseam measurements wanted. See size scale in center of page. Read "How to Measure" on Page 238. Shipping weight, 5 pounds 8 ounces.

39 G 1907—Part wool diagonal navy blue.. **$12.50**

39 G 1923—All Virgin Wool diagonal navy blue.......... **$19.50**

Size Scale for Suits Shown on This Page

Chest, inches	31	32	33	34	35	36
Waist, inches	27 to 29	28 to 30	29 to 31	29 to 32	29 to 32	30 to 33

Trousers inseam 27, 28, 29, 30, 31, 32 inches

$14.95

$16.95

A Bargain, Fellows!

The height of style, too. A three-button collegiate coat, six-button double breasted vest with broad lapels, full 20-inch cuff bottom trousers. A regular knockout. You'd have a hard time buying similar style and quality elsewhere for the money. Fine All Wool Cassimere in the new dark gray chevron weave. Coat full lined.

State chest, waist and trousers inseam measure. See size scale above. Read "How to Measure" on Page 238. Ship. weight, 5 lbs. 4 oz.

39 G 1915—Chevron striped dark gray...... **$14.95**

Diamond Weave All Wool

Dress up occasions, schooltime or business. You're always appropriately dressed in this finely tailored navy blue Suit of diamond weave All Virgin Wool Worsted. Stylish full cut. Dressy, broad shoulders; peak lapels. Cuff bottom trousers—the 19-inch width. Regular vest. Well made with half alpaca lining in coat.

State chest, waist and trousers inseam measure. See size scale above. Read "How to Measure" on Page 238. Shipping weight, 5 pounds 4 ounces.

39 G 1919—Diamond weave navy blue worsted **$16.95**

$8.95

$18.50

$18.95

$18.95

$15.00

A Lot of Style Here
Two-Piece Outfit

An ideal combination outfit of Blazer and Trousers for active young fellows. Smartness of style that appeals to every youth. Now being worn at colleges and high schools all over the country.

The blazer of heavy weight All Wool cloth keeps your upper body comfortable in chilly weather. Snug Collar can be buttoned up around the neck. Blazer is a lively plaid of blue, red, green and black.

Trousers are dark navy blue corduroy, full cut with 19-inch cuff bottoms. Slash pockets.

Save your dress up suit by wearing this handy outfit for sports or work.

State chest, waist and trousers inseam above. Read "How to Measure" on Page 238. Shipping weight, 5 pounds.

39 G 1931—Plaid blazer and navy blue trousers.... **$8.95**

One of Our Best
All Virgin Wool

In t. is LONGTIME Suit we present absolutely the best in style, in quality, in sturdiness. Although our price is only $18.50 we've spared no expense in making it one of the finest garments we've ever offered. It sells regularly elsewhere at about $25. The beautifully woven All Virgin Wool suiting will hold its shape exceedingly well and "Longtime" wear is assured.

Trim, smart lines tailored right into the coat. Front will hold its shape; pockets will not sag; collar and lapels fit perfectly. Coat half lined with strong fine alpaca and all seams taped. Collegiate 3-button coat, 6-button vest; trousers of full width, with 20-inch cuff bottoms.

State chest, waist and trousers inseam measure. See size scale above. Read "How to Measure" on Page 238. Shipping weight, 5 pounds 4 ounces.

39 G 1925— Medium brown glenn plaid...... **$18.50**

New Hollywood
Model for Youths

Designed by expert LONGTIME clothing authorities! What better proof could you have that here's the foremost creation in youths' Suits. We scoured the woolen markets of the country to get this wonderful textured fine virgin wool cloth with its new novelty weave. It's a rich shade of gray with a pin stripe to add life to the pattern.

Particular dressers will be attracted by the long rolling lapels of this 4-button, double breasted coat. Five-button vest and full cut cuff bottom trousers. Coat half lined with alpaca and shaped with haircloth and canvas interlining.

State chest, waist and trousers inseam measure. See size scale above. Read "How to Measure" on Page 238. Shipping weight, 5 pounds 4 ounces.

39 G 1927—Striped medium gray only...... **$18.95**

Collegiate Overcoat
Popular Yale Blue

If you asked us to pick out our most Collegiate Overcoat, we'd send you this model. It's the newest style for youths. Cut with a correctness, a degree of distinction never equaled before, even by our famous LONGTIME shops.

Don't think that style's its only feature though. You can rely on this warm, All Wool overcoating to shut out coldest winds.

Particular dark Yale blue is the most popular color this year. Style has dictated the double breasted, 6-button model. Broad shoulders; plain box back. Stylish warm collar. Yoke and sleeves lined with strong Venetian. Sewing and tailoring are proof of the best workmanship. Average length, 43 inches.

SIZES: Chest 31, 32, 33, 34, 35, 36 inches. State chest measure. Read "How to Measure" on Page 238. Shipping weight, 7 pounds 8 ounces.

39 G 2800— Dark blue only........ **$15.00**

Clothes That Make Records
for "LONGTIME" Service

$19.95

$18.95

Two Serges of Quality at Prices That Appeal
Both All Virgin Wool

Men, these Suits are not only the good looking kind, but the good looking "Longtime" wearing kind. Most clothing looks good when you put it on, but the real test of quality comes months later. That's why we justly point with pride to the service you'll get from this suit all through the first year and into the second. We know it's made right of fine All Virgin Wool Serge, and do not hesitate to recommend it to you.

As for value, just consider what R. C. Rector of Chesapeake, Ohio, writes: "Many have spoken of the perfect fit and quality of the goods, and have placed it in the $25 and $30 class."

This is a stronger statement than we wanted to make, but after you see the fine tailoring and feel the excellent serge, you too will say ours is a most moderate price.

Made of an extra fine quality close twilled All Wool serge—a material which has no superior for wear and dressiness in medium weight fabrics at this price. In navy blue or dark gray for practical wear the year 'round. Coat is full lined with strong alpaca and interlined with haircloth in front for permanent shapeliness. Vest is regular 5-button style and trousers have cuff bottoms that measure about 17 inches. Left hip pocket has a button. All strain points are reinforced and linings and pocket materials are of the best.

State chest, waist and trousers inseam measure. See size scale below. Read "How to Measure" on Page 238. Shipping weight, 6 pounds 6 ounces.

39 G 1005—Navy blue serge.
39 G 1007—Dark gray serge.
Each...............................$19.95

Real Value to Talk About
All Wool Worsteds

They say men rarely talk about their clothes, but wearers of these Suits are spreading enthusiastic praise about them everywhere. You'll feel that way about it, too, after you see this wonderful value. The low price for such quality, we believe, is amazing. Made of a warm, heavy weight All Wool worsted usually found only in $35 garments. Not the hard, wiry fabric so often used in suits today, but a high quality soft feeling cloth that looks well and makes an ideal wearing garment.

Choice of three desirable conservative dark patterns: striped dark blue, striped dark brown and striped black. They'll add dignity and a sense of well-being to your appearance for business or social wear.

Tailored in our own factory where we carefully supervise every detail of manufacture. Coat is full lined; vest is regular 5-button model; 17-inch cuff bottom trousers. A very desirable suit of guaranteed quality.

State chest, waist and trousers inseam measure. See size scale below. Read "How to Measure" on Page 238. Shipping weight, 6 pounds 8 ounces.

39 G 1130—Striped dark blue.
39 G 1134—Striped dark brown.
39 G 1138—Striped black. Each...$18.95

Size Scale for Suits Shown on This Page

Chest measure, inches....	35	36	37	38
Waist measure, inches....	30 to 32	30 to 34	32 to 35	33 to 36
Chest measure, inches....	39	40	42	44
Waist measure, inches....	34 to 37	35 to 38	37 to 40	40 to 42

Trousers inseam, cuff bottoms, 28 to 33 inches

$23.50

$17.95

$22.50

$15.95

Here's Economy, Men, in Two-Trousers Suits

Look neat, dress well and save money by wearing one of these two-trousers Suits. It's a real economy to own a suit with two pants, for a coat always outwears a single pair. Think of the convenience of having one pair always nicely pressed and ready to put on.

Two excellent "Longtime" wearing materials, in an all-year weight. One is a fine twilled All Wool navy blue serge; the other an All Wool pencil striped dark brown Worsted. Guaranteed not to fade. Through and through they're tailored for strenuous wear. Special sewing at strain points. Coat full lined with strong alpaca. Wear one and satisfy yourself of the really big value.

State chest, waist and trousers inseam measure. See size scale above. Read "How to Measure" on Page 238. Shipping weight, 7 pounds 12 ounces.

39 G 1703—Navy blue serge.
39 G 1707—Striped dark brown. Each...............................$23.50

Warm, Heavy Weight All Wool Suiting

Trim tailoring—that's for the fastidious man; serviceability—that's for the practical fellow; popular price—that's for everybody. Style is woven into every thread of the warm heavy weight All Wool suiting. It's a handsome pattern—medium shade of brown found elsewhere only in higher priced suits. Note the character—the graceful hang of the coat. Trousers are a conservative width with straight, hanging lines. Cuff bottoms.

Service is built into every feature. Coat full lined with long wearing material. Continuous suit production in our own factories and our cash purchase of enormous quantities of fabrics enable us to offer these garments at these attractively low prices.

State chest, waist and trousers inseam measure. See size scale above. Read "How to Measure" on Page 238. Shipping weight, 6 pounds 6 ounces.

39 G 1122—Striped medium brown only...............................$17.95

Young Men's Style All Wool Blue or Gray

Every inch a "Longtime" thoroughbred. To wear one of these Suits is to experience the most gratifying clothing satisfaction you've ever enjoyed. The fabrics alone will make you proud of your purchase. One is a fine finished All Wool worsted, noted for its excellent wearing qualities. The other, a smooth surfaced All Wool twilled cassimere, made by a mill renowned for the beauty of its materials. Both are medium weight—desirable for year 'round comfort.

Styled to fit unusually close around the collar and slightly form fitting at waist. Half lined with alpaca and shape tailored in to stay. Five-button vest; medium width cuff bottom trousers.

State chest, waist and trousers inseam measure. See size scale above. Read "How to Measure" on Page 238. Shipping weight, 6 pounds 6 ounces.

39 G 1125—Striped slate gray.
39 G 1152—Silver striped navy blue. Each...............................$22.50

All Wool Topcoat Pleasing Style and Fabric

Topcoats that are the vogue of the best dressers. When the chill is in the air, but it's not cold enough for an overcoat you'll appreciate its All Wool warmth. The price is so convincing and the quality measures up to such a fine high standard that you make a real saving if you take advantage of this value. You will admire its beautiful tailoring, its snug fitting collar, the easy drape effect over the shoulders. Whether your preference runs to the plain or plaid finish, you'll find your favorite here. The coat pictured is a medium gray with a harmonizing overplaid. The plain cadet blue (grayish blue) is the same style.

Tailored to the taste of the best dressers. Yoke and sleeves are lined with a fine silk serge. All seams are neatly taped. Straight hanging box back. Length, about 46 inches. Indeed a wonderful topcoat to own!

SIZES: Chest, 34 to 42 inches. State chest measure. See size scale above. Read "How to Measure," Page 238.

39 G 1801—Plain cadet blue.
39 G 1805—Medium gray overplaid. Each...............................$15.95

50

Tailoring for Thousands
Means Lower Prices for You

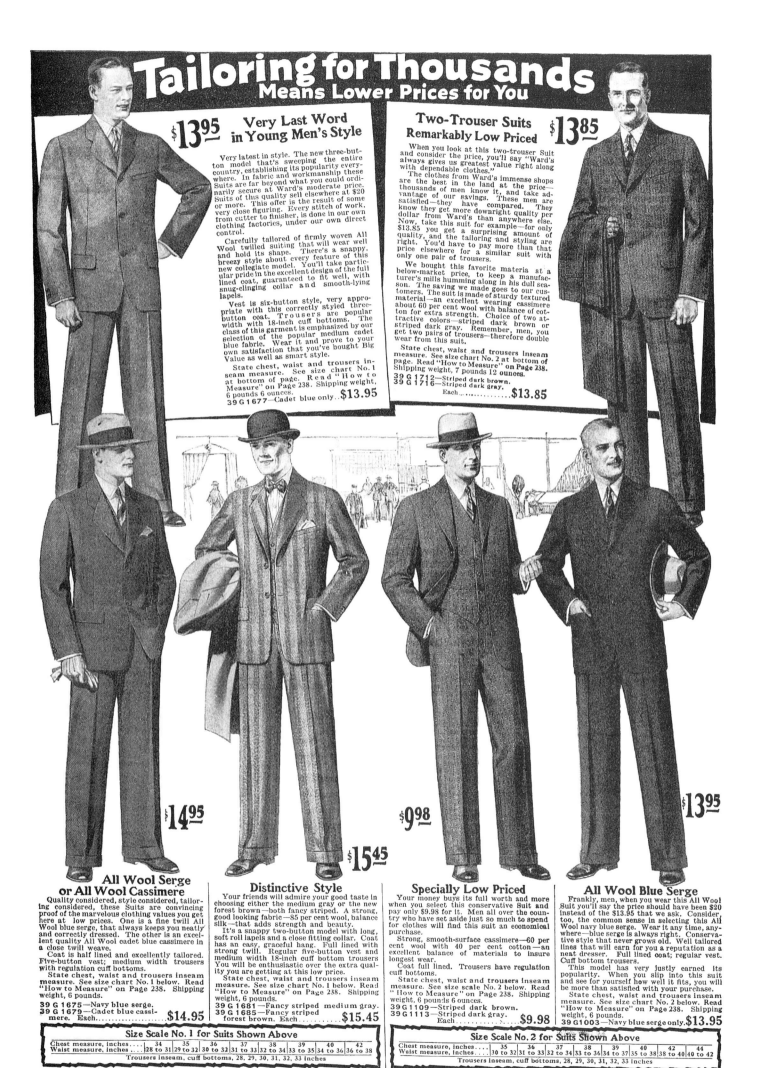

$13⁹⁵ Very Last Word in Young Men's Style

Very latest in style. The new three-button model that's sweeping the entire country, establishing its popularity everywhere. In fabric and workmanship these Suits are far beyond what you could ordinarily secure at Ward's moderate price. Suits of this quality sell elsewhere at $20 or more. This offer is the result of some very close figuring. Every stitch of work, from cutter to finisher, is done in our own clothing factories, under our own direct control.

Carefully tailored of firmly woven All Wool twilled suiting that will wear well and hold its shape. There's a snappy, breezy style about every feature of this new collegiate model. You'll take particular pride in the excellent design of the full lined coat, guaranteed to fit well, with snug-clinging collar and smooth-lying lapels.

Vest is six-button style, very appropriate with this correctly styled three-button coat. Trousers are popular width with 18-inch cuff bottoms. The class of this garment is emphasized by our selection of the popular medium cadet blue fabric. Wear it and prove to your own satisfaction that you've bought Big Value as well as smart style.

State chest, waist and trousers inseam measure. See size chart No. 1 at bottom of page. Read "How to Measure" on Page 238. Shipping weight, 6 pounds 6 ounces.
39 G 1677—Cadet blue only...$13.95

Two-Trouser Suits Remarkably Low Priced $13⁸⁵

When you look at this two-trouser Suit and consider the price, you'll say "Ward's always gives us greatest value right along with dependable clothes."

The clothes from Ward's immense shops are the best in the land at the price—thousands of men know it, and take advantage of our savings. These men are satisfied—they have compared. They know they get more downright quality per dollar from Ward's than anywhere else. Now, take this suit for example—for only $13.85 you get a surprising amount of quality, and the tailoring and styling are right. You'd have to pay more than that price elsewhere for a similar suit with only one pair of trousers.

We bought this favorite materia at a below-market price, to keep a manufacturer's mills humming along in his dull season. The saving we made goes to our customers. The suit is made of sturdy textured material—an excellent wearing cassimere about 60 per cent wool with balance of cotton for extra strength. Choice of two attractive colors—striped dark brown or striped dark gray. Remember, men, you get two pairs of trousers—therefore double wear from this suit.

State chest, waist and trousers inseam measure. See size chart No. 2 at bottom of page. Read "How to Measure" on Page 238. Shipping weight, 7 pounds 12 ounces.
39 G 1712—Striped dark brown.
39 G 1716—Striped dark gray.
Each...$13.85

$14⁹⁵ All Wool Serge or All Wool Cassimere

Quality considered, style considered, tailoring considered, these Suits are convincing proof of the marvelous clothing values you get here at low prices. One is a fine twill All Wool blue serge, that always keeps you neatly and correctly dressed. The other is an excellent quality All Wool cadet blue cassimere in a close twill weave.

Coat is half lined and excellently tailored. Five-button vest; medium width trousers with regulation cuff bottoms.

State chest, waist and trousers inseam measure. See size chart No. 1 below. Read "How to Measure" on Page 238. Shipping weight, 6 pounds.

39 G 1675—Navy blue serge.
39 G 1679—Cadet blue cassimere. Each...$14.95

$15⁴⁵ Distinctive Style

Your friends will admire your good taste in choosing either the medium gray or the new forest brown—both fancy striped. A strong, good looking fabric—85 per cent wool, balance silk—that adds strength and beauty.

It's a snappy two-button model with long, soft roll lapels and a close fitting collar. Coat has an easy, graceful hang. Full lined with strong twill. Regular five-button vest and medium width 18-inch cuff bottom trousers. You will be enthusiastic over the extra quality you are getting at this low price.

State chest, waist and trousers inseam measure. See size chart No. 1 below. Read "How to Measure" on Page 238. Shipping weight, 6 pounds.

39 G 1681—Fancy striped medium gray.
39 G 1685—Fancy striped forest brown. Each...$15.45

$9⁹⁸ Specially Low Priced

Your money buys its full worth and more when you select this conservative Suit and pay only $9.98 for it. Men all over the country who have set aside just so much to spend for clothes will find this suit an economical purchase.

Strong, smooth-surface cassimere—60 per cent wool with 40 per cent cotton—an excellent balance of materials to insure longest wear.

Coat full lined. Trousers have regulation cuff bottoms.

State chest, waist and trousers inseam measure. See size scale No. 2 below. Read "How to Measure" on Page 238. Shipping weight, 6 pounds 6 ounces.

39 G 1109—Striped dark brown.
39 G 1113—Striped dark gray.
Each...$9.98

$13⁹⁵ All Wool Blue Serge

Frankly, men, when you wear this All Wool Suit you'll say the price should have been $20 instead of the $13.95 that we ask. Consider, too, the common sense in selecting this All Wool navy blue serge. Wear it any time, anywhere—blue serge is always right. Conservative style that never grows old. Well tailored lines that will earn for you a reputation as a neat dresser. Full lined coat; regular vest. Cuff bottom trousers.

This model has very justly earned its popularity. When you slip into this suit and see for yourself how well it fits, you will be more than satisfied with your purchase.

State chest, waist and trousers inseam measure. See size chart No. 2 below. Read "How to Measure" on Page 238. Shipping weight, 6 pounds.

39 G 1003—Navy blue serge only...$13.95

Size Scale No. 1 for Suits Shown Above

Chest measure, inches....	34	35	36	37	38	39	40	42
Waist measure, inches....	28 to 31	29 to 32	30 to 32	31 to 33	32 to 34	33 to 35	34 to 36	36 to 38
Trousers inseam, cuff bottoms, 28, 29, 30, 31, 32, 33 inches								

Size Scale No. 2 for Suits Shown Above

Chest measure, inches....	35	36	37	38	39	40	42	44
Waist measure, inches....	30 to 32	31 to 33	32 to 34	33 to 36	34 to 37	35 to 38	38 to 40	40 to 42
Trousers inseam, cuff bottoms, 28, 29, 30, 31, 32, 33 inches								

More Quality Than These Prices Buy Anywhere

Every One a Style Bargain

Decidedly New!

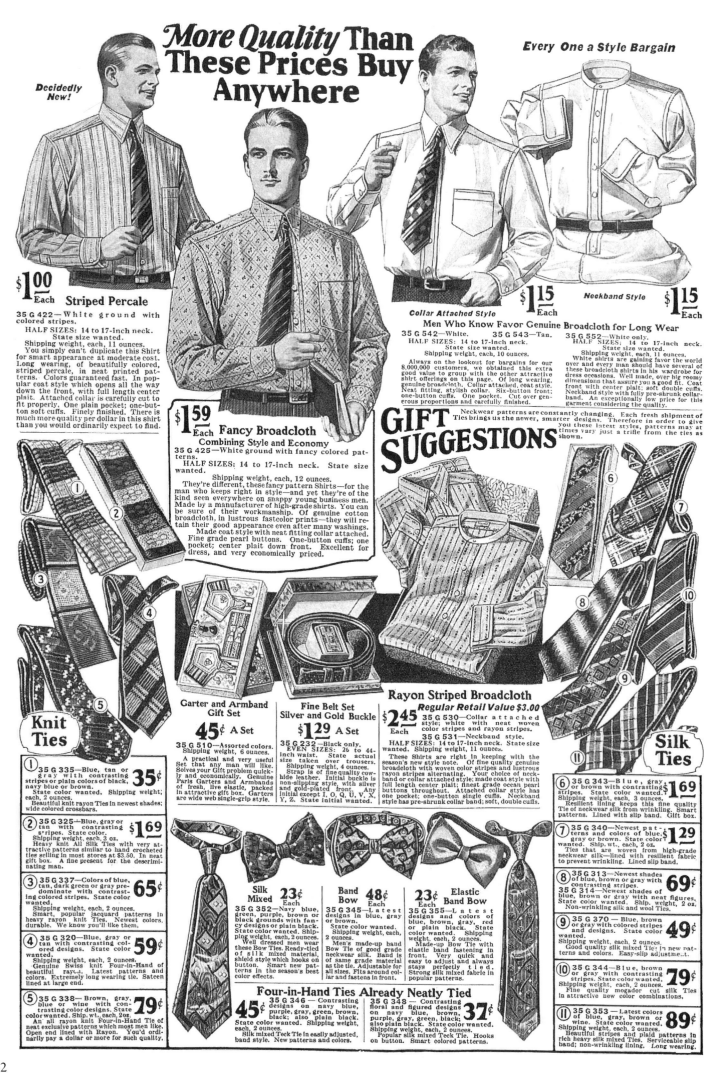

$1.00 Each — Striped Percale

35 G 422—White ground with colored stripes.
HALF SIZES: 14 to 17-inch neck.
State size wanted.
Shipping weight, each, 11 ounces.
You simply can't duplicate this Shirt for smart appearance at moderate cost. Long wearing, of beautifully colored, striped percale, in neat printed patterns. Colors guaranteed fast. In popular coat style which opens all the way down the front, with full length center plait. Attached collar is carefully cut to fit properly. One plain pocket; one-button soft cuffs. Finely finished. There is much more quality per dollar in this shirt than you would ordinarily expect to find.

$1.59 Each — Fancy Broadcloth
Combining Style and Economy

35 G 425—White ground with fancy colored patterns.
HALF SIZES: 14 to 17-inch neck. State size wanted.
Shipping weight, each, 12 ounces.
They're different, these fancy pattern Shirts—for the man who keeps right in style—and yet they're of the kind seen everywhere on snappy young business men. Made by a manufacturer of high-grade shirts. You can be sure of their workmanship. Of genuine cotton broadcloth, in lustrous fastcolor prints—they will retain their good appearance even after many washings. Made coat style with neat fitting collar attached. Fine grade pearl buttons. One-button cuffs; one pocket; center plait down front. Excellent for dress, and very economically priced.

Collar Attached Style — $1.15 Each
Men Who Know Favor Genuine Broadcloth for Long Wear

35 G 542—White.   35 G 543—Tan.
HALF SIZES: 14 to 17-inch neck.
State size wanted.
Shipping weight, each, 10 ounces.
Always on the lookout for bargains for our 8,000,000 customers, we obtained this extra good value to group with the other attractive shirt offerings on this page. Of long wearing, genuine broadcloth. Collar attached, coat style. Neat fitting, stylish collar. Six-button front; one-button cuffs. One pocket. Cut over generous proportions and carefully finished.

Neckband Style — $1.15 Each

35 G 552—White only.
HALF SIZES: 14 to 17-inch neck.
Shipping weight, each, 11 ounces.
White shirts are gaining favor the world over and every man should have several of these broadcloth shirts in his wardrobe for dress occasions. Well made, over big roomy dimensions that assure you a good fit. Coat front with center plait; soft double cuffs. Neckband style with fully pre-shrunk collarband. An exceptionally low price for this garment considering the quality.

GIFT SUGGESTIONS

Neckwear patterns are constantly changing. Each fresh shipment of Ties brings us the newer, smarter designs. Therefore in order to give you these latest styles, patterns may at times vary just a trifle from the ties as shown.

Knit Ties

① 35 G 335—Blue, tan or gray with contrasting stripes or plain colors of black, navy blue or brown. **35¢**
State color wanted. Shipping weight; each, 2 ounces.
Beautiful knit rayon Ties in newest shades; wide colored crossbars.

② 35 G 325—Blue, gray or tan with contrasting stripes. State color. **$1.69**
Shipping weight, each, 3 oz.
Heavy knit All Silk Ties with very attractive patterns similar to hand crocheted ties selling in most stores at $3.50. In neat gift box. A fine present for the descriminating man.

③ 35 G 337—Colors of blue, tan, dark green or gray predominate with contrasting colored stripes. State color wanted. **65¢**
Shipping weight, each, 2 ounces.
Smart, popular jacquard patterns in heavy rayon knit Ties. Newest colors, durable. We know you'll like them.

④ 35 G 320—Blue, gray or tan with contrasting colored designs. State color wanted. **59¢**
Shipping weight, each, 2 ounces.
Genuine Swiss knit Four-in-Hand of beautiful rayon. Latest patterns and colors. Extremely long wearing tie. Sateen lined at large end.

⑤ 35 G 338—Brown, gray, blue or wine with contrasting color designs. State color wanted. Ship. wt., each, 2oz. **79¢**
An all rayon knit Four-in-Hand Tie of neat exclusive patterns which most men like. Open end lined with Rayon. You'd ordinarily pay a dollar or more for such quality.

Garter and Armband Gift Set — 45¢ A Set

35 G 510—Assorted colors. Shipping weight, 6 ounces.
A practical and very useful Set that any man will like. Solves your Gift problem quickly and economically. Genuine Paris Garters and Armbands of fresh, live elastic, packed in attractive gift box. Garters are wide web single-grip style.

Fine Belt Set — Silver and Gold Buckle — $1.29 A Set

35 G 232—Black only.
EVEN SIZES: 26 to 44-inch waist. State actual size taken over trousers. Shipping weight, 4 ounces.
Strap is of fine quality cowhide leather. Initial buckle is non-slipping style, with silver and gold-plated front. Any initial except I, O, Q, U, V, X, Y, Z. State initial wanted.

Rayon Striped Broadcloth
Regular Retail Value $3.00 — $2.45 Each

35 G 530—Collar attached style; white with neat woven color stripes and rayon stripes.
35 G 531—Neckband style.
HALF SIZES: 14 to 17-inch neck. State size wanted. Shipping weight, 11 ounces.
These Shirts are right in keeping with the season's new style note. Of fine quality genuine broadcloth with woven color stripes and lustrous rayon stripes alternating. Your choice of neckband or collar attached style; made coat style with full length center plait; finest grade ocean pearl buttons throughout. Attached collar style has one pocket; one-button single cuffs. Neckband style has pre-shrunk collar band; soft, double cuffs.

Silk Ties

⑥ 35 G 343—Blue, gray or brown with contrasting stripes. State color wanted. **$1.69**
Shipping weight, each, 3 ounces.
Resilient lining keeps this fine quality Tie of neckwear silk from wrinkling. Smart patterns. Lined with slip band. Gift box.

⑦ 35 G 340—Newest patterns and colors of blue, gray or brown. State color wanted. Ship. wt., each, 2 oz. **$1.29**
Ties that are woven from high-grade neckwear silk—lined with resilient fabric to prevent wrinkling. Lined slip band.

⑧ 35 G 313—Newest shades of blue, brown or gray with contrasting stripes. **69¢**
35 G 314—Newest shades of blue, brown or gray with neat figures. State color wanted. Ship. weight, each, 2 oz.
Non-wrinkling silk and wool Ties.

⑨ 35 G 370—Blue, brown or gray with colored stripes and designs. State color wanted. **49¢**
Shipping weight, each, 2 ounces.
Good quality silk mixed Tie; in new patterns and colors. Easy-slip adjustment.

⑩ 35 G 344—Blue, brown or gray with contrasting stripes. **79¢**
Shipping weight, each, 2 ounces.
Fine quality mogador cut silk Ties in attractive new color combinations.

⑪ 35 G 353—Latest colors of blue, gray, brown or wine. State color wanted. **89¢**
Shipping weight, each, 2 ounces.
Beautiful stripes and plaid patterns in rich heavy silk mixed Ties. Serviceable slip band; non-wrinkling lining. Long wearing.

Silk Mixed — 23¢ Each

35 G 352—Navy blue, green, purple, brown or black grounds with fancy designs or plain black. State color wanted. Shipping weight, each, 2 ounces.
Well dressed men wear these Bow Ties. Ready-tied of silk mixed material, shield style which hooks on button. Smart new patterns in the season's best color effects.

Band Bow — 48¢ Each

35 G 345—Latest designs in blue, gray or brown.
State color wanted. Shipping weight, each, 2 ounces.
Men's made-up band Bow Tie of good grade neckwear silk. Band is of same grade material as the tie. Adjustable for all sizes. Fits around collar and fastens in front.

Elastic Band Bow — 23¢ Each

35 G 355—Latest designs and colors of blue, brown, gray, red or plain black. State color wanted. Shipping weight, each, 2 ounces.
Made-up Bow Tie with elastic band fastening in front. Very quick and easy to adjust and always stays perfectly tied. Strong silk mixed fabric in popular patterns.

Four-in-Hand Ties Already Neatly Tied

35 G 346—Contrasting designs on navy blue, purple, gray, green, brown, black; also plain black. State color wanted. Shipping weight, each, 2 ounces. **45¢**
Silk mixed Teck Tie in easily adjusted, band style. New patterns and colors.

35 G 348—Contrasting floral and figured designs on navy blue, brown, purple, gray, green, black; also plain black. State color wanted. Shipping weight, each, 2 ounces. **37¢**
Popular silk mixed Teck Tie. Hooks on button. Smart colored patterns.

Beau Brummel Shoes *for* Men
FINEST GOODYEAR WELT CONSTRUCTION

24 G 1455.. $5.98
SIZES: 6 to 11.
Widths C, D, E. State
size. Ship.wt.,2 lbs. 4oz.
Custom built Oxford for
winter wear–rich in quality. All Leather! Fine,
selected, tan calfskin uppers. Leather insole.
Leather heel with Good-
year lift. Special drifoot
wedge. They're $8 to $10
value.

Beau Brummel Custom Built Shoes
Made in a Factory Specializing in $10 Quality

24 G 1456—Tan calfskin.
24 G 1457—Black calfskin.............. $5.98
SIZES: 6 to 11. Widths C, D, E. State size wanted.
Shipping weight, 2 pounds 4 ounces.
Wear Custom Built Shoes for their fit—their comfort—their
wear—their appearance—they are equal to $8 to $10 shoes.
All Leather! Our very best quality. Tan or black calfskin uppers.
Heavy, single oak bend, leather sole, Goodyear welt. Leather in-
sole. Leather heel with Goodyear rubber lift. Calf leather lining.

24 G 1459—Tan calfskin.
24 G 1460—Black calfskin.............. $5.98
SIZES: 6 to 11. Widths B, C, D, E. State size wanted.
Shipping weight, 2 pounds 4 ounces.
Particular men are wearing them—Everywhere. You can tell
immediately by their lines, their workmanship, their weight, that
they're All Quality—All Leather! An $8 to $10 value! Tan or
black calfskin uppers—polish brilliantly—hold their shape.
Leather insole, counters, lining. Leather heel with Goodyear
rubber lift. Custom Built gives you our very best quality.

$5⁹⁸
*Choice of
6 Styles*

24 G 1458.. $5.98
SIZES: 6 to 11. Widths
C, D, E. State size. Ship.
wt., 2 lbs. 4 oz.
$8 to $10 value. All
Leather – Custom Built
Oxford. Rich, dark tan
calfskin uppers. Oak bend
leather soles. Goodyear
welt. Solid leather heel
with Goodyear rubber lift.

Beau Brummel STANDARD $5 to $6 Values

$3⁹⁸
*Choice of
10 Styles*

**Perfectly
Satisfied**
"The Beau
Brummel Shoes
are fine. I am per
fectly satisfied in
every way—style,
comfort, durabil-
ity. I never had
a pair of shoes I
like better."
A. E. Loomis,
Savoy, Mass.
Printed by
Permission

Popular Cherry or Black Patent
24 G 1445—Cherry tan patent leather.
24 G 1444—Black patent leather............. $3.98
SIZES: 6 to 12. Widths D and E. State size wanted.
Shipping weight, 2 pounds 4 ounces.
Follow the style, men! Wear patent leather Oxfords this
season. Beau Brummel Standard $5 to $6 values—$3.98!
Black or the new cherry tan on the popular square toe. Goodyear welt oak leather soles. Rubber heels. Beau Brummel
standards help you to dress better and more economically.

As Good as They're Good Looking
24 G 1453—Tan calf grain leather.
24 G 1454—Black calf grain leather.......... $3.98
SIZES: 6 to 12. Widths C, D, E. State size wanted.
Shipping weight, 2 pounds 4 ounces.
Any Beau Brummel Shoe you buy is quality through and
through! Swagger college styles like these of selected leathers
are $5 to $6 values. Oak leather soles, Goodyear welt. Rubber
heels. Perfect fit, reliable wear—and one of the best looking
styles of the year. At $3.98 you save money!

*Special
Dri-Foot
Wedge*

**Dri-Foot
Wedge**

Great Shoes for Winter Wear
24 G 1582—Tan calf grain leather.
24 G 1581—Black calf grain leather. $3.98
SIZES: 6 to 12. Widths D and E. State size.
Shipping weight, 2 pounds 8 ounces.
Two mighty good Shoes for winter wear.
They're Beau Brummel Standard, and
they're only $3.98! That they're big values—
you can be sure. All we can say is Wear Them. Long
service will prove all our claims. Built of sturdy, selected
leathers that look good, feel good, wear good. Tan or
black calf grain leather used in the uppers is equal to
that in most $5 and $6 shoes. Heavy single oak leather
soles, Goodyear welt. A special dri-foot wedge for
winter's dampness. Rubber heels.

24 G 1414—Tan calf grain leather.
24 G 1415—Black calf grain leather.......... $3.98
SIZES: 6 to 12. Widths C, D, E. State size wanted.
Shipping weight, 2 pounds 4 ounces.
It's new—full of dash and clever styling. The special dri-foot
wedge keeps out winter's dampness. Beau Brummel Shoes have
a nation-wide reputation for their well-fitting lasts and long
wearing leathers. Sturdy, selected calf grain uppers—tan or black.
Heavy oak leather soles, Goodyear welt. Rubber heels.

**Genuine
Calfskin**
24 G 1446—Tan calfskin.
24 G 1447—Black calfskin.......... $3.98
SIZES: 6 to 12. Widths D and E. State size wanted.
Shipping weight, 2 pounds 4 ounces.
Beau Brummel Oxfords bring you more quality—newer style—
utmost comfort—greater value. Two models of genuine full
grain calfskin. Oak bend leather soles with rolled edge. Goodyear welt. Rubber heels. Comfortable fitting toe, has all the
style young men demand. They're $5 to $6 values.

Beau Brummel SPECIAL $7 to $8 Values

$4⁸⁹ *Choice
of 6 Styles*

**The College Fellows
Are Wearing These**
24 G 1404—Tan.
24 G 1403—Black.......... $4.89
SIZES: 6 to 12. Widths C, D, E.
State size wanted.
Shipping weight, 2 pounds 4 ounces.
American college men want snap, dash,
"kick" in their Oxfords, and so they made
this style a big favorite for the season.
They're in the $7 to $8 class. Of fine tan
or black calf. Strong oak bend leather
soles. Goodyear welt. Goodyear rubber
heels. Combination last is perfection in
fit from toe to heel.

QUALITY–Inside and Outside
24 G 1591.................. $4.89
SIZES: 6 to 12. Widths C, D, E. State size.
Shipping weight, 2 pounds 8 ounces.
Beau Brummel Special Dress Shoe—made in a
factory specializing in shoes that retail for $7 to $8.
Quality leathers—shape-holding construction. Here's
a new style that gives keen delight to the young
fellow, and the square toe and combination last gives
the fit and comfort you've always wanted. Fine
tan calf leather uppers. Choice quality oak bend leather
sole. Goodyear welt. Goodyear rubber heels.

Handsome Black Calf Oxford
24 G 1406.................. $4.89
SIZES: 6 to 12. Width C, D, E. State size.
Shipping weight, 2 pounds 4 ounces.
A new Beau Brummel Special Oxford that will
certainly find a place in every man's wardrobe.
Made in a factory specializing in $7 to $8 shoes.
Rich, black calf leather that takes a beautiful glossy
polish. A patent leather eyelet trim adds dignity and
will appeal to the best dressed men. Choice quality
oak bend leather soles. Goodyear welt. Goodyear
rubber heels. Combination last hugs the heel and
fits the ball with glove-like perfection.

$4⁸⁹   **$4⁸⁹**

*See
Shoe Size Chart
Page 169*

A Dress Shoe of Real Style
24 G 1575.................. $4.89
SIZES: 6 to 12. Widths C, D, E. State size.
Shipping weight, 2 pounds 8 ounces.
Good Shoes like these have a quality "feel"
when you put your feet into them. There's something about the way they conform to the lines of
the foot that is only possible in finely made shoes.
It means more comfort—more wear—better appearance. Fine black calf uppers. Choice oak bend
leather soles. Goodyear welt. Goodyear rubber
heels. Combination last fits the heel and ball of
the foot with perfection. A $7 to $8 value.

So Much Style and Quality
24 G 1405.................. $4.89
SIZES: 6 to 12. Widths C, D, E. State size.
Shipping weight, 2 pounds 4 ounces.
The up-to-the-minute smartness of this model
is built right into its fine quality materials and
workmanship. You'll see it at a glance. It's a
winner, men! Holds its shape to the end. Close
fitting heel and ball because they're made over a
combination last. Fine tan calf leather uppers
polish brightly and always have that quality
appearance. Oak bend leather soles. Goodyear
welt. Goodyear rubber heels.

Light Weight Suits *for* All-Year Wear

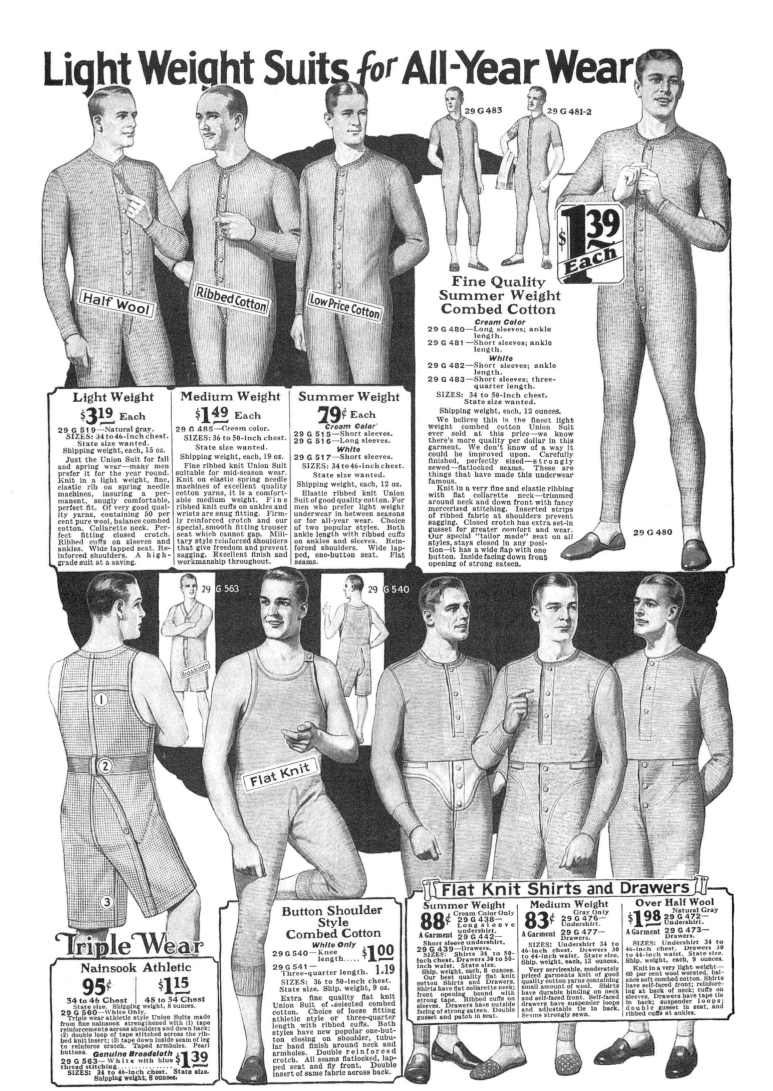

29 G 483 **29 G 481-2**

$1 39 Each

Half Wool **Ribbed Cotton** **Low Price Cotton**

Fine Quality Summer Weight Combed Cotton

Cream Color
29 G 480—Long sleeves; ankle length.
29 G 481—Short sleeves; ankle length.
White
29 G 482—Short sleeves; ankle length.
29 G 483—Short sleeves; three-quarter length.
SIZES: 34 to 50-inch chest. State size wanted.
Shipping weight, each, 12 ounces.

We believe this is the finest light weight combed cotton Union Suit ever sold at this price—we know there's more quality per dollar in this garment. We don't know of a way it could be improved upon. Carefully finished, perfectly sized—strongly sewed—flatlocked seams. These are things that have made this underwear famous.

Knit in a very fine and elastic ribbing with flat collarette neck—trimmed around neck and down front with fancy mercerized stitching. Inserted strips of ribbed fabric at shoulders prevent sagging. Closed crotch has extra set-in gusset for greater comfort and wear. Our special "tailor made" seat on all styles, stays closed in any position—it has a wide flap with one button. Inside facing down front opening of strong sateen.

29 G 480

Light Weight
$3 19 Each
29 G 519—Natural gray.
SIZES: 34 to 46-inch chest. State size wanted.
Shipping weight, each, 15 oz.

Just the Union Suit for fall and spring wear—many men prefer it for the year round. Knit in a light weight, fine, elastic rib on spring needle machines, insuring a permanent, snugly comfortable, perfect fit. Of very good quality yarns, containing 50 per cent pure wool, balance combed cotton. Collarette neck. Perfect fitting closed crotch. Ribbed cuffs on sleeves and ankles. Wide lapped seat. Reinforced shoulders. A high-grade suit at a saving.

Medium Weight
$1 49 Each
29 G 485—Cream color.
SIZES: 36 to 50-inch chest. State size wanted.
Shipping weight, each, 19 oz.

Fine ribbed knit Union Suit suitable for mid-season wear. Knit on elastic spring needle machines of excellent quality cotton yarns, it is a comfortable medium weight. Fine-ly reinforced crotch and our special, smooth fitting trouser seat which cannot gap. Military style reinforced shoulders that give freedom and prevent sagging. Excellent finish and workmanship throughout.

Summer Weight
79¢ Each
Cream Color
29 G 515—Short sleeves.
29 G 516—Long sleeves.
White
29 G 517—Short sleeves.
SIZES: 34 to 46-inch chest. State size wanted.
Shipping weight, each, 12 oz.

Elastic ribbed knit Union Suit of good quality cotton. For men who prefer light weight underwear in between seasons or for all-year wear. Choice of two popular styles. Both ankle length with ribbed cuffs on ankles and sleeves. Reinforced shoulders. Wide lapped, one-button seat. Flat seams.

29 G 563 **Broadcloth** **29 G 540**

Flat Knit

Triple Wear

Nainsook Athletic

95¢	**$1 15**
34 to 46 Chest	48 to 54 Chest

State size. Shipping weight, 8 ounces.
29 G 560—White Only.
Triple wear athletic style Union Suits made from fine nainsook strengthened with (1) tape reinforcements across shoulders and down back; (2) double loop of tape stitched across the ribbed knit insert; (3) tape down inside seam of leg to reinforce crotch. Taped armholes. Pearl buttons. **Genuine Broadcloth**
29 G 563—White with blue $1 39 thread stitching................
SIZES: 34 to 46-inch chest. State size. Shipping weight, 8 ounces.

Button Shoulder Style
Combed Cotton
White Only
29 G 540—Knee length..... **$1 00**
29 G 541—Three-quarter length. 1.19
SIZES: 36 to 50-inch chest. State size. Ship. weight, 9 oz.

Extra fine quality flat knit Union Suit of selected combed cotton. Choice of loose fitting athletic style or three-quarter length with ribbed cuffs. Both styles have new popular one-button closing on shoulder, tubular band finish around neck and armholes. Double reinforced crotch. All seams flatlocked, lapped seat and fly front. Double insert of same fabric across back.

Flat Knit Shirts and Drawers

Summer Weight
88¢ A Garment
Cream Color Only
29 G 438—Long sleeve undershirt.
29 G 442—Short sleeve undershirt.
29 G 439—Drawers.
SIZES: Shirts 34 to 50-inch chest. Drawers 30 to 50-inch waist. State size. Ship. weight, each, 8 ounces.

Our best quality flat knit cotton Shirts and Drawers. Shirts have flat collarette neck; front opening bound with strong tape. Ribbed cuffs on sleeves. Drawers have outside facing of strong sateen. Double gusset and patch in seat.

Medium Weight
83¢ A Garment
Gray Only
29 G 476—Undershirt.
29 G 477—Drawers.
SIZES: Undershirt 34 to 46-inch chest. Drawers 30 to 44-inch waist. State size. Ship. weight, each, 13 ounces.

Very serviceable, moderately priced garments knit of good quality cotton yarns containing small amount of wool. Shirts have durable binding on neck and self-faced front. Self-faced drawers have suspender loops and adjustable tie in back. Seams strongly sewn.

Over Half Wool
$1 98 A Garment
Natural Gray
29 G 472—Undershirt.
29 G 473—Drawers.
SIZES: Undershirt 34 to 46-inch chest. Drawers 30 to 44-inch waist. State size. Ship. weight, each, 9 ounces.

Knit in a very light weight 60 per cent wool worsted, balance soft combed cotton. Shirts have self-faced front; reinforcing at back of neck; cuffs on sleeves. Drawers have tape tie in back; suspender loops; double gusset in seat, and ribbed cuffs at ankles.

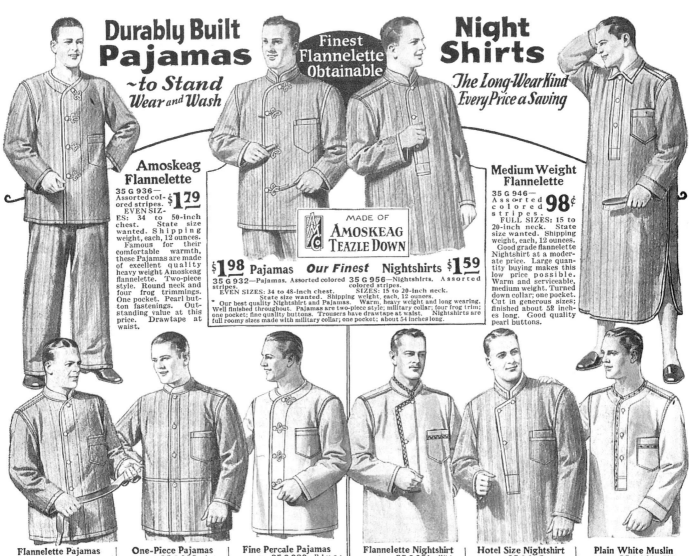

Durably Built Pajamas
~to Stand Wear and Wash

Finest Flannelette Obtainable

Night Shirts
The Long-Wear Kind Every Price a Saving

Amoskeag Flannelette

35 G 936—Assorted colored stripes. **$1⁷⁹** EVEN SIZES: 34 to 50-inch chest. State size wanted. Shipping weight, each, 12 ounces. Famous for their comfortable warmth, these Pajamas are made of excellent quality heavy weight Amoskeag flannelette. Two-piece style. Round neck and four frog trimmings. One pocket. Pearl button fastenings. Outstanding value at this price. Drawtape at waist.

MADE OF **AMOSKEAG TEAZLE DOWN**

$1⁹⁸ Pajamas *Our Finest* **Nightshirts $1⁵⁹**

35 G 932—Pajamas. Assorted colored stripes. EVEN SIZES: 34 to 48-inch chest. **35 G 956**—Nightshirts. Assorted colored stripes. SIZES: 15 to 20-inch neck. State size wanted. Shipping weight, each, 12 ounces.

Our best quality Nightshirt and Pajamas. Warm, heavy and long wearing. Well finished throughout. Pajamas are two-piece style; military collar; four frog trim; one pocket; fine quality buttons. Trousers have drawtape at waist. Nightshirts are full roomy sizes made with military collar; one pocket; about 54 inches long.

Medium Weight Flannelette

35 G 946—Assorted colored stripes. **98¢** FULL SIZES: 15 to 20-inch neck. State size wanted. Shipping weight, each, 12 ounces. Good grade flannelette Nightshirt at a moderate price. Large quantity buying makes this low price possible. Warm and serviceable, medium weight. Turned down collar; one pocket. Cut in generous sizes; finished about 52 inches long. Good quality pearl buttons.

Flannelette Pajamas
$1²⁹ **35 G 928**—Assorted stripes. EVEN SIZES: 34 to 48-inch chest. State size. Ship. wt., each, 12 ounces. Medium weight two-piece Pajamas for all year round wear. Made of soft flannelette, carefully finished. Stand-up, military collar; four-button front; one pocket. Cut full and roomy for comfort.

One-Piece Pajamas
$1⁴⁸ **35 G 933**—Assorted colored stripes. EVEN SIZES: 34 to 48-inch chest. State size. Shipping weight, each, 12 ounces. Look like ordinary suits. Pants sewed on to coat at waist. Serviceable, warm flannelette. Drop seat in trousers with three sewed-on buttons. Military collar.

Fine Percale Pajamas
$1³⁵ **35 G 939**—Blue; tan; white. EVEN SIZES: 34 to 48-inch chest. State size and color wanted. Shipping weight, each, 12 ounces. Mighty good looking and long wearing Pajamas of closely woven percale, with Rayon trimmed frogs; good quality pearl buttons; one pocket. Cut full; fast colors.

Flannelette Nightshirt
$1⁴⁵ **35 G 951**—White. **35 G 952**—Assorted stripes. SIZES: 15 to 20-inch neck. State size. Shipping weight, each, 12 ounces. Excellent quality heavy weight Amoskeag flannelette. About 54 inches long; military collar; braid trimmed; one pocket. Shoulders well reinforced.

Hotel Size Nightshirt
$1⁶⁵ **35 G 945**—Assorted stripes. SIZES: 15 to 20-inch neck. State size wanted. Shipping weight, each, 12 ounces. Heavy weight Amoskeag flannelette Nightshirt for the big man. Hotel size—cut about 58 inches long and extra full across shoulders and through chest.

Plain White Muslin
95¢ **35 G 961**—White. SIZES: 15 to 20-inch neck. State size. Ship. wt., each, 12 ounces. Good quality Nightshirts made of soft finished muslin. Comfortably roomy and full 52 inches long. Low neck, braid trim at neck and on pocket. Built for comfort and long wear.

New Shaded Patterns

A Gift of Quality and Comfort
With Slippers to Match

Big Value! Robe and Dressing Gown

Finest Blanket Robe
$9⁹⁸ **35 G 964**—Blue; brown; gray. SIZES: 34 to 48-inch chest. State size and color. Ship.wt., each, 4 lbs. Our most attractive shawl collar Robe—made of heavy weight double ombre or shaded Beacon blanket. Three large pockets. Collar, front and pockets trimmed with braid. Rayon rope girdle at waist. Sateen facing in yoke. Finely stitched.

Extra Quality Robe
$5⁹⁸ **35 G 969**—Blue; gray; brown. EVEN SIZES: 34 to 48-inch chest. State size and color wanted. Shipping weight, each, 3 pounds. An excellent value. Made of blanket cloth in shawl collar style; collar, front and pockets braid trimmed. Two pockets. Rayon and cotton rope girdle. Three-button closing. New patterns.

MADE OF GENUINE *Beacon* CLOTH

$6⁹⁸ **35 G 977**—Tan; blue; gray. EVEN SIZES: 34 to 48-inch chest. State size and color wanted. Shipping weight, each, 4 pounds. You are sure to please him by choosing this splendid Bathrobe for his holiday or birthday present. Its soft, warm, genuine Beacon blanket cloth of medium weight, and the genuine leather soled slippers to match, make a mighty fine outfit. Smart style, fine materials and good tailoring is evident throughout. Well made in every respect, and neatly trimmed around collar, cuffs, pockets and down entire front with lustrous corded braid. Long corded girdle at waist is of lustrous rayon. Strikingly new patterns enhance the beautiful color shades. Shawl collar; three roomy pockets. As serviceable as it is attractive—and a truly satisfying value which must be seen to be fully appreciated.

Good Blanket Cloth
$4⁹⁸ **35 G 971**—Blue; brown; gray. SIZES: Small, medium or large. State size and color. Shipping weight, each, 3 pounds. Men's low priced Bathrobe of good quality cotton blanket cloth in attractive patterns. Fine cord trimming around collar, pockets and cuffs. Rayon and cotton girdle. Two large pockets. Reinforced seams. Good grade buttons.

Rayon Dressing Gown
$12²⁹ **35 G 984**—Blue; wine; brown. EVEN SIZES: 34 to 48-inch chest. State size and color. Shipping weight, each, 3 pounds. A gift to please any man. He'll highly approve the style. Rayon and cotton overshot pattern. Collar facing and trim of pockets and cuffs is Skinner's satin. Silk mixed girdle. Cloth covered buttons to match. Very attractive.

Famous from Coast to Coast

Guaranteed To Wear 6 Months

24 G 1820—Brown.
24 G 1825—Black. **$3.35**

SIZES: 5 to 12. Wide width.
SIZES: 13 and 14, 75¢ extra.
State size. Ship. wt., 4 lbs.

The Wonder Work Shoes of All America!

Here's one letter picked at random from hundreds which we receive acclaiming these great shoes. W. G. Ledbetter of Grant, Ala., writes:

"I've been ordering these Shoes from you for the last fifteen years. I have been wearing my present pair for twenty-two months—the longest a pair of Shoes ever lasted me."

Only the toughest genuine leather is used in every part of these shoes. The upper is tanned like the famous old-fashioned "wang" leather, which makes it soft, extremely durable and solid acid resisting. Two heavy soles on each shoe, one of oak leather and the other of green chrome leather, both the same high quality. Solid leather heels, counters and insoles. These are, unquestionably, the most famous work shoes in America—the quality brings you $4 to $5 value for only $3.35 a pair. That's why we sell 100,000 pairs every year.

Ward's Six Months Guaranteed Work Shoes are the very best quality leather, and give you six months of service. Should they fail to wear six months, we guarantee to replace them with a new pair of shoes, charging you only for the number of days you had the old pair and crediting you with the number of days they failed to wear. This guarantee applies only to shoes number 24 G 1820 and 24 G 1825.

100,000 Pairs Sold Every Year

Guaranteed SOLID LEATHER

1—Soft, heavy, barnyard-proof leather uppers. 2—Solid leather counter. 3—Solid leather heel. 4—Strong full grain leather insole. 5—Triple stitched and reinforced with rivets. 6—Double soles, oak leather outsole and green chrome second sole of outsole quality from toe to heel. 7—Full vamp, not cut off under the tip, and hard box toe for protection against falling objects.

How to Order Shoes
See Page 169

$3.39

Moccasin Vamp—Goodyear Welt

24 G 1856—Brown Chrome Leather.
24 G 1857—Black Chrome Leather. **$3.39**
SIZES: 6 to 12. Wide width. State size.
Shipping weight, 3 pounds 2 ounces.

Feet that are always on the go will be free from discomfort if they are wearing a pair of these Goodyear welt shoes with moccasin vamp. Brown or black chrome tanned leather (known as elkskin). Wonder-Wear composition soles give extremely long wear and walking comfort. Solid rubber heels.

"I like my boots fine, so have worn them a lot since I received them. I haven't seen boots like them for the money any place around here. I wear them in fair weather and in mud, and it does not seem to hurt them at all."
Paul Stinar, Warren, Minn.
Printed by Permission

Our SPECIAL Farm Shoes

Famous Green Chrome Outsole Choice of Plain Toe or With Tip

$2.49

They're Saving Money for THOUSANDS of Men

24 G 1844—With tip. 24 G 1846—Soft plain toe.
SIZES: 5 to 12. Wide width. State size. Ship. wt., 3 lbs. 4 oz.

Now you can buy our Special Farm Shoes for only $2.49 a pair—it is like handing you a cash saving, because you **undoubtedly** would have to pay more for shoes like these in other stores. Next to our six-months guaranteed shoes, these are the most popular work shoes we sell. You'd pay at least $3 to $3.50 for them elsewhere. The uppers are brown, barnyard-proof grain leather, freshly tanned. Double soles—green chrome leather and oak leather. Solid leather heels. Solid leather insole.

$2.98

Famous "SEAMLESS" Work Shoe

24 G 1876......................$2.98
SIZES: 6 to 12. Wide width. State size wanted. Ship. wt., 3 lbs. 2 oz.

More and more men are changing to this Seamless Work Shoe. Once you wear them, you too will want to wear no other shoe! They are the strongest and most comfortable work shoe we have ever seen for tender, sensitive feet. One-piece uppers (except small inside piece) are brown chrome tanned leather (known as elkskin). Strong oak leather sole. Solid rubber heels. And a great "buy" at our price.

"The last few years I have bought my Hi-cut Shoes from Ward's because the price and quality are better than I get elsewhere. I find Ward's Hi-cut Shoes wear twice as long as the ones I used to buy elsewhere for the same price." — Theo. A. Gustafson, Norway, Mich.

Solid Leather Hi-cuts
Goodyear Welt

18-Inch Hi-cuts

Brown or Black **$7.89**

24 G 2042—Brown.
SIZES: 6 to 11; width C.
SIZES: 5 to 12; widths D, E, EE.
24 G 2038—Black.
SIZES: 5 to 12; width EE only. State size. Ship. wt., 6 lbs.

A Tower of Strength! Built of the best—Two of America's most famous hi-cuts in QUALITY and VALUE! All Leather in every part. Uppers are heavy soft, chrome tanned leather (known as elkskin), reinforced with strong stitching. Double soles of highest quality oak bend leather. Goodyear Welt sewed all around the heel. Solid leather heel, counter insole. Dri-foot wedge.

Our Best 16-Inch Hi-cut

24 G 2048........$6.98
SIZES: 5 to 11. State size wanted. Ship. wt., 5 lbs. 8 oz.
Solid leather in every part—uppers, soles, heels, counters, insoles. Double soles of heavy oak leather are genuine Goodyear welt sewed. Heavy, pliable brown chrome tanned leather (known as elkskin)—no other leather equals it for hi-cuts.

18-Inch—Double Soles

24 G 2041........$7.89
SIZES: 6 to 12. State size wanted. Ship. weight, 6 lbs.
Every part of this moccasin vamp Hi-cut is solid leather. The pearl color chrome leather uppers (known as elkskin) are reinforced and stitched to prevent sagging. Heavy, **double** oak leather soles, Goodyear welt. Dri-foot wedge. Many customers tell us they have never heard of a better hi-cut within $2 to $4 of our price.

16-Inch "Oil King"

24 G 2036........$7.69
SIZES: 6 to 12. Wide width. State size. Ship. wt., 6 lbs.
Now—the finest special built Hi-cut we've ever offered for hunting, hiking, mountain climbing—also for oil fields, lumber camps and all hard duty. Heavy, oil tanned, brown chrome leather uppers. Outside leather counter pocket. Leather insole. Heavy oak leather outsole and green chrome second sole. Goodyear welt. Oil tanned chrome leather tongue. Plain toe, army officer's style. A Super-Built hi-cut!

56

Coziest Warmth on Coldest Days

$2⁵⁹

24 G 4065 . . . . $2.59
SIZES: 3 to 9. Width EE.
No half sizes. State size.
Ship. weight, 1 lb. 12 oz.
Neat appearance and snug
warmth on coldest days
for women. Uppers are
soft black genuine
kid leather lined from
top to toe. Good leath-
er soles. Warm
gray felt. Good leath-
er soles. Rubber
heels. And at
this price, a
value that will
put a saving
back in your
pocket.

Warm Lined Black Kid Oxford

$1⁹⁸

Warm Lined from Top to Toe

Enjoy Its Warmth and Neatness
A Big Saving Is Yours at This Price

24 G 4063 . . . . $1.98
SIZES: 3 to 9. Width EE. No half sizes. State size
wanted. Shipping weight, 1 pound 8 ounces.
Now—women can step out into zero weather without
worrying about their feet getting cold. A full fleece lined
Oxford with the neat dressy appearance that every woman
likes. Uppers are black genuine kid leather. Good quality
leather soles and low rubber heels. A splendid cash saving
combined with coziest warmth and neatness.

Warm Lined from Top to Toe

Again—"Wonder" Warm Shoe

24 G 4038 . . . . $2.98
SIZES: 3 to 9. Width EE.
No half sizes. State size.
Ship. wt., 1 pound 13 ounces.
More than 10,000 women
bought these wool fleece lined
Shoes last winter and were delighted with their warmth.
Built over the popular, perfect
fitting, medium toe last. Soft,
comfortable black leather
uppers are full fleece lined
from top to toe. Durable
oak leather soles. Rubber
heels. A value that you'll
hardly duplicate ANY-
WHERE at our low prices.

$2⁹⁸

"I want to thank you for the wonderful Shoes you sent me a few weeks ago.
They fit me as perfectly as if my feet
were molded into them. Dealers here
tell me they could only sell a shoe of
this quality at a much higher price. I
have had trouble for years getting a
shoe to fit: now I know that I can always be fitted by your firm."
Mary I. Little, Warsaw, Ind.

Fleece Lined for Warmth

24 G 4064 . . . . $1.98
SIZES: 3 to 9. Width EE. No half
sizes. State size wanted.
Shipping weight, 1 pound 6 ounces.
Warmth—comfort—neat appearance
for women—and the price is remarkably low, only $1.98. Just what you
want if you're looking for an economically priced winter shoe.
The black genuine kid leather
vamps and black felt tops are
warm lined. Strong leather
soles. Rubber heels.

$1⁹⁸

$1⁹⁸

24 G 4067 . . . . $1.98
SIZES: 3 to 9. Width EE.
No half sizes. State size.
Ship. wt., 1 lb. 7 oz.
Women who wish to spend
only a small amount for
their warm Shoes will do
well to buy these, as
they are excellent val-
ues at our price. They
will bring warm com-
fort to your feet in
cold weather.
Soft black kid
leather vamps
and black felt
tops are warm
lined. Strong
leather soles and
rubber heels.

Wool Lined STOUT ANKLE Shoe or Oxford

Black Kid

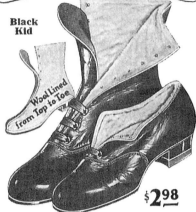

Wool Lined from Top to Toe

$2⁹⁸

24 G 4061— High Shoe. . $3.98 | 24 G 4066— Oxford . . . $2.98

SIZES: 3 to 9. Width EE. No half sizes. State size.
Shipping weights: Shoes, 1 lb. 13 oz.; Oxfords, 1 lb. 8 oz.
Your feet will be warm on the cold, frosty days if you
wear a pair of these high quality winter Shoes. Full,
roomy shapes for stout ankles. Your whole foot is sur-
rounded with thick sheep's wool from top to toe. Wool
fleece insole gives warmth and foot ease. Of black kid
leather. Strong leather soles. 1¼-inch rubber heels.

Men's *Everest* House Slippers

65¢ **$1¹⁹** **$1⁹⁸**

EEE Wide

$2²⁹

$1⁹⁵

Tan Kid—Leather Lined

24 G 3852—SIZES: 6 to 12. Width EE.
State size. Ship. weight, 1 lb. 8 oz. $2.29
At the end of a hard day's work give your feet
complete rest and relaxation. Slip them into
these Everest Slippers of tan soft genuine kid
leather. Flexible leather sole fastened by the
stitchdown process gives you a smooth and comfortable insole—free from tacks and stitches.
Soft leather lining all the way through. Elastic
gores at sides assure snug fit. Rubber heels.

Men, Women

24 G 3810 . . . . 65c
SIZES: 3 to 11. Width
EE. State size. No
half sizes. Ship. wt., 1 lb.
Comfortable Carpet
Slippers for men and
women, priced to save
you money. Of durable
quality carpeting mate-
rial in dark color combi-
nation. Leather and felt
sole; rubber heel lift. The
wear and comfort, at this
low price will please you.

Warm Gray Felt

24 G 4073 . . . . . . $1.19
SIZES: 6 to 12. Width
EE. No half sizes. State
size. Shipping weight,
1 pound 4 ounces.
When the day's work
is done slip your tired
feet into a pair of these
soft gray felt Everest
Slippers and they'll rest
in real comfort. Flexible
leather soles are durable
and give fine service. Rubber heels.

Soft Black Kid

24 G 3892 . . . . . . $1.98
SIZES: 6 to 12. Width
EEE. State size. Ship.
weight, 1 pound 8 ounces.
A soft black kid leather
Slipper especially designed for men with wide,
tender feet. There's ex-
tra width across the ball
assuring plenty of room.
Strong leather soles.
Low heels. Save at our
price and enjoy real
comfort, too.

Tan Kid—Flexible Sole

24 G 3802 . . . . $1.95
SIZES: 5 to 12. Width EE. State size.
Shipping weight, 1 pound 6 ounces.
A fine gift for father or brother. Brings
many hours of rest and comfort to tired feet.
They'll greatly appreciate a pair of these fine,
flexible Slippers of soft tan genuine kid.
Warm fleece lined. Oak leather soles are
stitchdown sewed for real flexibility. Rubber
heels. Remember him with a pair at Christmas time.

Very Soft Genuine Kid Leather

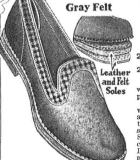

$1⁹⁸

A Fine Gift for Dad or Brother

24 G 3866—Brown $1.98
24 G 3867—Black 1.98
SIZES: 5 to 12. Width EE. State size wanted.
Shipping weight, 1 pound 8 ounces.
Fine looking and well made from soft genuine kid
leather—and they're leather quarter lined. Wide,
roomy soft toe gives soothing comfort to tired-out
feet. Good wearing leather soles. Rubber heels. From
$2.50 to $3 is the usual retail price for slippers like
these—therefore at $1.98 you are sure to save money.

Gray Felt

Men's and Women's

A Real Saving They're Only

$1⁰⁰

Leather and Felt Soles

24 G 4039—For men.
SIZES: 6 to 12. . . . . . $1.00
24 G 4036—For women.
SIZES: 3 to 8 . . . . $1.00
No half sizes. State size
wanted. Shipping weight, 1
pound 4 ounces.
Slippers that give excellent
wear, warmth and comfort, at
an extremely low price. One of
the leading values in our slipper
selection for men and women.
Soft, durable gray felt with a
checkered gray felt collar.
Leather outsole and thick felt
middle sole. Low rubber heels.
Make a fine holiday gift for
mother or father.

These Have Soft Cushion Soles

$1¹⁵

Soft and Light for Tender Feet

24 G 3918—Tan leather $1.15
24 G 3919—Black leather 1.15
SIZES: 6 to 12. No half sizes. State size wanted.
Shipping weight, 1 pound 4 ounces.
We believe they're the softest, easiest House Slippers you can buy at this low price. Pliable, durable
leather uppers are warm fleece lined. Padded cushion leather soles are soft and flexible—best for tired,
tender feet. Slip your feet into a pair and experience
the joy of real house slipper comfort.

Dependable Luggage
Ready for Any Trip

Hand Sewed Frame

$11.25

Leather Lining

Full Grain Cowhide

A stylish Bag for men or women—you will take real pride in its ownership. Its good quality is quickly apparent. Built to keep its original shape and neat appearance throughout hard usage. A roomy bag for week end trips or for one who travels constantly. Of heavy genuine top grain cowhide backed by heavy duck. Soft sheepskin lining with three pockets. Hand sewed, English style frame. Reinforced sewed corners. Brassed lock with key and lift fasteners. Heavy reinforcements in bottom and lower part of sides. Studs on bottom.

Size 18 by 10 inches. Shipping weight, 12 pounds.
447 G 820—Black.
447 G 822—Brown. Each............$11.25
Size 20 by 11 inches. Shipping weight, 13 pounds.
447 G 821—Black.
447 G 823—Brown. Each............$11.75

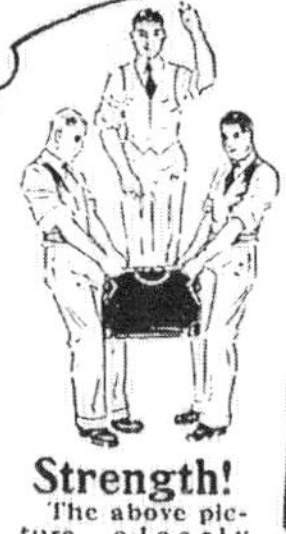

Strength!
The above picture clearly shows the strength of this Bag. We tested it in our own laboratory and found it would support a 145-pound man.

ONE of the greatest values ever offered anywhere. Built to stand the hard knocks it will receive when you travel on trains, in automobiles and taxicabs. Of fine quality, strong, smooth grain cowhide—not split. Securely riveted to frame and lined with soft tan sheepskin leather, with pockets on each side. Brassed key lock and catches; corners reinforced with cowhide, sewed on. Has eight brassed studs on bottom. Shipping weight, each, 11 pounds.

COLORS: Brown or black.
State color wanted.

Top Grain Cowhide

$7.50

Leather Lined

The Oxford Traveling Bag

447 G 870—Size 8¾ by 16 by 10 inches high........ $7.50
447 G 871—Size 9¾ by 18 by 12½ inches high........ 8.00
447 G 872—Size 10 by 20 by 12½ inches high........ 8.65

Same as above except of good quality black or brown heavy split cowhide with imitation leather lining. Will give very satisfactory service. Shipping weight, 11 pounds. State color wanted.
447 G 863—Size 9¾ by 18 by 12½ inches.................$4.98
447 G 864—Size 10 by 20 by 12½ inches................. 5.50

Individual Pockets

Genuine Cowhide

$13.85

Richly Embossed Bag

Quality through and through—a Bag you will be proud to own. Built to keep its shape throughout long, hard usage. Its selected top grain cowhide leather backed with heavy canvas has a rich hoarded (embossed) finish in black or brown. The inside arrangement is the delight of the traveler with its separate pockets for shaving soap, brushes and other articles. On the opposite side are three other larger pockets for shirts, stationery and other articles that should be protected from rumpling. Lined with strong plaid cloth and has sturdy double leather handles. Extra heavy solid brass hardware and flat key lock.

Size 18 by 10 inches. Shipping weight, 12 pounds.
447 G 828—Black.
447 G 830—Brown. Each.............$13.85
Size 20 by 11 inches. Shipping weight, 13 pounds.
447 G 829—Black.
447 G 831—Brown. Each............. $14.65

Genuine Walrus or Shark Grained Seal

Leather Lining

$18.95

Our Finest Traveling Bag

Will stand years of hard usage and still keep its original neat appearance. Almost impossible to wear out. Nicely lined with pigskin grained leather and has three neat inside gusseted pockets for carrying toilet articles, etc. Double leather handles securely stitched on. Heavy blued steel flat key lock and fasteners. Corners reinforced with body leather, sewed on. Handstitched to strong English frame and backed with heavy canvas. Brown only.
Size 18 by 10½ inches. Shipping weight, 13 pounds.
447 G 836—Genuine walrus.
447 G 838—Shark grained seal. Each...... $18.95
Size 20 by 11½ inches. Shipping weight, 14 pounds.
447 G 837—Genuine walrus.
447 G 839—Shark grained seal. Each..... $19.95

Strongly Made

Genuine Cowhide

$10.25

A strictly first quality Bag. We believe you cannot buy a bag that will give any more travel wear at anywhere near our price. Note its strength and sturdy construction. We know you will be delighted with this value. Full leather handle securely fastened on. Of genuine full grain cowhide, mahogany color, backed with heavy duck securely riveted to a strong steel frame. Heavy cowhide straps around outside give it added strength. Has brassed key lock and lift catches.
447 G 850—Size 18 by 9½ inches. Ship. wt., 12 pounds..$10.25
447 G 851—Size 20 by 10 inches. Ship. wt., 13 pounds.... 11.25

Good Grade Cowhide

$6.75

Of smooth finish split cowhide, lined with pig-grained imitation leather. Sewed English frame and interlining of heavy duck. Leather corners and leather handle. Brassed lock and lift-up fasteners. Three inside pockets.
Size 18 by 9½ inches. Shipping weight, 12 pounds.
447 G 844—Black.
447 G 846—Brown.
Each..................$6.75
Size 20 by 10 inches. Shipping weight, 13 pounds.
447 G 845—Black.
447 G 847—Brown.
Each.................. $7.25

Walrus Grained Cowhide

$3.25

A very low priced Traveling Bag and a remarkable value. Of black split cowhide—grained to resemble walrus, and riveted to a strong steel frame. Has brassed key lock and two lift catches. Strong handle. Lined with pig-grained (imitation) leather. Lining has two double pockets. Shipping weight, 9 lbs.
447 G 860—Black only.

Size 16 by 8½ inches..... $3.25
447 G 861—Black only.
Size 18 by 10 inches........ 3.65
447 G 862—Black only.
Size 20 by 10 inches........ 4.15

Cobra Grained Cowhide

$2.98

If you are looking for an inexpensive Traveling Bag that you can depend upon for good service, we recommend this one of cobra grained split cowhide. Most stores ask from $4.50 to $5.50 for the very same quality. Leather is riveted to a strong steel frame. Sewed leather corners. Brassed key lock, catches and bottom studs. Strong leather handle. Has keratol lining with double pocket. Shipping weight, 9 pounds.
447 G 808—Black only.

Size 18 by 9½ inches..... $2.98
447 G 809—Black only.
Size 20 by 10 inches..... $3.45

Cowhide Brief Cases

$5.95

Extra Heavy Fine Quality Leather

Especially designed for salesmen, business and professional people. May be used to carry papers, music, books and other similar articles. Of extra heavy grain cowhide, genuine walrus or shark grained seal. Has leather straps all around; gold-plated extension lock with name plate; leather partitions and three roomy pockets. Case is firmly sewed with lock stitching throughout. We are confident you will not be able to duplicate this same high quality elsewhere at our low prices. Size 16 by 11½ inches. Shipping weight, 4 pounds.
COLORS: Black or mahogany.
State color wanted.
47 G 498—Cowhide..................$5.95
47 G 496—Genuine walrus........... 8.25
47 G 497—Fine quality shark grained seal........................... 9.25

New Style Bag
Boar Grain Leather

$6.98

Here is the latest in Traveling Bags. Of new boar grain (embossed) leather that will give very good service. Besides being splendid for wear it is very neat—full cut and roomy. Leather is sewed to a heavy steel frame insuring a good, strong, substantial bag. Reinforced leather corners sewed on. Lined inside with plaid cloth and has three inside pockets. Has extra heavy brassed key lock and lift catches. Brassed studs on bottom give added protection. Leather handle securely fastened on.
Size 18 by 10½ inches. Shipping weight, 10 pounds.
447 G 865—Black.
447 G 866—Olive. Each...$6.98

Two Pockets

Serviceable quality, split cowhide or genuine top grain cowhide. Case has two pockets with dividing partition of leather. Nickeled key lock and buckles. Securely stitched. Size 10 by 15 inches. Shipping weight, 3 lbs. 8 oz.
COLORS: Black or brown. State color wanted.
47 G 500—
Split cowhide.......$2.75
47 G 502—
Top grain cowhide. 3.50

One Pocket

Case is securely stitched throughout. Nickeled key lock and two short straps with nickeled buckles. Has one pocket. Size 10 by 15 inches. Ship. wt., 2 pounds 8 oz. COLORS: Black or brown. State color wanted.
47 G 526—Split cowhide.... $1.85
47 G 527—Top grain cowhide...... 2.95

Two or Three Pockets

Has nickeled extension key lock. Securely stitched. 'Straps' all around. Size 16 by 11½ inches. Shipping weight, 3 pounds. COLORS: Black or brown. State color wanted.
47 G 521—Split cowhide with two pockets.... $2.98
47 G 499—Top grain cowhide with three pockets.... $4.35

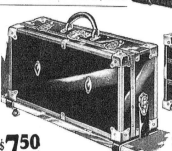

$7.50

Running Board Suitcase

Very convenient. Easy to put on and to remove. Clamps to the running board by two thumb-screws —no holes to bore. Of basswood covered with heavy enameled sheet metal; edges bound with sheet steel angles. Inside of lid has a composition dust-proof rubber collar. Has steel brassed bumpers, draw bolts and key lock. Size 15½ by 6¼ by 30 inches. Ship. weight, 23 pounds.
447 G 685—Dark blue only................... $7.50
447 G 686—Cover for above suitcase. Of black Cobra grained water-proof Fabrikoid . $2.00

$4.85

Metal Auto Suitcase

A sturdy Metal Suitcase, especially designed for automobile travel or may be used on camping trips and for general knock-about use. Of heavy basswood covered with strong enameled sheet metal; metal runners on top and bottom; heavy brassed key lock and draw bolts. Case has leather handle on top and also handle on one end for easy carrying. Size 16½ by 6¼ by 28 inches. Shipping weight, 21 pounds.
447 G 760—Black with maroon trimmings only...... $4.85

Men's Practical Gifts in Leather

3-Piece Gift Set

Name in 22-Karat Gold

A choice Gift Set. Excellent quality calfskin and furnished with a neat gift box. Billfold 4¾ by 3 inches folded, has one large pocket for bills, transparent cover for identification card and two small pockets. Key case, 3¾ by 2¼ inches, to match, has six swivel key hooks. Cigarette case, 3¼ by 3½ inches, is of same design with hand-laced edges. State name or initials and emblem wanted. Ship. wt., 12 oz.

547 G 1605—Brown calfskin. Per set........$5.75
547 G 1604—Same as above, except not hand-laced. Per set........3.50

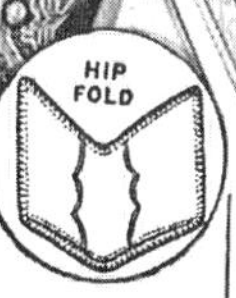

Genuine Calfskin Gift Set

Name in 22-Karat Gold

A very neat Billfold and Keycase Set in handsome box. Billfold 3 by 4⅞ inches folded, has one large pocket, one transparent section for identification card and two small pockets. Keycase 2¼ by 3¾ inches folded, has six swivel hooks. Brown calfskin with design and hand-laced edges or black pin seal with gold corners but without design and laced edges. State name or initials and emblem wanted. Shipping weight, 10 ounces.

547 G 1600—Brown calfskin. Hand-laced edges. Per set......$4.25
547 G 1601—Plain black. Pin seal, gold corners. Per set......3.25

Same as above, except with hipfold instead of regular three-fold type. See small picture above.

547 G 1607—Brown calfskin. Hand-laced edges. Per set......$4.50
547 G 1608—Plain black. Pin seal, gold corners. Per set......3.50

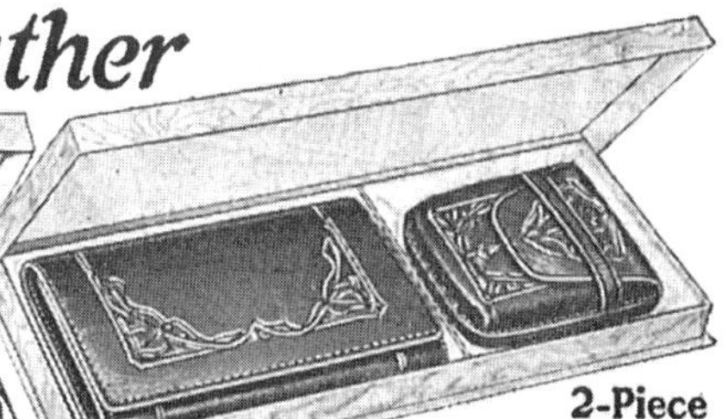

2-Piece Gift Set

Name in 22-Karat Gold

For the man who smokes—at a price far below that usually asked elsewhere. A regular $3.50 value. Billfold 4⅞ by 3 inches folded; has one large pocket, one transparent section and two small, miscellaneous pockets. Cigarette Case 3½ by 2¾ inches, to match. Sewed edges. State name or initials and emblem wanted. Shipping weight, 10 ounces.

547 G 1611—Brown calfskin. Per set........$2.75
547 G 1610—Black sheepskin. Per set........1.65
547 G 1612—Tan steerhide. Per set........4.25

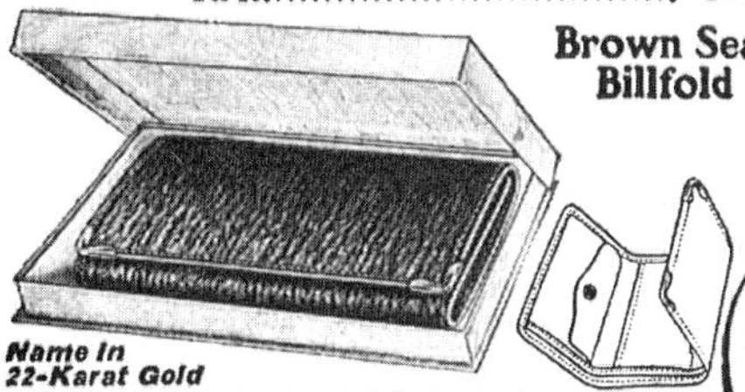

Brown Seal Billfold

Name in 22-Karat Gold

Genuine shark grain seal that will give excellent wear. Edges of fold ornamented by gold corners. Large pocket for bills, pocket for identification card or photo, and two small pockets. Size, folded, 3 by 4¾ inches. State name or initials and emblem wanted. Shipping weight, 8 ounces

547 G 1642—Brown. Each........$2.75
547 G 1643—Brown. Hand-laced edges, without gold corners. Each........3.00

~free~ Your Name or Initials and Emblem in Gold!

Where stated in the description of each article, we will imprint in 22-Karat gold leaf, in suitable size, without extra charge, any name or initials; also any emblem here shown. State emblem wanted. Print name or initials plainly in this manner: R. E. BEDFORD

SHRINE · MASONIC · ELKS · ODDFELLOW · MODERN WOODMEN · W.O.W. · WOODMEN OF THE WORLD · L.F.&E. · REDMEN · MOOSE · MACCABEE · K.C. · EAGLES · AMERICAN LEGION · YEOMEN · K.P. · RAILROAD MEN

Name in 22-Karat Gold

Big Value Set

Billfold 3 by 4¾ inches folded; has one large pocket for bills, two small card pockets and one window for identification or pass cards. Keycase 2¼ by 3¾ inches, is of same design and has six key hooks. State name or initials and emblem wanted. Shipping weight, 10 ounces.

COLORS: Black or brown. State color wanted.

547 G 1675—Sheepskin. Per set........$ .98
547 G 1677—Calfskin. Per set........1.89

Our Finest

Extra quality Billfold. Hand-laced edges. Size folded, 4¾ by 3 inches. State name or initials and emblem wanted. Shipping weight, 3 ounces.

547 G 1639—Brown calfskin........$1.98
547 G 1637—Tan steerhide........2.25
547 G 1638—Black morocco........2.50
547 G 1636—Tan pigskin........2.50

Genuine Black Pin Seal With Gold Corners

An attractive Billfold of genuine black pin seal—excellent for wear. Has one large pocket for bills, two small pockets for cards and one transparent section for passes, identification card, or photo. Gold corners. Size folded, 2¾ by 4½ inches. State name or initials and emblem wanted. Shipping weight, 3 ounces.

547 G 1687........85¢

A Handy Billfold

Contains all the toilet articles you would ordinarily have to carry loose in your pocket. Cobra grained sheepskin with embossed design. Holds mirror, comb, nail file, cuticle stick and has large pocket for bills. Size, 4¼ by 2¾ inches when folded. State name or initials and emblem wanted. Ship. wt., each, 4 oz.

547 G 1640—Black only........$1.00

Collectors' Billfold

A durable Case for carrying legal and other important documents. Of excellent quality cowhide. Size, 10½ by 4¾ inches. State name, initials and emblem wanted. Shipping weight, 12 ounces.

547 G 1649—Black. Three large and two small pockets........$1.45
547 G 1650—Black. Five large and four small pockets........1.95

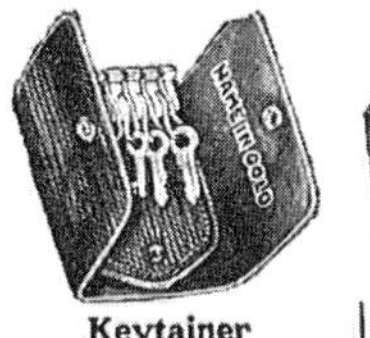

Keytainer

Has six key hooks that will accommodate twelve keys. Size, 3¼ by 2¼ inches. State name or initials and emblem wanted. Shipping weight, 3 ounces.

547 G 1645—Black sheepskin...43¢
547 G 1646—Black calfskin.....65¢
547 G 1647—Brown suede calf..85¢

Low Priced

Calfskin Billfold

Has one long pocket for bills, one transparent pocket for identification card and two small ones for cards. Size folded, 4¾ by 2¾ inches. State name or initials and emblem wanted. Ship. wt., 3 oz.

547 G 1633—Brown.......89¢
547 G 1634—Black.......89¢

Very Popular Billfold

Handy for carrying identification cards, etc. Has one large pocket for bills, a pocket with a flap for cards and room for four identification cards. Size folded, 3 by 4¾ inches. State name or initials and emblem wanted. Shipping weight, 3 ounces.

547 G 1690—Black sheepskin.....$1.15
547 G 1691—Brown calfskin......1.95

Combination Coin Purse and Billfold

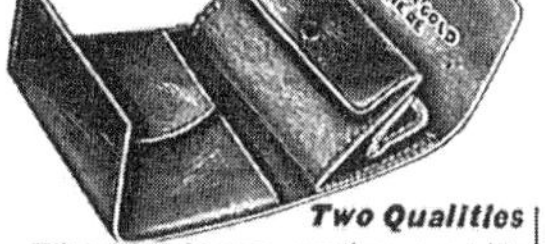

Two Qualities

Why take chances carrying your bills and change loose in your pocket when you can buy this Purse at such small cost? Has coin pocket with metal frame and spring catch. Two small pockets, bill roll. Snap button lock. Size, folded, 3½ by 2¾ inches. State name or initials and emblem wanted. Ship. wt., 3 ounces.

547 G 1652—Black sheepskin........$ .79
547 G 1653—Brown cordovan 1.39

New Style Billfold

A very popular two-fold style—far below the usual retail price. Very thin. Has one large pocket for bills, one pocket for cards, etc. Lined inside with very soft, pliable leather. Size, 4 by 4½ inches. State name or initials and emblem wanted. Shipping weight, 3 ounces.

547 G 1685—Black only. Morocco embossed sheepskin.....$1.39
547 G 1686—Genuine morocco...1.75

Money Belt

Campers, hunters and travelers carry your money in safety. With three pockets 3¼ inches wide. Center pocket is 8½ inches long and 2 end compartments are 3¼ inches long. Flaps fold tightly over pockets. Belt adjustable to any size waist. Shipping weight, each, 2 ounces.

47 G 1670—Tan goatskin..$1.10
47 G 1671—Gray suede calfskin........1.35

See Also Page 418

Cigarette Case

Keeps your cigarettes from being crushed. An exceptional value. Size, 3¼ by 2¼ inches. State name or initials and emblem wanted. Shipping weight, 3 ounces.

547 G 1668—Mahogany color 65¢
547 G 1669—Black morocco..98¢

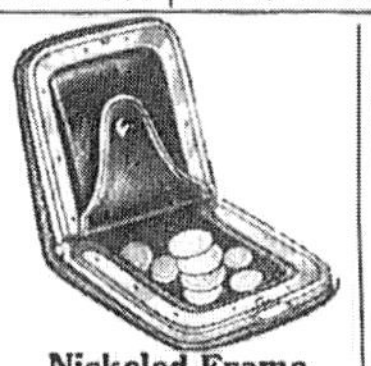

Nickeled Frame

Will make an excellent gift for dad or brother. Size folded, 3 by 3 inches. Shipping weight, 3 ounces.

47 G 1655—Smooth black sheepskin........39¢
47 G 1656—Brown calfskin..79¢

Button Snap Coin Purse

An all leather Coin Purse for a remarkably low price. Sewed edges Two pockets. Size, 3½ by 3 inches. Shipping weight, 3 ounces.

47 G 1663—Brown calfskin $.89
47 G 1664—Tan pigskin. 1.25

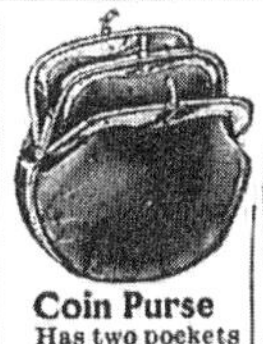

Coin Purse

Has two pockets and spring snap. Size, 3 by 3½ inches. Shipping weight, 3 ounces.

47 G 1658—Brown sheepskin..29¢
47 G 1659—Brown cowhide....42¢

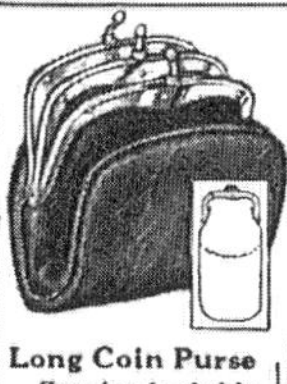

Long Coin Purse

Genuine buckskin. Long style. Has two compartments; nickeled frame and spring snaps. Size, 3¾ by 5¾ inches. Shipping weight, 3 ounces.

47 G 1661—Brown only.33¢

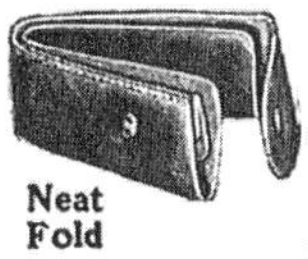

Neat Fold

This type of Billfold is very popular because of its small size. May be carried in any pocket. Has sewed edges and button snap. Size, folded, 1⅝ by 4 inches. Ship. weight, 2 ounces.

47 G 1679—Black sheepskin 29¢
47 G 1680—Brown calfskin. 55¢

Soft Collar and Necktie Case

A great traveling convenience. Keeps collars and ties from being mussed. A big value at our low price. Made of black rhino embossed leather. Moire lined. Size 4½ by 10½ inches. State name or initials and emblem wanted. Shipping weight, 12 ounces.

547 G 1614—Black only...$1.85

Gifts for the Man Who Travels

$3.50

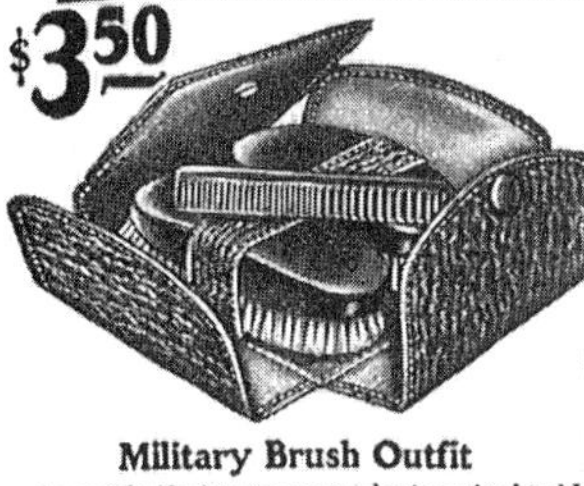

Military Brush Outfit

An outfit that every man who travels should own. Will make an excellent gift or present. May be had in two qualities—shark grain cowhide lined with smooth leather or cobra grain fabrikoid lined with pig grain (imitation) leather. The edges are neatly bound. Contains two military brushes and hard rubber comb. Size, about 5¼ by 1¾ by 5½ inches. Shipping weight, 1 pound 4 ounces.

COLORS: Black or brown. State color.

47 G 1455—Shark grain cowhide........$3.50
47 G 1456—Fabrikoid........2.75

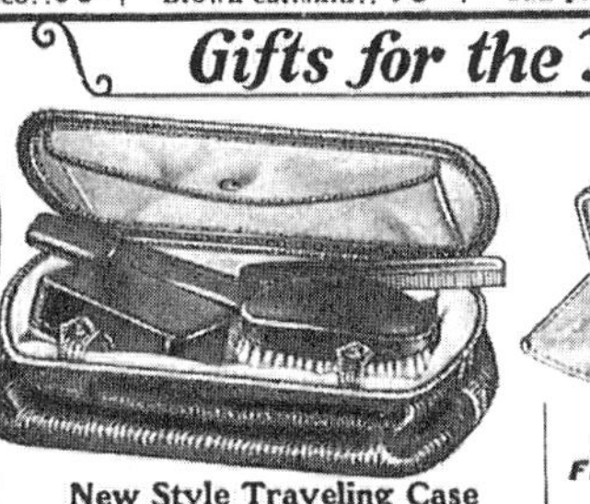

New Style Traveling Case

Can be used by both men and women. Holds bulky cold cream jars and bottles which cannot be carried loose. Of Dupont fabrikoid with sanitary washable rubber lining. Fitted with military brush, soap box, tooth brush box and comb. Size, about 5¼ by 2¾ by 10 inches. Shipping weight, 1¾ pounds.

COLORS: Black or brown. State color wanted.

47 G 1451—Complete........$3.95
47 G 1450—Case only........2.75

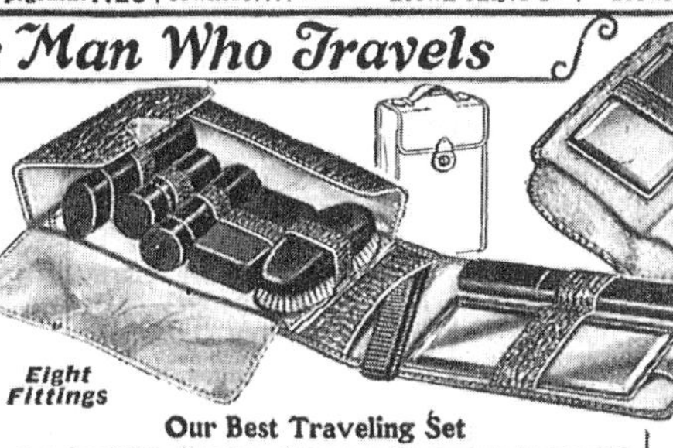

Eight Fittings

Our Best Traveling Set

Our finest Traveling Set. Of best quality shark grained cowhide lined with smooth leather. Nickel key lock. Its camera shape is of the latest design and will fit easily into any traveling bag or suitcase. Neat handle on top of case gives it a very attractive appearance. Set has eight inside fittings consisting of genuine ebony back military brush, mirror, comb, clothes brush, tooth paste tube, tooth brush tube, shaving soap box and soap box. Fittings of excellent quality. Size, about 6 by 2 by 9¼ in. Ship. wt., 2 lbs.

COLORS: Black or brown. State color wanted.

47 G 1454—Complete........$7.95

$6.25

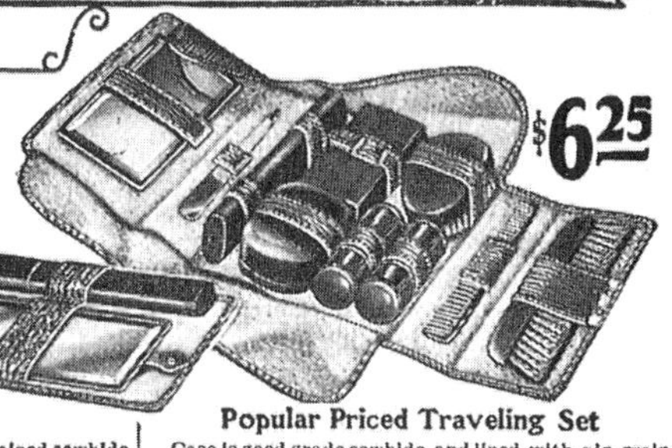

Popular Priced Traveling Set

Case is good grade cowhide and lined with pig grain (imitation) leather. Has nickel-plated key lock. Inside fittings consist of military brush, clothes brush, tooth brush holder, comb, mirror, nail file, shaving soap tube, soap box and safety razor box. Size, about 6½ by 1¾ by 8¼ inches.

COLORS: Brown or black. State color wanted. Shipping weight, 2¼ pounds.

47 G 1452—Cobra grained cowhide...$6.25
47 G 1453—Dupont Fabrikoid........4.95

Fine Heavy Weight Blazers

Fine Quality 28-Oz. All Wool — $6.95

The best you can get is always the least expensive in the long run. Measure this fine Blazer by this standard and you will be enthusiastic over your choice for a long time to come. It's a garment a man will always be proud to wear.

Its heavy weight 28-ounce All Wool mackinaw cloth will give you extraordinary wear — and comfort enough on coldest days.

Made by one of the country's leading blazer manufacturers. Neat notched collar, smart slash pockets with buttons, All Wool worsted knit bottom and adjustable cuffs. Choose from two handsome plaids such as you are sure to see wherever smart young fellows gather.

EVEN SIZES: Chest 34 to 46 inches. State chest measure. Read "How to Measure" on Page 238. Ship. wt., 3 lbs. 10 oz.
42 G 6407—Red, brown, blue and green plaid.
42 G 6409—Blue, tan, brown and gray plaid.
Each.................$6.95

Style—Service 28-Oz. All Wool — $5.95

You won't mind going out on frosty mornings when you have one of these heavy warm Blazers. It has established record sales during the past year because it so satisfactorily combines attractiveness, warmth and long wear. Heavy weight 28-ounce All Wool mackinaw cloth in beautiful patterns. Large convertible collar to button close around neck when the thermometer registers zero. Fancy All Wool worsted knit bottom. Two-button adjustable cuffs and two large patch pockets with buttoned-down flaps.

EVEN SIZES: Chest 34 to 46 inches. State chest measure. Read "How to Measure" on Page 238. Shipping weight, 3 lbs. 3 oz.
42 G 6419—Orange and gray plaid.
42 G 6421—Blue and brown plaid.
Each..............$5.95

Leather Trimmed 24-Oz. All Wool — $7.50

It's different! A beautiful plaid Blazer with dressy glove leather trimming on collar, pocket flaps and cuffs. That means extra service as well as extra style. The leather is a rich chocolate brown. The Blazer material is a handsome jacquard weave plaid in a combination of pleasing colors. Fancy All Wool worsted knit bottom. The heavy 24-ounce All Wool mackinaw cloth assures splendid warmth.

EVEN SIZES: Chest 34 to 46 inches. State chest measure. Read "How to Measure" on Page 238. Shipping weight, 2 lbs. 12 oz.
42 G 6415—Wine, brown, purple, and olive jacquard plaid.........$7.50

24-Oz. All Wool — A Special Value — $4.98

Even at this our lowest price you are assured a very desirable Blazer. For we never skimp or sacrifice on quality to offer a special price. Of 24-ounce All Wool mackinaw cloth. All wool worsted knit bottom. Convertible, notch style collar buttons closely around neck. Adjustable cuffs and generous sized patch pockets with buttoned-down flaps.

EVEN SIZES: Chest 34 to 46 inches. State chest measure. Read "How to Measure" on Page 238. Shipping weight, 3 lbs. 2 oz.
42 G 6413—Olive and gray with black and brown overplaid.$4.98

24-Ounce All Wool — Serviceable—Low Priced — $5.35

Think of all you get here for only $5.35. All Wool Blazers of the very finest 24-ounce mackinaw cloth. Made according to the same rigid specifications that we insist on for all our garments from highest price to lowest. Will stand a surprising amount of service for either sports or general wear. Style features usually found only on higher priced garments. Popular sports collar which is convertible. Has two outside patch pockets with buttoned-down flaps. All Wool worsted knitted bottom. You'll say it's out of the ordinary in value, considering its low price. We'll guarantee this big value to measure up to your expectations. If it doesn't, return it and get all your money back.

EVEN SIZES: Chest 34 to 46 inches. State chest measure. Read "How to Measure" on Page 238. Shipping weight, 3 lbs.
42 G 6423—Orange and black plaid.
42 G 6425—Wine and black plaid.
Each....................$5.35

Jack Frost — A New Garment 30-Oz. All Wool — $5.39

New! A Coat that's different than any utility garment ever offered. It pleasingly combines the most desirable features of the stag shirt and best liked points of the popular blazer. We gave it the Jack Frost label because it's such a fine value in a warm garment for winter wear. Made of 30-ounce All Wool mackinaw cloth and is 30 inches long. This preferred length plus its heavy weight makes it a desirable garment for work or general wear. Has a wide convertible collar that can be turned up to protect the ears from bitter winds and cold. Two generous sized pockets with flaps. You'll say, when you wear it, that you never expected so much genuine warmth and such all round comfort for the price.

EVEN SIZES: Chest 34 to 46 inches. State chest measure. Read "How to Measure" on Page 238. Shipping weight, 4 lbs. 4 oz.
42 G 6433—Blue and black plaid only...$5.39

Newest Sports Coat All Wool Plaid — $7.95

Every inch a champion. Bringing to you the very latest in Sports Coats. Created through demand for a general all round utility garment. You will like its comfortable fit the moment you slip into it. You will appreciate the warmth of the 30-ounce All Wool mackinaw cloth. The smart plaid is the most strikingly handsome pattern we ever offered. Note also that it has the popular notched collar. Four patch pockets with buttoned-down flaps. A half belt in back. 30 inches long—the approved length for general use or sports wear.

EVEN SIZES: Chest 34 to 46 inches. State chest measure. Read "How to Measure" on Page 238. Shipping weight, 4 lbs. 4 oz.
42 G 6569—Light gray with blue and red overplaid.........$7.95

The Nation's Most Popular Mackinaw — $9.75

Men—here's style that instantly "catches the eye" of all who see it. Stylish notch collar, popular all-around belt, two muff and two lower pockets with flaps and choice of two beautiful plaids make this Mackinaw an outstanding garment. Don't think that style's the principal feature,—we've kept in mind that men who wear this type of coat expect lots of warmth from it; so we have used All Wool heavy 34-ounce mackinaw cloth. Length, 35 inches. And besides all these features this garment is well made throughout to give extraordinary service.

EVEN SIZES: Chest 36 to 48 inches. State chest measure. Read "How to Measure" on Page 238. Shipping weight, 5 lbs. 6 oz.
42 G 6583—Blue, olive and maroon plaid.
42 G 6587—Brown, gray, maroon and green plaid. Each.....$9.75

Big Mackinaws for Sure Warmth!

$11⁴⁵ Leather Trimmed

Extra Heavy All Wool Mackinaw Overcoat

$12⁶⁵

Wear this Mackinaw Overcoat and experience the double satisfaction of warmth and dressiness. It's extra length for a coat of this kind—42 inches—protects your upper legs and gives it the appearance of an overcoat. Preferred by men everywhere because it outwears the usual overcoat and costs much less. You will admire its splendid construction of 38-ounce extra heavy All Wool Melton cloth. A very fashionable dark blue mixture. Its large shawl collar fits snugly about the neck, and affords protection to face and ears. Two muff pockets in which to keep your hands warm. Also two lower pockets with flaps. Tabs on sleeves. Double breasted style with half belt in back.

EVEN SIZES: Chest 36 to 46 inches. State chest measure wanted. Read "How to Measure" on Page 238. Ship. wt., 8 lbs. 12 oz.
42 G 6595— Dark blue mixture only. **$12.65**

$4⁹⁸

$12³⁹

Heavy All Wool-38-Ounce

One of our finest, warmest Mackinaws. When winter gets down to business in earnest you'll appreciate the heavy weight, long wearing, 38-ounce material—All Wool and closely woven. Finest workmanship throughout. Big shawl collar protects face and ears. Neat looking, double-breasted style. Cuffs on sleeves and all-around belt. Two lower patch pockets with flaps. One breast pocket with button-down flap. Length, 38 inches.
EVEN SIZES: Chest 36 to 46 inches. State chest measure. Read "How to Measure" on Page 238. Ship.wt., 7 lbs. 10 oz.
42 G 6579— Dark heather brown only....**$12.39**

Heavy Weight All Wool

Another fine quality Mackinaw of heavy weight 38-ounce All Wool with the added features of leather trimmed pockets. This prevents pocket edges from fraying—a great advantage to delivery men, railroad men, in fact anyone giving exceptional wear to their pockets. Two desirable colors, dark heather brown or dark Oxford gray. Convenient 38-inch length. Large shawl collar. Half belt in back. Double breasted style.
EVEN SIZES: Chest 36 to 48 inches. State chest measure. Read "How to Measure," on Page 238. Ship. weight, 8 lbs.
42 G 6593— Dark heather brown only......**$11.45**
42 G 6597—Oxford gray. Each............11.45

Warm, Sturdy Coat At a Low Price →

Here's the Coat for the man who wants a mackinaw but does not use a coat of this type enough to justify his buying a higher priced garment. Although our lowest priced—it's really an exceptional value. Made of 30-ounce material, about 30 per cent wool. Double breasted with all-around belt and neat shawl collar. Has tabs on sleeves. Two patch pockets with flaps.
EVEN SIZES: Chest 36 to 48 inches. State chest measure. Read "How to Measure" on Page 238. Ship. wt., 5 lbs.
42 G 6545— Dark brown plaid only.......**$4.98**

$5⁹⁵ Each Garment

$6⁹⁸

$2⁶⁹

Genuine Snugger Vest

The small amount of $2.69 never bought more solid comfort than you'll get from this Snugger Vest. After enjoying the protection of this closely knitted garment you'll wonder how it's possible to buy it at our remarkably low price. Wear it under your coat for added warmth in cold weather or without a coat in milder weather.

The closely knit double and twist cotton fabric has a heavy warm fleece lining of all wool. The vest clings to the shape of your body, shielding you from wind and cold. Closes with six snap fasteners. Has four pockets.

You can't possibly be fully aware of its welcome comfort until you wear one. You'll say it's the best protection against chest colds that you've ever had.

EVEN SIZES: Chest 36 to 48 inches. State chest measure. Read "How to Measure" on Page 238. Shipping weight, 14 ounces.
42 G 6473—Dark gray only..**$2.69**

All Wool Vests At a Very Low Price **$2⁴⁹**

Here's quality at a low price. In cutting the cloth for our all wool Overcoats pieces remain that we utilize in making these serviceable double breasted Vests. Furthermore, we make these garments in our own factory, eliminating the manufacturer's usual profit. The result is you can buy these warm, 30-ounce All Wool Mackinaw cloth vests at an exceptionally low price. Extra high neck; four patch pockets. Wear it on cool fall days to break the chill, and in winter to keep out cold winds. Men who spend considerable time outdoors get the utmost comfort from these garments. Those of you who are not familiar with the comfort of these vests should take the opportunity to get one while the price is so low.
EVEN SIZES: Chest 36 to 48 inches. State chest measure. Read "How to Measure" on Page 238. Shipping weight, 1 pound.
42 G 6429—Dark colors only. **$2.49**

Heavy Weight All Wool Suit

Extra warmth and extra wear in this All Wool Suit; stag shirt with either trousers or breeches, whichever you prefer. All sold separately. Worn extensively by hunters, loggers and others who spend a great deal of time outdoors. Made of 34-ounce all wool frieze material; has great strength and is more closely woven than ordinary mackinaw cloth. Stag shirt has regular shirt style collar. Trousers have straight bottoms. Breeches .ave laced bottoms.
State measure wanted. Read "How to Measure" on Page 238.
42 G 6453—Stag Shirt. Dark gray only. SIZES: Neck 15 16, 17, 18 inches. Shipping weight, 4 pounds 2 ounces...................**$5.95**
42 G 6443—Trousers. Dark gray only. SIZES: Waist 30, 32, 34, 36, 38, 40, 42, 44, 46, 48 in. Inseam 30, 32, 34 in. Ship. wt., 4 lbs. 2 oz....**$5.95**
42 G 6437—Breeches. Dark gray only. SIZES: Waist 30 32, 34, 36, 38, 40, 42, 44, 46, 48 inches. Inseam 24, 26, 28 inches. Shipping weight, 3 pounds 4 ounces.......................**$5.95**

Here's Value, Men! Heavy 32-Ounce Melton

Winter comfort is built into every feature of this moderately priced Mackinaw. It's one of our best sellers and you will say when you see it that it certainly is a remarkable value. We looked at hundreds of swatches, bargained with dozens of mill representatives before we made our choice. The result is this remarkably low price.

It's a firmly woven 32-ounce Melton cloth, about 85 per cent wool, that will give more service than you'd think possible at this low price. A shawl collar that will outwit the harshest winds. All-around belt and double breasted style. Coat is 34 inches long.

EVEN SIZES: Chest 36, 38, 40, 42, 44, 46 inches. State chest measure wanted. Read "How to Measure" on Page 238. Shipping weight, 4 pounds 2 ounces.
42 G 6553—Dark brown only......**$6.98**

61

Finer Qualities · Greater Values

Genuine Horsehide
Remarkable Value
In 27 or 30-Inch Lengths

$9⁸⁵

Ward's has arranged to offer you a positively remarkable value in this practical garment. To give you a genuine horsehide leather Coat of dependable quality at such a low price is certainly a wonderful achievement.

You'll say it's certainly worth a lot more than our low price. But we had to give the manufacturer a tremendous order to secure this big saving for you. We used the best wearing clothing leather it was possible to obtain. We lined the coat with good quality part wool Melton cloth, 25 per cent wool and the balance cotton for extra strength.

The collar is also horsehide leather and faced on the back with a fine thickset corduroy. Two-button adjustable cuffs lined with Melton cloth, sleeves unlined. Ventilation eyelets under arms. Two lower pockets with special turned leather edge double stitched for extra strength. Adjustable tab on each side of back. Made in lengths 27 inches and 30 inches: choose whichever best fits your requirements. Order a pair of HIKE-N-WORK horsehide breeches to complete your outfit.
SIZES: Chest 36, 38, 40, 42, 44, 46, 48 inches. State chest measure wanted. Read "How to Measure" on Page 238. Shipping weight, 5 pounds 2 ounces.
42 G 6932—
27-inch length coat..........$ 9.85
42 G 6934—
30-inch length coat.......... 10.85

Mr. J. H. Davis, Buyer of Leather Coats:
"The U. S. Bureau of Standards, after tests made of samples of horsehides sent them, advise that: 'These tests show side leather (horse fronts) to be approximately five times as strong and resistant to tearing as the butt leather.'"
E. H. HARVEY, Ward's Laboratory Chief.

Thickset Corduroy
Leather Lined

$7⁸⁵

Work outdoors in coldest weather and never mind the wind. With this thickset corduroy Vest about your body you can keep out winter blasts that would otherwise chill you through. Sleeves of unlined sheepskin glove leather, soft, pliable and easy to work in. Body lining of mahogany colored sheepskin leather matches sleeves. Ventilation eyelets under armpits. Worsted knit wristlets; collar of the same warm material. It's 25 inches long—the popular length for wear under other garments.
SIZES: Chest 36, 38, 40, 42, 44, 46, 48 inches. State chest measure wanted. Read "How to Measure" on Page 238. Ship. wt., 3 lbs. 2 oz.
42 G 6813—Drab brown....$7.85

Extra Warmth on Coldest Days

$4⁷⁹

You men who work outdoors and find Vest sleeves in your way, can't choose a more suitable garment than this. Sheepskin lining throughout to insure plenty of warmth all around the body. The lining comes to very edge of vest at one side covering entire chest. The outside is strong moleskin cloth for hard knockabout use. You'd never expect so much quality at this low price. It is 23 inches long—popular for wear under a suit or overcoat.

SIZES: Chest 36, 38, 40, 42, 44, 46, 48 inches. State chest measure wanted. Read "How to Measure" on Page 238. Shipping weight, 2 pounds 12 ounces.
42 G 6905—Drab brown only.$4.79

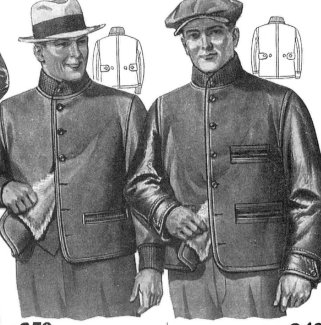

Fine Black Horsehide Sheepskin Lined

$16⁵⁰

Men, if you've never had a garment of black horsehide leather, you have overlooked the best wearing material ever put into work clothes. This horsehide coat style Vest has soft sheepskin lining throughout the body, a combination for wear and cold weather protection to suit most any need. Sleeves lined with black twill cloth. Coat style collar, also of horsehide leather. Two-button adjustable cuffs and inside knit wristlets. Two-piece adjustable back belt. Two lower and one breast pocket. Average length, 28 in.
SIZES: Chest 36, 38, 40, 42, 44, 46, 48 inches. State chest measure wanted. Read "How to Measure" on Page 238. Shipping weight, 8 pounds 2 ounces.
42 G 6908—Black horsehide (horse fronts) leather..........$16.50

Our Most Popular Horsehide Coat
Leather Lapels

$14⁹⁵

Our very finest!—and most popular Leather Coat. And no wonder. A better coat of this type would be difficult to find. The leather is genuine front quarter horsehide—there's nothing better for wear. The body lining is 22-ounce wool Melton cloth, 80 per cent wool, the most successful material known for lining work coats of this sort. We lined the sleeves with black twill cloth to prevent the leather from discoloring your shirt sleeves or underwear.
Collar and also the lapel are genuine horsehide leather. Knit wristlets and adjustable cuffs fit snugly. It's the right work length, 30 inches. Ventilation eyelets under each arm. Two muff pockets; two deep lower pockets with protecting flaps to button down, and an all-around belt to keep the coat snug to the body. You will be enormously pleased with the great satisfaction you get from this fine garment.
SIZES: Chest 36, 38, 40, 42, 44, 46, 48 inches. State chest measure wanted. Read "How to Measure" on Page 238. Shipping weight, 6 pounds 2 ounces.
42 G 6929—Black horsehide (horse fronts) leather..........$14.95

The Choice of Thousands of Men

$6⁷⁹

Men who must be outdoors in coldest weather say this garment is a wonder for comfort. Of stout moleskin, popular for its resistance to hard use and soil. For extreme protection the body is lined with sheepskin, extending to extreme edge on one side and sleeves with blanket cloth—no wonder it has been for years our most popular Vest. It's cut full with plenty of room for action. Collar and wristlets are wool knit material. Pockets have protection of corduroy beading on edge for extra wear. Adjustable tab and buttons on each side of back. Average length, 25 in.
SIZES: Chest 36, 38, 40, 42, 44, 46, 48 inches. State chest measure wanted. Read "How to Measure" on Page 238. Shipping weight, 4 pounds 2 ounces.
42 G 6909—Drab brown only. $6.79

Strong Moleskin Leather Sleeves

$9⁴⁹

Another wind-proof and cold-proof garment that is necessary to the outdoor man's equipment. To this sheep-lined Vest of tough long wearing moleskin cloth we've added the popular leather sleeves; unlined. They're of black sheepskin glove leather, pliable and easy to work in. Adjustable cuffs of the same material are lined with soft suede cloth. Sheepskin lining to very edge at one side of Vest safe-guards you against chest colds. Warm, worsted knit collar. Tabs and buttons on each side of back. Three pockets with leather trimmed edges. Average length, 25 inches.
SIZES: Chest 36, 38, 40, 42, 44, 46, 48 inches. State chest measure wanted. Read "How to Measure" on Page 238. Shipping weight, 4 pounds 10 oz.
42 G 6903—Drab brown only. $9.49

Nothing Better *for* HIKE-N-WORK

$5⁸⁵ Our Finest Moleskin

Our very best moleskin Breeches. Treated by a special process, they are shower-proof and no stains remain after drying. Leather patch reinforcements at knees. Double moleskin reinforcement on seat. Crotch and seat seams double sewed and taped. Two hip pockets with tabs and buttons. Button bottoms. State waist and inseam measurements. See size scale below. Shipping weight, 2 pounds 4 ounces.
42 G 5189—Spruce green (dark olive) only. **$5.85**

Horsehide Leather $9⁹⁵

You'll certainly receive full value from these wonderfully strong horsehide leather Breeches. They'll stand the hardest, longest kind of wear. Genuine front quarter horsehide leather—the most sturdy material used in outdoor work clothing. Wear them with one of our popular leather coats. Then you will be equipped with a suit that for long wear simply can't be out-classed. Entirely lined with strong khaki twill cloth. Two front, two hip and one watch pocket. Lace bottom style.
State waist and inseam measurements. See size scale below. Ship. wt., 4 lbs. 10 oz.
42 G 5158—Black leather only. **$9.95**

Leather Trimmed $5⁹⁸ Corduroy

Narrow ribbed, fine quality corduroy—the kind that's famous for long wear. Knee reinforcement patches of black horsehide leather. Strain points bar-tacked for added strength. Usual pockets, belt loops, and suspender buttons. Wear them with our fine corduroy or horsehide sheep-lined coats. Button bottoms.
State waist and inseam measurements. See size scale below. Shipping weight, 2 pounds 4 ounces.
42 G 5154—Brown.
42 G 5156—Blue...... **$5.98**

$2⁷⁹ Whipcord Sports Cloth

More popular every season. Snappy looking Oxford gray—will wear way beyond your expectations. You can't easily snag them. Medium-weight cloth. Strain points bar-tacked. Suspender buttons and belt loops. Lace bottom style.
State waist and inseam measurements. See size scale below. Shipping weight, 1 pound 12 ounces.
42 G 5183— Oxford gray only. **$2.79**

Bedford Cord $3⁶⁹ for Wear

If you have an eye for appearance as well as for wear, you will be well pleased with Bedford cloth. Makes a fine garment for sports wear or touring. Reinforcement patches on seat and knees. Suspender buttons; also belt loops. Button bottom style.
State waist and inseam measurements. See size scale below. Shipping weight, 2 pounds.
42 G 5181— Light olive only. **$3.69**

How to Order Breeches

Refer to the size chart to find the inseam lengths we furnish for a man of your waist measure. Then measure your leg in the manner shown in illustration to find which one of the lengths given in size chart best meets your requirements.

Be sure to state waist and inseam measure, also height and weight.

This Chart Shows Length of Inside Leg Seam Made in Each Waist Size										
Waist, Inches.	28	29	30	31	32	33	34	36	38	40	42
Inseam, Inches.	22–24	23–25	24–26	24–26	25–27	25–27	24–26–28	24–26–28	24–26–28	25–27	25–27

$2⁹⁸ Our Wonder Value Corduroy Breeches

The most popular Breeches we ever offered. And no wonder! Fine, thickset corduroy, shower-proofed, strongly constructed—and sold at a price that makes them one of the greatest values in the world. We buy thousands—that's the reason. Double reinforcement patches at knees where breeches usually first show wear. Seat and crotch seams double sewed and taped. Inner waistband and pockets of dyed drill to match corduroy. Belt loops; suspender buttons. Laced bottoms.
State waist and inseam measurements. See size scale at right. Shipping weight, 2 pounds 14 ounces.
42 G 5175— Drab brown only. **$2.98**

Sturdy Moleskin Unusual Bargain $2⁴⁸

An example of the remarkable values we offer in every moleskin garment. We are one of the largest users of moleskin cloth in the world. These Breeches are of good quality cloth and will give long satisfactory wear. Double seat extends to lower parts of legs—a feature desired especially by men who ride a great deal. Double stitched seams at seat and crotch. Bottom of fly, side pockets and belt loops bar-tacked. Laced bottoms.
State waist and inseam measurements. See size scale above. Shipping weight, 2 pounds 4 ounces.
42 G 5187—Drab brown only. **$2.48**

Long Wearing Whipcord Suit

Sportsmen—here's the Suit you'll find mighty practical for hunting, camping, touring. It's of pre-shrunk whipcord cloth, a material that resists snagging. The special finish makes it so attractive looking that many men prefer to have the three pieces—breeches and coat for wear about the camp, coat and trousers for wear on trips to town. Coat lined with sturdy khaki twill and has four handy pockets. We've reinforced the breeches where they get hardest use—at knees and seat. Popular button bottom trousers are strengthened in seat with double stitched seams. Strain points bar-tacked. Usual pockets, belt loops and suspender buttons on breeches and trousers.
State chest, waist and inseam measurements; also height and weight.
Coat SIZES: Chest 36, 38, 40, 42, 44 inches. Shipping weight, 4 pounds.
42 G 5831—Medium brown only.................. **$8.95**
Breeches: See size scale above. Shipping weight, 1 pound 14 ounces.
42 G 5231—Medium brown only................... **$4.75**
Trousers SIZES: Waist 30, 32, 34, 36, 38, 40, 42 inches. Inseam 29 to 34 inches. Shipping weight, 1 pound 12 ounces.
42 G 5233—Medium brown only................ **$3.85**

Finest Quality Moleskin Suit

There's no better cloth for a suit that must withstand rough wear than this excellent moleskin. And when it's made up in a three piece garment so well constructed as this—it is an ideal Work Suit. You get double the wear in the occasions change from breeches to trousers. Coat is Norfolk plaited style lined with good quality sateen. Breeches have double reinforcement at knees and bar-tacking at strain points. Usual pockets, belt loops, suspender buttons. Inner waistband and pocket material of pearl twill cloth. All strain points are bar-tacked. Trousers are strongly made throughout.
State chest, waist and inseam measurements; also height and weight.
Coat SIZES: Chest 36, 38, 40, 42, 44 inches. Shipping weight, 3 pounds 8 ounces.
42 G 5811—Gray and black striped only..... **$7.75**
Breeches: See size scale above. Shipping weight, 2 pounds 8 ounces.
42 G 5250—Gray and black striped only..... **$3.25**
Trousers SIZES: Waist 30, 32, 34, 36, 38, 40, 42 inches. Inseam 29 to 34 inches. Shipping weight, 2 pounds 8 ounces.
42 G 5252—Gray and black striped only..... **$2.75**

Great Cap Values

"Here's My Feature Value"

Says the Manager of Ward's Cap Store

39 G 606—Medium brown plaid.
39 G 608—Medium gray plaid. **$1.39**

SIZES: 6¾, 6⅞, 7, 7⅛, 7¼, 7⅜, 7½, 7⅝, 7¾. State size. Read "How to Measure" on Page 248. Shipping weight, 1 pound 3 ounces.

I wanted to give our customers a Cap that would be supreme in style and faultless in finish—one that I could offer without question as the greatest value in America. Here it is! Arrangements were made with one of the leading woolen manufacturers in the country to make the cloth. Being situated right in the heart of the sheep country he had the pick of the woolens. He set his looms to produce an exclusive, wonder wearing All Wool cloth in becoming color combinations.

To have the workmanship in keeping with this fine quality I sent this material to our very best cap manufacturer to style and shape it with all the skill at his command. Satisfied with the quality and workmanship I next turned my attention to price. By close figuring of cost I am proud to offer a cap of $2 style and quality for only $1 39. It's made for winter wear, too—the warm lined inband pulls down over the ears affording cold weather protection. I've had it lined with a good grade of lining. The visor is unbreakable, of course. Remember—in style, in quality, and in value here is the fullest measure of cap satisfaction.

L. J. STRETZ,
Manager Ward's Cap Store

All Wool—Low Priced

39 G 601—Assorted colors only. **89¢**

SIZES: 6¾, 6⅞, 7, 7⅛, 7¼, 7⅜, 7½, 7⅝, 7¾. State size. Read "How to Measure" on Page 248. Shipping weight, 1 pound.

When you see this Cap you'll readily agree that it looks like a lot more than just 89¢. Made of surplus ends of All Wool suiting in assorted colors and patterns. We cannot offer any special color or pattern but we guarantee you'll be pleased with what we send. All are full lined and have sanitary lined inbands to pull over ears. Unbreakable buckram visor.

Style—Wear—Value

39 G 602—Medium gray plaid.
39 G 604—Medium brown plaid. **$1.29**

SIZES: 6¾, 6⅞, 7, 7⅛, 7¼, 7⅜, 7½, 7⅝, 7¾. State size. Read "How to Measure" on Page 248. Shipping weight, 1 pound 2 ounces.

Embodying every new fashion idea of this season. Of All Wool suitings in attractive plaid patterns. Full lined with fine sateen. Unbreakable visor. Warm lined inband to cover ears.

Our Finest Winter Cap

39 G 646—Fancy medium brown plaid.
39 G 649—Fancy medium gray plaid. **$1.98**

SIZES: 6¾, 6⅞, 7, 7⅛, 7¼, 7⅜, 7½, 7⅝, 7¾. State size. Read "How to Measure" on Page 248. Ship. wt., 1 pound.

Expertly shaped by the best Cap makers in America for smooth stylish fit. The best of everything's gone into its making—exclusive All Wool novelty top coat fabrics of suberb quality, matched satin lining. The visor is unbreakable. Lined inband protects the ears.

Extra Quality Kersey

39 G 640—Light bluish gray.
39 G 643—Tan. **$1.95**

SIZES: 6¾, 6⅞, 7, 7⅛, 7¼, 7⅜, 7½, 7⅝, 7¾. State size. Read "How to Measure" on Page 248. Shipping weight, 1 pound 3 ounces.

Just a step ahead of style with the season's new plain finished kersey Cap. It's hand shaped and blocked. Made of fine quality All Wool kersey. Full lined with satin, and has unbreakable visor. Has warm inband to pull over ears.

New All Wool Patterns

39 G 626—Light gray plaid.
39 G 630—Light brown plaid. **$1.75**

SIZES: 6¾, 6⅞, 7, 7⅛, 7¼, 7⅜, 7½, 7⅝, 7¾. State size wanted. Read "How to Measure" on Page 248. Ship. weight, 1 pound.

Smartest style and pattern. Expertly tailored of All Wool suitings, enlivened by interwoven silk threads in harmonizing colors. The lining is of silk serge. Has a fur lined inband to pull down over the ears in cold weather. Visor is unbreakable.

Extra Heavy—All Wool

39 G 617—Dark brown.
39 G 621—Dark gray. **$1.35**

SIZES: 6¾, 6⅞, 7, 7⅛, 7¼, 7⅜, 7½, 7⅝, 7¾. State size wanted. Read "How to Measure" on Page 248. Ship. wt., 1 lb. 5 oz.

For the man who desires an extra warm, extra service Cap for winter wear. Made of heavy All Wool overcoatings. Warm lined inband. Full lined with a good quality lining. Has unbreakable visor.

Fine Quality Fur Caps

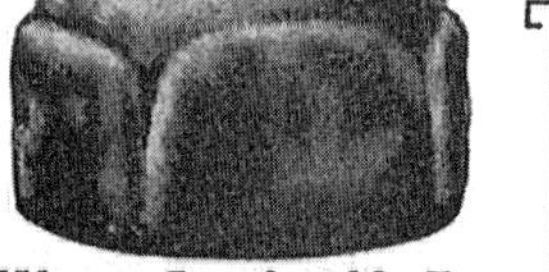

Warm, Serviceable Fur

39 G 901—Good quality coney fur. Black only................ **$2.98**
39 G 905—Fine quality coney fur. Black only.................. **3.95**
39 G 915—Select quality coney fur. Brown only................ **5.95**

SIZES: 6¾, 6⅞, 7, 7⅛, 7¼, 7⅜, 7½, 7⅝, 7¾. State size. Read "How to Measure" on Page 248. Shipping weight, 14 ounces.

Three grades, every one a superior value! All full lined. Fur is of fast dyed pelts of Belgian hare, noted for good wearing qualities. The brown cap is especially desirable because of the extra fine quality fur.

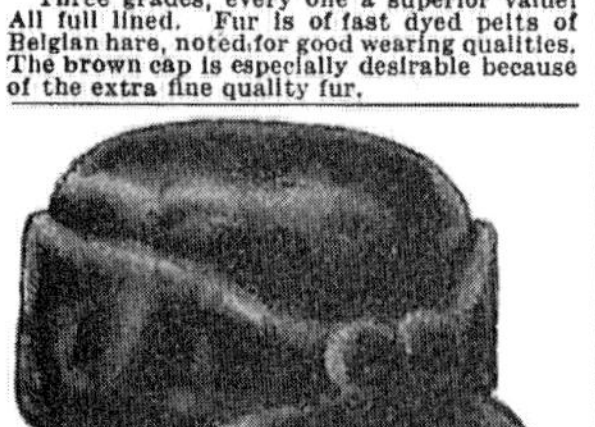

Driving Style Fur Cap

39 G 919—
Black coney fur only. **$6.45**

SIZES: 6¾, 6⅞, 7, 7⅛, 7¼, 7⅜, 7½, 7⅝, 7¾. State size. Read "How to Measure" on Page 248. Shipping weight, 14 ounces.

Men—here's exceptional value. Well shaped and built for many seasons wear. Black coney fur of especially fine quality. Full satin lined. Unbreakable visor. All-around pull-down band outside completely covers ears in wind or snowstorm. A Driving Cap of unusual merit to keep you warm in coldest weather!

Genuine Alaska Seal

39 G 921—Small pieced Alaska seal. Black only....... **$ 8.75**
39 G 929—Good quality large pieced Alaska Seal........ **11.85**
39 G 925—Extra fine select Alaska seal. Black only....... **15.95**

SIZES 6¾, 6⅞, 7, 7⅛, 7¼, 7⅜, 7½, 7⅝, 7¾. State size. Read "How to Measure" on Page 248. Shipping weight, 14 ounces.

U. S. government Alaska seal, the finest for Fur Caps. Lined with excellent grade satin. Flaps pull down for ear protection. Choice of three unusually fine values.

Smart, Becoming Styles for Fall Wear

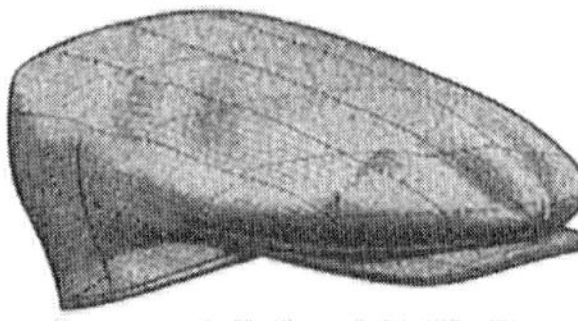

Lowest Priced Fall Cap

39 G 618—Light brown.
39 G 622—Medium gray. **$1.00**

SIZES: 6¾, 6⅞, 7, 7⅛, 7¼, 7⅜, 7½, 7⅝, 7¾. State size wanted. Read "How to Measure" on Page 248. Shipping weight, 14 ounces.

A striking example of the tremendous values we are offering in low priced men's Caps for Fall wear. The tailoring, style, colors—they all further emphasize the tremendous buying power of your clothing dollar at Ward's. Made of high-grade All Wool suitings. Has a genuine leather sweatband in front. No inband.

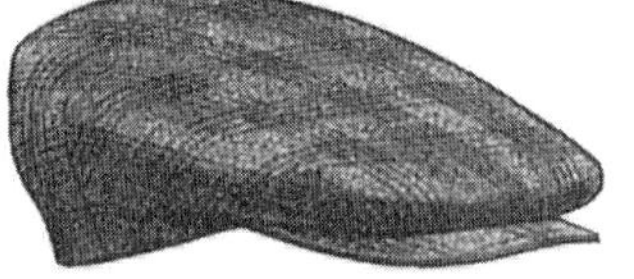

Latest Plaid Patterns

39 G 624—Medium brown.
39 G 632—Medium gray. **$1.49**

SIZES: 6¾, 6⅞, 7, 7⅛, 7¼, 7⅜, 7½, 7⅝, 7¾. State size wanted. Read "How to Measure" on Page 248. Shipping weight, 14 ounces.

You won't find more all round goodness and quality in a Cap at this price anywhere. Has the snappy style, perfect fit and sturdy quality young fellows are demanding today. One-piece top and is full satin lined. Has all-around genuine leather sweatband. No inband.

New College Style

39 G 662—Fancy gray plaid.
39 G 663—Fancy blue and gray plaid.
39 G 664—Fancy tan plaid. **$2.25**

SIZES: 6¾, 6⅞, 7, 7⅛, 7¼, 7⅜, 7½, 7⅝, 7¾. State size wanted. Read "How to Measure" on Page 248. Ship. weight, 1 pound.

With its new slightly smaller shape and peppy patterns—it's the king of the campus. Eight quarter style top. Hand shaped and full satin lined. Full leather sweatband; unbreakable visor of new water-proof cork. No inband.

Beautiful New Patterns

39 G 654—Fancy tan plaid.
39 G 656—Fancy bluish gray. **$1.85**

SIZES: 6¾, 6⅞, 7, 7⅛, 7¼, 7⅜, 7½, 7⅝, 7¾. State size. Shipping weight, 1 pound.

Has the snappy style discriminating dressers prefer. The pleasing weave with the plaid effect is truly beautiful. It's of sturdy All Wool suitings, full satin lined—has an unbreakable visor. is hand shaped and has a genuine full leather sweatband in front. No inband.

Smart—Adjustable Cap

39 G 650—
Medium brown plaid.
39 G 651—
Bluish gray plaid. **$1.69**

SIZES: To fit any head from 6¾ to 7½. Shipping weight, 1 pound.

We're selling more of these adjustable Caps every year. Many men prefer them to most any other type because they are so easily made to fit the head. Simply adjust the buckle to the proper size. The leather sweatband keeps the head comfortable. Only All Wool suiting material with the season's newest cross weave plaids are used. Unbreakable visor. Full satin lined.

It's Here, Fellows, the Latest

Popular Style

39 G 658—
Fancy brown.
39 G 660—
Fancy gray. **$2.00**

SIZES: 6¾, 6⅞, 7, 7⅛, 7¼, 7⅜, 7½, 7⅝, 7¾. State size. Read "How to Measure" on Page 248. Ship. wt., 1 lb.

It's a handsome All Wool pattern in a novelty twist weave. Hand blocked and shaped. Full satin lined. Unbreakable visor; genuine leather sweatband all around. Made by a manufacturer who produces caps renowned for smartness in style and fabrics. No inband.

Warm, Durable Work Caps

Best $1 Cap Anywhere $1.00

39 G 733—Tan only.
SIZES: 6¾, 6⅞, 7, 7⅛, 7¼, 7⅜, 7½, 7⅝, 7¾. State size. Read "How to Measure" on Page 248. Shipping weight, 1 pound 6 ounces.

One dollar never bought more quality or more wear than we have put into this phenomenal cap. Made of an exceptionally fine corduroy with a fur lined inside band to cover the ears in cold weather. The tie top is of double thickness all around—pull it down over the ears and under the chin for double cold protection. Full lined with soft chamois cloth.

"Engineer" Style 89¢

39 G 731—Melton. Dark blue.
39 G 732—Corduroy. Dark brown.
SIZES: 6¾, 6⅞, 7, 7⅛, 7¼, 7⅜, 7½, 7⅝, 7¾. State size. Read "How to Measure" on Page 248. Ship. wt., 1 lb. 3 oz.

Our price is so convincingly low that thousands will order this warm, serviceable engineers' cap for general wear. Choice of two heavy superior quality materials. Finest workmanship throughout. Cotton flannel lined. Outside slide band to cover the ears. Unbreakable visor.

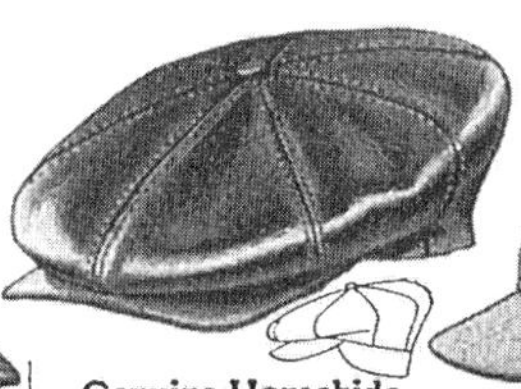

Genuine Horsehide $1.75

39 G 721—Black.
39 G 723—Brown.
SIZES: 6¾, 6⅞, 7, 7⅛, 7¼, 7⅜, 7½, 7⅝, 7¾. State size. Read "How to Measure" on Page 248. Ship. wt., 1 lb. 6 oz.

Here it is at last, Men! A genuine horsehide Cap—it's absolutely the strongest, longest wearing cap ever offered. Only the softest, most pliable and longest wearing skins were used. Full lined. Warm inband.

Water Repellent 79¢

39 G 703—Drab only.
SIZES: 6¾, 6⅞, 7, 7⅛, 7¼, 7⅜, 7½, 7⅝, 7¾. State size. Read "How to Measure" on Page 248. Shipping weight, 1 pound 3 ounces.

Without reserve we can truthfully state that this is the biggest money's worth of cap value ever offered for only 79¢. They're shower-proof too. Turn down the top over the ears and under the chin for cold weather protection. Sturdily constructed of warm heavy weight, good quality duck. Has a double fabric in the tie top and outside band. Full lined with flannelette. Unbreakable visor.

Genuine Horsehide $1.75

39 G 711—Black horsehide.
39 G 715—Brown horsehide.
SIZES: 6¾, 6⅞, 7, 7⅛, 7¼, 7⅜, 7½, 7⅝, 7¾. State size. Shipping weight, 1 pound 6 ounces.

The finest Judge style Cap ever offered. It's made of genuine horsehide—known everywhere for its toughness—strength and soft pliability of the skins. You can't tear it—nor can you wear it out. Caps of similar style sell elsewhere for a trifle less—but they are made of thin sciver leather. Warm sanitary lined inband. The visor is unbreakable. Full flannel lined.

Corduroy Hat $1.49

539 G 717—Light tan only.
SIZES: 6¾, 6⅞, 7, 7⅛, 7¼, 7⅜, 7½, 7⅝, 7¾. State size. Read "How to Measure" on Page 248. Shipping weight, 1 pound 8 ounces.

Last year we sold this hat for $1.79—the lowest price in America. Now we offer a still better hat at $1.49. Of double strength corduroy with warm lined inside band to cover ears. Full lined crown.

All Wool Judge Shape $1.49

39 G 741—Dark gray.
39 G 745—Dark brown.
SIZES: 6¾, 6⅞, 7, 7⅛, 7¼, 7⅜, 7½, 7⅝, 7¾. State size. Read "How to Measure" on Page 248. Shipping weight, 1 pound 3 ounces.

Although our price is amazingly low for an All Wool melton cloth Cap the quality and workmanship are of the best. Hand blocked. The unbreakable visor is of good grade canvas. Lined with cotton twilled serge. Has an inside band lined with fur.

Genuine Scotch Cap $1.00

39 G 729—Navy blue only.
SIZES: 6¾, 6⅞, 7, 7⅛, 7¼, 7⅜, 7½, 7⅝, 7¾. State size. Read "How to Measure" on Page 248. Shipping weight, 3 pounds 4 ounces.

"They're the most comfortable cold weather Caps I ever wore! Keep on making them." So writes William T. Styles of Palos Park, Ill. That's one of the reasons that we sell thousands of dozens of these genuine Scotch caps every year. This season we priced the cap lower than ever to break all records. Our customers demand the original and genuine Scotch cap because it's the only one giving absolute satisfaction in wear and warm comfort. Full lined. Inside band to cover ears.

Exceptional Value 89¢

39 G 705—Light tan corduroy.
39 G 707—Drab duck.
SIZES: 6¾, 6⅞, 7, 7⅛, 7¼, 7⅜, 7½, 7⅝, 7¾. State size. Shipping weight, 1 pound 4 ounces.

Here are two Judge shape Caps of remarkable quality at an unusually low price. One is fine grade narrow wale corduroy; the other a heavy water-repellent duck. Both are full lined and have leather visors. Have fur lined inbands.

Water-Proofed $1.55

39 G 727—Drab khaki only.
SIZES: 6¾, 6⅞, 7, 7⅛, 7¼, 7⅜, 7½, 7⅝, 7¾. State size. Read "How to Measure" on Page 248. Shipping weight, 1 pound 5 ounces.

Strong, finely twilled khaki, with cemented interlining. Construction of the best—seams taped and double stitched on the inside. Flannel lined for added warmth. In cold weather you'll be mighty glad to use the fur lined inband.

Silk Plush Fine Quality $1.79

39 G 753—Black plush only.
SIZES: 6¾, 6⅞, 7, 7⅛, 7¼, 7⅜, 7½, 7⅝, 7¾. State size. Read "How to Measure" on Page 248. Shipping weight, 1 pound 6 ounces.

The fine material, strong visor and sturdy lining of this dressy Judge shape Cap cannot be equalled at our low price. Made of a rich, heavy All Silk black plush. Unbreakable visor. It's hand blocked and full lined with black sateen. Warmly lined inside ear band.

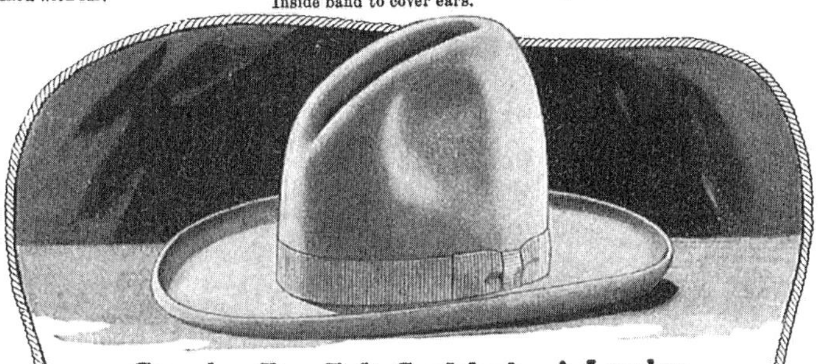

Genuine Fur Felt Carlsbad—A Leader $3.95

539 G 546—Black. 539 G 547—Dark brown. 539 G 548—Light tan.
SIZES: 6½, 6⅝, 6¾, 6⅞, 7, 7⅛, 7¼, 7⅜, 7½, 7⅝, 7¾. State size wanted. Read "How to Measure" on Page 248. Shipping weight, 3 pounds 4 ounces.

Before you buy your new Carlsbad investigate this famous value. There's a story about it that you should know. This great hat is a hobby, a special pride of our hat buyer. Every season he puts special effort behind it to improve the quality—to give you more and more for your money. He is a western man, has worn Carlsbads himself and knows what western men want. He has made this the best Carlsbad ever offered at the price. Thousands buy it. And no wonder. For real wearing quality and good looks there's nothing better sold at the price. Of good quality, smooth finished fur felt, it's carefully made and styled. The crown is 7 inches high and the brim 4 inches wide.

All Wool Black Melton $1.39

39 G 749—Black melton only.
SIZES: 6¾, 6⅞, 7, 7⅛, 7¼, 7⅜, 7½, 7⅝, 7¾. State size. Read "How to Measure" on Page 248. Shipping weight, 1 pound 3 ounces.

At first glance this Cap shows its superiority, and after months of hard use in all kinds of weather its real quality proves its worth. That's when you'll be glad you bought this cap. Made of a rich looking, All Wool black melton. Hand blocked. Full lined with a black twill. Unbreakable visor. Inband warmly lined.

Popular Wool Felt Carlsbad $1.98

539 G 515—Light tan.
539 G 517—Dark brown.
SIZES: 6¾, 6⅞, 7, 7⅛, 7¼, 7⅜, 7½, 7⅝. State size Read "How to Measure" on Page 248. Shipping weight, 3 pounds.

The quality of the wool felt is surprisingly good. Has genuine leather sweatband. Crown is 7 inches high; brim 4 inches wide.

Practical Work Hat—Wool Felt $1.45

539 G 587—Black. 539 G 589—Olive drab.
SIZES: 6¾, 6⅞, 7, 7⅛, 7¼, 7⅜, 7½, 7⅝. State size. Read "How to Measure" on Page 248. Shipping weight, 2 pounds 2 ounces.

Customers often tell us that their fathers bought the same hat—ordered it from us year after year. To make old friends like that and keep them is proof enough for anybody of the honest value offered. You may be sure we are careful to keep the quality right. The wool felt is a good grade, strong and unusually serviceable. Crown is 6 inches high; brim 3 inches wide.

The Dakota—Fine Fur Felt $3.95

539 G 501—Black.
539 G 505—Light tan.
SIZES: 6¾, 6⅞, 7, 7⅛, 7¼, 7⅜, 7½, 7⅝, 7¾. State size. Read "How to Measure" on Page 248. Ship. wt., 2 lbs. 10 oz.

There's a steadily increasing number of men sending to Ward's every year for the Dakota—because they have satisfied themselves that a better value can't be found. It's a fine, smooth finished fur felt with a broad stiff brim. Crown is 5¾ inches high and the brim 3½ inches wide.

Values That Won Us Leadership

One of Our Finest Overalls
Extra Heavy 8-Ounce White Back Denim

$1.19

From coast to coast this garment of time-proved quality and time-proved value is an old established friend of thousands. When men whose experience with Overalls covers many years and the wearing out of dozens of pairs—when these men say they're the best they ever wore for the price—then you have an endorsement to be depended upon.

"Best overalls I ever wore"—"Worth double your price"—"Couldn't duplicate the value anywhere"—"Has stood up under the hardest wear." Such expressions as these show what our customers think of them.

Only the highest quality extra heavy weight 8-ounce indigo blue, white back denim is used—the most durable and most popular overall material known. All seams are triple stitched and guaranteed against ripping—all pockets double sewed and bar-tacked. Two leg seams in the overalls for comfortable hang and fit. Self faced waist band for added wear. Every part of the garment that receives extra wear is strengthened. Details which might be considered small to the average man were given the most careful attention.

Jacket is three-seam style and has self faced cuffs. Four big pockets, one a combination for watch and pencil. In the overalls there are seven generous pockets—two front, two hip, one match or watch pocket in right front pocket, plier or rule pocket, and a combination pocket for watch and pencil on the bib. On the left side there's a hammer loop. The low back style has detachable suspenders with elastic inserts. The high back overalls are continuous—not sewed on. They are also made double thickness just the same as the low back suspenders—they won't twist.

If you can duplicate such fine quality, such fine workmanship at the price we ask—return the garments at our expense. As fair an offer as anyone could ask for.

EVEN SIZES: Chest 36, 38, 40, 42, 44, 46 inches. Waist 30, 32, 34, 36, 38, 40, 42, 44 inches. Inseam 30, 32, 34, 36 inches. State chest, waist and inseam measure. Read "How to Measure" on Page 238. Ship. wt., 2 pounds 2 ounces.

Jacket
42 G 6146—Indigo blue only............$1.19

Overalls
42 G 6150—Low Back. Indigo blue only.
42 G 6152—High Back. Indigo blue only.
Each...............$1.19

Low Back   High Back

$1.55 Double Seat Double Knees

Overalls for men whose work is unusually rough and hard on clothes. Double front patch extending below each knee and a double seat makes them give double duty service. Strong 2:20 white back blue denim, famous for its long wear. Extra service construction in three of the pockets, too—the lower half of the two hip and the plier pocket have double thickness of white back denim. There are three other pockets—a combination watch and pencil pocket on bib and two front pockets. Also has hammer loop on left leg. Continuous high back style cut right with pattern of overalls. All seams triple stitched to stand heaviest strain. Side gussets, all pockets and bottom of fly securely bar-tacked.
EVEN SIZES: Waist 30, 32, 34, 36, 38, 40, 42, 44 inches. Inseam 30, 32, 34, 36 inches. State waist and inseam measure wanted. Read "How to Measure" on Page 238. Shipping weight, 1 pound 12 ounces.
42 G 6156—Blue only......$1.55

$1.25 Riveted Overalls For Men and Youths

Six months ago we introduced these now famous riveted Overalls. Men everywhere quickly appreciated the ruggedness of these garments, built of strong, wear-resisting 8-ounce white back blue denim. They were pleased with the extra strength at bottom of fly, pockets and back strap, all of which are reinforced with copper rivets instead of the usual thread bar tacks. All seams are triple stitched with orange colored thread. Yoke back; strap and buckle. Two front and two hip pockets, also pocket in right front pocket, for watch or matches.
State waist and inseam measures. Read "How to Measure" on Page 238. Shipping weight, 2 pounds 12 ounces.

Youths' Sizes
42 G 6160—Waist, 26, 28, 30 inches. Inseam 26, 28, 30, 32 inches. Blue only............$1.15

Men's Sizes
42 G 6162—Waist 32, 34, 36, 38, 40, 42, inches. Inseam 30, 32, 34, 36 inches. Blue only.........$1.25

$1.95 Handy Allovers A Great Value

Sturdier, better quality than you could possibly get for this price anywhere. Fly front, extending from neck to bottom of fly, covers all front buttons, leaving no buttons exposed to catch in machinery. Unusually well constructed. Shirt band collar has two button extension tab. Back is three-seam style, legs two-seam style for better fit. All seams triple stitched. Has combination watch and pencil pocket, and pocket with button down flap on breast. Two front pockets, two hip and rule or plier pockets, also hammer loop. All pockets bar-tacked. Your choice of three of these sturdy materials. Any one you choose is a great value.
EVEN SIZES: Chest 36 to 46 inches. Inseam 30 (short), 32 (medium), 34 (long) inches. State chest and inseam measure. Read "How to Measure" on Page 238. Ship. wt., each. 2 lbs. 4 oz.
42 G 6193—Hickory stripe.
42 G 6194—Drab khaki twill.
42 G 6197—Blue white back denim. Each.............$1.95

$1.35 Genuine Stifel's Drill

This sturdy material is known for its long wearing quality. The pattern is Wabash stripe. Has a neat white stripe on blue background. Jacket is three-seam style with four patch pockets—one for watch and pencil. Shirt band collar with extension tab. Two-seam apron style low back overalls. Wide detachable suspenders with elastic inserts. Five pockets: Two front, two hip and one on bib for watch and pencil; also a rule or plier pocket. Side gussets, bottom of fly and all pockets bar-tacked. All seams triple stitched.
EVEN SIZES: Chest 36 to 46 in. Waist 30 to 44 in. Inseam 30 to 36 in. State measure wanted. Read "How to Measure" on Page 238. Shipping weight, 1 pound 4 ounces.
42 G 6188—Jacket. Blue with white stripe.
42 G 6192—Overalls. Blue with white stripe. Each....$1.35

STRONG! ~ Great Values, Too

46¢

59¢ 3 to 8 Years

69¢ 3 to 8 Years

77¢ 3 to 8 Years — A Garment

"Read My Story of Il Denim Superiority!"

Mothers, this is such important news about our boys' all denim "Pioneer" Overalls that I want to tell it to you myself. I've made them entirely of 2:20 white back blue denim, which I know will stand the hard use lively youngsters give it. I've even made the front pockets entirely of this same heavy weight denim. At the price they're the best overalls made for boys. I've sent the manufacturer strict instructions to make them exactly like our men's 2:20 denim overalls—just as roomy, just as comfortable, but in boys' sizes. Overalls have continuous high back suspenders which are one piece, (not sewed on as many others are). In the jacket I've put three pockets, one on breast for watch and pencil and two lower pockets. I put a combination pencil and watch pocket on bib; two hip; and the two in front of 2:20 white back denim in the overalls. They're all bar-tacked. All seams triple stitched. Mothers, this message is my wholehearted recommendation for these boys' sturdy overalls. I know you'll like them.

L. J. STRETZ, Manager Boys' Overalls Dept.

State size wanted. Read "How to Measure" on Page 252. Shipping weight, 1 pound 2 ounces.

42 G 6072—Jacket. Blue only.......77¢
SIZES: 3 to 8 years.................77¢
9 to 15 years.................87¢
42 G 6068—Overalls. Blue only.....77¢
SIZES: 3 to 8 years.................77¢
9 to 15 years.................87¢

Boys' Pioneer 2:20 White Back Blue Denim

A Great Bargain
It's been many years since we've been able to offer an Overall value as big as this. Nowhere else is it duplicated. Medium weight double and twist denim. Inseams triple stitched. Two front pockets and one hip are bar-tacked. The mothers of romping youngsters should buy several pairs at this low price.
SIZES: 3 to 8 years. State size wanted. Read "How to Measure" on Page 252. Ship. wt., 12 oz.
42 G 6008—Blue only...... **46¢**

New Hickory Cloth
New! Extra strong, wears long, washes especially well—that's Hickory stripe! Closely woven, medium weight—the tough fabric that son needs for the hard use he gives Overalls. Three pockets—two front, one hip. Fly and pockets bar-tacked. Inseams triple stitched. Mothers who are good judges of quality recognize here an unmatched value at our low price.
State size wanted. Read "How to Measure" on Page 252. Shipping weight, 12 ounces.
42 G 6002—Hickory stripe (blue and white) only.
SIZES: 3 to 8 years......... **59¢**
SIZES: 9 to 15 years.... **69¢**

Double Knees
Double thickness of denim at knees where boys give Overalls the hardest wear. Made of extra strong, medium weight double and twist denim. Well fitting two-seam style. Leg, bib and back seams triple stitched. Has two front pockets, two hip and one on bib for watch. Fly and pockets bar-tacked.
State size wanted. Read "How to Measure" on Page 252. Shipping weight, 14 ounces.
42 G 6060—Blue only.
SIZES: 3 to 8 years......... **69¢**
SIZES: 9 to 15 years......... **79¢**

Good Quality! High Back Style
Extraordinary Value! A quality not duplicated elsewhere at our low price. Overalls and Jackets of extra strong medium weight double and twist denim. The overalls are continuous high back style, a feature rarely found in garments at this price. Five pockets—two hip, two front and one on bib. The jacket has three large size pockets. Triple stitched seams. Pockets bar-tacked.
State size wanted. Read "How to Measure" on Page 252. Shipping weight, 14 ounces.
42 G 6064—Jacket. Blue only.
SIZES: 3 to 8 years... **62¢**
9 to 15 years... **72¢**
42 G 6066—Overalls. Blue only.
SIZES: 3 to 8 years... **62¢**
9 to 15 years... **72¢**

83¢ A Garment

88¢ A Garment — All Pockets Denim

Youths' Pioneer 2:20 White Back Blue Denim

Jacket **93¢** Overalls **$1.07**

$1.59 A Garment

Youths! Here's Value
Our youths' lowest price garments, but a big value! To prove what an unusual bargain in youths' Overalls is offered here we quote the letter of Mrs. John Borky of Ardmore, So. Dak., who says, "We could not purchase overalls of same quality here for less than double the amount." Made of medium weight extra strong double and twist denim. Pockets and fly bar-tacked. Seams of both overalls and jacket are triple stitched. Overalls have five pockets, one on bib for watch, two front and two hip. Jacket has three, one for watch on left breast and two lower pockets.
SIZES: Chest, 26 to 34 inches; waist, 26 to 31 inches; inseam, 26 to 32 inches. State chest, waist and inseam measure. Read "How to Measure" on Page 252. Ship. wt., each garment, 1 pound.
42 G 6078—Jacket. Blue only..... **83¢**
42 G 6082—Overalls. Blue only. ...**83¢**

Superior Value Famous the Country Over
Young fellows never wore more practical, sturdier Overalls! We know these "Pioneers" are the best value for the money and believe there are no better youths' overalls made. Entire garment, including pockets is entirely of 2:20 white back blue denim. Construction especially strong—just like that of our famous "Pioneers" for men. Continuous high back suspenders; cut right with pattern of garment. Seams triple stitched; pockets bar-tacked. Jacket has four pockets. Overalls have five, one on bib for watch and pencil—two front made of 2:20 white back denim and two hip.
State chest, waist and overall inseam measure. Read "How to Measure" on Page 252. Ship. weight, each garment, 1 pound 2 ounces.
42 G 6084—Jacket. EVEN SIZES: Chest, 26 to 34 inches. Blue only.
42 G 6086—Overalls. Waist, 26 to 31 inches. Inseam, 26 to 32 inches. Blue only.
Each garment. **88¢**

Double Seat—Double Knees
For double wear and extra service! One of our best values in Overalls and Jackets for youths! DOUBLE KNEES and DOUBLE SEAT make them wear longer. Wear resisting heavy weight white back denim. Overalls are attached suspender style; have two front pockets, two hip, one watch and pencil pocket on bib; pliers pocket on leg. Jacket has two lower and one breast pocket. Pockets and fly bar-tacked; seams triple stitched.
SIZES: Chest, 26 to 34 inches. Waist, 26 to 31 inches. Inseam, 26 to 32 inches. State chest, waist and inseam measure. Read "How to Measure" on Page 252. Ship. wt., each garment, 1 lb. 4 oz.
42 G 6070—Jacket. Blue only.....$ .93
42 G 6074—Overalls. Blue only. 1.07

Roomy, Serviceable Allovers
Best quality Boys' Allovers on the market at this remarkably low price. Complete protection from his shoe tops to his neck. Front buttons entirely covered with fly. Choice of three strong and durable materials; sturdy khaki twill, attractive hickory stripe (blue and white), and medium weight double and twist blue denim. We made them large and roomy. They assure you of excellent quality, workmanship and long wear. Seams triple stitched for extra strength. Six pockets—two breast (one for watch and pencil), two front and two hip. Pockets and fly are bar-tacked; crotch is reinforced.
EVEN SIZES: 6 to 16 years. State size wanted. Read "How to Measure" on Page 252. Shipping weight, 1 pound 9 ounces.
42 G 6092—Hickory stripe (blue and white).
42 G 6094—Drab khaki.
42 G 6098—Blue. Each $1.59

Every Boy Should Have *These* All-Weather Clothes

24-oz. All Wool Blazer In Smart Plaid Patterns Priced for a Big Saving

Fellows, they're here at last! The newer, smarter, Collegiate type Blazers! We instructed one of the best manufacturers to make us one of the most attractive garments ever sold—and here it is!

Recognized everywhere as the standard outdoor garment of the American boy. They are worn everywhere for every purpose. There are many reasons for this popularity. They're unequaled for hunting, skating, biking, school or general dress wear. Then, too, they're warm —the heavy weight 24-ounce All Wool mackinaw cloth is of that quality that assures long service. There's nothing like a warm blazer for wear when the ground is covered with snow. Two-button adjustable cuff. The knit bottom is of All Wool worsted. The combination of contrasting colors is most pleasing—green, tan and gray plaid. You'll see blazers of similar style and quality selling elsewhere for much more.

EVEN SIZES: 8 to 18 years. State size. Read "How to Measure" on Page 252. Shipping weight, 2 pounds.
42 G 6325—Green, tan and gray plaid.............................$3.98

$7.89

Our Very Best 30-oz. All Wool Mackinaw With Sheepskin Collar

The very latest and most sensible innovation of the year! A big, burly Mackinaw with a warm sheepskin collar. You'll find it one of the most satisfactory garments you ever owned. The first time you wear it the fellows will all say, "Gee—where did you get it—it sure is a beauty!" Mothers will find our price especially economical —only by volume buying and close figuring of cost could we manage to offer such an attractive value.

They are made by one of the best manufacturers of mackinaw coats in the country—your assurance of perfect tailoring. The 30-ounce All Wool mackinaw material will give a world of service and comfortable warmth. The big, warm collar is of thick, beaverized select sheepskin—it affords wonderful protection to the ears, neck, and face. The double-breasted style affords double protection in front. Two generous muff pockets keep hands warm in severe weather. You'll find this mackinaw just as serviceable and just as fine looking as the best garments shown in exclusive shops.

EVEN SIZES: 8 to 18 years. State size. Read "How to Measure" on Page 252. Shipping weight, 6 pounds 4 ounces.
42 G 6319—Brown, blue and gray plaid.......................$7.89

$5.59

Extra Heavy Weight

Sturdily constructed of one of the heavier blazer materials—30-ounce All Wool mackinaw cloth. Boys like its warmth—that's the big feature of this garment—it gives greater cold protection than most any other blazer. And fellows, they have that smart appearance and snappy style you like. Turn up the collar for storm protection—it's convertible. The knit bottom is All Wool worsted and fits snugly around the hips.

EVEN SIZES: 8 to 18 years. State size wanted. Read "How to Measure" on Page 252. Ship. wt., 2 pounds 9 ounces.
42 G 6337—Light brown, blue, olive and maroon plaid...........$5.59

$2.85

$3.45

$5.49

Two Big Raincoat Values

The material is best quality black rubber coating on white sheeting. The wide lapped over-seams are cemented and vulcanized. Three eyelets under each arm.
State size wanted. Read "How to Measure" on Page 252.
42 G 5603—Black only.
SIZES: 4, 6, 8, 10 years. Shipping weight, 2 lbs. 6 oz......$2.85

42 G 5605—Black only.
SIZES: 12, 14, 16, 18 years. Shipping wt., 2 lbs. 10 oz.....$3.19

Hat to Match
All seams are strongly stitched and taped.
SIZES: 6½, 6⅝, 6¾, 6⅞, 7, 7⅛, 7¼, 7⅜, 7½.
State size wanted. Read "How to Measure" on Page 248. Shipping weight, 8 ounces.
42 G 5609—Black only......49¢

Constructed of Asia cloth with a printed plaid lining and an interlining of rubber. All seams are sewed, strapped and cemented.
State size wanted. Read "How to Measure" on Page 252.
42 G 5651—Tan only.
SIZES: 4, 6, 8, 10 years. Ship. wt., 2 lbs. 2 oz......$3.45

42 G 5655—Tan only.
SIZES: 12, 14, 16, 18 years. Ship. wt., 2 lbs. 8 oz......$3.98

Hat to Match
Of the same high-grade material as the coat.
SIZES: 6½, 6⅝, 6¾, 6⅞, 7, 7⅛, 7¼, 7⅜, 7½.
State size wanted. Read "How to Measure" on Page 248. Shipping weight, 8 oz.
42 G 5659—Olive tan..49¢

Style—Quality— Warmth

A peppy Sports Blazer of a mighty fine quality 24-ounce All Wool mackinaw cloth. Two beautiful plaid patterns. They are so attractive that girls will be as pleased to wear them as the boys. Adjustable cuffs. The All Wool worsted knit bottom fits snugly about the waist.

EVEN SIZES: 8 to 18 years. State size. Read "How to Measure" on Page 252. Shipping weight, 2 pounds.
42 G 6339—Light gray with green overplaid.
42 G 6341—Tan with blue-green overplaid.
Each....................$5.49

$6.98

$5.69

$6.45

$3.98

Great for Cold Protection

Mackinaws are gaining in popularity everywhere —especially when they have the snap and style of this attractive model. Boys prefer them to the longer overcoats, as they are more convenient and allow greater freedom of action. They're warm— the 32-ounce All Wool mackinaw cloth has weight and thickness to keep you comfortable in the most severe weather. The color is very practical brown and blue plaid. Muff pockets are always popular—they keep the hands warm in coldest weather.

EVEN SIZES: 8 to 18 years. State size. Read "How to Measure" on Page 252. Shipping weight, 4 pounds 2 ounces.
42 G 6317—Brown and blue plaid..$6.98

Sturdy Material—Priced Right

A warm Mackinaw with the snappy style and clean cut appearance the boy will like and the good quality of material mothers demand. It's a very firmly woven 30-ounce mackinaw cloth of 80 per cent wool. For years we have used this fabric in boys' winter garments and long experience has proved that it gives unusual satisfaction and service. A big convertible notched collar for comfort in stormy weather. Double-breasted style with all around belt. Strongly constructed.

EVEN SIZES: 8 to 18 years. State size. Read "How to Measure" on Page 252. Shipping weight, 4 pounds 2 ounces.
42 G 6309—Dark brown only......$5.69

Heavy Weight All Wool

New! To meet this season's popular demand for blue we are offering this smart double-breasted well tailored Mackinaw. The material is a fine quality heavy weight All Wool 30-ounce melton in a beautiful navy blue shade. The boy is assured of a handsome, stylish garment; one that he will be proud to wear anywhere. Mothers will be well satisfied with the fine quality of the material at this economy price. Sturdily constructed in the popular double-breasted style with notched collar.

EVEN SIZES: 8 to 18 years. State size. Read "How to Measure" on Page 252. Shipping weight, 6 pounds 2 ounces.
42 G 6315—Navy blue only........$6.45

Serviceabl and Low Priced

Although this is our lowest priced Mackinaw its value welcomes comparison with garments selling elsewhere at higher prices. And fellows, you may rest assured that it's mighty neat appearing—the combination of contrasting colors is most pleasing. It's well made and strongly, too—the 30-ounce, 80 per cent wool material will give lasting service and warm comfort. You will be well satisfied with the wearing quality and pleased, too, with the money you saved.

EVEN SIZES: 6 to 16 years. State size. Read "How to Measure" on Page 252. Shipping weight, 4 pounds 4 ounces.
42 G 6301—Gray, blue and red plaid..$3.98

Lots More Warmth and Wear

$7 89

Fine Chinchilla Coat
Great for Cold Protection

Mothers! There's a world of warmth and good looks in this fine Chinchilla Coat. We've made it on the idea of giving your boy the greatest amount of protection against cold leg winds. An enormous purchase from a mill with a reputation of weaving only the better grades of chinchilla is the reason for this low price. You'll approve their mannish appearance—broad sturdy shoulders—and thick "hefty" material about 80 per cent wool. The convertible collar can be turned up in stormy weather to protect neck, ears and chin. It's double breasted, too—that assures double cold protection in front. There are four warm generous size pockets. Yoke and sleeves lined with a good grade plaid lining. Boys give their clothes rough wear, so we've bar-tacked all strain points. Our special low price will be of tremendous importance to the economy wise mothers.

SIZES: 5 to 9 years. State size wanted. Read "How to Measure" on Page 252. Shipping weight, 3 pounds 11 ounces.
40 G 4015—Cinnamon brown.
40 G 4019—Cadet blue.
40 G 4023—Medium gray. Each........ **$7.89**

Our Very Best
"Longtime" Overcoat for Boys

$8 85

It's our honest belief that style, workmanship and quality of material considered, this Coat would readily sell in the smartest shops as a feature value for $11 to $12. Made to our exact specifications of the finest "LONG TIME" All Wool material—a new superior quality that is causing enthusiastic comment the country over. Its sea blue or grayish brown herringbone effect is in the season's smartest patterns for young chaps. The sleeves and yoke are lined with a fine grade Venetian and the body is lined with a fancy plaid. Matched buttons strongly sewed on.

Turn up the collar in stormy weather—it's convertible. There is more dependable wear and winter comfort in this fine coat than we were ever able to offer at the price. You mothers know that the best is always so much the cheapest in the long run—that's the reason we so strongly recommend our best "LONG TIME" coat.

SIZES: 5 to 9 years. State size. Read "How to Measure" on Page 252. Ship. weight, 3 pounds 7 ounces.
40 G 4045—Sea blue.
40 G 4043—Grayish brown. Each........ **$8.85**

$4 85

Heavy and Warm **$5 85**

Your boy won't need any extra bundling if he's wearing one of these warm 32-ounce Melton cloth Overcoats. The extra heavy fabric is 85 per cent wool closely woven for added warmth. The double breasted coat buttons right up to the neck—giving warm protection all the way. There are warm lined muff pockets at the side, too—a feature that all the boys want. The high-grade attractive plaid body lining keeps the warmth in. Yoke and sleeves lined with cotton twill.

SIZES: 3 to 8 years. State size wanted. Read "How to Measure" on Page 252. Shipping weight, 3 pounds 6 ounces.
40 G 4105—Dark brown.
40 G 4109—Dark blue. Each.... **$5.85**

Popular Priced Chinchilla

Always in big demand. They're smart appearing, moderately priced and give exceptionally good service. Although this is our lower grade of chinchilla it represents an unequaled value at this low price. It's over 60 per cent wool and the balance cotton—an excellent combination for warmth and long service. Made in the popular, double breasted style with two set-in pockets. Full lined throughout with a durable twill.

SIZES: 3 to 8 years. State size wanted. Read "How to Measure" on Page 252 Shipping weight, 2 pounds 11 ounces.
40 G 4127—Navy blue.
40 G 4119—Cinnamon brown.
Each................ **$4.85**

Lowest Priced **$3 65**

There's a surprising amount of style, quality and warmth in this Overcoat at this sensible economy price. Sturdily constructed of a good medium weight 75 per cent wool material—bound to give more than a season's wear. The dark brown and dark blue colors are always so appropriate and sensible. Full lined for added warmth with a durable twill material. The all around belt adds to the attractiveness of the garment.

SIZES: 3 to 8 years. State size wanted. Read "How to Measure" on Page 252. Shipping weight, 2 pounds 9 ounces.
40 G 4103—Dark brown.
40 G 4101—Dark blue. Each.... **$3.65**

$6 95

$4 45

$3 98

$4 59

$4 98

Very Stylish All Wool

We strongly recommend this raglan style Overcoat to every mother that has difficulty in buying the right style of coat to properly fit her young son. We can say in all truth that for the price it's the best fitting, and best looking style of overcoat we know of for the little man. You'll see this same style displayed in the windows of the smartest shops everywhere.

It's warm as toast on winter days, too—the winter weight All Wool material was especially chosen because of its strength and wind breaking features. Turn up the convertible collar when sending sonny off to school—it'll keep his ears, neck and chin well protected. Body and sleeves fulllined with a quality of twill that assures long service. And when you consider price, you'll find ours to be an appreciable reduction from what you are usually asked to pay.

SIZES: 3 to 9 years. State size wanted. Read "How to Measure" on Page 252. Ship. wt., 3 lbs. 2 oz.
40 G 4009—
Fancy tan only........ **$6.95**

Snappy Style

Here's a letter typical of the thousands received from satisfied customers who have bought our Boys' Overcoats. "We were more than pleased with the little boy's coat we ordered from you recently. We feel as though we got more than our money's worth by sending to Ward's," says Mrs. La Cross of Flint, Mich.

Here's a coat that will give you the same satisfaction which Mrs. La Cross experienced. It has that neat, boyish appearance that all mothers approve. Its solid warmth permits sonny to play outdoors even in the coldest weather. The yoke and sleeves are a fine quality of twill. The material of 75 per cent wool has the thickness and sturdiness to carry it through two seasons of hard wear. Body lining of fancy plaid will further adds to its attractiveness and warmth.

SIZES: 3 to 8 years. State size wanted. Read "How to Measure" on Page 252. Shipping weight, 3 lbs.
40 G 4047—
Bluish gray only........ **$4.45**

All Wool Reefer

Mothers! Here's a thrift opportunity seldom, if ever, equalled in a boy's Overcoat. A manufacturer who was going out of business offered us thousands of yards of good All Wool overcoating material at 50 cents on the dollar. Of course, we snapped up his offer.

We secured a variety of beautiful colors and patterns any one of which will excite pleasing comment. We made them up with our usual fine workmanship into these attractive coats. Every feature that would possibly add to warmth and comfort was incorporated in this garment. Made reefer style and a trifle shorter than our regular overcoats. Full lined with a good grade twill.

SIZES: 3 to 9 years. State size wanted. Read "How to Measure" on Page 252. Shipping weight, 2 lbs. 9 oz.
40 G 4107—Assorted colors and patterns only.......... **$3.98**

Snappy Military Style

Here they are—military style Overcoats for the little fellows—they're the last word in overcoat smartness. Popular everywhere—mothers prefer them because they have that snap and dressiness far more becoming to sonny than most any other type of coat. They're warm, too—the coldest winds can't pierce them. Made of a fine navy blue melton cloth about 80 per cent wool—our laboratory tests have proved it the equal of fabrics in overcoats selling at much higher prices.

The military style idea is carried out all through the garment. Military brass buttons, a shield on left sleeve, and two rows of gold braid on both sleeves—details which will appeal to the younger lad. The excellent tailoring enables it to stand up under hard service. Has convertible collar and regular side pockets. Body of coat is lined with a fine finished, chamois red felt. Sleeves and yoke of a good grade twill.

SIZES: 3 to 9 years. State size wanted. Read "How to Measure" on Page 252. Shipping weight, 2 lbs. 9 oz.
40 G 4051—
Navy blue only............. **$4.59**

Economical—Durable

They're the very latest, mothers—these big, warm Overcoats with attractive fiber silk plush collars closely resembling Kolinsky fur. There's nothing quite their equal for either warmth or smart appearance. You have no doubt seen overcoats of this style and quality, but their price was usually much higher. Now we offer you a coat of equal value for only $4.98.

The 60 per cent wool chevlot overcoating has the strength to carry it through at least two seasons of rugged wear. The boy can turn up the convertible collar when he goes out in the cold—it gives great protection to the ears, cheeks, neck and chin. The coat is double breasted—that means double chest protection. The body is lined with good grade cotton plaid material which adds greatly to its warmth and appearance. Yoke and sleeves are lined with cotton twill.

SIZES: 3 to 8 years. State size wanted. Read "How to Measure" on Page 252. Shipping weight, 3 pounds 2 ounces.
40 G 4007—
Dark brown only.......... **$4.98**

69

This "Longtime" Idea Keeps the Boy Clothed
at Less Expense!

Style—Wear—Value!
All Wool—New Diamond Weave

$10.45 With Two Pairs Longies

"A good sound value for the money" —that's reason enough for thrifty mothers to order one of these serviceable Longie or Knicker Suits. The style and quality will impress you, and when you notice how it stands up under the boy's rough wear, you'll wonder how we can offer a Suit of such quality at a price so low.

We selected the All Wool winter weight twilled Cassimere material only after rigid tests had proved it to be sturdy and good wearing. You'll find its mannishly styled, single breasted model to be especially attractive, and most becoming. Carefully tailored even in the hidden places. The colors are sure to please—they're the very latest—a medium brown and a medium gray with a fancy stripe, both in the new birdseye diamond weave pattern. Coat is lined with strong cotton alpaca. With the coat and vest, you have a choice of two longies or a pair each of full lined knickers and golf knickers.

Read "How to Measure" on Page 252.

Coat—Vest—2 Knickers
SIZES: 5 to 15 years. State size, also chest and waist measure. Shipping weight, 3 pounds 9 ounces.
40 G 3415—Autumn brown.
40 G 3416—Medium gray.
Each.............. **$9.45**

Coat—Vest—2 Longies
SIZES: 10 to 16 years. State size, also chest, waist and trousers inseam measure. Shipping weight, 3 pounds 13 ounces.
40 G 3418—Medium brown.
40 G 3420—Medium gray.
Each.......... **$10.45**

40 G 3415

$7.75 With Vest

Sturdy—Stylish Diagonal Weave
We were determined to make this Suit an outstanding value. We've done it! We bought the piece goods way below present market prices. Extra pair of trousers means double wear—giving you satisfaction long after the price is forgotten. Diagonal weave, hard finished cassimere, about 40 per cent wool. Coat lining of strong cotton twill. Three-button coat with broad shoulders and snug fit at hips.
SIZES: 5 to 15 years. State chest, waist and trousers inseam measure; also height, weight and age. Read "How to Measure" on Page 252. Shipping weight, 3 pounds 12 ounces.
40 G 3443—Navy blue only................ **$7.75**

Every Suit Shown on This Page Has Two Pairs Pants

$8.45 With Vest

Long Wear—Bargain Price
At our low price—and that includes both longies and golf knickers—we consider it an absolutely unbeatable bargain. It's hard twisted cassimere—a sturdy cloth, 50 per cent wool—considered one of the strongest, longest wearing materials in the country today. There's attractiveness in the beautiful medium grayish brown, diamond weave pattern. Coat and knickers are strongly lined throughout.
SIZES: 8 to 16 years. State chest, waist and trousers inseam measure; also height, weight and age. Read "How to Measure" on Page 252. Ship. weight, 4 pounds.
40 G 3463 — Dark grayish brown with diamond weave only............ **$8.45**

$4.98

Our Lowest Priced Two Pants Suit
A value hard to beat! The lowest price imaginable for a serviceable two-knicker Suit. An outfit that lively son of yours can wear for school or for play—you may be sure he'll be well dressed in it.
Made of hard wearing winter-weight cassimere, about one-third wool with balance fine cotton for strength—attractive striped medium brown. Coat is a two-button, single breasted, notched lapel model. Two pairs of knickers double the life of outfit. Knickers and coat have strong cotton lining.
SIZES: 5 to 12 years. State chest and waist measures; also height, weight and age. Read "How to Measure" on Page 252. Shipping weight, 3 pounds 4 ounces.
40 G 3403—Medium striped brown only........... **$4.98**

$10.95 With Vest

Season's Smartest Style
Beautiful Patterns—All Wool
An attractive combination of basket and diagonal weave and handsome colors. One is a rich warm brown, the other a new lively shade of blue with a slight tinge of tan. We called on the leading woolen mills of the country, looked over thousands of swatches —then chose this winter weight All Wool twilled cassimere for its strength. Two pairs long pants. Coat is lined with strong striped alpaca.
SIZES: 8 to 16 years. State chest, waist and trousers inseam measure; also height, weight and age. Read "How to Measure" on Page 252. Shipping weight, 3 pounds 13 ounces.
40 G 3440—Rich brown.
40 G 3441—Blue and tan.
Each.......... **$10.95**

$13.95 With Vest

Our Best Two Pants Suit
All Wool Twilled Suiting
"The best two-trousers Suit bargain I ever saw," writes Vernie Huntwork of Union City, Ind. Fellows, you'd pay $20 and $25 for similar quality elsewhere. We bought the cloth at actual cost and had the garments made at a very low price because we kept the manufacturer busy during a slack season.
You'll get a surprising amount of wear from the finely finished All Wool cassimere. Retains its shape remarkably well. Color is the new Prussian blue. Coat lined with fine alpaca. Take this big step toward economy.
SIZES: 8 to 16 years. State chest, waist and trousers inseam measures; also height, weight and age. Read "How to Measure" on Page 252. Ship. wt., 3 lbs. 13 oz.
40 G 3467—
Prussian blue only.......... **$13.95**

$7.35

Low Priced Suit
All Wool Cassimere
Good quality, hard wearing and neat appearing—with two knickers for double service. The fabric is a sturdy All Wool cassimere in a very attractive medium brown with an overplaid—so much in favor this season, with the well dressed young fellows.
Boys like the extra pair of golf knickers—they're stylish, neat and bound to withstand their rough play. Coat and knickers fully lined. A value that offers unusual satisfaction for so low a price.
SIZES: 5 to 12 years. State chest and waist measure; also height, weight and age. Read "How to Measure" on Page 252. Shipping weight, 3 pounds 10 ounces.
40 G 3414—Medium brown only. **$7.35**

70

Now! "Longtime Suits" for That Rough-on-Clothes Boy of Yours

$6.98

Smart "Longtime" Outfit

Sweater included with coat and knickers of a new fabric of astounding strength!—Sturdy weave, hard surfaced cassimere, half wool, half cotton; every thread twisted to give cloth a wearing surface of surprising resistance. Shape retaining to a marked degree and as attractive a pattern as in any suit you ever saw. It's a medium brown with a fancy broken diamond weave of light gray.

Entire body of coat, as well as knickers full lined with cotton twill. "Nobby" buff and brown worsted and cotton slipover sweater instead of a vest. Just as smart as styles that older brother wears. Double sewed and taped at seat, crotch and inseam. A great value!

SIZES: 5 to 15 years. State chest and waist measure; also height, weight and age. Read "How to Measure" on Page 252. Shipping weight, 3 pounds 14 ounces.
40 G 3313—Medium brown only. $6.98

$6.95

A Remarkable Value! Special Fabric—Wool and Silk

Mothers, this Suit just shows you what can be done with a special fabric, specially tailored, to give you a value hard to find anywhere in the country except at Ward's. We're selling this Longie suit at $6.95 and the Knicker suit at $5.98. Look at garments similarly priced elsewhere and you'll see how they fall far short of Ward's "Longtime" Quality.

For instance, what other suits at this price can boast a cassimere that's 50 per cent All Wool and 50 per cent Silk—a fine, warm wear-resisting fabric we had woven during slack time, when production costs are lowest? You have no idea how that Silk brightens and beautifies the material. The fancy weave fabric with deep rich harmonizing shades in an interesting medium gray with popular lightening stripe and plaid will give proper pride of dress to that boy of yours. Just read these specifications which we sent the manufacturer—they tell the whole extra-value story in a nutshell.

"Carefully design in the latest six-button double breasted model. Cut with broad shoulder effect narrowing downward to snug fitting hips. Emphasize this athletic effect by making broad peak lapels. Give trousers special attention—make slightly wider and straight hanging with regular 1½-inch cuff bottoms. Line coats and knickers with a good grade of lining. Serge, reinforce and double stitch all seams, seat and inseam at crotch. No vest—the double breasted coat be amply warm for winter wear." They carried out our specifications to the very letter, and as a result you can buy a boys' suit of a quality we have never seen equaled at this price.

Longie Suit
SIZES: 8 to 16 years. State chest, waist and inseam measure; also height, weight and age. Read "How to Measure" on Page 252. Shipping weight, 3 pounds 4 ounces.
40 G 3347—Gray only. $6.95

Knicker Suit
SIZES: 5 to 12 years. State chest and waist measure; also height, weight and age. Shipping weight, 3 pounds 4 ounces.
40 G 3343—Gray only. $5.98

$6.95

All Wool Blue Serge

Lowest price in ten years. Good looking All Wool Blue Serge Suit, that meets every wish of the boy and his mother. We take special care in the construction of our serge suits—every seam is specially sewed because of the nature of all serge materials. All seams are strongly sewed and taped and double sewed at crotch, seat and inseam for extra strength. Coat and knickers are strongly lined with a good grade lining.

SIZES: 5 to 15 years. State chest and waist measure; also height, weight and age. Read "How to Measure" on Page 252. Shipping weight, 4 pounds.
40 G 3209—Navy blue only. $6.95

$5.69

$3.98

Champion

$7.65

$4.98

Here's Long Wear and Style

Here's the smart style the boys want, coupled with beauty of fabric and wearing qualities mothers demand. You'll find Suits of similar style and quality in the leading shops selling as feature values for much higher prices. Its neat double breasted model is favored the country over by the very smartest youngsters.

We selected this 65 per cent wool and 35 per cent cotton, heavy-weight cassimere because rigid tests proved it to be stronger and longer wearing than fabrics usually used in suits so reasonably priced. Its handsome bright medium blue color with a faint stripe lends the right touch to the ordinarily conservative blue. The tailoring, as usual, leaves nothing to be desired. The coat is fully lined with twill. No vest. Mothers, it's a big value!

SIZES: 5 to 15 years. State chest, waist and inseam measure; also height, weight and age. Read "How to Measure" on Page 252. Shipping weight, 3 pounds 4 ounces.
40 G 3309—Blue with stripe only. $5.69

Longies or Knickers

Our lowest priced two-piece Longie or Knicker Suits. Answering a nation-wide demand for suits of this kind, we introduced them in our last catalogue. Thousands of them were sold, and letters from our customers show that the suits gave remarkable service, considering the low price. While we have much finer suits, than these, we believe you will find it impossible to get the same satisfactory wear out of garments sold at this price anywhere else. The smart patterns and tailoring have produced garments of undeniable good looks and neat fit. Made of 40 per cent wool cassimere. Single breasted style. Coat and knickers full lined. Coat of longie suit full lined. Read "How to Measure" on Page 252.

Longie Suit
SIZES: 5 to 15 years. State chest and waist measure; also height, weight and age. Shipping weight, 2 pounds 6 ounces.
40 G 3301—Striped dark brown only. $3.98

Knicker Suit
SIZES: 5 to 12 years. State chest and waist measure; also height, weight and age. Shipping weight, 2 pounds 4 ounces.
40 G 3303—Striped dark brown only. $3.89

Genuine Stillson Worsted

The "Longtime" leader in boys' clothes. Young America has proved that genuine All Wool Stillson worsted outwears any boy's suit you could buy anywhere at any price. Of the same sturdy All Wool worsted cloth as used in our men's Stillson suits. Son can give his clothes the hardest possible use—Stillson suits are made to stand hard treatment. Seams and pockets are strongly sewed; belt loops bar tacked; coat full lined with durable twill. Knickers unlined.

Ask son's opinion of this Norfolk style—he'll soon tell you we have provided every desirable feature from neat lapels to all around belt and button down flap pockets.

Mothers, it's absolutely the biggest money's worth in boys' clothes.

SIZES: 6 to 16 years. State chest and waist measure; also height, weight and age. Read "How to Measure" on Page 252. Shipping weight, 3 pounds 8 ounces.
40 G 3216—Navy blue.
40 G 3222—Dark brown. Each. $7.65

Champion All Wool Worsted

A dominant value! A champion for long wear—winning the acclaim of thousands of boys and thousands of mothers. A Suit you'll call a wonder for wear, not only when it's first worn, but after many months of use. Son can climb fences, wrestle, play rough and tumble and this garment will hardly show any ill results.

Made of heavy, winter weight All Wool worsted, weighing full 20 ounces to the yard. Rich olive drab color. Pockets and strain points bar tacked to prevent ripping. Coat lined with durable twill. Knickers unlined.

Excellent tailoring. A mannish cut that son likes in clothes of his choice. We recommend this Champion suit as absolutely the very biggest value in the country at this low price.

SIZES: 6 to 16 years. State chest and waist measure; also height, weight and age. Read "How to Measure" on Page 252. Shipping weight, 3 pounds 8 ounces.
40 G 3318—Olive drab only. $4.98

They're All Hard on 'Em~Only "Longtime" Suits
Will Stand the Gaff

$4.69

$7.95

$5.89
With Vest

Handsome Patterns—Smart Style
Sturdy All Wool Fabric

The sturdy, stylish All Wool Cassimere Suits offered here undisputably prove our leadership in clothes for the boys of America. Exacting tests of the strong close weave enable us to guarantee a lasting life for the fabric in spite of the strains and hard service the boys unthinkingly give it. Our experienced suit men have rigidly supervised the tailoring and assure you complete satisfaction. The points of style, the attractive weave, and the pleasing colorings of these models are the kind usually found only in suits sold for much higher prices. The fancy striped pattern in a birds-eye diamond weave is offered in a choice of gray or rich autumn brown shades. The coat is full lined with cotton alpaca. In latest longie trouser style or with large roomy full lined knickers.

Ward's suits do NOT sacrifice material to give style at a moderate cost. Our enormous purchasing power enables us to save enough on large contracts to combine the style the boy must have with the serviceable materials that mother demands—two most important features for the price of one.

SIZES: 5 to 12 years. State size; chest and waist measure; also height, weight and age. Read "How to Measure" on Page 252. Shipping weight, 3 pounds 4 ounces.

Boys' Knicker Suit With Vest
40 G 3331—Brown.
40 G 3335—Gray.
Each............ **$7.95**

Boys' Longie Suit With Vest
SIZES: 10 to 16 years. Shipping weight, 3 pounds 6 ounces.
40 G 3337—Brown.
40 G 3339—Gray.
Each **$8.95**

40 G 3331 With Vest

40 G 3337 With Vest

40 G 3201

Brown Corduroy—Low Priced

This is our lowest price in years on a corduroy suit of this quality. We've made it one of the biggest values in the country at this price. Mothers who want to economize on clothing for their boys and still get a full measure of style and quality will order this corduroy Suit. Don't judge the garment by the price alone. It's a good drab brown corduroy, and will give long hard service. Reinforced at all strain points; good quality lining throughout.

SIZES: 5 to 15 years. State chest and waist measure; also height, weight and age. Read "How to Measure" Page 252. Shipping weight, 3 pounds 3 ounces.
40 G 3253—Drab brown **$4.69**

To Be Sure of Getting Right Size—State Chest, Waist and (for Longies Only) Trousers Inseam Measure; also Height and Weight. Refer to Size Scale on Page 252.

Practical Blue Serge

The young chap receives more style and smartness in this Suit than he ever thought possible at our low price. John La Rose of Cooks, Mich., writes: "The two suits I bought from you for my two boys cost only as much as I'd have to pay here for one. The boys like them very much, too."

Made from a good wearing wool mixed, Navy blue Serge that's 50 per cent wool. Both Longie and Knicker style. Coat and vest strongly lined with a good quality twill. Knickers full lined.

State chest, waist and (for longies) trousers inseam measure; also height, weight and age. Read "How to Measure" Page 252.
40 G 3204—Navy blue Serge Longie Suit with vest. SIZES: 5 to 15 years. **$5.89**
Ship. wt., 3 lbs. 8 oz...........
40 G 3201—Navy blue Serge Knicker Suit without vest. SIZES: 5 to 12 years. **$4.49**
Ship. wt., 2 lbs. 14 oz............

Vest Included
$10.95

$6.75

With Vest All Wool
$10.95

$5.98

Smart "Prep" School Style
Handsome All Wool Suiting

A model you'll see worn in all the style centers of the country. Three-button coat with the buttons widely spaced. Snug fitting at the shoulders; broadening at the bottom, giving a loose, stylish appearance. The small notched lapels fit close to the neck. Tailored in our own factory so we know it's right.

Made from an All Wool cassimere fabric that we've scientifically tested for long wear and found to be the equal in all ways of fabrics used in garments selling elsewhere for considerably more. Fully lined with guaranteed Gibraltar alpaca that will wear as long as the suit. Distinctive, rich autumn brown with a triple overplaid effect of blue—destined to be very popular this fall and winter. In fabric, quality and workmanship it's a garment for which you'd expect to pay a great deal more than our low price.

SIZES: 8 to 16 years. State chest, waist and trousers inseam measure; also height, weight and age. Read "How to Measure" on Page 252. Shipping weight, 3 pounds 4 ounces.
40 G 3391—Rich autumn brown... **$10.95**

Navy Blue College Corduroy
Fine Quality—A Big Value

Style and Snap! We've made this Longie Suit up-to-the-minute in style. The very popular model with easy hanging coat and attractive wide trousers. This fine quality, rich looking, Navy blue corduroy can be worn equally well for school or dress. And you know how corduroy wears—many mothers tell us that corduroy suits of similar style and quality have given their sons more than two seasons of satisfying wear. Coat is lined with strong Venetian. Remember, the corduroy used in this suit is an unusually fine grade—a quality seldom if ever found in other boys' suits sold at near our price. Excellent workmanship throughout.

No one can dispute the leadership in value at this remarkably low price. No vest.

SIZES: 8 to 17 years. State chest, waist and trousers inseam measure; also height, weight and age. Read "How to Measure" Page 252. Shipping weight, 3 pounds 2 ounces.
40 G 3271—Navy blue.......... **$6.75**

Boys! Here's Style and Value
Beautiful All Wool Fabrics

What do you think of this swagger Suit, fellows? One of the smartest and finest in our line! It's a big hit! You'll think so, too, when you see how good it really looks on you. Made of sturdy All Wool cassimere, selected after a long search of the most reputable mills in the country. Two of the newest fancy patterns. One a smart dark brown with a chevron stripe, the other a rich dark blue with chevron stripe. Its careful and painstaking tailoring was assured when we had it made to our own rigid specifications. Coat has neat looking broad lapels, squared at the shoulders and tapered at the hips; also full lined with a good grade alpaca. Wide, straight hanging, cuff-bottomed trousers.

SIZES: 8 to 16 years. State chest, waist and trousers inseam measure; also height, weight and age. Read "How to Measure" on Page 252. Shipping weight, 3 pounds 4 ounces.
40 G 3375—Walnut brown.
40 G 3378—Dark ocean blue.
Each **$10.95**

A Timely Outdoor Outfit
At a Money-Saving Price

The latest style Lumberjack Outfit for boys. Outfit consists of an All Wool Blazer of 24-ounce mackinaw cloth and corduroy Trousers. Blazer is specially processed to make it shower-proof. Heavy and warm for fall and winter wear. The longies are navy blue. Large and roomy for comfort—durable and strong for long wear.

The blazer is an attractive navy blue and black plaid pattern. The same quality would alone cost as much as the entire outfit in most stores. This good looking outfit is practical for school, hunting, skating, riding and all forms of outdoor sports.

SIZES: 6 to 16 years. State chest, waist and trousers inseam measure; also, height, weight and age. Read "How to Measure" on Page 252. Shipping weight, 3 pounds 4 ounces.
40 G 3398—Lumberjack outfit... **$5.98**

72

Styles That Boys Want

All Wool—Super Value
39 G 804—Brown.
39 G 805—Gray.
SIZES: 6⅜, 6½, 6⅝, 6¾, 6⅞, 7, 7⅛. State size wanted. Read "How to Measure" on Page 248. Ship. weight, 1 pound.

89¢

This Cap represents an amazing value for the money. Furthermore, it possesses the style and finish always associated with much higher priced caps. Of fine All Wool suitings in assorted stripes and checks. Sanitary lined inband to protect the ears. Unbreakable visor.

Good Quality Wool Felt
539 G 406—Light bluish gray.
539 G 408—Light tan.
SIZES: 6⅜, 6½, 6⅝, 6¾, 6⅞, 7, 7⅛. State size wanted. Read "How to Measure" on Page 248. Shipping weight, 2 pounds.

$1.59

Embodies all that is new in boys' Hat styles. A snap brim with that swank and swagger air so much desired by the smarter young fellows. Of a good quality wool felt which comes in the season's latest shades. Very attractive band. The sweatband is of genuine leather. A convincing value!

Snappy Style—Best Fur Felt
539 G 422—Pearl gray.
539 G 424—Light brown.
SIZES: 6⅜, 6½, 6⅝, 6¾, 6⅞, 7, 7⅛. State size wanted. Read "How to Measure" on Page 248. Shipping weight, 2 pounds.

$2.69

You can't improve in style, quality or price on this rakishly styled, snap brim Hat for boys. Especially styled by our master designers for the young fellow who wears only the better grade of garments. Made like our finest hats for men—of smooth finished, shape retaining fur felt. Has a genuine leather sweatband.

Our Big Dollar Special
39 G 826—Bluish gray.
39 G 828—Dark brown.
SIZES: 6⅜, 6½, 6⅝, 6¾, 6⅞, 7, 7⅛. State size wanted. Read "How to Measure" on Page 248. Shipping weight, 1 pound.

$1.00

Here's a value that tops them all! Beyond a doubt, we believe it's the biggest dollar's worth of value we or anyone else ever offered in a boys' winter Cap. Without exaggeration we examined thousands of samples before we finally chose this fine quality All Wool suiting material. The colors are the season's snappiest and newest. Warm lined inband to pull over the ears. Unbreakable visor.

A Very Low Price
39 G 803—Assorted colors only.
SIZES: 6⅜, 6½, 6⅝, 6¾, 6⅞, 7, 7⅛. State size wanted. Read "How to Measure" on Page 248. Shipping weight, 1 pound.

79¢

Our lowest priced winter Cap for boys. A special value made possible by utilizing surplus ends of All Wool suitings of assorted patterns and colors. Though low in price they're made with extreme care. We cannot offer any special color or pattern. Has warm lined inband to pull down over ears.

Heavy Winter Cap
39 G 855—Brown.
39 G 859—Gray.
SIZES: 6⅜, 6½, 6⅝, 6¾, 6⅞, 7, 7⅛. State size wanted. Read "How to Measure" on Page 248. Shipping weight, 1 pound 3 ounces.

$1.00

Just the Cap for cold weather wear and at an appreciable reduction in price from what is usually asked. Made of surplus ends of heavy All Wool overcoating in two desirable shades. Full lined with a good quality material. The sanitary lined inband protects the ears in severe weather. Exceptionally well tailored—it will give lasting service and warm comfort.

Famous Junior Carlsbad
539 G 404—Light tan.
539 G 405—Brown.
SIZES: 6⅜, 6½, 6⅝, 6¾, 6⅞, 7, 7⅛. State size wanted. Read "How to Measure" on Page 248. Shipping weight, 2 pounds 4 ounces.

$1.49

Here's exceptional value—the exact duplicate of our men's world famous Carlsbad Hat. Made of fine quality wool felt, the kind that will give wonderfully long service. The sweatband is of genuine leather. The crown is 6½ inches, the brim 3½ inches.

Lowest Priced Cap
39 G 810—Assorted colors.
SIZES: 6⅜, 6½, 6⅝, 6¾, 6⅞, 7, 7⅛. State size wanted. Read "How to Measure" on Page 248. Shipping weight, 1 pound.

69¢

They're equal in style and quality to Caps selling for considerably more elsewhere. Come in neat appearing assorted colors and patterns of All Wool suitings. Full lined with a good grade of twill. Have genuine leather sweatbands in front and unbreakable visors. Made without inband, this cap is designed for early fall wear. If our low price about matches the amount you choose to spend we are sure you will be enormously pleased with the value offered here.

Our Best for Early Fall
39 G 820—Tan.
39 G 821—Bluish gray.
SIZES: 6⅜, 6½, 6⅝, 6¾, 6⅞, 7, 7⅛. State size wanted. Read "How to Measure" on Page 248. Shipping weight, 1 pound.

98¢

Comfortable, stylish shaped Cap of All Wool suitings. The fancy new weaves and patterns, the fine quality and good looks are sure to win instant approval. Full lined and have genuine leather sweatband in front. No inband.

Sturdy Winter Corduroy
39 G 812—Seal brown.
39 G 814—Navy blue.
SIZES: 6⅜, 6½, 6⅝, 6¾, 6⅞, 7, 7⅛. State size wanted. Read "How to Measure" on Page 248. Shipping weight, 1 pound.

95¢

No wonder corduroy is popular—it wears so well—and besides it looks fine even after the longest service. Mothers will be glad to find such a serviceable Cap at our low price. Boys will like it because its snappy and smart. Well made of extra good quality sturdy corduroy in attractive colors. Substantially full lined. Sanitary lined inband pulls down and keeps the ears warm.

Genuine Horsehide
39 G 843—Black.
39 G 845—Cordovan brown.
SIZES: 6⅜, 6½, 6⅝, 6¾, 6⅞, 7, 7⅛. State size wanted. Read "How to Measure" on Page 248. Shipping weight, 1 pound 3 ounces.

$1.49

We are the first to offer the strongest, most serviceable Cap ever sold. Made of wonder wearing, first quality genuine horsehide leather. The soft, durable leather will give years of service. Remember—they're styled and built for extra wear and priced for sensible economy.

For Boys 3 to 7 Years

Best Child's Cap
39 G 881—Pearl gray.
39 G 885—Navy blue.
SIZES: 6, 6⅛, 6¼, 6⅜, 6½, 6⅝, 6¾. State size wanted. Read "How to Measure" on Page 248. Ship. weight, 14 ounces.

85¢

Something new and better for little chaps from three to seven. Of a fine grade of corduroy. Full lined—eight quarter style—leather faced visor is unbreakable. Warm lined inband.

A Great Value
39 G 875—Light brown.
39 G 877—Gray.
SIZES: 6, 6⅛, 6¼, 6⅜, 6½, 6⅝, 6¾. State size wanted. Read "How to Measure" on Page 248. Shipping weight, 14 ounces.

79¢

Saving for mothers—service for kiddies—value for all. Made to fit the little fellows from three to seven years. Full lined, and has an unbreakable visor. The sanitary lined inband protects the ears in cold weather.

For Cold Weather
39 G 895—Assorted colors only.
SIZES: 6, 6⅛, 6¼, 6⅜, 6½, 6⅝, 6¾. State size. Read "How to Measure" on Page 248. Ship. wt., 1 lb.

83¢

The kind of warm Cap the boy will be proud to wear. Made of assorted All Wool heavy mackinaw cloths. The band on the side slides down over the ears. Seams taped and double stitched for strength.

One of the Best
39 G 847—Light gray.
39 G 849—Light tan.
SIZES: 6⅜, 6½, 6⅝, 6¾, 6⅞, 7, 7⅛. State size wanted. Read "How to Measure" on Page 248. Shipping weight, 1 pound.

$1.45

Fellows! It's one of the finest, most stylish Caps you have ever seen. Styled with a smartness that could only be achieved by the best of cap makers. Its good looking patterns and colors mark it as a cap of distinction. Only fine cap materials were used. Lined with silk serge. The inband is warm lined for cold weather protection.

Very Latest—Quite Smart
39 G 889—Corduroy. Mole gray.
39 G 893—Cheviot. Navy blue.
SIZES: 6, 6⅛, 6¼, 6⅜, 6½, 6⅝, 6¾. State size wanted. Read "How to Measure" on Page 248. Shipping weight, 14 ounces.

69¢

Full lined and has unbreakable visor. Attractive insignia in front. Gold color cord across visor. Outside pull down for cold weather wear.

For Boys—3 to 16 Years
39 G 897—Dark brown.
39 G 899—Navy blue.
SIZES: Medium (3 to 8 years). Large (8 to 16 years). State size wanted. Read "How to Measure" on Page 248. Shipping weight, 7 ounces.

69¢

A fine knitted Cap that unbuttons in front and turns down, giving full protection to the neck, ears and throat. Has a fine fleece lining of pure worsted.

Our Best Boys' Dress Cap
39 G 851—Bluish gray.
39 G 853—Tan.
SIZES: 6⅜, 6½, 6⅝, 6¾, 6⅞, 7, 7⅛. State size wanted. Read "How to Measure" on Page 248. Shipping weight, 1 pound.

$1.49

Finest quality—smartest appearing Boys' Cap we ever offered. Priced for sensible economy, too. The beauty of the tailoring—snap of the style—freshness of the patterns really have to be seen to be fully appreciated. The very finest quality cap material was used. Full lined with rayon. The inband is warm lined.

Snappy Shirt Patterns —for Snappy Boys

Rayon Striped Broadcloth
$1.39 35 G 896—White with newest colored stripes and figures.
HALF SIZES: 12 to 14-in. neck. State size wanted. Shipping weight, 9 ounces.
Mothers who like colors on their boy will find these Shirts with lustrous Rayon stripes alternating with attractive colored figures a pleasing selection. Durable cotton broadcloth that will retain its good looks after repeated washings. Collar attached; coat style; pocket; one-button cuffs. All the regular fellows are wearing these shirts this Fall.

Flannel Shirts

Twilled Cotton Flannel
$1.15 35 G 947—Khaki. 35 G 948—Gray. 35 G 949—Brown.
HALF SIZES: 12 to 14-inch neck. State size wanted. Shipping weight, each, 6 ounces.
The exceptional wearing quality of this sturdy Shirt for boys recommends itself to economical mothers. Medium weight twilled cotton flannel, firmly woven. Closed front style; flat attached collar. Two large buttoned-through pockets. Faced sleeves.

One-Fourth Wool
$1.29 35 G 957—Khaki. 35 G 959—Gray.
HALF SIZES: 12 to 14-inch neck. State size wanted. Shipping weight, each, 10 ounces.
You'll have less worries about winter's colds and ills if your boy wears this Flannel Shirt—made of about ¼ wool. Closed front style; collar attached. Two large buttoned-through pockets. Colors are practical because they don't show soil easily. Washes excellently.

Imported English Broadcloth
$1.39 35 G 888—White. 35 G 889—Tan. 35 G 892—Blue.
HALF SIZES: 12 to 14-in. neck. State size wanted. Ship. weight, each, 8 ounces.
Great favorites with mothers—made of the same high quality Imported Broadcloth shirting, and with the same exacting care as our men's fine dress shirts. The fresh luster and almost everlasting wear of broadcloth delights both boy and mother. Collar attached; coat style; full length center plait. Pocket. One-button cuffs.

Boys Like the Smart Style

Fancy Broadcloth
$1.29 35 G 990—Blue, tan or gray with contrasting stripes and figures.
HALF SIZES: 12 to 14-inch neck. State size and color wanted. Shipping weight, 8 ounces.
Another most convincing proof of our wonderful values—genuine cotton Broadcloth Dress Shirts—that usually retail for $1.50 or more. These are excellent wearing shirts, and in the new dark patterns are especially attractive. Made in popular coat style with neat collar attached; one pocket; one-button cuffs.

Genuine Broadcloth
85¢ 35 G 863—White. 35 G 864—Tan.
HALF SIZES: 12 to 14-inch neck. State size wanted. Shipping weight, each, 8 ounces.
You will appreciate the good looks of this genuine cotton Broadcloth Dress Shirt, but not until you see the firm, even weave which means long, satisfactory wear, will you realize what a splendid value they are at this low price. Cut full and roomy in neat collar attached, coat style. Neatly finished; one pocket; one-button cuffs. Washes excellently.

Smart Shirtings
79¢ 35 G 904—Light grounds with contrasting checks.
HALF SIZES: 12 to 14-inch neck. State size wanted. Shipping weight, each, 8 ounces.
This value proves that it isn't necessary to pay a high price for a good quality Shirt. Of attractive looking extra high-grade percale in neat colorful patterns, guaranteed fast colors. Opens all the way down the front; neat attached collar. One pocket. Serviceable and good looking.

Shirts for Juveniles
6 to 10 Years

Cotton Broadcloth
35 G 982—White only. **75¢**
35 G 983—White with fancy colored stripes. **85¢**
AGES: 6, 7, 8, 9, 10 years. State age wanted. Shipping weight, each, 8 ounces.
You practice double economy in buying this Shirt—it is priced attractively low, and the firmly woven broadcloth insures extra long service. Choice of two styles: plain white or white grounds with neat colored patterns that will please the little fellow. Closed front; pocket.

Twill or Chambray
65¢ 35 G 885—Khaki twill. 35 G 887—Blue chambray.
AGES: 6 to 10 years. State age wanted. Shipping weight, each, 8 ounces.
Your choice of strong khaki twill or sturdy blue chambray in closed style. Juvenile Shirts. Both materials are widely used in making men's durable work shirts and will give excellent wear. Faced sleeves add longer life to shirt. One pocket; collar attached.

Twilled Flannel
95¢ 35 G 989—Khaki.
AGES: 6 to 10 years. State age wanted. Shipping weight, 9 ounces.
Juveniles' shirts made just like Dad's of fine quality, twilled cotton flannel, a firmly twisted thread fabric which is very durable. Neatly finished in every detail. Closed front style with attached collar; one pocket.

WORK SHIRTS

TUPELO Chambray

Strong Blue Chambray
69¢ 35 G 924—Blue only. HALF SIZES: 12 to 14-inch neck. State size wanted. Shipping weight, each, 6 ounces.
Here's a Work Shirt for the boy made just like Dad's famous Pioneer and it wears like iron. Two, big, buttoned-through pockets. Closed front style. Double shoulder yoke insures extra wear. Comfortable fitting collar attached.

Pioneer Junior
69¢ 35 G 925—Gray with fancy zigzag stripes.
HALF SIZES: 12 to 14-inch neck. State size wanted. Shipping weight, each, 6 ounces.
A Shirt you should buy for your boy because of its rugged, hard-wearing qualities. Of tough pliable Tupelo chambray—much used for men's work shirts. Closed front style; collar attached. Faced sleeves; two big buttoned-through pockets.

Strong Khaki Twill
75¢ 35 G 921—Khaki.
HALF SIZES: 12 to 14-inch neck. State size wanted. Shipping weight, 6 ounces.
Made from firmly twisted khaki twill, this Shirt stands hard knocks that would wear out ordinary shirts in no time. Closed front style; center plait; neat collar attached. Interlined cuffs and collar for comfort and added wear. Two large buttoned-through pockets.

Warm Nightshirt
79¢ 35 G 970—Assorted stripes only.
EVEN SIZES: 6 to 16 years. State size wanted. Ship. wt., 12 oz.
Flannelette that will keep your boy snug and warm—cut in extra full, roomy sizes. Firm material that will come through repeated washings in splendid shape. Three button front; flat collar and one pocket. All seams strongly attached with fine thread. Neatly finished.

Attractive Bathrobe
$3.29 35 G 975—Brown; gray blue.
EVEN SIZES: 6 to 16 years. State size and color wanted. Ship. wt., 2 lbs.
Your boy would be sure to appreciate a gift such as this. Beautifully patterned and colored Robe of soft finished blanketing. Comfortable heavy weight. Shawl collar, pockets and cuffs are edged with neat cord trimming. Girdle at waist is of lustrous rayon mixed with cotton.

Boys' Dress Suspenders
33¢ 35 G 263—Assorted colors. Length 32 inches. Shipping weight, 4 ounces.
Well made from fine quality fresh elastic webbing to give excellent service. Adjustable buckles. Leather ends.

35¢ 35 G 194—Fancy brown. EVEN SIZES: 24 to 30-inch waist. State size. Shipping weight, 4 ounces. Boys' cowhide Belt; wide style, (1¾-inch). Polished tongue buckle.

25¢ 35 G 226—Black. EVEN SIZES: 24 to 30-inch waist. State size. Shipping weight, 4 ounces. Embossed Belt; about 1¾ inches wide. Sturdy leather. Polished buckle.

45¢ 35 G 210—Tan. 35 G 224—Blue. EVEN SIZES: 24 to 30-inch waist. State size. Shipping weight, 4 ounces. Embossed grain cowhide Belt. About 1¾ inches wide. Nickeled buckle.

74

Boys'~They're for Long Wear~Dressy, Too!

See Shoe Size Chart on Page 169

$2.98 Boys' High Grade Welted Sole Shoes
Great for Wear

You're getting $4 quality in these shoes, and $4 style too! Made by a manufacturer who specializes in boys' high grade shoes. Uppers are of choice tan or black calf grain leather with the nationally famous Wear-proof lining. Handsomely finished with neat stitchings and perforations. Soles are extra heavy oak leather stitched by the new welted method that insures stronger construction and longer wear. Rubber heels. We're asking only $2.98 for this high quality—gives you a big saving! Ship. weight, 2 lbs.
SIZES: 1 to 6. State size wanted.
24 G 2279—Tan.
24 G 2280—Black.
Per pair.... $2.98

$2.89 Both Wear and Style for Boys

Every boy wants Oxfords that look like father's and big brother's. These are very handsome—of blonde grain leather with the popular collegiate square toe. Strong, long-wearing oak leather soles. Leather insole. Leather lining. Rubber heels. You get new style, sturdy quality, sensational value, for $2.89. Read above what Mrs. W. S. Forst, Bentonville, Ark., writes about the shoes she bought from Ward's for her boy. Ship. weight, 1 lb. 12 oz.
SIZES: 1 to 6. State size wanted.
24 G 2217.................... $2.89

$3.19 Boys—A Snappy Shoe for Winter

Everywhere—wide-awake young Americans prefer this type of shoe. Good quality tan calf grain leather—with stitching and perforations just like big brother's and dad's. Snappy wing tip that all college fellows wear. Extra heavy oak leather soles—sewed by the welted method—strongest sole fastening. Rubber heels. Made with a storm welt for winter wear. Ship. weight, 2 pounds.
SIZES: 1 to 6. State size wanted.
24 G 2256.................... $3.19

Fellows! These Have Everything~SERVICE~LOOKS~VALUE

$2.89

If your boy is unusually rough on shoes these will hold him much longer than an ordinary pair. Their long wear spells E-C-O-N-O-M-Y for mothers. Of sturdier materials—stronger brown or black grain leather uppers—heavier, sturdier oak tanned leather soles. Solid rubber heels. New square toe. Handsome appearance and sterling quality in every pair. Ship. weight, 2 pounds.
SIZES: 1 to 6. State size wanted.
24 G 2233—Brown leather.
24 G 2236—Black leather.
Per pair......... $2.89

Solid Rubber Heels

Extra Strong Oak Leather Soles

Smart mannish lines and good quality, make this Shoe a favorite among well dressed young fellows. Of brown or black grain leather. Notice the comfortable square toe and neat perforations. Soles especially tanned oak leather to give extra service. Solid rubber heels. If you paid a dollar more you couldn't buy stronger shoes and this style is a great favorite with boys. Ship. weight, 1 lb. 12 oz. State size.

Brown Grain Leather	
24 G 2200—Boys. SIZES: 1 to 6	$2.85
24 G 2201—SIZES: 9½ to 13½	2.29
Black Gunmetal Leather	
24 G 2204—Boys. SIZES: 1 to 6	2.85

Boys' Popular "SAMMIE" Shoe

$2.98 Strong Welted Oak Leather Sole

We've built this Boys' "Sammie" Shoe of solid materials through and through. Especially for hiking, school and every day! Constructed over the comfortable army style Munson last that's best for your boy's feet. Uppers are of durable brown chrome tanned leather, and are drill cloth lined. Oak bend leather soles fastened by the new welted construction—no better or stronger method of fastening soles to the uppers of boy's shoes. Rubber heels. At $2.98 a real value that saves you at least $1. Shipping weight, 2 pounds.
SIZES: 1 to 5½. State size wanted.
24 G 2260.................... $2.98

$3.19 Famous "GRO-CORD" Sport Soles

Handsome and sturdy for active boys. Uppers are of tan Russia grain leather, one of the popular new leathers of the season. Soled and heeled with nationally known "Gro-cord," found only on the better shoes. Quality all the way through, and value that wins friends for us. Ship. weight, 2 pounds.
SIZES: 1 to 6. State size.
24 G 2253...... $3.19

$3.19 The latest style in Oxfords for boys. Smart leather combination—tan grain leather with lighter tan embossed grain leather trimming. Has college style square toe. Soled and heeled with "Gro-Cord" composition, used only on the best shoes. Ship. weight, 1 lb. 12 oz.
SIZES: 1 to 6. State size.
24 G 2202..... $3.19

$2.59 Savings—Service—Style for Boys

Lower in price—good looking—fine for school or dress wear. These handsome high shoes are a fine example of the extra value Ward's gives in boys' Footwear. They'll certainly please, with their good appearance and the wonderful wear they give. Of sturdy tan or black grain leather with oak leather soles and solid rubber heels. Ship. weight, 2 lbs.
SIZES: 1 to 6. State size wanted.
24 G 2276—Tan.
24 G 2277—Black.
Per pair..................... $2.59

Fine Shoes for the Little Boys
Best for Growing Feet

$2.59 Two Snappy Oxfords

There's snappy smartness in the lines of these Oxfords that will appeal to every up-to-date young fellow. Sturdy calf grain leather uppers. Attractive perforations and stitching. Oak leather soles. Rubber heels. The limit in money-saving value combined with long wear! Ship. wt., 1 lb. 12 oz.
SIZES: 1 to 6. State size wanted.
24 G 2224—Tan.
24 G 2225—Black.
Per pair. $2.59

$2.19 For Active Youngsters

Mothers will certainly be happy over the longer wear these good looking Shoes will give. Strong black or brown grain leather uppers are lined. Oak leather soles and solid rubber heels. Correct shape toe for growing feet. Ship. weight, 1 lb. 8 oz.
SIZES: 9½ to 13½. State size.
24 G 2331—Tan.
24 G 2330—Black.
Per pair... $2.19

$1.98 They're Sturdy!

The little fellow wants stylish footwear, too. Here's a fine, durable Oxford of tan calf grain leather. Strong oak soles. Rubber heels. Best for growing feet, too. A $2.50 value at a substantial saving for you. Ship. weight, 1 lb. 6 oz.
SIZES: 9½ to 13½.
State size wanted.
24 G 2227..... $1.98

$1.98 Stitchdown Fiber Soles

Your healthy, active youngster needs staunch quality footwear like this. Of sturdy tan calf side leather full drill lined. Made over a broad toe last, best for growing feet. "Wonder Wear" composition soles, stitchdown sewed, are durable and flexible. Ship. wt., 1 lb. 8 oz.
SIZES: 9½ to 13½. State size.
24 G 2361—Shoe.
24 G 2205—Oxford.
Per pair. $1.98

$1.89 Low Priced—But Durable

You can rely on Ward's quality even at these low prices. Where else could you find such dependable value at such low cost? The black pebble leather tops and smooth leather vamps are neat and durable. Drill cloth lined. Strong leather soles. The sturdy materials and low prices make them ideal shoes to buy for your boy for everyday wear. Ship. wt., 2 pounds. State size.
24 G 2283—
SIZES: 1 to 5½............ $2.00
24 G 2384—
SIZES: 9½ to 13½........ 1.89

Wear-Wear-Wear! Built for Your Boy

$4.95

$3.98

$5.98

An Extraordinary Suit Value
Fine Winter Weight Cassimere
Newest Style and Pattern

You just bet your boy has ideas of his own in clothes preference. Just show him the picture of this manly little Suit—so much like daddy's—and he'll tell you how well he likes it.

L. O. Ross of Stockton, Ill., who has a growing boy to clothe, writes: "Both the youngster and myself are well pleased with the Suit, and I am sure I saved 30 per cent by purchasing from you." And Mr. Ross will find, just like thousands of fathers and mothers, that for sturdy wear this suit is hard to equal.

A Very Beautiful Pattern

Mothers, you've never seen a more handsome pattern nor a more cunning style for that youngster of yours. It's the most unusual and attractive combination of bluish gray in a plaid that's ever been offered our customers. We've added 25 per cent beautiful, lustrous silk to the 75 per cent pure wool winter weight cassimere to achieve this specially blended color and to add strength. Plenty of pockets where every lively boy wants them. The breast pocket is lined with a special colorful lining. Pull it out and it looks just like a pretty pocket handkerchief.

Sturdiness has not been overlooked. Fabric of suit and the strong twill lining of coat will stand plenty of hard wear. And still it's a very inexpensive garment.

SIZES: 4 to 9 years. Chest 23¼ to 27 inches. Waist 23 to 26 inches. State chest, waist and trousers inseam measure; also height, weight and age. See size scale and read "How to Measure" on Page 252. Shipping weight, 2 pounds 8 ounces.
40 G 3534—Fancy medium gray with blue overplaid $5.98

Two Rare Bargains in Most Becoming Styles

Mothers, you know that today boys' clothing must have lots of smart style. These attractive Junior Suits are very much "in style" and besides are offered at an unheard of low price. It's a new English model only recently introduced, but already immensely popular. It's about 80 per cent wool with 20 per cent silk to lend strength to the winter weight suiting of 55 per cent wool or a medium gray with faint overplaid and a beautiful pattern. Pants are full lined.
SIZES: 3 to 8 years. State chest and waist measure; also height, weight and age. See size scale and read "How to Measure" on Page 252. Shipping weight, 2 pounds 4 ounces.
40 G 3527—
Light brown with faint plaid.
40 G 3528—
Medium gray with plaid.... $4.95

"Get me this one, Mother!" Nine chances to one that's what your youngster will say about this newly designed Suit. It's so different, so individual in style, has so many trim looking features, that every mother's son wants it. Becoming to any small boy. All Wool, winter weight cassimere in a fancy tan plaid—a lively color that's very popular this year. Sleeves are unlined. Has a fancy tan cotton pongee waist that buttons to full lined pants. Fancy tie and sports belt included.
SIZES: 3 to 8 years. State chest and waist measure; also height, weight and age. See size scale and read "How to Measure" on Page 252. Shipping weight, 2 pounds 7 ounces.
40 G 3507—Fancy tan plaid. $3.98

How to Order Boys' Suits

To be sure of getting right size—state chest, waist and (for Longies only) trousers inseam measures. Also height, weight and age. Refer to size scale on page 252.

$5.65

Wool and Silk
Latest Colors
Popular Style

$3.79

Smart Norfolks New Styles
$5.89

In all the big cities of the country there's an unusually brisk demand for this Norfolk model this season. And mothers, 'a word to the wise'—ours are priced way below what others ask. Think of the service your boy will get from this strong winter weight suiting of 55 per cent wool and 45 per cent silk. Choice of a medium brown or a medium gray with faint overplaid and a beautiful pattern.
Shape retained by a canvas interlining. All seams doubly sewed and taped. Full lined throughout.
SIZES: 4 to 9 years. State chest and waist measure; also height, weight and age. See size scale and read "How to Measure" on Page 252. Shipping weight, 2 pounds 3 ounces.
40 G 3511—Fancy medium brown overplaid.
40 G 3512—Medium gray with overplaid........ $5.89

Big Values Eton Model

Again it's one of the best-liked Suits of the year. This Eton model continues steadily its leadership in popularity.
Choice of two desirable winter weight materials. One is a sturdy cassimere—about 40 per cent wool with neat brown stripes. The other is also cassimere about 85 per cent wool with the balance of silk in the pattern; it's a beautiful brown with a faint overplaid and check; sturdily made with good quality lining throughout entire garment.
SIZES: 3 to 8 years. State chest measure; also height, weight and age. See size scale and read "How to Measure" on Page 252. Shipping weight, 2 pounds 2 ounces.
40 G 3675—Part wool. Striped medium brown...... $2.98
40 G 3679—Wool and silk. Light brown with faint plaid. 3.98

Our Very Best Junior Suit
$5.98

Mothers who know the best is the least expensive in the long run will select this well made Junior Suit. Its sturdiness will save you a great deal of patching. To give it the wear resistance that playful, growing boys should have, we've combined this 85 per cent wool winter weight cassimere with 15 per cent silk. Has a faint plaid over the brown diamond fancy weave. Waist is fast dyed Peggy Cloth in an attractive brown and tan blazer stripe. Pants button to waist and have two side pockets. Coat has the style touch that alert youngsters appreciate. Coat and pants strongly lined.
SIZES: 4 to 9 years. State chest and waist measure; also height, weight and age. See size scale and read "How to Measure" on Page 252. Shipping weight, 2 pounds 6 ounces.
40 G 3518—Medium brown with fancy weave only......$5.98

One of our finest Juniors' Suits—a style leader! The old saying was, "Boys will be boys." Now they say "Boys will be stylish." They now demand just as appropriate and proper apparel as their older brothers. And here's the Junior Suit styled, cut and tailored just like older boys' clothing.
Made of winter weight cassimere 80 per cent wool and 20 per cent silk that will stand the rough tests a boy unknowingly gives his clothes every time he wears them.
Coat and knickers full lined. Fancy sports belt included.
SIZES: 5 to 9 years. State chest and waist measure; also height, weight and age. See size scale and read "How to Measure" on Page 252. Shipping weight, 2 pounds 2 ounces.
40 G 3519—Medium brown with stripe and diamond weave.
40 G 3523—Deep blue with stripe and diamond weave... $5.65

Low Priced Junior Suit

There's a surprising amount of quality and workmanship packed into this Suit at this amazing low price. Although one of our lowest priced garments, it's neat and stylish in appearance and will withstand a great amount of hard knocks and scuffling. You'll find it worth every cent of $3.79—and more. Sturdily constructed of 40 per cent wool, winter weight cassimere that's bound to give good service. The dark colors are good looking; either one a very practical choice for boys. Full lined throughout with strong material.
SIZES: 5 to 9 years. State chest and waist measure; also height, weight and age. See size scale and read "How to Measure" on Page 252. Shipping weight, 2 pounds 8 ounces.
40 G 3503—Dark brown mixture with subdued stripe.
40 G 3504—Bluish gray mixture with subdued stripe.
Each......................$3.79

76

Today's Boy Styles
Very Serviceable Too

$5⁹⁸

$2⁹⁸

$3⁴⁵

$1⁸⁹

Good Style Low Price $2²⁵

Here's a stylish, sturdy Suit. Waist is blue madras with fancy blue and white stripes. Pants are full lined; made of winter weight 80 per cent wool and 20 per cent cotton cassimere in a fancy pattern and plaid; one tan, the other bluish gray. Sports belt and imitation silk knitted tie with outfit.

SIZES: 3 to 8 years. State age. See size scale and read "How to Measure" on Page 252. Shipping weight, 1 pound 6 ounces.
40 G 3616—Tan with fancy plaid.
40 G 3618—Bluish gray plaid. Each.....$2.25

All Worsted Jersey

Here's the very latest model in Oliver Twist style. One of the season's smartest. Entire Suit is All Worsted Jersey. Pants are medium tan; full lined. Sweater style waist is tan, white and bright blue in a diamond weave. Fancy sports belt; two side pockets.

SIZES: 3 to 8 years. State age. See size scale and read "How to Measure" on Page 252. Shipping weight, 1 pound 9 ounces.

40 G 3686—Tan pants. Tan, white and blue fancy waist.................$2.98

All Wool Serge

Sailor ahoy! Every little fellow wants to wear this Sailor Suit, designed just like Jack Tar's, the defender of our flag on the seas. Has an extra pair of short pants that can be worn with any waist. Both pairs are well made and are fully lined.

Entire outfit is All Wool navy blue serge of a very good quality. Tailoring, sewing and trimmings are those equaled only in higher priced garments.

"That little boy is certainly well dressed and sensibly, too" is what other mothers will say about your kiddie when he wears this garment. It's an ideal Christmas gift!

SIZES: 3 to 8 years. State waist and trousers inseam measure, also height, weight and age. See size scale and read "How to Measure" on Page 252. Shipping weight, 2 pounds 4 ounces.

40 G 3603—
Navy blue serge only.. $5.98

This label, sewed inside every Ward's suit for boys, is your guarantee of quality.

Wool and Silk
Heaps of Warm Comfort
Brimful of Style
And Note the Low Price $3⁹⁸

It won't take your boy long to make friends with this outfit. He'll become so attached to it he'll want to play outdoors more so he can wear his Lumberjack Suit. It's a boon to sonny's health and the pride of every mother who has a growing youngster. You'll never imagine it possible to pack so much warmth into one garment, to make it so sturdy and then offer it at such a small amount.

Outfit made of strong, winter weight cassimere. Blazer is All Wool with a large plaid and fancy pattern of blue, tan and henna. Trousers are 80 per cent wool and 20 per cent silk for added sturdiness. They're medium brown with overplaid and fancy pattern. Have wide cuffs and belt loops. Straight cut and roomy like youngsters want them. They're unlined. Collar, cuffs and bottom of blazer trimmed with cassimere to match trousers.

Yes, mothers, you'll like this practical garment for the many uses your boy can make of it. Jacket may be worn over a shirt—then the outfit becomes a suit. Son can also turn up the sports collar, button it closely around his neck and wear a necktie.

Such a tremendous value that you should not miss the opportunity to purchase one at our unmatched low price.

SIZES: 4, 5, 6, 7, 8, 9 years. State chest, waist and trousers inseam measure; also height, weight and age. See size scale and read "How to Measure" on Page 252. Shipping weight, 2 pounds 6 ounces.

40 G 3695—Blue, tan and henna plaid blazer and medium brown trousers.................$3.98

Beautiful Patterns

Waist is All Wool plaid cassimere; All Wool worsted pants, collar and cuffs. Pants full lined and have two side pockets. Tie and belt.

SIZES: 3 to 8 years. State age. Ship. wt., 1 pound 9 ounces.
40 G 3682—Cadet blue pants; red, gray and green plaid blazer waist.

40 G 3680—Nile green pants; blue and henna blazer waist with green and red overplaid Each........$3.45

"Longtime" Wear

A big "LONGTIME" special—there's no end to the wear in this little garment. Low priced and durable to a marked degree. Strongly woven, winter-weight cassimere, 50 per cent wool, 50 per cent cotton. Attractive gray with a fancy pattern. Unlined.

SIZES: 3 to 8 years. State age. See size scale and read "How to Measure" on Page 252. Shipping weight, 1 pound 12 ounces.

40 G 3601—
Medium gray........$1.89

Mothers Who Want Their Sons
$2⁹⁵ Dressed Differently
Choose This New Style
Winter Weight Cassimere

New—one of the most stylish Oliver Twist Suits ever offered! The latest addition to our "young America" line of little boy's clothes. Designed by one of America's best known experts in children's clothing. It's so typically boyish that any little fellow will be tickled to wear one, and it's built to stand his rough play. Mother will take particular interest in the very low price we ask for such a practical and new innovation. Many features never before put in a garment for youngsters.

All Wool little vestee, decidedly different, protects sonny's chest where colds so often start. Collar attractively trimmed with All Wool broadcloth and fancily embroidered with silk in bright colors. Neat sailor tie. Cuffs of All Wool broadcloth to match collar; and the cute breast pocket—all make the garment very likeable.

Winter weight, it's the proper garment for little boys to wear now and for many, many months to come. The chevlot finished cassimere is 80 per cent wool and 20 per cent silk—a blending that makes a fine textured fabric for long wear. Two fancy patterns—one a medium brown, the other a dark bluish gray. Pants are full lined and have side pockets.

Of course you want one for your little son, especially at this remarkably low price.

SIZES: 3 to 8 years. State age. See size scale and read "How to Measure" on Page 252. Shipping weight, 1 pound 10 ounces.

40 G 3635—Fancy medium brown.
40 G 3637—Fancy bluish gray.
Each.........................$2.95

$2⁸⁵

$2⁹⁸

$2⁸⁵

$1⁴⁹

$2³⁵

Warmth for Cold Days

All Wool lumberjack style Waist with collar, cuffs and flaps of pockets of the same material as pants. Full lined pants with two side pockets made of a winter weight cassimere about 80 per cent wool and 20 per cent silk.

SIZES: 3 to 8 years. State age. Read "How to Measure" on Page 252. Shipping weight, 1 pound 12 ounces.

40 G 3622—Brown, maroon and silver gray and blue plaid blazer.

40 G 3624—Blue gray plaid pants; blue gray and tan plaid blazer.

Each.....................$2.85

Three-Piece Suit

Practical, sleeveless sweater of 70 per cent wool and 30 per cent Rayon. Tan chambray waist buttons to pants of All Wool Jersey. Outfit is ideal winter weight; pants full lined.

SIZES: 3 to 8 years. State age. See size scale and read "How to Measure" on Page 252. Shipping weight, 1 pound 11 ounces.

40 G 3626—Tan, maroon and silver sweater. Tan waist, medium brown pants.

40 G 3628—Purple, gray and silver sweater. Tan waist. Medium brown pants. Each.....................$2.98

Lowest Priced All Wool

An exceptional value. The first time in years we have been able to offer an All Wool Suit for so low a price. All Wool winter weight cassimere in choice of colors for both pants and shirt. Unlined. Collar and cuffs of same material as pants.

SIZES: 3 to 8 years. State age. See size scale and read "How to Measure" on Page 252. Shipping weight, 1 pound 7 ounces.

40 G 3660—Brown and maroon plaid shirt; brown plaid pants.
40 G 3662—Blue and henna plaid shirt; bluish gray plaid pants. Each.....$2.35

Warm Wool and Silk

A neat double breasted effect Middy Suit at a bargain price. Winter weight cassimere, about 85 per cent wool, remainder silk for strength. Beautiful patterns, one brown, the other bluish gray —both have a broken diamond weave and stripe. Full lined pants with side pockets. Cord and whistle with suit.

SIZES: 3 to 8 years. State age. See size scale and read "How to Measure" on Page 252. Shipping weight, 1 pound 10 ounces.

40 G 3664—Light brown with fancy pattern.
40 G 3666—Bluish gray with fancy pattern. Each.................$2.85

Well Made—Low Priced

Pants are good grade corduroy and unlined. They button to cotton flannel waist of harmonizing color. Collar and cuffs of corduroy. Wear much longer than you'd expect for the price.

SIZES: 3 to 8 years. State age. See size scale and read "How to Measure" on Page 252. Shipping weight, 1 pound 4 ounces.

40 G 3600—Dark golden brown pants; brown and blue waist.

40 G 3602—Navy blue pants; blue, tan and gray waist.................$1.49

For 1 to 4 Year Tots

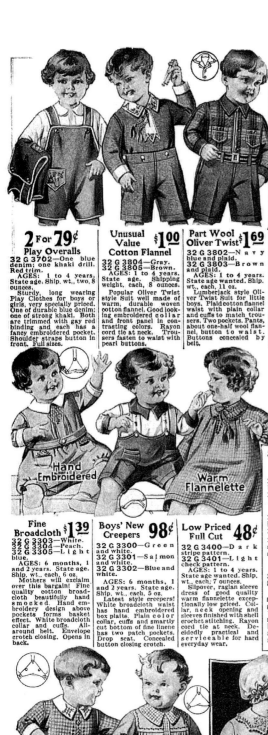

2 For 79¢
Play Overalls
32 G 3702—One blue denim; one khaki drill. Red trim.
AGES: 1 to 4 years. State age. Ship. wt., two, 8 ounces.
Sturdy, long wearing Play Clothes for boys or girls, very specially priced. One of durable blue denim; one of strong khaki. Both are trimmed with gay red binding and each has a fancy embroidered pocket. Shoulder straps button in front. Full sizes.

Unusual Value $1.00
Cotton Flannel
32 G 3804—Gray.
32 G 3805—Brown.
AGES: 1 to 4 years. State age. Shipping weight, each, 8 ounces.
Popular Oliver Twist style Suit well made of warm, durable woven cotton flannel. Good looking embroidered collar and front panel in contrasting colors. Rayon cord tie at neck. Trousers fasten to waist with pearl buttons.

Part Wool Oliver Twist $1.69
32 G 3802—Navy blue and plaid.
32 G 3803—Brown and plaid.
AGES: 1 to 4 years. State age wanted. Ship. wt., each, 11 oz.
Lumberjack style Oliver Twist Suit for little boys. Plaid cotton flannel waist with plain collar and front panel in contrasting colors. Two pockets. Pants, about one-half wool flannel, button to waist. Buttons concealed by belt.

Our Leader
Specially Priced Part Wool
32 G 3800—Navy blue.
32 G 3801—Brown.
AGES: 1 to 4 years. State age.
Shipping weight, each, 11 ounces. **$1.79**
Middy style, two-piece Suit carefully made of part wool flannel. Collar, cuffs, neck opening and pocket tops are trimmed with plaid flannel in pretty contrasting colors. Trousers on buttonhole waistband. Strong reinforced seams throughout.

Novelty Suit Priced Low $1.29
32 G 3806—Navy blue with plaid waist.
32 G 3807—Brown with plaid waist.
AGES: 1 to 4 years. State age wanted. Ship. weight, each, 10 ounces.
Attractive allover plaid flannel waist well made with contrasting tweed collar, cuffs and panel down side of waist. Tassel cord at neck. Warm, closely woven cotton tweed trousers. Pearl button trimmed. Drop seat. Long sleeves.

Oliver Twist or Middy Style $1.19
32 G 3808—Navy blue Oliver Twist Suit.
32 G 3809—Navy blue Middy style Suit.
AGES: 1 to 4 years. State age wanted. Shipping weight, each, 9 ounces.
Appealing style in good quality gaberdine, and very low priced. Collar, vestee, cuffs and pocket trimmed with rows of gold colored braid. Navy emblem on sleeve. Straight trousers on buttonhole waistband. Long sleeves.

Oliver Twist Chambray $1.00
Suits
32 G 3810—Blue.
32 G 3811—Tan.
AGES: 1 to 4 years. State age. Shipping weight, each, 7 ounces.
Ever so cute—and a big bargain! Boys' Oliver Twist Suit of serviceable chambray. White collar trimmed with hand embroidery; white cuffs and pocket trim. Waist has fancy side closing. Trousers fasten to waist with pearl buttons. Well made throughout. Long sleeves.

For Boys and Girls

Fine Broadcloth $1.39
32 G 3303—White.
32 G 3304—Peach.
32 G 3305—Light blue.
AGES: 6 months, 1 and 2 years. State age. Ship. wt., each, 6 oz.
Mothers will exclaim over this bargain! Fine quality cotton broadcloth beautifully hand smocked. Hand embroidery design above pockets forms basket effect. White broadcloth collar and cuffs. All-around belt. Envelope crotch closing. Opens in back.

Boys' New Creepers 98¢
32 G 3300—Green and white.
32 G 3301—Salmon and white.
32 G 3302—Blue and white.
AGES: 6 months, 1 and 2 years. State age. Ship. wt., each, 5 oz.
Latest style creepers! White broadcloth waist has hand embroidered box plaits. Plain color collar, cuffs and sleeves finished with shell crochet stitching. Rayon cord tie at neck. Decidedly practical and serviceable for hard everyday wear.

Low Priced Full Cut 48¢
32 G 3400—Dark stripe pattern.
32 G 3401—Light check pattern.
AGES: 1 to 4 years. State age wanted. Ship. wt., each, 7 ounces.
Slipover, raglan sleeve dress of good quality warm flannelette exceptionally low priced. Collar, neck opening and sleeves finished with shell crochet edging. Rayon cord tie at neck. Drop seat. Concealed button closing crotch.

Sturdy Quality Peggy-All 65¢
SHORT SLEEVES:
32 G 3703—Cadet blue chambray.
32 G 3704—Khaki. Each.... 65¢
LONG SLEEVES:
32 G 3716—Cadet blue chambray.
32 G 3717—Khaki.
32 G 3718—Blue stifel cloth; white stripes.
Each.................69¢
AGES: 2 to 6 years. State age wanted. Ship. wt., each, 8 oz.
Popular Play Suits of strong wash materials, gaily trimmed with turkey red linene on square neck, sleeves, belt and peg top trousers. Fullcut; reinforced seams. Has drop seat.

Chambray or Khaki 95¢
32 G 3782—Medium blue chambray with dark blue trim.
32 G 3783—Khaki with red trim.
AGES: 2 to 6 years. State age. Shipping weight, each, 7 ounces.
Durable little Play Suits. Trimmed with plain color binding and white embroidery pocket. Middy tie slips through loop in front. Bloomers button to waist. Elastic at knees. Well made.

Slipover Middy Suit 89¢
32 G 3761—Blue with white trim.
32 G 3762—Khaki with red tie.
AGES: 2 to 6 years. State age. Shipping weight, each, 8 ounces.
For everyday play wear you can't find a sturdier Middy Suit—nor a better bargain! Reinforced pocket tops have pearl button trim. Full cut bloomers with elastic at waist and knee. All seams double stitched.

Sturdy Overalls 48¢
32 G 3700—Navy blue stifel cloth with white stripes.
32 G 3701—Khaki cloth.
AGES: 1 to 6 years. State age wanted. Shipping weight, each, 6 ounces.
Durable knee length overalls—for either boy or girl. Trimmed with red bandings and pipings. Suspenders and side openings fasten with brass buttons. Two pockets.

Checked Gingham 89¢
32 G 3364—Pink.
32 G 3365—Blue.
32 G 3366—Maize.
AGES: 6 months, 1 and 2 years. State age wanted. Shipping weight, each, 5 ounces.
Babies' sturdy creepers of white checked gingham. White collar and cuffs. Collar and front are colorfully hand embroidered. All-around belt. Envelope flap crotch closing; patch pocket.

Strong Linene 95¢
32 G 3367—Light blue.
32 G 3368—Salmon.
32 G 3369—Pink.
AGES: 6 months, 1 and 2 years. State age wanted. Ship. weight, each, 6 ounces.
One of our prettiest and strongest Creepers at an almost unbelievably low price. Soft, durable fast color linene with smart zigzag stitch trimming front yoke. Collar, front tab effect, cuffs and top of pocket are of neat pin check pongette in blending color. Gathered below yoke. Has hand embroidered wreath in front. Full cut and well made with envelope crotch closing. All-around belt.

Save on Play Clothes at Ward's

Cashmere or Crepella $2.79
32 G 4005—Cream white cashmere. .$2.79
32 G 4006—Cream white crepella cloth.
.................$2.98
32 G 4007—Pink crepella cloth......$2.98
AGES: 1 to 3 years. State age. Shipping wt., each, 12 ounces.
Rich materials, about one-half wool in these stylish little walking length Coats. Hand embroidered collar and deep cuffs with Rayon crochet edging. Hand smocking trims front. Sateen lined; interlined. Three-button closing.

Half Wool Cashmere $2.69
32 G 4022—Infants' long coat. Length, about 26 inches. Infants' size only. Price..... $2.69
32 G 4023—Short walking length coat. AGES: 1 to 3 years only. State age. Price. .$2.79
Cream white only. Ship. wt., each, 13 oz.
Babies' warm Coats of cashmere, about one-half wool. Both styles have deep Rayon embroidered collar with scalloped edge and deep scalloped cuffs. Sturdy sateen lining; flannelette interlining. Close with two pearl buttons.

Cotton Cashmere $1.79
32 G 4003—Short walking length coat.
...............$1.79
AGES: 1 to 3 years. State age wanted.
32 G 4004—Infants' long coat. Length, 26 inches............$1.89
Cream white only. Ship. wt., each, 12 oz.
Serviceable and a real bargain! Both styles have deep collar embroidered and scalloped with silky Rayon. Scalloped cuffs. Sateen lining. Sateen interlining.

Stylish and Very Warm $2.49
32 G 4015—White.
32 G 4016—Brown.
32 G 4017—Red.
AGES: 1, 2, 3, 4 years. State age. Shipping weight, each, 1 lb. 2 oz.
Amazingly low priced! Service Coat in walking length style. The popular velveteen corduroy made in tailored belted style, with smart turnover collar. Double breasted effect, with two rows of fine quality pearl buttons, which also fasten the all-around belt. Quilted sateen lining.

Wonderful Value Chambray Creepers 49¢
32 G 3390—Blue.
32 G 3391—Pink.......49¢
AGES: 6 months, 1 and 2 years. State age. Shipping weight, each, 6 ounces.
Serviceable chambray Creeper with neat white binding on collar and cuffs. An exceptional bargain. Colorful tab trims front. Buttons in back and across bottom. All-around belt. Elastic at knees. Full sizes.

Stylish and Serviceable Yet Inexpensive 63¢
32 G 3306—Blue.
32 G 3307—Pink.
32 G 3308—Tan.
AGES: 6 months, 1 and 2 years. State age wanted. Shipping weight, each, 6 ounces.
Cunning little style of fine quality romper cloth. White fancy shaped collar; white cuffs. Attractively hand embroidered in front. Long sleeves. Full cut and well made. Two patch pockets. Envelope crotch closing.

How to Order
Short Coats
Our Coats are cut full size to fit the average age. State age size child wears. See "How to Order" on Page 87.
Long Coats
Long Coats come in one size only, about 26 inches in length.
Play Clothes
All other garments on this page are cut over our generous specifications and will fit the average age. State age size.

Warm Flannelette or Sturdy Sateen 49¢
32 G 3312—Flannelette; gray stripes. Each......49¢
32 G 3313—Flannelette; light checks. Each.....49¢
32 G 3311—Black sateen. Each...........59¢
AGES: 1 and 2 years. State age. Ship. wt., each, 6 oz.
Well made Creepers; colored bindings trim collar, cuffs and tabs. Buttons in back and across bottom. Elastic at knees. Long sleeves.

For Little Tots—1 to 6 Years

Warm Lumberjacks

Popular Model $1.25
31 G 445—Cardinal red.
31 G 446—Seal brown.
AGES: 3 to 6 years.
State age. Ship. weight, each, 13 ounces.

Dandy garment for the boy or girl who is hard on clothes! Woven closely of wool and sturdy cotton yarns, it stays neat and trim looking remarkably long. Has Byron collar and two pockets. Strongly reinforced.

Warm and Long Wearing $1.89
31 G 469—Brown; buff trimming.
31 G 470—Navy blue; gold trimming.
AGES: 3 to 6 years.
State age. Ship. weight, each, 1 pound 4 ounces.

Good looking and of a very good, warm texture. Knit from wool worsted and cotton yarns with the popular shawl collar that can be worn high around the neck and ears. Collar, front and the two pocket tops in contrasting color.

All Wool Flannel Very Handsome Plaid $1.98
31 G 481—Blue plaid combination.
31 G 482—Dark tan combination.
AGES: 3 to 6 years. State age. Shipping weight, each, 1 pound.

Handsome plaid Lumberjacket—marvelously warm and durable! In the style that the grown-up boys wear, it will appeal immensely to any youngster. Neatly made of All Wool flannel that stands up well under hard service. And it is priced almost unbelievably low! Cuffs and bottom fit snugly, as they are closely knit in the elastic stitch. Two pockets have button-down flaps.

Heavy—Storm-Proof Imitation Leather $3.48
31 G 463—Black with contrasting color trimming only.
AGES: 3 to 6 years. State age. Shipping weight, 1 pound 13 ounces.

Looks like a genuine leather Coat as the outside is made of a smooth, thick imitation leather. It is rain-proof and wind-proof and ever so snug and warm. Inside is a smartly striped, heavy knitted lining for extra warmth. Knitted collar, elastic knit cuffs and wristbands of strong cotton yarns. Two button-down flap pockets. Ordinarily it would cost you almost twice as much at other stores.

Flannel Lumberjack 98¢
31 G 436—Tan check.
31 G 437—Blue check.
AGES: 3 to 6 years.
State age. Shipping weight, each, 9 ounces.

Dashing plaids that will delight any lad or lassie! Warm as it is made of serviceable good weight cotton flannel. Very cute style with button-down flap pockets. Cuffs and waistband knit in elastic stitch.

Sturdy Coat Style $1.35
31 G 425—Maroon.
31 G 426—Seal brown.
AGES: 3 to 6 years.
State age. Ship. weight, each, 12 ounces.

Wonderful bargain in a wear-resisting Sweater Coat firmly knit from part wool yarns. Economical as it will save the children's clothes. Neatly made with double roll collar and cuffs and two pockets. Sturdily reinforced.

Part Wool $1.00
31 G 496—Blue combination.
31 G 497—Tan combination.
AGES: 3 to 6 years. State age. Ship. wt., each, 14 oz.

Exactly the style the college and high school boys wear! Good quality part wool yarns in a fancy, gaily colored pattern. Plain knitted collar, cuffs and bottom.

Wool Faced $1.98
31 G 447—Powder blue with combination trim.
31 G 448—Red with combination trim.
AGES: 3 to 6 years. State age. Shipping weight, each, 1 lb. 1 oz.

Rich worsted wool yarns form the outside, and the inside is woven of sturdy cotton yarns. Pretty and delightfully warm. Collar, pocket tops and bottom in contrasting color.

3-Piece Set $2.89
31 G 805—Seal brown.
31 G 806—Peacock blue.
31 G 807—Cardinal red.
AGES: 1 to 4 years.
State age. Shipping weight, each, 1 pound 7 ounces.

Youngsters can romp around warmly and in perfect comfort when they wear this sturdy well-fitting Suit. Firm, durable weave of part wool yarns. Reinforced coat has Byron collar and two pockets. Heavy, double knit cap. Leggings have draw string at waist, fitted ankles and strap at bottom of legs. Two pockets.

95¢ Smartly Tailored Fleeced Lumberjack
31 G 467—Tan and brown combination.
31 G 468—Cardinal red and black combination.
AGES: 3 to 6 years. State age. Shipping weight, each, 10 ounces.

Cunning winter-weight Lumberjack of durable cotton, heavily fleece lined. Has snug fitting knitted collar, cuffs and bottom. Two pockets.

All Wool Pullover $1.98
31 G 477—Camel tan with contrasting trim.
31 G 478—Cardinal with contrasting trim.
AGES: 3 to 6 years.
State age. Shipping weight, each, 15 ounces.

Pure worsted wool yarns give this Pullover Sweater snug warmth and a rich looking texture. Closely knit in the pretty drop-stitch effect. A popular style for boys and for girls, too. Contrasting stripes on sleeves, and snugly fitting bottom.

Cotton Coat Style 98¢
31 G 408—Buff with brown trim.
31 G 409—Red with navy blue trim.
AGES: 3 to 6 years.
State age. Shipping weight, each, 11 ounces.

Such a trim, pretty style! Even though it costs so little, it is knit very firmly of warm cotton yarns and it is carefully finished. Byron collar, front and pocket tops are in contrasting color. You'll agree that it's a remarkable value!

Heavy All Wool $2.48
31 G 489—Cardinal red with buff trim.
31 G 490—Buff with brown trim.
31 G 491—Navy blue with gold.
AGES: 3 to 6 years.
State age. Shipping weight, each, 1 lb. 3 oz.

Unusually heavy and warm, knit in the cardigan stitch from fine All Wool yarns. Good looking winter weight garment with collar, front, cuffs, pocket tops and bottom in contrasting color. A decidedly worthwhile value.

Astonishing Value in a 4-Piece Set—Popular Brushed Wool

$3.69
31 G 864—Buff.
31 G 865—Brown.
31 G 866—Peacock blue.
AGES: 1 to 4 years.
State age. Shipping weight, each, 2 pounds 1 ounce.

Mothers and youngsters will both be delighted with this Set, downily soft and amazingly warm. Part wool yarns, richly brushed, are firmly knit for long durability. Double knit Cap. Coat has snug fitting collar, all around belt, two pockets. Leggings have knitted draw cord at waist, fitted ankles and straps. Warm mittens.

Part Wool Coat Style $1.15
31 G 472—Cardinal red with navy blue.
31 G 473—Peacock blue with buff.
AGES: 1 to 3 years.
State age. Shipping weight, each, 9 ounces.

Gay little Sweater Coat in a very appealing style. Finely knit of part wool yarns into a warm and long wearing texture—it's a truly surprising value! Trimly fitting Byron collar. Pocket tops and front are in a contrasting color. Has two patch pockets.

All Wool New Style $1.59
31 G 441—Red combination.
31 G 442—Tan combination.
AGES: 1 to 3 years.
State age. Shipping weight, each, 9 ounces.

Latest style! Smart little Pullover Sweater, finely woven of All Wool worsted yarns. Especially warm and durable. The pretty stripes are in contrasting color. Has the dressy student collar—such a becoming style for youngsters—and close, trim fitting cuffs. Collar and cuffs in plain colors.

All Wool Belted Model $1.95
31 G 418—Buff.
31 G 419—White.
31 G 420—Red.
AGES: 1 to 3 years.
State age. Shipping weight, each, 13 ounces.

Because only very fine All Wool yarns are knit into this Sweater Coat, it will give extra warmth and marvelous service! Especially pretty, too, with its soft, fine texture and fancy knit panels in front. Cunning Norfolk style with close fitting Byron collar and all around belt. Pearl buttons.

All Wool Knit Cape $1.95
31 G 885—Pink.
31 G 886—Blue.
AGES: 1 to 3 years.
State age. Shipping weight, each, 15 ounces.

Exquisitely lovely Cape—any little girl will look adorable wearing it! And it's very soft and warm. Closely knit from finest All Wool yarns in the pretty link and link stitch. Silk buds are embroidered by hand on the collar, and down the front. Collar, wing sleeves and border are white. Knit cord ties; fluffy pompon balls.

Zephyr Wool $1.35
With Feet
31 G 851—Black.
31 G 815—White.
31 G 853—Red.
Without Feet
31 G 817—White.
31 G 818—Red.
AGES: 1 to 3 years.
State age. Shipping weight, each, 9 ounces.

Wise mothers will buy these specially fine, warm Leggings. Knit from soft, rich All Wool yarns in the pretty link and link stitch. Shiny buttons on sides and on legs below knees.

Fine Jersey $1.09
31 G 851—Black.
31 G 852—White.
31 G 853—Red.
31 G 854—Brown.
AGES: 1 to 6 years.
State age. Shipping weight, each, 13 ounces.

Unusually smart, long wearing Drawer Leggings of very good quality cotton jersey, warmly fleece lined. Durable elastic at waist and elastic foot straps assure a trimly snug fit. Knitted draw cord at waist, and fitted ankles.

Warm All Wool 84¢
Without Feet
31 G 801—White.
31 G 802—Red.
With Feet
31 G 803—White.
31 G 804—Red.
AGES: 1 to 3 years.
State age. Shipping weight, each, 8 ounces.

Dainty Leggings, finely knit of soft All Wool. Carefully made to fit trimly and comfortably and to last long. They'll keep baby's legs comfortably warm in coldest weather. Draw cord at waist.

Soft Warmth with Cunning Style

Famous KOZY WRAP
"THEY GROW"
FIRST A WRAP-THEN A COAT

Jap Satin

Embroidered Silk Bonnet 59¢
32 G 4211—White with blue trim.
32 G 4212—White with pink trim.
SIZES: 12 to 16 inches. For ages up to 4 years. Order face size; see "How to order." Shipping weight, 5 ounces.
Embroidered Jap silk. Ribbon and lace trim. Lined.

Cotton Duvetyn "Poke" Style 89¢
32 G 4425—Tan.
32 G 4426—Brown
32 G 4427—Copenhagen blue.
SIZES: 15 and 16 inches. For ages up to 4 years. Order face size; see "How to Order." Shipping weight, 6 ounces.
Shirred Rayon ribbon trim. Lined. Elastic in back.

Pretty Shirred Satin 48¢
32 G 4208—White with pink trim.
32 G 4209—White with blue trim.
SIZES: 12 to 16 inches. For ages up to 4 years. Order face size; see "How to Order." Shipping weight, 4 ounces.
Shirred Jap silk. Rayon braid and lace trim. Lined.

Coat Style "Kozy-Wrap" $5.29
32 G 2746—Cream white; blue trim.
32 G 2747—Cream white; pink trim.
Infants' size only. Shipping weight, each, 2 pounds.
Comfortable Bunting that keeps out the cold by patented hood, sleeves and flap. Adjustable so the child can wear it from birth to three years of age and it's easily changed into a coat. Detachable rubberized pad inside. Warm Kozy-Down cloth, double faced, with satin ribbon bound edges. Shoulders lined with white sateen. Sleeves have button flaps that serve as mittens. Sateen. lined hood ties with satin ribbon.

Bunting Style "Kozy-Wrap" $2.98
32 G 2748—White; light blue trim.
32 G 2749—White; pink trim.
Infants' size only. Shipping weight, each, 2 pounds.
Popular Bunting, priced amazingly low. A pretty Wrap that is easily converted into a walking length Cape by buttoning the lower flap on the inside. Made of warm double-faced elderdown bound with dainty colored satin ribbon. Buttons all the way down the front. Specially protects baby's hands, arms and feet from cold. Snug, pointed hood ties with satin ribbon.

Cashmere 59¢
32 G 4203—Cream white. SIZES: 12 to 16 inches. For ages to 4 years. Order face size; see "How to Order." Ship.wt., 5 oz.
Shirred ruffle; Rayon stitching. Lace and rosebud. Lined and interlined. Ribbon ties.

Silk Crepe de Chine 95¢
32 G 4213—White.
32 G 4214—Blue.
32 G 4215—Pink.
SIZES: 12 to 16 inches. For ages to 4 years. Order facesize; see "How to Order." Ship. weight, 5 ounces.
Shirred crepe de chine. Rosebud and ribbon trim. Lined.

Rayon $1.19
32 G 4200—Pink.
32 G 4201—Blue.
SIZES: 12 to 16 inches. For ages to 4 years. Order face size; see "How to Order." Ship. wt, 5 oz.
Shirred ruffle and rosebudtrim. Satin ribbon around face. Lined.

Imported Satin Bunting $3.39
32 G 2759—White with pink.
32 G 2760—White with blue.
Infants' size only. Shipping weight, each, 12 ounces.
One of the richest, daintiest Wraps you can buy anywhere for your baby! And exceptionally low priced for such wonderful quality. Lovely imported bunting of Japanese satin with delicate printed flower designs. Lined with dainty colored silk and beautifully quilted by hand. Buttons down front with satin covered buttons. Pointed hood ties snugly with satin bow draw.

Popular Priced Warm Bunting $1.69
32 G 2710—White; blue trim.
32 G 2711—White; pink trim.
Infants' size only. Shipping weight, each, 15 ounces.
Snug, flat elderdown to keep the baby perfectly warm. Arm openings and front are charmingly trimmed with colored satin ribbon and shell crochet edging to match. The becoming pointed hood is fitted with elastic and lined with sateen. Daintily faced with good quality satin ribbon. Pearl buttons down front.

Hand Embroidered

One-Half Wool Cashmere Sacque 65¢
32 G 2716—Pink trim.
32 G 2717—Blue trim.
Infants' size only. Ship. weight, each, 3 oz.
Soft, fine quality cream white cashmere sacque of about one-half wool. Daintily trimmed with colored hand embroidery and machine shell crochet edges. Finished with ribbon ties.

Amoskeag Flannelette Sacque 23¢
32 G 2708—White with blue trim.
32 G 2709—White with pink trim.
Infants' size only. Ship. wt., each, 4 oz.
This comfortabl little Sacque is ver low priced. Amoskea flannelette, with dainty shell crochet stitching on all edges. Long set-in sleeves. Ribbon tie.

Quilted Jap Satin Sacque $1.49
32 G 2795—Blue trim.
32 G 2796—Pink trim.
Infants' size only. Ship. wt., each, 4 oz.
Luxurious satin Sacque imported from Japan. Warmly hand quilted and has dainty printed floral designs; lined with soft silk in harmonizing color. Fastens with pretty frogs and tassels.

Poplin Bonnet 79¢
32 G 4202—Cream white only.
SIZES: 12 to 16 in. For ages to 4 yrs Order face size; see "How to Order." Ship. weight, 5 oz.
Ever so dainty! Silk and cotton poplin with lace edged ruffles. Lace around face. Ribbon ties. Lined and interlined.

Hand Embroidered Silk Crepe 45¢
32 G 2784—Pink.
32 G 2785—Light blue.
Infants' size only. Shipping weight, each, 2 ounces.
Lovely Imported Moccasins of fine crepe de chine. Hand made with dainty, colorful embroidery. Tied with double silk draw in front. Interlined.

Imported "Mary Janes" 69¢
32 G 2782—Light blue.
32 G 2783—Pink.
Infants' size only. Shipping weight, each, 3 ounces.
Imported silk crepe de chine Moccasins bound with silk and fastened with tiny silk covered buttons. Colorful hand embroidery. Silk lined; interlined.

Babies' Ear Cap 47¢
32 G 4210—White only.
SIZES: Small, medium, large; for ages up to 6 years. State size. Ship. wt., 2 oz.
If baby's ears are inclined to protrude, train them back with this adjustable Cap. Light cotton net. Bound and reinforced with tape. Laced back.

How to Order Bonnets

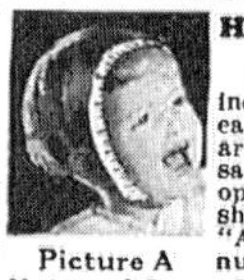

Picture A

Place tape one inch below front of ear and measure around face to the same position on opposite side as shown on picture "A." Order by number of inches.

Picture B

Hats and Caps—Measure around head, as shown on Picture "B." Number of inches will be the size.

All Wool Hand Made 79¢
31 G 847—White with pink.
31 G 848—White with blue.
Infants' size only. Ship. wt., each, 5 ounces.
Most exceptional value for such a cunning handmade Sacque! Yoke section closely crocheted. Lower section made to flare with wider stitches. Color trim and dainty cord tie.

All Wool Sacque 89¢
31 G 856—White with blue.
31 G 857—White with pink.
Infants' size only. Ship. wt., each, 6 ounces.
Has pretty zigzag pattern. Smart collar that may be buttoned high or low. Dainty, warm All Wool Sacque with narrow color trimming. Fastens in front with four pearl buttons.

Embroidered $1.39
31 G 812—White with pink.
31 G 814—White with blue.
Infants' size only. Ship. wt., each, 7 ounces.
Perfectly lovely for so little money! All Wool Sacque in close knit stitch with six hand embroidered buds trimming front. Colored border on neck, front and bottom. Two satin ribbon bow ties.

All Wool 3-Piece Set $1.69
31 G 921—White with pink.
31 G 922—White with blue.
Infants' size only. Ship. wt., set, 1 lb.
You're sure to be delighted with the remarkable value we are offering you in this lovely, warm Set—a Sacque, Cap and Bootees. Soft, carefully knit All Wool yarns with dainty colored Rayon outlining the fancy stitch inserts. Sacque has turnover collar and ties with ribbon bows. Cap and bootees also tie with ribbon. Such a welcome and inexpensive gift for the new baby!

Brushed All Wool $1.29
31 G 842—Pink with white.
31 G 843—Blue with white.
Infants' size only.
Ship. wt., each, 7 ounces.
Such a charming little Sacque! Made of soft, richly brushed All Wool. White revers are hand embroidered with dainty silk buds. Ribbon tie. White cuffs and bottom.

Dainty All Wool Sacque 98¢
31 G 855—White with pink.
31 G 863—White with blue.
Infants' size only. Ship. wt., each, 7 ounces.
Snug, warm Coatee made in the close link and link stitch. Five stripes of dainty colored Rayon each side of front. May be buttoned up high.

Adorable Warm Cape $1.19
31 G 893—Pink and white.
31 G 894—Blue and white.
SIZES: up to 1 year. Ship. wt., each, 7 ounces.
Dressy Cape in dainty colors. Knit from wool and rayon and reinforced with mercerized cotton yarn. Softly brushed collar, revers and arm openings have shell crochet stitching. Hand embroidered flowers. Cord Tie.

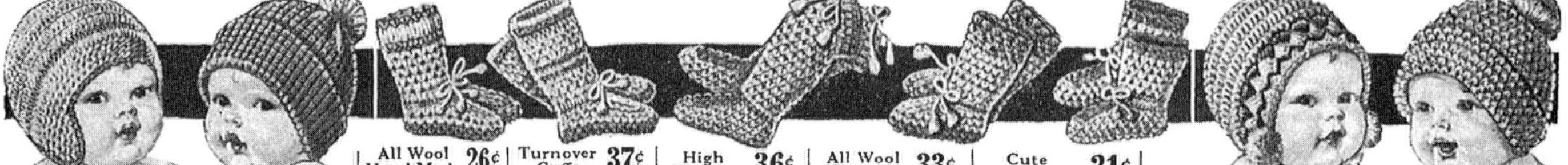

Silk Crochet Wool Lined 89¢
31 G 820—White with blue.
31 G 821—White with pink.
Infants' size only. Ship. wt., each, 6 oz.
Rich, lustrous Rayon Cap with earlaps. Color striping. All Wool knit lining. Cord ties.

Serviceable All Wool Cap 39¢
31 G 831—White.
31 G 832—Red.
Infants' size only. Ship. wt., each, 6 oz.
Double knit from soft, All Wool worsted yarns, this little Cap will give several times its low price in wear. Roll cuff. Pom on top.

All Wool Hand Made 26¢
31 G 874—White with pink.
31 G 875—White with blue.
Infants' size only. Shipping weight, each, 4 oz.
Warm All Wool crocheted Bootees with pretty colored striping at top and colored soles. Cord ties.

Turnover Cuffs 37¢
31 G 881—White with pink.
31 G 882—White with blue.
Infants' size. Shipping weight, each, 4 ounces.
Bootees of hand crocheted All Wool zephyr yarns. Colored soles, striping and ankle ties. Roll cuff.

High Bootees 36¢
31 G 883—White with pink.
31 G 884—White with blue.
Infants' size. Shipping weight, each, 4 ounces.
Fit snugly over Baby's knees. Hand crocheted All Wool zephyr yarns. Colored stitching and knee ties.

All Wool Bootees 33¢
31 G 891—White with pink.
31 G 892—White with blue.
Infants' size. Ship. wt., 4 ounces.
Beautifully hand crocheted from All Wool zephyr yarns with colored sole, tops and ankle ties. Warm and durable.

Cute Short Style 21¢
31 G 867—White with pink.
31 G 868—White with blue.
Infants' size only. Ship. wt., 4 oz.
Cunning All Wool Bootees, carefully hand crocheted from top to toe. Colored tops, insteps and ankle ties. Certainly low priced!

All Wool $1.29
31 G 844—White with pink.
31 G 845—White with blue.
Infants' size only. Shipping weight, each, 6 oz.
Dainty Rayon shell crochet edgings and cute pompons. Crocheted in drop stitch. Satin ribbon ties.

Two-Tone 49¢
31 G 849—White and pink.
31 G 850—White and blue.
Infants' size only. Shipping weight, 6 ounces.
All Wool Cap in fancy popcorn stitch. Double knit with turnback cuff. Two-tone pom.

Double Knit Warm Cap 45¢
31 G 878—Plain white.
31 G 879—White with pink.
31 G 880—White with blue.
Infants' size. Ship. wt., 6 oz.
Colored crown and stripings on cuff. Two-tone pompon. Double knit part wool, very serviceable.

For Baby All Wool $2.79
31 G 899—White.
31 G 900—Light blue.
31 G 901—Pink.
Shipping weight, each, 1 lb. 4 oz.
Warm, comfortable Shawl knit in fancy honeycomb stitch from soft All Wool yarns. Easily washed. Size, fringed, about 56 by 60 in.

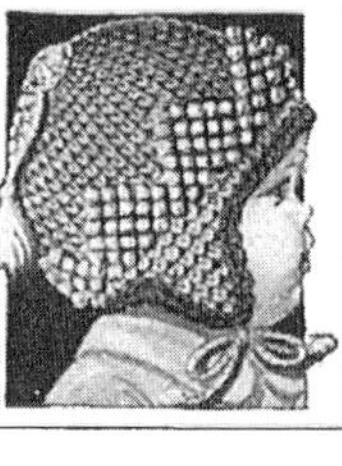

Fancy Stitch All Wool 69¢
31 G 872—White with blue.
31 G 873—White with pink.
Infants' size only. Ship. wt., each, 6 oz.
Warm and cozy and very durable—Cap of extra heavy, closely knit All Wool worsted yarns. Fancy stitch border. Colored edge. Snug earlaps with cord ties. Tassel on top.

Extra Fine Knit Cap 48¢
31 G 840—White with pink.
31 G 841—White with blue.
'nfants' size only Ship. wt, each., 6 oz.
Dainty All Wool in fancy stitch with color striped turnback cuff. Colored ribbon ties to match. A warm, serviceable Cap—wonderfully low priced.

Well Made for Baby

Warm, Long Gertrude Skirts
Part Wool Flannel
32 G 2660—Cream white only. Shipping weight, 4 ounces. Each..... **85¢**

Amoskeag Flannelette
32 G 2661—Flannelette. White only. Shipping weight, 5 ounces. Each.... **35¢**
Infants' size only. Long style—soft, fine materials. Dainty shell crochet edgings. Buttons at shoulders.

Soft Nainsook Slip and Skirt
32 G 2555—Long Bishop slip. Shipping weight, 3 ounces. Each..... **37¢**
32 G 2554—Long Gertrude skirt. Shipping weight, 3 ounces. Each..... **35¢**
White. Infants' size only.
Practical little garments. Sheer white nainsook Slip has lace edge on sleeves and neck. Skirt buttons at shoulder. Full cut.

Specially Priced Dress and Skirt
32 G 2590—Dress. Shipping weight, 3 ounces. Each..... **49¢**
32 G 2591—Skirt. Shipping weight, 3 ounces. Each..... **49¢**
White. Infants' size only.
Dress of good quality batiste. Has embroidered set-in yoke, lace edge on neck and sleeves and embroidery trimmed bottom. Long batiste skirt, buttons at shoulder with embroidery at bottom.

Lace Trimmed Dress and Skirt
32 G 2552—Dress. Ship. wt., 3 oz. Each..... **79¢**
32 G 2553—Skirt. Ship. wt., 3 oz. Each..... **59¢**
White only. Infants' size.
Good quality nainsook with embroidered yoke and panel down front. Embroidered ruffle. Lace trimmed neck and sleeves. Embroidery trimmed long Gertrude Skirt.

Fine Nainsook Dress and Skirt
32 G 2501—Dress. Ship. wt., 3 oz. Each..... **$1.79**
32 G 2502—Skirt. Ship. wt., 2 oz. Each..... **98¢**
White only. Infants' size only.
Dress is trimmed with beautiful hand embroidery and all edges are finished with dainty hand scalloping. Skirt edged with hand scalloping.

Lovely Dress and Skirt **$1.98**
32 G 2514—White. Infants' size only. Shipping weight, set, 5 ounces.
Price for set.... **$1.98**
Baby's fancy christening set of dainty soft nainsook. Dress has embroidered batiste yoke with lace insertion and ribbon rosettes. Embroidery and lace down front. Skirt ruffle trimmed with lace and insertion; lace edged neck and sleeves. Lace trimmed Gertrude Skirt to match.

Dainty and Fine Each **98¢**
32 G 2550—Long white dress. Shipping weight, 3 ounces. Each..... **98¢**
32 G 2551—Long white skirt. Shipping weight, 3 ounces. Each..... **98¢**
Infants' size only.
A marvelous value! Both pieces are hand made of fine quality nainsook. Dress has a plaited panel down the front and lovely hand embroidered designs in front below neck. Lace edged neck and sleeves are finished with tiny French knots. Long, hand made Gertrude Skirt has dainty lace edge at bottom.

AMOSKEAG FLANNELETTE

Flannelette Wrapper **39¢**
32 G 2624—White with pink trimming.
32 G 2625—White with blue trimming.
Infants' size only. Ship. weight, each, 5 oz.
Warm, cozy garment for the very tiny baby. Famous AMOSKEAG flannelette, with dainty colored shell crochet stitching on all edges. Sturdy and so economical. Satin ribbon ties. Well made and generously cut.

Soft Flannelette In Revers Style **41¢**
32 G 2616—White with pink trimming.
32 G 2617—White with blue trimming.
Infants' size only. Ship. weight, each, 5 oz.
A touch of pretty colored crochet edging on collar, sleeve, revers and bottom make this little Wrapper especially dainty. Well known Amoskeag flannelette that wears so splendidly. Carefully made in full sizes to give surprisingly long service. Satin ribbon tie.

Dainty Floral Pattern Revers **45¢**
32 G 2642—White with pink trimming.
32 G 2643—White with blue trimming.
Infants' size only. Shipping weight, each, ounces.
One of our daintiest Wrappers and very low priced for famous Amoskeag flannelette! The pretty floral patterned revers and cuffs are edged with shell crochet stitching. Ribbon tie.

Walking Length Flannelette Gown **48¢**
32 G 2604—White with blue trimming.
32 G 2605—White with pink trimming.
AGES: 1, 2, and 3 years. State age. Ship. wt., each, 6 oz.
Cozy, warm Amoskeag flannelette Gown. Collar and sleeves edged with tiny shell crochet stitching. Button front closing. Full cut and well made.

Bag Style Gown of Flannelette **43¢**
32 G 2676—White with pink trimming.
32 G 2677—White with blue trimming.
Infants' size only. Shipping weight, each, 5 ounces.
Delightfully warm Amoskeag flannelette Sleeping Bag with turn over collar, cuffs and neck opening edged with dainty colored shell crochet stitching. Satin ribbon tie. Protect Baby's feet by tying the tape snugly at the bottom.

Flannelette Nightgown **39¢**
32 G 2602—White with blue trimming.
32 G 2603—White with pink trimming.
Infants' size only. Ship. weight, each, 5 oz.
Amoskeag flannelette gown—and that means it's serviceable—priced at a genuine saving. Collar, cuffs and bottom edged with dainty shell crochet stitching. Two-button front closing. Well made and full cut.

Snug, Cozy Bag Style Gown **49¢**
32 G 2600—White with blue trimming.
32 G 2601—White with pink trimming.
AGES: 6 months, 1 and 2 years. State age. Ship. weight, each, 5 oz.
Gown of Amoskeag flannelette in the popular bag style for growing babies. Tie the tape at the bottom and the little feet are sure to keep warm. Gown has dainty shell crochet stitching at neck and turnback cuffs. Button front closing. Full roomy sizes nd exceptionally well made.

Embroidery Trimmed Amoskeag Flannelette **49¢**
32 G 2618—Long Skirt. Infants' size only. Shipping weight, 3 ounces. Each..... **55¢**
32 G 2619—Short Skirt. AGES: 6 months, 1 and 2 years. State age. Shipping weight, 3 ounces. Each..... **49¢**
White only.
Warm Gertrude Skirts of Amoskeag flannelette. Front of skirt is daintily trimmed with Rayon embroidery designs and shell crochet stitched edges. Buttons at shoulders.

How to Order Infants' Wear
All our garments are cut in full, roomy sizes.
For Baby's Short Dresses, measure from center of shoulder to bottom of hem and order by age.

Age	Length
6 months	About 20 in.
1 year	About 19 in.
2 years	About 20 in.

Short Skirts are one inch shorter than dresses.
Long clothes come in infants' size only; for infants up to 6 months. Dresses are about 24 inches long; skirts, 1 inch shorter. Gowns and Wrappers are about 27 inches ong from back of neck to bottom of hem.

Sleeping Bag **73¢**
32 G 2608—White only. One size. For babies up to 1 year. Ship. weight, 6 ounces.
Nationally famous "Arnold" Brand sleeping bag. Closely knit of combed cotton yarn, wonderfully warm and durable. Shell crochet edging at neck and tape drawstring. Bag style bottom ties with tape. Back closing.

Durable Short Skirts
Part Wool Flannel
32 G 2682—Cream white.

Amoskeag Flannelette **29¢**
32 G 2681—White.
AGES: 6 months, 1 and 2 years. State age. Ship. wt., each, 4 oz.
Wool mixed flannel or popular Amoskeag flannelette short Gertrude Skirts with shell crochet stitched edges. Buttons at shoulders.

Dress and Skirt Embroidery Trimmed
32 G 2503—Short dress. Shipping weight, 3 oz. Each..... **59¢**
32 G 2504—Short skirt. Shipping weight, 3 oz. Each..... **57¢**
AGES: 6 months, 1 and 2 years. State age wanted.
Lovely nainsook Dress with embroidered batiste yoke set in with hemstitching. Neck and sleeves lace edged. Bottom finished with embroidery hemstitched on ruffle. Gertrude Skirt to match has embroidery ruffle and buttons at shoulder.

Exquisitely Dainty Dress and Skirt
32 G 2510—Dress..... **$1.79**
32 G 2511—Skirt..... **.85**
White only. AGES: 1 and 2 years. State age. Ship. wt., 3 oz.
All hand made. Dress of fine batiste, has hand scalloping at neck and bottom and embroidered turnback cuffs. Front of dress has assorted hand embroidered designs and pin tucks on each shoulder in front with larger tucks in back. Nainsook Gertrude Skirt has all edges hand scalloped.

Lovely Batiste **$1.09**
32 G 2508—White with pink trimming.
32 G 2509—White with blue trimming.
AGES: 6 months, 1 and 2 years. State age. Ship. wt., each, 3 oz.
Charming Dress in the popular raglan sleeve style. Made of soft, fine batiste, with the neck and sleeves bound with pretty colored batiste and edged with dainty lace. Colored panels hemstitched into the front and exquisitely hand embroidered.

Dressy Frock and Skirt
32 G 2506—Short Dress..... **79¢**
32 G 2507—Short Skirt..... **59¢**
AGES: 6 months, 1 and 2 years. State age. White only. Ship. wt., each, 3 oz.
Skirt and Dress of sheer nainsook. Dress has embroidered yoke set in with lace insertion, and lace edged neck and sleeves. Embroidery ruffle at bottom and two rows of lace insertion. Gertrude Skirt has embroidery edge and lace insertion at bottom to match dress.

Ward's Special **$1.00**
32 G 2500—White only. AGES: 6 months, 1 and 2 years. State age. Shipping weight, 4 ounces.
Our most popular Hand Made Dress in the cunning Raglan style. Sheer nainsook with dainty embroidery and drawn work in front. Fine lace trims the high neck and elbow sleeves. Generous hem. Buttons in back. Remember—it's all hand made, smocked and hemstitched.

Beautiful Quality Batiste Dress **59¢**
32 G 2505—White only. AGES: 6 months, 1 and 2 years. State age. Shipping weight, 3 ounces.
You will wonder how Ward's can offer you this lovely Frock at such a low price. Fine quality batiste in a style suitable for either boy or girl. Collar colorfully embroidered. Hand smocking in dainty colors. Full cut with wide hem. French seams.

81

Waist Union Suits Comfytogs For Children 2 to 13 Years

COMFYTOGS offer unusual convenience and comfort to both children and mothers. They are practical Waist Union Suits knit from fine quality yarns, and are made in a variety of styles and sizes, giving you a wide selection. Deep flap under the roomy three-button drop seat, and an extra row of buttons at waistline for attaching outer-garments eliminates the separate waist. Where most waist union suits have but one strap over the shoulders, Comfytogs—in all but Dutch neck styles—have two. Buttons for attaching outer-garments are of genuine bone.

Order by Age Only

Heavy Weight for Winter Wear Contains Small Amount of Wool

Half Wool

Best Quality—Big Value

29 G 944—Cream color only.

2-3 and 4-5 years.........$2.15
6-7 and 8-9 years......... 2.45
10-11 and 12-13 years...... 2.75

State age.
Shipping weight, each, 13 ounces.
Our best quality Comfytogs—exceptionally well made in every respect. Finely finished—suitable for boys or girls. Knit in a fine elastic rib from one-half pure wool worsted, balance Peruvian cotton which has an extra long staple. Fabrics knit from it are famous for their long wearing qualities. Comfortable heavy weight ideal for coldest weather. Unbreakable bone buttons for attaching outer-garments are taped on tubular knit straps that reinforce back, shoulders and front. Other buttons are fine quality fish-eye pearl. Tubular knit button stay and buttonhole facing. Neat shell trim at neck. Three-button drop seat, fastening over deep flap has large comfortable gusset. Metal pin tubes for attaching hose supporters. Smooth, flatlocked seams.

Economy in Every Price

Special Style Extra Special Value

89¢ Each

29 G 942—Gray.
29 G 950—Cream white.
AGES: 2-3, 4-5, 6-7, 8-9, 10-11, 12-13 years.
State age. Shipping weight, each, 13 oz.

We want to call your attention to the still lower price we are making on these heavy weight Comfytogs, knit in a fine rib of good quality cotton containing a small amount of wool. Last year suits like these won the approval of over 100,000 mothers when they realized the splendid value Ward's was offering and bought.

These garments are quality made throughout to meet the demand for low priced but carefully finished underwear. Notice two knit straps over the shoulder. The drop seat on these suits has three buttons that prevent gaping and is made over a deep flap in back. Plenty of buttons for outer garments that are firmly sewed on. Button stay and buttonhole facing are tubular knit of self material. Buttons for attaching outer-garments are unbreakable bone. Metal pin tubes at sides for attaching hose supporters. All seams are smooth flatlocked. Extra large gusset.

Feature Value

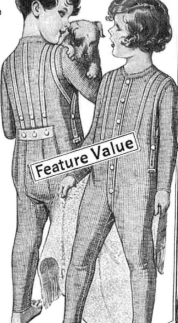

One-Fifth Wool

29 G 943—Cream color only.

2-3 and 4-5 years................ $1.28
6-7 and 8-9 years.................. 1.58
10-11 and 12-13 years............. 1.88

State age. Shipping weight, each, 13 ounces.
They are fine ribbed and very elastic. These heavy weight Comfytogs will keep the youngsters warm and cozy. Knit of excellent quality cotton, containing about 20 per cent wool worsted. Tubular knit straps reinforce front and back over shoulders. Taped on bone buttons for attaching outer-garments. Large gusset—three-button drop seat. Metal pin tubes for securing hose supporters. Flatlocked seams. Shell edging around neck.

Rayon Striped Small Percentage Wool

$1.00 29 G 967—Cream white only.
AGES: 2-3, 4-5, 6-7, 8-9, 10-11, 12-13 years.
State age. Shipping weight, each, 13 ounces.
Especially neat and attractive Comfytogs, fine ribbed knit in a heavy winter weight, of Rayon striped Peruvian cotton, with a small amount of pure wool for added warmth. Have much the appearance of silk and wool. Waist Union Suits such as these would cost about 50 per cent more at the average retail stores. High neck, long sleeve style with mercerized shell stitched neck. Tubular knit reinforcing straps over shoulders, front and back, and tubular knit button and buttonhole stays. Plenty of unbreakable bone buttons for attaching outer-garments, firmly sewed on. Tape covered metal pin tubes for securing hose supporters. Three-button drop seat. Flat seams.

Extra Heavy Fleeced Cotton

29 G 961
29 G 941
29 G 959
29 G 940
29 G 939
29 G 945

Lowest Priced Cotton Suits

Rayon Striped Cotton
Cream Color Only

79¢ 29 G 959—Dutch neck. Elbow sleeves, ankle length.
29 G 961—Dutch neck. Elbow sleeves, knee length.

AGES: 2-3, 4-5, 6-7, 8-9, 10-11, 12-13 years.
State age. Shipping weight, each, 11 ounces.
Attractively striped with Rayon, these fine ribbed cotton Comfytogs are priced low indeed for such good quality waist Union Suits. Knit in a medium heavy weight. Strongly reinforced over shoulders, front and back, with tubular knitted straps. Plenty of buttons for attaching outer-garments; back buttons securely taped on. Three-button drop seat fastens over deep flap so it will remain closed in any position. Tape loops at side for attaching hose supporters. Finished with neat edging of Rayon and mercerized crochet. Drawtape at neck.

Heavy Weight—Lightly Fleeced
Choice of Three Popular Styles
White Only

29 G 940—High neck, long sleeves, ankle length.
29 G 939—Dutch neck, elbow sleeves, ankle length.
29 G 941—Dutch neck, elbow sleeves, knee length.
AGES: 2-3, 4-5, 6-7, 8-9, 10-11, 12-13 years.
State age. Shipping weight, each, 13 ounces.

73¢ Each

Last year, at the low price of 83¢ each, these Comfytogs sold so rapidly that we had a hard time keeping the supply up to meet your demands. This year we have signed an even larger contract, enabling us to obtain a still lower price and again pass the saving along to you.

These little waist Union Suits are fine ribbed knit from good quality cotton yarn, and they're a wonderful value. Made in a comfortably heavy weight—slightly fleeced for warmth and smooth comfort. Well reinforced with strong tubular straps over shoulders, front and back. Bone buttons for attaching outer-garments are practically unbreakable. Metal pin tubes for attaching hose supporters. Three-button drop seat has an unusually large, comfortable gusset and fastens over a deep flap—remains closed in any position.

All sizes are cut over generous proportions—full and roomy. Smooth, flatlocked seams insure longer wear and provide against chafing tender skins.

Our Heaviest Cotton Comfytogs
White Only

29 G 945—High neck, long sleeves, ankle length.
AGES: 2-3, 4-5, 6-7, 8-9, 10-11, 12-13 years. State age. Shipping weight, each, 15 ounces.

89¢

Mothers know when they buy these heavy weight Comfytogs, they are buying real warmth and comfort for their children for the cold winter months. Elastic ribbed knit from good quality cotton, thickly fleeced inside for extra warmth. Reinforced over shoulders with tubular knit straps of the same good quality cotton. Taped-on buttons for attaching outer-garments. Three-button drop seat. Neat mercerized shell edging on flat collarette neck. Tape loops at sides for attaching hose supporters. Carefully finished in roomy sizes. Our low price means a worthwhile saving to you.

Boys' Winter Weight Cotton Union Suits!

Priced to make every penny count

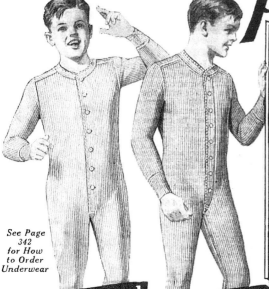

See Page 342 for How to Order Underwear

Heavy Weight

Extra Heavy Weight

Ribbed Cotton

Lightly Fleeced

6, 8, 10 Years	12, 14, 16 Years
66¢ Each	**86¢** Each

State age. Shipping weight, each, 14 ounces.

29 G 325—Cream color.
29 G 327—Gray mottled.

Boys' winter Union Suits that fit, at a great saving. Fine elastic ribbed knit of good quality cotton in a heavy weight, lightly fleeced. Made with reinforced inserts in shoulders; flat collarette neck; close fitting ribbed cuffs at wrists and ankles. Neck and front trimmed with fancy mercerized stitching. Closed crotch with large gusset in seat. Flatlocked seams.

Best Quality

$1.15

29 G 342—Light gray mottled only.
SIZES: 6, 8, 10, 12, 14, 16 years. State age. Ship. wt., each, 14 oz.

This is our best ribbed knit cotton Union Suit for boys, and our best bargain for their mothers who want the utmost in value. Extra fine quality yarns, knit into a comfortable heavy weight suit. Well fitting collarette neck; inserted ribbed strips across shoulders. Ribbed cuffs at wrists and ankles. Wide lapped one button seat. Closed crotch.

Flat Knit – Heavily Fleeced

6, 8, 10 Years	12, 14, 16 Years
69¢ Each	**89¢** Each

State age. Ship. wt., each, 15 ounces.

29 G 335—Jaeger tan only.

Every boy will like this warm, heavy weight cotton Union Suit with its soft, pure white fleece lining that is unusually comfortable. Thousands of mothers have found it to be a practical solution to their problem of warm, durable underwear for their boy. Reinforcement at back of neck adds to its wear. Ribbed cuffs on sleeves and ankles. Comfortable closed crotch with wide lapped seat that stays closed.

6, 8, 10 Years	12, 14, 16 Years
95¢ Each	**$1.15** Each

State age. Shipping weight, each, 16 ounces.

29 G 323—Silver gray only.

These are the best and heaviest flat knit Union Suits made and we know you will be well pleased with their warmth and service. Knit in an extra heavy weight from long staple cotton with a heavy pure white fleecing on the inside. Collarette neck fits snugly. Ribbed knit cuffs, very elastic and well fitting, are firmly sewed on the wrists and ankles. Closed crotch; wide lapped seat has one-button fastening.

Extra Heavy Fleecing

6, 8, 10 Years	12, 14, 16 Years
78¢ Each	**98¢** Each

State age. Ship. wt., each, 13 oz.
29 G 340—Gray only.

Active outdoor boys will appreciate this warm, heavy weight, ribbed knit cotton Union Suit and so will mothers who want to dress their boy well and warm at an economical price. An extra thread is knit into the back of the fabric and brushed to a thick soft fleece. Neat collarette neck fits snugly. Pearl buttons throughout. Closed crotch with roomy wide lapped seat. Smooth flatlocked seams. Very elastic ribbed knitting allows absolute body freedom. A wonderful bargain.

NITE WEAR FOR LITTLE TOTS

Sleepytime

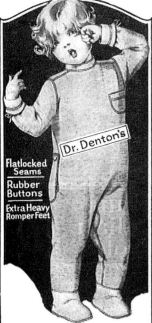

Dr. Denton's

Flatlocked Seams
Rubber Buttons
Extra Heavy Romper Feet

Our Own Special

Sleepytime

Flat Knit
Heavy Weight Cotton

1 year...$1.00		6 years..$1.50
2 years...1.10		7 years...1.60
3 years...1.20		8 years...1.70
4 years...1.30		9 years...1.80
5 years...1.40		10 years...1.90

State age. Shipping weight, each, 13 ounces.
29 G 981—Natural gray only.

Ages 1 and 2 open down back; 3 to 10 open down front.

The well known Dr. Denton Sleepers, made from medium heavy weight cotton jersey knitted cloth—containing a small percentage of wool. Soft fleecy finish inside and out. Ages 1 and 2 years have tie strings at cuffs. Three-button drop seat. Unbreakable rubber buttons. Flatlocked seams. All sizes made with extra heavy feet for longer wear.

Ribbed Knit Cotton

77¢ Each

AGES: 1, 2, 3, 4, 5, 6, 7 years. State age.

29 G 986—Gray only.

Shipping wt., each, 13 oz.

We have added another number to our popular "Sleepytime" brand. We have priced this low for such fine quality. Knit of soft ribbed knit cotton, brushed to a soft nap on both sides. Made in the convenient button front style that is easy to put on or take off. Roomy, three-button drop seat. Seat buttons taped on. The feet have double soles for longer wear. Tie strings at wrists. All smooth flatlocked seams. All bone buttons. Large gusset in seat insures roomy comfort.

Warm Sleepers Button in Back

1, 2, 3, 4, 5, 6 years	**82¢**
7, 8, 9, 10 years	**99¢**

State age. Ship. wt., each, 13 ounces.

29 G 982—Gray.
29 G 983—White.

This warm little Sleeper is one of the favorites of our "Sleepytime" family and rightly so, because it is such an unusual value. Made of fine cotton, lightly fleeced on both sides for additional warmth and comfort. Fastens down back and has three-button drop seat. All buttons are of strong unbreakable bone. One pocket. Sizes 1 to 4 years are made with tie strings at wrists. All sizes made with feet. Flat lock seams used throughout. Large gusset in seat.

Button Front Style

1, 2, 3, 4, 5, 6 years	**82¢**
7, 8, 9, 10 years	**99¢**

State age. Ship. weight, each, 13 ounces.

29 G 984—Gray only.

Popular style Sleepers, our famous "Sleepytime" brand, made of good quality knit cotton, lightly fleeced on both sides. Made and finished like garments for which you would pay almost twice this price. Made in the button front style which is easy for children to put on or take off, without assistance. Three-button drop seat. Buttons are made of bone. Sizes, 1 to 4 years have tie strings at wrists. Flatlocked seams throughout assuring comfort.

Slipper Foot

2, 3, 4, 5, 6 years	**$.89**
7, 8, 9, 10 years	**1.10**

State age. Ship. weight, each, 13 ounces.

29 G 985—Gray only.

Flat knit cotton Sleepers containing a small percentage of wool, our famous "Sleepytime" brand. Priced low for this fine quality. Made with special foot which can be unfastened and buttoned out of the way when the child walks around preventing them from becoming soiled. A feature all mothers will appreciate. Five-button drop seat. All buttons are of bone. Sizes, 2 to 4 years have tie strings at wrists. Large gusset in seat assures comfort.

Our Best "Sleepytime"

1 and 2 years	**$.98**
3, 4, 5, 6, 7 years	**1.09**
8, 9, 10, 11, 12 years	**1.35**

State age. Shipping weight, each, 13 ounces.

29 G 999—Gray only.

Our famous "Sleepytime" brand is growing in popularity every year, combining as it does fine quality at an economical price. Elastic ribbed fabric is knit from soft cotton and wool yarns containing more than the usual percentage of wool for garments selling for so low a price. Soft brushed finish inside and out. Made in the convenient button front style, with soles in the feet and tie strings at wrists. Roomy drop seat has taped on buttons. One pocket. Flatlocked seams. All buttons are bone. Priced low for such quality.

83

Guaranteed Factory-Tested
ELGIN, WALTHAM, NEW YORK STANDARD

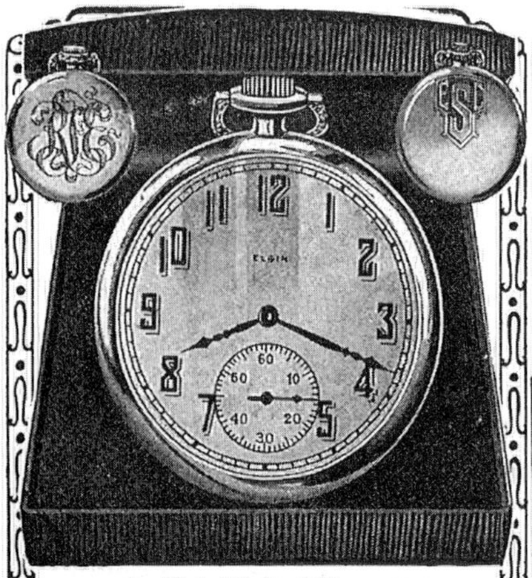

An Established Favorite

Plain polished with hand engraved monogram. Your choice of Ribbon Monogram as shown on the left, or Fancy Block as shown on the right. Open face 12-size; screw back and front, 10-Karat natural color gold filled case, guaranteed to wear 20 years. State initials, movement and style monogram wanted.

545 G 3799—15-J. Keystone-N.Y. Standard $10.95
545 G 3967—15-Jewel Admiral 12.50
545 G 3970— 7-Jewel Elgin or Waltham .. 12.85
545 G 3973—15-Jewel Elgin or Waltham .. 16.65
545 G 3974—17-Jewel Elgin or Waltham .. 19.50
545 G 3976—19-J. Waltham P. S. Bartlett 25.75

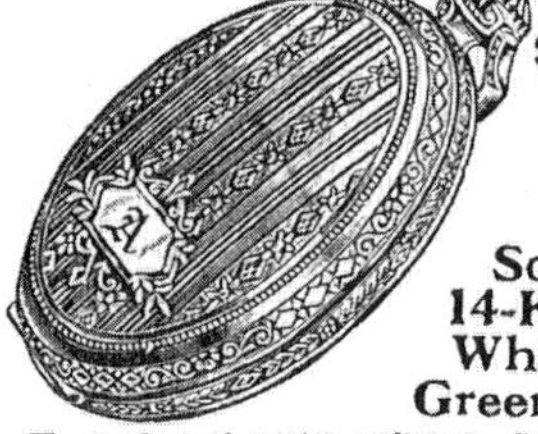

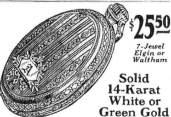

$25.50
7-Jewel Elgin or Waltham

Solid 14-Karat White or Green Gold

The product of master craftsmen. Solid 14-Karat gold, beautifully designed with hinged back; 12-size thin model. Any initial you desire will be engraved free of charge, in fancy old English letter as shown. State initial and movement wanted.

White Solid Gold
545 G 3841—15-J. Elgin or Waltham $29.50
545 G 3842—17-Jewel Elgin or Waltham . 31.85
545 G 3843—19-J. Waltham, P.S. Bartlett 37.98

Solid Green Gold
545 G 3844—7-Jewel Elgin or Waltham... $25.50
545 G 3845—15-Jewel Elgin or Waltham.. 29.50
545 G 3846—17-Jewel Elgin or Waltham .. 31.85

Expert Watch Repairing

We maintain a completely equipped Watch Repair Department, operated by skilled watchmakers. Send your watch by insured parcel post or express and we will immediately send estimate of cost of repairing.

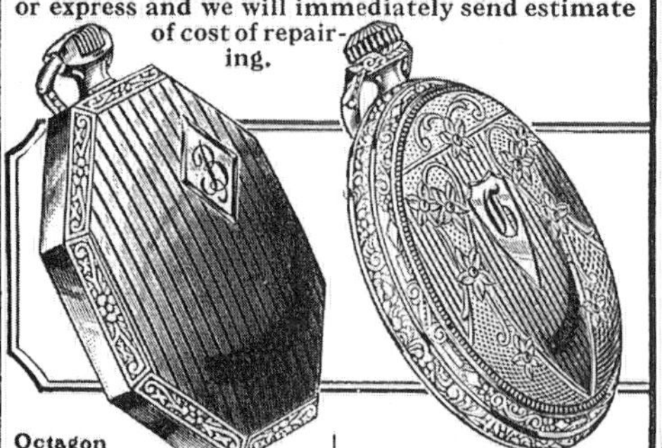

Octagon Shape

Men's 12-size open face Watch. Engraved 10-Karat green gold filled case, guaranteed to wear 20 years. State initials and movement.

545 G 3797—15-Jewel N.Y. Standard $13.98
545 G 3836—15-Jewel Admiral..... 15.25
545 G 3837—7-J. Elgin 16.65
545 G 3838—15-Jewel Waltham or Elgin...... $20.50
545 G 3839 — 17-J. Elgin or Waltham. $23.50

Handsome 12-size open face Watch in 10-Karat green gold filled case, guaranteed to wear 20 years. Screw front and back. State initials and movement.

545 G 3873—15-Jewel N. Y. Standard $11.95
545 G 3810—7-J. Elgin or Waltham... 14.48
545 G 3811—15-J. Elgin or Waltham.... 18.65
545 G 3812—17-J. Elgin or Waltham.... 21.25

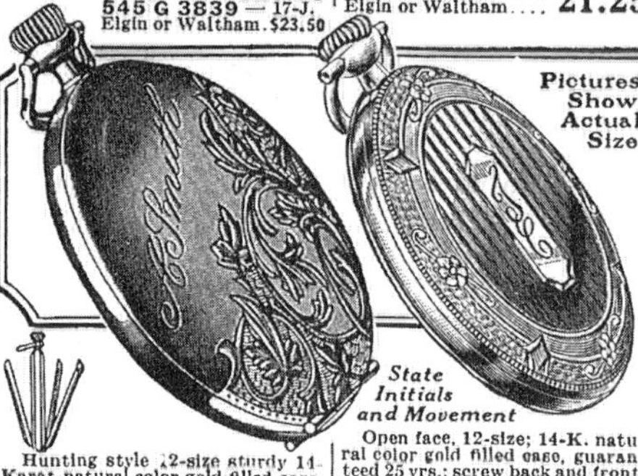

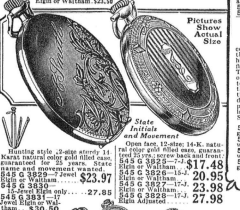

Pictures Show Actual Size

State Initials and Movement

Hunting style 12-size sturdy 14-Karat natural color gold filled case, guaranteed for 25 years. State name and movement wanted.

545 G 3829—7 Jewel Elgin or Waltham....... $23.97
545 G 3830—15-Jewel Elgin only.... ..27.85
545 G 3831—17 Jewel Elgin or Waltham... $30.50

Open face, 12-size; 14-K. natural color gold filled case, guaranteed 25 yrs.; screw back and front.

545 G 3825—7-J. Elgin or Waltham... $17.48
545 G 3826—15-J. Elgin or Waltham... 20.95
545 G 3827—17-J. Elgin or Waltham... 23.98
545 G 3828—17-J. Elgin Adjusted...... 27.98

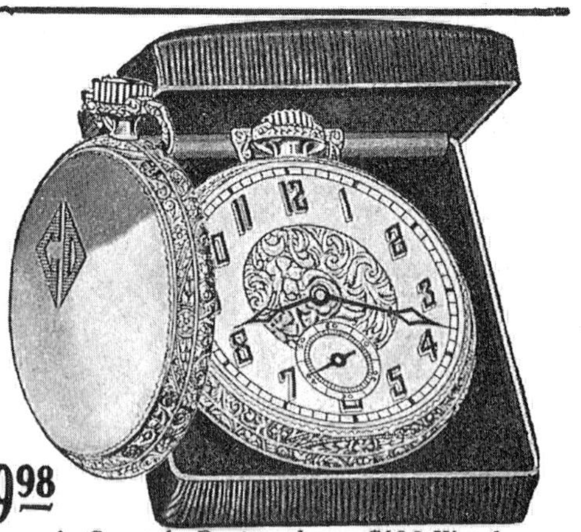

$9.98

As Smartly Designed as a $100 Watch

Designed throughout like the most expensive watches. A thin model 12-size with beautifully carved center, white or green, ten-year guaranteed gold filled case. A very striking silvered dial with fancy center and raised gilt numerals; gilt hands; in fact, many attractive features generally found in watches priced up to $100. And there is much more than appearance—the 15-Jewel Lanco movement is a good timekeeper, the product of one of Switzerland's foremost watchmakers and we guarantee it to give reliable service. It comes to you in a velvet lined leatherette gift case and is engraved with any initials desired in the very smart design shown above. State initials wanted.

545 G 4034—White gold filled.
545 G 4062—Green gold filled. Each $9.98

Genuine Elgin Streamline or Waltham Colonial

Nationally known and sold the country over for $40.00. Two extra thin models; 12-size open face with hinged back. Case is 14-Karat gold filled, guaranteed to wear 25 years. The 17-Jewel movements are the pride of both makers, and are timed and tested in the case before they leave the factory. Both models have beautiful silvered metal dials, specially designed for these watches. Come in plain back and engraved with any initials as shown free of charge. State initials wanted.

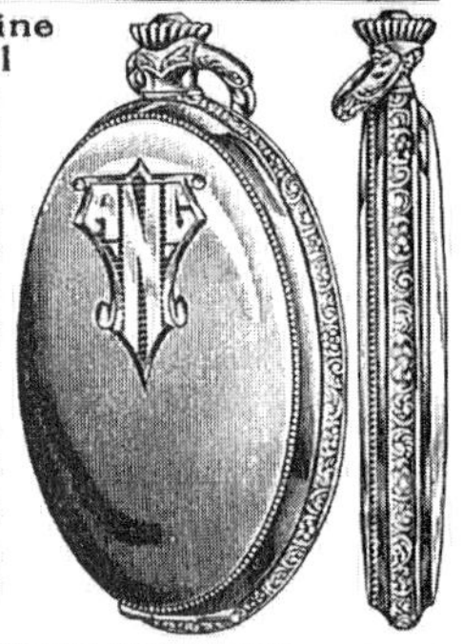

545 G 3942—Elgin Streamline, green gold filled.
545 G 3943—Elgin Streamline, white gold filled.
545 G 4245—Waltham Colonial, white gold filled.
545 G 4246—Waltham Colonial, green gold filled.
Each................ $32.50

Handsome Gift Case With Each Watch

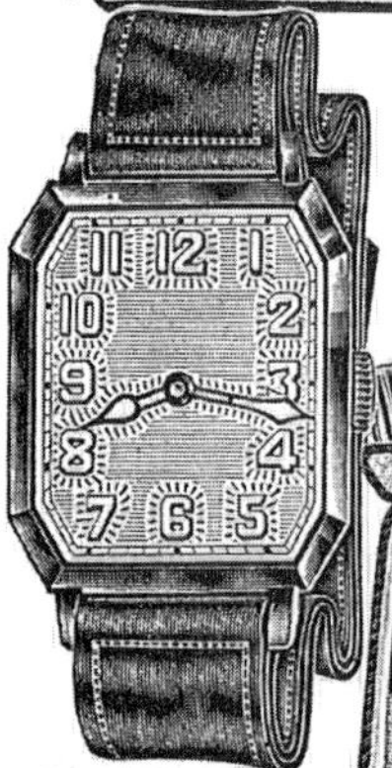

Attractive in design and a great favorite among men and boys everywhere. The dial has luminous hands and figures that show time in the dark. Reliable Swiss movement.

545 G 4163—15-Jewel silverine (nickel alloy) case.... $12.50
545 G 4164—6-Jewel white gold filled case guaranteed to wear ten years. $11.85
545 G 4165—15-Jewel white gold filled case guaranteed to wear ten years. $14.98

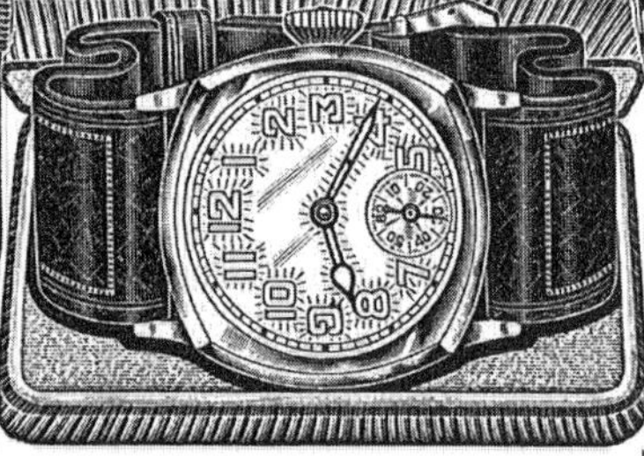

Men and boys appreciate this serviceable strap Watch fashioned in the popular cushion shape. Fitted with a 6-Jewel reliable Swiss movement. Luminous figures and hands; shows time in the dark. Handsome leatherette gift case.

545 G 4158—Silverine (nickel-alloy) case; 6-Jewel... $6.98
545 G 4283—White gold filled case guaranteed to wear ten years; 6-Jewel...................... $7.75

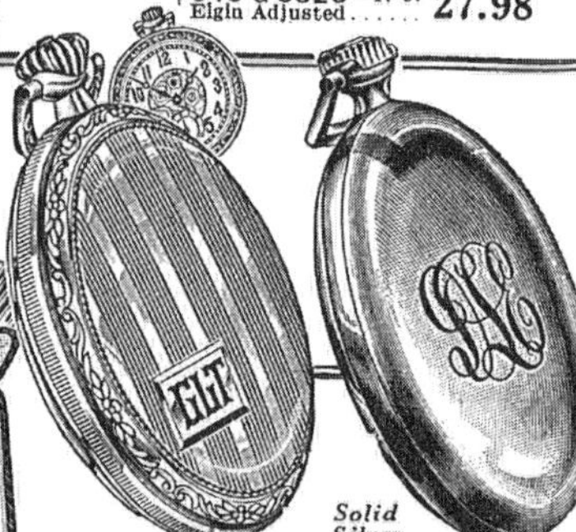

Open face 12-size Keystone-New York Standard. White or green gold filled case guaranteed to wear ten years. Artistic silvered dial. Any initials engraved free. State initials.

White Gold Filled
545 G 4224—15-Jewel...... $7.98
545 G 4223—7-Jewel....... 6.85

Green Gold Filled
545 G 4226—15-Jewel........ 7.98
545 G 4225 7-Jewel 6.85

Solid Silver

Plain polished. Open face 12-size thin model, screw back and front. State initials and movement.

545 G 4252—7-Jewel N.Y. Standard $9.98
545 G 4253—15-J. N.Y. Standard. $10.95
545 G 4254—7-Jewel Elgin or Walt. $14.95
545 G 4255—15-J. Elgin or Walt. $19.75
545 G 4256—17-J. Elgin or Walt. $21.50

The Very Latest Convenience

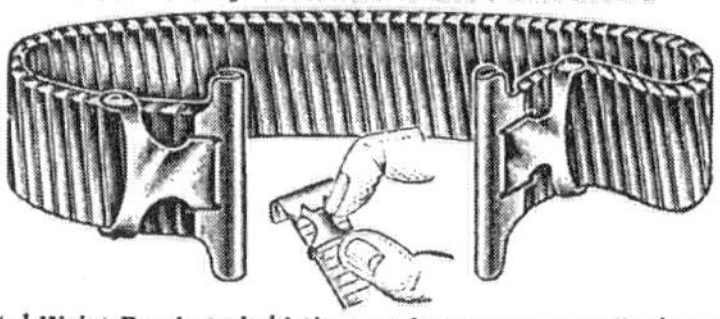

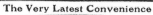

Metal Wrist Bands to hold the watch are now exceedingly popular. This one is very flexible with an expansion of about two inches and will fit most any man's wrist. Patent safety lock prevents loss of watch. Hook fasteners ⅝-in. wide. Ship. wt., 4 oz.

545 G 4297—Nickel-plated $1.45
545 G 4298—White gold filled 3.75
545 G 4299—Green gold filled 3.75

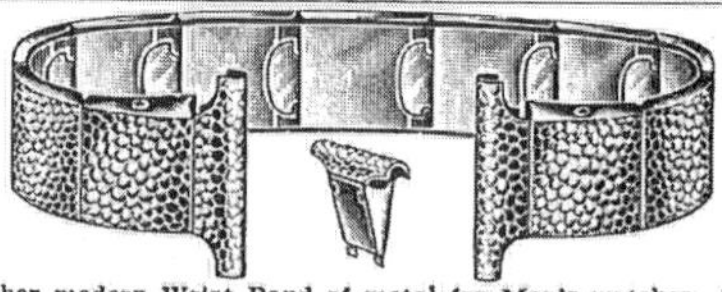

Another modern Wrist Band of metal for Men's watches. This one has detachable links, a splendid feature that allows shortening the band if necessary. Each link is large, with that massive square effect that is predominantly masculine in every respect. The safety end snaps for fastening to watch loops are ⅝ inch wide and will fit most any style wrist watch. Handsomely finished in nickel plate or green gold filled, in hammered effect as shown. Shipping weight, each, 4 ounces.

545 G 4300—Nickel plated.
545 G 4301—Green gold plate. Each.................. $1.48

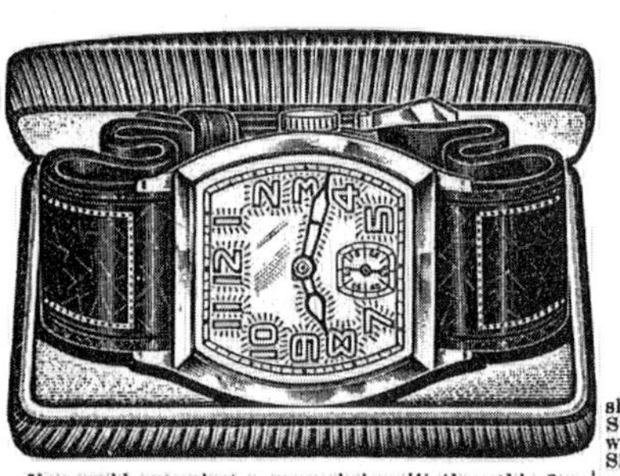

You could not select a more choice gift than this fine quality Swiss Strap Watch. It is medium sized and desirably neat in design. Luminous figures on dial and hands show time in the dark.

Silverine (Nickel Alloy) Case
545 G 4285— 6-Jewel........................ $7.98
545 G 4286—15-Jewel........................ 11.50

White Gold Filled, Ten-Year Case
545 G 4287— 6-Jewel........................ $10.85
545 G 4288—15-Jewel........................ 14.25

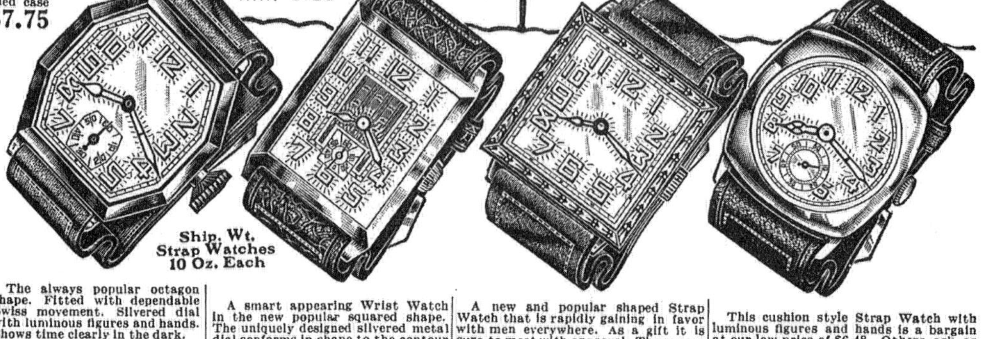

Ship. Wt. Strap Watches 10 Oz. Each

The always popular octagon shape. Fitted with dependable Swiss movement. Silvered dial with luminous figures and hands. Shows time clearly in the dark.

545 G 4166—6-Jewel; Silverine (nickel alloy) case.... $8.95
545 G 4167—6-Jewel; green gold filled case. $11.48
545 G 4168—15-Jewel; green gold filled case. $14.75

A smart appearing Wrist Watch in the new popular squared shape. The uniquely designed silvered metal dial conforms in shape to the contour of the case, and has a fancy ornamented center. Luminous figures and hands show time in the dark. Case is made of silverine (nickel alloy), with genuine leather strap. Fine quality Swiss movement that will render dependable service.

545 G 4289—6-Jewel $7.45

A new and popular shaped Strap Watch that is rapidly gaining in favor with men everywhere. As a gift it is sure to meet with approval. The square dial is silvered and has luminous figures and hands that clearly show time in the dark. Reliable Swiss movement.

545 G 4160—6-Jewel; silverine (nickel alloy) case.. $8.98
545 G 4161—6-Jewel; white gold filled case 11.96
545 G 4162—15-Jewel white gold filled case 14.95

This cushion style Strap Watch with luminous figures and hands is a bargain at our low price of $6.48. Others ask as much as $12 for equal quality. It has a 6-Jewel Swiss movement that is a dependable timekeeper for such a low price. The silverine (nickel alloy) case is highly polished and is fitted with genuine leather strap. For men or boys this watch will prove a mighty handy convenience and as a gift will be certain of appreciation.

545 G 4284............... $6.48

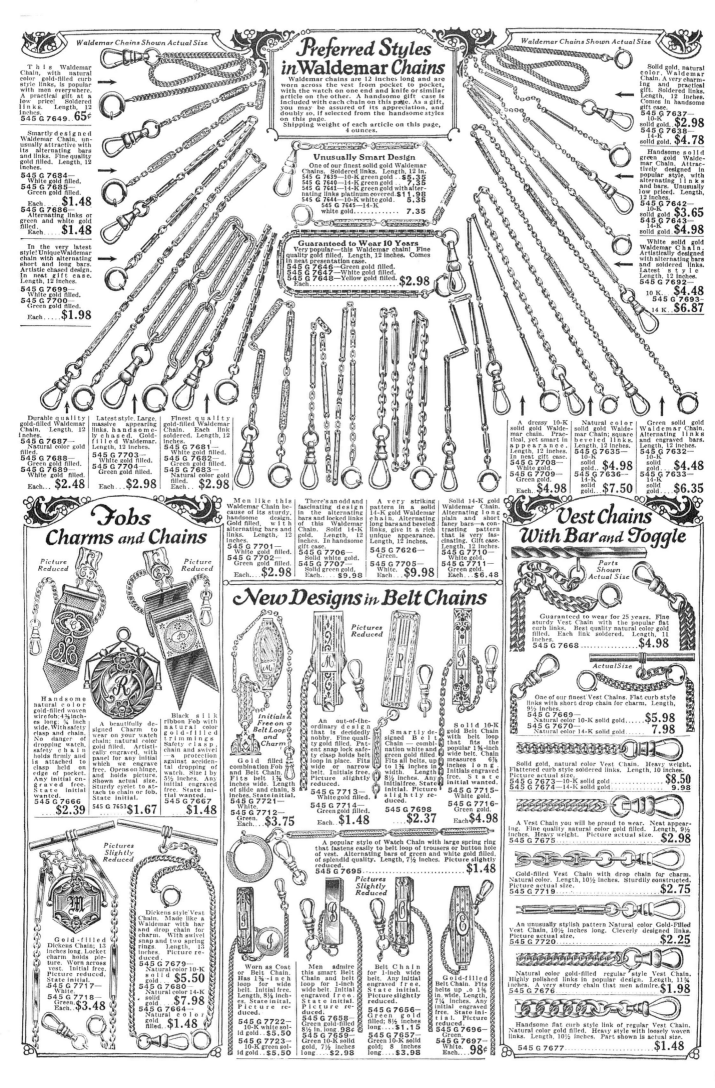

Preferred Styles in Waldemar Chains

Waldemar Chains Shown Actual Size

Waldemar chains are 12 inches long and are worn across the vest from pocket to pocket, with the watch on one end and knife or similar article on the other. A handsome gift case is included with each chain on this page. As a gift, you may be assured of its appreciation, and doubly so, if selected from the handsome styles on this page.
Shipping weight of each article on this page, 4 ounces.

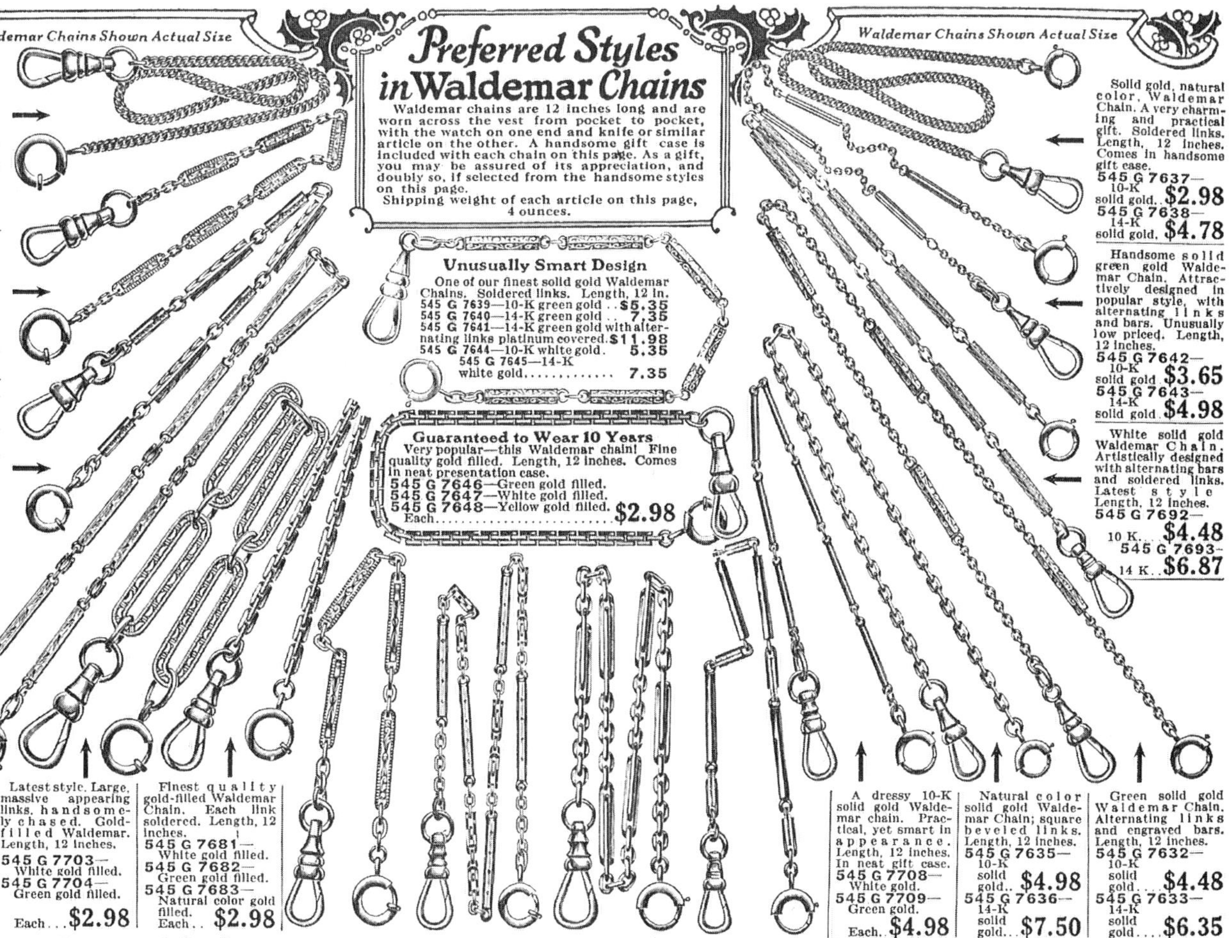

This Waldemar Chain, with natural color gold-filled curb style links, is popular with men everywhere. A practical gift at a low price! Soldered links. Length, 12 inches.
545 G 7649..65¢

Smartly designed Waldemar Chain, unusually attractive with its alternating bars and links. Fine quality gold filled. Length, 12 inches.
545 G 7684—White gold filled.
545 G 7685—Green gold filled.
Each.....$1.48
545 G 7686—Alternating links or green and white gold filled.
Each.....$1.48

In the very latest style! Unique Waldemar chain with alternating short and long bars. Artistic chased design. In neat gift case. Length, 12 inches.
545 G 7699—White gold filled.
545 G 7700—Green gold filled.
Each.....$1.98

Unusually Smart Design
One of our finest solid gold Waldemar Chains. Soldered links. Length, 12 in.
545 G 7639—10-K green gold..$5.35
545 G 7640—14-K green gold.. 7.35
545 G 7641—14-K green gold with alternating links platinum covered.$11.98
545 G 7644—10-K white gold. 5.35
545 G 7645—14-K white gold........... 7.35

Guaranteed to Wear 10 Years
Very popular—this Waldemar chain! Fine quality gold filled. Length, 12 inches. Comes in neat presentation case.
545 G 7646—Green gold filled.
545 G 7647—White gold filled.
545 G 7648—Yellow gold filled.
Each.........................$2.98

Waldemar Chains Shown Actual Size

Solid gold, natural color, Waldemar Chain. A very charming and practical gift. Soldered links. Length, 12 inches. Comes in handsome gift case.
545 G 7637—10-K solid gold. $2.98
545 G 7638—14-K solid gold. $4.78

Handsome solid green gold Waldemar Chain. Attractively designed in popular style, with alternating links and bars. Unusually low priced. Length, 12 inches.
545 G 7642—10-K solid gold. $3.65
545 G 7643—14-K solid gold. $4.98

White solid gold Waldemar Chain. Artistically designed with alternating bars and soldered links. Latest style. Length, 12 inches.
545 G 7692—10 K. $4.48
545 G 7693—14 K..$6.87

Durable quality gold-filled Waldemar Chain. Length, 12 inches.
545 G 7687—Natural color gold filled.
545 G 7688—Green gold filled.
545 G 7689—White gold filled.
Each... $2.48

Latest style. Large, massive appearing links, handsomely chased. Gold-filled Waldemar. Length, 12 inches.
545 G 7703—White gold filled.
545 G 7704—Green gold filled.
Each...$2.98

Finest quality gold-filled Waldemar Chain. Each link soldered. Length, 12 inches.
545 G 7681—White gold filled.
545 G 7682—Green gold filled.
545 G 7683—Natural color gold filled.
Each.. $2.98

Men like this Waldemar Chain because of its sturdy, handsome design. Gold filled, with alternating bars and links. Length, 12 inches.
545 G 7701—White gold filled.
545 G 7702—Green gold filled.
Each....$2.98

There's an odd and fascinating design in the alternating bars and locked links of this Waldemar Chain. Solid 14-K gold. Length, 12 inches. In handsome gift case.
545 G 7706—Solid white gold.
545 G 7707—Solid green gold.
Each.....$9.98

A very striking pattern in a solid 14-K gold Waldemar chain. Alternating long bars and beveled links, give it a rich unique appearance. Length, 12 inches.
545 G 7626—Green.
545 G 7705—White.
Each....$9.98

Solid 14-K gold Waldemar Chain. Alternating long plain and short fancy bars—a contrasting pattern that is very fascinating. Gift case. Length, 12 inches.
545 G 7710—White gold.
545 G 7711—Green gold.
Each...$6.48

A dressy 10-K solid gold Waldemar chain. Practical, yet smart in appearance. Length, 12 inches. In neat gift case.
545 G 7708—White gold.
545 G 7709—Green gold.
Each..$4.98

Natural color solid gold Waldemar Chain; square beveled links. Length, 12 inches.
545 G 7635—10-K solid gold.. $4.98
545 G 7636—14-K solid gold..$7.50

Green solid gold Waldemar Chain. Alternating links and bars. Length, 12 inches.
545 G 7632—10-K solid gold.. $4.48
545 G 7633—14-K solid gold....$6.35

Fobs Charms and Chains

Picture Reduced

Picture Reduced

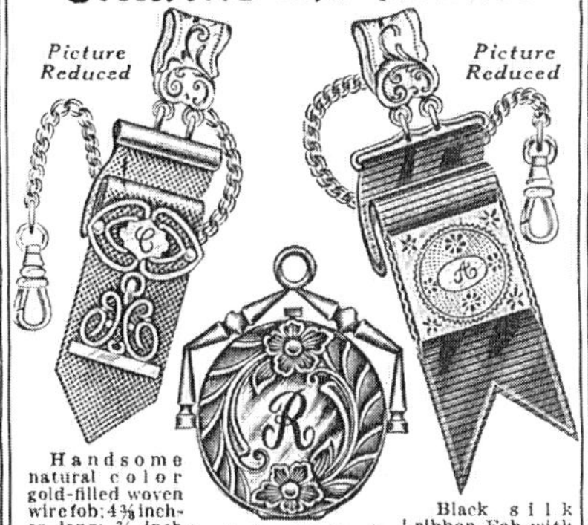

Handsome natural color gold-filled woven wire fob; 4⅜ inches long; ¾ inch wide. With safety clasp and chain. No danger of dropping watch, safety chain holds firmly and is attached to clasp held on edge of pocket. Any initial engraved free. State initial wanted.
545 G 7666
....$2.39

A beautifully designed Charm to wear on your watch chain; natural color gold filled. Artistically chased, with panel for any initial which we engrave free. Opens on hinge, and holds picture. Shown actual size. Sturdy eyelet to attach to chain or fob. State initial.
545 G 7653 $1.67

Black silk ribbon Fob with natural color gold-filled trimmings. Safety clasp, chain and swivel —a protection against accidental dropping of watch. Size 1 by 5½ inches. Any initial engraved free. State initial wanted.
545 G 7667
....$1.48

Pictures Slightly Reduced

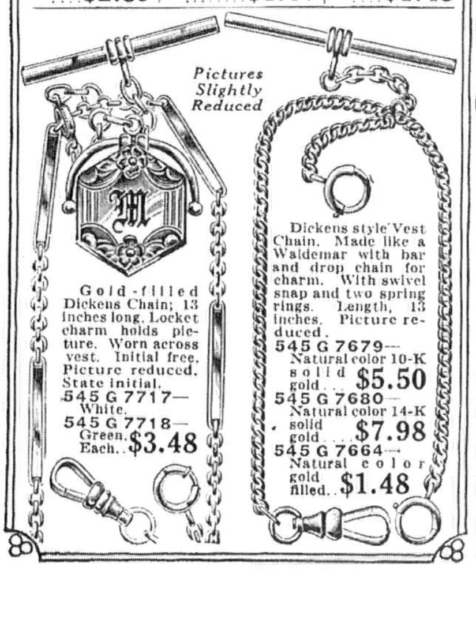

Gold-filled Dickens Chain; 13 inches long. Locket charm holds picture. Worn across vest. Initial free. Picture reduced. State initial.
545 G 7717—White.
545 G 7718—Green. Each..$3.48

Dickens style Vest Chain. Made like a Waldemar with bar and drop chain for charm. With swivel snap and two spring rings. Length, 13 inches. Picture reduced.
545 G 7679—Natural color 10-K solid gold.... $5.50
545 G 7680—Natural color 14-K solid gold.... $7.98
545 G 7664—Natural color gold filled..$1.48

New Designs in Belt Chains

Pictures Reduced

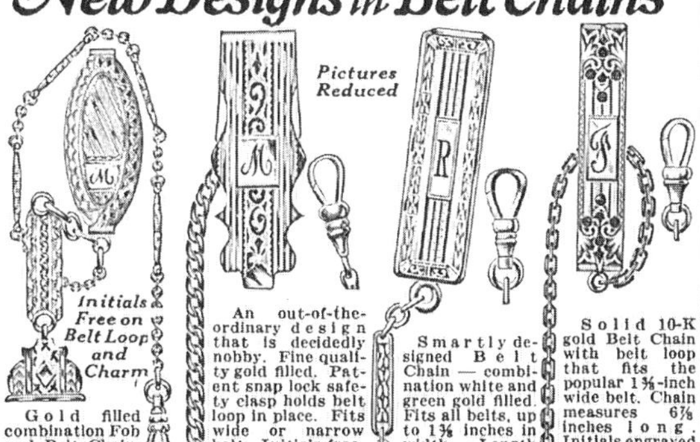

Initials Free on Belt Loop and Charm

Gold filled combination Fob and Belt Chain. Fits belt 1¾ inches wide. Length of slide and chain, 8 inches. State initial.
545 G 7721—White.
545 G 7712—Green. Each....$3.75

An out-of-the-ordinary design that is decidedly nobby. Fine quality gold filled. Patent snap lock safety clasp holds belt loop in place. Fits wide or narrow belt. Initials free. Picture slightly reduced.
545 G 7713—White gold filled.
545 G 7714—Green gold filled.
Each..$1.48

Smartly designed Belt Chain — combination white and green gold filled. Fits all belts, up to 1⅜ inches in width. Length 8½ inches. Any initial free. State initial. Picture slightly reduced.
545 G 7698
....$2.37

Solid 10-K gold Belt Chain with belt loop that fits the popular 1⅜-inch wide belt. Chain measures 6⅞ inches long. Initials engraved free. State initial wanted.
545 G 7715—White gold.
545 G 7716—Green gold.
Each $4.98

A popular style of Watch Chain with large spring ring that fastens easily to belt loop of trousers or button hole of vest. Alternating bars of green and white gold filled, of splendid quality. Length, 7½ inches. Picture slightly reduced.
545 G 7695......................$1.48

Pictures Slightly Reduced

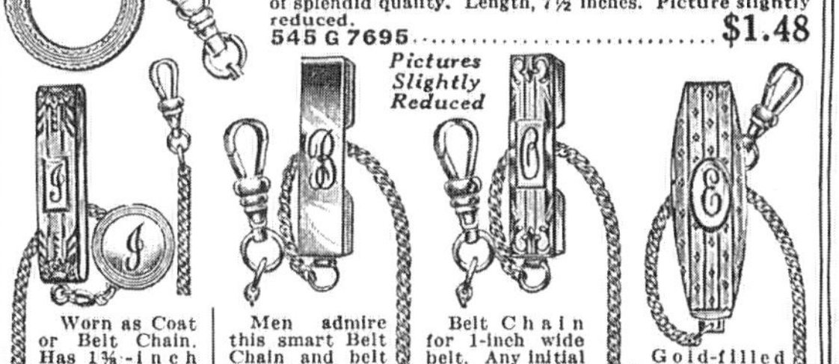

Worn as Coat or Belt Chain. Has 1⅜-inch loop for wide belt. Initial free. Length, 8⅛ inches. State initial. Picture reduced.
545 G 7722—10-K white solid gold..$5.50
545 G 7723—10-K green solid gold..$5.50

Men admire this smart Belt Chain and belt loop for 1-inch wide belt. Initial engraved free. State initial. Picture reduced.
545 G 7658—Green gold-filled 8½ in. long..98¢
545 G 7659—Green 10-K solid gold, 7½ inches long....$2.98

Belt Chain for 1-inch wide belt. Any initial engraved free. State initial. Picture slightly reduced.
545 G 7656—Green gold filled; 8½ inches long....$1.15
545 G 7657—Green 10-K solid gold; 8 inches long....$3.98

Gold-filled Belt Chain. Fits belts up to 1⅜ in. wide. Length, 7¼ inches. Any initial engraved free. State initial. Picture reduced.
545 G 7696—Green.
545 G 7697—White.
Each....98¢

Vest Chains With Bar and Toggle

Parts Shown Actual Size

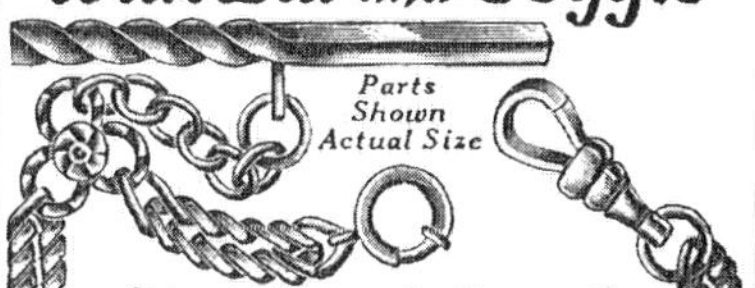

Guaranteed to wear for 25 years. Fine sturdy Vest Chain with the popular flat curb links. Best quality natural color gold filled. Each link soldered. Length, 11 inches.
545 G 7668.................$4.98

Actual Size

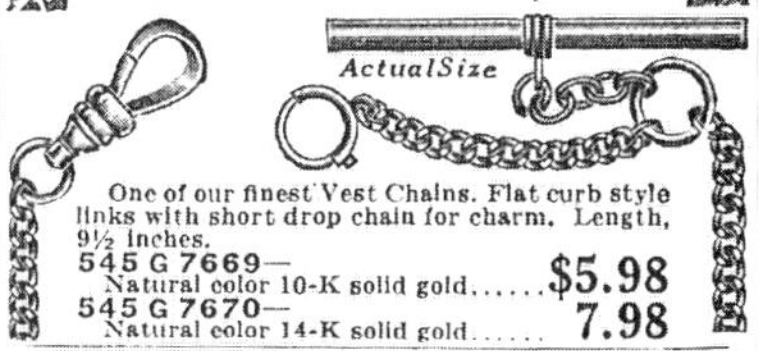

One of our finest Vest Chains. Flat curb style links with short drop chain for charm. Length, 9½ inches.
545 G 7669—Natural color 10-K solid gold......$5.98
545 G 7670—Natural color 14-K solid gold...... 7.98

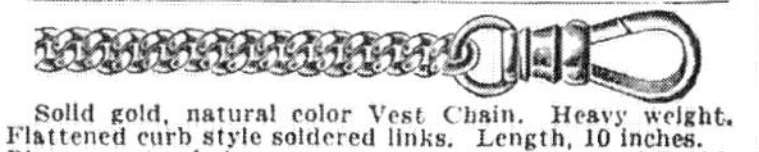

Solid gold, natural color Vest Chain. Heavy weight. Flattened curb style soldered links. Length, 10 inches. Picture actual size.
545 G 7673—10-K solid gold.............. $8.50
545 G 7674—14-K solid gold.............. 9.98

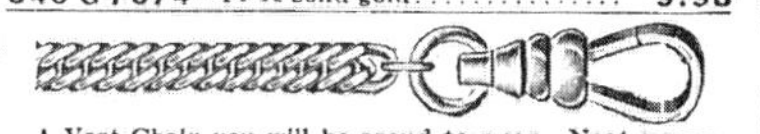

A Vest Chain you will be proud to wear. Neat appearing. Fine quality natural color gold filled. Length, 9½ inches. Heavy weight. Picture actual size.
545 G 7675.......................... $2.98

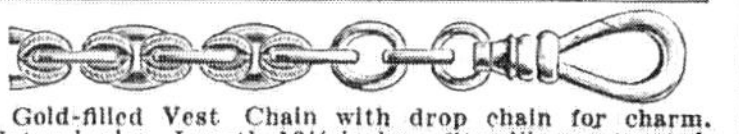

Gold-filled Vest Chain with drop chain for charm. Natural color. Length, 10½ inches. Sturdily constructed. Picture actual size.
545 G 7719.......................... $2.75

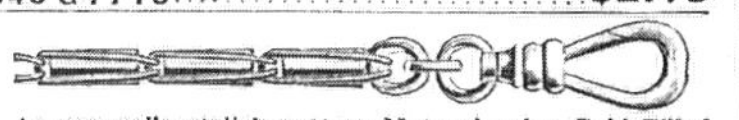

An unusually stylish pattern Natural color Gold-Filled Vest Chain, 10½ inches long. Cleverly designed links. Picture actual size.
545 G 7720.......................... $2.25

Natural color gold-filled regular style Vest Chain. Highly polished links in popular design. Length, 11¾ inches. A very sturdy chain that men admire.
545 G 7676.......................... $1.98

Handsome flat curb style link of regular Vest Chain. Natural color gold filled. Heavy style with loosely woven links. Length, 10½ inches. Part shown is actual size.
545 G 7677.......................... $1.48

USEFUL GIFTS THAT APPEAL TO MEN

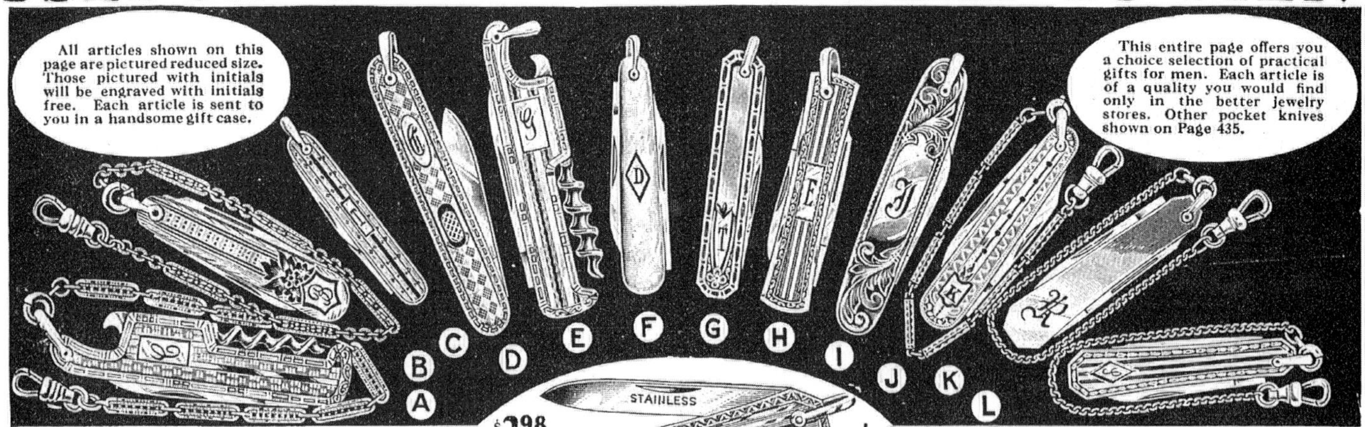

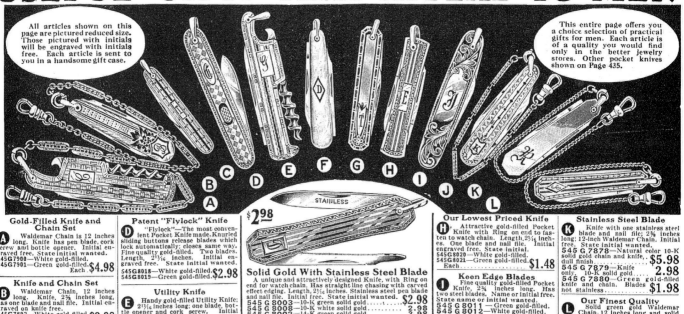

All articles shown on this page are pictured reduced size. Those pictured with initials will be engraved with initials free. Each article is sent to you in a handsome gift case.
This entire page offers you a choice selection of practical gifts for men. Each article is of a quality you would find only in the better jewelry stores. Other pocket knives shown on Page 435.
A
B
C
D
E
F
G
H
I
J
K
L

Gold-Filled Knife and Chain Set

A Waldemar Chain is 12 inches long. Knife has pen blade, cork screw and bottle opener. Initial engraved free. State initial wanted.
545G7900—White gold-filled.
545G7901—Green gold-filled. Each . $4.98

Knife and Chain Set

B Waldemar Chain, 12 inches long. Knife, 2⅜ inches long, has one blade and nail file. Initial engraved on knife free.
545G7892—White gold-filled.
545G8014—Green gold-filled. $2.98

Midget Size

C Popular small size, 2⅛ inches long; two blades. Initial free.
545 G 8010—Solid 10-K white gold. Stainless steel. $2.48
545 G 8009—Solid 10-K green gold. Stainless steel $2.48
545 G 8006—Natural color gold filled; 2 blades; not stainless. $1.48

Patent "Flylock" Knife

D "Flylock"—The most convenient Pocket Knife made. Knurled sliding buttons release blades which lock automatically; closes same way. Fine quality gold-filled. Two blades. Length, 2 13/16 inches. Initial engraved free. State initial wanted.
545G8018—White gold-filled.
545G8019—Green gold-filled. $2.98

Utility Knife

E Handy gold-filled Utility Knife; 2 11/16 inches long; one blade, bottle opener and cork screw. Initial engraved free. State initial.
545G8016—White gold-filled.
545G8017—Green gold-filled. $3.98

Pearl With Gold Shield

F Real pearl handle; 14-K solid gold shield and gold ring on end. Stainless steel blade and nail file. Length, 2¼ inches. Initial free. State initial wanted.
545 G 8015 .... $2.98

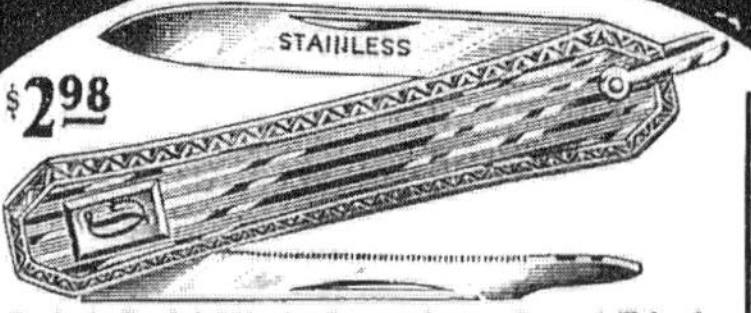

$2.98
STAINLESS

Solid Gold With Stainless Steel Blade

A unique and attractively designed Knife, with Ring on end for watch chain. Has straight line chasing with carved effect edging. Length, 2 1/16 inches. Stainless steel pen blade and nail file. Initial free. State initial wanted.

545 G 8003—10-K green solid gold	$2.98
545 G 8008—10-K white solid gold	2.98
545 G 8002—14-K green solid gold	3.98
545 G 8001—14-K white solid gold	3.98

Effective Design

G Smartly patterned, gold-filled Pocket Knife with Ring on end for watch chain. Has one blade and nail file. Initial engraved free. Length, 2 5/16 inches. State initial wanted.
545 G 8022—White gold-filled.
545 G 8023—Green gold-filled. Each $1.98

Shipping Weight on All Knives, 4 Oz. Each

Our Lowest Priced Knife

H Attractive gold-filled Pocket Knife with Ring on end to fasten to watch chain. Length, 2 5/16 inches. One blade and nail file. Initial engraved free. State initial.
545G8020—White gold-filled.
545G8021—Green gold-filled. Each $1.48

Keen Edge Blades

I Fine quality gold-filled Pocket Knife, 2¾ inches long. Has two steel blades. Name or initial free. State name or initial wanted.
545 G 8011—Green gold-filled.
545 G 8012—White gold-filled.
Each $1.98

Smartly Engine Turned

J White 10-K solid gold Waldemar Chain, 12 inches long and 10-K solid white gold Knife, 2⅜ inches long. Has one blade and one nail file. Initial free. State initial.
545 G 7891—Knife and chain $6.98
545 G 8013—Knife only. 3.35

Stainless Steel Blade

K Knife with one stainless steel blade and nail file; 2⅜ inches long; 12-inch Waldemar Chain. Initial free. State initial wanted.
545 G 7878—Natural color 10-K solid gold chain and knife, dull finish $5.98
545 G 7879—Knife only, 10-K solid gold 2.98
545 G 7880—Green gold-filled knife and chain. Blades not stainless $1.98

Our Finest Quality

L Solid green gold Waldemar Chain, 12 inches long and solid green gold Knife, 2 5/16 inches long. Initial free. State initial wanted.
545 G 7876—14-K solid green gold knife with stainless steel blade and nail file, and 14-K solid gold chain. $7.98
545 G 8007—14-K solid green gold knife only 3.87
545 G 7877—Similar to above but green gold-filled. Knife and chain set; not stainless steel $2.27

POCKET COMBS

All Pocket Combs Shown Reduced Size

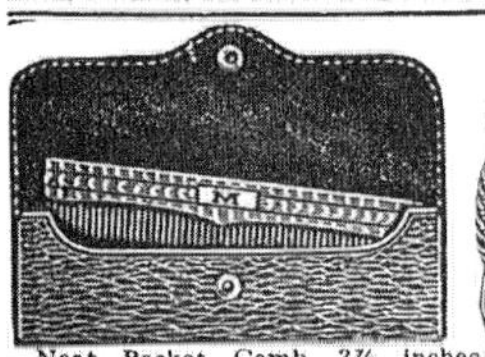

Neat Pocket Comb, 3⅞ inches long. Gold-filled mounting. Genuine blue leather case. Initial free. Ship. weight, 3 ounces.
545G8104—White gold-filled.
545G8107—Green gold-filled. Each $1.87

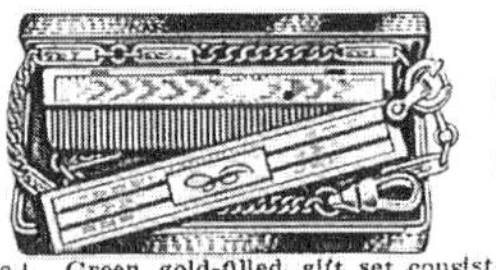

Green gold-filled gift set consisting of a 12-inch Waldemar Chain and engraved Folding Pocket Comb. Length of comb, closed, 3 inches. Initial free. Ship. wt., 3 ounces.
545 G 7881—Per set $3.98

Folding Pocket Comb is green gold filled. Has engine-turned front with engraved border; ring on end for watch chain. Length closed, 3½ inches. Any initial free. State initial wanted. Shipping weight, 3 ounces.
545 G 8101 .... 98¢

State Initial Wanted

Sterling silver Folding Pocket Comb in neat gift case. Length, 3 1/16 inches. Initial engraved free on attractive panel. Has beautiful chased effect. Any initial free. Shipping weight, 3 ounces.
545 G 8103 .... $2.25

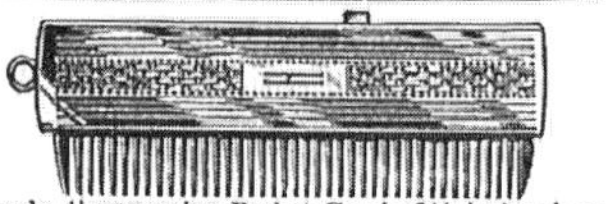

Handy disappearing Pocket Comb, 3⅛ inches long. Fine quality gold filled. Slide knob at top opens and closes comb. Any initial free. State initial wanted. Shipping weight, 3 ounces.
545 G 8108—White gold-filled.
545 G 8109—Green gold-filled.
Each $2.48

BELT BUCKLES

All Belt Buckles Shown Reduced Size

Ship. wt., 6 oz. each

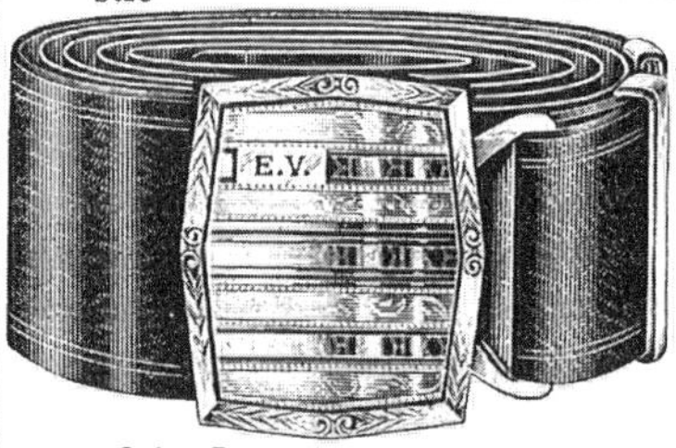

E.V.

Other Belts Shown on Page 295

Solid Sterling Silver With 14-Karat Gold Inlay

Wide Belt Included

The very latest style in Belt Buckles. Fits 1⅜-inch belt. Sterling silver with inlaid stripe of solid 14-K green gold in a combination of dull and bright finish. This two-tone effect is most artistic and attractive. Genuine black cowhide belt, 1⅜ inches wide is included. Any initial engraved free. As a gift, or for your own use, this outfit is attractive as well as practical. You will appreciate its smart appearance.
WAIST SIZES: 30 to 46 inches. State waist size and initial wanted.
545 G 7959 .... $4.98

Black cowhide Belt; Buckle, 1 inch wide.
WAIST SIZES: 30 to 46 inches. State size and initial.
545 G 7952—Sterling silver $3.48
545 G 7954—Natural color 10-K solid gold. 13.98

Artistically fashioned Belt Buckle, sterling silver, with black cowhide, 1-inch belt. Any initial free.
WAIST SIZES: 30 to 46 inches. State size and initial.
545 G 7956 .... $1.98

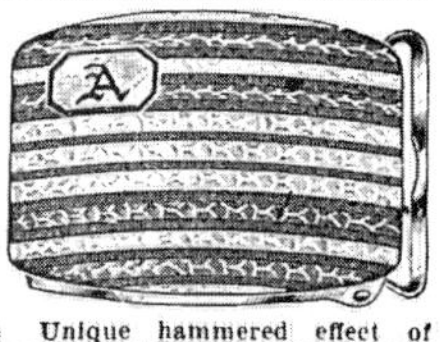

Unique hammered effect of sterling silver with stripes of green 14-K solid gold inlaid. Black cowhide, 1-inch belt included.
WAIST SIZES: 30 to 46. State size and initial.
545 G 7951 ...... $3.98

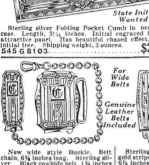

For Wide Belts

Genuine Leather Belts Included

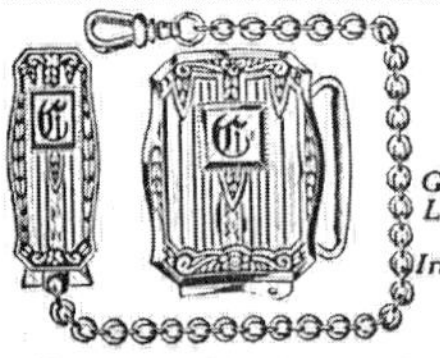

New wide style Buckle. Belt chain, 6⅝ inches long. Sterling silver. Black cowhide belt, 1⅜ inches wide. Initial engraved free.
WAIST SIZES: 30 to 46 inches. State initial and waist size wanted. Shipping weight, 6 ounces.
545 G 7893 .... $2.98

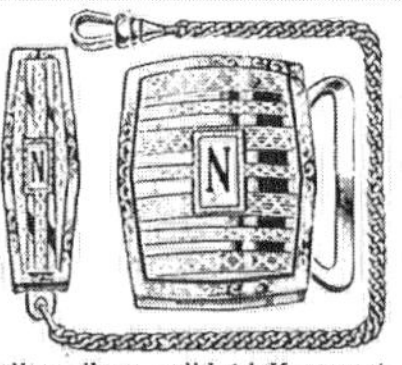

Sterling silver, solid 14-K green gold striped Belt Buckle; Belt Chain, 6⅞ inches. Black cowhide Belt, 1⅜ inches wide. Initial engraved free.
WAIST SIZES: 30 to 46 inches. State waist size and initial wanted. Shipping weight, 6 ounces.
545 G 7895 .... $6.98

Wide style Belt Buckle; Belt Chain, 6¾ inches long. Sterling silver. Black cowhide Belt, 1⅜ inches wide. Initial engraved free.
WAIST SIZES: 30 to 46 inches. State waist size and initial wanted. Ship. wt., 6 oz. $3.98
545 G 7894 ....

R.K.

Sterling Silver

Sterling silver Buckle with genuine cowhide leather Belt; 1 inch wide. Initials engraved free.
WAIST SIZES: 30 to 46 inches. State size and initial wanted.
545 G 7958
$2.98

Wide Belt

Sterling silver Buckle; inlaid stripes of solid 14-K green gold. Black cowhide belt, 1⅜ inches wide.
WAIST SIZES: 30 to 46 inches. State size and initial.
545 G 7960
...... $3.48

MEN'S DRESS SETS *Make Practical Gifts*

Lasting Quality

New style Wide Belt Set with Cuff Links. High quality white gold-filled. Belt Chain, 8 inches long with belt slot. Belt buckle with 1⅜-inch wide black cowhide belt. Nice presentation case included. Initial free.
WAIST SIZES: 30 to 46 inches. State size and initial wanted. Shipping weight, 7 ounces.
545G7888—Per set. $5.98

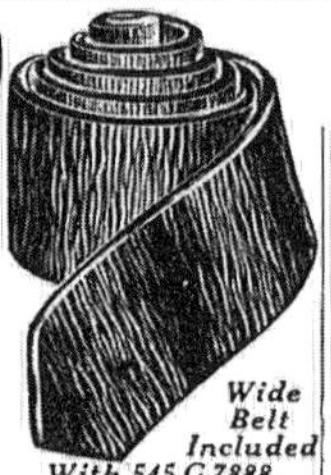

Wide Belt Included With 545 G 7888, 545 G 7889, 545 G 7904, 545 G 7905

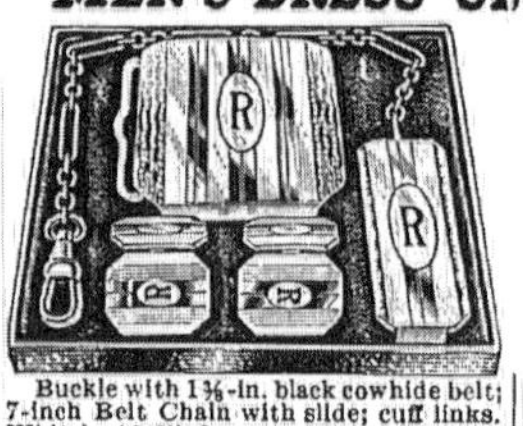

Buckle with 1⅜-in. black cowhide belt; 7-inch Belt Chain with slide; cuff links. White gold filled.
WAIST SIZES: 30 to 46 in. State size and initial. Ship. wt., 7 ounces.
545 G 7889—Per set $4.48

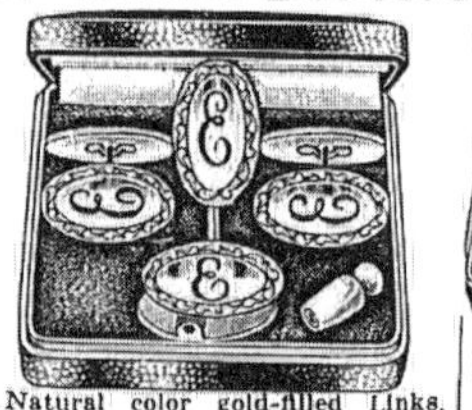

Natural color gold-filled Links, Tie Clasp and Scarf Pin. Initials engraved free. State initial. Shipping weight, 5 ounces.
545 G 7886—Per set... $2.87

Fine quality gold filled. Buckle, pair of Cuff Links, Belt Chain and Waldemar Chain. Black cowhide Belt 1⅜ inches wide.
WAIST SIZES: 30 to 46 inches. State size and initial. Ship. wt., 7 oz.
545 G 7904—White gold-filled.
545 G 7905—Green gold-filled.
Per set $9.98

Distinctive Set

A correct jewelry outfit for men. Consists of fine quality gold-filled Waldemar Chain, Pocket Knife with fine steel blade and pair of Cuff Links; all matched in design. Any initial engraved free. State initial wanted. Shipping weight, 7 ounces.
545 G 7902—White gold-filled.
545 G 7903—Green gold-filled.
Per set $4.98

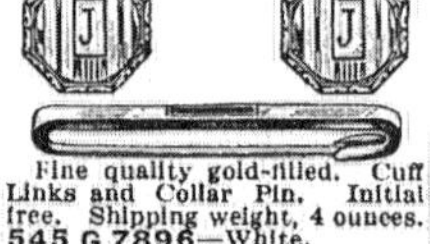

Fine quality gold-filled. Cuff Links and Collar Pin. Initial free. Shipping weight, 4 ounces.
545 G 7896—White.
545 G 7897—Green. Per set $1.98

Natural color gold-filled set for men. Consists of Scarf Pin with safety clutch and Cuff Links. Any initial engraved free. State initial. Shipping weight, 5 ounces.
545 G 7890—Per set $2.25

Natural color gold-filled Dress Set, consisting of Scarf Pin with safety clutch, Tie Clasp and Cuff Links. Any initial free. State initial. Shipping weight, 5 ounces.
545 G 7887—Per set $1.48

Gold-filled Cuff Links and Collar Button Set. A practical gift at a low price. State initial. Shipping weight, 5 ounces.
545 G 7898—White.
545 G 7899—Green. Per set .... 98¢

FOR MISSES

Materials and Tailoring
Say "Quality" to The Touch

For Descriptions and Sizes See Opposite Page

Mandel Fur

10 G 578
All Wool
Buxkin
Suede
$29.98

Manchurian Wolf Dog

Mandel Fur

Mandel Fur

Mandel Fur

10 G 582
All Wool
Suede
Velour
$17.98

10 G 588
All Wool
Estrella
Bolivia
$29.98

10 G 594
All Wool
Chamo
Suede
$19.98

Mandel Fur

Mandel Fur

Moufflon Fur

Mandel Fur

10 G 600
All Wool
Suede
Velour
$14.98

10 G 606
All Wool
Buxkin
Suede
$19.98

10 G 610
All Wool
Buxkin
Suede
$27.98

10 G 616
All Wool
Buxkin
Suede
$22.98

FOR MISSES The Critical New York Style Experts
Acclaim These New Designs

14 G 370
All Silk
De Luxe
Crepe Satin
$14.98

14 G 376
All Silk
De Luxe
Crepe Satin
$14.95

14 G 352
All Wool
Flannel
$7.98

14 G 358
All Wool
Poiret
Sheen
$12.98

14 G 364
All Silk
De Luxe
Flat Crepe
$14.98

14 G 382
All Silk
De Luxe
Crepe Satin
$13.98

14 G 388
All Silk
De Luxe
Flat Crepe
$13.98

14 G 394
Quality
All Silk
Flat Crepe
$9.98

14 G 400
All Silk
De Luxe
Crepe Satin
$16.95

14 G 406
All Silk
De Luxe
Flat Crepe
$13.98

*These Dresses are also Furnished
in Each of the Colors Described
on Opposite Page.*

Smart Things *for* Housewear
Superior Values—Every One

Also Furnished in Each of the Colors Described on Opposite Page

36 G 86
Foulard
Pongette
Regular and Extra Sizes
$1.98

36 G 112
Novelty
Cotton
Serge
$2.49

36 G 80
Rayon
Striped
Cotton
Serge
$2.59

36 G 82

36 G 84

36 G 92
Novelty
Gingham
$1.94

Misses
36 G 106
Mercerized
Broadcloth
$1.98

3 G 118

36 G 120

36 G 116
Checked
Flannel
$1.98

Hand
Embroidered
36 G 98
Broadcloth
or
Black Sateen
$1.95

36 G 122
Peter Pan
Print
$2.98

36 G 128
Mercerized
Broadcloth
$1.98

36 G 704
Beacon Cloth
$5.95

36 G 710
Blanket
Cloth
Regular Sizes $2.89 *Extra Sizes* $3.59

Velveteen
Corduroy
36 G 718
Unlined
$4.95

Lined
$6.95

Now Everybody Can Afford~
Lingerie of Lustrous Silk or Rayon

Descriptions on Opposite Page

C Rayon $1.98

E Rayon $1.59

A Lustersheen $2.98

B Radium Silk $3.98

D Rayon Vest 89¢ Bloomers $1.49

F Rayon $1.98

H Finest Rayon $2.49

J Rayon $2.49

K Rayon $1.98

L Rayon "Triad" $1.89

M Rayon $1.49

N Rayon $1.98

O Rayon $1.59

P Heavy Crepe de Chine $2.98

R Rayon Vest 69¢ Bloomers 98¢

S Heavy Crepe de Chine $4.98

T Super-Rayon Vest 98¢ Bloomers $1.69

U Rayon $2.98

V Glove Silk Vest $1.49 Bloomers $1.98

Coats *and* Hats ~ 1 to 4 Years
Dresses ~ 2 to 6 Years

A
Coat
$5⁴⁹~

B
Coat
$4⁹⁵~

C
Coat
$5⁹⁸~

D
Coat
$5⁸⁹~

E
Coat
$3⁸⁹~

F
Coat
Chinchilla
$5⁹⁸~
Kersey
$4⁸⁹~

H
Coat
$4⁹⁸~

J
Coat
$2⁹⁸~

K
Coat
$3⁹⁸~

L
Coat
$3⁵⁰~

M
Coat
$3⁹⁵~

Boys
Suits
1 to 4
Years

N
Coat
$3⁹⁸~

O
$2⁹⁸~
All Wool

P
$2⁸⁹~

R
$1²⁹~

S
$1⁰⁰~

T
$1⁸⁹~

MADE OF GENUINE
SILKETTE
AN ALL COTTON FABRIC
REG. U.S. PAT OFF

U
$3⁹⁸~

V
$2⁸⁹~

W
$1⁹⁸~

X
Charming
Two-Pantie
Dress
$1⁰⁰~

Y
$1⁴⁹~
Hand
Embroidered

Z
$2⁹⁸~
Hand
Embroidered

Newest *and* Best In Sweater Styles

A $6~75

B $7~39

C $5~25

D $4~95

E $2~98

F $4~99

Jersey Lind

For Descriptions See Opposite Page

Misses' 7 to 14 Years

H $3~98

J $3~25

K $4~85

L $4~98

M $2~95

N $2~79

Warm Knit Wear for Children

Boys' Blizzard Cap 69¢
31 G 542—Buff.
31 G 543—Cardinal red.
31 G 544—Navy blue.
One size only; for ages 3 to 6 years. Ship. wt., each, 6 oz. Warm and durable, as it's closely knit of part wool yarns. Soft brushed wool inside. Can be buttoned down around the neck to protect throat.

O $4~98

P $2~59

R $1~98

S $2~95

T $1~85

All Wool Fancy Stitch 55¢
31 G 539—White with blue.
31 G 540—White.
31 G 541—Red.
One size only; for ages 3 to 6 years. Ship. wt., each, 6 oz. Finest All Wool worsted yarns double knit in a fancy block stitch. Unusually elastic, it keeps its trim shape. Ever so warm and durable. Deep roll cuff. Fine for boys or girls.

27¢ Costs Little Firmly Knit
31 G 533—Brown with buff.
31 G 534—Red with navy blue.
One size only; for ages 3 to 6 years. Ship. wt., each, 6 oz. Isn't it jolly looking with its smart stripes around the top and border! Double knit from wool and cotton yarns in the strong cardigan stitch, it is soft and warm. Our price offers a genuine saving. Suitable for boys or girls.

U $2~98

For Other Children's Sweaters See Page 93

Rope Stitch Soft and Warm 46¢
31 G 500—Red.
31 G 510—Buff.
31 G 514—Brown.
One size only; for ages 3 to 6 years. Shipping weight, each, 6 ounces. Rich looking and warm, as it is knit in the heavy rope stitch from soft, part wool yarns. Just the style that grown-ups wear—it's sure to appeal to any boy or girl. Has deep roll cuff.

NEW from New York

$4.98
Choose and Be PROUD!
24 G 363—SIZES: 2½ to 8. Widths B, C, D, E. State size wanted. Ship. weight, 1 lb. 8 oz.
An applique of hand-painted, imported leather lends a colorful touch of Paris to this alluring Slipper. Has slender straps, and a 2½-inch covered spike heel. The new combination narrow-in-the-heel last. Lined with light genuine kid leather—will not discolor hose.

$4.39
Black Patent or Satin Step-ins
24 G 368—Black satin.
24 G 367—Black patent.
SIZES: 2½ to 8. Widths C, D and E. State size wanted. Ship. weight, 1 lb. 8 oz.
A Colonial of gracious chic in Skinner's satin or black patent. Large square buckle, cut steel trimmed. 2-inch covered Spanish heels, with rubber lifts. Snug fit elastic. Concealed by buckle. Light leather lining.

$4.89
Patent with Smart Gray Trim
24 G 377—SIZES: 2½ to 8. Widths C, D and E. State size wanted. Ship. wt., 1 lb. 4 oz.
The Gypsy Slipper — New from New York! Notice the extremely graceful lines that cling to every curve of the foot. Patent leather with gray reptile embossed grain leather, appliqued on vamp and quarters. The 2 inch covered heel has rubber lift. Light leather lining protects silk hose from discolor. A model that's in the mode of the moment.

The Vogue in the East
24 G 376.............$4.98
SIZES: 2½ to 8. Widths B, C, D, E. State size wanted. Ship. wt., 1 lb. 8 oz.
The quaint smartness of "gingham" occupies such a leading place that we used it as a leather trim on this entrancing black patent leather Pump. The new combination last hugs the heel and arch. Fashionable 2½-inch spike heel and graceful curving arch. Light genuine kid leather lining.

Here Vogue and Value Meet!
24 G 393.............$2.98
SIZES: 2½ to 8. Widths C, D, and E. State size wanted. Ship. wt., 1 lb. 4 oz.
A prominently popular one-strap. It's so smart, in all the fashion-newness of black patent. So convenient, because it goes perfectly with any costume. Fine binding of black and white. Has 1¼-inch covered military heel. Light leather lining.

$4.98
New York's Newest
With 2½-Inch Heel
24 G 365—SIZES: 2½ to 8. Widths B, C, D, E. State size wanted. Ship. weight, 1 lb. 8 oz.
New—and of a charm distinctively New York! Gay cerise leather, flecked with white, makes a bright buckle and underlay. The Slipper is of black patent leather with a 2½-inch covered spike heel, round toe and a beautifully curved arch. Combination last is narrow in heel. Snug fit elastic under buckle. Genuine kid leather lining.

"Strip" Pumps—More Chic Than Ever
24 G 369—With 1¼-inch military heel.
24 G 370—With 2½-inch Louis heel.............$3.79
SIZES: 2½ to 8. Widths B, C, D, E. State size wanted.
Shipping weight, 1 pound 8 ounces.
Shining patent, unadorned, reflects the mode for smart black! Your choice of the new, smart, graceful 2½-inch covered spike heel; or the popular 1¼-inch military covered heel—rubber lifts. Narrow heel combination last. The new vamp will please Milady—for it actually makes the foot look smaller. Light leather lining.

How to Order Shoes
See Page 169

$3.98
Black Patent Favorite
24 G 354—SIZES: 2½ to 8. Widths C, D and E. State size wanted. Ship. wt., 1 lb. 4 oz.
Simple lines lend slim elegance to the foot that wears this Slipper. Of rich black patent in the single strap style, with a dainty buckle fastening. New 2-inch medium Spanish covered heels are very dressy. Finished with a light rubber toplift. Light leather lining will not stain hose. Rich in quality, big in value and in the height of fashion in the cities everywhere.

$3.98
A Dainty Two-Tone
24 G 375—SIZES: 2½ to 8. Widths D and E. State size wanted. Ship. wt., 1 lb. 8 oz.
A clever Tie of youthful charm presented by the hand of fashion. Quarter saddle of fashionable tan reptile grain leather harmonizes with vamp and heel of rosy tan kid. Tear shaped cutouts at the D'Orsay sides. Ribbon tie. The 1¼-inch covered heel has a light rubber lift. Light leather lining. Gives chic and charm to the foot—and also a foot-flattering smallness.

Black and White Is Correct
$4.29
A Striking New Pattern
With 2½-Inch Heel
24 G 379—SIZES: 2½ to 8. Widths B, C, D and E. State size wanted. Ship. wt., 1 lb. 8 oz.
Decidedly new—and of course from New York! Many dots on the quarters and bow of this dashing patent leather Pump lend new zest to the vogue for black and white.
The high 2½-inch spike heel and rounded vamps are of plain black patent. High curved arch and graceful D'Orsay sides. An elastic concealed underneath the bow gives a close, fine fit. The light gray genuine kid lining is soft and will not stain hose. Light rubber heel lifts. Now you can have the trim daintiness you want and at only $4.79.

$4.89
New York Bows to Its Beauty
24 G 366—SIZES: 2½ to 8. Widths B, C, D, E. State size wanted. Ship. weight, 1 lb. 4 oz.
Introducing one of New York's most popular and chic new Ties. Of black patent with smart green paisley inlay on vamp and tongue. The 2½-inch covered heel, curving arch and round toe give the foot a small dainty appearance. Combination last is narrow in the heel. Light colored genuine kid lining.

$3.98
Two Styles That Won New York
24 G 371—Rose blush calf.
24 G 372—Black patent.
SIZES: 2½ to 8. Widths C, D and E. State size wanted. Ship. weight, 1 lb. 8 oz.
Waterlily iridescent leather trims black patent or mesh-embossed grain leather on rose blush calf. Adjustable buckle. Has 1¼-inch military heel rose blush and patent covered, rubber lifts. Light leather lining.

$4.98
Patent with "Gingham" Applique
24 G 374 — SIZES: 2½ to 8. Widths B, C, D and E. State size wanted. Ship. wt., 1 lb. 8 oz.
Old fashioned "gingham" returns as one of the smartest decorative leathers! Here it lends rare chic to a black patent leather one strap. Combination last fits the heel snugly. Has the new 2½-inch covered spike heel, and rounding toe. Leather heel lifts; light genuine kid leather lining.

Black Suede with Patent
24 G 380.............$3.79
SIZES: 2½ to 8. Widths D and E. State size. Ship. wt., 1 lb. 8 oz.
Chosen for its foot-flattering lines, simple rich design and fine materials. Soft-napped black suede with a dainty trim of shining patent leather. Smooth fitting combination last; low-cut D'Orsay sides and 1¼-inch military heel has a rubber top lift. Light leather lining will not stain light hose.

Black Patent—The Trim Is New!
24 G 373.............$3.89
SIZES: 2½ to 8. Widths C, D and E. State size wanted. Ship. wt., 1 lb. 8 oz.
Futuristic applique on the toe and sides stamps this conventional patent leather one strap as "definitely different." Gray grain leather, embossed in a checkered design, alternates with black patent on the toe and quarters—very unusual! The 2-inch covered heel has a rubber lift. Light leather lining.

Europe's Best Quality *and* Style
Washable Fabrics

Washable Fabrics IMPORTED 59¢ to $1.35

BEAVER
OAK
BROWN
SAND
GRAY

Lined Gloves

Ultra Smart
Unlined Kid Gloves

Wool Skating Gloves

Everest Slippers *for* Everybody

98¢

New Leather Slippers for Women
24 G 3931—Blue leather.
24 G 3932—Tan leather.
Per pair...................98¢
SIZES: 3 to 8. No half sizes. State size wanted.
Shipping weight, 12 ounces.
In the new sabot style and ever so pretty! With a handsome trim of gold and black checkered leather. Durable leather uppers are soft and easy for real comfort. Soft padded leather soles. Cozy lining is of fawn colored felt.

Brown Felt Hi-lo
24 G 4045......98¢
SIZES: 3 to 8. No half sizes. State size. Ship. wt., 12 ounces.
Button up the top and it's a practical house Shoe as well as a cozy bedroom Slipper. Soft, warm brown felt, with a light tan collar. Padded cushion leather sole—comfortable and durable.

Brocaded Satin
97¢
24 G 3910—SIZES: 3 to 8. No half sizes. State size wanted. Ship. wt., 12 ounces.
Tan satin is brocaded with a blue futuristic design flecked with gold. Blue and gold braid, and a smart rosette give a dainty finish. Soft padded leather soles.

High Back Juliets
24 G 3902—Brown.
24 G 3904—Old rose.
24 G 3903—Heather, brown trim.
24 G 3901—Sapphire blue.
$1.25
SIZES: 2½ to 9. State size. Ship. wt. 12 oz.
Juliet style Slippers with high backs to keep the ankles warm. The fur plush trimming is thick and warm. Excellent quality felt, in four attractive colors. Soles of flexible leather; rubber heels. They're $1.75 to $2 values. An ideal Christmas gift.

24 G 3906—Copenhagen blue
24 G 3907—Old rose.
Per pair...$1.15
SIZES: 3 to 8. No half sizes. Ship. weight, 12 ounces.
Ever popular — this style in two pretty colors—Copenhagen blue or old rose. Matching collar of velvet is checkered in black. Soft, brown padded leather sole.

Dainty Styles of Fine Felt
24 G 3909—Old rose.
24 G 3908—Copenhagen blue.
Per pair.............$1.00
SIZES: 3 to 8. No half sizes. Shipping weight, 12 ounces.
Two of our prettiest Slippers, and so moderately priced! Your choice of old rose or Copenhagen blue—both popular shades. A matching collar of quilted satin and a silk bow provide a rich trim for the warm, durable felt uppers. Soft, padded leather soles are warm and comfortable underfoot. You'll be proud to wear these slippers.

$1.00

Great Value 72¢
Choice of Five Colors
24 G 3914—Kelly green; cerise trim.
24 G 3915—Old rose; silver trim.
24 G 3912—Turquoise blue; silver trim.
24 G 3911—Lavender; fawn trim.
24 G 3913—Brown; fawn trim.
SIZES: 3 to 8. No half sizes. State size wanted. Ship. wt. 12 ounces.
QUALITY FIRST—then low price! Warm, cozy Slippers in two contrasting shades of felt are ornamented with fluffy pompons and ribbon trim. Of heavy, full-bodied felt. Soft padded soles are of brown leather. An ideal Christmas gift.

Smart New Design
24 G 3917—SIZES: 3 to 8. No half sizes. State size. Ship. weight, 12 ounces.
Black and white checked velvet is smartly dainty with the lining of black rayon silk. A fluffy pompon gives a smart finish. Tan leather padded soles are soft and comfortable.

$1.35

Everest Slippers for Children

24 G 3937—SIZES: 11 to 2.....$1.09
24 G 3938—SIZES: 5 to 10.......98
No half sizes. State size wanted.
Ship. weight, 6 ounces.
Cozy Bunny Slippers of Sheeps-wool will keep the kiddies' feet as warm as toast. Red binding all around the sole keeps them from rippling. Give them for Christmas and they'll be happy.

Moveable Eyes

24 G 3922—
12 to 2......95¢
24 G 3923—9 to 11.89¢
24 G 3924—5 to 8...79¢
No half sizes. State size. Ship. wt., 6 oz.
Bootie Slipper has lamb's wool collar. Excellent quality. Padded leather sole.

24 G 3925—
12 to 2.....89¢
24 G 3926—9 to 11.79¢
24 G 3927—5 to 8...79¢
No half sizes. State size. Ship. wt., 6 oz.
This Bunny moves his eyes. Tan felt with painted figures. Tan leather padded sole.

24 G 4120—
12 to 2.....75¢
24 G 4121—9 to 11.67¢
24 G 4122—5 to 8...59¢
No half sizes. Ship. wt., 6 oz.
Warm red felt Slippers with padded leather soles. Light tan felt collar. Priced low.

Boys' Slippers

24 G 4071..$1.00
SIZES: 1 to 5. No half sizes. State size. Ship. wt., 6 ounces.
Delight your boy with a Christmas pair. Gray felt uppers. Flexible, strong stitchdown leather soles. Rubber heels.

24 G 3921...98¢
SIZES: 1 to 5. No half sizes. State size. Ship. wt., 6 oz.
Your boy will want to wear these every minute—they're so easy and warm. Durable brown felt. Checkered Hi-lo collar. Padded leather sole.

24 G 4074—
1 to 5.........92¢
24 G 4075—9 to 13.79¢
No half sizes. State size. Ship. wt., 6 oz.
It makes a big hit with boys—the cozy brown felt has baseball players stenciled in color. Padded sole is of strong leather.

Black Satin
24 G 3900—$1.98
SIZES: 3 to 8. No half sizes. State size. Ship. wt., 12 ounces.
"Mules" so pretty—they'll make lovely Christmas gifts! Of black satin with pink satin lining. Covered heel. Light weight leather sole. Braided trim. Pink Rosette.

Old Rose
24 G 3905—$1.49
SIZES: 3 to 8. No half sizes. State size. Ship. wt., 12 ounces.
A very high grade Slipper, of excellent quality old rose felt. Finished with a fancy trimming and rosette. Covered heel. Padded brown leather sole is soft under foot.

Black Patent
24 G 3920—$1.59
SIZES: 3 to 8. No half sizes. State size. Ship. wt., 12 ounces.
Something new in a lounging Slipper — glossy black patent trimmed with paisley colored leather. Smart with any color robe. Soft blue felt lining. Soft padded leather sole.

Gold Trim
24 G 3916.....85¢
SIZES: 3 to 8. No half sizes. State size. Ship. wt., 12 ounces.
Unusually pleasing! Of blue felt, with a trim of gold checkered cloth and a rosette. Has a warm, soft sole, of brown padded leather. Makes a pleasing Christmas gift and is an excellent value.

For Women and Children
24 G 3933—
For Women.....$1.00
24 G 3934 — For Children, 12 to 2.....95¢
24 G 3935—9 to 11.89¢
24 G 3936—5 to 8...79¢
No half sizes. State size. Ship. wt., 12 oz.
Big value! Of very durable soft tan leather in the popular two-tone combination. Soled with soft brown padded leather. Very restful.

Two Tone Gray Felt
$1.19
24 G 4110—SIZES: 3 to 8. No half sizes. State size. Ship. wt., 12 oz.
Enjoy cozy comfort at a saving when you select this Two tone felt Slipper. Gray felt in two contrasting shades. Lightweight leather sole. Easy and durable. The 1-inch leather heel has rubber lift.

Leather Soles
24 G 4106—Brown.
24 G 4107—Blue.....$1.19
SIZES: 2½ to 8. State size. Ship. wt., 12 ounces.
Two very big sellers of good quality wool-back felt prettily trimmed with silk ribbon and pompon. Extra long wearing flexible oak leather soles, 1-inch rubber heels. Cozy and warm.

Extra Wide
24 G 4112.....$1.09
SIZES: 2½ to 9. State size. Ship. wt., 12 oz.
Extra wide for stout feet—light, roomy and ideal for house-wear. They'll give real comfort. Brown felt uppers are soft and warm; leather soles are flexible. Low heel has rubber lift, and they're low priced.

Gray Felt
$1.00
24 G 4002—SIZES: 2½ to 8. State size. Ship. wt., 12 ounces.
For real economy and true comfort you could scarcely make a better selection. The soft gray felt and flexible stitchdown leather sole are very restful to tender feet. Low rubber heel. An example of good, dependable quality at a low money-saving price.

Men's *Everest* Slippers

$1.49

$1.95

An Ideal Gift for Men

Leather Sole Hi-lo
24 G 3928.....$1.49
SIZES: 6 to 12. State size. No half sizes. Ship. weight, 1 pound.
They're new, men! If you've been on your feet a great deal you'll appreciate the comforting relaxation these Slippers give. Good quality brown felt; popular Hi-lo style. Strong oak leather soles; rubber heels.

Patent Leather
24 G 3929.....$1.95
SIZES: 6 to 12. No half sizes. State size. Ship. wt., 1 pound.
Nothing would please him more than a pair of these handsome and durable Slippers for Christmas. Of good-quality black patent leather with a lining of quilted rayon. Soft padded brown leather sole.

Flexible Sole
24 G 4059...$1.19
SIZES: 6 to 12. No half sizes. State size. Ship. wt., 1 lb. 4 oz.
Tired feet enjoy great comfort in a pair of these. The soft, warm gray felt is of good-wearing quality. Flexible leather sole is stitchdown sewed. Low heel has a rubber lift. A big value for the money.

Soft Tan Leather
24 G 3930.....$1.29
SIZES: 6 to 12. No half sizes. State size. Ship. wt., 1 pound.
Any man will be pleased with the rich appearance and comfort of these Slippers. Surprise him with a pair at Christmas time! Of soft golden brown kid, with a warm felt lining. Padded soft brown leather sole.

Two Popular Styles
24 G 4060—Brown.
24 G 4056—Gray.
Per pair..............93¢
SIZES: 6 to 12. No half sizes. State size. Ship. wt., 1 pound.
After a long strenuous day there's nothing so restful as a cozy pair of house Slippers. These of good quality, and unusual ease, are warm and snug fitting. Of soft, brown or gray felt with a neat checkered collar. The full cushioned sole is of brown leather, thickly padded, and as comfortable as a stocking. They're favorites with the men—and no wonder! Give him a pair.

Every Man Likes Hi-los
24 G 4055—Brown.
24 G 4054—Gray.
Per pair..............$1.19
SIZES: 6 to 12. No half sizes. State size. Shipping weight, 1 pound.
Wear a pair of these snug, easy Slippers and make your evenings at home a real pleasure. The Hi-lo collar buttons up warmly around the ankles. Of durable felt with soft padded leather soles. He'll enjoy every minute he wears them. You couldn't make a finer selection for his Christmas gift—and at our low money-saving price, it is an excellent value!

The Junior Miss Strolls in New York Style
Nature-Patterned for Growing Feet

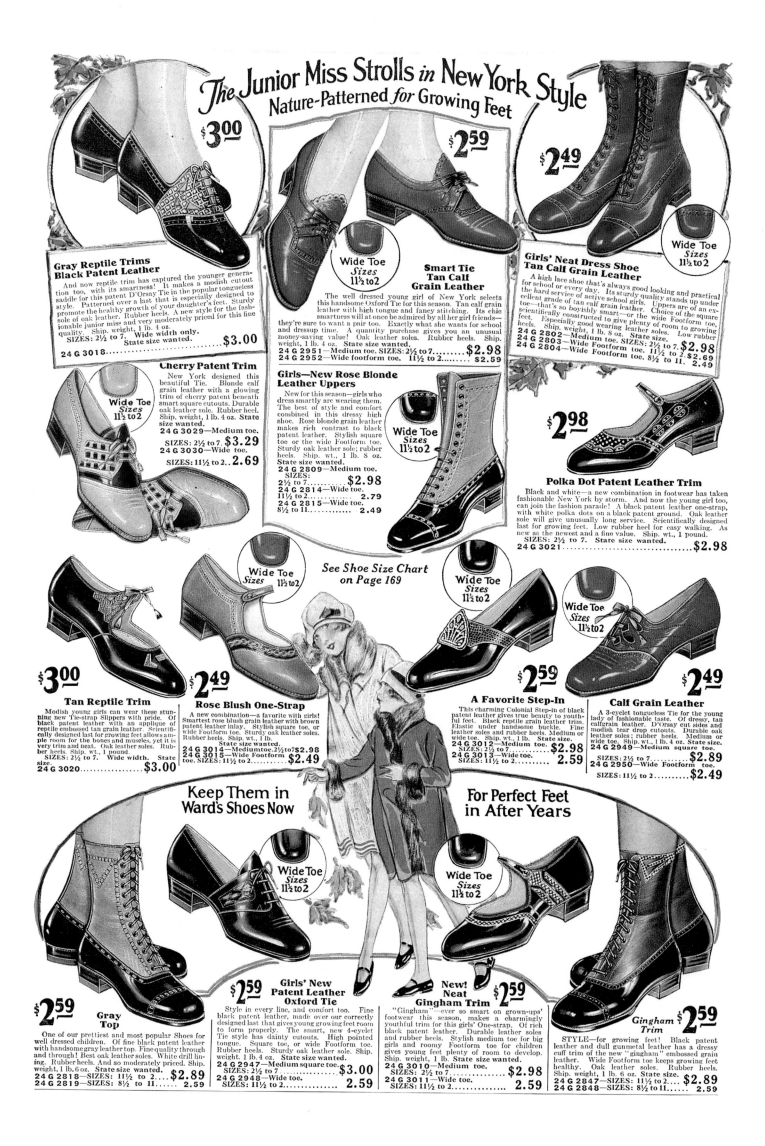

$3.00

Gray Reptile Trims Black Patent Leather

And now reptile trim has captured the younger generation too, with its smartness! It makes a modish cutout saddle for this patent D'Orsay Tie in the popular tongueless style. Patterned over a last that is especially designed to promote the healthy growth of your daughter's feet. Sturdy sole of oak leather. Rubber heels. A new style for the fashionable junior miss and very moderately priced for this fine quality. Ship. weight, 1 lb. 4 oz. **Wide width only.**
SIZES: 2½ to 7. State size wanted.
24 G 3018...................................$3.00

Cherry Patent Trim

Wide Toe Sizes 11½ to 2

New York designed this beautiful Tie. Blonde calf grain leather with a glowing trim of cherry patent beneath smart square cutouts. Durable oak leather sole. Rubber heel. Ship. weight, 1 lb. 4 oz. State size wanted.
24 G 3029—Medium toe.
SIZES: 2½ to 7. **$3.29**
24 G 3030—Wide toe.
SIZES: 11½ to 2.. **2.69**

$2.59

Smart Tie Tan Calf Grain Leather

Wide Toe Sizes 11½ to 2

The well dressed young girl of New York selects this handsome Oxford Tie for this season. Tan calf grain leather with high tongue and fancy stitching. Its chic smartness will at once be admired by all her girl friends—they're sure to want a pair too. Exactly what she wants for school and dressup time. A quantity purchase gives you an unusual money-saving value! Oak leather sole. Rubber heels. Ship. weight, 1 lb. 4 oz. State size wanted.
24 G 2951—Medium toe. SIZES: 2½ to 7...... **$2.98**
24 G 2952—Wide footform toe. 11½ to 2........ **$2.59**

Girls—New Rose Blonde Leather Uppers

New for this season—girls who dress smartly are wearing them. The best of style and comfort combined in this dressy high shoe. Rose blonde grain leather makes rich contrast to black patent leather. Stylish square toe or the wide Footform toe. Sturdy oak leather sole; rubber heels. Ship. wt., 1 lb. 8 oz. State size wanted.
24 G 2809—Medium toe.
SIZES:
2½ to 7............ **$2.98**
24 G 2814—Wide toe.
11½ to 2............ **2.79**
24 G 2815—Wide toe.
8½ to 11............ **2.49**

Wide Toe Sizes 11½ to 2

$2.49

Girls' Neat Dress Shoe Tan Calf Grain Leather

Wide Toe Sizes 11½ to 2

A high lace shoe that's always good looking and practical for school or every day. Its sturdy quality stands up under the hard service of active school girls. Uppers are of an excellent grade of tan calf grain leather. Choice of the square toe—that's so boyishly smart—or the wide Footform toe, scientifically constructed to give plenty of room to growing feet. Especially good wearing leather soles. Low rubber heels. Ship. weight, 1 lb. 8 oz. State size.
24 G 2802—Medium toe. SIZES: 2½ to 7. **$2.98**
24 G 2803—Wide Footform toe. 11½ to 2. **$2.69**
24 G 2804—Wide Footform toe. 8½ to 11. **2.49**

$2.98

Polka Dot Patent Leather Trim

Black and white—a new combination in footwear has taken fashionable New York by storm. And now the young girl too, can join the fashion parade! A black patent leather one-strap, with white polka dots on a black patent ground. Oak leather sole will give unusually long service. Scientifically designed last for growing feet. Low rubber heel for easy walking. As new as the newest and a fine value. Ship. wt., 1 pound.
SIZES: 2½ to 7. State size wanted.
24 G 3021...................................$2.98

See Shoe Size Chart on Page 169

$3.00

Tan Reptile Trim

Modish young girls can wear these stunning new Tie-strap Slippers with pride. Of black patent leather with an applique of reptile embossed tan grain leather. Scientifically designed last for growing feet allows ample room for the bones and muscles, yet it is very trim and neat. Oak leather soles. Rubber heels. Ship. wt., 1 pound.
SIZES: 2½ to 7. Wide width. State size.
24 G 3020...................................$3.00

$2.49

Rose Blush One-Strap

Wide Toe Sizes 11½ to 2

A new combination—a favorite with girls! Smartest rose blush grain leather with brown patent leather inlay. Stylish square toe, or wide Footform toe. Sturdy oak leather soles. Rubber heels. Ship. wt., 1 lb.
State size wanted.
24 G 3014—Medium toe. 2½ to 7. **$2.98**
24 G 3015—Wide Footform toe. SIZES: 11½ to 2... **$2.49**

$2.59

A Favorite Step-In

Wide Toe Sizes 11½ to 2

This charming Colonial Step-in of black patent leather gives true beauty to youthful feet. Black reptile grain leather trim. Elastic under handsome buckle. Fine leather soles and rubber heels. Medium or wide toe. Ship. wt., 1 lb. State size.
24 G 3012—Medium toe. SIZES: 2½ to 7............. **$2.98**
24 G 3013—Wide toe. SIZES: 11½ to 2......... **2.59**

$2.49

Calf Grain Leather

Wide Toe Sizes 11½ to 2

A 3-eyelet tongueless Tie for the young lady of fashionable taste. Of dressy, tan calfgrain leather. D'Orsay cut sides and modish tear drop cutouts. Durable oak leather soles; rubber heels. Medium or wide toe. Ship. wt., 1 lb. 4 oz. State size.
24 G 2949—Medium square toe.
SIZES: 2½ to 7............. **$2.89**
24 G 2950—Wide Footform toe.
SIZES: 11½ to 2......... **$2.49**

Keep Them in Ward's Shoes Now

For Perfect Feet in After Years

Wide Toe Sizes 11½ to 2

Wide Toe Sizes 11½ to 2

$2.59
Gray Top

One of our prettiest and most popular Shoes for well dressed children. Of fine black patent leather with handsome gray leather top. Fine quality through and through! Best oak leather soles. White drill lining. Rubber heels. And so moderately priced. Ship. weight, 1 lb. 6 oz. State size wanted.
24 G 2818—SIZES: 11½ to 2.... **$2.89**
24 G 2819—SIZES: 8½ to 11.... **2.59**

$2.59
Girls' New Patent Leather Oxford Tie

Style in every line, and comfort too. Fine black patent leather, made over our correctly designed last that gives your growing feet room to form properly. The smart, new 4-eyelet Tie style has dainty cutouts. High pointed tongue. Square toe, or wide Footform toe. Rubber heels. Sturdy oak leather sole. Ship. weight, 1 lb. 4 oz. State size wanted.
24 G 2947—Medium square toe.
SIZES: 2½ to 7.................. **$3.00**
24 G 2948—Wide toe.
SIZES: 11½ to 2.............. **2.59**

$2.59
New! Neat Gingham Trim

"Gingham"—ever so smart on grown-ups' footwear this season, makes a charmingly youthful trim for this girls' One-strap. Of rich black patent leather. Durable leather soles and rubber heels. Stylish medium toe for big girls and roomy Footform toe for children gives young feet plenty of room to develop. Ship. weight, 1 lb. State size wanted.
24 G 3010—Medium toe.
SIZES: 2½ to 7.............. **$2.98**
24 G 3011—Wide toe.
SIZES: 11½ to 2.............. **2.59**

$2.59
Gingham Trim

STYLE—for growing feet! Black patent leather and dull gunmetal leather has a dressy cuff trim of the new "gingham" embossed grain leather. Wide Footform toe keeps growing feet healthy. Oak leather soles. Rubber heels. Ship. weight, 1 lb. 6 oz. State size.
24 G 2847—SIZES: 11½ to 2.... **$2.89**
24 G 2848—SIZES: 8½ to 11...... **2.59**

A New Quality in Service to Men

39 G 2828
$24.75

39 G 2816

39 G 2818
$17.75

39 G 2837
$28.50

39 G 2815
$19.95

39 G 2846
$21.75

39 G 2879

39 G 2855

39 G 2871

Special

39 G 2821

39 G 2875
$26.50

39 G 2851
$19.85

39 G 2867
$22.50

39 G 2817
$19.95

More Than Fine Fabrics ~ Longtime Tailored, Too !

for Men
and Young Men

All Suits on This Page
34 to 42-Inch Chest

39 G 1721
2 Pants Suit
$16⁷⁵~

39 G 1627
I Pants Suit
$13⁵⁰~

39 G 1687
$21⁸⁵~

39 G 1669
$22⁹⁵~

39 G 1617
$22⁰⁰~

Special

39 G 1637
$17⁵⁰~

39 G 1655
$19⁸⁵~

39 G 1689
$21⁵⁰~

39 G 1633
$17⁸⁵~

39 G 1691
$22⁵⁰~

39 G 1693

Finest Flannel Shirts and Lumberjacks

Here Ward's Values Always Lead

Men's Sizes Only

Warmth-Quality-Price Weight-Patterns-Saving

A Heavy All Wool $4.89

B Heavy All Wool $4.79

C Extra Heavy All Wool $5.69

D Looks Like Leather $3.79

How to Order Men's Lumberjacks

Order the same size Lumberjack as the shirt you wear. If you wear size 16 shirt, order size 16 lumberjack.

E Medium Wt. Half Wool $2.59

F Heavy Part Wool $2.98

G About 60% Wool $3.29

H Fine Corduroy $2.89

J Looks Like Leather $2.79

K Army Style Part Wool $2.19

L All Wool Buffalo $3.79

M Finest Broadcloth Finish $2.98

N Medium Wt. All Wool $3.98

P About 40% Wool $2.79

R Our Finest All Wool $4.79

Today ~ the Best Styles *for* Men

Heavy Shaker Knit

College Style Sweaters *for* Boys 7 to 14 Years

For Descriptions See Opposite Page

Ages 3 to 6 Years

B $2.98
D $3.95
E $4.50
A $4.98
H $3.98
C $4.69
J $3.85
F $3.89
L $3.98
M $5.95
N $7.50
K $4.69
O 98¢
X $1.98
P 79¢
R $2.45
Y $1.98
T $3.98
U $2.98
V $2.59
S $1.39
W $2.98
Z CAP 69¢ ZZ LUMBERJACK $2.48

Colorful Cottons
More Than 100 Patterns

Wide Woven Romper Cloth
Neat New Patterns—Yarn Dyed
16¢ A Yard

STURDY—decidedly! Thousands of mothers say, "It's simply great for kiddies' play clothes. Wears and wears." Here are fifteen interesting patterns are woven in—not printed on—colorful patterns at this price. Yarn dyed the neat, colorful patterns easily. Shipping weight, per yard, 4 ounces. Clear, sensible colors; won't show soil easily. Shipping weight, per yard, 4 ounces.

16 G 3245—PATTERNS AND COLORS: As pictured. State pattern number wanted.

Fast Colors—Prints and Plain
55¢ A Yard

Width of prints, 32 inches Width of plain colors, 35 inches Nationally famous Peter Pan—extra fine fabric—guaranteed fast color. In brilliant new prints and clear solid colors. Same fabric you see in better shops. Same prints and children's wear in the better shops. Only Ward's can sell it to you by mail; we bring you substantial savings over the usual price! Shipping weight, per yard, 4 oz.

16 G 3159—PATTERNS AND COLORS: As pictured; also plain white. State pattern number wanted.

Colorful New Fancy Ginghams
Serviceable—Standard Quality
15½¢ A Yard

Width, about 32 inches There's a crisp freshness in Ginghams you find in no other fabric! Here are fifteen interesting patterns to choose from, all in clear, high colors and the season's newest designs. Excellent value— full standard quality. They wash and wear longer. Shipping weight, per yard, 4 ounces.

16 G 3129—PATTERNS AND COLORS: As pictured. State pattern number wanted.

Ward's Famous Chambray
13¢ A Yard

Width, about 28 inches "My husband insists upon Country Side for all his work shirts," writes an old customer friend from Geneva, Ill. Just one of thousands of sensible men! They've time-tested Country Side Chambray Shirting and say it gives greatest satisfaction, longest wear for every penny it costs. Our own brand, excellent weight, enduring weave. Patterns that men and boys like—won't show soil easily. Just as desirable for women's house dresses and children's clothes. Keeps its firm, close texture through frequent laundering. A wonder value! Shipping weight, per yard, 4 oz.

16 G 3270—PATTERNS AND COLORS: As pictured. State pattern number wanted.

Our Finest Zephyr Ginghams
Guaranteed Fast Colors
32¢ A Yard

Width, about 32 inches Beautiful quality, fine-weave Zephyr Gingham in fascinating patterns and clear, plain colors. All are guaranteed fast color—tub them frequently without fear. Soft, silky texture, fine enough for your best wash frocks. Shipping weight, per yard, 4 ounces.

16 G 3174—PATTERNS AND COLORS: As pictured. State pattern number wanted.

New Fast Color Glorio Cloth
35¢ A Yard

Width, about 35 inches "So fine that I want to back it with my own personal recommendation! Beautiful colors, guaranteed fast to boiling and sunlight. Extra fine weave of long combed cottons, fine spun and highly mercerized. Soft as fine pongee, sturdy as best gingham."

W.W. May Manager Dry Goods Department.

16 G 3156—COLORS: As pictured. State color wanted. Ship. weight, per yard, 3 oz.

Fast Color Service Suiting
Looks Like Linen—Durable!
32¢ A Yard

Width, about 36 inches Enduring, linen-like weave—our own time-tested Tu Crest. Colors are vat dyed and guaranteed fast to washing. The ideal economy fabric for children's dresses and play suits, for popular smocks and colorful allover aprons. Tubbing only renews the clear, fresh colors and brings out the linen-like texture. Shipping weight, per yard, 5 oz.

16 G 3450—COLORS: As pictured. State color wanted.

Gay Comforter Challis
New Patterns—Brilliant Colors
14¢ A Yard

Width, about 36 inches Fresh, cheery colors in these delightful new designs. Think what attractive comforters they'll make at small cost. Use them to renew old comforters or to make warm, downy new ones. Fine batts are shown on Page 147. A good weight weave of long staple cottons. Shipping weight, per yard, 3 oz.

16 G 3320—PATTERNS AND COLORS: As pictured. State pattern number wanted.

New Comforter Cretonnes
Gay Colors—Standard Quality
16¢ A Yard

Width, about 36 inches Best value you'll find in bright new Comforter Cretonnes. Delightful designs in vivid colors. Newest and best for making warm, cozy comforters. Good weight, full standard quality. Very decorative for sun-porch draperies. A few yards made into a slip cover will transform a couch or chair. Ship. wt., per yard, 3 oz.

16 G 3316—PATTERNS AND COLORS: As pictured. State pattern number wanted.

Yard Wide Printed Flannelette
27¢ A Yard

Soft, warm Cotton Flannelette with softly fleeced nap on one side, firm plain weave on the other. Delightful patterns to please all the family. Good weight. Shipping weight, per yard, 5 oz.

16 G 3223—PATTERNS AND COLORS: As pictured. State pattern number wanted.

Big Value Percale
Full Standard Quality
13½¢ A Yard

Width, about 36 in. Same standard quality Percale we have offered for years. Same big value that's made it the popular choice of thousands. Now in wide array of the season's gay, new patterns; old favorites, too. A sturdy, full count weave, exceptionally serviceable. Ship. weight, per yard, 4 oz.

16 G 3203—PATTERNS AND COLORS: As pictured. State pattern number wanted.

Tubfast Kiddiana Kloth
Gay Patterns—Stay Bright and Fresh
25¢ A Yard

Width, about 32 inches Fascinating prints, new and brilliantly colorful! Soft, fine-weave Kiddiana Kloth, guaranteed fast to constant tubbing. Charming for little folks' and grownups' frocks. Delightful patterns—the season's newest and best. Ship. weight, per yard, 4 oz.

16 G 3208—PATTERNS AND COLORS: As pictured. State pattern number wanted.

Fancy Dress Prints
Distinctive New Styles
16¢ A Yard

Width, about 36 in. Smartest, newest patterns you ever saw, in the vivid, high colors that fashion favors. Extra quality, fine-yarn Dress Prints. Comes through many washings fresh and crisp. At our special price, it's a value to tell your friends about. Ship. weight, per yard, 4 ounces.

16 G 3205—PATTERNS AND COLORS: As pictured. State pattern number wanted.

Popular and Useful Gift Jewelry

Your Choice $1.98

Solid 14-Karat Gold Throughout

These emblems are 14-K solid gold throughout, including screw post and fastener. Enameled emblems are colored in true fidelity.

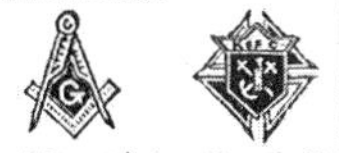

Masonic Button, blue enameled. Green gold. 545 G 7239 ..$1.98

K. of C. Button, enameled. 545 G 7240 $1.98

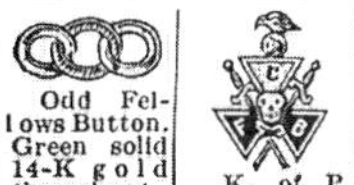

Odd Fellows Button. Green solid 14-K gold throughout. Heavy weight. 545 G 7238 $1.98

K. of P. Button. 14-K green solid gold. Enameled. 545 G 7243 ..$1.98

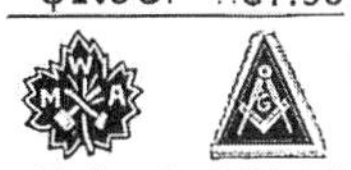

Modern Woodmen. Solid 14-K gold. Enameled. 545 G 7241 $1.98

Solid 14-K gold, platinum top emblem in genuine onyx. 545 G 7236 $1.98

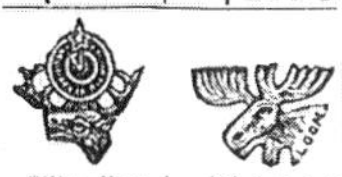

Elks Button. 14-K natural gold. 545 G 7257 $1.98

Moose Button. 14-K green gold. 545 G 7242 $1.98

Diamond Set Scarf Pins

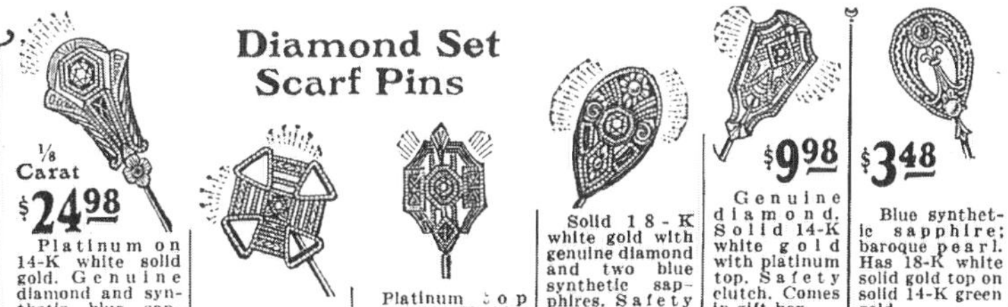

1/8 Carat $24.98

Platinum on 14-K white solid gold. Genuine diamond and synthetic blue sapphire.
545 G 3414—1/8 carat .. $24.98
545 G 3415—3/16 carat .. $39.98
545 G 3427—1/4 carat .. $58.75

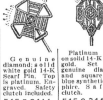

Genuine diamond; solid white gold 14-K Scarf Pin. Top is platinum. Engraved. Safety clutch included. 545 G 3411 .. $5.48

Platinum top on solid 14-K white gold. Set with genuine diamond and square cut blue synthetic sapphire. Safety clutch. 545 G 3410 .. $9.98

Solid 18-K white gold with genuine diamond and two blue synthetic sapphires. Safety clutch. 545 G 3419 .. $12.50

$9.98 Genuine diamond. Solid 14-K white gold with platinum top. Safety clutch. Comes in gift box. 545 G 3408 .. $9.98

Shipping Weight on Scarf Pins, 4 Ounces Each | All Pictures Actual Size

Solid Gold Scarf Pins

$3.48 Blue synthetic sapphire; baroque pearl. Has 18-K white solid gold top on solid 14-K green gold. 545 G 7155 .. $3.48

Genuine opal with sparkling fiery color. Green 10-K solid gold Scarf Pin. Gift box. 545 G 7154 .. $1.87

Solid 10-K natural color gold Scarf Pin. Set with red synthetic ruby. Safety clutch and gift box. 545 G 7152 .. $1.78

Sure Protection for Scarf Pin or Bar Pin

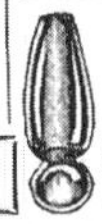

This Safety Clutch prevents loss of scarf pin or bar pin. Holds firmly. Sent free with each scarf pin listed on this page. Slips on very easily. Gold filled. 545 G 7153 .. 15¢

Safety Clutch Included With Each Scarf Pin

Diamond Set Emblems

The most cherished gift you can give to a lodge brother is his Emblem. And what could be more appropriate than one of these fine diamond set buttons or pins! Those shown in this group are exceptionally fine both in quality and design. Shipping weight, each, 2 ounces.

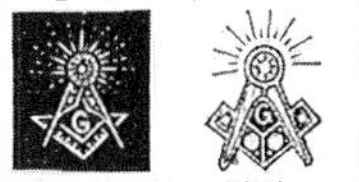

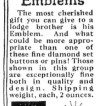

Solid 14-K white gold; platinum top. Genuine diamond. 545 G 7235 $4.98

Platinum on 14-K solid white gold. One large and two small diamonds. 545 G 3426 $24.95

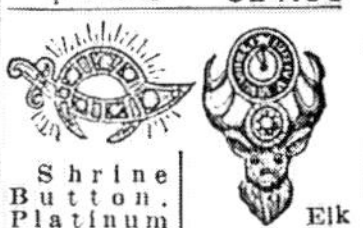

Shrine Button. Platinum top on 14-K solid white gold. Six diamonds. 545 G 3424 $24.95

Elk Button. Platinum on 14-K white gold. Genuine diamond. 545 G 3425 .$19.98

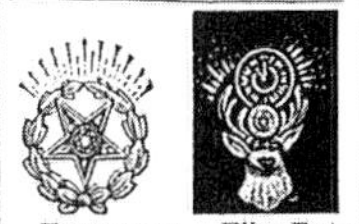

Eastern Star Pin; 14-K white solid gold. Genuine diamond. 545 G 7273 $4.98

Elks Button. Platinum on 14-K solid gold. Genuine diamond. 545 G 7232 $4.98

Solid Gold Emblem Pins and Buttons

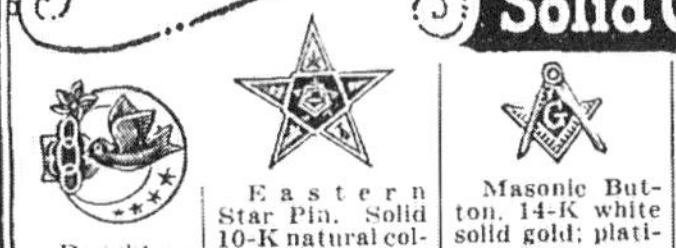

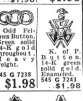

Daughters of Rebekah Pin. Solid 14-K gold. 545 G 7254 Green gold; enameled $1.48
545 G 7274 Solid 14-K white gold. $1.48

Eastern Star Pin. Solid 10-K natural color gold. 545 G 7279 .. 98¢

Masonic Button. 14-K white solid gold; platinum top. 545 G 7244 .. 87¢

Rebekah, and Odd Fellows Pin. 545 G 7275 14-K white solid gold. $1.98
545 G 7276 14-K green solid gold. $1.98

You Can Depend on the Quality

The Emblem Buttons and Pins shown in this group are all solid gold; the fastenings, such as screw parts, backs, pins, joints and catches are gold filled. This does not in any way affect the wearing quality of the emblem itself, which is solid gold. Most of these emblems are enameled in colors, and all of the pins are fitted with safety clasps. A neat gift case is included with each button or pin.

Shipping Weight on All Emblems, 2 Ounces Each

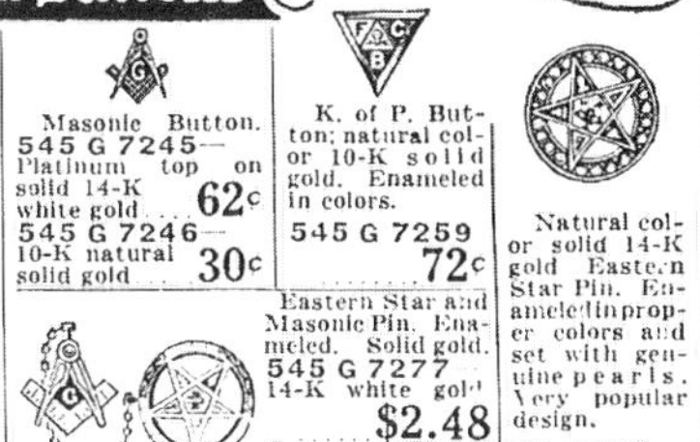

Masonic Button. 545 G 7245—Platinum top on solid 14-K white gold .. 62¢
545 G 7246—10-K natural solid gold .. 30¢

K. of P. Button; natural color or 10-K solid gold. Enameled in colors. 545 G 7259 .. 72¢

Eastern Star and Masonic Pin. Enameled. Solid gold. 545 G 7277 14-K white gold $2.48
545 G 7278—14-K green gold $2.48

Natural color solid 14-K gold Eastern Star Pin. Enameled in proper colors and set with genuine pearls. Very popular design. 545 G 7247 $3.65

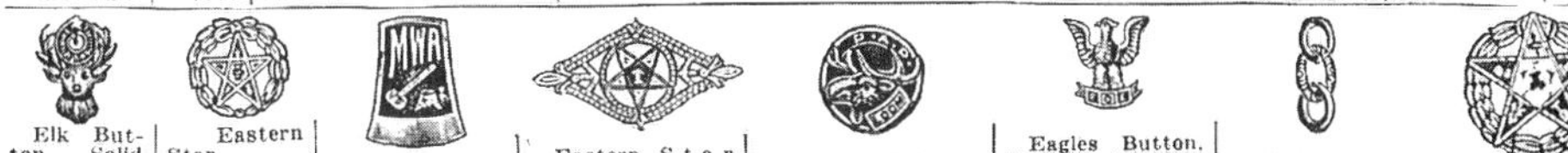

Elk Button. Solid 14-K white gold. Stone set eyes; enameled dial. A favorite size among the Elks. 545 G 7280 ..$1.48

Eastern Star. 545 G 7261 14-K green solid gold. $1.50
545 G 7262 14-K white solid gold. ..$1.50

M. W. A. Button. Enameled in colors. Solid 10-K natural color gold. 545 G 7263 .. 75¢

Eastern Star brooch Pin; 14-K white solid gold, platinum top. Emblem is enameled in colors and set in artistic circle. 545 G 7256 .. $2.98

Loyal Order of Moose Emblem Button. Raised emblem. Enameled. Solid 10-K natural color gold. A very popular size and design. 545G7264 98¢

Eagles Button. F. O. E. inlaid in colored enamel. Solid 10-K natural color gold. The emblem is faithfully reproduced. 545 G 7265 .. 69¢

14-K green solid gold. Odd Fellows Button. Finely finished and neatly engraved. 545 G 7251 .. 89¢

Eastern Star Pin. Enameled. 545 G 7266—14-K green gold .. $1.98
545 G 7267—14-K white gold .. $1.98

Solid Gold Emblem Rings

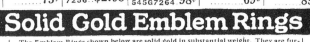

The Emblem Rings shown below are solid gold in substantial weight. They are furnished in sizes 7 to 13 unless otherwise stated. Read "How to Order" on Page 413.

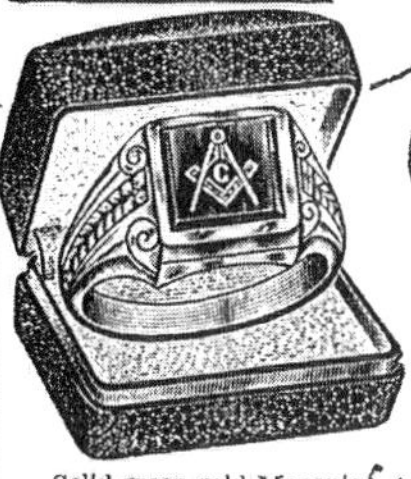

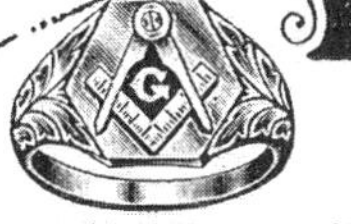

Solid 10-K green gold. Neatly engraved sides. Enameled. SIZES: 7 to 13. State size wanted.
545 G 6055—Masonic.
545 G 6056—I. O. O. F.
545 G 6314—K. of C.
Each .. $4.98

Solid green gold Masonic Ring beautifully engraved, and set with synthetic ruby incrusted emblem of solid gold. SIZES: 7 to 13. State size wanted.
545 G 6044 10-K solid gold $ 9.98
545 G 6045—14-K solid gold 11.98

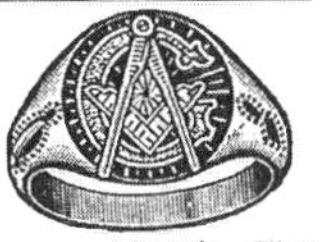

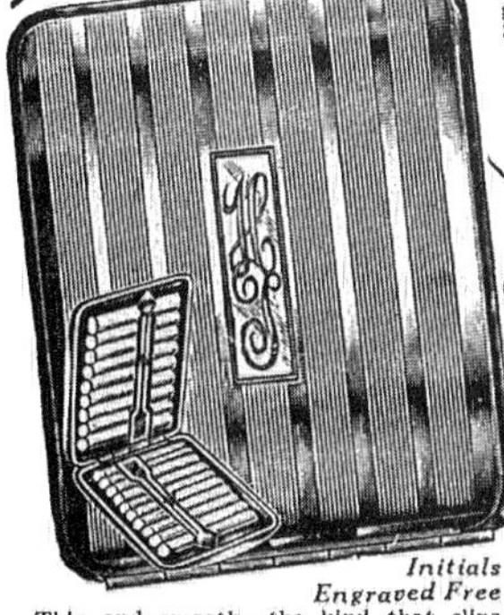

Masonic Ring. Solid green gold with raised white gold emblem. SIZES: 7 to 13. State size.
545 G 6091 10-K .. $6.98
545 G 6092 14-K .. $8.98

All Rings Shown Actual Size

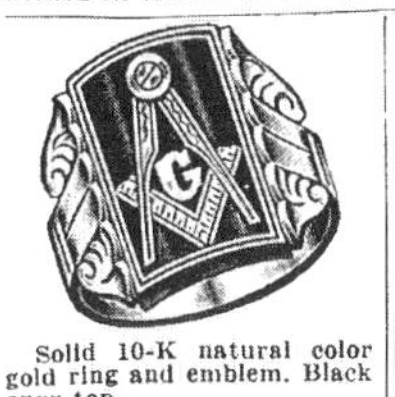

Solid 10-K natural color gold ring and emblem. Black onyx top. SIZES: 7 to 13.
545 G 6046—Masonic .. $8.98
545 G 6047—Odd Fellows .. 8.98
545 G 6049—Masonic with 6 genuine diamonds .. $15.98

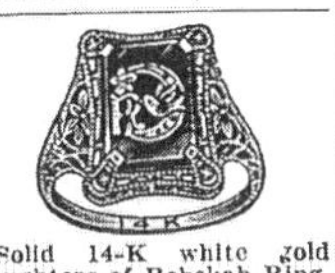

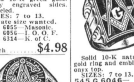

Solid 14-K white gold Daughters of Rebekah Ring. Genuine black onyx. SIZES: 4 to 7. State size. 545 G 6089 .. $5.75

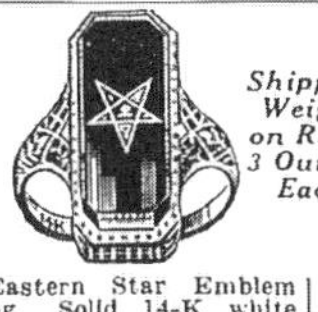

Shipping Weight on Rings 3 Ounces Each

Eastern Star Emblem Ring. Solid 14-K white gold. Genuine black onyx with raised 14-K white gold emblem enameled in colors. SIZES: 3 to 7. State size. 545 G 6310 .. $4.98

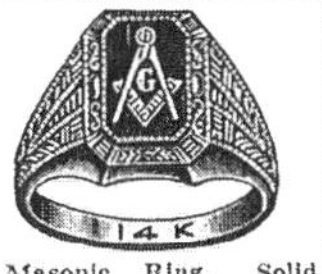

Masonic Ring. Solid green gold. White gold border. Synthetic ruby; white gold encrusted emblem. SIZES: 7 to 13.
545 G 6087 10-K .. $6.65
545 G 6088—14-K .. 8.25

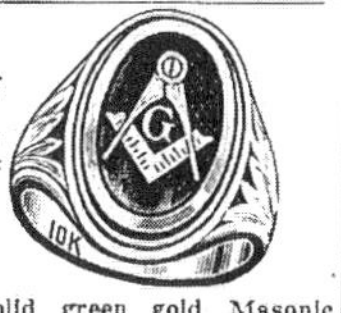

Solid green gold Masonic Emblem Ring. Full oxidized, rich, dull finish. Genuine black onyx with encrusted white gold masonic emblem. A large massive ring, smartly designed in the very latest style. Leatherette gift case. SIZES: 7 to 13. State size wanted.
545 G 6312—10-K $9.98
545 G 6313—14-K 12.50

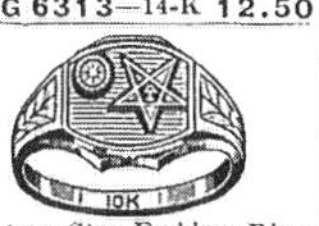

Eastern Star Emblem Ring. Solid 10-K white gold neatly engraved sides. Raised emblem in enameled colors. Genuine diamond in platinum setting. SIZES: 4 to 9. State size. 545 G 6311 .. $9.98

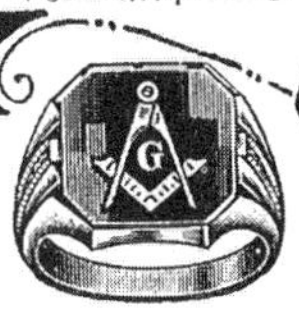

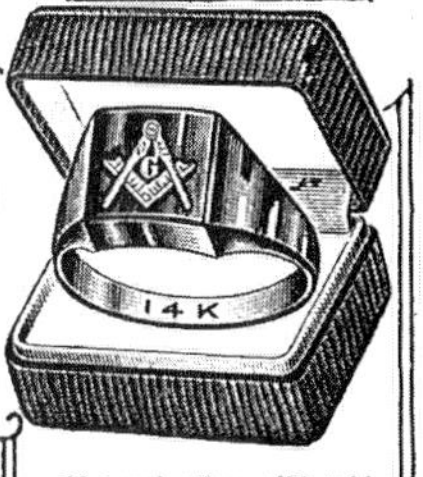

Masonic Ring large and massive in appearance. 10-K green solid gold. Genuine Black Onyx. Encrusted white gold emblem. SIZES: 7 to 13. State size. 545 G 6093 $6.98

Natural color solid gold Masonic Emblem Ring. Plain polished finish. Emblem is gold encrusted into synthetic red ruby. SIZES: 7 to 13.
545 G 6152—10-K solid gold .. $7.78
545 G 6153—14-K solid gold .. 8.98

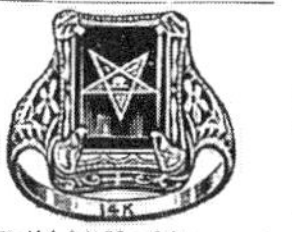

Solid 14-K white gold Eastern Star Ring. Genuine black Onyx. Raised emblem. Enameled in proper colors. SIZES: 4 to 7. State size wanted. 545G 6090 $5.75

Gift Case With Each Ring

Cigarette Lighters and Cases

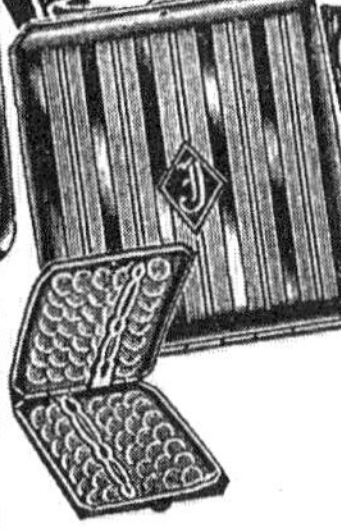

Initials Engraved Free

Thin and smooth—the kind that slips easily into the vest pocket. The back and front are engine turned in straight line effect. Inside is gold plated. Holds a full package of 20 cigarettes. Length, 4¼ inches; width, 3¼ inches. Any initials free. Ship. wt., 9 oz. State initials wanted.
546 G 4280—Nickel silver .. $1.75
546 G 4281—Silver plated .. 2.25

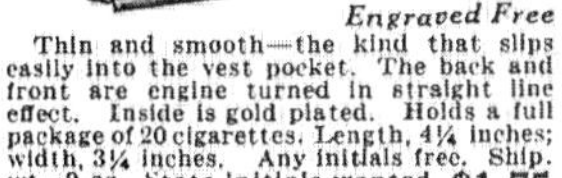

Popular Square Shape

Handsomely engine turned. Inside of case is gold plated. Holds 18 cigarettes, 9 on each side. Spring joint, snap catch. Size, 3⅜ by 3 inches. Any initial engraved free. Shipping weight, each, 9 ounces. State initial wanted.
546 G 4288—Nickel silver .. $1.18
546 G 4289—Silver plated .. 1.80

Two Color Finish

A thin, curved case that will easily slip into a vest pocket. Handsome gold embossed border and floral design with nickel silver or silver plated body. Inside is gold plated. Easily opened by push snap at top of case. Spring joint. Width, 2⅞ inches; length, 3¾ inches. Any initials engraved free. Ship. wt., each, 9 oz. State initials wanted.
546 G 4297—Nickel silver .. $2.75
546 G 4298—Silver plated .. 3.25

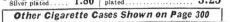

Other Cigarette Cases Shown on Page 300

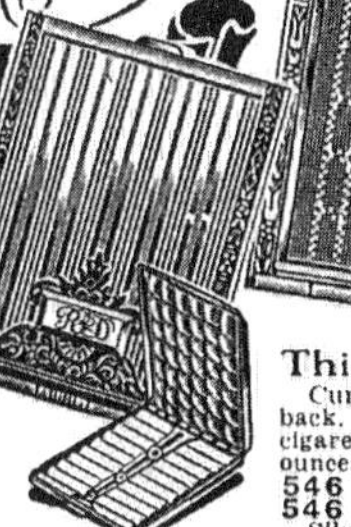

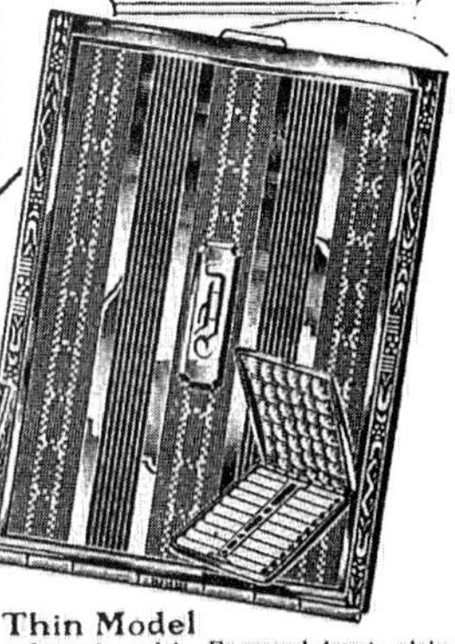

Thin Model

Curved model. Engraved front, plain back. Gold lined inside. Holds ten cigarettes. Shipping weight, each, 9 ounces. State initial.
546 G 4294—Nickel silver .. $1.45
546 G 4295—Silver plated .. 1.89
546 G 4296—Sterling silver, similar design .. 6.89

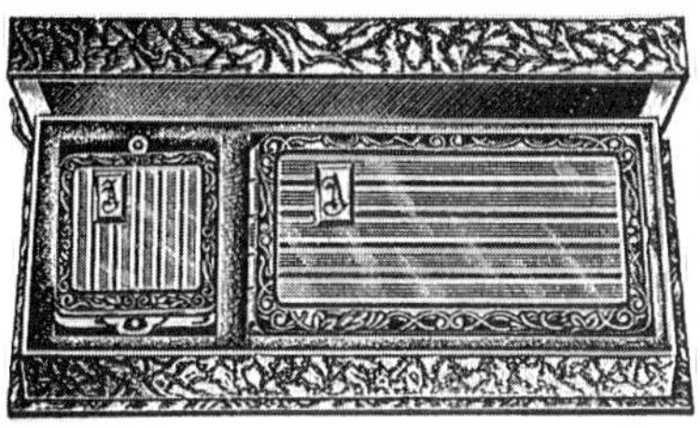

Combination Gift Set

A sure way to please a man! Give him this attractive set consisting of a thin model Cigarette Case 4⅛ by 3 inches, that holds 10 cigarettes, and a Match Case, 1¾ by 2¼ inches, that holds one book of paper matches. Both pieces are matched in design with an embossed border in attractive deep carved effect, and a straight line engine turned center. Match case is fitted with a ring loop to be worn on end of watch chain. The complete set is sent to you in an attractive cloth lined gift case. Shipping weight, per set, 1 pound. State initials wanted.
546 G 4299—Nickel silver. Per set .. $2.75
546 G 4300—Silver-plated. Per set .. 3.59

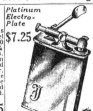

Platinum Electro-Plate $7.25

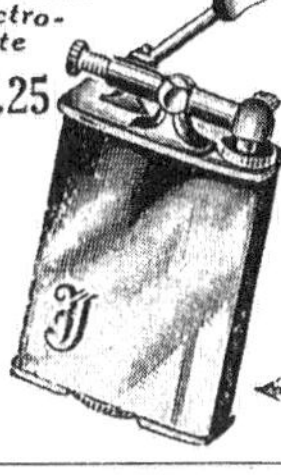

Automatic Lighter

Clark W G G

The new and improved Genuine Clark lighter! Not an experiment but a real practical lighter that will not fail. Large thumb wheel operates the smaller concealed sparking wheel—just a touch and it lights. Magazine carries flint which is kept at proper tension against sparking wheel, by an adjusting screw. Snuffer arm fits closely over wick, prevents evaporation. Best results are obtained with the use of high test gasoline or a high-grade benzine. Shipping weight, 10 ounces.

545 G 6846—Platinum electro-plate on white metal. Equal to most lighters selling for $10. Any initial engraved free. .. $7.25

545 G 6847—Green gold-filled end and fitting; genuine alligator grained leather covered body. Equal to many lighters selling for $17.50. $9.50

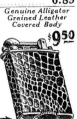

Genuine Alligator Grained Leather Covered Body $9.50

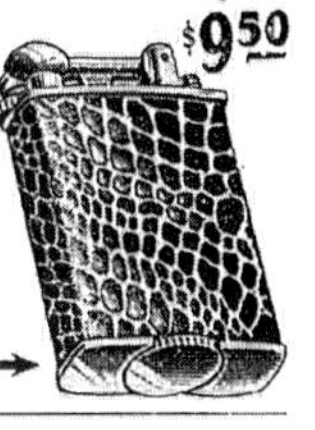

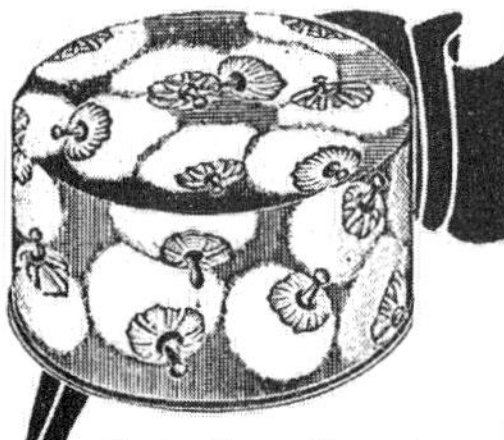

LES PARFUMS COTY IMPORTED FROM PARIS

Every woman knows that the perfumes and toilet articles manufactured under the Coty trademark are among the loveliest of toilet preparations and made by one of the most widely known perfumers of Paris. They come in beautiful packages that make attractive gifts for all occasions.

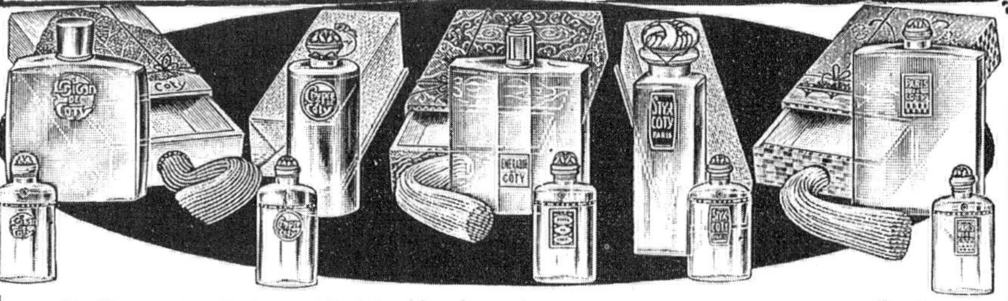

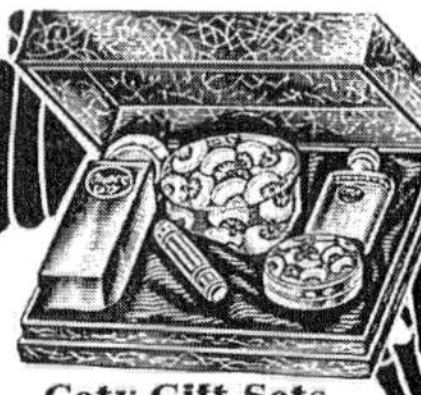

Coty Face Powder

Regular $1.00 Size

Shipping weight, per box, 4 ounces. COLORS: White; flesh; brunette; or ochre rose (a daylight shade). State color wanted.
53 G 2519—L'Origan Face Powder.
53 G 2552—Paris Face Powder.
53 G 2555—Chypre Face Powder.
53 G 2645—Styx Face Powder.
53 G 2523—Emeraude Face Powder. (White, Flesh, or Brunette only).
Per box .... 89¢

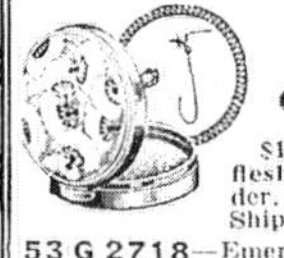

Coty Powder Compacts

$1.00 size with flesh color cake powder, mirror and puff. Ship. weight, 6 oz.
53 G 2718—Emeraude Compact.
53 G 2528—L'Origan Compact.
53 G 2717—Paris Compact.
53 G 2716—Chypre Compact.
53 G 2650—Styx Compact.
Each .... 89¢

Refills (Each with Puff). Shipping weight, 2 ounces.
53 G 2721—Emeraude.
53 G 2522—L'Origan.
53 G 2720—Paris.
53 G 2719—Chypre.
53 G 2651—Styx. Each ... 42¢

Coty Perfumes: Shipping weights: 2-ounce bottle, 12 ounces; other sizes, 7 ounces.

Parfum L'Origan

53 G 2527—¼ ounce. 89¢
53 G 2525—$2.00 ½ ounce Size $1.76
53 G 2526—$3.75 1 ounce Size 3.39
53 G 2513—2 ounces. $7.00 size. In gift box with silk tassel. $6.49

Chypre

53 G 2706—¼ ounce. 89¢
53 G 2707—$2.00 ½ ounce Size $1.76
53 G 2708—$3.75 1 ounce Size 3.39
53 G 2709—2 ounces. $6.75 size. Beautiful gift box $6.25

Emeraude

53 G 2710—¼ ounce. 89¢
53 G 2711—$2.00 ½ ounce Size $1.76
53 G 2712—$3.75 1 ounce Size 3.39
53 G 2713—2 ounces. $7.00 size. In gift box with silk tassel. $6.59

Styx

53 G 2646—¼ oz. $1.00
53 G 2647—$2.25 ½ ounce Size 1.85
53 G 2648—$4.10 1 ounce Size 3.49
53 G 2649—2 ounces. $8.60 size. Beautiful bottle in gift box. $7.49

Parfum Paris

53 G 2701—¼ ounce 89¢
53 G 2702—$2.00 ½ ounce Size $1.76
53 G 2703—$3.75 1 ounce Size 3.39
53 G 2704—2 ounces. $6.75 size. In gift box with tassel $6.25

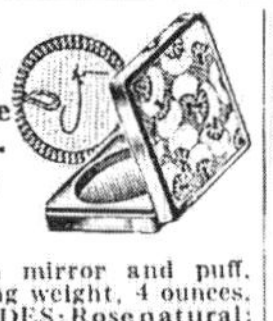

Coty Rouge Compact

With mirror and puff. Shipping weight, 4 ounces. SHADES: Rose natural; light geranium, or orange.
53 G 2549—$1.25 size $1.12

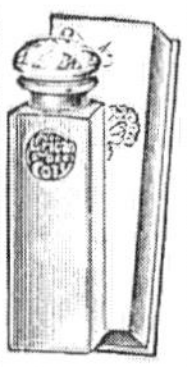

Coty Toilet Water

Regular $4.00 size

Four-ounce crystal bottle with ground glass stopper. In gift box. Shipping weight, each, 1 lb.
53 G 2622—Emeraude.
53 G 2515—L'Origan.
53 G 2620—Paris.
53 G 2621—Chypre.
53 G 2652—Styx.
Each ... $3.49

L'Origan Sachet Powder

53 G 2610—Shipping wt., 8 ounces. $1.90 Size $1.69

L'Origan Talcum

53 G 2529—Shipping wt., 12 ounces. $1.00 Size 89¢

Brilliantine L'Origan

53 G 2611—Shipping wt., 8 ounces. $1.50 Size $1.29

Eau de Coty Cologne

53 G 2550—Shipping wt., 6 ounces. $1.00 Size 89¢

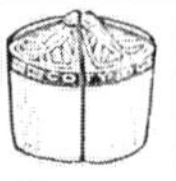

Creme Coty

Vanishing cream. Shipping weight, jar, 6 ounces.
53 G 2553 $1.00 size .. 89¢

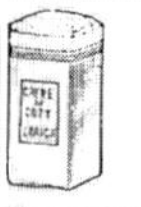

Colcreme Coty

Cold Cream. Shipping wt., jar, 6 ounces.
53 G 2554 $1.00 size .. 89¢

Coty Gift Sets

Ship. weight, 1 pound 10 ounces. ODORS: L'Origan; Chypre; Emeraude; Styx; Paris.
53 G 2683—Contains ½ ounce Perfume; 4 ounces Toilet Water; flesh Face Powder; Powder Compact and medium shade Lipstick $6.49
53 G 2686—Contains ¼-ounce Perfume; 4 ounces Toilet Water and Powder Compact $5.75

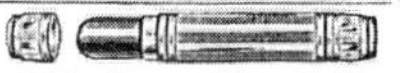

L'Origan Lipstick

Shipping weight, 2 ounces. COLORS: Light; medium, or dark. State color wanted.
53 G 2612—$1.00 Size ... 89¢

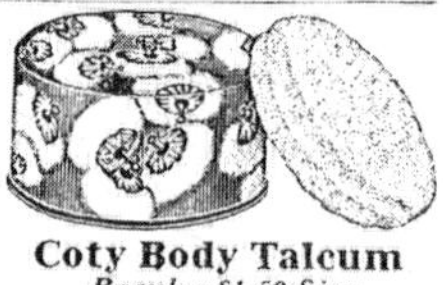

Coty Body Talcum

Regular $1.50 Size

"After the bath" powder. Large size boxes. Scented with delightful Coty odors. Each with beautiful puff. Ship. wt., box, 12 oz.
53 G 2530—L'Origan.
53 G 2565—Chypre.
53 G 2524—Emeraude.
53 G 2564—Styx.
53 G 2623—Paris.
Each $1.33

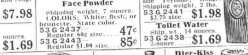

Djer-Kiss

"My masterpiece," says M. Kerkoff, the manufacturer. "Into it, as in one bewitching bouquet, I blend the very spirit and charm of my gay Paris."

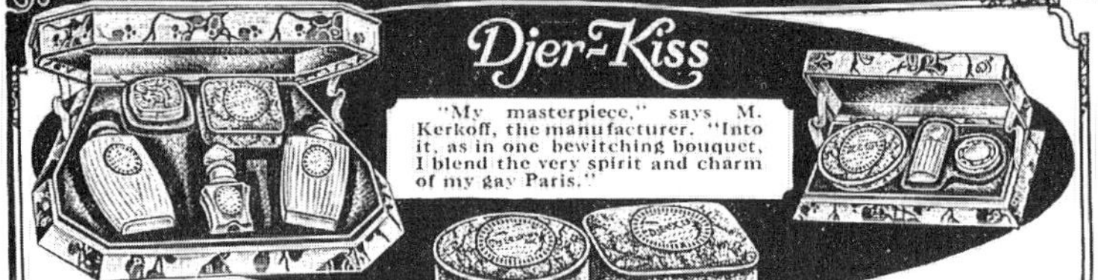

5-Piece Gift Set

Contains Toilet Water; Perfume; large size Face Powder; Talcum; loose powder and rouge Vanity.
53 G 2446—$12.00 size. Ship. wt., 3 lbs. $7.98

Perfume

Shipping weight, 12 ounces.
53 G 2439—1-oz. bottle. $2.00 Size $1.69

Face Powder

Shipping weight, 7 ounces. COLORS: White; flesh, or brunette. State color.
53 G 2437—Regular 60¢ size ..... 47¢
53 G 2443—Regular $1.00 size .... 85¢

3-Piece Gift Set

Face Powder; vanity size Perfume; Rouge. Shipping weight, 2 lbs.
53 G 2441—$2.75 size ... $1.98

Toilet Water

Ship. wt., 14 ounces.
53 G 2438—3-ounce $1.69

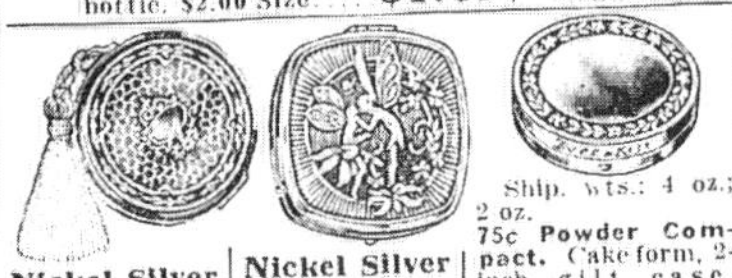

Nickel Silver

In gift box. Ship. wt., 6 oz.
53 G 2453—Powder (Naturelle) $1.69
53 G 2448—Cake Powder. Flesh, white, or brunette. $1.29

Nickel Silver Double

Loose Powder Vanity (flesh powder) and medium Rouge in satin gift box. Ship. wt., 12 oz.
53 G 2426— $2.19

Ship. wts.: 4 oz.; 2 oz.
75¢ **Powder Compact.** Cake form, 2-inch gilt case. White; flesh; brunette.
53 G 2445 .. 59¢
50¢ **Rouge Compact** SHADES: Light; medium; dark; poppy; orange; raspberry.
53 G 2444 ... 42¢

Djer-Kiss Talcum

Ship. wt., 6 ounces.
53G2436 35¢ size. 27¢

Djer-Kiss Brilliantine

Ship. wt., 7 oz.
53 G 2434—Solid. 75¢ size.
53 G 2435—Liquid. 75¢ size. Each ...... 59¢

Djer-Kiss Creams

Regular 75¢ Sizes

Shipping wt., jar, 10 ounces.
53 G 2432—Vanishing Cream.
53 G 2449—Cold Cream.
53 G 2433—Tissue. Cream. Each .... 59¢

Djer-Kiss Sachet

Shipping weight, 8 oz.
53 G 2447—Regular $1.00 size. 85¢

TRE-JUR

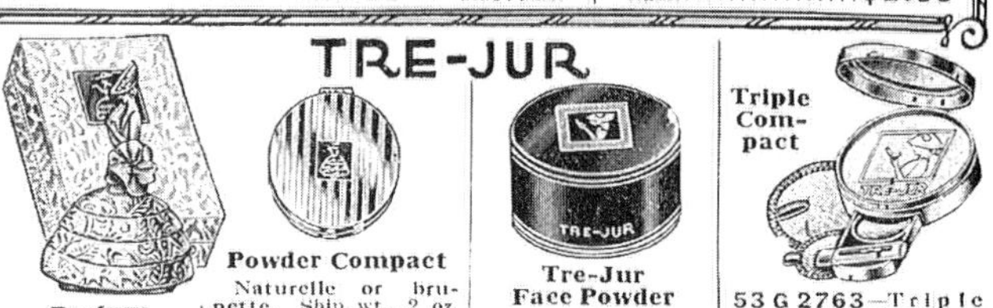

Parfum Suivez-Moi

"Follow Me" Girl-shaped bottle. Ship. wt., 4 oz.
53 G 2764—About ¼ oz. $1.00 size. 57¢

Powder Compact

Naturelle or brunette. Ship. wt., 2 oz.
53 G 2762—Regular 50¢ size. 43¢

Loose Powder Compact

White; flesh; rachel. Ship. wt., 2 oz.
53 G 2768—Regular 50¢ size. 43¢

Tre-Jur Face Powder

Shipping weight, per box, 6 ounces. COLORS; White; flesh, or rachel. State color wanted.
53 G 2766—50¢ size ...... 43¢

Triple Compact

53 G 2763—Triple Compact (medium rouge; flesh powder; medium lipstick). Ship. wt., 7 oz. $1.25 size ... $1.09
53 G 2769—Double Compact. Flesh Powder; Medium Rouge. Ship. wt., 6 oz. $1.00 size 83¢

50¢ Rouge Compact

COLORS: Orange; raspberry, or poppy. Ship. wt., 2 oz. 50¢ size.
53 G 2761 .... 43¢

Tre-Jur Lipstick

SHADES: Orange; medium; raspberry; poppy red. Shipping weight, 2 ounces.
53 G 2767—50¢ size ... 43¢

Jean de Parys

BOTTLED AND BOXED IN PARIS

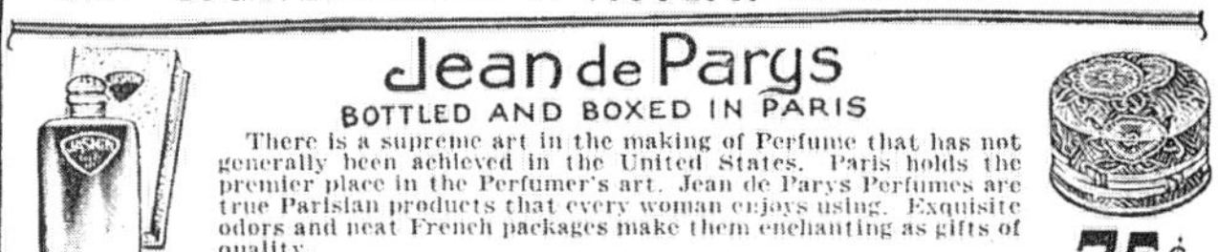

There is a supreme art in the making of Perfume that has not generally been achieved in the United States. Paris holds the premier place in the Perfumer's art. Jean de Parys Perfumes are true Parisian products that every woman enjoys using. Exquisite odors and neat French packages make them enchanting as gifts of quality.

Parisian perfume of similar quality usually costs you more than twice as much as Ward's asks for this brand.

75¢

Bouquet de Fleurs

A delightful flower blend. Ship. weight, 7 ounces.
53 G 2923—2 ounces ... $4.98
53 G 2922—1 ounce 2.49
53 G 2921—½ ounce ... 1.37

Parfum Jasmin

True odor of the jasmine flower. Ship. weight, 7 ounces.
53 G 2920—2 ounces $4.98
53 G 2919—1 ounce 2.49
53 G 2918—½ ounce ... 1.37

Ambre de Patna

So delightful it cannot be described. Ship. weight, 7 ounces.
53 G 2917—2 ounces $4.98
53 G 2916—1 ounce 2.49
53 G 2915—½ ounce 1.37

Poudre

Soft and clinging Face Powder, made in Paris. Shipping weight, 7 ounces. COLORS: White; flesh, or brunette. State color wanted.
53 G 2914—Reg. $1.00 ... 75¢

Max Factor's

COSMETICS OF THE STARS

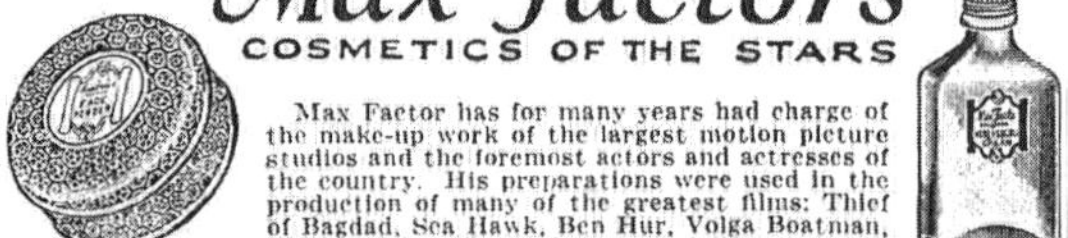

Max Factor has for many years had charge of the make-up work of the largest motion picture studios and the foremost actors and actresses of the country. His preparations were used in the production of many of the greatest films: Thief of Bagdad, Sea Hawk, Ben Hur, Volga Boatman, Old Ironsides, Mare Nostrum and others.

Mr. Factor's aims have been to make preparations that may be applied very thinly and smoothly and to achieve a make-up that would remain all day without the need of retouching. His success in the professional field has now been followed by the perfection of cosmetics that accomplish the same aims for the non-professional woman.

Face Powder

Spreads smoothly and adheres. Ship. wt., 8 oz. White; flesh; natural, or rachel. $1.00 size.
53 G 2993 89¢

Powder Foundation

For the woman with a dry skin. Before applying powder, apply little dabs of Powder Foundation. Spread smoothly. Ship. wt., 1 lb. White; flesh; natural; rachel.
53 G 2991 $1.00 size 89¢

Dry Rouge

Gives a natural appearance that cannot be detected. State shade. Shipping weight, 6 oz. SHADES: Day (light orange for white skin); blondeen; natural; light raspberry; medium raspberry; raspberry (brunette).
53 G 2994 .. 43¢

Lipstick

Water-proof. Ship. wt., 4 oz. SHADES: Light; medium; dark.
53 G 2996 50¢ size ... 43¢

Skin and Tissue Cream

For sagging muscles. Apply three times a week. Shipping weight, per jar, 1 pound.
53 G 2990 89¢

Eye Shadow

Makes eyes appear larger and more brilliant. Shipping weight, 4 ounces. COLORS: Gray; brown; blue. State color.
53 G 2998 43¢

Eyebrow Pencil.

SHADES: Black or brown. Ship. wt., 2 oz.
53 G 2999 43¢

Honeysuckle Cream

A lotion that serves as a powder base for oily skin. Ship. wt., 1 lb.
53 G 2992—$1.00 size .. 89¢

Cleansing Cream

Shipping wts.: 14 ounces; 1 lb.
53 G 2987—Solid ..... 89¢
53 G 2986—Liquid .... 89¢

Lemon Creams

Shipping wts.: 14 ounces.; 1 lb.
53 G 2989—Solid ...... 89¢
53 G 2988—Liquid ..... 89¢

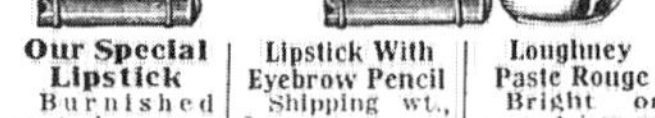

Our Special Lipstick

Burnished metal case. Water-proof. Ship. wt., 2 oz.
53 G 2568—Cherry .. 27¢
53 G 2569—Orange. 27¢

Lipstick With Eyebrow Pencil

Shipping wt., 2 ounces.
53 G 2566—Black eyebrow pencil ..... 37¢
53 G 2567—Brown eyebrow pencil ..... 37¢

Loughney Paste Rouge

Bright or medium shade. Shipping weight, 2 ounces.
53 G 2216 $1.00 size .... 69¢

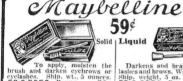

Maybelline

59¢

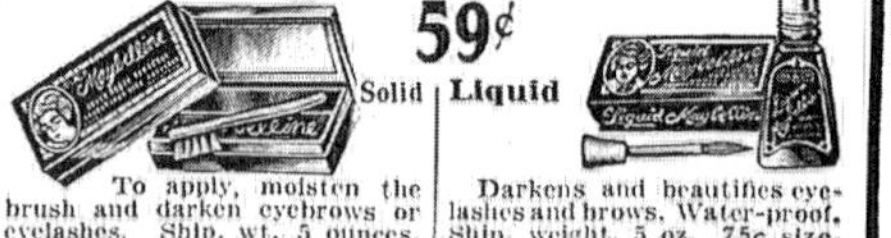

Solid

To apply, moisten the brush and darken eyebrows or eyelashes. Ship. wt., 5 ounces.
53 G 2956—Brown ..... 59¢
53 G 2957—Black ..... 59¢

Liquid

Darkens and beautifies eyelashes and brows. Water-proof. Ship. weight, 5 oz. 75¢ size.
53 G 2954—Brown ... 59¢
53 G 2955—Black .... 59¢

Deodorants

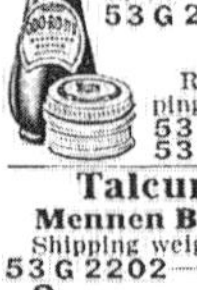

Odo-ro-no

A widely used liquid for destroying body odors. Shipping weight, 10 ounces.
53 G 2120—2-ounce size .... 49¢

"Mum"

Removes odor of perspiration. Shipping weight, 8 ounces.
53 G 2122—½-ounce jar ...... 23¢
53 G 2124—1-ounce jar .... 43¢

Talcum Powders

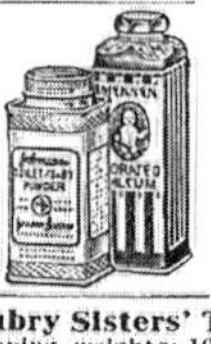

Mennen Borated Talcum

Shipping weight, 1 pound.
53 G 2202—4⅛-ounce cans. 2 Regular 25¢ cans ...... 39¢

Johnson's Baby Powder

Keeps skin cool. Use after bath. Shipping weight, 2 cans, 1 pound.
53 G 2203—25¢ can ... 2 for 39¢

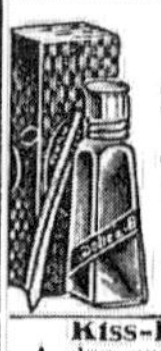

Delica-Brow

Darkens eyebrows or lashes. Shipping weight, 4 ounces. COLORS: Black or brown.
53 G 2238—About ½ ounce. $1.00 size ... 83¢
53 G 2239—About ¼ oz. 75¢ size ..... 67¢

42¢

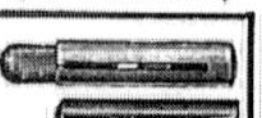

Kiss-Proof Lipstick

Water-proof. Stays on well and blends with any complexion. In neat gunmetal case. Shipping weight, 2 ounces.
53 G 2170 .... 42¢

Kiss-Proof Rouge

A dry compact Rouge, that blends with any complexion. Made by the makers of the Kiss-Proof lipstick. Shipping weight, 4 ounces.
53 G 2240—Compact .... 75¢ size 67¢

Kiss-Proof Face Powder

An excellent soft clinging powder. Shipping weight, 6 ounces. COLORS: White; flesh; brunette. State color wanted.
53 G 2241—Regular $1.00 box ...... 83¢

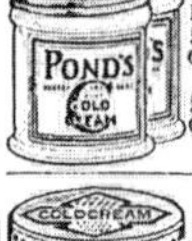

Pond's Two Creams

Shipping weight, per jar, 1 lb. 2 oz.
53 G 2134—Cold Cream, 3½-oz. jar. 60¢ size .... 49¢
53 G 2132—Vanishing Cream, 4-ounce jar. 65¢ size .... 49¢

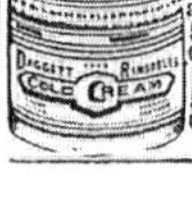

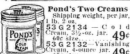

Daggett & Ramsdell's

Shipping weights: 2 lbs. and 1 lb. 2 oz.
53 G 2103—Cold Cream, 8-ounce jar. $1.00 size .... 83¢
53 G 2104—Vanishing Cream, 4-ounce jar. 60¢ size .... 48¢

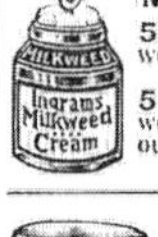

Ingram's Milkweed Cream

53 G 2136—Ship. weight, 1 lb. 2 oz. $1.00 size ... 87¢
53 G 2137—Ship. weight, 1 pound 8 ounces. $1.75 size. $1.55

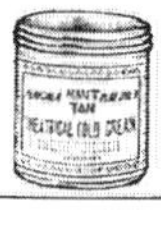

Haut Ton Theatrical Cream

Soothing, healing, and cleansing. Shipping wt., 2 lbs. 4 oz.
53 G 2367—75¢ size ..... 67¢

Creme Elcaya

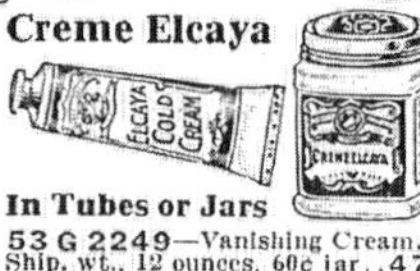

In Tubes or Jars

53 G 2249—Vanishing Cream. Ship. wt., 12 ounces. 60¢ jar .. 47¢
53 G 2250—Vanishing Cream. Ship. wt., 4 ounces. 25¢ tube. 19¢
53 G 2251—Cold Cream. Ship. wt., 12 ounces. 60¢ jar .. 47¢
53 G 2252—Cold Cream. Ship. wt., 4 ounces. 25¢ tube. 19¢

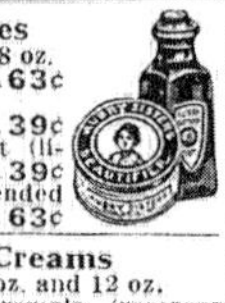

Aubry Sisters' Toiletries

Shipping weights: 10 ounces; 8 oz.
53 G 2853—75¢ Cold Cream . 63¢
53 G 2852—50¢ Vanishing Cream .... 39¢
53 G 2851—50¢ Liquid Tint (liquid rouge; medium shade) .... 39¢
53 G 2850—Beautifier (blended cream and powder) .... 63¢

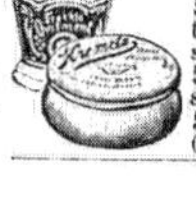

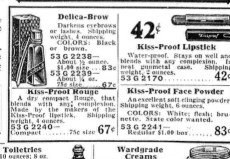

Berry Creams

Ship. wts.: 10 oz. and 12 oz.
53 G 2977—Kremola (removes tan; makes skin soft) $1.25 size $1.09
53 G 2976—Cream Balm (massage cream and skin food) .... 83¢
53 G 2978—Freckle Ointment (fragrant; snow white) .... 53¢

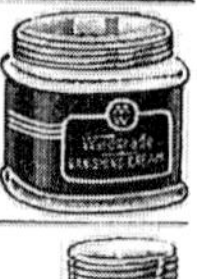

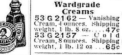

Wardgrade Creams

53 G 2162—Vanishing Cream, 4 ounces. Shipping weight, 1 lb. 8 oz. .... 47¢
53 G 2157—Cold Cream, 8 ounces. Shipping weight, 1 lb. 12 oz ... 65¢

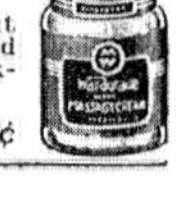

Wardgrade Massage Cream

Opens pores; brings out dirt; makes skin clean and glowing. Clears face of blackheads. Ship. wt., 1 lb. 2 oz.
53 G 2168—4½-oz. jar .... 37¢

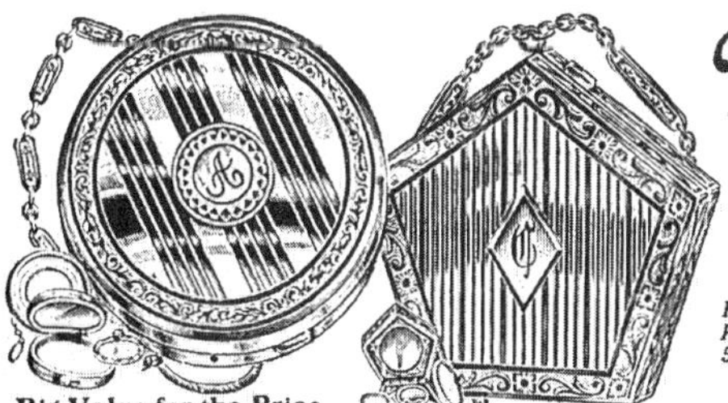

Fashionable Compacts in Latest Designs

It is the accessory that stamps the smart woman. The Compact is as necessary to the modern costume as the purse. The styles we offer are the newest, the quality found only in the better shops of New York and Chicago; but our prices are far lower. Every compact, except the loose powder models, comes with standard size powder and rouge fillers, refills of which may be purchased without difficulty at most stores carrying toilet goods. Shipping weight on all Compacts, 8 ounces each.

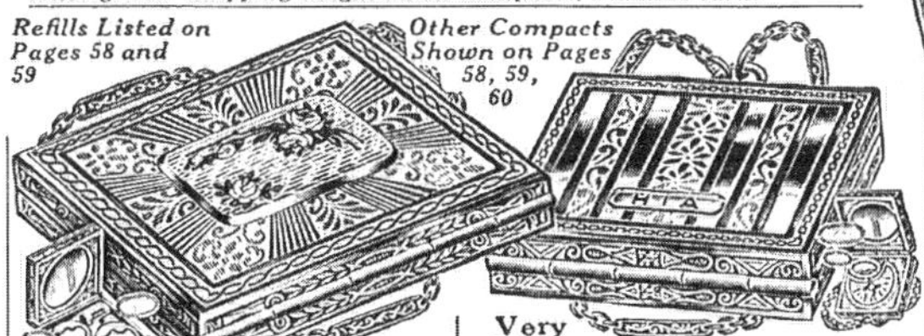

Refills Listed on Pages 58 and 59

Other Compacts Shown on Pages 58, 59, 60

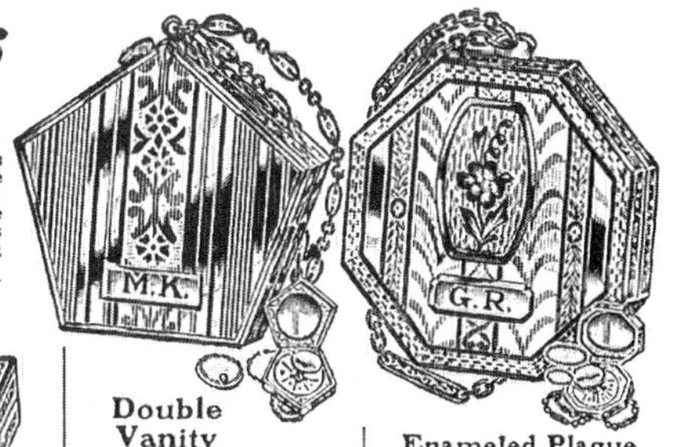

Big Value for the Price
Of course every woman uses powder! Neatly designed Compact, with 4-inch chain. Priced low! Nickel-plated, bright finish. Includes standard size rouge, compact, powder, mirror and two puffs. Diameter, 2 inches. Engraved free. State initial.
545 G 6822 .... 98¢

Loose Powder Model
Smart looking Compact, modestly priced. Of a solid white metal through and through, closely resembling white gold. Complete with mirror, puffs, rouge, and compartment for loose powder; 10-inch chain. Size, 2¼ by 2¼ inches. Initial engraved free. State initial.
545 G 6838 ...... $2.98

Exquisite!
To see this Compact is to want it! A lovely accessory that contains everything the modern young woman requires—powder and rouge, lipstick, eyebrow pencil, and mirror. Case is white gold filled, inlaid with green gold border and rays. Hand painted colored enamel plaque on sterling. Size, 2½ in. square; 10-in. chain.
545 G 6845 .... $9.98

Very New!
Select this lovely Compact with the confidence that it is correct in every detail. Case is white gold filled, with brocade effect panels and border of green gold; 10-inch chain. Mirror, puffs, rouge and compartment for loose powder. Size, 2 by 2 inches. Any initials engraved free. State initials wanted.
545 G 6841 .... $6.50

Double Vanity
No more puffs and scattered powder in your purse! Sterling silver case, handsomely engraved; 10-inch chain. Complete with rouge, mirror and two puffs. You add your own preferred loose powder. Size, 2$^{3}/_{16}$ by 2$^{3}/_{16}$ inches. Any initials engraved free. State initials.
545 G 6828 .. $7.25

Enameled Plaque in Pastel Colors
An exquisite bit of useful jewelry. Sterling silver ornament enameled in dainty pastel colors—white metal case, decorated with green gold. Compact has mirror, puffs, rouge and space for loose powder. Size, 2 inches across. Initials engraved free. State initials.
545 G 6839 .... $4.98

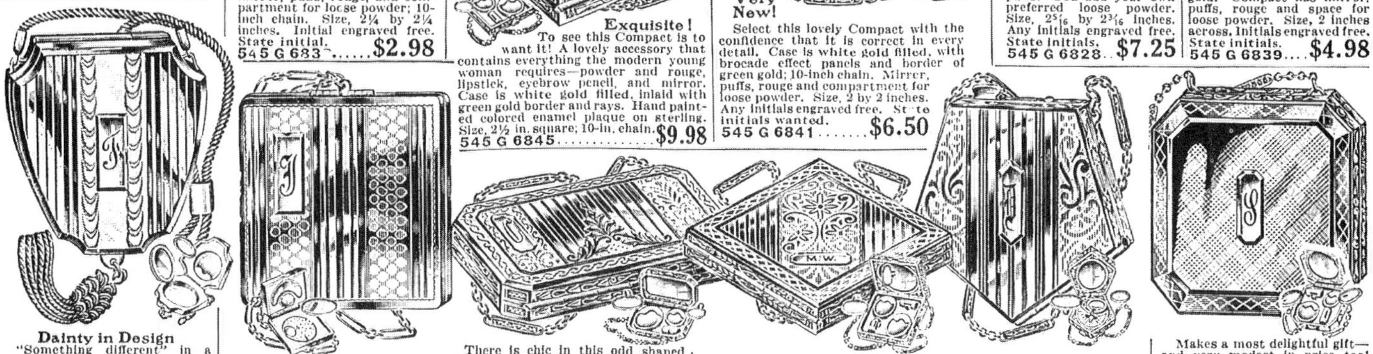

Dainty in Design
"Something different" in a Vanity. Brightly polished case with black silk tassel at bottom and 13-inch silk cord. Powder and rouge compacts; puffs and hinged mirror. Size, 2$^{1}/_{16}$ by 2$^{5}/_{16}$ inches. State initial wanted.
545 G 6830—Nickel plated $2.25
545 G 6827—Sterling silver 5.98

A most popular inexpensive Compact—at our price a remarkable value! Solid white metal that will wear indefinitely. Trim design on front and back; 10-inch chain. Has mirror, rouge, puffs and loose powder sifter. Size, 2¼ inches square. Any initial free. State initial.
545 G 6837 .... $1.48

There is chic in this odd shaped Compact—a design new and captivating! Engraved; with chain. Complete with mirror, compact powder, puffs, rouge, lipstick. Size, 2⅞ by 1¾ in.
545 G 6843—White gold filled, with green gold decorations $6.50
545 G 6844—Sterling silver with green gold decorations $8.50

"Wonderfully attractive" best describes this smart Compact. White gold filled with tapestry design running through center; border of green gold. Deep carved effect on edges. Has mirror, compact powder, puffs, rouge, lipstick and eyebrow pencil. Size, 3½ inches square. Any initials free. State initials.
545 G 6842 .... $7.50

A style of Compact shown only in the better shops. White gold filled case, handsomely engine turned. Excellent workmanship throughout. Has rouge, puffs, mirror and container for loose powder. Size, 2¼ by 2¼ inches. Any initial free. State initial.
545 G 6840 ...... $4.98

Makes a most delightful gift—and very modest in price too! Daintily designed vanity Compact of highly polished white metal resembling white gold; 10-inch chain. Has standard size rouge, powder, lipstick, eyebrow pencil, mirror and two puffs. Size, 2½ by 2½ inches. Any initial engraved free. State initial wanted.
545 G 6824 .... $3.75

Dainty Brooch Pins

Pictures Slightly Reduced

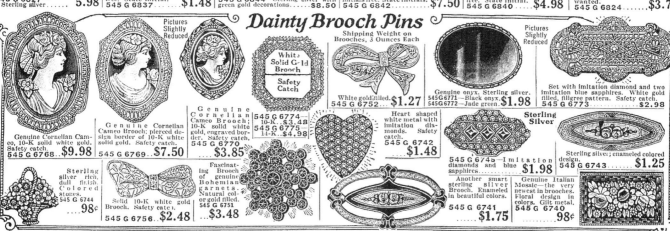

Shipping Weight on Brooches, 3 Ounces Each

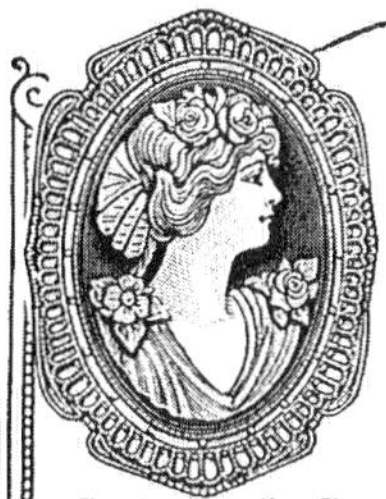

Genuine Cornelian Cameo, 10-K solid white gold. Safety catch.
545 G 6768 .. $9.98

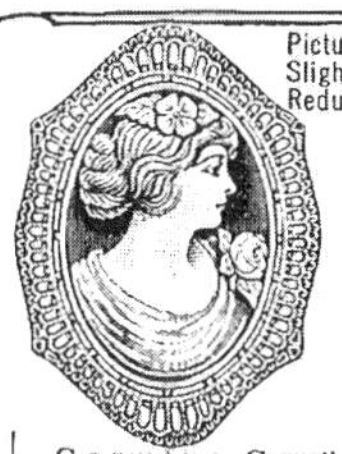

Genuine Cornelian Cameo Brooch; pierced design border of 10-K white solid gold. Safety catch.
545 G 6769 .... $7.50

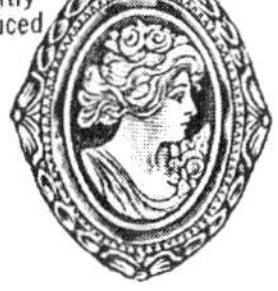

Genuine Cornelian Cameo Brooch; 10-K solid white gold, engraved border. Safety catch.
545 G 6770 ..... $3.85

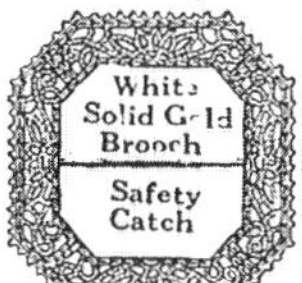

545 G 6774—10-K .. $3.48
545 G 6775—14-K .. $4.98

White gold filled .. $1.27
545 G 6752 .... $1.27

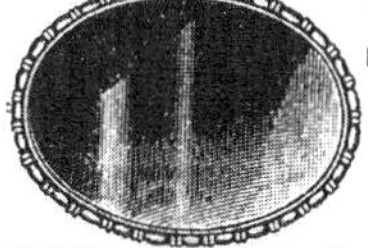

Genuine onyx. Sterling silver.
545 G 6771—Black onyx ..
545 G 6772—Jade green .. $1.98

Pictures Slightly Reduced

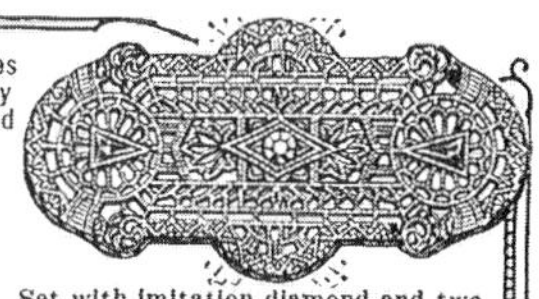

Set with imitation diamond and two imitation blue sapphires. White gold filled, filigree pattern. Safety catch.
545 G 6773 .... $2.98

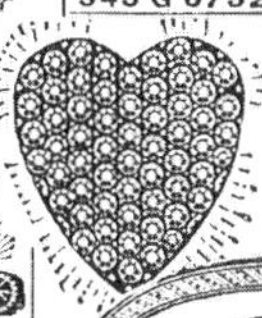

Heart shaped white metal with imitation diamonds. Safety catch.
545 G 6742 .... $1.48

Sterling Silver

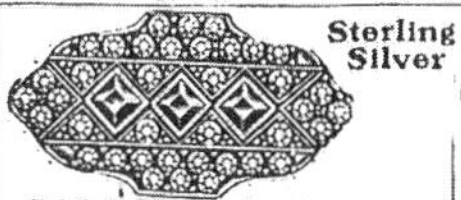

545 G 6745—Imitation diamonds and blue sapphires $1.98

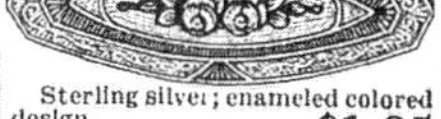

Sterling silver; enameled colored design.
545 G 6743 .... $1.25

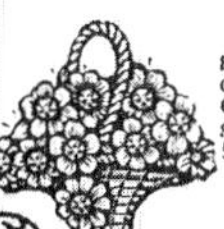

Sterling silver rich, dull finish. Colored stones.
545 G 6744 .... 98¢

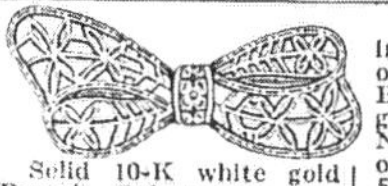

Solid 10-K white gold Brooch. Safety catch.
545 G 6756 .. $2.48

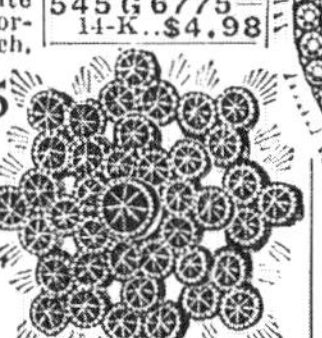

Fascinating Brooch of genuine Bohemian garnets. Natural color gold filled.
545 G 6751 .... $3.48

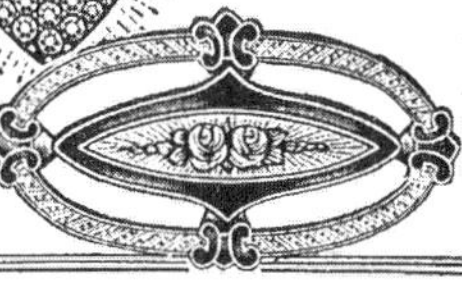

Another smart sterling silver Brooch. Enameled in beautiful colors.
545 G 6741 ...... $1.75

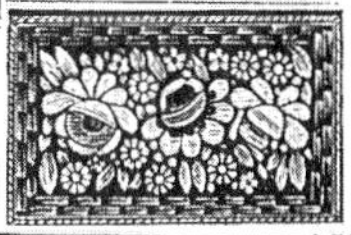

Genuine Italian Mosaic—the very newest in brooches. Floral design in colors. Gilt metal.
545 G 6740 ...... 98¢

Artistic Bracelets

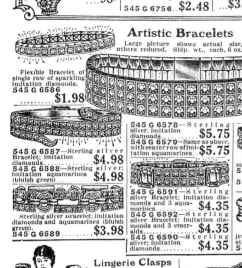

Large picture shows actual size, others reduced. Ship. wt., each, 6 oz.

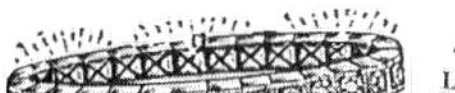

Flexible Bracelet of single row of sparkling imitation diamonds.
545 G 6586 .... $1.98

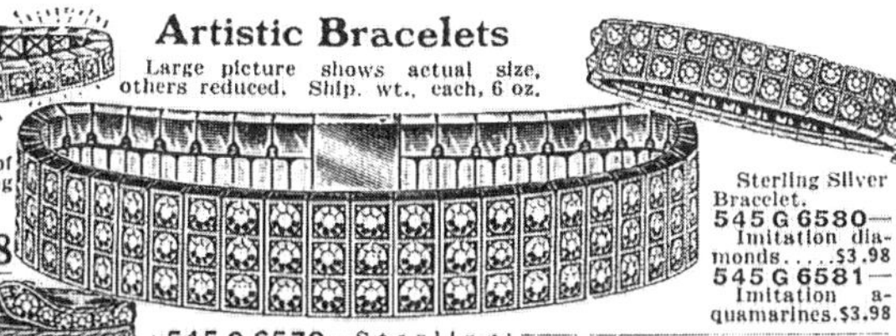

Sterling Silver Bracelet.
545 G 6580—Imitation diamonds $3.98
545 G 6581—Imitation aquamarines .. $3.98

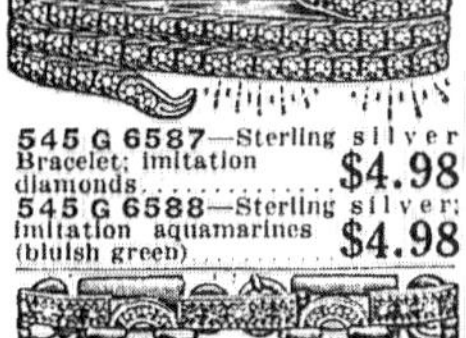

545 G 6587—Sterling silver Bracelet; imitation diamonds $4.98
545 G 6588—Sterling silver; imitation aquamarines (bluish green) $4.98

Sterling silver Bracelet; imitation diamonds and aquamarines (bluish green).
545 G 6589 .... $3.98

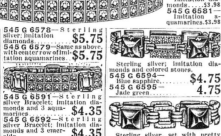

545 G 6578—Sterling silver; imitation diamonds $5.75
545 G 6579—Same as above, with center row of imitation aquamarines .. $5.75

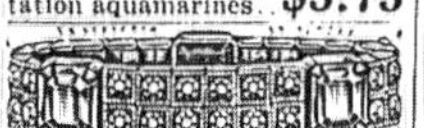

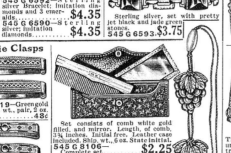

545 G 6591—Sterling silver Bracelet; imitation diamonds and 3 aquamarines $4.35
545 G 6592—Sterling silver Bracelet; imitation diamonds and 3 emeralds $4.35
545 G 6590—Sterling silver; imitation diamonds $4.35

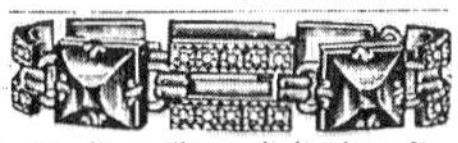

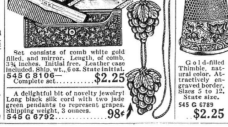

Sterling silver; imitation diamonds and colored stones.
545 G 6594—Blue sapphire $4.75
545 G 6595—Jade green 4.75

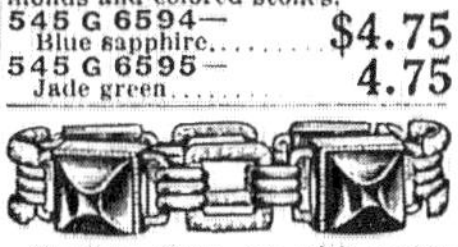

Sterling silver, set with pretty jet black and jade green stones.
545 G 6593 .. $3.75

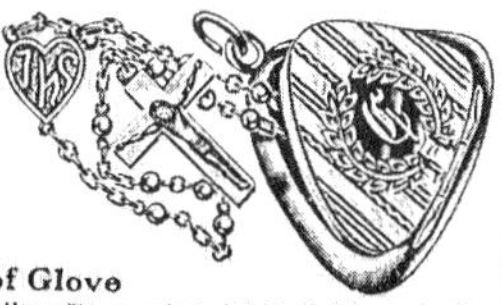

$2.48

Easily Carried Inside of Glove
Sterling silver Rosary in brightly finished sterling silver case. Any initial engraved free on case. The 11-inch rosary has a 2½-inch drop.
545 G 6821 .... $2.48

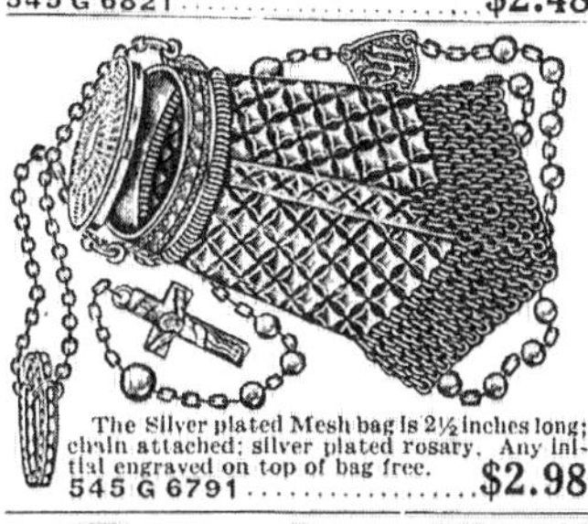

The Silver plated Mesh bag is 2½ inches long; chain attached; silver plated rosary. Any initial engraved on top of bag free.
545 G 6791 .... $2.98

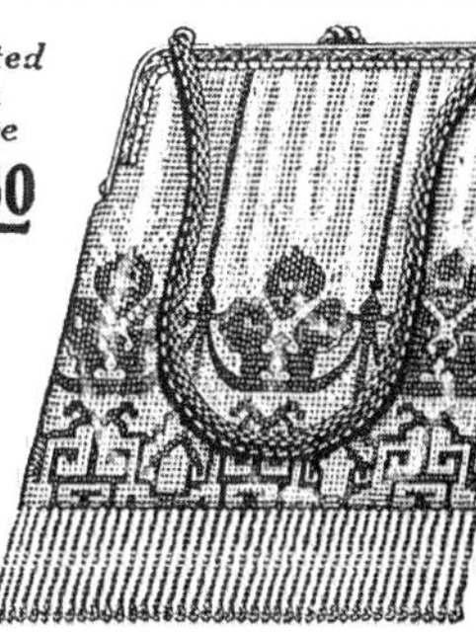

Imported from France

$12.50

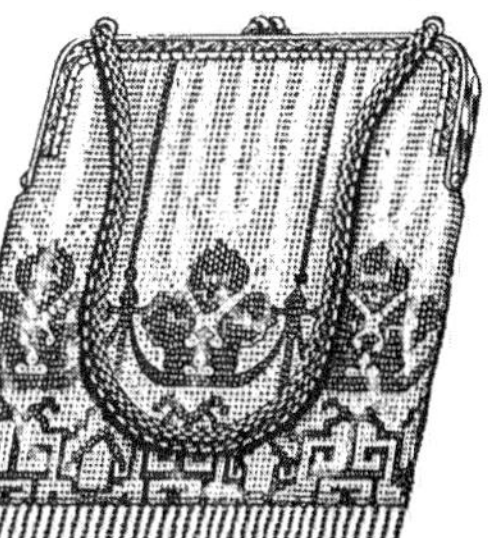

To Enhance Your Best Costume A Beaded Bag of Chic Design

Direct from France comes this stunning Beaded Bag—the handiwork of expert needleworkers. Steel cut beads on all metal frame. Beautiful flower motif in pastel shades on a background of gold color and effective harmonizing fringe. Lining of excellent quality French silk has pocket for small coin purse. Size of bag, 4½ by 8 inches. Shipping weight, 1 pound.
545 G 6790 .... $12.50

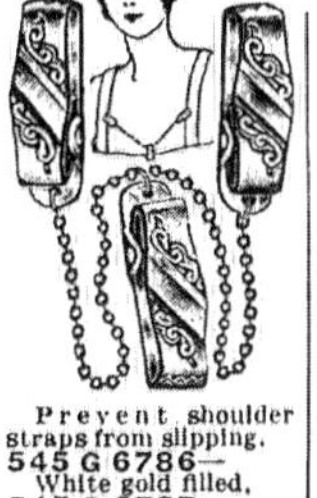

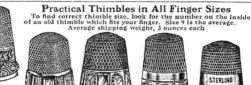

Prevent shoulder straps from slipping.
545 G 6786—White gold filled,
545 G 6787—Green gold filled. Each .. 98¢

Lingerie Clasps

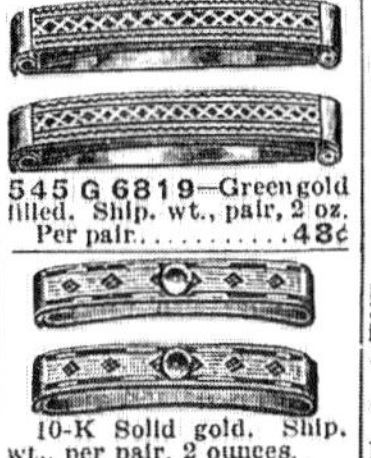

545 G 6819—Green gold filled. Ship. wt., pair, 2 oz. Per pair .... 48¢

10-K Solid gold. Ship. wt., per pair, 2 ounces.
545 G 6817—White gold.
545 G 6818—Green gold.
Per pair .... 98¢

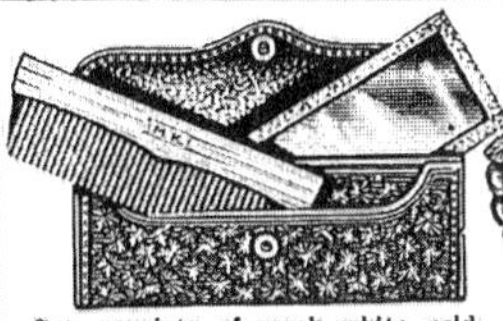

Set consists of comb white gold filled, and mirror. Length, of comb, 3¾ inches. Initial free. Leather case included. Ship. wt., 6 oz. State initial.
545 G 8106—Complete set $2.25

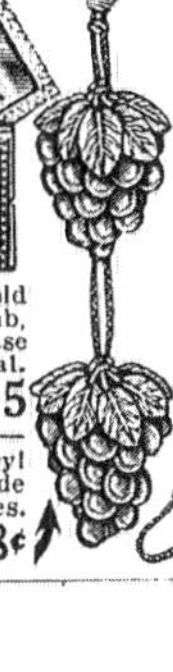

A delightful bit of novelty jewelry! Long black silk cord with two jade green pendants to represent grapes. Shipping weight, 3 ounces.
545 G 6792 .... 98¢

Practical Thimbles in All Finger Sizes

To find correct thimble size, look for the number on the inside of an old thimble which fits your finger. Size 9 is the average. Average shipping weight, 3 ounces each

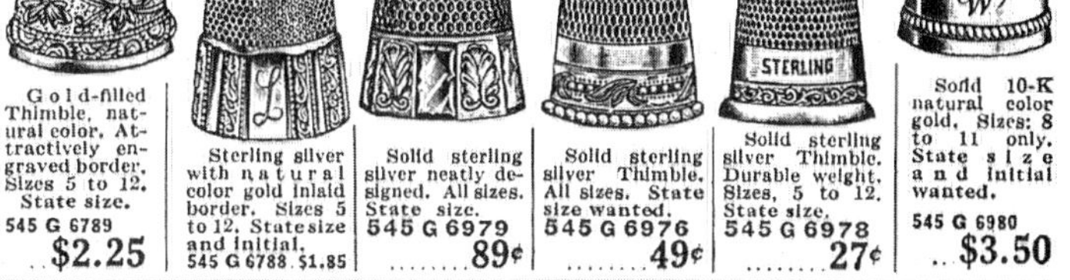

Gold-filled Thimble, natural color, Attractively engraved border. Sizes 5 to 12. State size.
545 G 6789 .. $2.25

Sterling silver with natural color gold inlaid border. Sizes 5 to 12. State size and initial.
545 G 6788 . $1.85

Solid sterling silver neatly designed. All sizes. State size.
545 G 6979 .... 89¢

Solid sterling silver Thimble. All sizes. State size wanted.
545 G 6976 .... 49¢

Solid sterling silver Thimble. Durable weight. Sizes, 5 to 12. State size.
545 G 6978 .... 27¢

Solid 10-K natural color gold. Sizes: 8 to 11 only. State size and initial wanted.
545 G 6980 .. $3.50

This Season Brings Wrist
Swiss Watches Noted *for* Quality

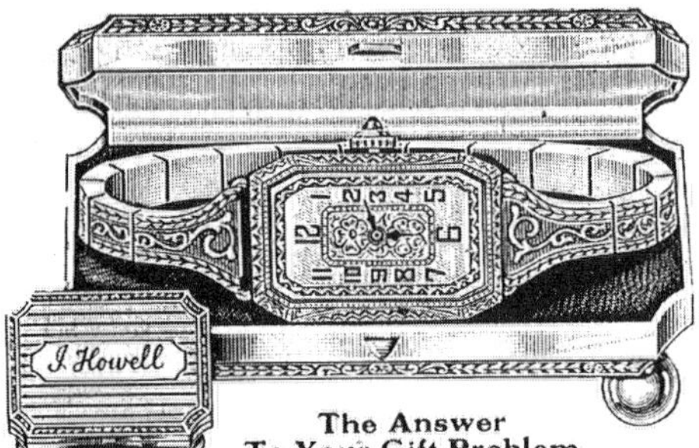

The Answer To Your Gift Problem

A Gift Set of unquestioned beauty and utility. Gracefully designed case of solid white gold, delicately engraved on top and sides. Metal bracelet is white gold filled and very flexible, with full expansion and detachable links. The fine 15-Jewel Swiss movement will keep accurate time. Enclosed in silver-plated presentation case of exquisite design, with any name desired engraved free on cover. State name wanted.

545 G 3671—14-K solid white gold. $19.98
545 G 3636—18-K solid white gold. 23.50

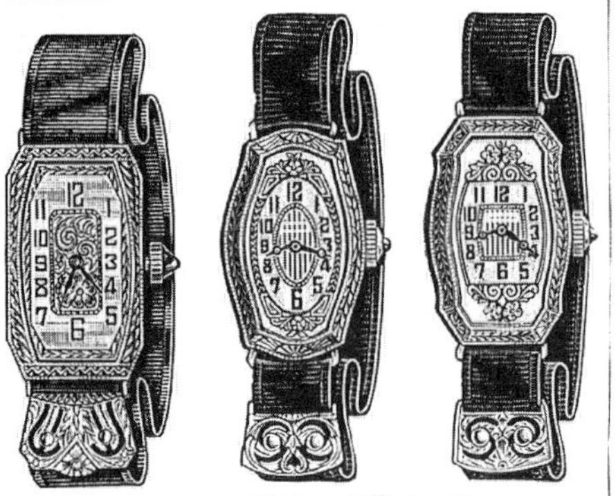

This is the kind of watch one wears and shows with delight! A pleasing design in the popular rectangular style. White gold filled case guaranteed 10 years. Fine Swiss movement. Silvered dial. Heavy black silk ribbon with gold-filled clasp.
545 G 3631—
6-Jewel. . $9.50
545 G 3672—
15-Jewel. . $13.25

18-Jewel Winton Movement

A Wrist Watch that is distinctively flattering to the hand. White 14-K solid gold case, beautifully engraved on top and sides. Sapphire pendant; 18-Jewel Winton movement. Silvered dial. White gold clasp—black silk ribbon.
545 G 3715
. . . . . $26.25

This lovely Watch is made of 14-K solid white gold, exquisitely engraved on top and sides. Fitted with 18-Jewel Winton movement of guaranteed dependability. Artistic workmanship is apparent in the unusually rich looking dial.
545 G 3717
. . . . . $26.85

Every Wrist Watch shown on this page is pictured actual size. With each watch we include an attractive gift case. Safe delivery guaranteed. Written guarantee. Shipping weight, each watch, 10 ounces.

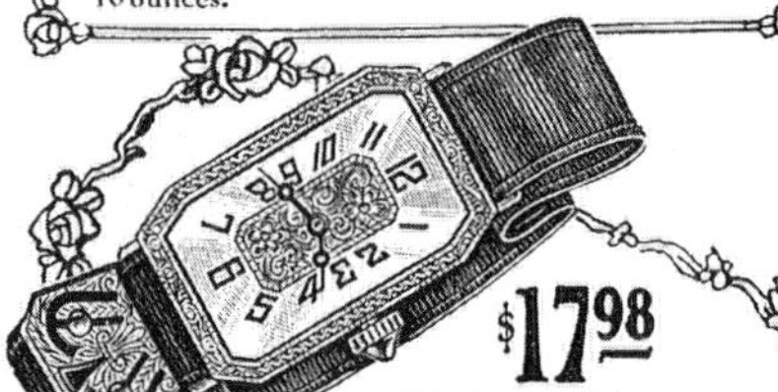

$17.98

Fashionable, Serviceable Swiss Watch

"It is with pleasure that I recommend to you this Swiss Bracelet Watch. It is a graceful expression of the watchmaker's craft, combining beauty with life-long wear. The fashionable rectangular case is skilfully made of 14 or 18-K solid white gold, closely resembling platinum, richly engraved on front and sides, with neat border on back. Has a reliable 15-Jewel Swiss movement; platinum finish dial. Heavy black silk ribbon with solid white gold clasp."

Thos. F. Connell,
Manager Jewelry Department

545 G 3632—14-K solid gold. $17.98
545 G 3633—18-K solid gold. 21.50

RARE beauty and dependable quality are apparent in every Bracelet Watch shown on this page. The intricately designed cases represent the finest workmanship of American craftsmen, and they are fitted with the highest quality Swiss movements that it is possible to obtain in each particular price range.

The strict supervision we maintain in the selection of these watches, combined with our large purchases, enables us to offer, at all times, the highest qualities and at prices that save you fully one-half over what you would have to pay locally. Every watch is timed and tested in the case before being shipped, and is guaranteed free from mechanical imperfections.

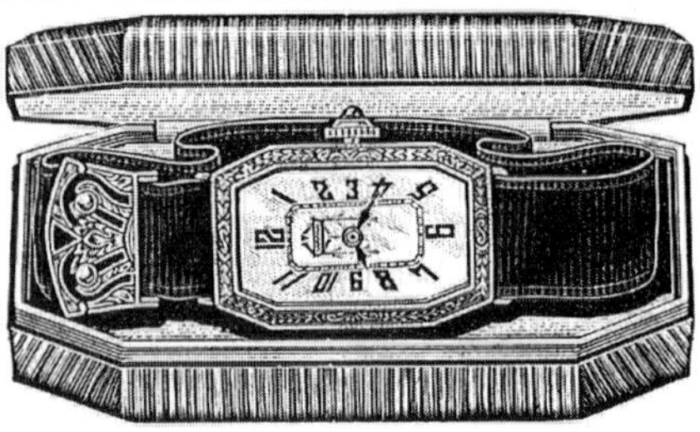

Always in Good Taste

This Watch adds style appeal to wearing qualities. It will give service every hour of the day, year in and year out. The case is made of white 14-K gold filled, richly engraved on front and sides; guaranteed to wear 25 years. Fine Swiss movement. Silvered dial. Popular rectangular shape. Comes complete with black silk ribbon with gold-filled clasp. Leatherette gift case.

545 G 3598— 6-Jewel Swiss movement. $10.98
545 G 3599—15-Jewel Swiss movement. 15.45

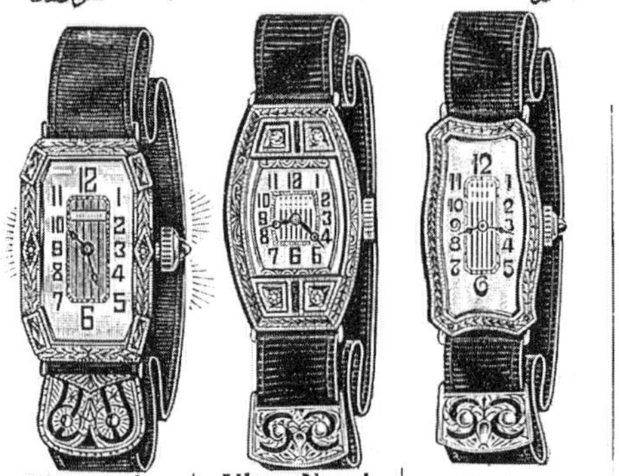

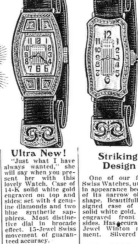

Diamond Studded

Beautiful, practical and appropriate for any gift occasion. Exquisitely made Bracelet Watch, set with two genuine diamonds and four blue synthetic sapphires. The case is 14-K white solid gold, closely resembling platinum and is beautifully engraved on top and sides. Has reliable 15-Jewel Swiss movement and silvered dial.
545 G 3661
. . . . $29.50

Ultra New!

"Just what I have always wanted," she will say when you present her with this lovely Watch. Case of 14-K solid white gold engraved on top and sides; set with 4 genuine diamonds and two blue synthetic sapphires. Most distinctive dial in brocade effect. 15-Jewel Swiss movement of guaranteed accuracy.
545 G 3714
. . . . . . $38.95

Striking Design

One of our finest Swiss Watches, unique in appearance because of its narrow oblong shape. Beautifully designed case of 14-K solid white gold, hand engraved front and sides. Has accurate 15-Jewel Winton movement. Silvered dial.
545 G 3718
. . . . $29.25

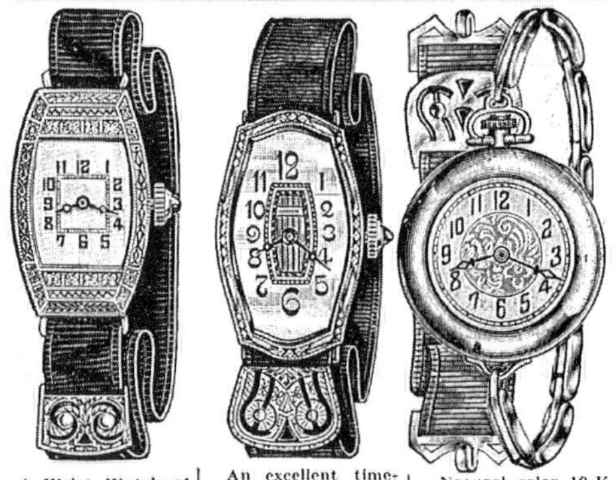

A Wrist Watch of beauty and utility. Specially designed case makes it appear smaller than it actually is. Solid 14-K white gold case with engraved top and sides. 15-Jewel Swiss movement.
545 G 3719
. . . . . . $24.50

An excellent timekeeper in a handsome design. Solid 14-K white gold, hand engraved on top and sides. Plain back, silvered dial. Has 15-Jewel Swiss movement. Black silk ribbon with 14-K white gold clasp.
545 G 3665
. . . . . . $17.35

Natural color 10-K gold-filled case, guaranteed to wear 20 years. 15-Jewel Swiss movement; Black silk ribbon wristband with gold-filled clasp, also adjustable expansion Link Bracelet.
545 G 3551
. . . . $12.48

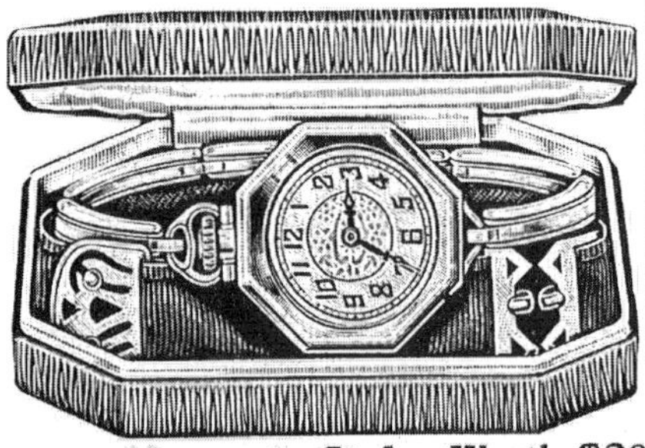

Always in Style—Worth $20

The simplicity of design in this Watch will appeal to those who are lovers of simple beauty. A thoroughly accurate and reliable timepiece. The case is the popular octagon style of 10-K natural gold filled. Guaranteed to wear 20 years. Has 15-Jewel Swiss movement. Watch comes complete with silk ribbon wristband with gold-filled attachment and also an expansion Link Bracelet, to be worn as preferred. All in attractive leatherette gift box.
545 G 3587. . . . . $12.50

Three Unusual Values

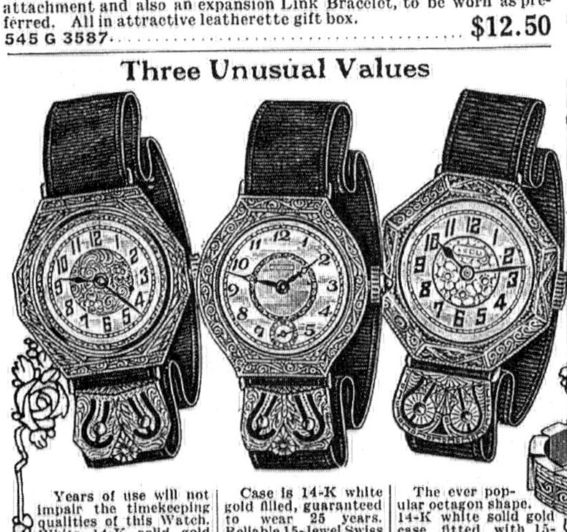

Years of use will not impair the timekeeping qualities of this Watch. White 14-K solid gold case, engraved front and back. High-grade 15-Jewel Swiss movement. Silvered dial with easily read numerals. Black silk ribbon with 14-K solid white gold clasp.
545 G 3594
. . . . $15.98

Case is 14-K white gold filled, guaranteed to wear 25 years. Reliable 15-Jewel Swiss movement; second hand white gold-filled clasp on black silk ribbon.
545 G 3668—
Each. . $14.75
545 G 3680—
6-Jewels. White gold-filled case, guaranteed 10 years. . . . $11.75

The ever popular octagon shape. 14-K white solid gold case fitted with 15-Jewel Swiss movement. Engraved front, plain back. Fancy silvered dial with easily read numerals. Black silk ribbon with 14-K solid white gold clasp.
545 G 3593
. . . . $15.50

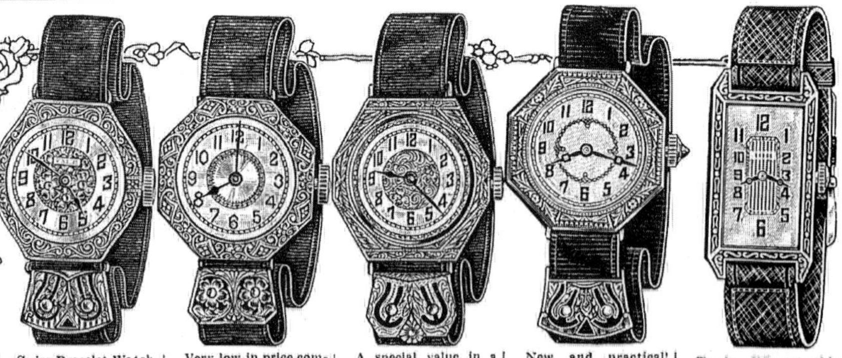

Swiss Bracelet Watch. Has white gold-filled case with hand carved effect on front; guaranteed to wear 10 years. Plainback. Brocade effect on dial. In neat leatherette gift case.
545 G 3601—
15-Jewel. . $11.45
545 G 3612—
6-Jewel. 8.45

Very low in price compared to the service it gives. White gold-filled case guaranteed 10 years. Front has appearance of hand carving. Black silk ribbon with white gold-filled clasp.
545 G 3600—
6-Jewel. . . . $7.35
545 G 3602—
15-Jewel. 10.65

A special value in a thoroughly practical Wrist Watch. White gold-filled case and clasp, guaranteed to wear 25 years. Engraved front, plain back. Fine quality 15-Jewel movement. Silvered dial. Black silk ribbon.
545 G 3596
. . . . $12.95

New and practical! Just the Watch for a school girl. Non-breakable crystal. White gold-filled case guaranteed 10 years. Has dependable 6-Jewel Swiss movement.
545 G 3720 $8.50

To be different this Bracelet Watch has a leather wristlet. Reliable 6-Jewel movement. Case of white gold-filled carved effect on front and sides. Guaranteed to wear 10 years. Raised gold numerals.
545 G 3721
. . . . $13.35

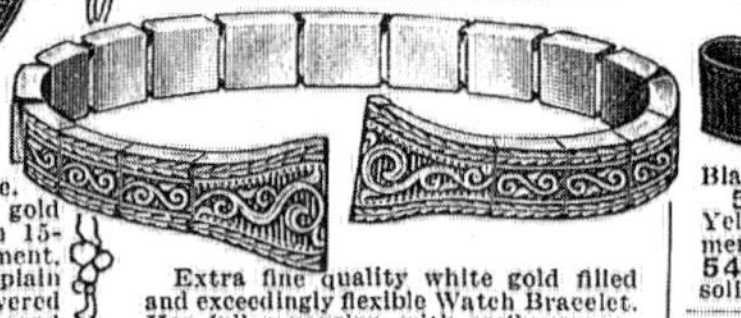

Extra fine quality white gold filled and exceedingly flexible Watch Bracelet. Has full expansion, with easily removable links. Easily attached and fits any size wrist. Ship. wt., each, 4 oz.
545 G 3673—For all watches using ribbon 7/16 inch or wider.
545 G 3713—With 3/8-inch straight ends.
545 G 3709—With 3/8-inch curved ends.
Each. $2.85

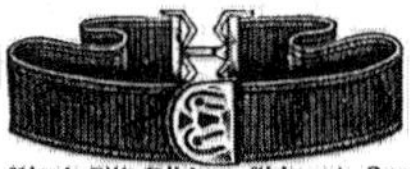

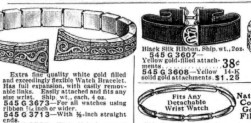

Black Silk Ribbon. Ship. wt., 2oz.
545 G 3607—
Yellow gold-filled attachments. . . . . 38¢
545 G 3608—Yellow 14-K solid gold attachments. $1.25

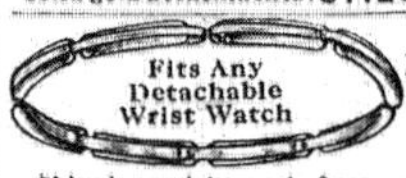

Natural Color Gold Filled

Shipping weight, each, 2 ounces.
545 G 3605—Plain. . . . . 50¢
545 G 3606—Engraved. . . . . 55¢

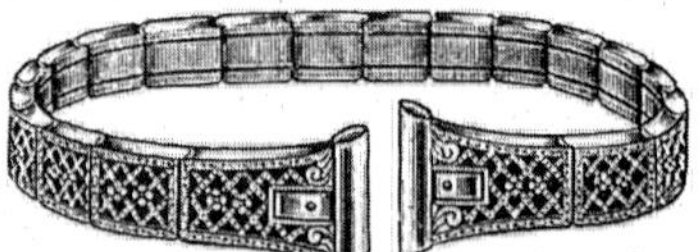

Flexible metal Watch Bracelet with easily removable links. Shipping weight, each, 4 ounces.
545 G 3610—Yellow gold filled for convertible Watch style, 545 G 3587, shown above.
545 G 3609—White gold filled, for all watches using ribbon 7/16 inch or wider.
545 G 3711—White gold filled with 3/8-inch straight ends.
545 G 3712—White gold filled with 3/8-inch curved ends.
Each. $1.75

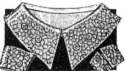

91

Smart! Gift Purses from 5th Avenue

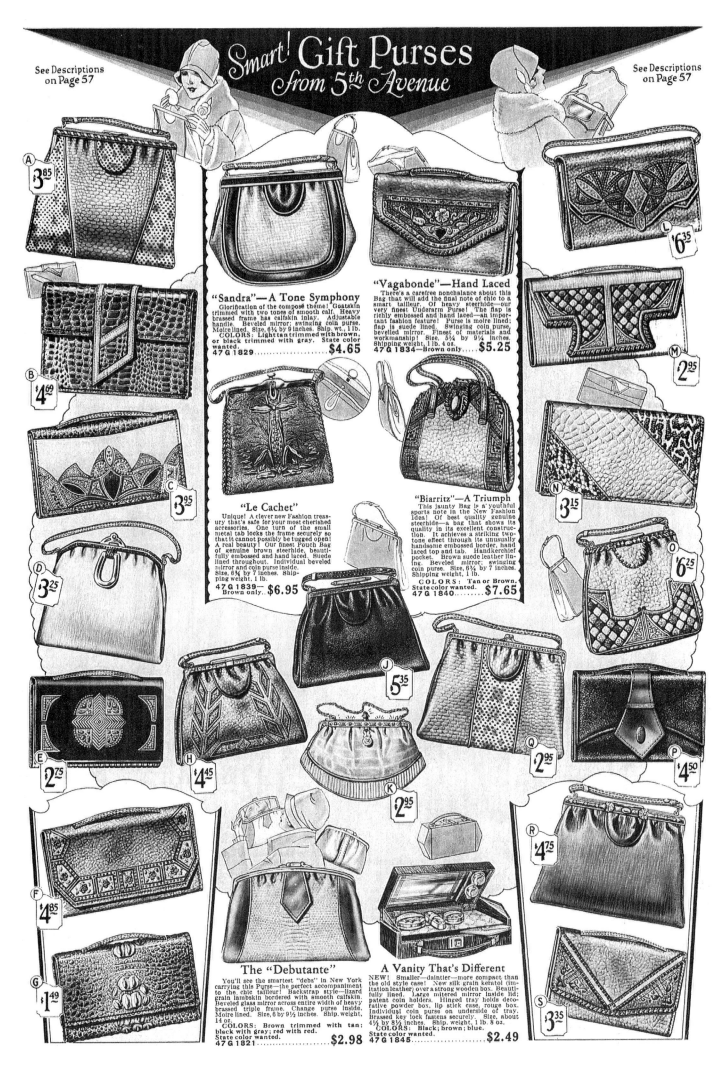

A $3.85

B $4.69

C $3.95

D $3.25

E $2.75

F $4.85

G $1.49

"Sandra"—A Tone Symphony

Glorification of the composé theme! Goatskin trimmed with two tones of smooth calf. Heavy brassed frame has calfskin inlay. Adjustable handle. Beveled mirror; swinging coin purse. Moiré lined. Size, 6¼ by 9 inches. Ship. wt., 1 lb.
COLORS: Light tan trimmed with brown, or black trimmed with gray. State color wanted.
47 G 1829........................$4.65

"Le Cachet"

Unique! A clever new Fashion treasury that's safe for your most cherished accessories. One turn of the small metal tab locks the frame securely so that it cannot possibly be tugged open! A real beauty! Our finest Pouch Bag of genuine brown steerhide, beautifully embossed and hand laced. Suede lined throughout. Individual beveled mirror and coin purse inside. Size, 6¾ by 7 inches. Shipping weight, 1 lb.
47 G 1839— Brown only..$6.95

"Vagabonde"—Hand Laced

There's a carefree nonchalance about this Bag that will add the final note of chic to a smart tailleur. Of heavy steerhide—our very finest Underarm Purse! The flap is richly embossed and hand laced—an important fashion feature! Purse is moiré lined; flap is suede lined. Swinging coin purse, bevelled mirror. Finest of materials and workmanship! Size, 5¼ by 9¼ inches. Shipping weight, 1 lb. 4 oz.
47 G 1834—Brown only.....$5.25

"Biarritz"—A Triumph

This jaunty Bag is a youthful sports note in the New Fashion idea! Of best quality genuine steerhide—a bag that shows its quality in its excellent construction. It achieves a striking two-tone effect through an unusually handsome embossed border, hand laced top and tab. Handkerchief pocket. Brown suede leather lining. Beveled mirror; swinging coin purse. Size, 6¾ by 7 inches. Shipping weight, 1 lb.
COLORS: Tan or Brown. State color wanted.
47 G 1840........$7.65

L $6.35

M $2.95

N $3.15

O $6.25

H $4.45

J $5.35

K $2.95

Q $2.95

P $4.50

R $4.75

S $3.35

The "Debutante"

You'll see the smartest "debs" in New York carrying this Purse—the perfect accompaniment to the chic tailleur! Backstrap style—lizard grain lambskin bordered with smooth calfskin. Beveled glass mirror across entire width of heavy brassed triple frame. Change purse inside. Moiré lined. Size, 6 by 9½ inches. Ship. weight, 14 oz.
COLORS: Brown trimmed with tan; black with gray; red with red. State color wanted.
47 G 1821........................$2.98

A Vanity That's Different

NEW! Smaller—daintier—more compact than the old style case! New silk grain keratol (imitation leather) over a strong wooden box. Beautifully lined. Large mitered mirror inside lid; patent coin holders. Hinged tray holds decorative powder box, lip stick case, rouge box. Individual coin purse on underside of tray. Brassed key lock fastens securely. Size, about 4½ by 8½ inches. Ship. weight, 1 lb. 8 oz.
COLORS: Black; brown; blue. State color wanted.
47 G 1845........................$2.49

Descriptions of Purses on Page 56

A "Marilyn." A fashion triumph overnight! Best quality soft, pliable goatskin in Hudson seal grain and ultra chic water snake grain trimming. Heavy gilded frame, richly chased. Adjustable handle. Moire lining. Beveled mirror swinging coin purse. Size, 8 by 9 inches. Shipping weight, 1 pound 4 ounces.
COLORS: Tan or gray. State color wanted.
47 G 1827—Each $3.85

B The "Yvette." Highest fashion laurels go to this Bag of smooth, shiny brown calf in ultra smart alligator grain. Outside handkerchief pocket. Strap is bordered with light tan reptile grain leather. Excellent moire lining. Beveled mirror. Coin purse. Unusually fine quality! Size, 6¾ by 10 in. Ship. wt., 1 lb.
47 G 1832—Brown only $4.69

C The "Marcelle." Alligator grained goatskin with front flap handkerchief pocket of beautifully embossed calfskin. Inside metal frame; mirror; coin purse. Size, 5½ by 10 in. Ship. wt., 1 lb.
COLORS: Tan or brown. State color wanted.
47 G 1830—Each $3.95

D The "Duet." Two color tones add interest to this smooth genuine calfskin Bag with frame covered in lizard grain leather. Lively ivorette tab. Beveled mirror; swinging coin purse. Moire lined. Size, 7¼ by 8¼ inches. Shipping weight, 1 pound.
COLORS: Black trimmed with gray or tan trimmed with brown. State color wanted.
47 G 1825—Each $3.25

E The "Gloria." Dignity—beauty—chic—in this Purse of smooth cowhide with beautifully embossed flap. Handkerchief pocket on the back. Flap leather lined. Inside metal frame. Mirror; change purse. Size, 5¾ by 8¾ inches. Ship. weight, 1 pound.
COLORS: Black or light brown. State color.
47 G 1817—Each $2.75

F The "Sunset." Captivating! Color harmony so rich beckons attractive warmth to the costume of today! Of good quality tan steerhide—embossed in rich autumn hues. Suede lined flap. Handkerchief pocket. Inside metal frame. Beveled mirror; change purse. Size, 5½ by 10 inches. Ship. wt., 1 lb.
47 G 1822—Tan only $4.85

G The "Vivian." Of seal leather embossed to resemble fashionable horn back alligator. Handkerchief pocket on back. Individual mirror. Inside metal frame. Moire lined flap. Size, about 5¼ by 9 inches. Shipping weight, 1 pound.
47 G 1823—Brown only $1.49

H The "Chanel." A style originated by the famous French designer! Very feminine—of genuine steerhide, richly embossed. Covered frame. Adjustable handle. Iridescent moire lined. Beveled mirror; swinging coin purse. Size, 6¼ by 8¾ inches. Shipping weight, 14 ounces.
COLORS: Brown or tan. State color.
47 G 1833—Each $4.45

J The "Bijou." A gem of fashion and beauty—smartly conservative—the very best quality of black pin seal relieved by a bright touch of color on the cylinder lock. Covered frame. Adjustable strap handle. Quality moire lining. Beveled mirror; swinging coin purse inside. Size, 6¼ by 9 in. Ship. wt., 1 lb.
47 G 1835—Black only $5.35

K The "Alice." Of silk and Rayon moire, with its pretty shirring and gold piping. Colorful jewels ornament the frame. Gilt chain. Rayon lined; with individual beveled mirror and coin purse. Size, 5 by 8 inches. Shipping weight, 12 ounces.
COLORS: Black; gray; beige. State color.
47 G 1824—Each $2.95

L The "Lorelei." Feminine vanity is pardonable when Milady combines her fastidiousness with good judgment! Of embossed steerhide. Handkerchief pocket in back. Outside flap suede leather lined. Inside flap with wide beveled mirror conceals secret pocket underneath. Another pocket holds two compacts and lip stick holder. Metal frame and inside coin purse. Size, 6 by 8½ inches. Shipping weight, 1 pound 4 ounces.
COLORS: Brown or tan. State color wanted.
47 G 1836—Each $6.35

M The "Hiawatha." There's an Indian air about the stunning hand laced flap and handsome embossing of this new Underarm model. Handkerchief pocket on back. Flap leather lined. Individual mirror; change purse; inside metal frame. Size, 5½ by 10 inches. Shipping weight, 1 pound 4 ounces.
COLORS: Brown or tan. State color wanted.
47 G 1820—Each $2.95

N The "Ritz." True to its name, this stunning Purse will be seen only with the most fashionable people. Of alligator grain leather, cleverly trimmed with water snake grain. Back strap and handkerchief pocket. Leather lined flap. Inside metal frame; mirror. Size, 6 by 10 inches. Shipping weight, 1 pound.
COLORS: Tan; red; blue. State color wanted.
47 G 1819—Each $3.15

O The "Melody." Of genuine steerhide. It sounds the favored color notes in Fashion's autumn medley! New block bottom. Embossed. Hand laced tab. Colorful brassed frame. Adjustable handle. Iridescent quality moire lining. Mirror; swinging coin purse. Size, 7 by 9 inches. Shipping weight, 1 pound 4 ounces.
COLORS: Tan or brown. State color wanted.
47 G 1841—Each $6.25

P The "Nocturne." Its smart simplicity brings into relief the rich quality of the genuine pin seal, ornamented by a strap and pull tab of smooth black calf. Handkerchief pocket. Leather lined flap. Moire inner lining. Mirror; change purse. Size, 5¾ by 8½ inches. Shipping weight, 1 pound.
47 G 1831—Black only $4.50

Q The "Sunny." The gayety of youth is translated into smartness by this New York Bag of Hudson grain lambskin, with front panel reptile grained. Chased gilded frame. Moire lining; beveled mirror; swinging coin purse. 7 by 9½ in. Ship. wt., 1 lb.
COLORS: Brown, tan or gray. State color wanted.
47 G 1818—Each $2.95

R The "Magnolia." With one accord New York has welcomed this new fashion idea. Soft calfskin of excellent quality—roomy enough for the hundred and one trivials a woman likes to carry—yet slender and graceful in appearance. Ornamented brassed frame. Adjustable handle. Moire lining. Beveled mirror; swinging coin purse. Size, 7 by 10 inches. Ship. weight, 1 pound.
COLORS: Black; brown; tan. State color wanted.
47 G 1826—Each $4.75

S The "Florence." Antique finish lends unusual richness to the strong genuine steerhide leather. Quality and style—in the hand lacing and cleverly embossed design. Suede leather lined flap. Beveled mirror. Inside metal frame. Size, 5¼ by 8½ in. Shipping weight, 1 pound.
47 G 1828—Brown only $3.35

Rare Values

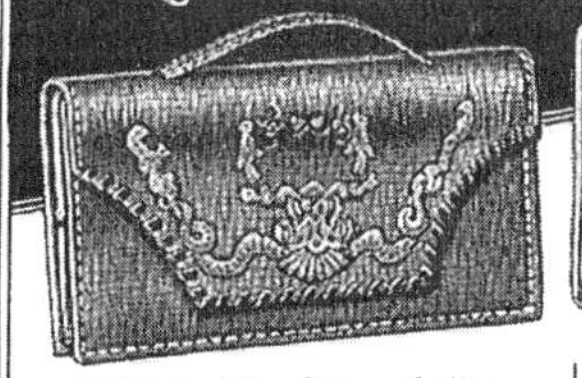

Chic! Hand Laced Flap

Style that intrigues your interest is fashioned into this chic Purse, with its beautifully embossed and hand laced flap. Crepe grained real leather. Individual mirror; coin purse on metal frame. Size, 5¼ by 9 inches. Ship. weight, 1 lb.
COLORS: Black; brown; tan.
State color wanted.
47 G 1809—Each $1.89

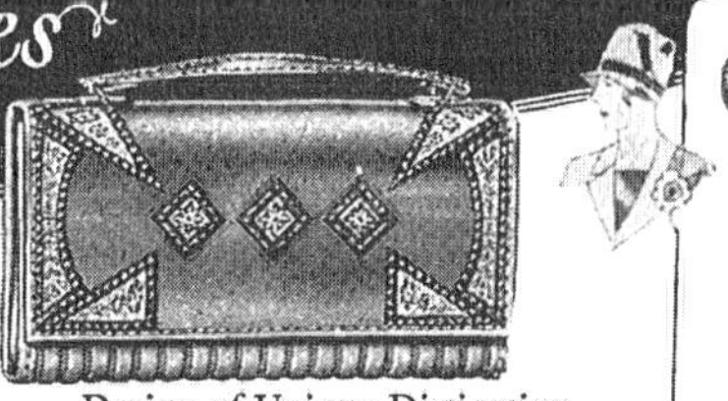

Design of Unique Distinction

An oddly shaped design—richly embossed on genuine smooth cowhide leather accents the smartness of this handsome Underarm Bag! Handkerchief pocket on back. Splendid for wear—and a value hard to improve! Size, about 5¼ by 9½ inches. Shipping weight, 1 pound.
COLORS: Black; brown; tan.
State color wanted.
47 G 1812—Each $1.98

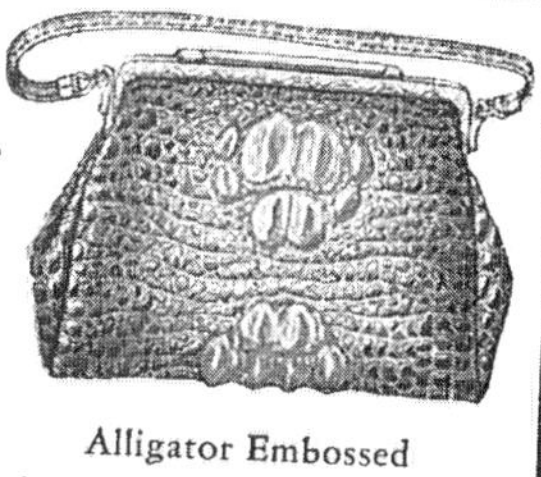

Alligator Embossed

An unusual value—this smart tan Pouch Bag of seal leather gains swagger distinction through its blended horned back alligator grain embossing. A style that many smart women choose. A purse you can depend on for good wear; trimly lined—with a swinging coin purse and individual mirror. White metal frame. Size, about 5¾ by 9¼ inches. Shipping weight, 10 ounces.
47 G 1801—Brown only....... 98¢

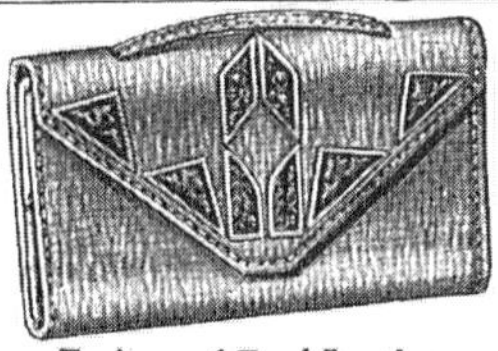

Embossed Real Leather

Simplicity spells C-h-a-r-m in this conservative Underarm Bag of crepe grain real leather, with its odd shaped flap handsomely embossed. Flap moire lined. Individual inside mirror; metal frame coin purse. You'll agree—an outstanding value! Size, about 5 by 8½ inches. Shipping weight, 1 pound.
COLORS: Brown; tan; black.
State color wanted.
47 G 1803—Each......... $1.59

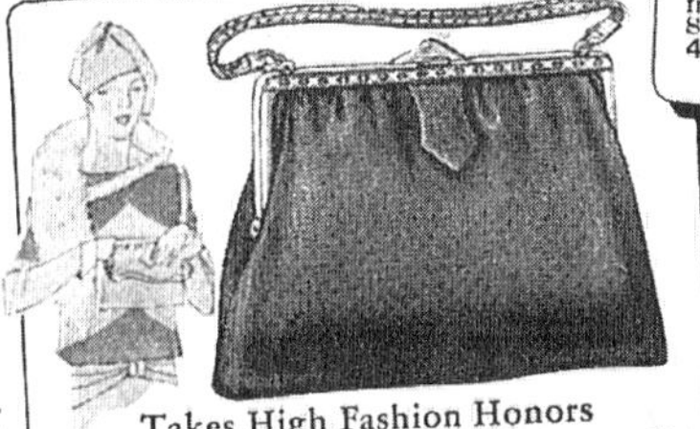

Takes High Fashion Honors

Genuine calfskin leather—a Bag whose quality does credit to its fashionable design! Never before have we been able to sell so good a genuine calf pouch at such an extremely low price! Mounted on a heavy brassed frame, beautifully embossed. Has moire lining, individual swinging coin purse and mirror. Size, about 6 by 9 inches. Shipping weight, 1 pound.
COLORS: Black or tan. State color.
47 G 1806—Each.................... $1.95

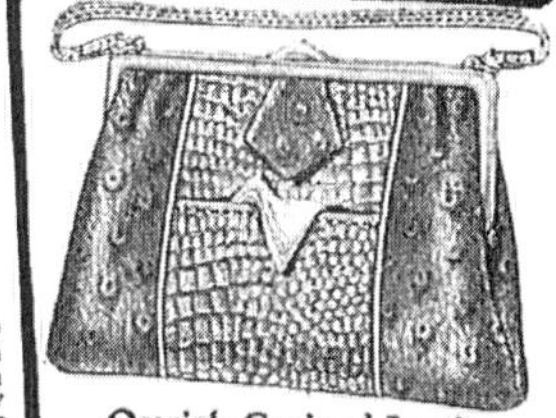

Ostrich Grained Leather

An outside pocket from which your handkerchief will peep—just one of its many smart features! Real leather, grained like genuine ostrich. Front panel of tan alligator grain. Moire lined. Mirror; swinging coin purse. Size, 6½ by 9 in. Ship. wt., 1 lb.
47 G 1807—Tan only.... $2.35

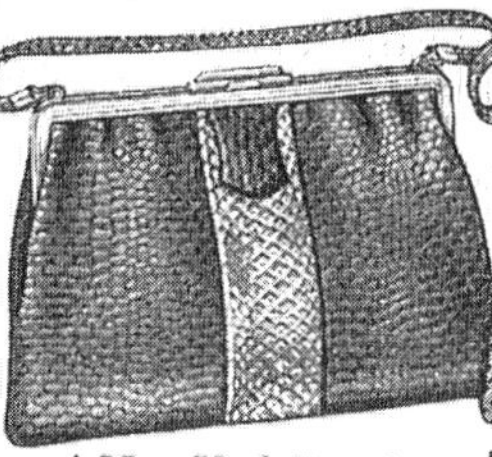

A New York Favorite

Reptile—the latest Fifth avenue craze—reflected in this Bag with front panel embossed like water snake. Hudson seal grained leather. Moire lined. Mirror; swinging coin purse. 6¼ by 10 in. Ship. wt., 1 lb.
COLORS: Black; tan; gray.
State color wanted.
47 G 1804—Each..... $1.57

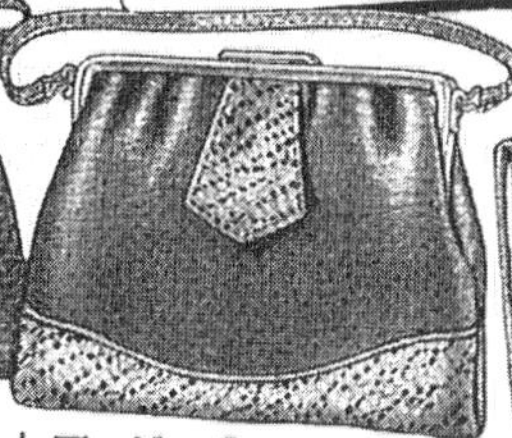

The New Compose Theme

This swagger soft leather Bag provides gold piping and reptile grain leather to attain ultra chic entirety. Moire lined. Mirror; swinging coin purse. 6½ by 9 inches. Shipping weight, 1 pound.
COLORS: Tan; black; gray.
State color wanted.
47 G 1811—Each..... $1.87

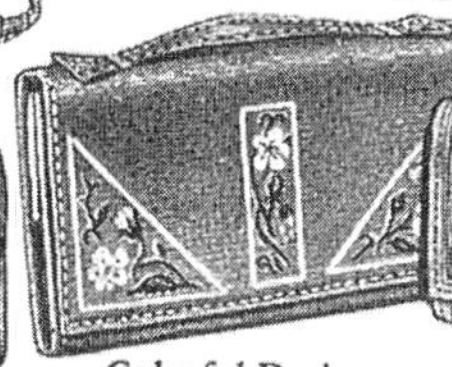

Colorful Design

Of long wearing keratol, with stencilled design on the flap. Individual mirror; inside metal frame. Moire lined flap. Size, 5¼ by 8½ inches. Shipping weight, 1 pound.
COLORS: Tan or black.
State color wanted.
47 G 1800—
Each .... 75¢

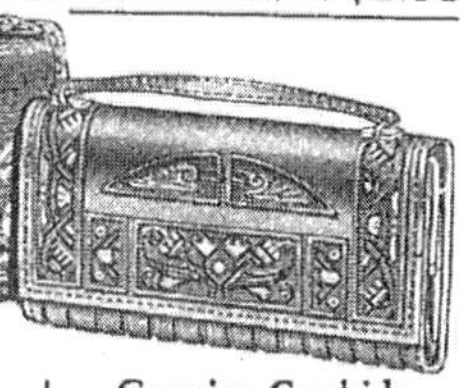

Genuine Cowhide

Tuck Fashion under your arm! Genuine Cowhide, doubly smart because of its handsome embossed flap. Mirror; metal frame coin purse. Neat lining. 4⅜ by 8¼ inches. Shipping weight, 1 pound.
COLORS: Black or brown.
State color wanted.
47 G 1810—
Each............ $1.45

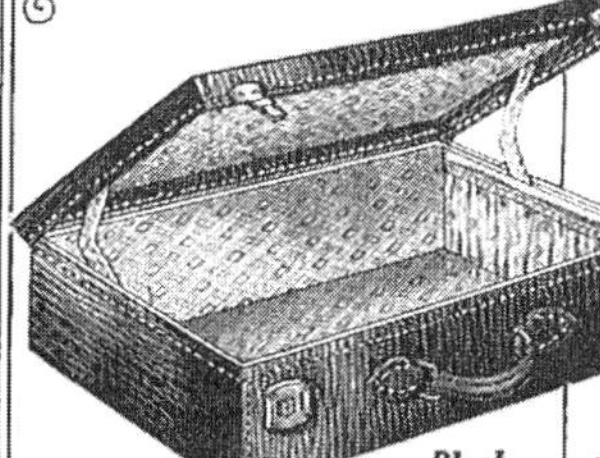

Black Only

Women's Overnight Case

Cobra grained Du Pont Fabrikoid (imitation leather) backed by a layer of chipboard. Securely stitched. Built on an inside steel frame. Brocaded lining. Full stitched hinge; two brassed key locks. Size, 12¼ by 22 inches without fittings. Ship. wt., 8 pounds.
447 G 770—
Black only.............. $4.25

Overnight Case With Fittings

Like Case above except built on a wood frame with padded top. Fittings: tooth brush holder, soap box, nail file, mirror, shoe hook, buffer, brush and comb of lustrous blue pearl effect on amber colored back. Shipping weight, 12 pounds.
447 G 771—Black only. $10.35

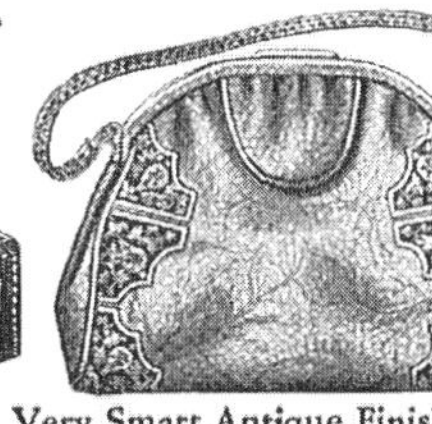

Very Smart Antique Finish

New York's newest fashion fancy—this new leather Pouch Bag of tan, blended in rich antique finish. Splendid value! Moire lined. Mirror; swinging coin purse. Size, 6½ by 8¾ inches. Shipping weight, 1 pound.
47 G 1805—Tan only.............. $2.79

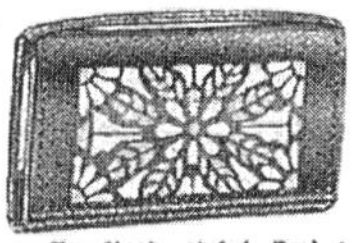

For little girls! Imitation leather. Mirror; coin purse. 3½ by 6⅛ in. Ship. wt., 8 ounces.
COLORS: Red; blue; brown. State color.
47 G 1814—
Each........... 45¢

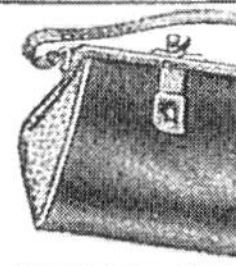

Kiddie's sheepskin Pouch Bag. Mirror. 3½ by 5¾ in. Ship. wt., 4 oz.
COLORS: Blue; green; red.
47 G 1815—
Each.......... 39¢

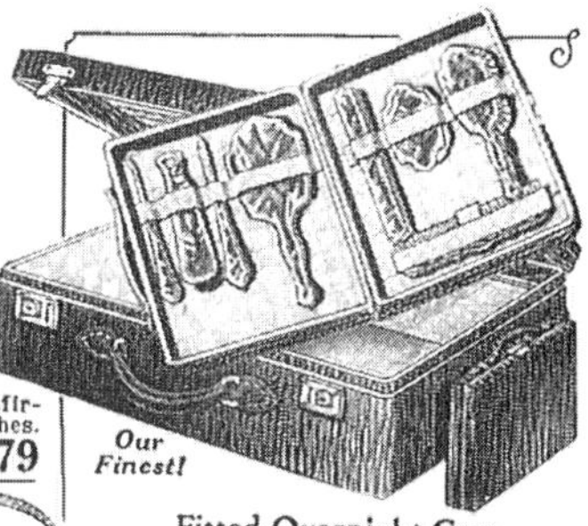

Our Finest!

Fitted Overnight Case

Genuine top grain cowhide over basswood frame. Padded top, sewed leather hinges. Two brassed locks. Fittings of pearly maize color on solid imitation amber back. Hair brush, comb, mirror, soap box, nail file, shoe horn, shoe hook, tooth brush holder. Removable tray, when closed makes separate case. Rayon lining. Size, 12 by 22 inches. Shipping weight, 13 pounds.
447 G 772—Black only.
Complete................ $18.95
447 G 773—Case only, without inside tray and without fittings. Ship. wt., 10 pounds 8 ounces.. $13.25

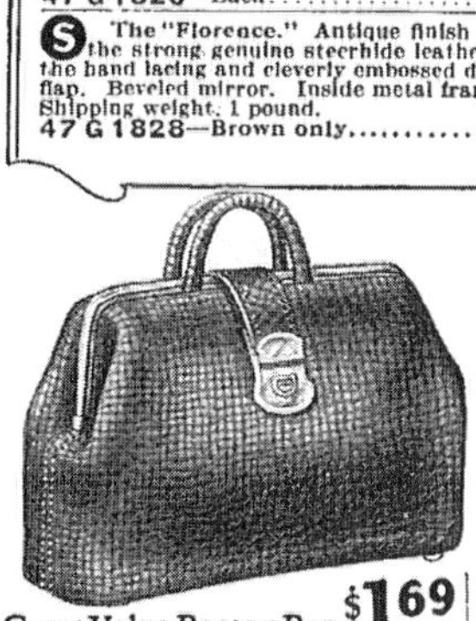

Great Value Boston Bag $1.69

A very good grade—for short trips or shopping. Heavy split cowhide—hand boarded (embossed) and built on overlapping steel frame. Brassed extension lock. Bottom reinforced with fiber board. Size, 15 by 9 by 5¾ inches. Mahogany color only. Shipping weight, 3 pounds.

Split Cowhide
47 G 471—Cloth lined.......... $1.69
47 G 474—Rubberized cloth lined. 1.89

Top Grain Cowhide Leather
Same construction as above except of best quality full cowhide leather. Same quality usually sells for $4.50 to $5.50.
47 G 488—Cloth lined.......... $3.75
47 G 489—Brown leather lined... 4.65

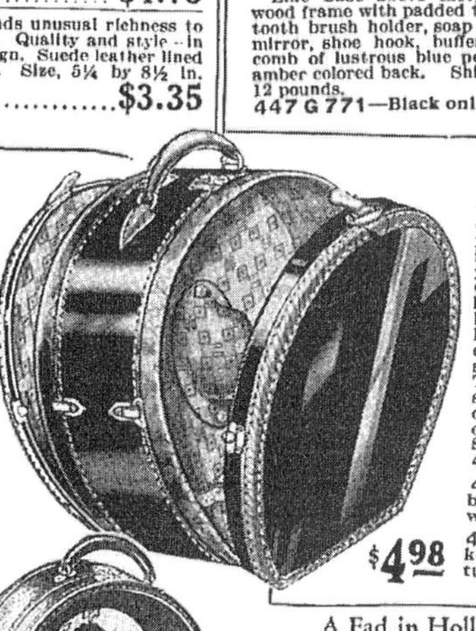

$4.98

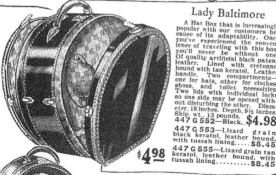

Lady Baltimore

A Hat Box that is increasingly popular with our customers because of its adaptability. Once you've experienced the convenience of traveling with this box, you'll never be without one! Of quality artificial black patent leather. Lined with cretonne, bound with tan keratol. Leather handle. Two compartments—one for hats, other for clothes, shoes, and toilet necessities. Two lids with individual locks so one side may be opened without disturbing the other. Diameter, 18 inches. Depth, 9½ inches. Ship. wt., 13 pounds.
447 G 552—Black.. $4.98
447 G 553—Lizard grain black keratol, leather bound, with tussah lining..... $8.45
447 G 555—Lizard grain tan keratol, leather bound, with tussah lining.......... $8.45

Pullman Style $2.79

Isn't it trim looking! Once you see it you will agree with us that it would be hard to find a better or neater Hat Box anywhere at this low price. A most convenient size—for, in addition to your hats, you can pack other apparel in it very satisfactorily. Of good black enameled sheeting, backed with fiber board. Bound with tan keratol and lined with cretonne. Has leather handle. Inside frilled pocket. Removable hat form. Wonderfully inexpensive! Size, depth, 9 inches; diameter, 18 inches. Shipping weight, each, 8 pounds.
447 G 568—Black only $2.79
447 G 565—Same as above but heavy quality black enameled drill. Has beautiful brocaded silk and cotton lining. Edges bound with gray color cowhide. Depth, 9 inches; diameter, 18 inches.............. $5.95

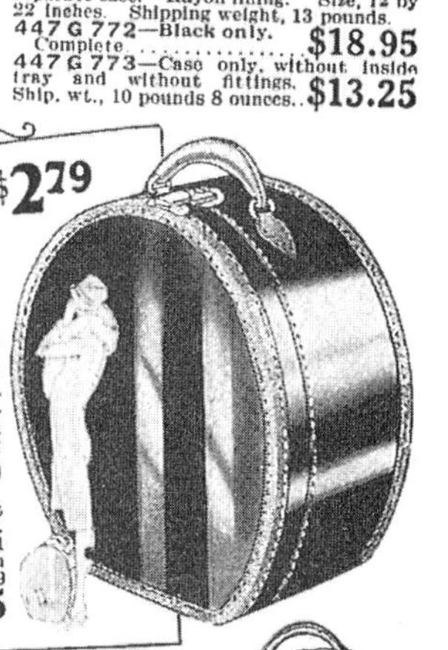

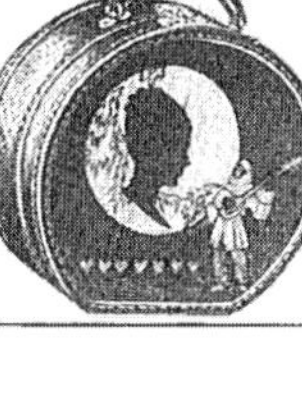

A Fad in Hollywood

Ever so smart—with its bright, four-color design on the lid! Black enameled pebbled grained cloth over strong fiber-board. For shopping, babies' needs and overnight trips. Washable lining. Brassed fasteners. Leather handle riveted on. Size, 11 by 4½ inches. Shipping weight, 2 pounds 8 ounces.
47 G 576—Black only.............. 98¢

For Other Bags and Cases, See Pages 166 and 167

Hollywood Box for Juveniles

Gaily decorated lid in child rhyme designs. Good quality black enameled pebbled grain cloth backed by heavy chipboard. Edges neatly bound with Keratol, carefully stitched. Fastens with brassed metal catch. Sturdy handle. Size, 7 by 3½ inches. Ship. wt., 1 lb.
47 G 1816—Assorted colors with bright designs.................. 55¢

$3.98 A Complete Money-Saving Assortment

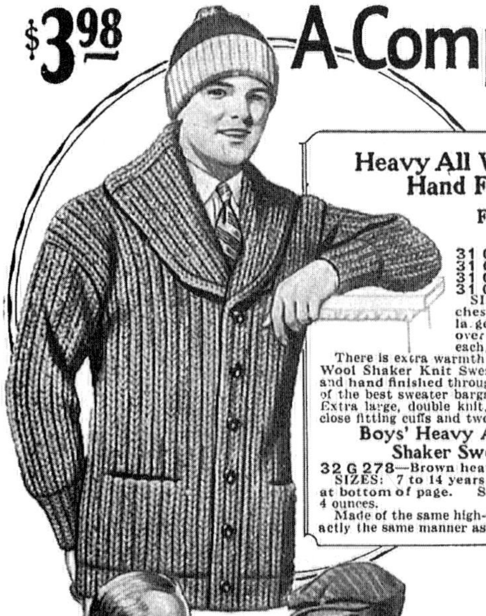

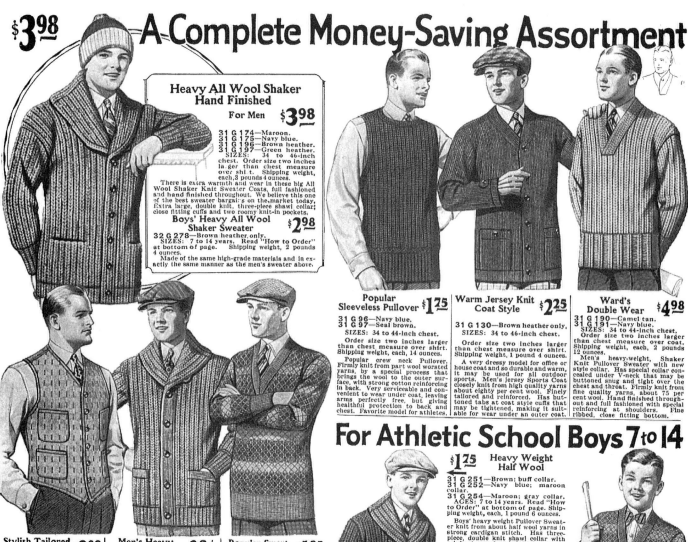

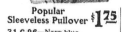

Heavy All Wool Shaker Hand Finished

For Men $3.98

31 G 174—Maroon.
31 G 175—Navy blue.
31 G 196—Brown heather.
31 G 197—Green heather.

SIZES: 34 to 46-inch chest. Order size two inches larger than chest measure over shirt. Shipping weight, each, 3 pounds 4 ounces.

There is extra warmth and wear in these big All Wool Shaker Knit Sweater Coats, full fashioned and hand finished throughout. We believe this one of the best sweater bargains on the market today. Extra large, double knit, three-piece shawl collar; close fitting cuffs and two roomy knit-in pockets.

Boys' Heavy All Wool Shaker Sweater $2.98

32 G 278—Brown heather only.
SIZES: 7 to 14 years. Read "How to Order" at bottom of page. Shipping weight, 2 pounds 4 ounces.

Made of the same high-grade materials and in exactly the same manner as the men's sweater above.

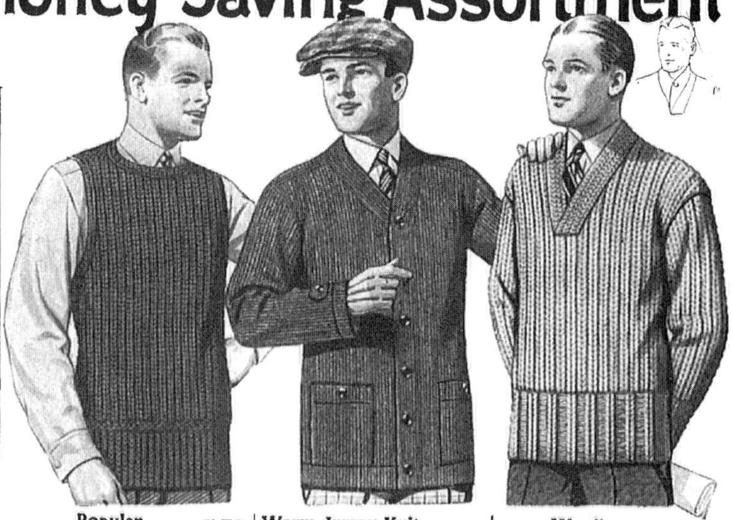

Popular Sleeveless Pullover $1.75

31 G 96—Navy blue.
31 G 97—Seal brown.
SIZES: 34 to 44-inch chest.

Order size two inches larger than chest measure over shirt. Shipping weight, each, 14 ounces.

Popular crew neck Pullover. Firmly knit from part wool worsted yarns, by a special process that brings the wool to the outer surface, with strong cotton reinforcing in back. Very serviceable and convenient to wear under coat, leaving arms perfectly free, but giving healthful protection to back and chest. Favorite model for athletes.

Warm Jersey Knit Coat Style $2.25

31 G 130—Brown heather only.
SIZES: 34 to 46-inch chest.

Order size two inches larger than chest measure over shirt. Shipping weight, 1 pound 4 ounces.

A very dressy model for office or house coat and so durable and warm, it may be used for all outdoor sports. Men's Jersey Sports Coat closely knit from high quality yarns about eighty per cent wool. Finely tailored and reinforced. Has buttoned tabs at coat style cuffs that may be tightened, making it suitable for wear under an outer coat.

Ward's Double Wear $4.98

31 G 190—Camel tan.
31 G 191—Navy blue.
SIZES: 34 to 44-inch chest.

Order size two inches larger than chest measure over coat. Shipping weight, each, 2 pounds 12 ounces.

Men's heavy-weight, Shaker Knit Pullover Sweater with new style collar. Has special collar concealed under V-neck that may be buttoned snug and tight over the chest and throat. Firmly knit from fine quality yarns, about 75 per cent wool. Hand finished throughout and full fashioned with special reinforcing at shoulders. Fine ribbed, close fitting bottom.

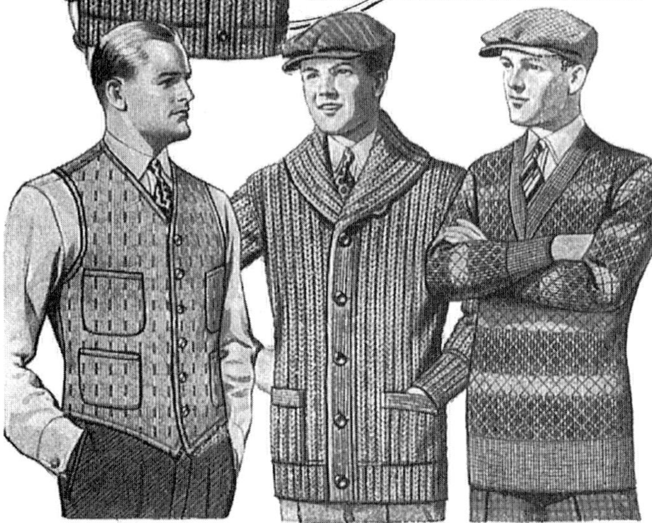

Stylish Tailored All Wool Vest $3.89

31 G 62—Light oxford heather.
31 G 63—Dark brown heather.

SIZES: 34 to 46-inch chest. Order size two inches larger than chest measure over shirt. Shipping weight, each, 1 pound 4 ounces.

Exceptionally popular with well dressed men because of its fine tailored appearance. A model selling elsewhere for almost double our low price. Firmly knit from fine quality, All Wool yarns in a smooth finish resembling wool broadcloth. Plain color trim. Very durable.

Men's Heavy Weight Cotton 98¢

31 G 159—Brown mixture.
31 G 160—Oxford (medium gray).
SIZES: 36 to 46-inch chest.

Order size two inches larger than chest measure over shirt. Ship. wt., each, 1 pound 12 ounces. Knit in heavy ribbed stitch. Double knit, three-piece collar.

Boys' Heavy Cotton

31 G 217—Oxford gray.
31 G 218—Brown mixture. 95¢

AGES: 7 to 14 years. Read "How to Order Boys' Sweaters" below. Ship. wt., each, 1 lb. 4 oz. Same as above with extra button and loop on shawl collar.

Popular Smart Half Wool $1.95

31 G 194—Powder blue combination.
31 G 195—Tan combination.
SIZES: 34 to 44-inch chest.

Order size two inches larger than chest measure over shirt. Shipping weight, each, 1 pound 8 ounces.

Very dressy model in pleasing color combinations and fancy patterns. An attractive sports Sweater on which we know we are saving you money. Firmly knit of about half wool and worsted yarns. Has plain knit trim on V-neck and on close fitting, elastic knit cuffs and bottom. A splendid value.

For Athletic School Boys 7 to 14

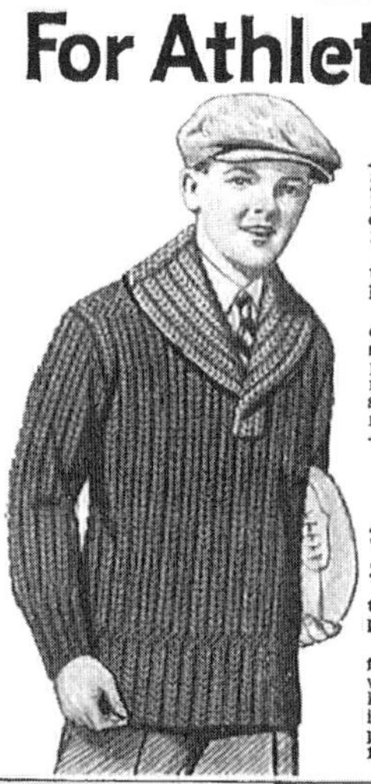

$1.75 Heavy Weight Half Wool

31 G 251—Brown; buff collar.
31 G 252—Navy blue; maroon collar.
31 G 254—Maroon; gray collar.

AGES: 7 to 14 years. Read "How to Order" at bottom of page. Shipping weight, each, 1 pound 6 ounces.

Boys' heavy weight Pullover Sweater knit from about half wool yarns in strong cardigan stitch. Has three-piece, double knit shawl collar with reinforcing and rack knitting across shoulders to prevent stretching. Well made to stand lots of hard service.

Medium Weight Half Wool $1.75

31 G 270—Powder blue combination.
31 G 271—Tan combination.

AGES: 7 to 14 years. Read "How to Order" at bottom of page. Shipping weight, each, 1 pound 1 ounce.

Just the collegiate model boys want for school wear. Dressy, medium-weight, Cricket Sweater, very durably knit from about one-half wool yarns in attractive color combinations. Has plain knit trim at V-neck and snug fitting cuffs and bottom.

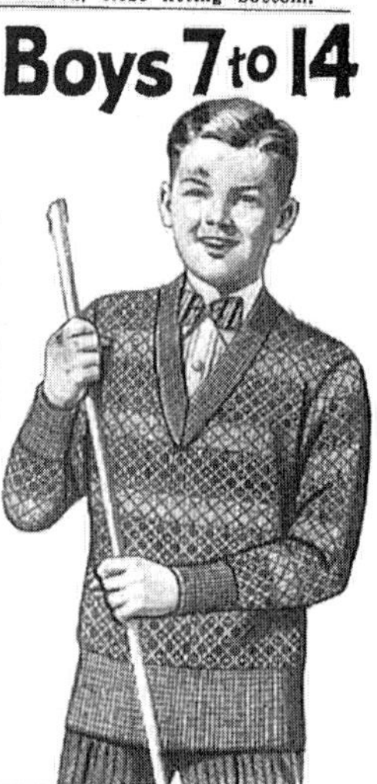

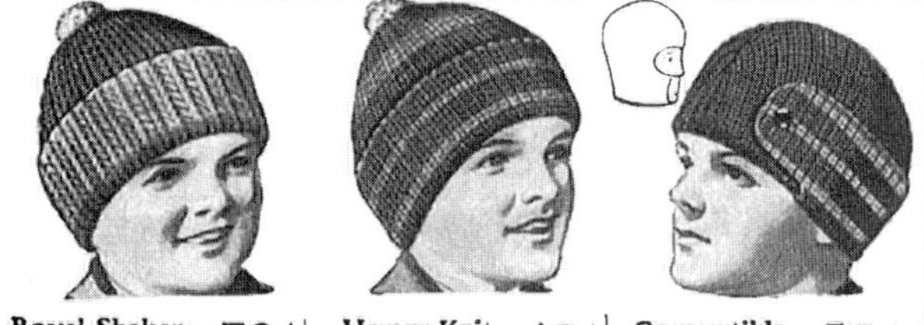

Boys' Shaker All Wool 79¢

31 G 554—Brown with buff cuff.
31 G 555—Navy blue with red cuff.
31 G 556—Plain white.

Boys' size only. Ship. weight, each, 7 ounces. Warm, durable heavy weight, Shaker Knit All Wool Hockey Cap.

Heavy Knit Half Wool 42¢

31 G 535—Red with navy blue trim.
31 G 536—Brown with buff trim.
31 G 537—Maroon.
31 G 538—Navy blue.

Boys' size only. Ship. weight, each, 7 ounces. About one-half wool. Heavy cardigan stitch. Very warm.

Convertible Part Wool 59¢

31 G 501—Black with orange stripes.
31 G 502—Navy blue with red stripes.
31 G 503—Maroon with gold stripes.

Boys' size only. Ship. weight, each, 7 ounces. May be buttoned down to protect cheeks and throat.

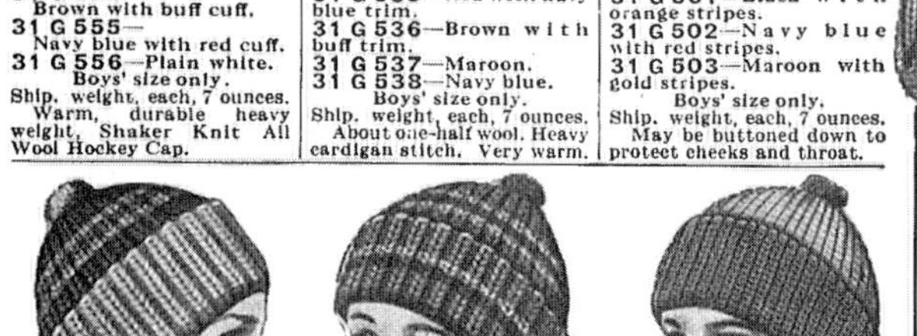

Double Knit Hockey Cap 39¢

31 G 567—Brown with contrasting trim.
31 G 568—Maroon with contrasting trim.
31 G 569—Navy blue with contrasting trim.

Boys' size only. Ship. weight, each, 7 ounces. Fine for all outdoor, cold weather sports. Good quality, firmly knit, part wool.

Heavy Rope Stitch All Wool 49¢

31 G 570—Maroon with trim.
31 G 571—Black with trim.
31 G 572—Brown with trim.

Boys' size only. Ship. weight, each, 7 ounces. Heavy, warm All Wool Cap for hard everyday wear. Has contrasting color trim. Low price for such good quality.

Cardigan Stitch Part Wool 45¢

31 G 573—Navy blue with red.
31 G 574—Black with orange.
31 G 575—Brown with buff.

Boys' size only. Ship. weight, each, 7 ounces. Well knit from strong part wool yarns. Contrasting, snug fitting, deep roll cuff.

Boy's Sweaters Built for Hard Wear

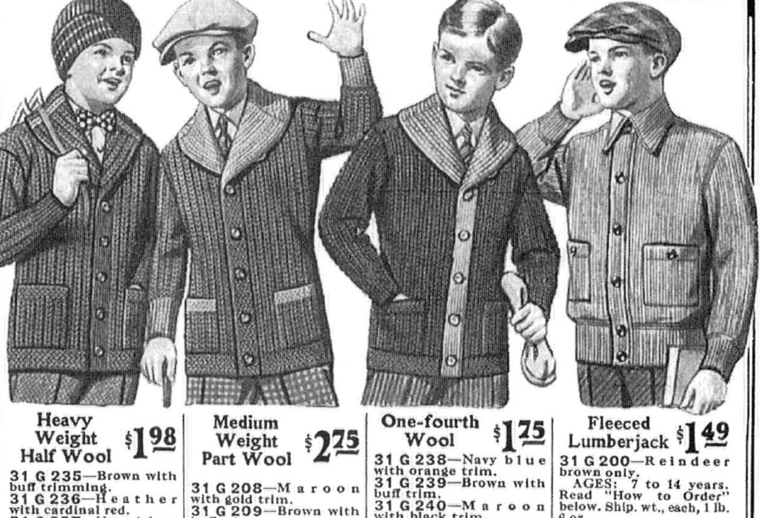

Heavy Weight Half Wool $1.98

31 G 235—Brown with buff trimming.
31 G 236—Heather with cardinal red.
31 G 237—Navy blue with orange.

AGES: 7 to 14 years. Read "How to Order" at right. Shipping weight, each, 1 pound 8 ounces.

Serviceable, heavy-weight long wearing Coat Sweater firmly knit in cardigan stitch from about one-half wool yarns. Has large shawl collar with contrasting color trim.

Medium Weight Part Wool $2.75

31 G 208—Maroon with gold trim.
31 G 209—Brown with buff trim.
31 G 210—Navy blue with orange trim.

AGES: 7 to 14 years. Read "How to Order" at right. Shipping weight, each, 1 pound 7 ounces.

Strongly knit from about 45 per cent worsted yarns in elastic cardigan stitch. Contrasting color trim on collar, pocket tops, cuffs.

One-fourth Wool $1.75

31 G 238—Navy blue with orange trim.
31 G 239—Brown with buff trim.
31 G 240—Maroon with black trim.

AGES: 7 to 14 years. Ship. wt., each, 1 lb. 8 oz. Contrasting trim on collar, facing, pockets.

Fleeced Lumberjack $1.49

31 G 200—Reindeer brown only.

AGES: 7 to 14 years. Read "How to Order" below. Ship. wt., each, 1 lb. 6 oz.

Closely woven cotton jersey cloth heavily fleeced. Double knit cuffs and bottom.

How to Order Boys' Sweaters

Order by age corresponding to measure over blouse.

Ages.	Chest measure.
7 to 8 years.	26¼ inches.
9 to 10 years.	27¾ inches.
11 to 12 years.	29¼ inches.
13 to 14 years.	30¾ inches.

# of Quality Winter Knit Wear

$3.95

Ward's All Wool Heavy Weight Champ
Special Price Value

31 G 107—Maroon.
31 G 108—Navy blue.
31 G 109—Brown.
SIZES: 36 to 46-inch chest. Order size two inches larger than chest measure over shirt. Shipping weight, each, 3 pounds.

Built specially warm and durable for the active outdoor man. Will stand lots of hard, rough usage and still retain its snug fit after long wear. A big heavy weight model that sells elsewhere for far more than our extremely low price.

Firmly and evenly woven in heavy rope stitch from strong All Wool yarns. Has extra large, double knit shawl collar. A strip of rack knitting across the shoulders and strong reinforcing at all points of strain keep this sweater from stretching and add many months to its satisfactory wearing service. Rack knit trim on pocket tops and close fitting bottom and cuffs.

Famous Ranger "A" Lumberjack

Warmth Without Weight

31 G 139—Reindeer brown only.
SIZES: 34 to 46-inch chest. Order size two inches larger than chest measure over shirt. Shipping weight, 1 pound 8 ounces.
$1.69

Easiest of knitted garments to wear and very popular with sportsmen because of its great warmth without bulkiness. Has that fine tailored appearance of models selling for twice our low price. Made of closely woven jersey cloth, heavily fleeced on inside and practically wind-proof. Close fitting, double knit wrists and bottom. Two pockets.

All Wool Sportjack Jerseys

Men's With Front Opening	Boys' With Front Opening
31 G 182—Green.	31 G 212— Maroon.
31 G 183—Navy.	
31 G 184—Maroon.	31 G 213—Navy.
31 G 186—Brown.	31 G 214—Brown.
Each....$2.59	Each....$2.39
Plain Collar	**Plain Collar**
31 G 170—Gray.	31 G 222—Navy.
31 G 171—Navy.	
31 G 172—Maroon.	31 G 223— Maroon.
31 G 173—Brown.	31 G 224—Brown.
Each....$2.49	Each....$2.29

SIZES: 34 to 44-inch chest. Order size larger than chest measure over shirt. Shipping weight, each, 12 ounces.

AGES: 7 to 14 years. Read "How to Order" Page 104. Shipping weight, each, 9 ounces.

Popular Jerseys of fine, flat knit, All Wool worsted yarns very closely woven. Suitable for all outdoor sports. Very durable. Very close fitting with double knit collar and cuffs.

Read "How to Order" Page 104.

How to Order Men's Sweaters

Order size two inches larger than actual chest measurement over shirt. A roomy size will give much better service than one that fits too snugly. In taking chest measure, be careful not to pull the tape too tightly nor let it slip down in the back.

Medium Weight All Wool
$2.98

31 G 168—Maroon (dark red).
31 G 169—Navy blue.
SIZES: 34 to 46-inch chest. Order size two inches larger than chest measure over shirt. Shipping weight, 2 pounds 6 ounces.

You men of the outdoors need a Sweater for winter, one that is warm and one that will stand the hard knocks of rough work or strenuous play.

Note the quality of this sweater in the firm and even elastic cardigan stitch, the warmth and softness of the strong All Wool yarns and the large, five-piece shawl collar. The rack knitting on the shoulders insures longer wear without stretching. Rack knit trim on pocket tops and bottom. We recommend this sweater for lasting satisfactory service and invite rigid price comparison on sweaters of equal quality sold elsewhere.

$2.98

All Wool Scarfs

Boys' 59¢

31 G 504—Brown.
31 G 505—Buff.
31 G 506—Royal blue.
Shipping weight, each, 6 ounces.
Warm, heavy Scarf of soft All Wool yarns. Brushed finish; fringed ends. Size, fringed, 5½ by 45 inches.

Men's 89¢

31 G 507—Gray.
31 G 508—Brown.
31 G 509—Buff.
Shipping weight, each, 8 ounces.
Good looking, soft, warm All Wool with richly brushed finish. Knotted fringe ends. Size, 9 by 55 inches. Splendid gift items.

Cardigan Knit Part Wool Coat
$1.95

31 G 73—Navy blue.
31 G 74—Maroon (dark red).
31 G 75—Brown.
31 G 76—Green heather.
SIZES: 36 to 46-inch chest. Order size two inches larger than chest measure over shirt. Shipping weight, each, 1 lb. 8 oz.

There is wonderful value in this durable, medium weight Sweater Coat and it is very low priced for such high quality. Firmly woven in cardigan stitch from about one-fourth wool yarns. Large five-piece shawl collar with extra loop and button. Two roomy pockets and double-knit cuffs.

Medium Weight V-Neck Style
$1.89

31 G 140—Gray.
31 G 141—Navy blue.
31 G 142—Brown.
SIZES: 34 to 46-inch chest. Order size two inches larger than chest measure over shirt. Ship. weight, each, 1 pound 10 ounces.

Splendid, low priced Sweater, very popular because of its general utility. Finely tailored with extra strong seams. Very warm and durable. Evenly and firmly knit from good quality yarns, about one-fourth wool, with rack knitting at bottom, on pocket tops and across the shoulders to keep it from stretching.

Finest All Wool Worsted
$8.98

31 G 103—Brown.
31 G 104—Navy blue.
31 G 105—Camel tan.
31 G 106—White.
SIZES: 36 to 46-inch chest. Order size two inches larger than chest measure over shirt. Ship. weight, each, 3 lbs. 8 oz.

Our finest Sweater Coat, well worth the difference in cost because of the best quality, All Wool worsted yarns used, the even Shaker Knit stitch, the hand finishing throughout and the full fashioning. Has extra large shawl collar and two roomy, non-sagging knit-in pockets. Ribbed cuffs.

Big Values for the Outdoor Youth

All Worsted and Rayon
$2.89

31 G 233— Gray combination.
31 G 234— Buff combination.
SIZES: 34 to 36-inch chest. Order size two inches larger than chest measure over shirt. Shipping weight, each, 1 pound 12 ounces.

Popular cricket style Pullover Sweater of smooth knit wool worsted and Rayon in attractive color combinations and fancy block pattern. Plain color trim on V-neck and close fitting, ribbed cuffs and bottom.

Honor Style Pullover
$2.95

31 G 265—Navy blue with orange trim.
31 G 266—Maroon with gold trim.
SIZES: 34 to 36-inch chest. Order size two inches larger than chest measure over shirt. Shipping weight, each, 1 pound 8 ounces.

Popular Athletic style. The favorite model used by many colleges for Honor Sweaters. Durably knit of warm, wool worsted yarns firmly plaited over a strong cotton back. Large shawl collar; color stripe on chest.

All Wool Crew Neck Pullover
$2.98

31 G 267—Navy blue with new crew neck.
31 G 268—Maroon with navy blue trim.
SIZES: 34 to 36-inch chest. Order size two inches larger than chest measure over shirt. Shipping weight, each, 1 pound.

Latest style Pullover with new crew neck. Closely knit from warm, All Wool worsted yarns in elastic cardigan stitch. Fancy knitted band striped in contrasting color goes all around neck.

All Wool Shaker Knit
$3.45

31 G 263— Red with buff trim.
31 G 264— Buff with brown trim.
SIZES: 34 to 36-inch chest. Order size two inches larger than chest measure over shirt. Shipping weight, each, 2 pounds 10 ounces.

Hand finished throughout and full fashioned. Handsome, durable, well made Shaker Knit All Wool Sweater Coat. A good, warm, heavy weight that will give long service. Double-knit shawl collar.

Knit Caps for Men and Boys
All Wool Hockey Cap

31 G 643—Brown with buff trimming.
31 G 644—Black with orange trimming.
31 G 645—Maroon (dark red).
31 G 646—Brown.
65¢

SIZES: Men's or boys'. State size. Ship. wt., each, 7 oz.

Know real winter comfort by wearing a knitted Hockey Cap. Splendid for winter driving, skating or any outdoor activity. The deep roll cuffs afford warm protection to the ears and cheeks. Made in heavy jumbo stitch from warm All Wool yarns, closely knit to stand hard wear. Will keep its snug, close fit without stretching. Color stripe on cuff. Knitted caps make highly appreciated winter gifts.

Men's or Boys' All Wool 45¢

31 G 597— Navy blue with orange.
31 G 598— Green with red.
31 G 599— Brown with green.
SIZES: Men's or boys'. Shipping weight, each, 7 ounces.
Knit in fancy stitch from warm All Wool yarns. Has design on top in contrasting color. Deep roll cuff.

Men's or Boys' All Wool 89¢

31 G 564— Green with red design.
31 G 565— Royal blue with white.
31 G 566— Brown with buff design.
SIZES: Men's or boys'. Shipping weight, each, 7 ounces.
Medium weight durable Cap with fancy designs on top and contrasting color stripe on deep roll cuff.

Part Wool Rope Stitch 59¢

31 G 697—Brown with contrasting color trim.
31 G 698—Royal blue; contrasting color trim.
31 G 699—Maroon with contrasting color trim.
Men's size only. Shipping weight, each, 7 ounces.
Warm Hockey Cap knit in heavy rope stitch with fancy design. A good, serviceable cap priced very low.

And Ward's Quality Makes These Genuine Values

All Wool Worsted

Wonder Value!
All Wool $2.98

Never Before Offered at This Price

All Wool Worsted

Our Best

Popular Tuxedo Style $4.98

31 G 354—Dark tan.
31 G 357—Navy blue.
SIZES: 34 to 46-inch bust. Order size two inches larger than bust measure over dress.

Shipping weight, each, 2 pounds.

Decidedly the favorite model of thousands of women because it gives such variety to a wardrobe. It's charming worn over a blouse or just a vestee of lace or silk! Buttoned up close it makes a warm, serviceable Sweater Coat. Finely knit from rich All Wool worsted yarns in a fancy drop-stitch that gives it a tailored appearance. A remarkably durable quality in a close ribbed stitch. Two buttons on sleeves, pockets and belt.

Smartly Tailored $4.98

31 G 297—Dark tan.
31 G 298—Powder blue.
31 G 299—Black.
SIZES: 34 to 46-inch bust. Order size two inches larger than bust measure over dress.

Shipping weight, each, 1 lb. 13 oz.

In the fashionable city sports shops you will see Sweater Coats in this becoming double breasted style. But there they cost almost twice the low price we ask. Beautifully knit in a fine rib stitch from soft All Wool worsted yarns with a charming effect of shadow striping. Carefully tailored throughout. Daintily bound with Rayon braid in harmonizing color. Has neatly set-in pockets.

Serviceable and Economical for Knockabout Wear $2.98

31 G 340—Cardinal red.
31 G 341—Navy blue.
SIZES: 34 to 46-inch bust. Order size two inches larger than bust measure over dress.
Shipping weight, each, 2 pounds.

For hard, knockabout service, snug warmth and a trim appearance, we highly recommend this All Wool Sweater. Buying it while our price is so low is genuine economy, as such a bargain can be offered but seldom, even at Ward's. Firmly knit in the popular cardigan stitch, it will keep its shape very well. You'll like the large, double knit shawl collar that may be worn either turned down or buttoned up high around the neck. Rack knitting across the shoulders, pocket tops and front gives added strength and a pretty trimming. The close fitting cuffs are knit in a fine ribbed stitch. Has two roomy patch pockets.

Don't judge the quality of the sweater by its low price. It is really a most exceptional bargain value. Only once in a long while can you buy a sweater like this at such a saving.

Astrakan Cloth Looks Like Fur $3.98

31 G 325—Tan.
31 G 326—Brown.
SIZES: 34 to 44-inch bust. Order size two inches larger than bust measure over dress.

Shipping weight, each, 1 lb. 14 oz.

Perfectly stunning—rich, fur-like cloth, fashioned in the smartest style imaginable! And it's so delightfully soft and warm. All Wool, tightly curled yarn, is woven onto a strong cotton back for the outside. The lining is fine jersey cloth. Soft, downy brushed wool collar, cuffs and band around the bottom. All edges are bound with silky Rayon braid. Collar may be worn low or high.

Our Best Sweater Superb Quality $8.98

31 G 372—White.
31 G 373—Camel tan.
31 G 377—Maroon.
SIZES: 34 to 46-inch bust. Order size two inches larger than bust measure over dress.

Shipping weight, each, 3 pounds.

Absolutely an unrivaled bargain! Big stores on Fifth Avenue charge about $12 for heavy Sweaters like this—and they are worth it, for they will give nearly a lifetime of service. Finest, soft, All Wool worsted yarns are evenly knit in the shaker stitch. Double knit set-in pockets and shawl collar that may be worn high or low. Hand finished throughout and it fits superbly. Facing and bottom edge have wide hems.

Rich Looking, Warm Beaver Cloth Shawl $6.95

31 G 946—Gray.
31 G 947—Brown.
Shipping weight, each, 3 pounds.
It will be your pride and delight for years! Luxuriously soft, heavy beaver cloth, about 85 per cent pure wool. Think of the marvelous protection and warmth it will give you! Beautiful border and yarn fringe all around. Size, including fringe, about 72 inches square.

Medium Weight Half Wool Beaver Cloth

31 G 935—Gray.
31 G 936—Brown. Each.... $3.45
Shipping weight, each, 2 pounds 8 ounces. Same style as above, medium weight. Size, including fringe, about 60 by 64 inches.

Soft, Warm Shoulder Shawl 85¢

31 G 923—Gray.
31 G 924—Brown.
Size, including fringe, about 37 inches square.
Shipping weight, each, 10 ounces. Each.... 85¢

Larger Sizes In Same Quality

31 G 925—Gray.
31 G 926—Brown.
Sizes, including fringe, about 42 inches square.
Shipping weight, each, 1 lb. 4 oz. Each...... $1.19

Two convenient sizes—slip these shawls around your shoulders when you feel chilly or wish to go outdoors. Woven closely from about 25 per cent wool yarns into a comfortably warm, medium weight. Striped borders and soft fringe all around give them an attractive appearance. You'll agree that they are an astonishing bargain for so low a price when you see how lovely and fine they are.

Closely Woven All Wool Shawl Light; Warm and Comfortable $3.15

Size, 62 inches square
31 G 930—Gray.
31 G 931—Brown. Each.... $3.15
Shipping weight, each, 1 pound.

Size, 62 by 116 inches
31 G 932—Gray.
31 G 933—Brown. Each.... $6.38
Shipping weight, each, 1 pound 10 ounces.

Ever so soft and supple—very comfortable to wear! And its finely woven All Wool yarns will easily keep out all the chill and dampness. Pretty and tailored looking with its smart plaid border, soft wool fringe all the way around and smooth finish. An amazing bargain at our price as it will give years of splendid service.

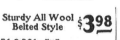

$1.98

Two Splendid Values $2.98

Half Wool Sweater

31 G 311—Brown.
31 G 312—Cardinal red.
SIZES: 34 to 46-inch bust. Order size two inches larger than bust measure over dress.
Ship. wt., each, 1 lb. 10 oz.
Surprising offer of a finely tailored, warm, winter-weight Sweater Coat at an exceedingly low price. It is firmly knit from about half wool yarns in an even rib stitch, with a double shawl collar, snug fitting cuffs and two roomy patch pockets. A practical, inexpensive winter weight garment.

Heavy Cotton $1.15

31 G 346—Brown mixture.
31 G 364—Oxford gray.
SIZES: 34 to 44-inch bust. Order size two inches larger than bust measure over dress.
Shipping weight, 1 lb. 10 oz.
Same style as above, firmly knit heavy cotton.

Regular and Extra Sizes $3.98

31 G 393—Cardinal red with trimming.
31 G 394—Navy blue with trimming.
REGULAR SIZES: 36 to 46-inch bust. Each...... $3.98
EXTRA SIZES: 48, 50, 52-inch bust. Each...... $4.98
Order size two inches larger than bust measure over dress.
Shipping weight, each, 2 pounds.

Has the smart, attractive appearance that pleases a woman for street and sports wear. It is also snugly warm and of an astonishing durability. Closely knit in a fancy stitch from fine yarns, about one half wool. Even after you give it strenuous wear, it will keep its evenness of texture and trim, smart shape. Rows of stitches knit in silky Rayon of a contrasting color trim the collar, cuffs, pocket tops and bottom. You can button the collar up high around the neck. Its beauty and wear-resisting qualities are all out of proportion to its low price.

Ward's "Aristocrat" All Wool

With Straight Flattering Lines

31 G 315—Green.
31 G 316—Buff.
31 G 317—Jockey red. $4.95
SIZES: 34 to 44-inch bust. Order size two inches larger than bust measure over dress.
Shipping weight, each, 1 pound 14 ounces.

What a graceful, distinguished style! If you wish to look more slender, this is a very wise choice as it has been designed to give the long, slim lines that are so fashionable. So cleverly is it woven in a new fancy stitch that it looks as if there were tucking both in front and back, on the sleeves and across the bottom. Very soft and warm. Closely knit in a fine ribbed stitch of splendid All Wool worsted yarns. Has a trim Byron collar that may be worn open or buttoned and is always becoming. Carefully tailored with close fitting cuffs and two neat patch pockets.

$4.95

Sturdy All Wool Belted Style $3.98

31 G 361—Buff.
31 G 362—Cardinal red.
31 G 363—Oxford gray.
SIZES: 34 to 46-inch bust. Order size two inches larger than bust measure over dress.
Shipping weight, each, 2 lbs. 2 oz.

For hard, general wear we are positive you can't find a more satisfactory Sweater at so moderate a price. Only fine quality All Wool yarns of long wearing strength are knit into its heavy weight cardigan stitch texture. It will be warm and protecting in winter, fall and spring. Trimly tailored and carefully finished throughout—a decidedly good-looking sweater coat. Close rack knitting finishes the shoulders, pocket tops, facing and bottom. Has a large shawl collar that may be buttoned high around the neck and ears whenever you want extra warmth. Two-button belt and two roomy pockets.

Dainty, New Slipover $1.98

31 G 286—Powder blue combination.
31 G 304—Rose beige (buff) combination.
SIZES: 34 to 42-inch bust. Order size two inches larger than bust measure over dress.
Shipping weight, each, 1 pound.

Lovely enough for practically any occasion! Just slip it on over almost any skirt and you'll have a delightfully smart and fashionable ensemble! Silky and fine, it is woven in a very dainty stitch from Rayon, All Wool worsted and cotton yarns. It will wear splendidly. So tailored looking with its plain colored student collar and close fitting, turned back cuffs. Much of its charm is due to its soft, harmonious color combinations. At any other store you would have to pay considerably more for such a perfectly beautiful sweater.

96

Satisfaction *Plus* Is Woven Into Every Sweater

All Wool

All Wool

$3.95

Heavy Weight All Wool

Hand Crocheted

All Wool Greatsweater $5.95

Heavy and Warm

31 G 350—White.
31 G 351—Cardinal red.
31 G 352—Brown.
31 G 353—Navy blue. $5.95
Each
WOMEN'S SIZES: 34 to 46-inch bust. Order size two inches larger than bust measure over dress. Ship. wt., 2 lbs. 10 oz.

Girls' All Wool Sweaters
31 G 635—Cardinal red.
31 G 636—White.
31 G 637—Brown.
31 G 638—Navy blue. $4.69
Each
AGES: 7 to 14 years. State age. Shipping weight, 2 lbs. 7 oz.
So superb in quality that they will give years of satisfaction! All Wool yarns are woven in a pliable rope stitch. Rack knit facings on collar front and pocket tops. Well finished and strongly reinforced. Has large shawl collar that may be rolled high. Sateen lined pockets.

All Wool Tuxedo Sports Coat $4.89

31 G 355—Brown heather.
31 G 356—Blue heather.
SIZES: 34 to 50-inch bust. Order size two inches larger than bust measure over dress. Ship. weight, each, 2 lbs. 3 oz.
Marvelously practical—you can button it up and wear it as a coat or sweater, or in the Tuxedo style with a blouse or vestee of lace or silk. Ideal for sport or more dressy occasions! Buttons and loops concealed beneath the revers make it easy for you to close the front when you wish. Amazingly durable and warm, it is made of smooth, heavy jersey cloth very finely knit from soft All Wool yarns. Such a trim, neatly tailored style—and in colors that will harmonize with any costume. May be worn with or without belt. Two large patch pockets.

Amazing Value in a Sweater Coat

31 G 387—Cardinal red.
31 G 388—Navy blue. $3.95
SIZES: 34 to 46-inch bust. Order size two inches larger than bust measure over dress. State size. Ship, weight, each, 2 pounds 8 ounces.
Especially popular with our customers and an extraordinary bargain! That's because its All Wool texture stands up marvelously well under hard service although this Sweater costs so little. Finely knit in the sturdy rope stitch, it is heavy and comfortably warm and will keep its trim, snug fit. You will like the big adjustable shawl collar that may be worn either high or low. Rack knit bottom, shoulders and pocket tops. Has, durable shaker knit front. Strongly reinforced at all points of strain and well finished. While our price is so amazingly low it's a genuine economy to order this splendid sweater. Thoroughly dependable in quality, it will give you real satisfaction.

Hug-Me-Tight for Cozy Warmth

With Sleeves
31 G 391—Black.
31 G 392—Orford gray. $2.59
Without Sleeves
31 G 389—Black.
31 G 390—Oxford gray. $1.85
SIZES: 34 to 48-inch bust. Order size two inches larger than bust measure over dress. State size. Shipping weight, each, 12 ounces.
Delightfully snug and warm to wear in the house on cool days, and under a coat when outside. Closely knit in the elastic cardigan stitch from choice yarns about one-half worsted wool. Carefully made to give lasting satisfaction and to fit trimly and comfortably. It's sure to be acceptable as a gift! A band at the waist and at the top of each shoulder, knitted in a fancy stitch, gives a pretty contrast. All edges are finished in a dainty knitted lace effect. Has cloth covered buttons.

All-Wool Hug-Me-Tight $1.89

31 G 322—Gray with orchid trim.
31 G 323—Black with orchid trim.
SIZES: 34 to 46-inch bust. State bust measure. Shipping weight, each, 8 ounces.
Dainty and soft, it has an intimate charm all its own! Just as finely and carefully made as if you had crocheted it yourself. All Wool worsted yarns, rich and lustrous, knit in lovely block stitch with edging, border and tassels of pretty orchid colored yarns. Such snug, warm comfort it will bring Mother or Grandmother if she slips it on when she's a little chilly, or wears it under her coat. It will keep draughts away from her shoulders and back, and looks very pretty and becoming. Of a thoroughly dependable wearing quality, it will last for years. Perfectly delightful for a gift—one that is sure to be appreciated. Looks as if it cost far more than $1.89.

Warm, Durable Sweaters *for* School Girls 7 to 14 Years

Half Wool

All Wool

All Wool $2.89

All Wool

Heavy Part Wool $1.95

Tremendously Popular All Wool Service Coat

31 G 662—Cardinal red with buff trimming.
31 G 663—Powder blue with gray trimming.
Each $2.89
AGES: 7 to 14 years. State age. Shipping weight, each, 1 pound 4 ounces.
Girls will love its trim, smart style! And their mothers will be delighted with the warmth and long service it gives. Closely knit in the cardigan stitch from heavy All Wool yarns of uniform strength, it will stand up under hard wear at school and play. Reinforced at places that receive particular strain to prevent stretching or sagging. Carefully made to fit very snugly and neatly. Collar and front are rack knit in a contrasting color. Rack knitting also at cuffs, shoulders, bottom and pocket tops. You'll agree that our price is far lower than other stores would ask for a Sweater of this splendid quality.

Charming and So Serviceable $2.79

31 G 515—Powder blue with buff trimming.
31 G 516—Brown with orange trimming.
31 G 517—Cardinal red with buff trimming.
AGES: 7 to 14 years. State age. Shipping weight, each, 1 pound 3 ounces.
It's easy to have daughter well dressed for school when you can buy this pretty, long wearing Sweater at so low a price! And it will keep her snug and warm. Knit in a close, even stitch from about one-half worsted wool yarns by a special process so that all the cotton is brought to the inner surface. Pretty color combinations in clear rich shades. Neatly tailored for a smooth, trim fit. Has button belt and two roomy patch pockets.

All Wool Heavy Sweater $2.98

31 G 620—Buff.
31 G 621—Cardinal red.
31 G 622—Powder blue.
AGES: 7 to 14 years. State age. Shipping weight, each, 1 pound 6 ounces.
Luxuriously rich and warm! That's because its soft All Wool yarns are firmly knit into its strong cardigan stitch. Will hold its shape and stand up under lots of wear and tear. And it is very attractive with its large shawl collar, two-button belt and rack knit trimming on shoulders, pocket tops and bottom.

A Good Durable Sweater $1.98

31 G 577—Peacock blue with buff trimming.
31 G 578—Cardinal red with navy blue.
AGES: 7 to 14 years. State age. Ship. weight, each, 1 pound 2 ounces.
Active girls will get real warmth and decidedly good service from this sturdy Sweater Coat. Firmly knit in the cardigan stitch from part wool yarns. It fits well and will last long. Collar, pocket tops and front in contrasting color. A decidedly worthwhile value.

Heavy Part Wool $1.95

31 G 494—Cardinal red.
31 G 495—Peacock blue.
AGES: 7 to 14 years. State age. Ship. weight, each, 1 pound 8 ounces.
Good-looking and amazingly durable! Firmly knit of part wool yarns. Large shawl collar and two pockets. Rack knitting trims shoulders, pocket tops, bottom and front.

Heavy Cotton 95¢

31 G 563—Medium gray.
31 G 593—Brown mixture.
AGES: 7 to 14 years. State age. Ship. wt., 1 lb. 7 oz.
Durable ribbed cotton weave. Shawl collar has extra button and loop to button close around neck.

A New Appealing Jacquard Pattern in a Splendid All Wool Lumberjack for Girls $3.95

31 G 624—Light blue combination.
31 G 649—Tan combination.
AGES: 7 to 14 years. State age. Shipping weight, each, 1 pound 4 ounces.
Wearing this strikingly beautiful Lumberjack will give any girl a tremendous thrill! At play, or in the school room it will look so pretty and distinctive, because of the unusual richness of its jacquard pattern in lovely colors. All Wool worsted yarns, very closely woven, give it marvelous durability, a comfortably soft texture and snug warmth. A popular style, with elastic knit close fitting striped bottom, cuffs, and pocket flaps that button down. Colored buttons.

Stunning Lumberjack Coat for Girls With Gaily Colored Navajo Patterns $2.79

31 G 733—Buff combination.
31 G 734—Light blue combination.
AGES: 7 to 14 years. State age. Shipping weight, each, 1 pound 2 ounces.
Of course every girl wants at least one smart Lumberjack—and this is such a good-looking one! Closely knit of about one-half wool yarns, with many of its interesting Navajo designs in silky Rayon threads. Ideal for sports or everyday wear—all the school girls like them. It will keep its fresh, new appearance amazingly long and it's delightfully snug and warm. Finely ribbed double cuffs and waistband at bottom make it fit trimly. Collar that may be worn either high or low and two patch pockets with knit tops.

97

For Housewear
Women Everywhere Talk About Ward's Values ~

Polka Dot Percale
Extraordinary Value

36 G 74 Work-a-day clothes can be most attractive—that is proved by this lovely Apron Dress of blue and gold Polka Dot Percale, trimmed with gold rickrack braid. And to add to the pleasure of wearing it is the knowledge that so far as we know you would not be able to purchase its equal at anywhere near our low price of only 84¢. Roomy pockets. Tie back sash.

REGULAR SIZES: Small (34 to 36 bust); medium (38 to 40 bust); large (42 to 44 bust). State size.
EXTRA SIZES: (46 to 48 bust) or (50 to 52 bust). State size. Ship. wt., 12 oz.
36 G 74—Navy blue with gold dots only..**84¢**

36 G 74
Percale
Regular and
Extra Sizes
84¢

Roguish Little Apron
Gingham, Percale or Sateen

36 G 301 Smart and attractive Apron to protect one's pretty frocks without hiding them. Made in a charming style, with piping dividing the skirt into tiers and outlining the edges and pockets. A tie-sash at back. You will want more than one of these, for it comes in three different combinations: Black Sateen with orange piping; Assorted Dark Percale, or Blue Checked Gingham—each with pipings of white. This model comes in one size only. Ship. wt., 8 ounces.
36 G 301—Black sateen with orange binding.......**75¢**
36 G 303—Assorted dark percale with white binding.
36 G 305—Blue checked gingham with white binding..................**64¢**

36 G 301 | 36 G 303
Sateen | Percale or Gingham
75¢ | **64¢**

36 G 194
Sateen
Regular and
Extra Sizes
$1.95

Hand Embroidered

Black Sateen
Saves Laundering

36 G 194 Attractiveness goes hand in hand with utility in this hand-embroidered Apron Frock. Black Sateen, a marvel of durability, is a striking background for the brightly colored Hand Embroidery. Inverted side plaits. Sash back. Novel cuffs.
REGULAR SIZES: Small (34 to 36 bust); medium (38 to 40 bust); large (42 to 44 bust). State size.
EXTRA SIZES: (46 to 48 bust) or (50 to 52 bust). State size. Shipping weight, 1 pound.
36 G 194—Black only..**$1.95**

36 G 196
Amoskeag
Gingham
$1.95

Unusually Pretty
Amoskeag Gingham

36 G 196 A smart, fast color, fancy Gingham Frock that makes a most attractive street costume. The flattering V-front is accented by white piping which also trims the flap pockets. White pearl buttons on vestee and pocket flaps. Tie-back sash.
WOMEN'S AND MISSES' SIZES: 34, 36, 38, 40, 42, 44-inch bust; 16, 18, 20, 22 years. State size. Shipping weight, 1 lb.
36 G 196—Copenhagen blue.
36 G 198—Lavender.
36 G 200—Coral Rose. **$1.95**

INDIAN HEAD

Indian Head Cloth—the invincible, iron-strong, linen-like material famed the country over for its durability—has been used for making this "Reversible" Apron and Frock.

We invite you to join the ranks of thousands and thousands of housewives, physicians' assistants and nurses who yearly send to Ward's for this type of double service Apron or spic-and-span Dress, made from this unrivaled tub material. Read the wonderful Laboratory test of this famous cloth, at top of Page 138.

36 G 189
INDIAN HEAD
$1.84

Reversible Front Apron Dress
36 G 189 It will wear almost endlessly! The reversible feature gives even added service. Merely reversing the closing gives you a fresh, clean front, the part of a frock that always soils first. Shawl collar, stitched-back cuffs, large patch pockets.
SIZES: Small (34 to 36 bust); medium (38 to 40 bust); large (42 to 44 bust). State size. Shipping weight, 1 pound 4 ounces.
36 G 189—White only,...................$1.84

36 G 91
INDIAN HEAD
$1.59

Durable Apron Frock
36 G 91 Choice of professional women whose duties demand white, and of the housekeeper who prides herself on looking spotless about the home. Patch pockets set above inverted plaits. Reinforced open neck, double collar and cuffs. Kimono sleeves. Tie-back sash.
SIZES: Small (34 to 36 bust); medium (38 to 40 bust); large (42 to 44 bust). State size. Ship. wt., 1 lb.
36 G 91—White only,...................$1.59

36 G 202
Mercerized
Broadcloth
$1.98

Reversible Front Smock Dress
More Popular Than Ever
36 G 202 Soft finish, fine quality Broadcloth is used in this exceedingly nice Smock with smooth fitting raglan shoulders and tailored panel back. Three shoulder tucks add fullness at each side of front, and a smart buttoned belt holds the smock trimly at the hips. Two pockets. Novelty buttons on belt and cuffs. A two-in-one smock (reversible front) that will give endless satisfaction. Simply reverse the front and you have a clean frock. Becoming to all figures.
SIZES: Small (34 to 36 bust); medium (38 to 40 bust); large (42 to 44 bust). State size. Shipping weight, 1 lb.
36 G 202—Copenhagen blue.
36 G 204—Rose.
36 G 206—Green. **$1.98**

Smock of Crisp Chambray
Assorted Checked Gingham Trimming
36 G 10 Your pretty frock will be grateful for the protection of this good-looking Smock, and your appearance won't be one whit less charming, for both the colors and lines of this popular garment are delightfully feminine. It has infinite laundry saving possibilities as an apron, a house coat, a garden smock. Conveniently roomy pockets, and sleeves that can be rolled back if desired.
SIZES: Small (34 to 36 bust); medium (38 to 40 bust); large (42 to 44 bust). State size. Shipping weight, 12 oz.
36 G 10—Copenhagen blue.
36 G 12—Lavender.
36 G 14—Tan. **89¢**

36 G 10
Chambray
89¢

Serviceable Dresses for House, Kitchen or Garden

Regular and Extra Sizes

Sateen Foulard Dress—Extra Sizes
With Slenderizing Skirt Panel Effect

36 G 142 Fine Quality Cotton Foulard $2.95

36 G 142 The New Idea has permanently invaded our morning and house dresses in a way thousands have already noted. The standard of our materials, the method of finishing, has been noticeably raised—to give you the utmost satisfaction you demand, and are certain to receive in all our New Idea dresses.

This charming Sateen Frock is figured in a delightfully fashionable foulard pattern, which makes it quite appropriate for afternoon calls or callers, or for the street. Nicely styled on trig, slenderizing lines—with a convertible collar which closes to the throat with buttons and loops. Fitted cuffs finish the long, modish sleeves. Contrasting pipings accent the unique pockets and trim skirt-panel lines. Shoulder tucks and inverted plaits let in admirable ease, and a self-sash belts it becomingly in to your figure.

EXTRA SIZES: 39, 41, 43, 45, 47, 49, 51, 53-inch bust. State size wanted. Shipping weight, 1 pound 10 ounces.
36 G 142—Navy blue and tan.
36 G 144—Black and white. Each.................... $2.95

36 G 16 Gingham $1.00

Good Value! Extra Sizes!
Always Reliable Checked Gingham

36 G 16 House Dress of excellent value in Checked Gingham. The bias skirt panels and the two pockets are unusual. The neckline is finished with collar of white pique and black ribbon bow. The sleeves are set in made for comfort. Tie sash at back.

REGULAR AND EXTRA SIZES: 36, 38, 40, 42, 44, 46, 48, 50, 52, 54-inch bust. State size wanted. Shipping weight, 12 ounces.
36 G 16—Blue.
36 G 18—Black.
36 G 20—Lavender. Each. $1.00

Regular and Extra Sizes

36 G 156 Linene $1.79

Hand Embroidered

36 G 162 Amoskeag Gingham $1.84

36 G 168 Striped Cotton Serge $1.98

36 G 146 Mercerized Broadcloth $1.89

Extra Sizes!

Broadcloth Dress Polka Dot Trimming
Piping on Front Panel—Neat Crochet Buttons

36 G 146 Graceful, and well made from lustrous and soft Broadcloth. Will always be soft and lustrous. Polka dot material in selftone is used for the tie and collar combination and the cuffs of the long sleeves. Piping outlines the front panel effect where unique pockets are placed. Crochet buttons and an attractive ornament buckle on tie add distinction to this charming frock.

EXTRA SIZES: 39, 41, 43, 45, 47, 49, 51, 53-inch bust. State size wanted. Ship. weight, 1 pound 12 oz.
36 G 146—Copenhagen.
36 G 148—Lavender.
36 G 150—Green.
Each.......... $1.89

36 G 152 Mercerized Broadcloth $1.77

Good Quality Linene
Slenderizing Long Lines Soutache Braid Trimming

36 G 156 Utility Dress that is very neat. Made of good quality Linene in attractive colors. Trimmed with Soutache braid on the long shawl collar, cuffs and V-shaped pockets. An unusual and becoming neckline. Shawl collar ends in buttoned tab.

REGULAR SIZES: Medium (38 to 40 bust); large (42 to 44 bust).
EXTRA SIZES: (46 to 48 bust) or (50 to 52 bust.) State size wanted. Shipping weight, 1 pound.
36 G 156—Copenhagen blue.
36 G 158—Lavender.
36 G 160—Rose. Each...$1.79

Amoskeag Gingham
Hand Embroidered—With Fancy Stitched Trimming

36 G 162 An exceptionally fine House Dress of Amoskeag Gingham with hand embroidered design on the front, and fancy stitching on collar, cuffs and pockets. Extra fullness given by side plaits. Sash tie at back. Good lines for stout women.

REGULAR SIZES: Medium (38 to 40 bust); large (42 to 44 bust).
EXTRA SIZES: (46 to 48 bust) or (50 to 52 bust.) State size wanted. Shipping weight, 1 pound 4 ounces.
36 G 162—Blue.
36 G 164—Green.
36 G 166—Heliotrope. Each......... $1.84

Striped Cotton Serge
Navy Blue Sateen and Fancy Braid Trimming

36 G 168 Straightline one-piece Dress of Striped Cotton Serge, for house or general wear. Stripe and panel effect give the desired long line. Navy blue sateen and fancy braid trim the cuffs, pockets and panel, while metal buttons show on the blouse and pocket tabs.

EXTRA SIZES: 39, 41, 43, 45, 47, 49, 51, 53-inch bust. State size wanted. Shipping weight, 1 pound 4 ounces.
36 G 168—Navy blue striped serge only..... $1.98

Stunning Striped Broadcloth—Extra Sizes
Smart Black Ribbon Tie at Collar
Slenderizing Effect—Sash Ties at Back

36 G 152 The desired slenderizing effect is produced in this lustrous, gay striped Broadcloth Dress that will please the woman of fuller figure. She will find an effective contrast given by plain colored broadcloth on collar, pocket trimming and piping, and an unusual effect of line by having the pockets and panel cut crosswise. A black ribbon bow finishes the collar, and a sash ties at the back. Attractive buttons trim the pocket tabs and panel at the waistline.

EXTRA SIZES: 39, 41, 43, 45, 47, 49, 51, 53-inch bust. State size wanted. Shipping weight, 1 pound 2 ounces.
36 G 152—Tan and blue.
36 G 154—Tan and lavender. Each................. $1.77

Slenderizing Panel Dress—Extra Sizes
For Indoor and Outdoor Wear
Strongly Woven Cotton Checks

36 G 170 Practical Dress that will stand hard wear and still look well—that's why this neat, good looking model of strong Woven Cotton check is so popular with countless women for home and street wear. Black braid trims the full length panel and pockets effectively. The long sleeves are finished with cuffs. A black ribbon tie confines V-shaped neck. Self sash belt.

EXTRA SIZES: 39, 41, 43, 45, 47, 49, 51, 53-inch bust. State size wanted. Shipping weight, 15 ounces.
36 G 170 Black and white woven check only. Each................ $1.95

36 G 170 Woven Cotton Check $1.95

Our Best 4-Buckle Galosh

Now—We've Cut Prices for Women, Children $2.59

A better grade, better looking 4-buckle Galosh made of sturdy quality materials. Gives protection to your feet and shoes in wet, cold weather. Soft, fast color black cashmerette uppers are reinforced and fleece lined. Strong, corrugated rubber soles. It will stand comparison with any $3.50 galosh on the market. Hold their shape longer—wear longer—fit better. Shipping weights: Women's, 2 pounds 7 ounces; children's, 1 pound 11 ounces.

For Women. SIZES: 2½ to 9. Order half size larger than shoe.
26 G 4456—Round toe, low heel........ $2.59
26 G 4457—Pointed toe, military heel .. 2.59

For Girls and Children. Round toe. Order one size larger than shoe.
26 G 4451— 11 to 2.................. $2.19
26 G 4452— 6 to 10½.............. 1.98

26 G 4457
Pointed Toe
High Heel

Low Priced, Stylish and Dependable

Save MORE! Prices Are Reduced $1.69

This well made 4-buckle Galosh is absolute proof of Ward's reliable quality and extremely low prices. One-piece seamless uppers of durable black cloth. Fresh, live rubber soles and bright rubber reinforcement. Has the appearance of higher priced galoshes and is perfect fitting. WE BELIEVE it is America's biggest bargain in galoshes. Shipping weights: Women's, 2 pounds 7 ounces; girls' and children's, 1 pound 11 ounces. State size wanted.

26 G 4446
Pointed Toe
High Heel

26 G 4447 and 26 G 4448
Misses' and Children's
Broad Toe
Low Heel

For Women. SIZES: 2½ to 9. Order half size larger than shoe.
26 G 4446—Pointed toe, military heel............$1.69
26 G 4445—Round toe, low heel.. 1.69

For Girls and Children Broad Toe and Low Heel
Order Size Larger Than Shoe
26 G 4447—SIZES: 11 to 2.. $1.65
26 G 4448—SIZES: 6 to 10½.. 1.59

This Toe and Heel
Women's 26 G 4445

Women's All Rubber Arctic $2.69

$2.29

Girls—On or Off in a Jiffy
They're Popular Everywhere

Popular automatic fastening Galosh for girls. On or off in a hurry. Strong, warm black cashmerette uppers reinforced with bright black rubber. Sturdy rubber soles. There's a saving here that will please mothers. Broad toe, low heel. Order one size larger than shoe. State size wanted. Shipping weight, 2 pounds 2 ounces.
26 G 4497—For Misses. SIZES: 11 to 2........... $2.59
26 G 4498—For Children. SIZES: 6 to 10½........... 2.29

Ideal for Wet Weather
Light and Water-Tight

Women's all black rubber 4-buckle Arctic. Special design and construction, gives you a light weight Arctic that you will enjoy wearing because of its comfort. Absolutely water-proof, assuring positive protection in slushy weather. Is strongly reinforced and also warmly lined. Will fit over round toe, low heel shoes. An ideal winter arctic. Order one size larger than shoe. Shipping weight, 4 pounds 6 ounces.
26 G 4458 .... $2.69

Women's and Children's Two-Buckle Arctic

Warmth—Service—Protection $1.79
At Special Reduced Prices

Buy these fine, warm two-buckle Arctics at our reduced prices. Wear them to prevent wet feet and also to protect your shoes. Black cashmerette tops are fast color and strongly reinforced. Wide rubber reinforcement around the vamp and heel. Strong rubber soles and heels. Order women's half size larger and girls' and children's one size larger than shoe. State size. Shipping weights: Women's and girls', 2 pounds 4 ounces; children's, 1 pound 10 ounces.
26 G 4430—For Women. SIZES: 2½ to 9.............. $1.79
26 G 4550—For Girls. SIZES: 11 to 2............. 1.75
26 G 4555—For Children. SIZES: 5 to 10½........... 1.59

Women's and Girls'

One-Buckle Arctics

In cold, wet weather this Arctic gives warmth, protection good fit and long wear. Heavy, soft black cashmerette tops are warmly lined. Bright black rubber reinforcement. Broad toe, low heel. Order women's half size larger and girls' and children's one size larger than shoe. State size wanted. Ship. wts.: Women's and girls, 2 pounds; children's, 1 lb.
26 G 4500—For Women. SIZES: 2½ to 9........ $1.29
26 G 4585—For Girls. SIZES: 11 to 2.. 1.15
26 G 4590—For Children. SIZES: 4 to 10½.. .98

Fine Light Arctic

For Women

Women's light-weight dress Arctic. Its neatness, warmth and service are sure to please you. The black jersey cloth uppers are fast color. Durable rubber sole and heel. For broad toe, low heel shoes. Order half size larger than shoe. Shipping weight 1 pound 10 ounces.
SIZES: 2½ to 9. State size wanted.
26 G 4540..................... $1.49

Men's and Boys' Arctics—Guaranteed First Quality—Greater Values Than Ever

Men's Warm 4-Buckle Arctics

$1.95 $2.39 $2.95    $1.69

Heavy Rolled Sole

A pair of these big, strong one-buckle Arctics will give you long service, comfort and protection when the weather is cold and wet. Black cashmerette tops are warmly lined. Rolled edge rubber soles and heels are solidly vulcanized to the uppers. It's an extremely big value at our price. Wide toe. Order one size larger than shoe. Shipping weight, 2 pounds 6 ounces.
SIZES: 6 to 13. No half sizes. State size wanted.
26 G 4440................. $1.95

Gives you real cold, wet weather protection for your feet. Light-weight cashmerette uppers are warmly lined, and reinforced around the vamp with bright black rubber. Popular with motorists. Strong, corrugated rubber soles and heels. There's a sure saving for you at our price. For low heel, wide toe shoes. Order half size larger than shoe. Ship. wt., 2 pounds 10 ounces.
SIZES: 6 to 13. State size wanted.
26 G 4455 $2.39

Warmth for your feet in any kind of winter weather—long wear, too. Get yourself a pair of these four-buckle Arctics for those chores that take you out into the wet and slush. Heavy, black cashmerette uppers are warm lined. Have thick, rolled edge soles and heels for heaviest work. Low heel, broad toe. Order one size larger than shoe. Shipping weight, 3 pounds 9 ounces.
SIZES: 6 to 13. No half sizes. State size.
26 G 4470 $2.95

Men's Light Weight Arctic

Business men, outdoor men—are wearing this light-weight, dress Arctic to keep their feet warm and dry every day through the winter. Durable, black jersey cloth is warmly lined and strongly vulcanized to the bright rubber vamp. Strong, fresh, live rubber soles. A value that saves you money. Wide toe. Order half size larger than shoe. Shipping weight, 2 pounds 6 ounces.
SIZES: 6 to 13. State size wanted.
26 G 4490................. $1.69

Men's and Boys' 1-Buckle Arctic

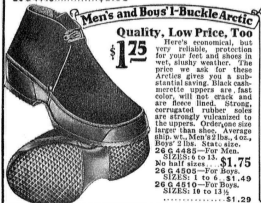

Quality, Low Price, Too

$1.75

Here's economical, but very reliable, protection for your feet and shoes in wet, slushy weather. The price we ask for these Arctics gives you a substantial saving. Black cashmerette uppers are fast color, will not crack and are fleece lined. Strong, corrugated rubber soles are strongly vulcanized to the uppers. Order one size larger than shoe. Average ship. wt., Men's 2 lbs., 4 oz., Boys' 2 lbs. State size.
26 G 4485—For Men. SIZES: 6 to 13. No half sizes.....$1.75
26 G 4505—For Boys. SIZES: 1 to 6..$1.49
26 G 4510—For Boys. SIZES: 10 to 13½......$1.29

Men's Heavy All Rubber Arctic

SPECIAL $1.79

We're saving you money on this all black rubber one-buckle Arctic. When the ground is wet or frozen they'll keep your feet perfectly dry and comfortable. Heavy, plain edge soles and heels. For wide toe, low heel shoes. Order one size larger than shoe. Shipping weight, 3 pounds 6 ounces.
SIZES: 6 to 13. No half sizes. State size wanted.
26 G 4475..................... $1.79

Men's and Boys' 2-Buckle Arctic

 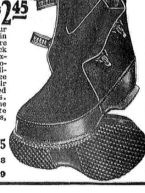

You're Sure to Save Here $2.45

In cold, wet and slush your feet will be warm and dry in these Arctics. The uppers are strong, closely woven black cashmerette in the full excluder style giving more protection and warmth than ordinary arctics. They are fleece lined which adds to their warmth. Strong, corrugated rubber soles and heels. Wide toe, low heel. Order one size larger than shoe. State size wanted. Ship. wt.: Men's, 2 lbs. 8 oz.; boy's, 2 lbs. 4 oz.
26 G 4420—For Men. SIZES: 6 to 12. No half sizes.....$2.45
26 G 4425—For Boys. SIZES: 1 to 6..... 1.98
26 G 4435—For Boys. SIZES: 10 to 13½.. 1.89

Absolute Storm Protection

Chicago Style Police Coat — $7 85

Gives satisfactory protection in wet and stormy weather. Black rubber with double cape over back, front and shoulders. One inside pocket; also billy pocket. Badge loops in front. Seams are lapped, cemented and vulcanized. Length, about 50 inches.

EVEN SIZES: Chest 36, 38, 40, 42, 44, 46, 48 inches. State chest measure. Read "How to Measure" on Page 238. Shipping weight, 5 pounds.
42 G 5455—Black only...........$7.85

Universal Style Fireman's Coat — $6 49 — 46 Inch

Our 42 G 5449 is durable rubber coated material. For a garment of extra quality and length, we recommend 42 G 5447. Double coating of rubber. Seams cemented and vulcanized.
EVEN SIZES: Chest 36 to 48 inches. State chest measure. Read "How to Measure" on Page 238. Ship. wt., 7 lbs. 12 oz.
42 G 5447—Black only...............$7.85
Extra quality; 48-inch length.
42 G 5449—Good quality; 46-inch length. Black only.................6.49

Extra Quality Black Rubber — $4 88

Coat of dull finished black gum rubber lined with white sheeting. Corduroy tipped collar. Cape over outside of back; ventilation eyelets underneath. Lapped, cemented and vulcanized seams. Average length, 48 inches.
EVEN SIZES: Chest 36 to 48 inches. State chest measure. Read "How to Measure" on Page 238. Ship. wt., 4 lbs. 2 oz.
42 G 5425—Black only...............$4.88

Sou'wester Hat to Match
SIZES: 6¾ to 7¾. State size. Read "How to Measure" on Page 248. Ship. wt., 6 oz.
42 G 5401—Black only...............69¢

Exceptional Value Here — $3 69

Choose this durable, black rubber Coat for general wear. White Sheeting lined. Wide lapped, cemented and vulcanized seams. Average length, 48 inches.
EVEN SIZES: Chest 36 to 48 inches. State chest measure. Read "How to Measure" on Page 238. Shipping weight, 4 pounds.
42 G 5421—Black only...............$3.69

Water-Proof Cape Cap to Match
SIZES: 6¾ to 7¾. State size. Read "How to Measure" on Page 248. Ship. wt., 10 oz.
42 G 5409—Black only...............95¢

Black Rubber Leggings — $1 75

Thoroughly waterproof. Fine for washing automobiles and wagons or for wear in dairies and creameries —they'll keep your legs dry and protect your clothing. Straps at bottom fit under sole of shoe and those at top fasten to adjustable belt at waist. Outside length about 32 inches. Shipping weight, 1 pound 3 ounces.
42 G 5413—Black only $1.75

Cape Ann Slicker Hat — 69¢

Our best water-proof slicker Hat. Heavy weight flexible oiled material which will not crack. Domet flannel lining; adjustable chin strap.
SIZES: 6¾ to 7½. State size. Read "How to Measure" on Page 248. Shipping weight, 9 ounces.
42 G 5517—Black only.69¢

Water-Proof Oil Dressing — 27¢

This protective liquid a mighty big seller! Especially prepared for water-proofing and re-coating oiled clothing, slickers, horse and wagon covers or other fabrics. Contents, one pint. Shipping weight, per can, 1 pound 8 ounces.
42 G 5501—Black.
42 G 5505—Yellow.
Per can....................27¢

Oiled Slicker Hat — 48¢

A big value! Brim is double thickness, moderately stiff.
SIZES: 6¾ to 7½. State size. Read "How to Measure" Page 248. Ship. wt., 6 ounces.
42 G 5509—Black.
42 G 5513—Yellow.
Each.....................48¢

Double Coated Rubber Apron — $1 68

Gives that needed clothes protection for work around cars and machinery. Heavy weight black rubber, double coated on heavy weight jean —it wears well. Very serviceable too, for men who work around liquids. A big value, men!
Size, 34 by 48 inches. Shipping weight, 2 pounds.
42 G 5417—Black only....$1.68

$1 79 Each Garment

$2 85 Each Garment

Made Extra Long for Extra Protection — $3 69

In rainy, windy and all kinds of disagreeable weather you'll appreciate its complete protection. There's a double thickness of oiled slicker cloth throughout the entire garment. It's the kind of coat you need when you must be out in the rain for hours.
Popular storm fly front to waistline. Lined collar and storm tab. Made extra roomy for greater working comfort. Wristlets in sleeves keep out rain. Our price is exceptionally low. Average length, 56 inches.
SIZES: Chest 36, 38, 40, 42, 44, 46, 48 inches. State chest measure. Read "How to Measure" on Page 238. Shipping weight, each, 5 pounds 2 ounces.
42 G 5569—Black.
42 G 5573—Yellow. Each..$3.69

Black or Yellow Jacket or Overalls

For long wear and dependable service they're hard to equal at this low price. Overalls are apron style with large bib and attached suspenders. Jacket about 30 inches long. Serviceable storm fly front. Double thickness oiled slicker sheeting gives double protection. Greater value than you'd expect for this money.
SIZES: Chest 36, 38, 40, 42, 44, 46, 48 inches. Waist 30, 32, 34, 36, 38, 40, 42, 44 inches. State chest and waist measure. Read "How to Measure" on Page 238. Ship. wt., each, 3 lbs.
Overalls
42 G 5521—Black.
42 G 5525—Yellow. Each..$1.79
Jacket
42 G 5537—Black.
42 G 5541—Yellow. Each..1.79

Extra Quality Oiled Slicker, Overalls or Jacket

Overalls are apron style; have double thickness of material throughout with patches at knee and double seat. Adjustable suspenders. Jacket has triple thickness of fabric in front, back and shoulders; corduroy collar; wristlets in sleeves; patches on elbows. Average length of jacket, about 30 inches.
SIZES: Chest 36, 38, 40, 42, 44, 46, 48 inches. Waist 30, 32, 34, 36, 38, 40, 42, 44 inches. State chest and waist measure. Read "How to Measure" on Page 238. Ship. wt., each, 3 lbs.
Jacket
42 G 5561—Black only.
Overalls
42 G 5565—Black only.
Each garment.........$2.85

Pommel Slicker Riding Coat — $4 19

The unusual value has made big sales for this Slicker Coat during the past year. Owners tell us they wouldn't part with theirs. Extra long garment with double thickness of oiled fabric. Can be buttoned up around the legs and has extension front and gusset back which cover saddle completely—features liked by men who ride. Also has a take-up button in skirt which quickly converts it into a walking garment. Average length, about 58 inches.
SIZES: Chest 36, 38, 40, 42, 44, 46, 48 inches. State chest measure. Read "How to Measure" on Page 238. Shipping weight, 6 pounds.
42 G 5597—Black.
42 G 5599—Olive drab.
Each...........$4.19

Our Very Best Black Slicker — $5 19

They're made especially for you men who demand the strongest, longest wearing best quality oil Slicker made. They'll outwear two ordinary slickers—proving that the best is always the least expensive in the end. Deservingly popular for besides being extra roomy and of highest quality the price is exceedingly low. Double and triple thickness of sheeting throughout. Storm fly front. Epaulets on shoulders. Outside patch on front of sleeves. Wristlets in sleeves.
You save by ordering here. Average length, about 56 inches.
SIZES: Chest 36, 38, 40, 42, 44, 46, 48 inches. State chest measure. Read "How to Measure" on Page 238. Shipping weight, 6 pounds 2 ounces.
42 G 5589—Black only...........$5.19

RAINCOATS
Style Calls for Gay Colors to Brighten Dull Days

Popular Oil Skin Slicker
Women's and Girls' Sizes

10 G 922 Practical, sturdy and positively rain-proof—three reasons why you may select with confidence this inexpensive raincoat. Roomy enough to wear over another wrap. Notice the very large flap pockets. Smart little leather strap to adjust the snug corduroy lined collar.

WOMEN'S SIZES: 32, 34, 36, 38, 40, 42 and 44-inch bust; length, about 46 and 48 inches. State size wanted. Ship. wt., 3 lbs.
10 G 922—Olive green.
10 G 924—Yellow.
10 G 926—Red. $3.69

GIRLS' SIZES: 6, 8, 10, 12 and 14 years. Length, 30, 33, 39, 41, 43 in. State size. Ship. wt., 2 lbs.
10 G 928—Olive green.
10 G 936—Yellow.
10 G 938—Red. $2.98

Fine Quality Leatheroid Raincoat

10 G 956 Fine, smooth Leatheroid, heavier than leatherette. Will neither spot nor crack. All seams cemented and reinforced. Corduroy lined strap collar. Flap Patched pockets. Button tab cuffs.

MISSES' AND WOMEN'S SIZES: 14, 16, 18, 20 yrs.; 32, 34, 36, 38, 40, 42 and 44 bust; length, 46 and 48 in. State size. Ship. wt., 2 lbs. 12 oz.
10 G 956—Leather brown.
10 G 958—Green.
10 G 960—Light navy blue.
10 G 962—Red. $3.98

EXTRA SIZES: 39, 41, 43, 45, 47, 49, 51 and 53 bust; length, about 48 inches. State size wanted. Shipping weight, 3 lbs. 4 oz.
10 G 964—Leather brown.
10 G 966—Green.
10 G 968—Light navy blue.
10 G 970—Red. $4.95

10 G 922 Oil Slickers $3.69 Women's Size
Girls' Sizes 10 G 928 $2.98

The Leatherette Trench Coat

10 G 940 The raincoat now becomes a part of the smart wardrobe. Flashing new shades, mannishly stunning of line, and essentially a waterproof protection. This swagger Trench Coat of soft pliable Leatherette will neither spot nor crack. All seams fully cemented. A double breasted notch collar model, adjustable belt and bellows pockets. The stitched suede back leatherette is a heavier coat for more severe weather.

MISSES' AND WOMEN'S SIZES: 14, 16, 18, 20 years; 32, 34, 36, 38, 40, 42 and 44 bust; length, 44 and 48 inches. State size. Ship. wt., 4 lbs. 4 oz.

Leatherette	Suede Back
10 G 940—French blue.	10 G 948—French blue.
10 G 942—Green.	10 G 952—Green.
10 G 944—Leather.	10 G 954—Leather.
10 G 946—Black. $6.49	10 G 958—Black. $6.98

10 G 940 Leatherette Trench Coat $6.49

Extra Sizes Also

Serviceable Hood Cape

Red Riding Hood's Cape was never so securely rain-proofed. Roomy Cape—with attached elastic drawn hood gayly faced with plaid. Sheltering arm vents.
Ages, years........ 6 8 10 12 14
Length, inches..... 30 33 39 41 43
State size wanted. Ship. wt., 1 lb.

Rubber Surface Fabric
10 G 930—Red.
10 G 932—Blue.
10 G 934—Green.
10 G 961—Pansy. $1.49

Bombazine
10 G 825—Navy blue.
10 G 839—Tan. $1.00

$1.49

Leatheroid Coat, Cap

Even the keen dampness will hardly be felt' in this smooth, soft leatheroid Raincoat. Little Billie Burke hat to match, snugly fitted with elastic at back. Corduroy faced collar with leather strap to adjust it. Raglan sleeves; big flap pockets; regulation sleeve tabs. All seams fully cemented. Umbrella not included.
Ages, years........ 6 8 10 12
Length, inches..... 30 33 39 41 43
State size wanted. Shipping wt., 2 lbs.
10 G 980—Blue.
10 G 982—Red.
10 G 984—Green.
10 G 990—Leather. $3.79

$3.79

Complete Rainy Day Outfit

Such a complete outfit, she will long for lots of rainy schooldays. The sparkling Rubber Surface Fabric of this serviceable Coat is lovely in any of its fashionable shades. Everything she needs; elastic fitted cap; strap carryall bag, with rain-proof flaps.
Ages, years........ 6 8 10 12 14
Length, inches..... 30 33 39 41 43
State size wanted. Shipping weight, 1 lb. 4 oz.
10 G 977—Red.
10 G 979—Blue.
10 G 981—Green.
10 G 983—Pansy. $3.49

$3.49

Extra Sizes Also

Excellent Style—Rich Colors—Rain-Proof

Looks like a frosted silk—this inexpensive Rubber Surface Fabric. Comes in rich mellow tones. Fashion adopts it for style, color, and makes it superior to its mere rain-proof possibilities. Corduroy lined collar with adjustable strap. Large flap pockets.

MISSES' AND WOMEN'S SIZES: 14, 16, 18, 20 years; 32, 34, 36, 38, 40, 42 and 44 bust; length, 46 and 48 in. State size wanted. Ship. wt., 1 lb. 4 oz.
10 G 901—Red.
10 G 903—Blue.
10 G 905—Green.
10 G 963—Pansy. $2.75

EXTRA SIZES: 39, 41, 43, 45, 47, 49, 51, 53 bust; length, about 48 inches. State size wanted. Shipping weight, 1 lb. 12 ounces.
10 G 972—Red.
10 G 974—Blue.
10 G 976—Green.
10 G 978—Pansy. $3.98

$2.75

Stunning Leatherette Model—Hat to Match

You could not find a more sensible choice—this Leatherette Raincoat which will not spot or crack. A style coat as well, with its Military collar, corduroy lined and strap adjusted; raglan sleeves; big flap pockets and sportive sleeve bands. Stunning hat to match—sold separately.

MISSES' AND WOMEN'S SIZES: 14, 16, 18, 20 years; 32, 34, 36, 38, 40, 42 and 44 inches; length, 46 and 48 inches. State size wanted. Ship. wt., 3 lbs. 8 oz.

Leatherette Coat	Hat to Match
10 G 992—French blue.	10 G 892—French blue.
10 G 994—Black.	10 G 894—Black.
10 G 996—Red.	10 G 896—Red.
10 G 998—Green. $5.49	10 G 898—Green. $1.29

10 G 956 $3.98

Extra Sizes Also

$5.49

Outing and Sports Wear

Blazer All Wool 15 G 38 $3.49

Blazer Khaki Jean 15 G 37 $1.98

Tweed Knickers 15 G 833 $2.59

Khaki Knickers 15 G 611 95¢

Shirt Broadcloth 15 G 10 $1.00

Girl's Plaid Lumber Jacket
All Wool Plaid, well made. Buttoned cuffs with plackets. Convertible collar. Pockets. GIRLS' SIZES: 7, 8, 10, 12, 14 years. State size. Read "How to Order" on Page 51. Shipping weight, 1 pound 8 ounces.
15 G 38—Medium blue and red plaid.
15 G 40—Rust and brown plaid. $3.49

All Wool Tweed Knickers
Warm and sturdy! Just the thing for active outdoor sports! Has mannish cut, well tailored with swagger hip closing. Pockets and sport belt.
GIRLS' SIZES: 7, 8, 10, 12, 14 years; 25, 26, 27, 28 and 29 inches waist. State size. Read "How to Order" on Page 51. Ship. wt., 1 lb. 4 oz.
15 G 833—Gray mixture.
15 G 835—Tan mixture. $2.59

Khaki Jean Blazer for Girls
Great fun for outdoor girls to wear this sporty Blouse of good quality Khaki! Knitted cotton hip band. Comfortable and serviceable. Patch pockets. Button cuffs.
GIRLS' SIZES: 7, 8, 10, 12, 14 years. State size wanted. Read "How to Order" on Page 51. Shipping weight, 12 ounces.
15 G 37—Khaki Jean. $1.98

Khaki Jean Cloth Knickers
They'll save other clothes! Reinforced for hard wear. Pocket, belt, two-button cuff.
GIRLS' SIZES: 7, 8, 10, 12, 14 years; 25, 26, 27, 28 and 29 inches waist. State size wanted. Read "How to Order" on Page 51. Shipping weight, 10 ounces.
15 G 611—Khaki tan only. 95¢

Serviceable Broadcloth Shirt Waist
Every sportswoman will admire this Shirt, so trimly tailored. Long sleeves, buttoned cuffs; pockets, knitted tie. Wears well!
WOMEN'S AND MISSES' SIZES: 34, 36, 38, 40, 42, 44-inch bust. 16, 18, 20, 22 years. State size. Read "How to Order" on Page 51. Shipping weight, 12 ounces.
15 G 10—White.
15 G 12—Tan. $1.00

Carefully Tailored Riding Breeches
In khaki, corduroy or whipcord. Two side openings, slot pockets, reinforced seat. Detachable belt and knee lacing.
MISSES' AND WOMEN'S SIZES: 24 to 34 inches waist. State size. Read "How to Order" on Page 51. Ship. wt., 1 lb. 12 oz.
10 G 986—Brown corduroy. $2.95
10 G 988—Tan whipcord.
10 G 837—Khaki tan. $1.59

Blazer All Wool 15 G 34 $3.98

Khaki Shirt Regular Size 15 G 219 95¢ **Extra Sizes** $1.19

Riding Breeches Corduroy or Whipcord 10 G 986 $2.95 **Khaki** $1.59

10 G 900 Khaki or Cotton Tweed 95¢ **Extra Sizes** $1.19

10 G 908 All Wool Tweed Corduroy or Whipcord $2.89 **Wool Mixed Tweed** $1.89 **For Extra Sizes See Descriptions**

2 Piece Khaki Jean 15 G 700 $1.89

10 G 402 Genuine Leather $14.95

Tomboy Outfit Sturdy and Serviceable
Little girls who play as hard as little boys will enjoy this sturdy two-piece Play Suit that will stand hard wear! The well tailored shirt has long sleeves with buttoned cuffs, a convertible collar to be worn opened or closed, and a convenient patch pocket. The skirt is reinforced with well made gores that will give extra wear. It has a slot hip pocket and opens at side. A fancy belt, finished with leather ends and a buckle, is run through loops of Khaki at the waist.
GIRLS' SIZES: 7, 8, 10, 12, 14 years; 25, 26, 27, 28 and 30 inches waist. Read "How to Order" on Page 51. State size wanted. Shipping weight, 1 pound.
15 G 700—Khaki Jean $1.89

All Wool Plaid Blazer
As sporty and well tailored as any sports lover could desire—as comfortably warm as All Wool should be—and strong enough for hard rough treatment! Ideal for sports wear—that's why it's such a favorite. Convertible plain collar and patch pocket tops. The cuffs and waistband are wool knitted.
WOMEN'S AND MISSES' SIZES: 34, 36, 38, 40, 42, 44 inch bust. 16, 18, 20, 22 years. State size. Read "How to Order" on Page 51. Ship. wt., 1 lb. 10 oz.
15 G 34—Tan, brown or gray plaid.
15 G 36—Brick and black plaid. $3.98

Khaki or Cotton Tweed Knickers
Women everywhere choose Knickers for camping, and all rough outdoor wear, because they're so wonderfully practical. Cut full to give ample room for freedom. Two slot pockets, side openings and buttoned knee closing.
MISSES' AND WOMEN'S SIZES: 24 to 34 inches waist. State size wanted. Read "How to Order" on Page 51. Shipping weight, 1 pound.
10 G 900—Khaki tan.
10 G 902—Gray tweed. 95¢
EXTRA SIZES: 35 to 41 inches waist. State size wanted. Read "How to Order" on Page 51. Shipping weight, 1 pound 4 ounces.
10 G 904—Khaki tan.
10 G 906—Gray tweed. $1.19

Khaki Cloth Sport Shirt
Because it will endure the strain, this strong Shirt is popular for the most energetic sports! Mannish collar, black sateen tie, buttoned cuffs and patch pocket.
MISSES' AND MISSES' SIZES: 34, 36, 38, 40, 42, 44-inch bust. 16, 18, 20, 22 years. State size wanted. Read "How to Order" on Page 51. Ship. wt., 14 oz.
15 G 219—Khaki tan only. 95¢
EXTRA SIZES: 46 to 54 inches bust. State size. Read "How to Order" on Page 51. Ship. wt., 16 oz.
15 G 221—Khaki tan only. $1.19

Tweed, Corduroy or Whipcord Knickers
A big value! Excellent Knickers cut full and roomy. Two slot pockets and buttoned side openings. Knee closing with button. Detachable belt.
MISSES' AND WOMEN'S SIZES: 24 to 34 inches waist. State size wanted. Read "How to Order" on Page 51. Shipping weight, 1 pound 12 ounces.
All Wool Tweed
10 G 908—Gray tweed. $2.89
10 G 910—Tan tweed.
Wool Mixed Tweed
10 G 912—Gray. $1.89
10 G 914—Tan.
Corduroy
10 G 916—Brown. $2.89
Whipcord
10 G 918—Tan.
EXTRA SIZES: 35 to 41 inches waist. State size wanted. Read "How to Order" on Page 51. Shipping weight, 2 lbs. 5 ozs.
10 G 920—Gray Wool Mixed Tweed. $2.39

Gaily Colored Jacket
The smart thing to wear for cold or stormy weather—this jacket in red, blue or green Genuine Leather—lined with All Wool Plaid for additional warmth! Two roomy side pockets fastened with button closed flaps. Adjustable tabs on the sleeves are a protection against bad weather. An all around adjustable belt and snappy yoke at back give the coat a fine finish. Length about 30 inches.
MISSES' AND WOMEN'S SIZES: 14 to 20 years; 32 to 44 inches bust. State size wanted. Read "How to Order" on Page 51. Ship. wt., 3 lbs.
10 G 402—Red.
10 G 404—Blue.
10 G 406—Green. $14.95

Colorful and Stylish
for Rain or Shine

Extra Fine All Silk
With Brass Frame
$5.49

520 G 803—COLORS: Navy blue; black; red; green; purple. State color wanted.

Rich color tones are brought to the costume by the glowing silk of these Umbrellas! The color enameled on the handle and the fine silk wrist cord matches the silk. In lovely contrast are the bright brass rod and hollow turned brass frame. The handle has the color and transparency of amber—rib tips and stub end match. 16-ribbed, of course—all the newer umbrellas insist on that. And unusually chubby—only 23½ inches. Spread, 34¼ inches. Shipping weight, 2 pounds.

All Silk in Rich Colors
Our Great Special
$3.95

520 G 805—COLORS: Navy blue; purple; black; green; red. State color.

All silk in lovely vivid colors covers this finely made Umbrella; and the same color is carried out in the silk wrist cord and in the enameled amber-like handle. The handle itself has matching rib tips and end. Black paragon 10-rib steel frame, well made and strong. And the price is amazingly low. Stub size—about 24 inches; spread, about 35 inches. Shipping weight, 2 pounds.

Modish 16-Rib Frame
All Silk Umbrella
$4.69

520 G 804—COLORS: Navy blue; purple; black; green; red. State color.

Perfect accord of color is achieved in this Umbrella with handle enamel-trimmed in colors to match the satin edged silk covering. The heavy silk wrist cord, arranged in the new way is in the same color. Sunny amber-like handle with matching rib tips and end. Up-to-the-minute 16 ribbed construction. Black paragon steel frame. A real "find" at only $4.69. Stub length, about 23 inches; 34¼-inch spread. Shipping weight, 2 pounds.

Our Finest Rich All Silk 16-Rib Umbrella
$7.95

Stubby 23-Inch Length

Handle of Striking Beauty

520 G 800—COLORS: Navy blue; red; black; green; purple. State color wanted.

Beautiful enough and fine enough to carry with the smartest costume. Rich, striking colors for the gay note that Fashion demands. Unusually lovely amber-like handle, rib tips and end—all to match—of rich amber color with silvery, pearlized finish. Special Handikup feature holds tips neatly in place when closed.

The extra heavy silk taffeta, with twin border stripes of satin, has matching color enameled on the handle; the same color is repeated in the flat braided silk wrist cord. Brass rod and beautifully made 16-rib brass hollow turned frame make a sunny contrast against the bright silk covering and reveal it as the newest of umbrellas. Short stubby size—only about 23 inches—to hang on the wrist; just right to slip into your suitcase. Has 34-inch spread in popular new semi-flat shape. A charming gift—ultra smart, extra fine. Ship. wt., 2 pounds.

Colorful Heavy All Silk
Gayly Decorated Handle
$6.98

520 G 801—COLORS: Navy blue; red; black; green; purple. State color wanted.

A smart costume note in radiant colors for rain or shine! Even the handle is rich in appearance with its colored carvings and matching Handikup that holds tips trigly when umbrella is closed. The color of the handle is repeated in stub end, rib tips and silk wrist cord—all to match the heavy satin edged taffeta covering. Fine construction—brass rod and hollow turned 16-rib brass frame. Popular stub length—about 23 inches—smart to carry; easy to pack in a suitcase. Spread, 34½ inches. Shipping weight, 2 pounds.

Fine All Silk
With Handikup
$4.98

520 G 802—COLORS: Navy blue; red; black; green; purple. State color wanted.

A color to match the fine satin-edged silk covering is enameled on the clear amber-like handle to bring bright beauty to this Umbrella. Special Handikup feature—the lower part of the handle forms the Handikup—usually found only on most expensive models. The silk wrist cord also repeats the color of the silk. Black paragon steel frame in the popular 10-rib style. Amber trim on rib tips and stub end. In the short, chubby size—about 23¾ inches long. 35½-inch spread. A dress accessory—smart, colorful, practical! Shipping weight, 2 pounds.

Bradford Cloth Rich Colors
Amber Trim
$2.48

520 G 816—COLORS: Navy blue; red; black; green; purple. State color.

A finely imported cotton taffeta which looks much like silk but is stronger and more serviceable—is used for this practical, good-looking Umbrella. Very strong 10-rib black paragon steel frame with amber color tips and end. The trimming on the amber-like handle and the cord loop matches the cover. Well made—well finished—rain-proof! Stub length, about 24 inches. Spread, about 36½ inches. Shipping weight, 2 pounds.

Fine Cotton Taffeta Paragon Steel Frame
$1.69

520 G 814—COLORS: Navy blue; red; black; green; purple. State color.

Here's proof of Ward's great values! Good quality cotton taffeta in deep, rich colors covers a 10-rib black paragon steel frame. The amber-like handle is trimmed in color to match the taffeta and has a matching cord loop. Amber color trim. Length, about 24 inches. Spread, about 36 inches. Shipping weight, 2 pounds.

Silky Bradford Cloth 16 Ribs—Brass Rod
$3.48

520 G 818—COLORS: Navy blue; red; black; green; purple. State color wanted.

A smart dress accessory! Fine, lustrous Bradford cloth—that famous long-wearing fabric which looks so much like silk—is in rich colors to match the wrist cord, wood bead and the enamel on the handle. The brass rod and hollow-turned brass frame are in sunny contrast. Sunfast; rain-proof. Length, about 24 inches; spread, about 34½ inches. Shipping weight, 2 pounds.

16-Rib—Paragon Frame
Amber Color Trim
$2.85

520 G 817—COLORS: Navy blue; red; black; green; purple. State color.

All the features of the newest Umbrellas are included in this one of extra fine silky finish cotton taffeta, finished with a 2-inch fancy border. It has the smart 16-rib black paragon steel frame with amber color trim; the new 23-inch stub size; and a handle and cord colored to match the cover. A fine umbrella, made to stand hard wear. Rain-proof. Spread, 35 inches. Prepare now for rainy day! Shipping weight, 2 pounds.

Cotton Taffeta
Well Made—Rain-Proof
$1.98

520 G 815—COLORS: Navy blue; red; black; green; purple. State color wanted.

Richly colored, lustrous cotton taffeta Umbrella with carved handle, wrist cord and bead tip all in matching color. The 10-rib black paragon steel frame has amber-color trim. A thoroughly well-made, rain-proof umbrella. Length, about 25½ inches; spread, about 36 inches. Ship. wt., 2 pounds.

Child's Umbrella
In Gay Colors
$1.25

520 G 809—COLORS: Red; blue; green. State color.

Children love pretty colors—they'll be delighted with this little 22-inch umbrella of silky finish colored cotton taffeta. It's strong, too, with a seven-rib black paragon steel frame. The amber-like handle has a bead cord to make it easier to carry. Amber trim. An umbrella that will please any child. And it's just as practical as it is pretty. Spread, when open, about 30½ inches. Shipping weight, 1 pound 8 ounces.

Rain-Proof Cotton Taffeta
Ⓐ $1.85

520 G 810—Black only. Men's serviceable rainproof Umbrella of good quality cotton taffeta. Strong 10-rib black paragon steel frame. Prince of Wales style handle with carved end. Unusually practical—at a very low price! Length, about 34 inches. Spread, about 42 inches. Ship. wt., 2 lbs. 8 oz.

Bradford Cloth Hardwood Handle
Ⓑ $2.39

520 G 811—Black only. Men's rain-proof Umbrella of fine quality mercerized cotton taffeta over a strong 10-rib black paragon steel frame. Prince of Wales style hardwood handle. Strongly made and well finished. Length, about 34 inches. Spread, about 41 inches. Shipping weight, 2 pound 8 ounces.

Silk and Cotton Malacca Handle
Ⓒ $5.48

520 G 813—Black only. Our finest Umbrella for Men! Heavy, imported half silk and half cotton taffeta, beautifully silky and lustrous, covers this strong well-made 10-rib paragon steel frame. Tape edge. Beautiful Malacca handle. Silk case. Length, about 34 inches; spread about 40½ inches. Ship. wt., 2 pounds 8 ounces.

Extra Fine Quality Mercerized Cotton
Ⓓ $2.85

520 G 812—Black only. This imported cotton taffeta is so fine and highly mercerized that it looks almost like silk. Absolutely rain-proof—the manufacturer calls it "wear-proof." Strong 10-rib paragon steel frame. Tape edge. Hardwood handle. Length, about 34 inches. Spread, about 40½ inches. Shipping weight, 2 pounds 8 ounces.

Women's Children's Men's
Three Super Values
For All the Family ## 98¢ Each

You'll wonder how these good practical Umbrellas can be sold at this amazingly low price! It is possible only because of Ward's enormous purchasing power. They have strong 7-rib black paragon steel frames covered with serviceable black cotton taffeta with a tape edge. The women's and children's umbrellas have fancy handles; the men's is the bent Prince of Wales style. All are well made and well finished—very fine values. Shipping weight, 2 pounds.

For Women
520 G 806—Black only.
Length 31 in.
Spread 39 in.
Each... 98¢

For Children
520 G 808—Black only.
Length 24½ in.
Spread 31 in.
Each... 98¢

For Men
520 G 807—Black only.
Length 34 in.
Spread 39 in.
Each... 98¢

The Mode in Blouses
for Fall and Winter

15 G 14
All Silk Ponqee
$3.69

15 G 24
Cotton Flannel
98¢

(Regular Sizes) $2.49   Extra Sizes $2.95

15 G 35 Mercerized Broadcloth $1.00

15 G 67 Mercerized Broadcloth $1.00

All Silk Pongee
Sizes 40 to 54

15 G 14 There is no substitute for All Silk Pongee for service and good looks. If you choose this for your good blouse, you may be confident that it will retain its soft silken beauty throughout its long life. For Pongee is well known to be laundry-proof and always lives up to its reputation.

The collar is finished with a string tie of self material. Three rows of filet patterned Val lace on each side of a row of sparkling pearl buttons make the simulated vestee, and the same lace trims the turnback cuffs. Equally suitable for small and large sizes.

REGULAR AND EXTRA SIZES: 40, 42, 44, 46, 48, 50, 52, 54-inch bust. State bust measure. Read "How to Order" on Page 51. Ship. wt., 14 ounces.
15 G 14—Natural tan only.... $3.69

Good Quality Broadcloth
Vest Overblouse

15 G 35 The tailored woman's favorite! And no wonder, for its smart mannish lines, excellent cut and expert workmanship lend an enviable trimness. It is fashioned of a soft finish, good quality Broadcloth, with fancy collar and simulated pockets. Self belt buttons in back. Wide tailored cuffs button in the approved masculine manner.
WOMEN'S AND MISSES' SIZES: 32, 34, 36, 38, 40, 42, 44-inch bust. State bust measure. Read "How to Order" on Page 51. Shipping weight, 14 ounces.
15 G 35—White.
15 G 73—Tan. $1.00

Dressy Brocaded Costume Blouse
Trimmed With Braid and Novelty Buttons

15 G 16 The silky texture and luster of this pretty Brocaded Rayon and Cotton makes a costume Blouse that is quite as attractive as pure silk and far less expensive. Plain Rayon is used for the bib vestee and bands on collar and cuffs. Trimmed with braid and fancy metal buttons. Black ribbon tie. Wide hip band closes at one side.
REGULAR SIZES: 34, 36, 38, 40, 42, 44-inch bust. State bust measure. Read "How to Order" on Page 51. Shipping weight, 14 ounces.
15 G 16—Navy blue.
15 G 18—Tan. $2.49
EXTRA SIZES: 46, 48, 50, 52, 54-inch bust. State bust measure. Read "How to Order" on Page 51. Shipping weight, 1 pound.
15 G 20—Navy blue.
15 G 22—Tan. $2.95

Tailored Blouse
Fine for Service

15 G 67 There are months of fine service ahead for this tailored Overblouse of good quality Broadcloth. The well-fitting mannish collar, cuffs and patch pocket have true, tailor-made dash that is further emphasized by the knit tie. Slightly shirred front and smooth fitting shoulders. Fastened with pearl buttons.
WOMEN'S AND MISSES' SIZES: 34, 36, 38, 40, 42, 44-inch bust. State bust measure. Read "How to Order" on Page 51. Shipping weight, 14 ounces.
15 G 67—White.
15 G 71—Tan. $1.00

Outdoor Shirt
Cotton Flannel

15 G 24 The outdoor woman grows enthusiastic over this Sports Shirt to play in and work in, for it is an all around utility style that always looks well. This is the type of shirt that the sports woman chooses for camping and motoring. It keeps her comfortably warm and is slow to show soil. Of a good quality Cotton Flannel with smart tailored collar, turned back cuffs and convenient patch pocket. Neatly finished with taped strings at waistline. A knitted tie is included with the blouse. So much comfort and service for the small sum of 98¢!
WOMEN'S AND MISSES' SIZES: 34, 36, 38, 40, 42, 44-inch bust. State bust measure. Read "How to Order" on Page 51. Ship. wt., 8 oz.
15 G 24—Gray only. 98¢

15 G 43 Lonsdale Jean $1.19

15 G 102 Khaki Jean $1.00

15 G 106 Lonsdale Jean 98¢

15 G 741 Khaki Jean $1.29

15 G 747 Khaki 94¢

One-Piece Khaki Play Suit
Drop-Seat Back

15 G 741 Unhampered play hours are in store for the girl who wears this sturdy, almost soil-proof Khaki Play Suit. So easy to slip into, and roomy everywhere. Buttons conveniently down the front, has roomy set-in belt, long sleeves, athletic collar and snappy patch pocket. The bloomers are laid in trim plaits over the trim hips, gathered into elastic at knees, and the drop-seat back buttons neatly over the blouse.
GIRLS' SIZES: 7, 8, 10, 12, 14 years; 25, 26, 27, 28, 29-inch waist. State size. Read "How to Order" on Page 63. Shipping weight, 14 ounces.
15 G 741—Khaki tan only.. $1.29

Best Quality Middy
Taped in Regulation Style

15 G 43 Middy of famous white Lonsdale Jean, with navy blue collar and cuffs taped in regulation style, and a beautiful red and blue emblem on the left sleeve. Jaunty black tie. Wide hipband. Also in solid white.
GIRLS' AND MISSES' SIZES: 7, 8, 10, 12, 14, 16, 18, 20, 22 years. State size. Read "How to Order" on Page 51. Shipping weight, 12 ounces.
15 G 43—White with blue collar and cuffs.
15 G 45—Solid White. $1.19

White Lonsdale Jean
Very Durable for School Wear

15 G 106 All White Middy Blouse in girls' and misses' sizes. Of nationally known Lonsdale Jean that she can use and use without wearing it out. Ideal to wear for school and athletic meets, when youthful vanity is almost as important as the game. Slot pocket, two-button cuffs. Black tie.
GIRLS' AND MISSES' SIZES: 7, 8, 10, 12, 14, 16, 18, 20, 22 years. State size. Read "How to Order" on Page 51. Shipping weight, 10 ounces.
15 G 106—White only. 98¢

Attractive Sports Middy
Practical Khaki Jean Cloth

15 G 102 Long woodland tramps, Indian summer outings—all the vigorous outdoor play of the Fall season calls for a sports middy like this of Khaki Jean in which the wearer can wholeheartedly participate in all the fun. Neat three-button hip band; two-button tailored cuffs. Black tie.
GIRLS' AND MISSES' SIZES: 7, 8, 10, 12, 14, 16, 18, 20, 22 years. State size. Read "How to Order" on Page 51. Shipping weight, 12 ounces.
15 G 102—Khaki Jean only. $1.00

Two-Piece Khaki Play Suit
Black Sateen Tie

15 G 747 What a glorious time the kiddies have, togged out in play clothes like this. Mother will welcome it, too, knowing that in both color and texture, Khaki will stand a lot of hard usage. The two-piece style is very practical, as a different blouse or other bloomers may be substituted when desired. Black tie slips under front tab. Double collar; stitched hip band. Full cut bloomers with elastic waistband and knees.
GIRLS' SIZES: 7, 8, 10, 12, 14 years. State size. Read "How to Order" on Page 63. Shipping weight, 14 ounces.
15 G 747—Khaki only. 94¢

15 G 740 All Wool Plaid $2.69

15 G 744 All Wool Serge $1.98

Sports Skirt
Colorful Plaid

15 G 740 A bright, colorful All Wool Plaid that children love so well is kilted all around in alternating knife and box plaits. The muslin waist, made detachable to simplify the problem of tubbing, buttons on to the smooth fitting band of the skirt. A splendid skirt to wear with middies or blazers.
GIRLS' SIZES: 7, 8, 10, 12, 14 years. State size wanted. Read "How to Order" on Page 63. Shipping weight, 1 pound 8 ounces.
15 G 740—Blue mixed.
15 G 742—Green mixed. $2.69

Plaited Skirt
Popular Navy Blue Serge

15 G 744 A very practical and economical Skirt for school wear! Nothing can take its place for wear with her numerous tub middies, and it is equally suitable with lumberjackets and sweaters for winter wear. All Wool Serge, generously plaited all around and with detachable muslin waist for easy laundering.
GIRLS' SIZES: 7, 8, 10, 12, 14 years. State size. Read "How to Order" on Page 63. Shipping weight, 1 pound 8 ounces.
15 G 744—Navy blue only. $1.98

Save Good Clothes

"Just What a Boy Needs" Writes V. F. Heidemann

This father who speaks so highly of these garments, lives in Brandt, S. Dakota. Playing rough and tumble won't hurt these Allovers. They're made for extra tough wear. A quality that surprises every mother who takes advantage of this remarkably low price. Choose from two equally strong fabrics; one a medium weight indigo blue denim; the other khaki cloth. Both carefully made; all seams triple stitched; all strain points bar-tacked. Drop seat style. Low priced beyond all expectations. SIZES: 3 to 8 years. State size. Ship. weight, each, 1 pound; 2 pairs, 2 pounds.
40 G 3946—Indigo blue denim. Each $ .85
40 G 3950—Tan khaki. 2 Pairs 1.59

85¢

Triple Sewed Seams

75¢

95¢

89¢ Double Knees
Great big grownup men's style Allovers for little boys. Strong and wear resistant; remarkably low priced.
Made of "Giant Hickory"—a medium weight cotton material that will wear and wear. Double knees and drop seat. They wash beautifully.
SIZES: 3 to 8 years. State size. Ship. wt., 1 lb. 1 oz.
40 G 3972—Blue striped.
40 G 3974—Brown striped.... 89¢

89¢ Strong Denim
Thoughtful mothers dress their youngsters in Allovers. These are especially strong—of 2:45 white back blue denim—a very sturdy material for the hard use happy youngsters give it. Its button front enables son to put garment on alone. Drop seat. Mothers take advantage of these savings.
SIZES: 3 to 8 yrs. State size. Ship. wt., 1 lb. 2 oz.
40 G 3922—Blue denim only.. 89¢

87¢ Double Duty
Little boys like yours can't "go through at the knees" in these Allovers for a long time. Double thickness of denim at knees gives this added protection. Double material at seat, too! Entire garment is fast color, indigo blue denim of medium weight. Cotton. Drop seat. Mothers everywhere will order these big values.
SIZES: 3 to 8 years. State size. Ship. wt., 1 lb.
40 G 3918—Blue denim only. 87¢

Ready for the Kickoff $3.45 →
"Signals: 40-G41-08." The ball is snapped and away he goes for a long end run and a touchdown. Healthy fun in this Football Outfit. Pants and shirt of strong duck. Helmet of smooth sheepskin. Imitation leather belt. Pants and helmet heavily padded. Football and stockings not included.
EVEN SIZES: 6 to 16 years. State size. Shipping weight, 3 pounds.
40 G 4108—Tan duck only..........$3.45

67¢

Double Knees ↑
Value unmatched! Labor savers for mothers and knee savers for sonny. Rough and tumble falls won't wear these All-overs through at knees as quick as in other garments because of double thickness of material. Of extra strong, light weight blue pin check material. Drop seat. Horn not included.
SIZES: 3 to 8 years. State size. Ship. wt., 13 oz.
40 G 3985—Blue pin check only...... 67¢

Real Value
Choice here of Stifel's blue and white drill, khaki drill or blue denim—all durable materials. Fast color trimmings. Drop seat. All seams double stitched.
SIZES: 2 to 8 years. State size. Ship. wt., 1 lb.
40 G 3912—Blue denim.
40 G 3916—Stifel's striped blue drill.
40 G 3920—Khaki drill. Each......... 75¢
Two colors or two of any one. 2 for $1.43

Two for One Price
Here's two pairs for the price others charge for one. Sturdy weight, strong construction, comfortable fit. One is blue and white Stifel's drill, the other a hard wearing blue denim. Both are medium weight and double stitched.
SIZES: 2 to 8 years. State size. Ship. wt., 2 pairs, 1 lb. 2 oz.
40 G 3966—Blue denim.
40 G 3968—Stifel's blue drill. 2 pairs 89¢

Heavy Weight
Extra heavy weight, better made, neatly trimmed Allovers. Choice of two materials; one a strong 2:20 white back denim, the other a good weight fast color khaki jean. Both have fast color blue jean cuffs, collar and trimming. Drop seat.
SIZES: 3 to 8 years. Ship. wt., 1 lb. 4 oz.
40 G 3987—Blue denim.
40 G 3993—Khaki jean. Each.............. 95¢

Dandy Gifts for Young America

$3.25

$3.89

"Black Pirut" Suit
Boys and girls wear this Pirut Outfit for playtime. Black sateen bloomers have elastic waistband and bottoms. Waist and sash black and orange striped cotton flannel. Genuine pirut hat with name Black Pirut. Oilcloth leggings with red leatherette flaps. Carved wood cutlass.
EVEN SIZES: 4 to 16 years. State size. Ship. wt., 2 lbs.
40 G 4106—Black Pirut outfit........... $3.25

Tom Mix Outfit
Of strong khaki, except chaps which are cotton flannel. Imitation leather plates on chest of shirt. Includes Wool felt Jr. Carlsbad western hat, bandanna, popgun, leather holster and belt, lariat and pin autographed by Tom Mix. All decorations fast color.
EVEN SIZES: 4 to 14 years. State size. Ship. wt., 3 lbs. 4 oz.
40 G 4142—Tan khaki only....$3.89

$2.88

Arrest Him!
A regular officer of the law—that's what son will say he is. Coat, long pants and cap are good grade Navy blue cotton drill. Coat trimmed with metal buttons. Equipment includes hat, shiny star, billy club, belt, toy pistol and holster.
EVEN SIZES: 4 to 14 years. State size. Shipping weight, 2 lbs. 14 oz.
40 G 4120—Navy blue only.......$2.88

$1.48

Bring on the Rodeo
A toss of the lariat and he's roped a wild horse. Mother will be pleased to see the many hours of happiness she gives son for such little expense. Although it's our lowest priced Cowboy Suit it's made very carefully. It's good cotton khaki. Included in outfit are shirt, long pants with imitation leather fringe, hat, red bandanna, lariat, pistol, holster and belt.
EVEN SIZES: 4 to 14 years. State size. Ship. wt., 2 lbs. 3 oz.
40 G 4100—Tan only.......$1.48

Go Gettem Cowboy
He'll be the star of the kiddies' wild west show in this Cowboy Suit. Cotton flannel shirt with large plaids of blue and green. Long cowboy pants of khaki drill. Two front pockets and trimmings down side of legs are genuine leather. Campaign hat with band of cotton flannel. Outfit includes lariat, large toy pistol, leather holster, belt and bandanna.
EVEN SIZES: 4 to 14 years. State size. Ship. wt., 2 lbs.
40 G 4116—Cowboy outfit....$2.49

40 G 4132 $1.97
40 G 4124 97¢

Heap Big Chief
"Whoopee! Me scare um pale face." We recommend the $1.97 outfit, our best Indian Suit. It's good weight tan khaki. Head dress has 12 highly colored feathers. The other suit is of lighter weight khaki. Also has colored trimmings and feather head dress. State size.
40 G 4132—EVEN SIZES: 4 to 14 years. Best quality. Tan only. Ship. wt., 1 pound 8 ounces....$1.97
40 G 4124—EVEN SIZES: 4 to 14 years. Good quality. Tan only. Ship. weight, 1 pound 4 ounces....97¢

Stylish, Warm Overgaiters for Men and Women

Ten-button black cloth Overgaiter for men. Fleece lined. No half sizes. Ship. wt., 6 oz. SIZES: 6 to 12.
27 G 5021 ....89¢

For Men
Men's stylish five-button Overgaiter in fawn color or black. Ship. wt., 4 oz. SIZES: 6 to 12. No half sizes. State size.
27G5161— Fawn color felt...$1.25
27G5160— Black cloth...75¢

Women's good quality black cloth ten-button Overgaiters. Ship. wt., 5 oz. SIZES: 3 to 8. No half sizes. State size.
27 G 5030 ....89¢

For Women
Black, Brown, Gray, Fawn
Women's fine quality ten-button Overgaiters with strap and buckle that fit snugly under arch. Well made, dressy and splendid values. Ship. wt., 5 oz. SIZES: 3 to 8. No half sizes. State size wanted.
27 G 5034—Black.
27 G 5043—Brown.
27 G 5039—Gray.
27 G 5041—Fawn.
Per pair.....$1.19

Women's and Children's Leggings

Order Overgaiters and Women's and Children's Leggings Same Size as Shoes

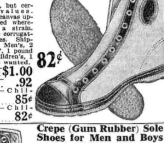

Ex- tend Above the Knee

Children's brown jersey cloth Leggings. Neat, snug fitting and warm. Reach above the knee. Priced to save. Ship. wt., 5 oz. SIZES: 4 to 10 years. No half sizes. State size.
27 G 5143.....65¢

Black jersey cloth Leggings, fleece lined. Button over the knee. Fit snugly. Shipping weight, 6 ounces. No half sizes. State size wanted.
27 G 5005—For Women. SIZES: 3 to 8. Per pair.....89¢
27 G 5010—For Girls. SIZES: 11 to 2. Per pair.....79¢
27 G 5015—For Children. SIZES: 3 to 10. Per pair.....65¢

For Basket-Ball or Everyday Wear

For Men, Boys, Children
Strong Rubber Soles
Low priced, but certainly good values. Strong white canvas uppers, reinforced wherever there's a strain. Durable crepe corrugated rubber soles. Shipping weights: Men's, 2 pounds; boys', 1 pound 12 ounces; children's, 1 lb. 8 ounces. State size wanted.
26 G 4285—Men's, 6 to 11...$1.00
26 G 4286—Boys', 1 to 6...92¢
26 G 4287—Children's, 11 to 13½...85¢
26 G 4288—Children's, 6 to 10½...82¢

82¢

Crepe (Gum Rubber) Sole Shoes for Men and Boys
$1.39
A high-grade Shoe with crepe rubber (pure gum) soles. Extremely long wear and genuine foot comfort are features of this crepe sole sports shoe, and a value you cannot match anywhere. Durable weight, white canvas uppers are reinforced with fiber rubber. Shipping weights: Men's, 2 pounds; boys', 1 pound 8 ounces. State size wanted.
26 G 4265—Men's, 6 to 11...$1.49
26 G 4266—Boys', 1 to 6...1.45
26 G 4267—Boys', 11 to 13½...1.39

Men's and Boys' Popular Basket-Ball Shoe
Non-Slip Sole

Basket-ball players prefer this higher grade Shoe because it is made with the famous slip-proof ebony black rubber soles. Extra thick for longer dependable service. Also popular for everyday wear. Superior grade white canvas uppers are reinforced along the eyelets, soles and on the ankle. Ship. weight, 2 pounds 4 ounces. State size wanted.
26G4210—Men's, 6 to 12...$1.85
26G4211—Boys', 2½ to 6...$1.69

Fine Leather Puttees

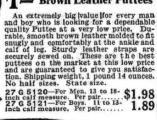

Puttees Do Not Come in Half Sizes

High-Grade Puttees
Genuine cowhide leather Puttees in the spring steel, hook fastening style. Ship. wt., 2 lbs. SIZES: 13 to 18-inch calf measure. State size.
27 G 5105— Brown...$2.98
27 G 5106— Black...2.98

Our Very Best Puttees
Superior quality brown genuine horse hide leather. Molded to fit perfectly in the strap style. $5 values. Ship. wt., 2 pounds. SIZES: 13 to 18-inch calf measure.
27 G 5112...$3.95

Well made, genuine cowhide leather strap Puttees. Ship. wt., 2 lbs. SIZES: 13 to 18-inch calf measure. State size.
27G5107— Brown...$2.98
27G5108— Black...2.98

Our very best Brown genuine horse-hide Puttee with leather strap and steel catch fastener. Ship. wt., 2 pounds. SIZES: 13 to 18-inch calf measure.
27G5110...$3.95

$1.98 Men's and Boys' Brown Leather Puttees
An extremely big value for every man and boy who is looking for a dependable quality Puttee at a very low price. Durable, smooth brown leather molded to fit snugly and comfortably at the ankle and calf of leg. Sturdy leather straps are securely sewed on. These are the best puttees on the market at this low price and are guaranteed to give you satisfaction. Shipping weight, 1 pound 14 ounces. No half sizes. State size.
27 G 5120—For Men, 13 to 18-inch calf measure. Per pair...$1.98
27 G 5121—For Boys, 11 to 13-inch calf measure. Per pair...1.89

Canvas Footwear for Everybody

See Also Page 634

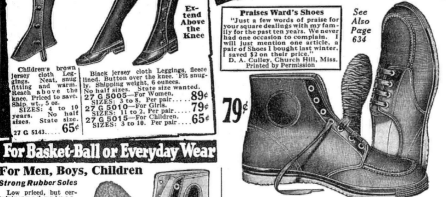

79¢

Men's and Boys'—Strong Rubber Soles
For everyday wear—for sports—for gymnasium, basketball, tennis—get a pair of these new, popular Indian style Moccasin toe Shoes or Oxfords. Durable quality, closely woven brown duck will stand lots of wear and tear. Crepe-corrugated rubber soles are sturdy, slip-proof and very comfortable to the feet. Rubberized reinforcement along eyelets and on the ankle. Average shipping weight, 1 pound 8 ounces. State size.

High Shoes		Oxfords	
26G4236—Men's 6 to 12...$1.00		26G4222—Men's 6 to 12...$1.00	
26G4237—Boys' 1 to 6...89		26G4223—Boys' 1 to 6...89	
26G4238—Boys' 11 to 13½...79		26G4224—Boys' 11 to 13½...79	

Rubber-Soled Canvas Footwear

Strong Rubber Soles

Average Ship. Wt., 1 Lb. 4 Oz.

57¢ **56¢**

Black Canvas Oxfords		White Canvas Oxfords	
26 G 4293—For Men 6 to 12...75¢		26 G 4253—For Men 6 to 12...75¢	
26 G 4294—For Boys and Girls. 1 to 6...67¢		26 G 4254—For Boys and Girls. 1 to 6...65¢	
26 G 4295—For Boys and Girls 11 to 13½...59¢		26 G 4255—For Boys and Girls. 11 to 13½...63¢	
26 G 4296—For Women 2½ to 8...67¢		26 G 4256—For Women 2½ to 8...67¢	
26 G 4297—For Children 6 to 10½...57¢		26 G 4257—For Children 6 to 10½...56¢	

Black Canvas Shoes		White Canvas Shoes	
26 G 4230—For Men 6 to 12...87¢		26 G 4206—For Men 6 to 12...85¢	
26 G 4231—For Boys and Girls. 1 to 6...79¢		26 G 4207—For Boys and Girls. 1 to 6...79¢	
26 G 4233—Boys and Girls. 11 to 13½...75¢		26 G 4208—Boys and Girls 11 to 13½...75¢	
26 G 4234—Women 2½ to 8...79¢		26 G 4209—For Women 2½ to 8...79¢	

Leggings and Puttees for Men and Boys

Brown Canvas
Durable, shapely spring and lace Leggings for men. Leather strap fastening under the arch of shoe. Ship. wt., 9 oz. SIZES: 14 to 18-inch calf measure. No half sizes. State size.
27 G 5096 Per pair...95¢

A Saving on Every Price
Brown canvas hook and lace Leggings for men and boys. They're priced low. Ship. wt., 6 oz. No half sizes. State size.
27 G 5095— 14 to 18-inch calf measure...85¢
27 G 5070— 11 to 13-inch calf, Per pair...75¢

Durable brown canvas Puttees for men and boys. Ship. wt., 5 oz. No half sizes.
27 G 5128— Men, 14 to 18-inch calf measure. Per pair...75¢
27 G 5129— Boys, 11 to 13-inch calf measure. Per pair...69¢

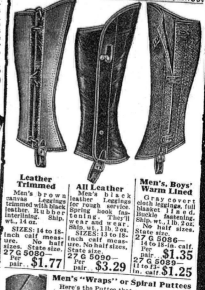

Leather Trimmed
Men's brown canvas Leggings trimmed with black leather. Rubber interlining. Ship. wt., 14 oz. SIZES: 14 to 18-inch calf measure. No half sizes. State size.
27 G 5080 Per pair...$1.77

All Leather
Men's black leather Leggings for rough service. Spring hook fastening. They'll wear and wear. Ship. wt., 1 lb. 2 oz. SIZES: 13 to 18-inch calf measure. No half sizes. State size.
27 G 5090 Per pair...$3.29

Men's, Boys' Warm Lined
Gray covert cloth Leggings, full blanket lined. Buckle fastening. Ship. wt., 1 lb. 2 oz. No half sizes. State size.
27 G 5086— 14 to 18-in. calf. Per pair...$1.35
27 G 5089— 11 to 13-in. calf...$1.25

Men's "Wraps" or Spiral Puttees
Here's the Puttee that a great many outdoor workmen are wearing. They keep the legs warm as well as protect them from dirt, dust and brush. They're the well known army style spiral puttee of fine quality mixture of wool and brown felt. Our price is very low. Ship. wt., 6 ounces.
27 G 5113...85¢

Men's and Boys' Heavy Canvas Work Shoes

Thick Tire Tread Rubber Soles Wear and Wear
$1.59
Many men prefer these comfortable heavy brown canvas Work Shoes. Just the shoe to wear when you're out in the field or for any other everyday working purpose. The uppers are of very durable brown duck lined with white canvas. Thick tire tread rubber soles will wear and wear—thoroughly vulcanized to the uppers. Solid rubber heels. Army style toe with rubber cap. Smooth insoles. Shipping weight, 2 lbs. State size wanted.
26 G 4246—Men's. SIZES: 6 to 12...$1.75
26 G 4247—Boys'. SIZES: 1 to 6...$1.59

Women's Canvas Rubber-Soled Footwear

92¢

One-Strap and Shoe
Wear these economically priced black canvas Shoes or Slippers for chores around the house or for shopping. Black canvas uppers and strong rubber soles and rubber heels. Ship. wt., 1 lb. 4 oz. SIZES: 2½ to 8. State size.
26 G 4298— One-strap...$1.00
26 G 4252—Shoes...1.48

Durable Trimming
Many women wear these for tennis, gymnasium or around the house. They'll save money for you. Very comfortable and fit snugly. Strong white canvas uppers reinforced along eyelets, on the toe and ankle. Durable corrugated rubber sole. Lace to toe style. Shipping weight, 1 pound 8 oz. SIZES: 2½ to 8. State size.
26 G 4289...92¢

108

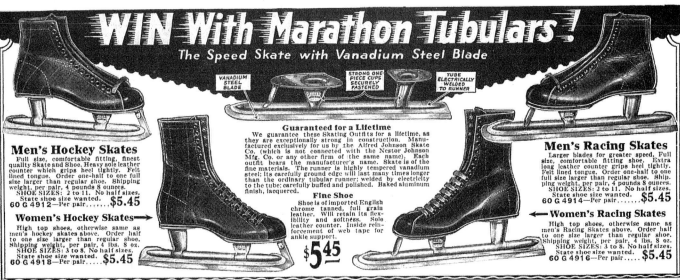

This Sleeping Doll Wants a Mama

So precious in her dainty white organdie dress and bonnet with rose colored ruffles and silk ribbon—any little mother would love this 'Century' Ma-ma Doll. Sleeping eyes, long lashes and tiny open mouth. Sewed mohair wig. Hard-to-break composition head and arms; ¾ composition legs. Cotton-stuffed body. Pink petticoat and bloomers, pink mercerized hose, pink slippers. She's 24 inches tall. Shipping weight, 6 pounds.
449 G 2644—Blonde.
449 G 2444—Brunette.
Each.............$4.89

Effanbee Advertised Doll

This Ma-ma Doll is proud of her pink organdie dress with its ruffles and rosettes. Combination petticoat, white hose, slippers. Hard-to-break composition head, arms, legs; cotton-stuffed body. Sleeping eyes, lashes. Sewed mohair wig. She's 19 inches tall. Shipping weight, 4 pounds 8 ounces.
449 G 2680—Blonde.
449 G 2480—Brunette.
Each.............$4.89

Petite "Ma-ma" Doll
Nationally Advertised

Lovable—isn't she? All dressed up in her white organdie dress with pink and white dotted hem and trimming. Ruffled cap. Combination petticoat, white hose, pink slippers. Composition head, arms and legs; cotton-stuffed body. 17 inches tall. Mohair wig. Shipping weight, 3 pounds.
449 G 2659—Blonde.
49 G 2459—Brunette.
Each.............$3.48

"Gem" Quality Doll

Rose pink voile dress has black stitched hem. Petticoat and bloomer combination. Composition head, arms and legs; sleeping eyes with lashes, mohair wig, "Ma-ma" voice. Cotton stuffed. She's 18 inches tall. Shipping weight, 4 pounds.
Each.............$3.79

Each With Six Photographs

Effanbee's Beautiful Dancing Dolls

"How do you do! I am Rose Mary as slender and graceful as a real little girl—and almost as lively. I'll dance or walk if you lead me. I have sleeping eyes with long lashes, and a cunning open mouth. My sewed wig has long, silky brown curls of real human hair. Mary Sue, my sister, is just like me, except she wears her fluffy golden hair in the latest ringlet bob. This is our third year at Ward's and already we have made thousands of little girls happy. Notice our hard-to-break composition head and legs, and our full composition arms so beautifully shaped, and jointed at the shoulders. We're dressed in dainty sheer white dotted voile with lace edged ruffles of pink organdie, pink petticoat, pink hose and slippers. Each of us comes with a set of six photographs for you to give your friends.

Can Say "Ma-ma"

Mary Sue With Golden Bob				Rose Mary With Dark Brown Curls			
Article Number	Height	Ship. Wt.	Each	Article Number	Height	Ship. Wt.	Each
449 G 2617	26 in.	7 lbs.	$9.98	449 G 2678	26 in.	7 lbs.	$9.98
449 G 2616	23 in.	6 lbs.	8.98	449 G 2677	23 in.	6 lbs.	8.98
449 G 2615	21 in.	6 lbs.	7.59	449 G 2676	21 in.	5 lbs.	7.59
449 G 2614	18 in.	4 lbs.	5.98	449 G 2675	18 in.	4 lbs.	5.98

A Beautifully Dressed Doll

Dolly Dimple

Sleeping Eyes With Lashes

Three Sizes

Dotty's wearing one of the prettiest outfits in all Doll Land—we've noticed ever so many of the other dolls taking fashion notes on her dress. No wonder she looks so happy and confident—for an artist designed this dainty frock of lacelike voile with its butterfly pockets, bow tie, and cunning red buttons. Her pretty hat very becomingly matches her dress. Combination underwear, socks and shoes with bow ties. Sleeping eyes, mohair wig, hard-to-break composition head, legs and jointed arms. New slender cotton-filled body. She'll call you "Ma-ma." Shipping weights: 3, 4½, and 6 pounds.

Article No.	Dress	Height	Each
449 G 2672	Blue	23 inches	$4.19
449 G 2671	Peach	21 inches	3.79
449 G 2670	Pink	18 inches	2.98

23 Inches Tall

Sleeping Eyes

$4.19
"Royal" Make

Wonderfully Low Price

Annabelle won the beauty prize at a recent Dolly's ball! When she speaks, she says "Ma-ma." She has a French human hair wig, rose petal bob with silk bows. Sleeping eyes with lashes; open mouth, teeth and tongue. Hard-to-break composition head, legs and arms. Slim cotton-stuffed body. Dainty organdie dress is of flowered pink with blue satin sash. Pink petticoat and combination. White slippers and hose. She's 23 inches tall. Shipping weight, 5 pounds.
449 G 2685—Blonde.
449 G 2485—Brunette. Each..$4.19

A New Doll Year This $3.48

Non Breakable

Madame Hendren Special

Betty Ann with her new boyish bob, steps in the smartest doll circles. Her head, of extra heavy celluloid, was modelled by a European genius—and her painted light brown curly hair is cleverly embossed. Her skin is of soft velvety texture and waterproof tint. Glass eyes. Composition legs; jointed arms. Very light. White organdie dress trimmed in pale green voile, black edging. Hat to match. Combination suit and underskirt. Shoes; mercerized socks. Blue or brown eyes. State choice.

Article Number	Hgt. In.	Ship. Wt.	Each
449 G 2531	19	4 lbs.	$5.00
49 G 2532	14	2 lbs.	3.48

Beautiful Deluxe Make Jointed American "Ma-ma" Doll

21 Inches Tall

As ladylike as she's pretty, though the perky pink bow on her wig of real human hair makes her look quite saucy! Hard-to-break composition head, pretty arms, legs with jointed knees. Sleeping eyes with lashes, open mouth, teeth. Her cotton-stuffed body is slim and graceful. The sleeves and scallops of her peach color silver cloth dress are smartly trimmed with peach satin ribbon. Pink silk streamers and flowers at neck. White shoes, hose. She's 21 inches tall. Shipping weight, 5 pounds.
449 G 2612........$7.79

Treasure Set Handy Bag 89¢

Any little girl would love this Charleston Bag of extra heavy fiberboard with leatherette edging, real hinges and suitcase snaplock. Bag is finished in black with colored picture design on cover. Has fancy colored lining. Real leather handle. Adorable little twin babies, 4 inches long, are of pink celluloid, with movable arms, painted eyes, mouth and hair. So cunning in their dainty silk trimmed pink blanket pocket. A beautiful present to give a little girl—handy for use in carrying school lunches—or as a shopping bag. Shipping weight, 1 lb. 8 oz.
49 G 2557..89¢

$4.98

Like a Real Baby

20 inches tall. Wears pink and white or blue and white soft combed wool coatee, hood and bootees, embroidered with pink and blue silk flowers. Has hard-to-break composition baby head and arms. Painted hair, and sleeping eyes. Cotton-stuffed body and soft baby legs. White organdie dress; petticoat, and canton flannel diapers. Shipping weight, 4 lbs. 8 oz.
449 G 2654—Doll with pink jacket.
449 G 2454—Doll with blue jacket.
Each.............$4.98

$5.48

27 Inches Tall Simply Wonderful

Gwendolyn's as wonderful a Dolly as any little girl could hope to possess! You can actually make over little girls' clothes to fit her. "Royal" quality. Real human hair wig sewed on cloth foundation. Pretty bandeaux. Sleeping eyes with lashes. Hard-to-break composition head, arms and legs. Cotton-stuffed body. Lace-trimmed blue rayon dress; rayon combination suit. White socks and shoes. She's 27 inches tall. Ship. wt., 7 lbs.
449 G 2658—Blonde.
449 G 2458—Brunette.
Each.............$5.48

27-Inch Doll $2.79

Here is Rosalie (standing at the right). A dear little playmate for you—and about your size. Pretty and slender, with hard-to-break composition head, hands and legs, mohair wig, painted eyes, and crying voice. Dainty pink striped organdie dress; combination underwear. Clever cap to match. Slender type; 27 inches tall. Shipping weight, 6½ lbs.
449 G 2674—Blonde.
449 G 2474—Brunette. Ea..$2.79

20 Inches Tall

Flowered Crepe Dress

Adorable! Her silk finish crepe dress is in pale blue. Blue silk bandeaux with flower. Blue petticoat and combination suit. Rose petal bob of mohair sewed on cloth. Hard-to-break composition head, arms and legs. Cotton-stuffed body. Sleeping eyes, open mouth. "Ma-ma" voice. She's 20 inches tall. Shipping weight, 4½ lbs.
449 G 2664—Blonde.
449 G 2464—Brunette—$3.79

This 17-Inch Sleeping Doll $1.69

Gloria knows what color becomes her most—so she chose this crisp canary yellow organdie hat and lace-trimmed dress. Yellow sateen combination. Mercerized socks; pretty slippers. Go-to-sleep eyes; mohair wig. Crying voice. Hard-to-break composition head, hands and legs, with dimpled knees. She's 17 inches tall. Shipping weight, 2 pounds.
49 G 2560—Blonde.
49 G 2460—Brunette. Each........$1.69

Feature Value $2.48

Martha Ann stands head and shoulders OVER ANY DOLL VALUE WE HAVE EVER BEEN ABLE TO OFFER! Can you believe it,—she actually has wonderful big eyes that go to sleep, a real Ma-ma voice and a mohair wig! She has grown quite tall—a full 20½ inches. Has hard-to-break composition head, arms and dimpled composition legs. Smiling open mouth. Blue rickrack trims her pretty dress and hat of rose pink Rayon. Rose pink sateen combination. Mercerized socks and button slippers. Shipping weight, 4 pounds.
449 G 2554—Blonde.
449 G 2484—Brunette. Each........$2.48

Small circle shows the sleeping eyes, open mouth, mohair wig and rayon hood of this sweet chubby doll.

20 Inches Tall Goes to Sleep $1.89

Great big eyes, rosy cheeks, fluffy mohair wig and winning personality—that's Suzanne! She's 20 inches tall. Has hard-to-break composition head, hands and legs. Tiny open mouth. Crying voice. Light blue organdie dress with lace trimming. White socks and slippers. Ship. wt., 3 pounds.
449 G 2559—Blonde.
449 G 2469—Brunette. Each........$1.89

Costs So Little! $1.29

She's 18 inches tall, and exceptionally cute in her figured blue organdie dress and bonnet. Hard-to-break composition head and hands; tinted cheeks; painted eyes and hair. Crying voice. Cotton-filled legs. Shipping weight, 2 pounds.
49 G 2535....$1.29

Has Crying Voice 98¢

Hard-to-break composition head and arms. Painted eyes. Mohair wig. 16 in. high. Her pink organdie dress is trimmed with lace and bows of blue ribbon. Bonnet matches. Ship. wt., 1 lb. 8 oz.
49 G 2561—Blonde.
49 G 2461—Brunette. Each........98¢

15-Inch Doll 98¢

A healthy looking youngster with chubby cheeks and bright eyes! Goes to sleep; has crying voice. Hard-to-break composition head and hands. Her dainty dress and bonnet are fashioned of peach color organdie. White underslip; socks and slippers. Shipping weight, 1 pound 8 ounces.
49 G 2578...98¢

Squeeze Her and She Cries 65¢

Mighty cute and a full 16 inches tall! Cunning lifelike painted eyes, hair and features. Her lace trimmed colored organdie dress has bloomers and cap to match. White cloth on legs looks like socks, black cloth feet. Hard-to-break composition head and arms. Crying voice. Shipping weight, 1 pound.
49 G 2574....65¢

A Big Sleeping Baby $1.98

He's 16 inches tall; 24½ inches with dress. Hard-to-break composition head with real sleeping eyes. Tinted cheeks and hair. Soft cotton body and curved baby legs. Tiny pink celluloid hands. Long white lace trimmed organdie dress. Long white underskirt, lace trimmed; white stockings. Crying voice. Pillow not included. Shipping weight, 2 pounds.
49 G 2541.......$1.98

Lovable Year Old Smiling Baby $2.62

No, little girl, she is not a real live baby, though she looks like one! Her fat dimpled little hands are always heading straight for her rosy open mouth, because she's just cutting some teeth. She has big eyes that go to sleep, and a crying baby voice. Hard-to-break composition head with painted hair, and chubby composition arms. Soft cotton body and curving baby legs—she'll sit up alone, for she's about a year old! Her sleeveless dress is of white lace trimmed organdie. Petticoat; flannelette diaper; knitted bootees, and white ruffled baby cap. Pillow not included.

Article Number	Height	Shipping Weight	Each
49 G 2566	14 inches	2 pounds	$2.67
449 G 2567	16 inches	4 pounds	3.45

18-Inch Baby Doll $2.89

Honey's always just the same happy and jolly, as a nice healthy one-year-old baby should be! Her soft baby-shaped cotton body is jointed at the hips so she can sit up. She has sleeping eyes, open mouth, painted hair, and crying baby voice. Hard-to-break composition head and full length arms. Her white organdie dress is daintily trimmed with lace, and rayon silk jacket and cap are braid trimmed. She has white underslip, flannelette diaper, white stockings; white shoes. Pillow not included. Shipping weight, 4 pounds.
449 G 2565 ....$2.89

Semi-English Type—Newest Design $17.50

Royal Luxury for the Luckiest Doll in the Neighborhood!

Some little girl has a wonderful dolly that she just adores—a dolly for whom nothing is too good! How wonderful to roll her down the street in luxurious comfort—the envy of all other dolls! This new Carriage is the most fashionable English style—and priced at $8 to $12 under the usual retail price! It's a real bargain, too.

Has large 13-inch artillery wood wheels set close together. Rubber tires are ⅝ inch in diameter. Nickel-plated hub caps. Has heavy tubular pushbar extending all the way to the front axle with the top 6 inches heavily nickel plated. The side panels of the carriage and hood are wood, sanded with an automobile body finish. Panels are outlined with round woven fiber reed rolls and braid. Top is of same reed. Has glass windows in each side.

Carriage is finished in the fashionable London smoke gray with gold stripes and royal blue reed work. Lined throughout with gray leatherette, water-proof and washable. The sides, front and seat are exceptionally well padded. Has reclining back. Leather strap holds dolly in. Adjustable hood fixtures, footbrake. Gears allow body of carriage to be turned around so that the little mother can look at her baby doll. Length of body not including reclining back, 23¾ inches. Width inside, 11 inches. Height for top of hood, 37½ inches; to top of pushbar, 31 inches. Will hold a 28-inch doll comfortably. Shipping weight, 43 pounds. Not mailable.
148 G 3398.................$17.50

13-Inch Wheels

$12.98

13-Inch Wheels

Our Big Special Doll Carriage $9.98

The little girl who receives this Doll Carriage will be proud and happy for a long, long time. It's designed after the handsome big carriages for real live babies; wonderfully comfortable for dolly to ride in, and very convenient for little mothers to wheel. It will carry dolls up to 24 inches tall.

Made entirely of fine round fiber reed. Beauty rolls on hood and body. The transparent windows in the hood have nickel-plated frames. Adjustable sliding hood fixtures. Heavy artillery wood wheels, 11 inches in diameter, have about ¾-inch rubber tires and nickel-plated hub caps. Reclining back.

Beautifully finished in rich golden tan with cream colored wheels and gear. The carriage is upholstered in cream colored rep corduroy. Has leather hold-in strap. The tubular pushbar extends to the front axle. Double footbrake. Length of body, 22½ inches. Height to top of hood, 34 inches; height to top of pushbar, 28 inches. Inside width of carriage, 10¼ inches. Shipping weight, 28 pounds. Not mailable.
148 G 3400.........................$9.98

FULL PUSH BAR
BALLOON TIRES
ARTILLERY WHEELS

Our Finest Reed Doll Carriage $12.98

Same Luxurious Fittings of a Fine Baby Buggy

To delight the hearts of all little girls! An unusually beautiful Carriage of best quality material—De Luxe construction throughout. Large enough for our largest Rose Mary or Mary Sue dolls, or any 28-inch doll. Body and hood of finest machine woven round fiber reed with beauty rolls on body and hood. Glass windows in hood with nickel-plated frames. The entire body and hood are upholstered in dark golden brown velvet corduroy, with padded seat, back and sides. Wind curtain included is made of same high quality corduroy.

Oversize artillery wood wheels about 13 inches in diameter have ¾-inch balloon tires and nickel-plated hub caps. Full tubular pushbar extending to front axle. Reversing gear permits body to be swung around so that baby faces the little mother as she strolls through the park. Extra strong frame and double footbrake. Hood is mounted on rod with sliding attachments. Wheels have the patented snap on attachment used almost exclusively on baby buggies. Length of body, 26¼ inches; height to top of hood, 36½ inches; height to pushbar, 32 inches. Inside width, 10½ inches. Finished in two coats of rich cafe-au-lait enamel (coffee cream color). Cream wheels and gear. Shipping weight, 42 pounds. Not mailable.
148 G 3399.........................$12.98

Storm Cover

Picture above shows the storm curtain in position with body reversed; it is of the same corduroy as the carriage upholstering. Other features are footbrake, sliding hood fixtures, hood windows, reversing body, reclining back, tubular pushbar, corduroy lining and heavy wood artillery wheels.

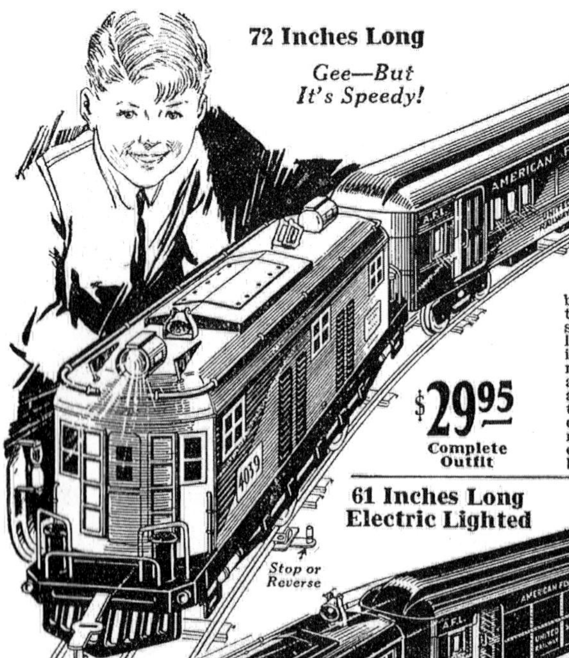

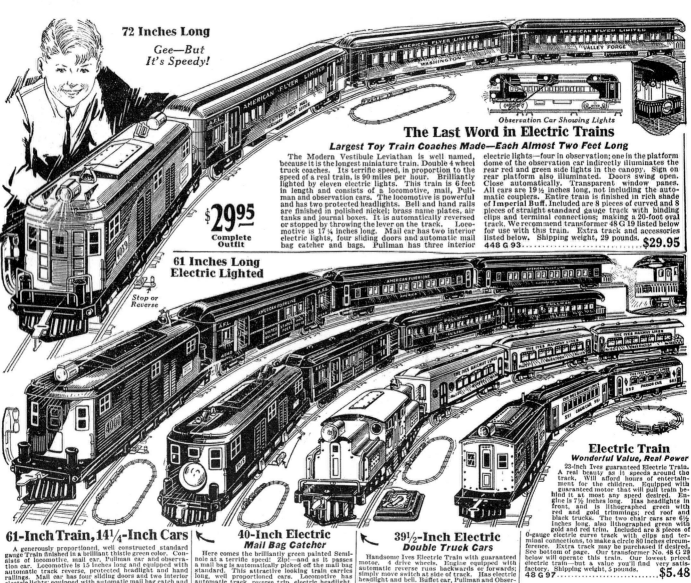

72 Inches Long

Gee—But It's Speedy!

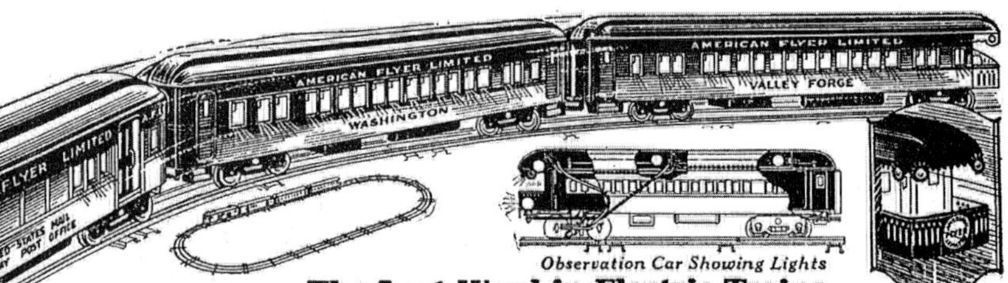

Observation Car Showing Lights

The Last Word in Electric Trains

Largest Toy Train Coaches Made—Each Almost Two Feet Long

$29.95 Complete Outfit

Stop or Reverse

The Modern Vestibule Leviathan is well named, because it is the longest miniature train. Double 4 wheel truck coaches. Its terrific speed, in proportion to the speed of a real train, is 90 miles per hour. Brilliantly lighted by eleven electric lights. This train is 6 feet in length and consists of a locomotive, mail, Pullman and observation cars. The locomotive is powerful and has two protected headlights. Bell and hand rails are finished in polished nickel; brass name plates, air tanks and journal boxes. It is automatically reversed or stopped by throwing the lever on the track. Locomotive is 17¼ inches long. Mail car has two interior electric lights, four sliding doors and automatic mail bag catcher and bags. Pullman has three interior electric lights—four in observation; one in the platform dome of the observation car indirectly illuminates the rear red and green side lights in the canopy. Sign on rear platform also illuminated. Doors swing open. Close automatically. Transparent window panes. All cars are 19½ inches long, not including the automatic couplers. Entire train is finished in rich shade of **Imperial Buff.** Included are 8 pieces of curved and 8 pieces of straight standard gauge track with binding clips and terminal connections; making a 20-foot oval track. We recommend transformer 48 G 19 listed below for use with this train. Extra track and accessories listed below. Shipping weight, 29 pounds.
448 G 93 .... **$29.95**

61 Inches Long Electric Lighted

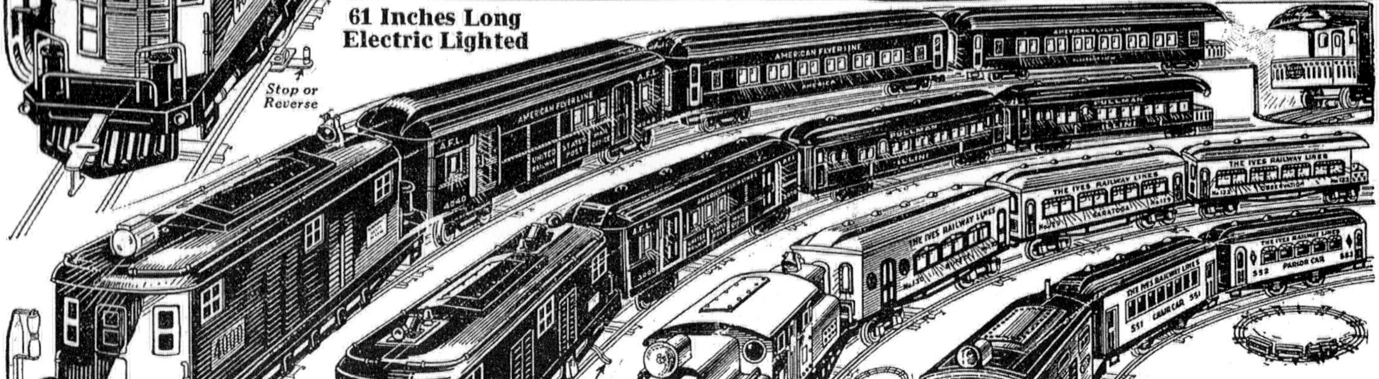

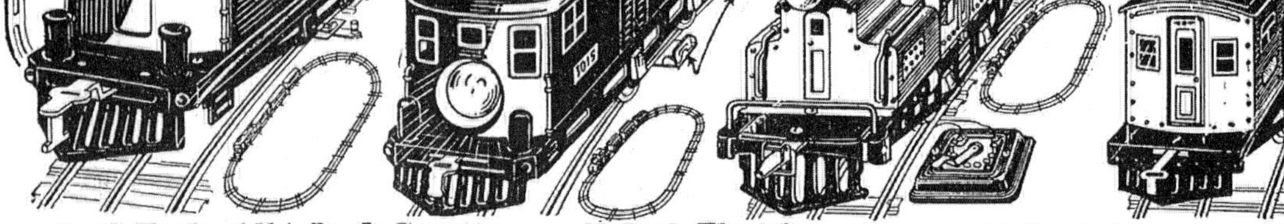

Electric Train

Wonderful Value, Real Power

23-inch Ives guaranteed Electric Train. A real beauty as it speeds around the track. Will afford hours of entertainment for the children. Equipped with guaranteed motor that will pull train behind it at most any speed desired. Engine is 7½ inches long. Has headlights in front, and is lithographed green with red and gold trimmings; red roof and black trucks. The two chair cars are 6½ inches long, also lithographed green with gold and red trim. Included are 8 pieces of 0-gauge electric curve track with clips and terminal connections, to make a circle 80 inches circumference. Extra track may be purchased if desired. See bottom of page. Our transformer No. 48 G 29 below will operate this train. Our lowest priced electric train—but a value you'll find very satisfactory. Shipping weight, 5 pounds.
48 G 97 .... **$5.48**

61-Inch Train, 14¼-Inch Cars

A generously proportioned, well constructed standard gauge Train finished in a brilliant thistle green color. Consists of locomotive, mail car, Pullman car and observation car. Locomotive is 15 inches long and equipped with automatic track reverse, protected headlight and hand railings. Mail car has four sliding doors and two interior electric lights; equipped with automatic mail bag catch and bags. Pullman car has two interior lights; observation car has brass platform railings—one interior and one platform electric light, and transparent window panes. All cars are 14¼ inches long, not including automatic couplers—and have vestibule, steps, air tanks and 3-point suspension on double trucks. Entire length of train, 61 inches; eight pieces of curved and eight pieces of straight Standard gauge track with reverse attachment, binding clips and terminal connections making a 212-inch oval. We recommend Transformer 48 G 19 below, for use with this train. Shipping weight, about 27 pounds.
448 G 94 .... **$22.50**

40-Inch Electric

Mail Bag Catcher

Here comes the brilliantly green painted Seminole at a terrific speed! Zip!—and as it passes a mail bag is automatically picked off the mail bag standard. This attractive looking train carries long, well proportioned cars. Locomotive has automatic track, reverse trip, electric headlight, nickel railings, brass name and number plates and brass journal boxes with red painted pilots and red wheels. Each car is 9¼ inches long equipped with four-wheel trucks, brass vestibule steps and one interior electric light. Mail car has four sliding doors. Observation car has polished brass railings and canopy trim. Eight pieces curved and eight pieces straight 0-gauge tracks, clips and terminal connections, track—forming 164-inch oval. We recommend Transformer 48 G 32 below for use with this train. Ship. weight, 18 pounds.
448 G 95 .... **$13.48**

39½-Inch Electric

Double Truck Cars

Handsome Ives Electric Train with guaranteed motor. 4 drive wheels. Engine equipped with automatic reverse runs backwards or forwards; simply move switch at side of track. Has electric headlight and bell. Buffet car, Pullman and Observation car, each 9 inches long and each electric lighted. Double truck coaches with automatic couplers. Train is finished in orange with maroon outlined windows and black ironwork at the bottom. Included are eight pieces of curved track and four pieces of 0-gauge straight track which make oval 120 inches round. Track clips. Extra track may be added to this outfit. See bottom of page for extra accessories. We recommend our transformer No. 48 G 32 below, for operatng this train. Shipping weight, 12 pounds.
48 G 96 .... **$8.98**

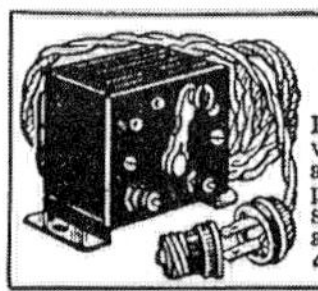

Transformer for 110-Volt Alternating Current

Four speeds, 25 watts. From 6 to 8 volts in half-volt steps. Has 6-foot cord and two-piece attaching plug. Screw into lamp-socket. Shipping weight, about 2 pounds.
49 G 29....... **$1.98**

0-gauge track is 1⅜ inches from center to center of outside rails. Standard wide gauge is 2¼ inches from center to center of outside rails.

Reliably Built Transformers

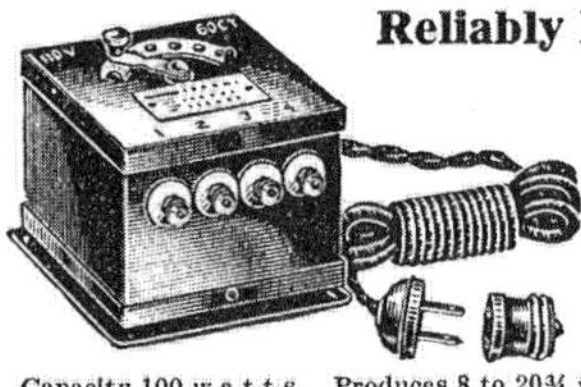

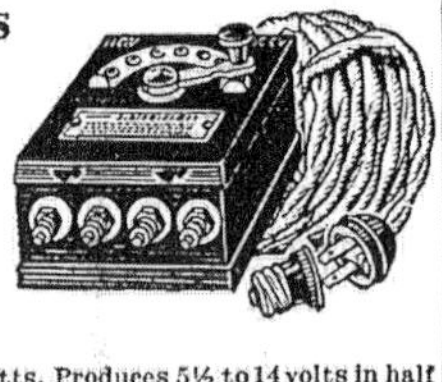

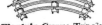

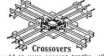

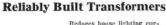

Reduces house lighting current to a lower voltage for operating electrical toys and small motors. Replaces batteries. Regulates the voltage, thus eliminating rheostats for speed control. Safe, economical. With long cord and 2-piece plug. For 105 to 110-volt, 60-cycle alternating current only.

Capacity 100 watts. Produces 8 to 20¾ volts in ¾-volt steps. Gives eighteen speeds. Size, 3⅜ by 4 by 4 inches long. Shipping weight, 6 pounds.
48 G 19 .... **$4.98**

Capacity 75 watts. Produces 5½ to 14 volts in half volt steps. Gives 15 speeds. Size, 3⅛ by 3⅞ by 4 inches long. Shipping weight, 4 pounds.
48 G 32 .... **$2.98**

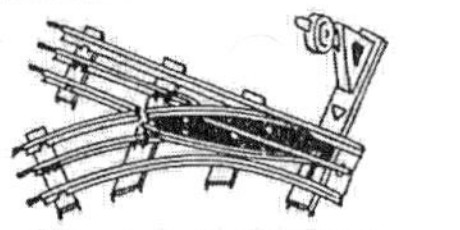

Electric Switches

48 G 53—0-gauge (1⅜ inches wide). Size, 11 by 5½ inches. Ship. wt., 1 pound 8 ounces. Per pair. **$1.98**
48 G 83—Standard wide gauge (2¼ inches wide). Size, 14¾ by 8 in. Ship. wt., 2 lbs. 8 oz. Pair.... **$4.48**

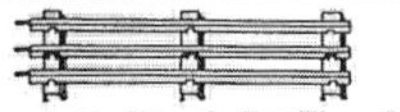

Electric Straight Track

Each section, 10 inches. Shipping weight, 12 ounces.
48 G 24—0-gauge (1⅜ inches wide). 4 pieces.................. **45¢**
48 G 82—Standard wide gauge (2¼ in. wide). 14 in. long. 2 Pieces.. **54¢**

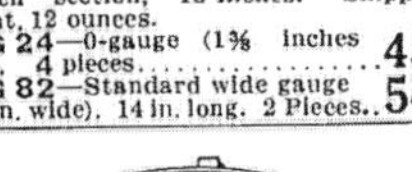

Electric Curve Track

10-inch sections.
48 G 25—0-gauge (1⅜ inches wide). 4 pieces. Ship. weight, 12 ounces... **45¢**
48 G 81—Standard wide gauge (2¼ inches wide). 14 inches long. 2 pieces. Shipping weight, 12 ounces......... **54¢**

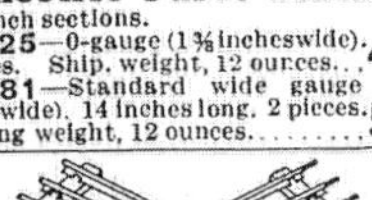

Crossovers

To add to your present tracks. Shipping weights, 12 oz. and 1 lb. 8 oz.
48 G 54—0-gauge (1⅜ in. wide). Each.......................... **87¢**
48 G 80—Standard wide gauge (2¼ inches wide). Each.......... **98¢**

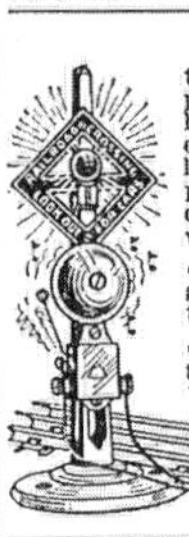

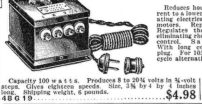

Red light and electric alarm bell. Approaching train rings highly polished nickel-plated bell and lights red light. One piece of track included. Shipping weight, 14 ounces.
48 G 84—For 0-gauge track.... **$2.98**
48 G 86—For wide gauge track..... **$3.35**

Double Electric Street Lamp

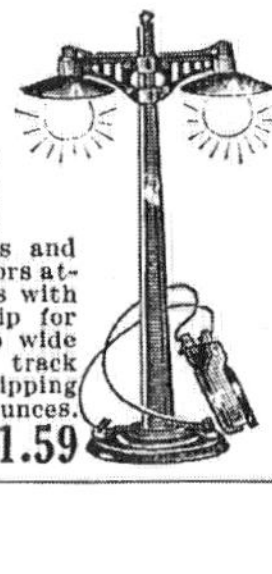

White metal post, 10¼ inches high. Two frosted bulbs and green reflectors attaching wires with universal clip for attaching to wide or 0-gauge track included. Shipping weight, 12 ounces.
48 G 85. **$1.59**

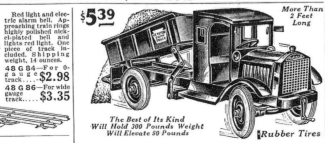

$5.39

More Than 2 Feet Long

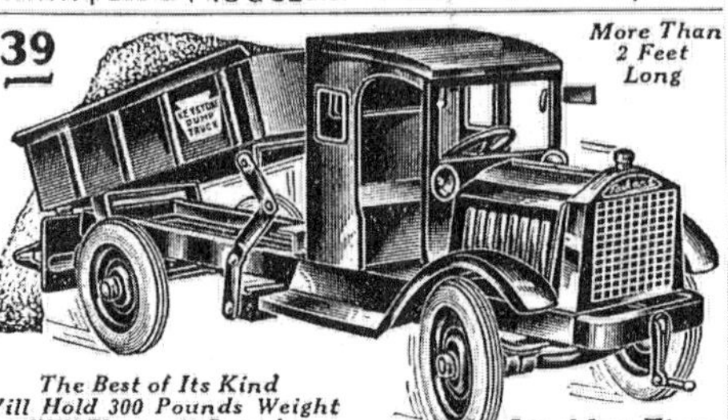

The Best of Its Kind
Will Hold 300 Pounds Weight
Will Elevate 50 Pounds

Rubber Tires

Packard Dump Truck

A $7.50 value. One of the finest toys you have ever seen. Built exactly like a Packard truck. Made of automobile body cold rolled steel in gauges 22 to 14. U-beam chassis—can be pulled along safely with full-grown man standing in it. The 4¾-inch steel disc wheels are guaranteed to run for hundreds of miles; solid rubber tires. Body elevates with crank in front of radiator; will raise a load up to 50 pounds in weight. Body will hold at any angle; elevating mechanism and supports of strongest construction. Length over all, 26½ inches; height, 10½ inches. Truck body is 15¼ by 8½ inches. Dumplifts 6½ inches from chassis. Protruding headlights; heavy steel steering knuckles operated by wheel in cab. Packard radiator. Stop and go signal arm. Small chute gate in tail board permits unloading. Black enameled cab and body, red chassis and wheels. Shipping weight 14 pounds.
448 G 1212 .... **$5.39**

$3.69

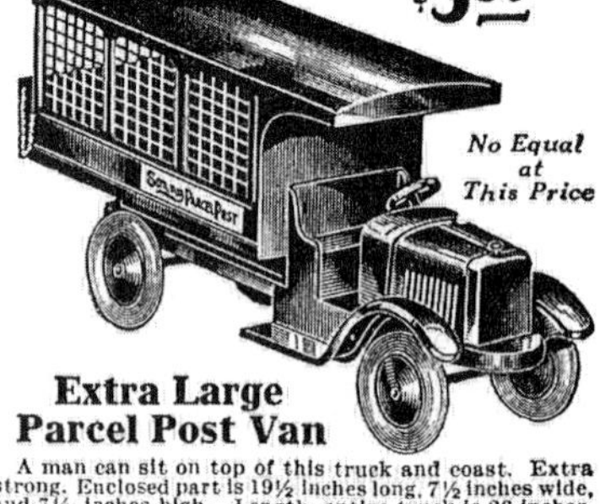

No Equal at This Price

Extra Large Parcel Post Van

A man can sit on top of this truck and coast. Extra strong. Enclosed part is 19½ inches long, 7½ inches wide, and 7¼ inches high. Length, entire truck is 26 inches, height 11½ inches. Made of heavy auto body steel with U-shaped steel beams. Steel bottom, crown fenders. Body enameled green; chassis black, and wheels red. Shipping weight, 18 pounds.
448 G 1218 .... **$3.69**

$5.00

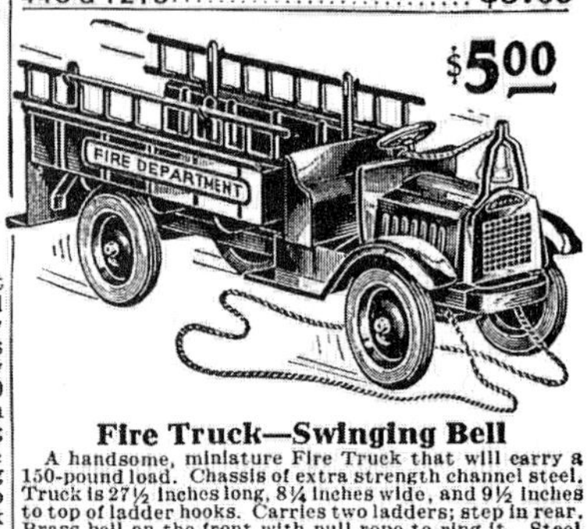

Fire Truck—Swinging Bell

A handsome, miniature Fire Truck that will carry a 150-pound load. Chassis of extra strength channel steel. Truck is 27½ inches long, 8¼ inches wide, and 9½ inches to top of ladder hooks. Carries two ladders; step in rear. Brass bell on the front with pull rope to ring it. Steel disc wheels with black rubber tires. Finished in bright red enamel. Shipping weight, 12 pounds.
448 G 1271 .... **$5.00**

High Speed!-Low Speed!

REAL GEAR-SHIFT AUTO

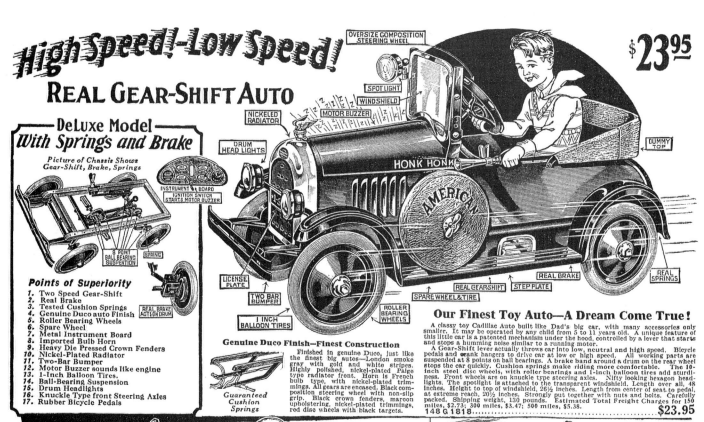

$23.95

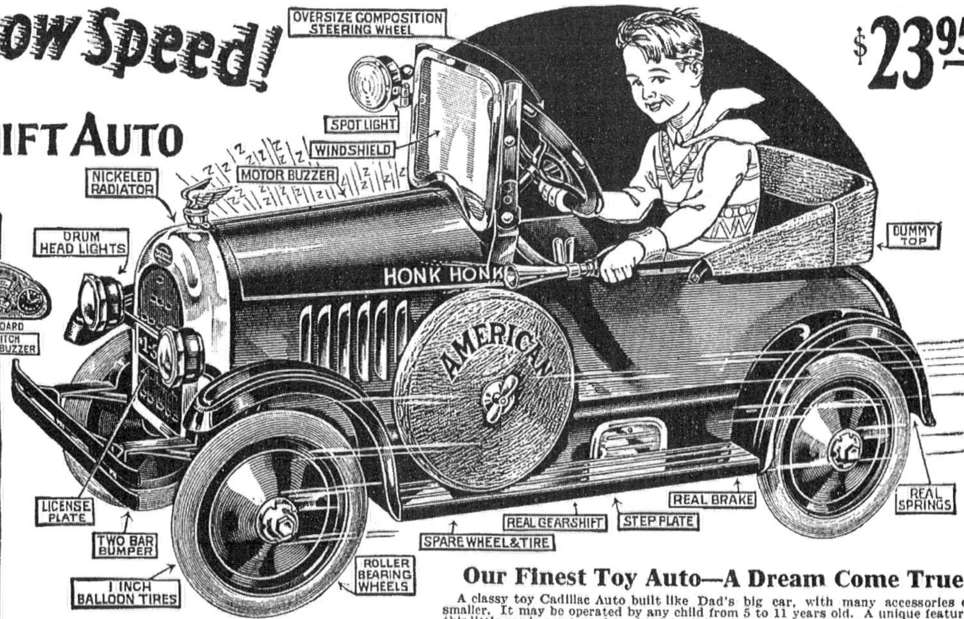
OVERSIZE COMPOSITION STEERING WHEEL
SPOT LIGHT
WINDSHIELD
MOTOR BUZZER
NICKELED RADIATOR
DRUM HEAD LIGHTS
DUMMY TOP
HONK HONK
AMERICAN
LICENSE PLATE
TWO BAR BUMPER
1 INCH BALLOON TIRES
ROLLER BEARING WHEELS
SPARE WHEEL&TIRE
REAL GEARSHIFT
STEP PLATE
REAL BRAKE
REAL SPRINGS

DeLuxe Model
With Springs and Brake

Picture of Chassis Shows Gear-Shift, Brake, Springs

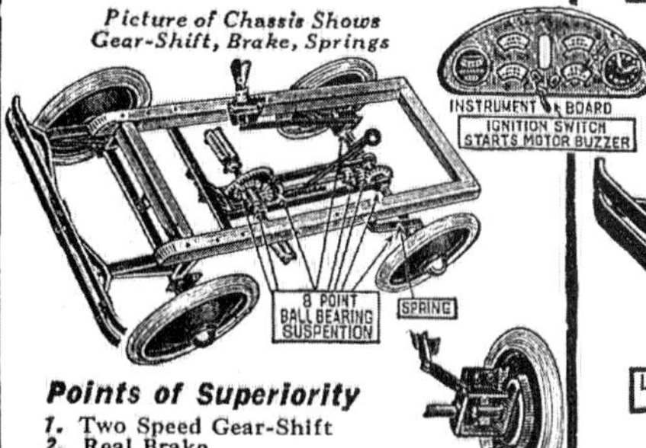
INSTRUMENT BOARD
IGNITION SWITCH STARTS MOTOR BUZZER
8 POINT BALL BEARING SUSPENTION
SPRING
REAL BRAKE ACTS ON DRUM

Points of Superiority

1. Two Speed Gear-Shift
2. Real Brake
3. Tested Cushion Springs
4. Genuine Duco auto Finish
5. Roller Bearing Wheels
6. Spare Wheel
7. Metal Instrument Board
8. Imported Bulb Horn
9. Heavy Die Pressed Crown Fenders
10. Nickel-Plated Radiator
11. Two-Bar Bumper
12. Motor Buzzer sounds like engine
13. 1-Inch Balloon Tires.
14. Ball-Bearing Suspension
15. Drum Headlights
16. Knuckle Type front Steering Axles
17. Rubber Bicycle Pedals

Genuine Duco Finish—Finest Construction

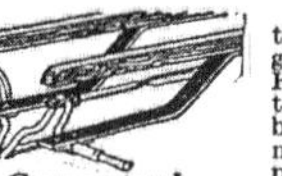

Guaranteed Cushion Springs

Finished in genuine Duco, just like the finest big autos—London smoke gray with gold and white stripes. Highly polished, nickel-plated Paige type radiator front. Horn is French bulb type, with nickel-plated trimmings. All gears are encased. Black composition steering wheel with non-slip grip. Black crown fenders, maroon upholstering, nickel-plated trimmings, red disc wheels with black targets.

Our Finest Toy Auto—A Dream Come True!

A classy toy Cadillac Auto built like Dad's big car, with many accessories only smaller. It may be operated by any child from 5 to 11 years old. A unique feature of this little car is a patented mechanism under the hood, controlled by a lever that starts and stops a humming noise similar to a running motor.

A Gear-Shift lever actually throws car into low, neutral and high speed. Bicycle pedals and crank hangers to drive car at low or high speed. All working parts are suspended at 8 points on ball bearings. A brake band around a drum on the rear wheel stops the car quickly. Cushion springs make riding more comfortable. The 10-inch steel disc wheels, with roller bearings and 1-inch balloon tires add sturdiness. Front wheels are on knuckle type steering axles. Nifty looking hexagon headlights. The spotlight is attached to the transparent windshield. Length over all, 48 inches. Height to top of windshield, 26½ inches. Length from center of seat to pedal, at extreme reach, 20½ inches. Strongly put together with nuts and bolts. Carefully packed. Shipping weight, 130 pounds. Estimated Total Freight Charges for 150 miles, $2.73; 300 miles, $3.47; 500 miles, $5.38.

148 G 1818..$23.95

$16.50

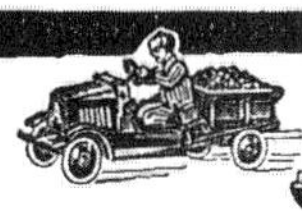

Nearly 5 Feet Long

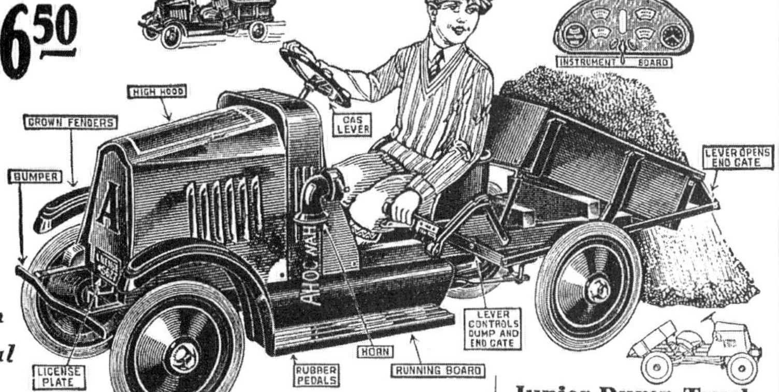
INSTRUMENT BOARD
HIGH HOOD
CROWN FENDERS
GAS LEVER
BUMPER
LEVER OPENS END GATE
AHOOWAH
LEVER CONTROLS DUMP AND END GATE
HORN
LICENSE PLATE
RUBBER PEDALS
RUNNING BOARD

Easy to Run

Powerful

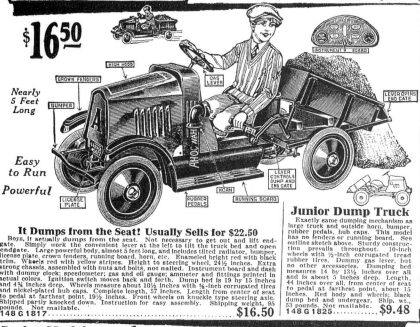

It Dumps from the Seat! Usually Sells for $22.50

Boys, it actually dumps from the seat. Not necessary to get out and lift endgate. Simply work the convenient lever at the left to tilt the truck bed and open endgate. Large powerful body, almost 5 feet long, and includes tilted radiator, bumper, license plate, crown fenders, running board, horn, etc. Enameled bright red with black trim. Wheels red with yellow stripes. Height to steering wheel, 24½ inches. Extra strong chassis, assembled with nuts and bolts, not nailed. Instrument board and dash with dummy clock; speedometer; gas and oil gauge; ammeter and fittings printed in actual colors. Ignition switch moves back and forth. Dump bed is 19 by 15 inches and 4¾ inches deep. Wheels measure about 10½ inches with ⅝-inch corrugated tires and nickel-plated hub caps. Complete length, 57 inches. Length from center of seat to pedal at farthest point, 19½ inches. Front wheels on knuckle type steering axle. Shipped partly knocked down. Instruction for easy assembly. Shipping weight, 95 pounds. Not mailable.

148 G 1817..$16.50

Junior Dump Truck

Exactly same dumping mechanism as large truck and outside horn, bumper, rubber pedals, hub caps. This model has no fenders or running board. See outline sketch above. Sturdy construction prevails throughout. 10-inch wheels with ½-inch corrugated tread rubber tires. Dummy gas lever, but no other accessories. Dumping bed measures 14 by 13½ inches over all and is about 5 inches deep. Length, 44 inches over all, from center of seat to pedal at farthest point, about 15 inches. Red body and wheels; black dump bed and undergear. Ship. wt., 53 pounds. Not mailable.

148 G 1825..............$9.48

Rear Spring

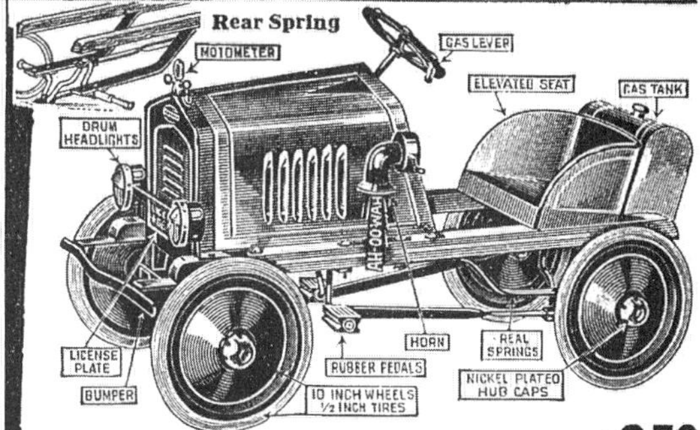
MOTOMETER
GAS LEVER
ELEVATED SEAT
GAS TANK
DRUM HEADLIGHTS
AHOOWAH
LICENSE PLATE
BUMPER
RUBBER PEDALS
HORN
REAL SPRINGS
NICKEL PLATED HUB CAPS
10 INCH WHEELS ½ INCH TIRES

Boys! It's a Hudson—and Only $8.79

Speed down the street in one of these big Hudson Super-Six Toy Automobiles and watch them all make way for you. You'll be proud of its flashing finish—pea green body with wheels trimmed darker green. A big purchase enables us to offer this little beauty at such a remarkably low price. We don't believe you can equal this value at anywhere near the $8.59 we ask.

The high-grade, enamel finish is protected by a heavy coat of water-proof varnish. Horn and drum headlights are black enameled. Embossed, steel radiator front has a Hudson name plate, and hood with vents in the sides just like big cars. All parts securely bolted and braced—not nailed. Regular equipment includes dummy gas tank; shelf with clip and oil can under hood, also bottle of oil. Heavy, double disc wheels 10 inches wide with ½-inch corrugated tires let you take the bumps easily and smoothly. Excellent cushion springs on rear axle increase the riding comfort of this dandy machine. They are a feature on practically all our toy automobiles. Front wheels work on knuckle type steering axles. Length, 39 inches; height, 24 inches. It is 18 inches from the center of seat to the farthest point the pedals reach. Ship. weight, 38 lbs. Not mailable.

148 G 1803..$8.79

Dodge Model

$6.50

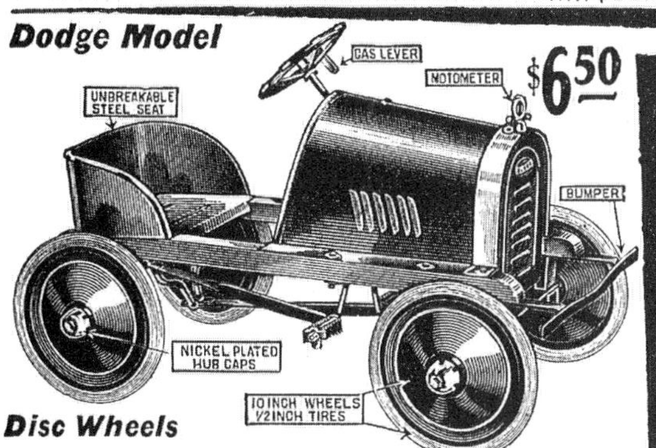
GAS LEVER
MOTOMETER
UNBREAKABLE STEEL SEAT
BUMPER
NICKEL PLATED HUB CAPS
10 INCH WHEELS ½ INCH TIRES

Disc Wheels

Superior Quality—Extraordinary Value

A speeder for the little fellows. Light in weight—and oh how it can travel! Healthful exercise and good times for children 3½ to 6 years old. A strong, sturdy, handsome toy. Six sets of bolts, nuts and washers hold the auto body and steel hood to chassis. Finished in glossy, red enamel trimmed in yellow with a high gloss varnish coat. Steel radiator, hood, seat, and running gear. Front wheels are on knuckle type steering axles. Dummy gas lever. Steel bumper; nickel-plated hub caps. Height to top of steering wheels, 22 inches. Length over all, 37 inches. Furnished with steel double disc wheels or steel spoke wheels as described below. Shipped partly knocked down. Easy to assemble by following our instructions.

Disc Wheel Model

Has 10-inch steel disc wheels, ½-inch corrugated rubber tires. Length from center of seat to pedal at farthest point, 16½ inches. Shipping weight, 33 pounds. Not mailable.

148 G 1831............$6.50

Spoke Wheel Model

Has 9¾-inch double spoke, steel wheels; ⅜-inch corrugated rubber tires. Length from center of seat to pedal at farthest point, 16½ in. Ship. wt., 28 lbs. Not mailable.

148 G 1832..........$4.98

$11.98

With Roller Bearings

Snappy Model

Lots of Pep and Speed

Note the Special Features

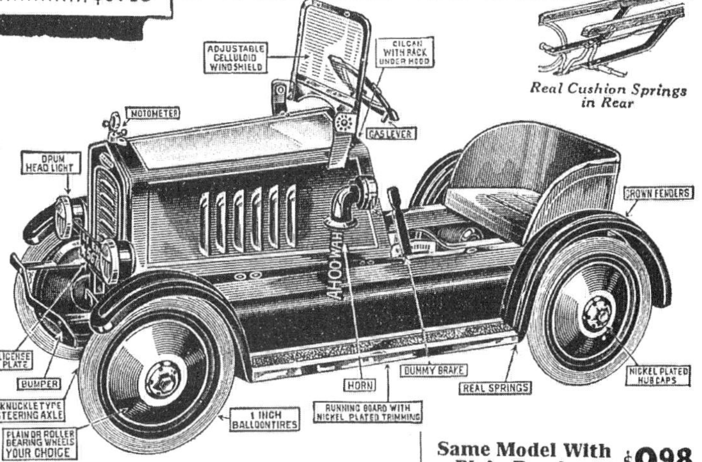
ADJUSTABLE CELLULOID WINDSHIELD
OILCAN WITH RACK UNDER HOOD
MOTOMETER
GAS LEVER
DRUM HEAD LIGHT
AHOOWAH
CROWN FENDERS
LICENSE PLATE
BUMPER
KNUCKLE TYPE STEERING AXLE
PLAIN OR ROLLER BEARING WHEELS YOUR CHOICE
1 INCH BALLOONTIRES
HORN
RUNNING BOARD WITH NICKEL PLATED TRIMMING
DUMMY BRAKE
REAL SPRINGS
NICKEL PLATED HUB CAPS

Real Cushion Springs in Rear

Step on it! Let's go! A racy model that w ll give all the boys a run for their money. A delight to any boy who owns it. Built for speed, with the features of a big car included. A big bargain at our low price, too. Light in weight, but sturdily and strongly built for long service.

Has roller bearings of high quality steel. The body and wheels are Yale blue with sky blue panels and yellow trim. Fenders, horn, headlights, steering wheel, undergearing and springs are black. The cushion springs add much to the riding comfort of the car. Has a fine quality steel hood firmly bolted to the chassis and supported with steel braces. The entire car is securely braced throughout with sturdy steel rods. Loud outside horn, drum headlights, license plate, bumper and aluminum motometer. Steel radiator front with Hupmobile nameplate. Adjustable windshield. Dummy gear-shift; shelf with clip and oil can inside hood. Bottle of oil included. Front wheels on knuckle type steering axles. Height to top of windshield, 27 inches. Length over all, 40 inches. Roller-bearing wheels, 10¾ inches in diameter with 1-inch corrugated balloon tires. Shipping weight, 46 pounds. Not mailable.

148 G 1816..$11.98

Same Model With Plain Bearings $9.98

Another snappy little roadster that will make the other fellows all want a ride. This model is exactly the same in every feature as the one described at left, except that it has plain bearings. Wheels, 10 inches in diameter with ⅝-inch corrugated rubber tires. Only finest quality and best workmanship is used throughout. Guaranteed to stand your inspection. Carefully packed at our factory so that every car will reach you in first class condition. A beautifully running car. Ship. weight, 46 lbs. Not mailable.

148 G 1815..............$9.98

114